SOCIAL PROBLEMS
Second Edition

Consulting Editor

Michael McKee
St. Mary's College

SOCIAL PROBLEMS

Second Edition

IAN ROBERTSON

Random House
New York

Second Edition

987

Copyright © 1975, 1980 by Random House, Inc.

All rights reserved under International and Pan-American Copyright Conventions. No part of this book may be reproduced in any form or by any means, electronic or mechanical, including photocopying, without permission in writing from the publisher. All inquiries should be addressed to Random House, Inc., 201 East 50th Street, New York, N.Y. 10022. Published in the United States by Random House, Inc., and simultaneously in Canada by Random House of Canada Limited, Toronto.

Library of Congress Cataloging in Publication Data

Robertson, Ian, 1944–
  Social problems.

First ed. by M. McKee and I. Robertson.
  Includes bibliographies and index.
  1. Sociology. 2. Social problems. 3. United
States—Social conditions. 4. Social psychology.
  Social problems.
          I. Title.
HM51.M198 1980   301   79-25968
          ISBN 0-394-32025-5

Cover illustration: **Robert Rauschenberg. Estate. 1963.**
Philadelphia Museum of Art: Given by Friends of the Museum.

Text design: James L. McGuire

Picture research: Alan Forman

Manufactured in the United States of America.
Composed by Typothetae Book Composition, Palo Alto, Ca.

Printed and bound by Von Hoffman Press, Inc., St. Louis, Mo.

Since this page cannot legibly accommodate all the copyright notices, the pages following the Index constitute an extension of the copyright page.

Preface

I have prepared this new edition of the text with several goals in mind. The main goal, of course, was to offer a clear description and analysis of major American social problems. But I felt that if the book were to be truly effective, it should do more. The problems that our students study today will change in the future, and new, unforseen problems will doubtless emerge during their lifetimes. An important task of a social problems text, then, is to equip students with the lasting sociological perspective and skills that can enable them to make sense of future developments. Specifically, a text should teach the theoretical approaches that provide the essential framework for analysis; it should emphasize the role of human action—particularly that of social movements—in creating and solving social problems; it should demonstrate the complexity and interrelatedness of social problems (for example, the recurrent tendency for an attempted solution in one area to create a new problem elsewhere); and it should instill a sense that they can indeed be solved, although this optimism should be tempered with a realistic awareness of the difficulties involved. These are the goals I have tried to achieve.

Changes in the present edition
I had fondly imagined, when I began this revision, that my task would consist essentially of updating and polishing the earlier work. I soon found that I was grievously mistaken: developments in both society and sociology have been such that the book has been almost entirely rewritten for the present edition. Many of the changes in the text are designed to fulfill the goals outlined above. Thus, I have given more attention to theory in this edition, and have tried to better integrate it into the text narrative. I have also clarified and expanded upon the role of social movements in the field of social problems, and have included appropriate illustrations throughout the book. There is also a new epilogue on "Solving Social Problems," in which I discuss some of the difficulties implicit in confronting the problems, including those posed by their complexity and interrelatedness.

Other changes reflect new trends in society and new concerns among sociologists. Statistical and other material has been fully updated throughout from the most current sources. There is one entirely new chapter, on the important topic of Health Care, and the chapter in the first edition dealing with the life cycle now becomes a virtually new chapter on Aging. In addition, all of the other chapters include new material of current interest: for example, the chapter on Work now deals with unemployment; the chapter on Crime has an expanded discussion of violence; the chapter on Race and Ethnic Relations gives more attention to Hispanics and to such topical issues as busing and affirmative action; that on Environment and Resources gives greater emphasis to the energy crisis; that on problems of The Family, to new alternatives to traditional marriage; that on the abuse of Drugs, to such newly fashionable drugs as "angel dust"; that on Mental Disorders, to the urban "psychiatric ghettos."

Organization

The basic organization of the first edition was well received by users, and I have retained it in this revision. The book is divided into four parts. The first, "Introduction," provides a thorough orientation to the sociological approach to social problems. The second, "Society in Transition," deals with problems that arise largely from rapid social change: Population, Environment and Resources, Work, The Cities. The third unit, "Inequality in Society," deals with problems linked to the unequal distribution of wealth, power, and other resources: Government and Corporations, Poverty, Race and Ethnic Relations, Sex Roles. The fourth, "Private Troubles and Public Issues," concentrates more on problems that often manifest themselves at a highly personal level: The Family, Aging, Health Care, Mental Disorders, Crime and Violence, Sexual Variance, and the abuse of Drugs. I have taken great care, however, to arrange chapter content and cross-references in such a way that if instructors so wish, they can readily omit some chapters or, after covering the Introduction, can follow a quite different chapter sequence.

Theory

I have been especially anxious to avoid what I consider the fundamental flaw of many texts in the field—the neglect of sociological theory. Too often, the theories that should provide the basis for an understanding of current and future social problems are given a perfunctory recitation in an introductory chapter, and then applied either sporadically or not at all in the rest of the book. The student may thus be left with an understanding little deeper than might be gleaned from newsmagazines, plus a conviction that sociology is just "common sense" and its theory irrelevant to the world. I believe that sociological theory, properly presented, can be readily understood by today's students, and I have tried to demonstrate its utility by applying it systematically to each problem discussed in the book. Three theoretical approaches are used: functionalist theory, which sees problems as a result of social disorganization; conflict theory, which sees them as a result of competing interests and

values; and deviance theory, which sees them as a result of the violation of important norms. I have used these approaches flexibly, applying one or more of them, as appropriate, to each problem.

Learning aids

The book includes a number of features that are intended to help in the learning process. These are:

Consistent organization. Each chapter follows the same basic, three-part organization. The first part, "The Problem," gives a short overview of the nature and dimensions of the problem in question. The second part, "Analyzing the Problem," is the main section of the chapter. It always opens with a discussion and application of one or more of the theoretical approaches, and then goes on to investigate the problem in detail, using evidence from all relevant sources. The third part, "Confronting the Problem," outlines and evaluates solutions that have been or might be attempted. Experience with a similar chapter organization in the first edition showed that students found this structure useful and developed learning expectancies based on it.

Important terms. All important terms are italicized and defined where they first appear. The terms and definitions are then listed at the end of the chapter for further review.

Illustrations. The book is liberally illustrated with photographs, tables, and charts, each selected to reinforce or to amplify material in the narrative.

"Voices." A new feature of this edition are the boxed "Voices"—authentic, first-person accounts of the impact of a specific social problem on an individual's life. These "Voices" are intended to add personal interest and immediacy to the text discussion.

Summaries. At the end of every chapter there is a numbered, point-by-point summary for reviewing purposes.

Suggested readings. Every chapter includes an annotated list of suggested readings, including both classic sources and current contributions to the field.

Glossary. In addition to the end-of-chapter lists of terms, there is a glossary at the end of the

book, containing all the important terms and
their definitions.

Thanks

I am happy to thank the many colleagues and
students who, in writing or in person, have offered me their encouragement, suggestions, and
criticisms. Their comments have been an important resource for me in this revision. In addition,
I am especially grateful to the various teachers
and specialists who either gave detailed critiques
of the first edition in the light of their classroom
experience, or who commented on various drafts
of the manuscript for the present edition. They
were:

Susan Hasselbart, Florida State University;
James Sweet, University of Wisconsin; William
Feigelman, Nassau Community College; Neal
Garland, University of Akron; Morris Forslund,
University of Wyoming; Paul W. Goodman,
University of Texas at El Paso; James E. Smith,
University of Miami; George Ritzer, University
of Maryland; Bernard Beck, Northwestern Uni-
versity; Michael Goldstein, University of Los
Angeles; Richard Robbins, University of Mas-
sachusetts; Christopher Hurn, University of
Massachusetts; Anthony Orum, University of
Texas; Rex A. Campbell, University of Missouri;
Kirsten A. Grønbjerg, Loyola University; Erich
Goode, SUNY at Stoneybrook; Daniel Hodges,
University of Oregon; Richard Burkey, Univer-
sity of Denver.

This revision has benefited immeasurably
from the insights and suggestions of these review-
ers. I am, of course, solely responsible for the
final book.

Lastly, I must thank Barry Fetterolf at Random House for his encouragement, and my
editors, Jeannine Ciliotta and Marilyn Miller,
for their skill, patience, and unflagging humor.

Ian Robertson

Contents

SOCIAL PROBLEMS
Second Edition

1

INTRODUCTION

Social problems are "social" in the sense that they originate in human social behavior and have an undesirable impact on human social life. We study these problems in order that we may understand them and, armed with this understanding, try to solve them. And it is because these problems are social—rather than, say psychological or physical—that they are best investigated through the discipline of sociology, the scientific study of human society and social behavior.

Sociological analysis of the problems yields results that are often far richer, more accurate, and even more disconcerting than those obtained by "common sense" and random personal impressions. This unit provides an introduction to sociology—its concepts, theories, and research methods—and to the basic insights that form the sociological approach to social problems.

1
The Sociology of Social Problems

We are a restless society—pioneering social and technological change at a rate unprecedented in human history, torn by conflicts over basic social goals, yet sustained by the vision of a bright future and of our country as the best hope of humanity. We are also a society of paradoxes—a nation committed to human equality, yet tolerating profound inequalities; a country possessed of spectacular natural beauty, but also with one of the worst pollution problems in the world; a society of high ideals, but with a long and harsh record of social injustice; a people of material affluence for the many, but poverty and squalor for the few. This is the stuff of which social problems are made.

All societies have social problems, of course, but it seems that the basic features of American society generate problems more complex and more numerous than those many other nations must confront. Our society is often dislocated by rapid and uneven social change. It contains a diverse population whose differing backgrounds and interests lead to eternal tensions and conflicts. It includes various groups, which, despite their loyalty to the common culture, reject or deviate from some basic social beliefs and practices. Yet we are an optimistic people, convinced of our collective ability to solve our problems. As we shall see, the discipline of sociology has contributed significantly to our sense that we can change the social environment, and it continues to contribute to the design of programs for change.[1]

WHAT IS A SOCIAL PROBLEM?

At first sight, it hardly seems necessary to ask what a social problem is: the answer would appear to be self-evident. But a moment's thought suggests that the issue is not quite so simple. Is witchcraft a problem in American society? Although you probably don't think so, some people do. Is discrimination against women a problem? Today most people think it is, but a few years ago, when there was far more sexual inequality, very few people regarded sex discrimination as a social problem. Is homosexuality a problem in the United States? Millions of people believe it is, but millions of other people think that the problem is not homosexuality but prejudice against homosexuals. Obviously, the question is more complicated than it might seem.[1]

What is a social problem, then? Here is a

---

[1]For discussions of some difficulties in defining a social problem, see Irving Tallman and Reece McGee, "Definition of a Social Problem," in Erwin O. Smigel (ed.), *Handbook on the Study of Social Problems* (Chicago: Rand McNally, 1971); John I. Kitsuse and Malcolm Spector, "Toward a Sociology of Social Problems: Social Conditions, Value Judgments, and Social Problems," *Social Problems*, 20 (1972), 407–419; and Jerome G. Manis, *Analysing Social Problems* (New York: Praeger, 1976.)

definition: *A social problem is whatever a signifi-cant part of the population perceives as an undesirable gap between social ideals and social realities and believes can be eliminated by col-lective action.* This definition contains several distinct ideas that will lead us to a clearer understanding of the nature of social problems.

1. A social condition becomes a social problem only when it is publicly perceived as one. The mere existence of a social condition such as poverty, government corruption, or drug abuse is not enough to make it a social problem. It becomes a problem only when people perceive it as problematic. Sometimes a condition exists for decades or even centuries before it is regarded as a problem. From time immemorial, women have been regarded as inferior to men, and conse-quently have been refused equal opportunity in many areas of life. It is only recently that a significant part of the population has perceived this condition as undesirable. The combination of this social condition and the new public perception of it has made discrimination against women a social problem in modern America. Similarly, it is likely that many social conditions that are not regarded as problems today will become social problems in the years ahead as public perceptions change. Sociologists some-times try to identify these "latent" problems[2] in order to predict the social concerns of the future.

The public's perception of a social problem naturally depends to a great extent on how visible the problem is. For this reason, groups that are newly aware of some problem try to bring it to public attention, often by dramatic methods. Social movements such as those for civil rights, women's liberation, or tax reduction try to publicize their grievances, because they realize that unless the situation they complain of is widely perceived as a social problem, no social action will be taken to solve it. The success of their efforts to make a problem visible depends largely on the willingness of the mass media,

particularly newspapers and TV, to publicize it. The media have an important function in mod-ern societies: by focusing on newsworthy activi-ties of aggrieved groups, they increase public awareness of emerging social problems and thus help set the agenda for remedial social action. In the United States the news media do not merely report events; they also offer commentary and do investigative reporting, uncovering and publiciz-ing social problems that might have escaped attention. An obvious example was the exposure of the Watergate scandal, which focused atten-tion on the problem of government corruption, with major consequences.

2. Social problems involve a gap between social ideals and social realities. All social problems involve a widespread perception of the differ-ence between the real—what is—and the ideal—what ought to be. The ideals of any society are based on the values of its people. *Values* are socially shared ideas about what is desirable, right, and proper, such as beliefs concerning free speech, the sanctity of marriage, or the need for equal opportunity. Naturally, values vary greatly from one society to another, and among dif-ferent groups and individuals within a society. Because social values are always changing, the gap between particular social ideas and particu-lar social realities also changes—sometimes clos-ing, sometimes widening—with the result that new social problems seem to emerge and old ones disappear.

The issue of environmental pollution is an example of how changing ideals lead to the emergence of a new social problem. There is nothing new about the ravaging of the environ-ment. It has been an accepted feature of the American scene for nearly two hundred years, with some of the worst destruction occurring long before the modern ecology movement came into being. But social ideals have suddenly moved ahead of social reality. We are now increasingly aware of the damage we are doing to the environment and are often disturbed by practices—such as the dumping of industrial wastes into rivers—that we ignored or tolerated before. The result is that environmental pollu-tion, a subject that did not even appear in social

[2]Robert K. Merton, "The Sociology of Social Problems," in Robert K. Merton and Robert Nisbet (eds.), *Contemporary Social Problems*, 4th ed. (New York: Harcourt Brace Jovan-ovich, 1976), p. 13.

Power is unequally distributed in society. Some people have much more influence than others in defining social problems and in determining public policy toward the problems.

problems textbooks a few years ago, is now regarded as a serious social problem.

On the other hand, some social conditions that were perceived as major problems a few decades ago have become less problematic, not because the reality is any different, but because social ideals have adjusted to the reality. For example, premarital sex was perceived as a major problem in the 1940s and 1950s, but opinion polls show that attitudes relating to sexual conduct have now become much more tolerant. The gap between the ideal and the real has lessened, and the issue is not generally considered a serious social problem any longer.

3. *Social problems must be perceived as problems by a significant part of the population.* No matter how undesirable a social condition may seem to a few people, it cannot be regarded as a social problem until it is perceived as such either by significant numbers of people or by people who occupy significant positions of power and influence in society. Thus the "desecration" of the Sabbath by Sunday sports is not generally regarded as a social problem in the United States. Although recreational activities on Sundays are repugnant to some, these people are not sufficiently numerous, nor do they occupy enough positions of power and influence, for their viewpoint to carry much weight. American society contains many groups that find some social condition or other undesirable, but unless their perception is widely shared or is endorsed by influential individuals, the society will not regard that condition as a social problem.

For example, when the United States first became involved in the Vietnam war, an insignificant minority of Americans saw our intervention as an affront to American ideals. Although support for antiwar protestors gradually increased, by the mid-1960s opinion polls still showed that their views were rejected by the great majority of Americans. Around that time, however, people occupying positions of considerable power or influence began to speak out against the war—senators, members of Congress, editors of major newspapers, presidents of large corporations, religious leaders. With this new impetus, opposition to the war developed rapidly among a significant part of the population. Feeling grew so intense that President Johnson's reelection seemed unlikely, and he withdrew from the 1968 presidential campaign. Shortly thereafter, Richard Nixon was able to win the election largely on a promise to end a war that had been strongly supported by most Americans, including himself, only two years previously.

4. To be regarded as a social problem a social condition must be considered capable of solution through collective action. All societies experience conditions that they consider undesirable, such as disease, war, or famine. But people regard these conditions as social problems only when they believe that they can do something about them. If the conditions are defined as a part of the natural order—an unavoidable feature of life, an act of God, or an inevitable result of human nature—then people will not view them as social problems because they consider them unchangeable.

Many of our current social problems have at one time or another fallen into the latter category. Mental disorders, for example, have, until recently, been explained as the result of congenital defects, moral deficiencies of the individual, or even possession by evil spirits; therefore, people did not feel that social action could have much effect on mental disorder. In contrast, most people now accept that at least some mental disorders are caused by social stresses that could be reduced through collective action. Similarly, poverty was usually regarded in the past as natural and inevitable. The poor were believed to be shiftless, idle, and entirely responsible for their own plight. Today, poverty is widely thought to be the result, at least partially, of the way wealth is distributed. People believe that governments can manipulate their economies to reduce or eliminate poverty. The condition is thus defined as a problem that can be solved by collective action.

"Collective action" refers to any steps taken by people acting in concert, such as strikes by labor unions, new laws passed by legislatures, private lobbying or public-relations advertising by industrial corporations, street demonstrations by organized interest groups, or massive national campaigns by antiabortionist or pro-civil rights movements. The need for collective action arises when it is impossible for individuals, acting as individuals, to solve a social problem—although they may be able to personally escape its effects. For example, individuals can sometimes escape from poverty through their own efforts, but the overall social problem of poverty will persist unless it is effectively confronted by collective social action.

A SOCIOLOGICAL APPROACH

There are many different ways of looking at social problems. The economist, the artist, the psychologist, the novelist, and the theologian all look at social problems from their own distinctive perspectives. But because these problems are social—rooted in the structure and workings of society—it is the sociologist who is uniquely equipped to analyze them.

Sociology is the scientific study of human society and social behavior. The discipline is scientific in that it relies for its analysis on rigorous logic, hard facts, and testable theories. Its body of accumulated scientific knowledge, some of which contradicts commonsense assumptions, provides powerful tools for investigating the causes and effects of social problems. Of course, the sociologist may use perspectives and information from other disciplines: historical facts, psychological theories, or even the impressions of poets can help to illuminate a particular problem. But ultimately the sociologist analyzes social problems within a framework of theory and research that is distinctively a sociological one.

All social problems fall within the boundaries of the discipline, even though they may initially seem to be purely individual in their causes or effects. One of the most important sociological insights is that an inescapable relationship exists between the plight of the apparently isolated individual and the overall social context in which that person lives. One of the founders of modern sociology, Emile Durkheim (1858–1917), graph-

Private troubles and public issues are inextricably linked. The heroin addict's problem may seem purely personal—but it can only be fully understood in terms of social pressures toward addiction and social opportunities for becoming an addict.

ically illustrated this relationship in a classic study of suicide.[3]

Suicide is surely one of the most individualistic acts that we are capable of. If someone commits suicide, we usually try to explain it in terms of biography and psychology: we ask what stresses that person was subjected to, and what impact they had on his or her particular personality. This method of explanation may be adequate for many purposes, but as Durkheim showed, it is incomplete. He painstakingly studied statistics for different regions of Europe and found that the suicide rate varied among different areas and different population groups in a consistent way over the years. For example, people in urban areas were more likely to commit suicide than people in rural areas; Protestants were more likely to commit suicide than Catholics; single people were more likely to commit suicide than individuals living in family groups. The common factor behind these differences, Durkheim found, was the extent to which the individual was integrated into social bonds. Individuals living in certain social contexts are more likely to feel lonely and isolated than individuals in other contexts, so the rate of suicide is higher among the former.

Durkheim also compared suicide in modern society with suicide in some traditional societies where it was an expected act under certain circumstances. In ancient Rome and in a traditional society like Japan, for example, people who had been disgraced were expected to take their own lives, and with that act regain their honor. In traditional Indian society a widow was often expected to immolate herself on her husband's funeral pyre. In essence, what Durkheim found was that whereas people in modern societies may kill themselves because they have weak links with their community and no expectations made of them, people in certain traditional societies sometimes killed themselves because they had strong links with a community that expected them to do so. However, in either case, deeply influential social forces can be seen in this apparently individualistic act.

---

[3]Emile Durkheim, *Suicide* (Glencoe, Ill.: Free Press, 1964), originally published in 1897.

Although the suicide of a specific person may still be explained in terms of individual circumstances, the total rate of suicide has to be explained in sociological terms. The same is true of any other social problem, such as alcoholism, sexism, violence, crime, overpopulation, or racial discrimination. These problems all involve individuals, but their form and extent is influenced by the social context in which they occur. As C. Wright Mills observed, it is fundamental to the sociological perspective that one should grasp this essential link between "private troubles" and "public issues"—between the fate of individuals and the social forces that surround them.[4]

SOME SOCIOLOGICAL CONCEPTS

Science assumes that there are regular, predictable patterns in the universe. If social life were a random, haphazard affair, it could not be subjected to scientific analysis. But, in fact, society is remarkably orderly and predictable under most circumstances. Although all societies constantly change, all have an underlying pattern of social relationships, a *social structure*. This structure and the social processes that maintain and change it can be analyzed through the use of a few basic but important sociological concepts.

Culture. In sociological usage, the word *culture* refers to all shared products of human society, whether material or nonmaterial. Material culture includes physical objects such as paintings, airplanes, houses, nuclear reactors, arrows, and toothbrushes. Nonmaterial culture includes less tangible human products, such as language, values, political systems, religious beliefs, music, racial prejudice, and the rules of baseball. Taken together, the material and nonmaterial aspects of culture provide the way of life for a society.

A basic sociological insight is that our conception of reality is socially constructed. Human beings do not all perceive the same universe:

rather, their perceptions are colored by the culture in which they happen to live. In the Europe of the Middle Ages, people "knew" that the earth was flat, because that was the information their culture offered them. Likewise, we "know" that the earth is round—not because each of us has conducted personal experiments to prove it, but because we automatically accept the information our own culture offers us. People who live exclusively in a given culture, whether in the United States or in an Amazon jungle tribe, tend to take their culture for granted. They lack an "outsider's" view of it and regard their own cultural practices as "normal," as expressions of "human nature." This means that they tend to judge other cultures by the standards of their own—and not surprisingly, they may conclude that other peoples' way of life is strange, perhaps bizarre, or even immoral. This type of thinking is *ethnocentric*. Ethnocentrism not only prevents people from seeing other cultures objectively; it also prevents them from seeing their own culture clearly.

Within a large, mass society such as the United States there are a number of *subcultures*, groups that participate in the overall culture but also have their own distinctive life styles and values. Membership in a subculture also colors one's view of reality: the subculture of Wall Street stockbrokers probably takes a view of American social reality markedly different from that of the subculture of Los Angeles Hell's Angels. Each subculture thus tends to be ethnocentric in relation to other subcultures, judging them by its own standards and implicitly assuming that its own way of life is superior to, and perhaps more "normal" than, the others'. The relevance of this fact to social problems is obvious: different groups view the same social conditions in very different ways, and may sharply disagree over what is a problem and what is a solution.

Norms. Every human society constructs its culture out of an infinite range of possibilities that exist in every area of life, from musical forms to clothing styles. Although each culture or subculture includes only a small segment of these possibilities, its members view this segment as

---

[4]C. Wright Mills, *The Sociological Imagination* (New York: Oxford University Press, 1959).

appropriate and all other possibilities as inappropriate. There are many ways a man can appear in public—wearing pants, a kilt, a loincloth, war paint, or nothing at all—but in any society some of these will be considered acceptable and others will cause, at the minimum, raised eyebrows.

Judgments about correct or "normal" behavior are guided by social *norms*, the formal or informal rules that prescribe the appropriate behavior for a given situation. These norms are so taken for granted that we rarely notice them—unless they are broken, as when people pick their nose in public or wear colorful clothes at a funeral. Deviations from norms may be penalized with anything from mild social disapproval to a sentence of death, depending on the importance society places on conformity to the norm in question. Some relatively weak norms, called *folkways*, consist of the ordinary customs and conventions of society, such as saying "hello" when answering the telephone, or eating with utensils rather than with one's fingers. People disapprove violations of the folkways, but they are not morally outraged by them. Other norms, called *mores*, are much stronger, in that society attaches moral significance to them. In our culture, public nudity, armed robbery, the desecration of the flag, and contempt for religious symbols all excite a strong reaction. Many norms, particularly mores, are encoded in *laws*, which are formal rules backed by the power of the state. The strongest norms of all are *taboos*, or prohibitions against behavior that is considered loathsome and almost unthinkable, such as cannibalism or incest. Taboos have such power that laws may not be necessary to enforce them: many American states, for example, have no laws against cannibalism.

Conformity to norms ensures the smooth working of social relationships. Most people conform to most norms most of the time because conformity is usually a habit that is taken for granted. When important norms are violated by individuals or groups in society—for example, property norms by thieves, chastity norms by prostitutes, or drug-abuse norms by college students—the deviations are likely to be defined by the dominant culture as social problems. Obviously, social tensions arise when what is "normal" to one group is considered "abnormal" by another.

Status. The concept of *status* refers to position in society. Each of us has many statuses—son, black person, woman, student, roommate, teacher, and so on. Some of these statuses are *ascribed* to us by society; that is, they are assigned to us on grounds over which we have little or no control. Other statuses are *achieved* by us, at least partly, through our own efforts or failings. Examples of achieved statuses are those of senator, prison convict, and college graduate. In a society that offers maximum opportunity for people to attain their potentials, most statuses will be achieved. In a more restrictive society, ascribed statuses become barriers to the fulfillment of individual talent. If some part of the population, such as a racial minority, is prevented from gaining achieved statuses because of its members' ascribed status, a social problem is likely to result. And if some statuses rank so much higher than others that wealth, power, and prestige are believed to be unfairly shared, this inequality is likely to be defined as a social problem also.

Role. This sociological concept is taken directly from the theater: a *role* is the part played by a person occupying a particular status in society. The distinction between role and status is a simple one: you occupy a status; you play a role. Each social status is surrounded by norms that prescribe how the role or roles attached to it ought to be played. A person with the status of president of the United States is expected to play such roles as head of state or commander in chief; a woman with the status of mother is expected to play one role in relation to her child, another as a PTA member, and so on. When a section of the population is restricted to low-status positions, its members are inevitably restricted to playing menial roles. This situation, for example, is what the social problem of sex roles is all about. Women have traditionally been confined to such roles as housewife or secretary rather than those of family breadwinner or corporation executive.

Institutions. Each society has to meet the social needs of its members: goods must be produced, law must be enforced, recreation must be provided, children must be taught the knowledge they will need later in life, and so on. To meet these requirements, each society creates *institutions*—stable patterns of norms, statuses, and roles that center on fulfilling some social need. Major social institutions are the family, which regulates sexual behavior and provides for the care of children; education, which transmits knowledge from one generation to the next; religion, which provides shared rituals and beliefs; the economy, which organizes the production and distribution of goods and services; and the political system, which maintains social order. There are also countless lesser institutions, such as prostitution, which provides a means of sexual outlet, or sport, which meets a need for recreation.

Because institutions are very stable, they tend to change slowly—sometimes too slowly to adjust to changing social needs. When this happens, established institutional patterns may become irrelevant, oppressive, or damaging to society. For example, the traditionalist societies of the developing world have always had the institution of the large family, mainly because the infant death rate in these societies was so high that only about half the children survived into adulthood. Although the introduction of modern sanitary, nutritional, and medical standards has slashed the infant death rate in these societies, the institutionalized high birth rate has persisted. The result has been a population explosion that is now a grave social problem and a threat to the human future.

Socialization. An individual born into any culture must learn to follow its norms, occupy certain statuses, play the appropriate roles, and participate in the society's institutional life. This learning process is called *socialization*—a lifelong experience in which each of us acquires a personality and learns the culture of the society.

Our capacity for socialization is unequaled in the animal world. The behavior of lower animals is governed almost entirely by instincts: a worm learns virtually nothing during its entire life; its behavior consists of rigid responses that are genetically programmed. As the level of animal life grows higher, instinct becomes steadily less important, and learning exerts more and more influence on behavior. In human beings, learning is supremely important, accounting for virtually all our behavior. In fact, most modern psychologists reject the view that we have any instincts, or complex inborn behavior patterns. We have a few simple, inborn reflexes (such as withdrawing our hands from a hot surface) and a few basic drives for food, sex, and self-preservation. Even then, our drives, unlike those of lower animals, are nonspecific. We have to learn what is edible and what is not, what is sexually appropriate behavior and what is inappropriate, and how to go about surviving generally. Our personalities, values, knowledge, and social behavior depend largely on our learning experiences, which, in turn, are determined by the society into which we are born. Various agencies of socialization—the family, the mass media, the peer group, the schools—socialize us into acceptable patterns of behavior, until this behavior comes to seem "natural," "normal," or even to appear as "instinctive."[5]

[5]The view that some human social behavior may be genetically determined has recently reappeared as one of the assumptions of sociobiology, a new science devoted to the unified study of all social animals. Some sociobiologists believe that genes may determine quite specific behaviors, while others believe that they may supply only broad potentials, with the content of actual behavior being supplied by culture. Sociobiological analysis of human behavior is thus far essentially speculative, and based primarily on inference and extrapolation from the behavior of other social animals. Human beings, however, differ radically from other species, which lack both culture and our highly evolved cerebral cortex. For these reasons, most social scientists appear to reject the sociobiological view as being based on inadequate evidence and faulty analogies. For a detailed presentation of sociobiological principles, see Edward O. Wilson, *Sociobiology: the New Synthesis* (Cambridge, Mass.: Harvard University Press, 1975). A briefer account is provided in David P. Barash, *Sociobiology and Behavior* (New York: Elsevier, 1977). Marshall Sahlins offers a critique of sociobiology in *The Use and Abuse of Biology* (Ann Arbor, Mich.: University of Michigan Press, 1976). Various viewpoints are gathered in Michael S. Gregory, Anita Silvers, and Diane Sutch (eds.), *Sociobiology and Human Nature: An Interdisciplinary Critique and Defense* (San Francisco: Josey-Bass, 1978); and in Arthur L. Caplan (ed.), *The Sociobiology Debate: Readings on Ethical and Scientific Issues* (New York: Harper & Row, 1978).

Socialization is the lifelong process by which we acquire personality and learn the culture of our society. The precise content of the socialization process differs according to such factors as social class or ethnic group membership.

In a large modern society with its many subcultures, the content of socialization varies a great deal from one group to another. An important effect of this is that people in different social positions perceive social conditions according to very different personal experiences and values. Consequently, there is often fierce dispute about the causes, effects, and possible solutions of social problems.

Power. The concept of power is an important one in sociology, and especially in the sociology of social problems. Essentially, *power* is the ability to control the behavior of others, even without their consent. Power implies the ability to participate effectively in a decision-making process; those who cannot influence decisions, however much they may be affected by them, are therefore powerless. Power can be exercised in many different ways—legally or illegally, subtly or blatantly—and can derive from many sources.

The power of the antiwar movement in the 1960s derived from its depth of support among the American people. The power of large corporations derives from their immense political and economic influence, the power of government bureaucrats, from the official statuses they hold, the power of a rioting mob, from the fear of its destructiveness.

When different groups or interests come into conflict, the outcome favors the more powerful party. Since the social arrangements in any society will therefore tend to reflect the perceived interests of the most powerful groups, those arrangements are likely to be regarded as a social problem by the less powerful groups. To change the situation, the weaker groups will usually have to take corrective action to alter the balance of power to some degree. Typically, they must organize themselves to apply pressure through whatever tactics are open to them—friendly persuasion, media advertising, private lobbying of legislators, strikes, demonstrations, riots, and so on. Eventually, a weak group may persuade members of the powerful group of the rightness of its claims—or at least convince them that it would be costly to ignore these claims any longer. In some cases the balance of power might shift enough that the formerly weak group gains access to positions of power.

How this process works can be seen in the following example. For generations there has been conflict—sometimes open, sometimes subtle—between blacks and whites in the United States. The whites have always been the more powerful of the two groups, and social arrangements have therefore tended to benefit them, denying blacks equal opportunity in, among other things, employment, housing, and education. But in the late 1950s and 1960s, blacks and sympathetic whites formed the civil rights movement, thereby deriving power from their organization, their numbers, and the moral force of their claims. By using a variety of tactics, they were able to persuade those in power either that their demands were just or that ignoring these demands would prove more inconvenient than attempting to meet them. While American race relations still leave much to be desired, the substantial improvements that have taken place since the 1950s would probably not have occurred without the application of pressure by the formerly weak group. In certain Northern cities and some Southern states, too, the balance of power between the two groups is now shifting as black voters begin to outnumber white.

C. Wright Mills writes of the scientific understanding of society as "the sociological imagination."[6] To Mills, sociology is a form of greater human awareness, a transcendence of ethnocentrism, a profoundly liberating experience. It enables people to fully comprehend the social surroundings they had always taken for granted. The sociological imagination allows us to see that social conditions, seemingly laws of nature, are really human products—created in the past and capable of being modified now and in the future. Thus social ills are suddenly perceived

afresh, to be collectively dealt with rather than simply endured.

SOCIAL PROBLEMS AND SOCIAL MOVEMENTS

Social problems are "created" by making a significant part of the population aware of a gap between social ideals and social reality. An important sociological insight is that such awareness is brought about largely through the efforts of a *social movement*—a large number of people who join together to initiate or resist some social or cultural change. These movements, such as the civil rights movement, the peace movement, the women's liberation movement, the ecology movement, and the consumer movement, are crucially important in identifying social problems, publicizing them, campaigning for their solutions, and in some cases fully or partially solving them.[7]

Social movements arise when some people become dissatisfied with a particular social condition and feel that it can and should be changed. The members of the movement, however scattered they may be, begin to act collectively in a conscious way, typically by forming an organization or several related organizations to achieve their objectives. Most would-be movements are unsuccessful; they never number more than a handful of people, make little or no impact on public perceptions, and eventually disappear. Other movements attract mass membership, capture public attention through their campaigns, persuade a significant part of the population that their viewpoint is correct, propose specific programs for change, and participate in solving the problem.

A number of sociologists have pointed out that social problems and social movements have an intertwined "natural history" or "life cycle," in which each influences developments in the other. Analyzing the relationship between several social problems and the social movements that arose to confront them, Malcolm Spector

[6]*Op. cit.*

[7]See Armand L. Mauss and Julie Camile Wolfe (eds.), *This Land of Promises: The Rise and Fall of Social Problems in America* (Philadelphia: Lippincott, 1977).

and John Kitsuse conclude that there are four basic stages through which the "life cycle" typically passes—assuming the movement lasts long enough to complete the cycle.[8]

The first stage is *agitation*, in which the new movement tries to transform "private troubles into public issues" by arousing public opinion. In most cases these efforts are unsuccessful. There are many possible reasons for failure. The movement's complaints may be demonstrably false. The movement itself may be composed of people too powerless to make much public impact. Or it may use counterproductive tactics that offend rather than persuade. And, of course, it may face opposition from a more powerful movement and be overwhelmed in the competition for support.

The second stage is *legitimation and cooptation*. The life cycle of both the movement and the problem changes when government or other established authorities are forced by the increasing success of a social movement to accept the legitimacy of its claims. At this point the movement becomes respectable: its members, who might previously have been regarded as cranks or subversives, are now seen as responsible reformers. Government and other institutions begin to coopt, or absorb, the movement's policies and sometimes its leading members—apparently on the principle that "if you can't beat them, get them to join you." Thus, when the civil rights movement became a national force, government commissions and agencies invited its leaders to participate in their policy planning. Similarly, corporations have now recognized the legitimacy of the women's movement and are hastily inviting prominent women to join their boards of directors, at least in token numbers. The principal effect of this cooptation is that government and other established organizations take control of the handling of the problem. How they actually deal with it varies from one situation to another. They may "cool out" issues, for example, by deliberately or unintentionally

allowing them to become bogged down in committees, commissions, conferences, and token reforms, until the problem recedes from public attention; or they may take direct and effective action to confront and perhaps solve the problem.

The third stage is *bureaucratization* and *reaction*. A characteristic of large organizations such as government departments is that they become more engrossed in day-to-day administrative problems than in the long-range task of reaching the goals they were originally set up to achieve. Yet failure to deal with the problem rarely leads to the dissolution of the agency responsible for solving it. In fact, even though the problem may remain virtually unchanged, or get worse, the agency may prosper and grow, demanding still more funds and more officials on the grounds that its lack of impact on the problem is due to inadequate staff and budget. Gradually, the organization comes to focus less on solving the problem and more on dealing with complaints about its failure to do so.

The fourth stage is the *reemergence of the movement*. At this point, awareness of the initial problem is rekindled, but this time it is coupled with dissatisfaction over existing policies and programs. The original movement may regroup and launch renewed campaigns, or there may arise new movements promoted by people who see themselves as the victims of bureaucratic bungling. Thus, even though some changes will have been made as a result of the campaigns of the original social movement, the problem may be only partially solved, and dissatisfaction may persist. (See Figure 1.1).

An understanding of the role of social movements and of the difficulties they face is important for two reasons. First, it enables us to see how, through collective social action, people can change their society. Second, it enables us to see some of the difficulties involved in the task of alleviating social problems, and to appreciate why they are never quickly solved, no matter what the urgency. Throughout this book we shall refer to the efforts of social movements to define and confront social problems, and in the epilogue we shall discuss more fully the difficulties of solving them.

[8]Malcolm Spector and John I. Kitsuse, "*Social Problems: A Reformulation,*" *Social Problems,* 21 (1973), 145–149, and *Constructing Social Problems* (Menlo Park, Calif.: Cummings, 1977).

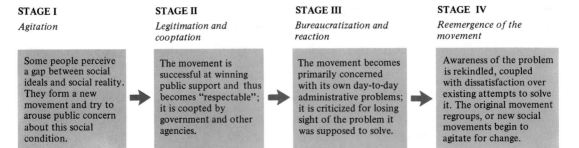

STAGE I	STAGE II	STAGE III	STAGE IV
Agitation	*Legitimation and cooptation*	*Bureaucratization and reaction*	*Reemergence of the movement*
Some people perceive a gap between social ideals and social reality. They form a new movement and try to arouse public concern about this social condition.	The movement is successful at winning public support and thus becomes "respectable"; it is coopted by government and other agencies.	The movement becomes primarily concerned with its own day-to-day administrative problems; it is criticized for losing sight of the problem it was supposed to solve.	Awareness of the problem is rekindled, coupled with dissatisfaction over existing attempts to solve it. The original movement regroups, or new social movements begin to agitate for change.

FIGURE 1.1 **The life cycle of social movements and social problems.** Social problems and the social movements that arise to solve them usually have an intertwined history, or "life cycle," because developments in one influence developments in the other. This chart shows a fairly typical "life cycle," although of course many variations are possible. The most common departure from the model is for fledgling social movements to die out at an early stage from lack of public support.

SOCIAL PROBLEMS: THEORY AND RESEARCH

Like all sciences, sociology consists of two inter-related elements, theory and research. Both are essential to the sociological enterprise. Theory without research may become little more than abstract speculation, unrelated to the real world. Research without theory can produce a collection of facts that are meaningless, for they cannot be interpreted. We will look first at the theoretical tools sociologists use to analyze social problems, and then at the basic methods of social-problems research.

THEORIES OF SOCIAL PROBLEMS

A *theory* is a statement that explains a relationship between facts or concepts. Suppose that students who use heroin tend to drop out of college. A theory attempts to explain the relationship between the fact of heroin use and the fact of dropping out of college. If the theory is a sound one, it can do more than explain why particular heroin-using students drop out: it can be generalized to other cases and can be used to predict that the same basic relationship will always exist under the same conditions. Different sociologists, of course, may come up with different theories to explain a relationship between facts. One may theorize that students who

use heroin are so affected by the drug that they lose interest in college; another may theorize that they have to leave college to earn the money to support their habit; another may theorize that both factors, and/or other factors, are responsible. A theory that has not been confirmed by research is called a *hypothesis*. Further research aimed at getting the relevant facts will confirm or disprove the hypothesis.

Some sociological theories are narrow in scope and are statements about very specific issues, such as the relationship between suicide rates and place of residence or heroin use and dropping out of college. Others are more abstract and serve to orient the sociologist in terms of a general approach to an entire range of issues. Different theoretical approaches throw different light on the same problem, and it is often fruitful to use several of them in combination. Sociologists who analyze social problems usually use one or more of the following: the functionalist approach, the conflict approach, or the deviance approach.

The Functionalist Approach

Herbert Spencer (1820–1903), one of the founders of sociology, developed a theory about society that may strike us a bit far-fetched today: he compared societies to living organisms. Spencer pointed out that the various organs of an animal, such as the heart, brain, liver, and lungs, are all interdependent—each has its own job to do, but together they ensure the survival of the organism itself. In the same way, he argued, the various parts of a society, such as the state, the economy, or the family, are also interdependent and contribute to the survival of the society. Emile Durkheim used this idea in his own social analysis, although he did not press the analogy between societies and living organisms. His basic approach to any feature of society, such as the existence of religion or education, was to ask what *function*, or effect, it had in maintaining the social system as a whole. Religion, he concluded, has the function of cementing society by providing shared moral beliefs; education has the function of ensuring social continuity by passing down cultural knowledge from one generation to the next.

Durkheim's approach was adopted by the American sociologist Talcott Parsons[9] and became highly influential, particularly during the 1940s and 1950s. Parsons argued that every society has a structure consisting of interrelated parts, such as insititutions, statuses, roles, and norms, and that each of these has a function in maintaining the stability of the society as a whole. Under ideal conditions, he claimed, society has a tendency to be in balance, or equilibrium, with its various elements smoothly organized into a stable system. The society works because all the parts fit together and serve their functions. This "structural functionalist" approach is generally referred to as *functionalism.*

How do social problems arise in this stable, self-regulating, organized system? Mainly through some parts of the system becoming *dysfunctional* in certain respects, that is, coming to have negative rather than positive effects elsewhere in the society.[10] For example, rapid industrialization has been functional for American society because it has generated the huge wealth on which our way of life depends. But it has also been dysfunctional in its pollution of the environment and its depletion of natural resources, with such adverse effects on other parts of society that a social problem has resulted. When some part of society becomes dysfunctional in this way, the social equilibrium is upset. The result is *social disorganization*, a situation in which society is imperfectly organized to maintain its stability and achieve its goals.

There can be many reasons for social disorganization. Most frequently, however, its underlying cause is social change, particularly rapid change. Changes in any one part of the system disrupt the equilibrium and must be compensated for by changes elsewhere in the system. Often these compensating adjustments do not take place fast enough, and the society becomes disorganized as a result.

Dramatic examples of this kind of social disorganization are found in some developing nations, where modern technology has made the once functional culture, norms, statuses, roles, institutions, and socialization processes of these previously "primitive" societies hopelessly outmoded. Population numbers soar as modern medicine and sanitation reduce the death rate; shantytowns spring up as farmers are lured to urban areas by the promise of new jobs in industry; folkways and mores that once regulated community life are abandoned but are not satisfactorily replaced; power shifts from one group to another as traditional political institutions are overturned, often by revolutions or coups d'état. The pace of social change is uneven, resulting in what William Ogburn calls *culture lag*, the tendency for a society to be disorganized because some of its parts have not "caught up" with changes elsewhere.[11]

American society, too, is vulnerable to disorganization caused by rapid social change. One

[9]Talcott Parsons, *The Structure of Social Action* (New York: McGraw-Hill, 1937); and *The Social System* (Glencoe, Ill.: Free Press, 1951).

[10]Robert K. Merton, *Social Theory and Social Structure*, 2nd rev. ed. (New York: Free Press, 1968); see, also, Mark Abrahamson, *Functionalism* (Englewood Cliffs, N.J.: Prentice-Hall, 1978).

[11]William F. Ogburn, *Social Change* (New York: Viking, 1950).

reason is that the society is a highly complex structure in which change in one area can have multiple effects in other interdependent areas. A second reason is that the society is changing at a rate probably unprecedented in human history. In the traditional societies of the past, social change was slow, and people expected their children to live much the same lives as their own grandparents had. The Industrial Revolution shattered this expectation. Today we take constant social change for granted and expect that our children will live in a world very different from our own, one that would have been unimaginable to our grandparents. According to the anthropologist Margaret Mead, the speed of social change is now so great that, in a sense, our parents have no children and our children no parents: the discontinuity between the cultures into which each generation is born is so extreme that they live in what are virtually different worlds.[12]

A functionalist analysis of social problems is thus based on the following assumptions: (1) Ideally, a society is a stable, well-organized system in which each part has a useful function in maintaining social stability; (2) Largely as a result of social change, the system is thrown out of balance and into disorganization, with some of its parts having negative or dysfunctional effects on some other parts of society or on the society as a whole; (3) Efforts to solve social problems must therefore focus on organizing society effectively once more.

As you will see in later chapters, this approach is often useful for the understanding of social problems. A major criticism of functionalism, however, is that it tends in practice to be inherently conservative. Because of their focus on social stability, functionalists may be tempted to dismiss changes (or demands for changes) as unwelcome disruptions, even if those changes would be necessary and beneficial in the long run. In solving social problems, too, there may be a tendency for the functionalists to confuse the task of reorganizing society with the task of reorganizing the way it was—in other words, to

try to restore the equilibrium of the status quo rather than trying to arrive at a new and different equilibrium. The emphasis on what is functional to society as a whole may also lead the sociologist to neglect an important possibility: that something which has an overall functional effect may be highly dysfunctional to particular groups within society.

The Conflict Approach

Writing over a century ago, Karl Marx (1818–1883) declared, "The history of all hitherto existing societies is the history of class conflict."[13] Every society, he argued, is divided into two or more social classes, one of which dominates and exploits the others economically. The dominant class is able to translate its economic power into social and political power as well, thus enabling itself to maintain its position and protect its interests. The social and cultural arrangements of any society therefore reflect the interests of the ruling class, and social problems such as poverty and discrimination can be understood in this light. While few Western sociologists accept that virtually every social problem can be reduced to a conflict between classes, many find a kernel of truth in Marx's view. To understand why some social problems arise and persist, they argue, we have to ask an important question: Who benefits?

The *conflict* approach emphasizes the struggles between different groups as a permanent feature of social life and an important source of change. "Conflict" does not necessarily imply outright violence, nor is it restricted to conflict between classes. It includes both disagreement over values and competition for scarce resources such as power, wealth, or prestige. It can involve any groups that feel they have interests to maintain or defend—rich versus poor, old versus young, black versus white, students versus faculty, manufacturers versus consumers, city dwellers versus suburbanites, and so on. On any social issue, some groups stand to gain and some

---

[12]Margaret Mead, *Culture and Commitment* (New York: Natural History Press, 1970).

[13]See Tom Bottomore and Maxmilian Rubel (eds.), *Karl Marx, Selected Writings in Sociology and Social Philosophy* (Baltimore, Md.: Penguin, 1964).

stand to lose. A certain measure of conflict between these groups is inevitable, but the outcome will always favor the stronger group.

Thus conflict theorists see many social problems as created and perpetuated by the actions of interest groups working for their own advantage. To fully understand the problem of pollution, for example, we must recognize that powerful corporations earn large profits from manufacturing processes that harm the environment, and that in the name of their financial interests, these corporations use their influence to prevent or delay effective but costly antipollution control. To understand why millions of Americans live below the poverty line while millionaires can use legal loopholes to avoid paying any taxes, we must recognize that the wealthy have far more influence over government economic policy than the poor. To understand why health services are so expensive and so unequally distributed, we must recognize that physicians, through the powerful American Medical Association, have fought for many years to prevent reforms that would benefit the public but might harm their own perceived interests.

In a small, traditional society there is usually a strong consensus on values: people live very similar lives and share the same beliefs and interests, so the potential for conflict is limited. But in a vast, heterogeneous society such as the United States, with its wide spectrum of opinions, occupations, life styles, classes, subcultures, and minorities, the potential for conflict over values and interests is much greater. And different groups may not only take a different view of the same problem: they may also have different problems. To complicate matters, the United States is a highly unequal society, and the relative few who occupy powerful statuses exert much more influence than others in defining norms and values, in determining which social problems get priority, and in deciding how they should be solved. The positions of power in American society are those at or near the top of the hierarchy in politics, the mass media, corporations, and government bureaucracies. Such positions are generally held by wealthy, white, male, middle-aged, Protestants of Anglo-Saxon background. These people do not necessarily act

as a "conspiracy," but like any other group, they tend to take their own values for granted and to promote their own interests. For this reason, our social arrangements are more likely to benefit them than people who are nonwhite, female, old, Catholic, of Mexican background, or poor.

Thus a conflict analysis of social problems is based on the following assumptions: (1) Different groups have different values and interests to defend. In the attendant conflict, success for one group may become a problem for another; (2) Efforts to solve social problems must therefore include attempts by disadvantaged groups to wrest changes from those in power; (3) A certain amount of conflict can be beneficial to society, because it acts as a stimulus for necessary social changes.

Conflict theorists reject the functionalist idea that society is normally a stable, well-organized system in which each part serves to maintain social order. Instead, they see society as an arena of constant conflict and change, in which something that is "functional" for one group may be "dysfunctional" for another. In turn, an important criticism of the conflict approach is that it is too narrowly focused: by emphasizing the more politically controversial aspects of society, it tends to overlook other possible sources of social problems.

The Deviance Approach

From a sociological point of view, *deviance* is any behavior that violates important social norms and consequently is negatively valued by large numbers of people. Various forms of deviance, such as prostitution and crime, become social problems because most of the population regards these behaviors as repugnant or threatening—an affront to their values or a danger to social order. In small, traditional communities, deviance occurs fairly infrequently: people are socialized into similar values and norms and tend to abide by them unquestioningly. In a heterogeneous modern society, however, deviance may be much more common. People in different subcultures are socialized into different and even contrasting value systems, and what seems normal behavior to one group (such as lower-class juveniles in search of "kicks") may be regarded as deviant by the dominant culture.

Earlier in the century, sociologists tended to blame deviants for most social problems. They assumed that deviance is an intrinsic characteristic of the deviants themselves—that there is something "wrong" with them. This notion, which is still widely shared by the public, is a rather ethnocentric one; that is, it takes the values and norms of middle-class America for granted and then views any deviation from them as sick, wicked, or immoral. The difficulty with this attitude, of course, is that behavior which seems deviant in one time or place may seem perfectly normal, acceptable, and appropriate in another. Accordingly, most sociologists are careful to use the term "deviant" in a strictly neutral way to refer to behavior that does not conform to specified social norms, usually (but not necessarily) those of the dominant culture. Applied in this way, the word does not carry any moral judgment.

In analyzing deviant behavior, sociologists often make use of either of two explanations of deviance—one influenced by the functionalist approach, the other by the conflict approach. Robert Merton, a leading functionalist, explains deviance in terms of what he calls *anomie*, a situation in which social norms cease to be meaningful or effective.[14] Since people in such a state are no longer guided by these norms,

---

[14]Robert K. Merton, "Social Structure and Anomie," *American Sociological Review*, 3 (1938), 672–682.

Some form of social conflict is involved in all social problems, for there is always controversy over the nature, causes, and solutions of the problems. But according to conflict theorists, these social tensions may have a beneficial result: the campaigns of and competition between opposing interests can lead to needed change.

their behavior may become deviant. In Merton's view, deviance results from a specific form of social disorganization—a discrepancy between socially approved goals and the availability of socially approved means of achieving them. For example, in the United States there is a socially approved goal of becoming rich. But socially approved means of becoming rich (such as high-paying jobs) are not available to everyone. If some people value the goal but lack approved means to achieve it, they may pursue the goal by socially disapproved means—such as stealing. Similarly, sexual satisfaction is an approved social goal in American society, but the socially approved means of achieving it (within marriage) is not available to everyone. Some people may therefore seek the goal through disapproved, deviant means, such as prostitution. The cause of deviance is thus located primarily in the structure of society itself: by denying certain categories of the population access to approved means of achieving approved goals, society exerts pressure on them to deviate.

Howard Becker, a sociologist influenced by the conflict approach, explains deviance in terms of what he calls *labeling*, the process by which some people successfully apply to others the label "deviant."[15] In this view, there is no such thing as deviance per se, because everyone is deviant from the viewpoint of someone else: the deviant is merely someone to whom others have attached a label such as "whore," "weirdo," "crook," or "nut." In any conflict among groups over norms and values, it is the stronger group, not the weaker, that has the power to make the label "deviant" stick. The dominant culture's view of marijuana use is that it is a social problem caused by deviant drug users. From the point of view of marijuana smokers, the problem is that other people have successfully labeled them as a problem. Similarly, pornography is usually defined as a social problem arising out of sexual deviance, but from the viewpoint of the pornographers and their customers the problem is that other people are imposing their values on them.

In some sense at least, then, a deviant is the victim of a conflict of values; if individuals who are regarded as deviants had greater power, they would be considered "normal" and their accusers would be labeled "deviant."

The deviance approach to social problems is thus based on the following assumptions: (1) Most people conform to social norms most of the time, but some people violate important norms; (2) Such a violation is regarded by the rest of society as a social problem because it offends the values of the dominant culture and disrupts normal social expectations; (3) Efforts to solve social problems caused by deviance must therefore focus either on discouraging the deviance (for example, by providing deterrents to crime), or by redefining the behavior so that it is no longer regarded as deviant (for example, by decriminalizing marijuana use).

The anomie explanation has the advantage of showing why some forms of deviance occur, but it is open to the criticism that it ignores the process by which certain people are defined as deviant by others. The labeling explanation has the virtue of illuminating this process, but it does not explain why people should violate social norms even before they are labeled by others. The labeling explanation is also criticized for encouraging an indiscriminate sympathy for the underdog as the victim of labeling by the powerful. Although this victimization may exist in some cases of deviant behavior, certain forms of deviance (such as crime and violence) are so disruptive that they do present serious social problems, and the extreme relativism of labeling theory may obscure this fact. In addition, many social problems cannot be usefully analyzed from the deviance approach. This is the case, for example, with overpopulation in traditional societies, which results from conformity to, not deviation from, the large-family norm of these societies.

The functionalist, conflict, and deviance approaches all start from different assumptions and ask different questions. But this does not necessarily mean that they are always contradictory. Rather, they focus on different aspects of social reality, and they can often be used in combination to increase our understanding of social

---

[15]Howard S. Becker, *Outsiders: Studies in the Sociology of Deviance* (New York: Free Press, 1963).

problems. As we look at specific social problems in later chapters, we shall often use more than one approach to analyze them. Table 1.1 summarizes the three approaches.

Table 1.1   Theoretical Approaches to Social Problems: A Comparison

	Functionalist Approach	Conflict Approach	Deviance Approach
Basic Assumptions	Ideally, society is a stable, well-organized system in which each part functions to maintain social equilibrium, or balance.	Society is an arena of tension, disagreements, and other conflicts over the different values and interests of various social groups.	Society is for the most part orderly because most people follow most social norms most of the time. Yet some important norms are sometimes violated.
Source of Social Problems	Largely as a result of uneven social change, the system is thrown out of balance and into social disorganization. Some part of the system is thus dysfunctional rather than functional.	Powerful groups are able to ensure that social arrangements reflect their own interests and values, but inequality and injustice may result. Success for one group may be a problem for another.	Through such social processes as anomie or labeling, some people learn deviant behavior. This behavior becomes problematic because it disrupts social life.
Solutions to Social Problems	The necessary adjustments must be made to the social system to bring it into equilibrium once more, thus eliminating the dysfunctional effects of social disorganization.	Disadvantaged groups must form social movements or make other attempts to apply power and bring about social change. Conflict can thus be beneficial for society.	Either the deviant behavior must be discouraged, or the behavior must be socially redefined so that it is no longer regarded as deviant.
Criticisms	There is a risk that functionalist analysis may be inherently conservative: the focus on social stability may blind the analyst to the need for change, even if change is disruptive.	Conflict analysis is narrowly conceived: it focuses only on more politically controversial aspects of social problems and overlooks other potential sources and solutions.	The deviance approach has limited applicability, because many problems do not involve deviant behavior at all. Also, there is no universally accepted theory of deviant behavior.

RESEARCH ON SOCIAL PROBLEMS

Sociological research aims at finding out what is happening in the social world and why. It is only through this research that we can gain an accurate picture of specific problems. Certainly such a picture cannot be based on people's personal beliefs and impressions. Each of us sees only a tiny part of the social world, and each of us is exposed to a limited number of interpretations of the things we see. These personal impressions cannot be generalized to apply to the entire society, for they are sometimes biased, wildly inaccurate, or influenced by beliefs that are nothing more than myths. For example, many people believe that a high proportion of welfare recipients could work if they really wanted to. But research shows that less than 2 percent of people on welfare are employable able-bodied males; most recipients are aged, children, or mothers with young children. Many people believe that pornography encourages sex crimes. But research shows that convicted sex offenders tend to have had much less exposure to pornography than nonoffenders. Many people believe that a child's scholastic performance is strongly influenced by the amount of money spent on school facilities. But research shows that expenditure on facilities has little influence; what matters most is the family and social-class background of the child. "Commonsense" beliefs about social problems cannot be taken for granted. They must be tested by research.

In many cases sociological research involves merely tracking down facts that are already available—in historical documents, in government reports and other official sources of data, or in the published findings of sociology and related fields. Frequently, however, the facts are unavailable and will have to be discovered by one of three methods. Each method has its advantages and disadvantages, and each is more appropriate for some issues than for others. Often all three can be applied to the same problem, for like the theoretical approaches, they are not necessarily mutually exclusive. The three research methods used by sociologists are the case study, the survey, and the experiment.

The Case Study

A *case study* is an intensive examination of a particular social phenomenon—a riot, gang behavior, life in a mental hospital, and so forth. The researcher carefully studies the subject, often as a participant-observer who takes part in the life of the group under study and keeps detailed records of significant trends and events. The researcher then analyzes the data and draws conclusions that may help in understanding similar cases.

William Chambliss conducted a case study of two juvenile gangs in the same town, the lower-class Roughnecks and the middle-class Saints.[16] The Roughnecks were constantly in trouble with the police, whereas the Saints had clean records and were regarded by the community as good, if high-spirited, adolescents. Yet Chambliss found that the Saints took part in as much delinquent behavior as the Roughnecks. They were able to get away with their mischief partly because they had access to cars and could commit their delinquent acts out of view of the community; and if they were caught, they behaved contritely and were let off with a warning. The Roughnecks, on the other hand, "hung out" around the center of town, where their behavior was more easily observed. When they were caught, they antagonized the police by their resentful manner, and so were frequently arrested.

As a result of different public perceptions, only one of two delinquent gangs was designated "delinquent"—a label that had a powerful influence over the later careers of the gang members. The findings of this case study are supported by a great deal of other evidence suggesting that, contrary to popular belief, lower-class youths do not commit more delinquent acts than middle-class youths; they are simply more likely than middle-class youths to be arrested and convicted (see Chapter 13, "Crime and Violence").

The case-study method can provide rich insights and "real life" information that other methods may overlook. But because it relies heavily on the skills and interpretations of the researcher, the case study may be distorted by a

---

[16]William J. Chambliss, "The Saints and the Roughnecks," *Society*, 11 (1973) 24–31.

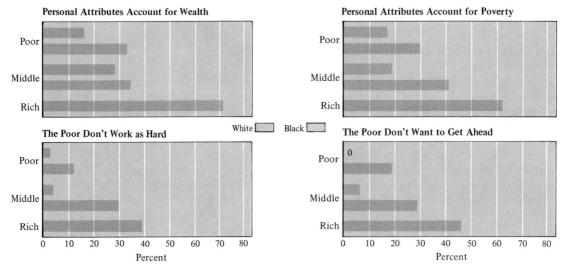

Personal Attributes Account for Wealth

Poor

Middle

Rich

The Poor Don't Work as Hard

Poor

Middle

Rich

0 10 20 30 40 50 60 70 80
Percent

Personal Attributes Account for Poverty

Poor

Middle

Rich

White ▢ Black ▢

The Poor Don't Want to Get Ahead

Poor 0

Middle

Rich

0 10 20 30 40 50 60 70 80
Percent

FIGURE 1.2 **Beliefs about personal attributes as a cause of income (in percent).** Why are some people rich and others poor? As this chart shows, there are widely differing beliefs about the answer to this question—with the rich and the poor not only holding different opinions on the subject, but also taking the viewpoint that best supports their own interest.

Like most people, the respondents in this survey tend to see the world from the narrow vantage point of their own social status and so have quite different ideas about the causes of poverty.
Joan H. Rytina et al., "Income and Stratification Ideology", *American Journal of Sociology* 75, January 1970, 703–716.

researcher's conscious or unconscious bias. Another disadvantage of the method is that the findings of a single case study are an inadequate basis for proving anything about the subject matter in general. The case may have been exceptional in some unknown way, and generalizations to apparently similar cases may be invalid.

The Survey

A *survey* is a method of discovering facts or opinions by putting questions to members of a population. The "population" may consist of any social category—American women, citizens of Dallas, triplets born between 1950 and 1955, lawyers with incomes of over $50,000, or the entire nation. It is often impractical and unnecessary to survey every single member of such a population, so the questions are usually asked of a small sample drawn randomly from the entire category. Provided that those sampled members are fully representative of the entire category, the responses can be generalized to the population as a whole. A properly chosen sample of 3,000 voters can be used to predict a presidential

election result to within a couple of percentage points of the final outcome, but a poorly chosen sample of 3,000,000 voters could produce a hopelessly inaccurate prediction.

In one survey (Figure 1.2), Joan Rytina and her colleagues tried to find out what beliefs people in various income groups have about poverty. When the richest group in their survey was asked to agree or disagree with the statement "The poor don't get ahead," 46 percent of them agreed. But when poor whites were asked the same question, only 19 percent agreed, and when poor blacks were asked, none of them agreed. Some 39 percent of the richest group felt that "the poor don't work as hard," whereas only 13 percent of poor whites and only 3 percent of poor blacks agreed with the statement. An overwhelming 72 percent of the richest group felt that "personal attributes account for wealth," but only 34 percent of the poor whites and only 17 percent of the poor blacks agreed.[17] This

[17]Joan H. Rytina *et al.*, "Income and Stratification Ideology," *American Journal of Sociology* 75 (January 1970), 703–716.

study convincingly demonstrates the sociological principle outlined earlier in this chapter: people in different social positions will tend to see the same problem quite differently, and usually in accordance with their own interests. The findings of the survey also imply that the rich and the poor might take very different views on how to go about solving the problem of poverty.

Surveys are also useful for tracing changes in public attitudes over time. A 1968 survey of blacks in large Northeastern and Midwestern cities, conducted by the Survey Research Center of Michigan University, found that 46 percent of the subjects believed that there would "always be a lot of racial prejudice and discrimination in the United States." When the New York Times–CBS poll asked the same question of a similar group in 1978, the proportion agreeing with the statement had actually risen, to 53 percent. This finding may seem surprising in the light of the many recent improvements in the status of black Americans. What has happened, it seems, is that improvement in race relations has slowed since the sixties, while black hopes and expectations have continued to rise. From the point of view of blacks, the gap between social ideals and social reality remains. Surveys can also be used to test the public response to proposed solutions to social problems. Recent opinion polls show that a majority of Americans favor school integration, but that an even larger majority opposes busing, which is probably the only way of achieving school integration. This apparently contradictory finding obviously presents a problem to policy-makers, but at least they are aware of public opinion on the issue (see Chapter 8, "Race and Ethnic Relations").

The survey is not as useful as the case study for penetrating analyses of social problems, and it can often be expensive to conduct. There are also many difficulties involved in obtaining an accurate survey. For example, some people might refuse to answer questions, some might fail to understand them, and some might not tell the truth. Any such flaws can bias the findings. The method is, however, a vital source of information on social characteristics and opinions, and is especially useful for measuring social trends over time.

The Experiment

The *experiment* is a carefully controlled method for tracing the influence of one variable on another. A *variable* is simply any characteristic that can differ across time or space or from one individual or group to another: for example, social class, age, a sense of humor, suicide rates, hair color, or prejudice. Suppose a researcher wants to trace the influence of one variable, TV violence, on another variable, agressive behavior in children. The researcher could assemble two groups of children who are similar in all relevant respects, such as age, sex, social class, and so on. One group, the "experimental" group, would then be exposed to TV violence, while the other group, the "control" group, would not. The level of aggression in each group would then be measured, and if the experimental group's proved significantly higher than the control group's, the researcher could conclude that the TV violence was responsible. The researcher could then publish these findings with a full account of the methods used, so that other researchers could attempt to replicate the study—that is, repeat it to see if they get the same results.

The experimental method is often useful in social-problems research. Robert Rosenthal wanted to test the influence of one variable, teacher expectations, on another variable, pupil achievement.[18] Would pupils do better in school merely because their teachers expected that they would? To find out, Rosenthal told teachers in one school that he had developed a test that would predict future "spurts" in children's achievement. He tested the children and then gave the teachers a list of those who were likely to "spurt ahead" in the coming year, with instructions that this information should not be revealed to anyone. In fact, the test was a fake that could make no predictions whatever; the likely "spurters" had been selected at random. There were thus two groups of children in the school, the experimental group of "spurters" of

[18]Robert Rosenthal and Leonore Jacobson, *Pygmalion in the Classroom: Teacher Expectation and Pupils' Intellectual Development* (New York: Holt, Rinehart and Winston, 1968).

whom the teachers now had high expectations, and the control group consisting of the rest of the children. A year later, Rosenthal found that there actually were significant academic gains among the "spurters," showing that teacher expectations had subtly influenced performance. This finding was important, since other research has shown that teachers generally have higher expectations of middle-class children than lower-class children.

Rosenthal's study aroused a great deal of interest, and several other researchers have attempted to replicate it. Their results have been mixed, however, and in most cases the "self-fulfilling prophecy" that Rosenthal discovered did not occur.[19] The reasons for the failure are not clear. It might be, for example, that there were flaws in Rosenthal's original experiment; or it might be that teachers in later experiments have guessed that *they* are the real subjects and have not allowed the prophecy about academic "spurts" to influence them. Research on the issue is continuing, but the attempts to replicate the study do illustrate the scientific nature of the enterprise—the determination not to take anything for granted but rather to uncover facts and test theories through rigorous research.

The experimental method is especially valuable because it allows a carefully controlled scientific analysis of problems that may be difficult to study in everyday life, where so many

other influences can distort the processes involved. But the method is useful only for rather narrowly defined issues involving a small number of variables, and there is always the possibility that people may behave differently in the real world than they do in the laboratory or other carefully controlled experimental environments.

THE PROBLEM OF BIAS

If everyone saw the world in exactly the same way, there would be no disagreement about social problems. But as we have seen, people interpret the world from the viewpoint of their own subculture, norms, and values, and can thus reach radically different conclusions about the same phenomenon. Sociologists are perhaps more aware of this problem of bias than others, for they are trained to recognize the relativity of values and to be as objective as possible. Ironically, this critical detachment often leads to charges of bias when the sociologist's findings do not support the interests of the dominant culture. Howard Becker speaks of a "hierarchy of credibility":

> We provoke the suspicion that we are biased in favor of the subordinate parties . . . when we tell the story from their point of view. . . . We provoke this charge when we assume, for the purposes of our research, that subordinates have as much right to be heard as superordinates, that they are as likely to be telling the truth as they see it as superordinates, that what they say about the situation has a right to be investigated and have its truth or falsity established, even though responsible officials assure us that it is unnecessary because the charges are false.
> We can use the notion of a *hierarchy of credibility* to understand this phenomenon. In any system of ranked groups, participants take it as given that members of the highest group have the right to define things the way they really are. . . . Therefore, from the point of view of the well-socialized participant in the system, any tale told by those at the top intrinsically deserves to be regarded as the most credible account obtainable. . . . We are, if we are proper members of the group, morally bound to accept the definition imposed on reality

[19]See, for example, Ray C. Rist, "Student Social Class and Teacher Expectations: The Self-Fulfilling Prophecy in Ghetto Education," *Harvard Education Review*, 40 (August 1970), 411–451; Robert L. Thorndike, "Review of *Pygmalion in the Classroom*," *American Educational Research Journal*, 5 (November 1968), 708–711; Robert Rosenthal, "Empirical Versus Decreed Validation of Clocks and Tests," *American Educational Research Journal*, 6 (November 1969), 689–691; William J. Gephart, "Will the Real Pygmalion Please Stand Up?" *American Educational Research Journal*, 7 (May 1970), 473–474; Theodore Barber *et al.*, "Five Attempts to Replicate the Experimenter Bias Effect," *Journal of Consulting and Clinical Psychology*, 3 (February 1969), 1–6; Theodore Brameld, "Education as Self-Fulfilling Prophecy," *Phi Delta Kappan*, September 1972, pp. 8–11, 58–61; and John W. Ritchie, "The Magic Feather: Education and the Power of Positive Thinking," *Teachers College Record*, 78 (May 1978), 477–486.

by a superordinate group in preference to the definitions espoused by subordinates.[20]

In applying theories and research methods, sociologists must, in fact, deal with the problem of their own biases. Like everyone else, their values are influenced by the time and place in which they happen to live; sociologists are not exempt from socialization.

To what degree can the sociologist avoid unconscious bias? There is no general consensus among sociologists on this question other than their acknowledgment that absolute objectivity is impossible. No matter how scrupulously unbiased the sociologist tries to be, some unconscious values and assumptions are bound to intrude into research and theory. Personal values might determine, for example, what subjects the sociologist chooses to investigate, which theoretical approaches are used to analyze them, and how the findings are interpreted. Indeed, some sociologists argue that they should make no attempt to eliminate bias, that they should instead make definite value judgments and conduct research in accordance with their personal values and social commitments. The majority of sociologists probably reject this view and consider that research will be guarded against gross distortions of reality by adherence to three basic rules: (1) make every effort to be aware of personal biases and to exclude them from research; (2) distinguish between fact and opinion in research; and (3) make research methods, data, and findings available for the critical scrutiny of the profession and the public.

THE PLAN OF THIS BOOK

Of the many problems that American society faces, sixteen have been selected for analysis in this book. These particular problems have been chosen because on the basis of opinion polls, news-media coverage, and sociological writings, they appear to be of major concern to both the general public and sociologists. Each problem is discussed in a separate chapter.

To clarify your understanding of the problems, every chapter is structured according to the same basic format, consisting of three main sections. The first, "The Problem," is a brief statement about the problem at hand and is intended simply to orient you to the most basic issues involved. The second section, "Analyzing the Problem," is the main part of each chapter. It always opens by discussing the relevance of the functionalist, conflict, or deviance approach (or some combination of these) to the problem and then presents a detailed analysis of the most relevant facts, theories, and research. The third section, "Confronting the Problem," discusses possible solutions, including those that have been, or are being, attempted. Each chapter closes with a point-by-point summary for reviewing purposes, a glossary, and a list of suggestions for further reading. There is also a full glossary at the end of the book.

Although each problem is covered in a separate chapter, you will be able to trace common themes running throughout the book. One theme is the relevance of the conflict, functionalist, or deviance approaches to the understanding of social problems. A second is the role of social movements in identifying social problems, arousing public concern, and searching for solutions. A third is the interrelatedness of social problems—that is, the fact that different problems often have similar origins, and that any one problem often has implications for several others. A fourth theme is the frequent tendency of attempts at solving one problem to create other unforeseen problems. Finally, the epilogue discusses the process of solving social problems, using illustrations from earlier chapters to analyze some of the difficulties involved.

[20]Howard S. Becker, "Whose Side Are We On?" *Social Problems* (Winter 1967), 239–247.

SUMMARY

1. A social problem exists when a significant part of the population perceives an undesirable gap between social ideals and social realities and believes that this gap can be eliminated by collective action.

2. Sociology is the scientific study of human society. Although social problems may affect individuals, they are rooted in social conditions and must be studied sociologically.

3. Some basic sociological concepts are culture (the shared products of society); norms (informal rules that prescribe appropriate behavior); status (a position in society); role (the part played by a person in a particular status); institutions (the stable clusters of norms, statuses, and roles centered on some social need); socialization (the process by which people learn culture); and power (the ability to control the behavior of others, even without their consent).

4. Social movements play a vital part in defining and sometimes solving social problems. The problems and the movements may have an interlinked life cycle in which each influences developments in the other.

5. Theory is essential if social problems are to be interpreted. According to the functionalist ap-proach, society is a system in which, ideally, each part functions to maintain overall stability; but largely through social change the system can be thrown into social disorganization, with dysfunctional effects. The conflict approach emphasizes that competition among groups seeking their own interest is a source of social problems and of social change. The deviance approach sees some social problems as the result of behavior that violates important social norms and is negatively valued as a result. Two explanations of deviance are that it results from anomie or from labeling.

6. Research on social problems is essential to discover facts about social life. The case study is an intensive examination of a particular phenomenon. The survey is a device for questioning members of a population about their characteristics or opinions. The experiment is a carefully controlled procedure for tracing the influence of one variable on another. Each of these tools has its advantages and disadvantages.

7. Everybody has unconscious biases. Sociologists are more likely to provoke the charge of bias if they give credence to the views of low-status groups. By taking careful precautions, sociologists can minimize unconscious bias in their work.

GLOSSARY

Achieved status. A status that is gained by the individual at least partly through his or her own efforts or failings.

Anomie. A state in which social norms have ceased to be meaningful or effective, often resulting in deviant behavior.

Ascribed status. A status assigned to the individual by society on arbitrary grounds over which the individual has little or no control.

Case study. An intensive examination of a particular social phenomenon.

Conflict approach. A theoretical approach that emphasizes conflict among competing groups as an important influence on social and cultural arrangements and as a source of social change.

Culture. All the shared products of human society, comprising its total way of life.

Culture lag. The tendency for society to be disorganized because some of its parts have not adjusted to changes elsewhere in society.

Deviance. Any behavior that violates important social norms and is therefore negatively valued by large numbers of people.

Dysfunction. A negative effect that one element in a system has on the rest of the system or on some other part of the system.

Ethnocentrism. The tendency for members of one group to assume that their own values, attitudes, and norms are superior to those of other groups and to judge other groups accordingly.

Experiment. A carefully controlled method for tracing the influence of one variable on another.

Folkways. The ordinary customs and conventions of society; conformity to these norms is expected, but people are not morally outraged by violations of them.

Function. The effect that one element in a system has on the rest of the system or on some other part of the system.

Functionalism. A theoretical approach that sees society as an organized system, in which each part ideally has a useful function in maintaining social stability.

Hypothesis. A tentative theory that has not been confirmed by research.

Institution. A stable pattern of norms, statuses, and roles that centers on some social need.

Labeling. The social process by which some people successfully attach the label "deviant" to others.

Law. A formal rule that is backed by the power of the state.

Mores. Morally significant social norms, violations of which are considered a serious matter.

Norms. Formal or informal rules that prescribe the appropriate behavior in a given situation.

Power. The ability to control the behavior of others, even without their consent.

Role. The part that a person occupying a particular status plays in society.

Social disorganization. A situation in which society is imperfectly organized for the maintenance of social stability and the achievement of social goals.

Social movement. A large number of people who join together to initiate or to resist some social or cultural change.

Social problem. Whatever a significant part of the population perceives as an undesirable gap between social ideas and social realities and believes can be eliminated by collective action.

Social structure. The underlying pattern of social relationships in a society.

Socialization. The lifelong experience through which the individual acquires personality and learns the culture of the society.

Sociology. The scientific study of human society and social behavior.

Status. A position in society.

Subculture. A group that participates in the overall culture of a society but also has its own distinctive life styles and values.

Survey. A method of discovering facts or opinions by questioning members of a population.

Taboo. A powerful social prohibition against behavior that is considered loathsome or unthinkable.

Theory. A statement that explains a relationship between facts or concepts.

Values. Socially shared ideas about what is desirable, right, and proper.

Variable. Any characteristic that can differ across time or space or from one person to another.

FURTHER READING

BECKER, HOWARD S. *Outsiders: Studies in the Sociology of Deviance.* New York: Free Press, 1963. Becker presents a series of studies of different kinds of "deviance." In each case his analysis is based on the "labeling" theory—that deviance is not so much a characteristic of the people deemed deviant as a social process by which some individuals are labeled as deviant by others.

BERGER, PETER L. *Invitation to Sociology: A Humanistic Perspective.* New York: Doubleday, 1963. A short and elegantly written introduction to sociology, this work includes an absorbing analysis of what Berger calls "the sociological perspective."

CLINARD, MARCHALL B., and ROBERT F. MEIR. *The Sociology of Deviant Behavior.* 5th ed. New York: Holt, Rinehart and Winston, 1979. This text provides a comprehensive and detailed overview of social deviance.

EVANS, ROBERT R. (ed.). *Social Movements: A Reader and Source Book.* Chicago: Rand McNally, 1973. A useful selection of sociological articles on social movements in general and some social movements in particular.

FREEMAN, JO. *The Politics of Women's Liberation: A Case Study of an Emerging Social Movement and Its Relation to the Policy Process.* New York: David McKay, 1977. An insightful study of one social movement, from its origins to its later inclusion in government policy-making.

HOROWITZ, IRVING L. (ed.) *Society.* New Brunswick, N.J.: Transaction Inc., Rutgers: The State University. A useful periodical containing readable articles on a variety of sociological topics, including many social problems. It provides an up-to-date means of complementing texts and other course materials.

MEAD, MARGARET, *Culture and Commitment.* New York: Natural History Press, 1970. A famous anthropologist examines the impact of rapid cultural and technological change on modern society.

MERTON, ROBERT K., and ROBERT NISBET (eds.). *Contemporary Social Problems.* 4th ed. New York: Harcourt Brace Jovanovich, 1976. A sophisticated text that analyzes social problems as issues of either deviance or social disorganization. Merton's introductory chapter is the definitive statement of the functionalist approach to social problems.

MILLS, C. WRIGHT. *The Sociological Imagination.* New York: Oxford University Press, 1959. Writing from a conflict perspective, Mills analyzes the "sociological imagination" and elaborates the connection between "private troubles" and "public issues." The book includes a spirited critique of functionalism.

SKOLNICK, JEROME H., and ELLIOTT CURRIE (eds.). *Crisis in American Institutions.* 4th ed. Boston: Little, Brown, 1979. A collection of articles on social problems, written from the conflict perspective. The introduction provides a critical analysis of other approaches and an argument for the conflict approach.

SPECTOR, MALCOLM, and KITSUSE, JOHN I. *Constructing Social Problems.* Menlo Park, Calif.: Cummings, 1977. A study of the role of social movements in creating and defining social problems, with an analysis of the "life cycle" of problems and movements.

U.S. DEPARTMENT OF COMMERCE. *Statistical Abstract of the United States.* Published annually by the U.S. Bureau of the Census. Contains a great deal of easily accessible data on many aspects of American society and is a useful source for statistics on a variety of social problems.

WEINBERG, MARTIN S., and EARL RUBINGTON (eds.). *The Solution of Social Problems.* 2nd ed. New York: Oxford University Press, 1977. A selection of articles on solving social problems by writers using different theoretical approaches.

2
SOCIETY IN TRANSITION

Social change has always been a central focus of sociology; indeed, the discipline grew out of the attempts of nineteenth-century thinkers to understand the various changes that were disrupting their societies. Those changes were ushered in by industrialism, which is still the dominant social force in the modern world. Our preindustrial ancestors expected that their children would live much the same lives as their grandparents had lived; but in the modern industrial era, change is so rapid that we hardly dare speculate about the kind of world our children will inhabit.

We often think of change as "progress" toward something better, and this faith is certainly justified in many areas of life. Yet change can also bring wrenching dislocation to the social world. In this unit we explore problems brought about by change in the fields of population growth, environment and resources, work, and our cities.

2
Population

THE PROBLEM

In approximately the time it takes you to read this sentence, four people, three of them children, will die from the effects of malnutrition. According to the U.N. Food and Agriculture Organization, of the 4.2 billion people on earth, nearly half a billion are malnourished or undernourished and as a result, are currently dying at the rate of at least 10 million each year. The number of the underfed is rising, both in absolute terms and as a proportion of the total world population; and famines are expected to cause tens of millions of deaths annually before the end of the century. The problem is the growth in the human population: One out of every twenty people who have ever lived is alive today—and the population is expected to double within the next four decades. It is doubtful whether the planet has the resources to support such growth. If the present rate of increase were to be maintained, there would be a hundred people for every square yard of the earth's surface—including the oceans—within less than a thousand years. Obviously, the limited ability of the planet to support an indefinitely expanding human population will put a stop to growth long before that point.[1]

EFFECTS OF POPULATION GROWTH

Unchecked population growth in an environment of limited space and natural resources must inevitably lead to social disruption and human misery on a scale that we can scarcely imagine. But population growth also has many other indirect consequences, several of which we shall encounter in later chapters. In particular, overpopulation is implicated in the following social problems:

Health Problems. In a poor country, overpopulation means malnutrition for many or most of the inhabitants. Malnutrition has direct effects on the body and the mind, stunting physical growth, damaging the brain, and directly causing a number of diseases. It also lowers resistance to all other diseases. Overpopulation puts a strain on medical resources, because services are spread ever more thinly as population increases. A poor and overpopulated country may also be unable to maintain satisfactory standards of public hygiene and sanitation, so infectious diseases and epidemics spread more readily.

Ecological Problems. Human populations need raw materials to survive, yet all our natural resources—such as food, fibers, fuels, minerals, and fresh water—are limited in quantity. The habitable areas of the planet are also finite, and as populations increase, there will be more pressure on living space, more despoiling of the countryside, and more destruction of the habitats of other species. Moreover, the higher a society's standard of living, the more damage its members do to the environment as they consume ever more goods and dispose of ever more wastes. At present, only a minority of the world's population lives in the *developed countries*—the

[1]See *Current History* issue on population and food resources, vol. 68 (June 1975); Shirley F. Hartley, *Population Quantity versus Quality* (Englewood Cliffs, N.J.: Prentice-Hall, 1972); *Scientific American* issue on the human population, vol. 231, (September 1974); Jean Mayer, "The Dimensions of Human Hunger," *Scientific American* (September 1976) 40–49; *New York Times*, March 15, 1978, p. 6.

fully industrialized nations such as those of North America, Europe, and Japan. Yet the less industrialized, predominantly agricultural *developing countries* of Africa, Asia, and Latin America hope one day to achieve a level of industrialization comparable to our own. The ecological effects of an increasingly industrialized global population of many billions would be incalculable.

Economic Problems.   Whether the overpopulated developing countries will ever achieve the living standards of the developed nations is doubtful, because economic progress in these countries tends to be canceled out by the increased population, leaving the people no better off than before. Poorer countries may find it almost impossible to accumulate the investment capital they need to industrialize and improve living standards.

Political Problems.   In an age of rising expectations, a large poor population is a threat to political stability. People who are hungry, poorly clothed, and miserably housed are likely to be politically restless. Law and order too often come to look as though they have been designed to protect the interests of the rich—among nations as well as among individuals. Overpopulation can threaten conflict within and even between nations.

Educational Problems.   A fast-growing population contains a very high proportion of school-age children. The financial burden on a poor country of providing enough schools—let alone improving their quality—is almost insupportable. The result is that in many countries a majority of children simply do not go to school. Despite international campaigns against illiteracy in the past few decades, there are now more illiterate people in the world than at any time in history. As a result, millions of people are denied opportunities to fulfill their human potential.

Until fairly recently there was little public awareness of the consequences of rapid population growth. When writers of the 1950s and 1960s became convinced of the seriousness of the problem, they often adopted a "doomsday" approach to call attention to it. The titles of some of their books are suggestive: *Standing Room Only, Our Crowded Planet, The Challenge to Man's Future, The Population Bomb.*[2] The prophecies of these critics are bleak, typically employing mathematical logic—sometimes carried to the point of absurdity—to show the impossibility of indefinite population growth.

Isaac Asimov, for example, calculates that at the current rates of increase the total mass of the human population would equal the mass of the earth by the year 3530 and the mass of the entire universe by 6826.[3] What, he asks, are the outside limits of population that could possibly be reached? Since the limit of animal life depends on the availability of edible plant life, Asimov hypothesizes a situation in which the entire planet is occupied exclusively by humans and a single plant food—unicellular algae, which can be consumed in its entirety by human beings and, in turn, can feed on human wastes and finely chopped human corpses. Under these circumstances the earth could theoretically support a population of 40 trillion, or about 200,000 persons per square mile. Asimov calculates that we would reach that number by 2436, less than five hundred years from now. These calculations do not take into account other factors such as energy requirements, pollution, or the social breakdown that might result from progressively intense crowding of people into less and less space.

Rapid population growth is clearly one of the most urgent social problems of the twentieth century. There can be no question that, unless expansion is checked, our very way of life is liable to a fundamental and unwelcome change. Some experts believe it may already be too late to avert a catastrophe; they are pessimistic because the

[2]Karl Sax, *Standing Room Only: The World's Exploding Population* (Boston: Beacon Press, 1960); Fairfield Osborn (ed.), *Our Crowded Planet: Essays on the Pressures of Overpopulation* (New York: Doubleday, 1962); Harrison Brown, *The Challenge to Man's Future* (New York: Viking, 1954); Paul R. Ehrlich, *The Population Bomb* (New York: Ballantine, 1968).
[3]Isaac Asimov, "The End," *Penthouse Magazine,* (January 1971), 26–28, 56.

population problem, to a greater extent than most other social problems, is certain to grow more serious the longer we wait to take effective action. Moreover, the effects of population growth can be more far-reaching than those of most other social problems, with consequences that touch directly or indirectly on practically every aspect of personal and social life.

ANALYZING THE PROBLEM

Sociologists can usefully analyze the problem of rapid population growth from both the functionalist and the conflict approaches, for each highlights different aspects of the problem.

The Functionalist Approach

Seen from the functionalist approach, the problem of rapid population growth lies in social disorganization resulting from rapid and uneven social change. The reason for the population explosion is not, as might be thought, that people are now having more children than ever before. On the contrary, the reason is that people are now living, on average, much longer than before. As a result, the ratio of births to deaths has been dramatically altered, leading to a huge population increase.

The global population has always been fairly stable. In the words of the seventeenth-century English philosopher Thomas Hobbes, life in traditional, preindustrial societies was "poor, nasty, brutish, and short." In the Bronze Age, *life expectancy*—the number of years the average newborn would live—was an estimated eighteen years. By the time of the Roman Empire, it had increased to about twenty-five or thirty years. By the beginning of the twentieth century, average life expectancy was forty years.[4] In the United States today it is over seventy years.

Average life expectancy was short in traditional societies because as many as half of the children died before the age of five, mostly from infectious diseases. Under these conditions a high birth rate was functional for the family among peoples who lived by horticulture or agriculture: each new family member represented another productive worker in the fields. The high birth rate was also functional for the society as a whole, for it counterbalanced the high death rate.

Social change has radically altered this situation. The Industrial Revolution began in Europe some 250 years ago, and since that time the formerly agricultural societies of Europe, North America, and Japan have been transformed into developed, industrial societies. These societies differ in important respects from traditional ones. In an industrial society, large numbers of children are no longer functional for the family: if anything, they are an economic burden on the parents, for they have to be fed, clothed, and educated, and by the time they enter the work force, they are almost ready to form families of their own. In addition, because industrial societies have high standards of sanitation, nutrition, and medicine, and therefore a low infant death rate, they have little need for large families. Consequently birth rates have tended to decline as industrialization proceeds. This process has taken place over many generations, allowing time for social values concerning large families to adjust to changing circumstances.

The newly developing nations, however, have been thrust into the modern world with a dramatic suddenness that has resulted in social disorganization. Vaccination programs and other medical services have sharply reduced the death rate, particularly among infants, and life expectancy has greatly increased. But because these changes have taken place within the space of a generation or two, social values concerning the desirability of large families have not yet ad-

[4]Robert C. Cook, "How Many People Have Ever Lived on Earth?" *The Population Bulletin*, 18 (February 1962), 15; Thomas McKeown, *The Modern Rise of Population* (New York: Academic Press, 1977).

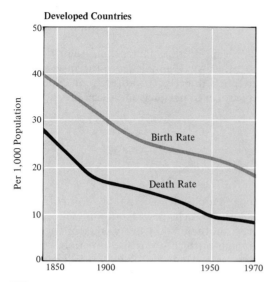

Developed Countries

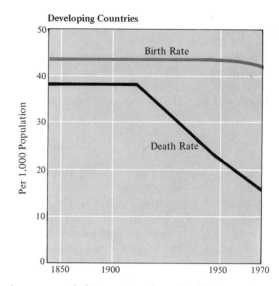

Developing Countries

FIGURE 2.1 **Birth rates and death rates in developed and developing countries.** In the developed countries, the decline in the death rate over the past century has been accompanied by a parallel decline in the birth rate. In the developing countries, however, there has been a rapid decline in the death rate during the course of this century, but the birth rate has remained almost constant. The result is massive population growth in the developing countries.
(International Demographic Statistics Center, Bureau of the Census.)

justed to the new conditions. Most people in these societies are still engaged in agriculture, so large families remain an asset. Also, many of these societies lack a system of social security, and parents hope for a number of children who will support them in old age. The social practice of having many children continues, even though on the whole it is now dysfunctional rather than functional for the societies concerned.

The Conflict Approach

The conflict approach highlights the fact that there are often severe disagreements over the desirability of controlling population growth. Population control runs counter to the values and the interests of many individuals, social movements, and governments. In fact, to many people and governments abroad, and even to some people in the United States, the population problem simply does not exist. There are many reasons for this attitude, of which these are some of the more recurrent ones:

Traditional Values. Large families and growing tribes have always been regarded as fundamentally good for the society, and social customs in many parts of the world continue to encourage early marriage, to prize a large family, and to stress the domestic role of the woman as mother and child-rearer. Obviously, it is very difficult to change in the course of a few decades values that have held sway throughout history. Moreover, human reproduction and family size have traditionally been regarded as a private affair and the prerogative of parents. People tend to resist any suggestion of interference as an invasion of liberty and privacy.

Nationalist Feelings. Many nations or ethnic groups believe that their military strength or political influence is enhanced by a large population. Some developing countries regard themselves as underpopulated because they fail to see their situation in a global context. In the supposed interests of economic growth, for example, Argentina is attempting to double its population by the end of the century (to this end the

Argentinian government issued a decree in 1974 restricting the use of contraceptives). In the overpopulated and desperately poor country of Bangladesh, the first minister of family planning was a father of eighteen children who was opposed to population control in principle. His first official act was to curtail family-planning programs. Many citizens of Bangladesh feel that their country can be secure only if it has as many people as China—a country with sixty-seven times its land area and comparably greater natural resources. Only 6 percent of the fertile couples in Bangladesh practice any method of birth control.[5]

Religious Objections. Religious values often affect attitudes toward population growth and birth control. Some major religions have traditionally objected to sex for pleasure rather than procreation, and these doctrines influence both governments and individuals. The Roman Catholic Church is influential in many overpopulated areas, particularly Latin America, and has always opposed both contraception and abortion.[6] Some sects of the Islamic religion reject birth control, and there is opposition to family planning in many traditionalist Muslim societies of the Middle East and North Africa. "To have many children is to be blessed by Allah," an old proverb runs. Hinduism and Buddhism are generally noncommittal on the subject and do not have doctrines against birth control. However, in the countries where these religions are influential, there have been particularly strong social and economic pressures for large families.

Preoccupation with Other Problems. The indirect effects of rapid population growth are easily overlooked as such, for they come bearing other labels: poverty, unemployment, illiteracy, disease, and crime. These immediate, visible problems can obscure the significance of anything so distant and abstract as world population trends. In particular, inhabitants of developed countries may see little connection between the

size of their own populations, which may enjoy high standards of living, and the plight of millions elsewhere in the world. Also politicians tend to think in terms of immediate results and the next election. There are few votes and little popularity to be gained by designing policies for the next generation, let alone the next century, so the population problem is placed low on the agenda of national priorities.

The population problem is thus embroiled in issues of social conflict, particularly conflict over values. In some developing nations, governments advocating birth control policies meet stout resistance from their traditionalist peoples. In other countries, governments believe that the poverty of their inhabitants is the result not of overpopulation but rather of a global imbalance in the distribution of wealth. They feel that if they had a greater share of the wealth now concentrated in the hands of a few industrialized societies, their large populations would not be such a problem. In many nations such issues as abortion or the use of contraceptives by unmarried teen-agers arouse intense value conflicts. In the United States some social movements, such as the Planned Parenthood Association and the Zero Population Growth organization, argue for population limitation. They are opposed by religious organizations such as the Catholic and Mormon churches and by social movements such as the antiabortion Right to Life movement.

THE ELEMENTS OF DEMOGRAPHY

To analyze the problem of population growth, sociologists draw on concepts from *demography,* a subdiscipline of sociology that studies the size, composition, growth rates, and distribution of human populations. Accurate information on population trends is important to social and economic planning in any modern society, and the demographer is trained to assemble the relevant statistics, to explain them, to compare them, and to project them into the future.

No human population is ever completely

[5]"World Environment Newsletter," *World,* May 8, 1973, p. 38.
[6]"Birth Control Blues," *Time,* February 4, 1974, p. 54.

stable. The two most important factors directly affecting population growth or decline are the birth rate and the death rate, which are expressed as statistical measures: the *birth rate* is the number of births per year per thousand members of the population; the *death rate* is the number of deaths per year per thousand members of the population. A third factor, *migration rate*—the number of people entering or leaving the population per year per thousand members of the population—may also be important in specific populations. Immigration, legal and illegal, is still a significant factor in American population growth, accounting for perhaps two-thirds of our annual population increase. Migration, of course, has no effect on the total human population. The *growth rate* is a measure of how fast the size of a population is increasing (or declining); it is determined by subtracting the number of deaths from the number of births and then expressing this figure as an annual percentage.

By applying these measures to a particular society, we can get a good idea of its demographic characteristics and trends. Bangladesh, for example, has a birth rate of 47 per thousand, a death rate of 20 per thousand, and an annual growth rate of 2.7 percent. The United States, in contrast, has a relatively low birth rate of 15.3 per thousand, a death rate of 8.8 per thousand, and a growth rate of 0.6 percent. A few parts of Europe, such as Austria and both East and West Germany, actually have negative growth rates, meaning that their populations are shrinking.[8]

The contrasting statistics for Bangladesh and the United States represent a pattern of striking

---

[7]World Environmental Fund, "Population Estimates, 1977," Washington, D.C., 1977.

Table 2.1   Population Growth in Selected Countries, 1978

Country	Total Pop. (millions)	Birth Rate	Death Rate	Rate of Natural Increase (%)	Years to Double Pop.	Pop. Under 15 (%)	Per Capita GNP (U.S. $)
U.S.	216.8	15.3	8.8	0.6	116	24	7,890
Canada	23.6	16	7	0.9	77	26	7,510
U.K.	56.0	12	12	0.0	–	23	4,020
France	53.4	14	10	0.3	231	24	6,550
Sweden	8.3	12	11	0.1	693	21	8,670
E. Germany	16.7	12	14	−0.2	–	21	4,220
W. Germany	61.3	10	12	−0.2	–	21	7,380
U.S.S.R.	261.0	18	9	0.9	77	25	2,760
India	634.7	34	14	2.0	35	40	150
Bangladesh	85.0	47	20	2.7	26	43	110
China	930.0	22	8	1.4	50	33	410
Japan	114.4	16	6	1.0	69	24	4,910
Taiwan	16.9	26	5	2.1	33	35	1,070
S. Korea	37.1	24	7	1.7	41	39	670
Mexico	66.9	42	8	3.4	20	46	1,090
Cuba	9.7	21	5	1.5	46	37	860
Brazil	115.4	36	8	2.8	25	42	1,140
Ireland	3.2	22	10	1.1	63	31	2,560

Source: Adapted from the *1978 World Population Data Sheet* (Washington, D.C.: The Population Reference Bureau, 1978); U.S. Bureau of the Census, *Statistical Abstract of the U.S., 1978* (Washington, D.C.: U.S. Government Printing Office, 1978).

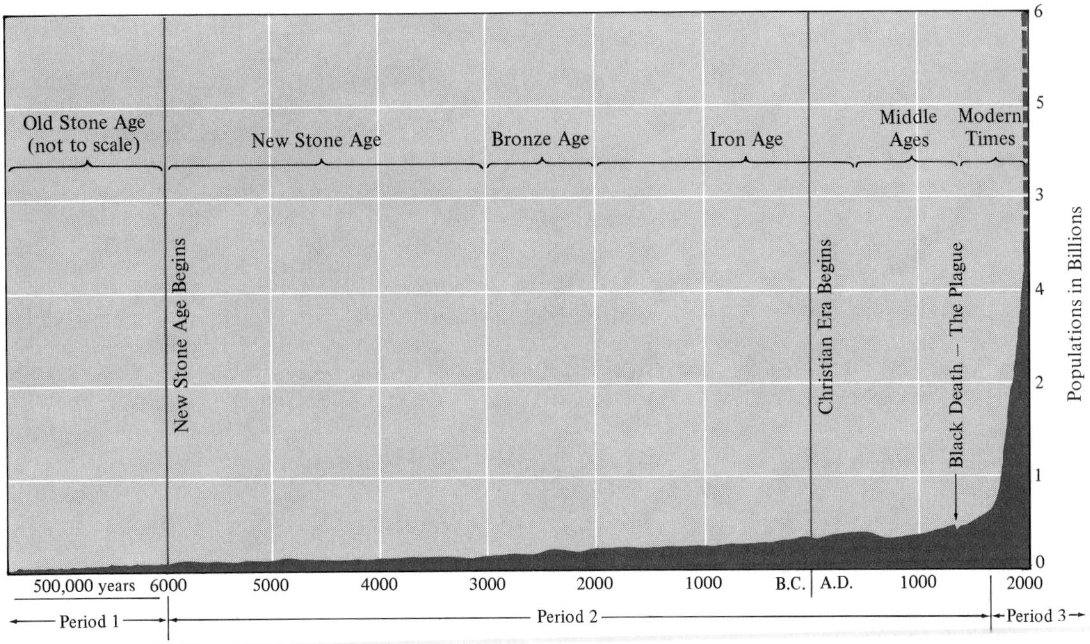
Old Stone Age
(not to scale)
New Stone Age
Bronze Age
Iron Age
Middle Ages
Modern Times
New Stone Age Begins
Christian Era Begins
Black Death – The Plague
Populations in Billions
0
1
2
3
4
5
6
500,000 years
6000
5000
4000
3000
2000
1000
B.C.
A.D.
1000
2000
Period 1
Period 2
Period 3

FIGURE 2.2 **Population throughout history.** After increasing at a slow and fairly steady pace for hundreds of thousands of years, human population growth has suddenly exploded. Although the recent growth curve shown in this graph is unprecedented in our history, it is familiar to biologists as preliminary, in all other species, to a drastic population collapse. (Adapted from Population Reference Bureau, "How Many People Have Ever Lived on Earth?" *The Population Bulletin*, V. 18, n. 1, February 1962, p. 5; *World Population Data Sheet* [Washington, D.C.: The Population Reference Bureau, 1978].)

and consistent differences between the developed and the developing countries of the world. Low birth rates—those below 20 per thousand—are found exclusively in the developed areas of North America, Europe, and Japan. Birth rates over 35 per thousand are characteristic of the large developing nations, although a few smaller nations of Asia and Latin America fall somewhere in between (see Table 2.1).

A useful concept in the analysis of population growth is that of *doubling time*—the number of years required for a given population to double its size. Until recently, doubling time has been a matter of centuries. Today, in most nations, it takes less than a single lifetime. According to demographers' rough estimates of the population of the human species at various points in history (Figure 2.2), the total human population during the Stone Age, when people were hunting and gathering for subsistence, was probably not more than 10 million. By the beginning of the Christian era the number had grown to about 250 million. A thousand years later, the total population was about 300 million, and by 1650 it had risen to half a billion. In the two centuries to 1850, it doubled to a billion. The next doubling, to the 2 billion mark, took only eighty years and was completed around 1930. The most recent doubling to 4 billion was completed in less than fifty years; and if present growth rates continue, the next doubling will take only forty-one years.

---

[8] 1978 *World Population Data Sheet* (Washington, D.C.: The Population Reference Bureau, 1978); U.S. Bureau of the Census, *USA Statistics in Brief, 1978* (Washington, D.C.: U.S. Government Printing Office, 1978).

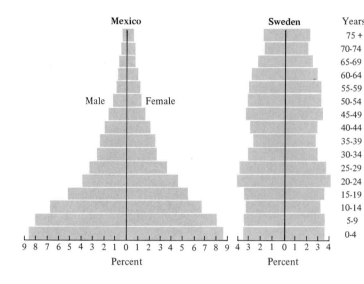

Mexico   Sweden

Male   Female

9 8 7 6 5 4 3 2 1 0 1 2 3 4 5 6 7 8 9   4 3 2 1 0 1 2 3 4

Percent   Percent

Years
75 +
70-74
65-69
60-64
55-59
50-54
45-49
40-44
35-39
30-34
25-29
20-24
15-19
10-14
5-9
0-4

FIGURE 2.3 **Age structure in Mexico and Sweden.** There are major differences in the age structures of the developing and the developed countries. Like most poor, overpopulated nations, Mexico is "bottom heavy" with children; while in Sweden, as in other developed countries, the proportion of children to adults is far smaller. When Swedish children grow up and reproduce, their country's population structure will change only a little, but in Mexico, the same process will produce a huge population explosion. (United Nations Demographic Yearbook.)

This rapid growth rate means that by the year 2000, within the lifetime of most readers of this book, the earth may be supporting a population of approximately 7 billion, close to three times as many as when most of these readers were born.[9]

Why does doubling time accelerate in this way? Consider a population of 10,000 increasing at 3 percent a year. In ten years the population would have increased, not by 30 percent to 13,000, but by about 34 percent to 13,439. This happens because population growth is *exponential*; that is, the increase for each period is based not on the original figure but on the figure for the preceding period. Thus, even at a growth rate of 1 percent—slightly more than the present rate in the United States—a population would double itself in seventy years. At 1.7 percent—the current world rate—it would double in forty-one years. At 3.4 percent, the current rate in Mexico, the population would double itself in a mere twenty years. In practice, of course, very high birth rates will not lead to continued exponential growth and ever shorter doubling times; they will lead to high death rates as people succumb to the effects of malnutrition, disease, and even wars.

One further factor complicates this gloomy picture: the *age structure* of the populations of the developing nations. The age structure refers to the proportions of different age groups within a population. Figure 2.3 shows typical age structures for a developed country and a developing country, in this case, Sweden and Mexico, respectively. Characteristically, the age structure of Mexico is "bottom heavy" with young people. In the most developed countries of the world, roughly a quarter of the population is under fifteen: in Sweden the figure is 21 percent, in Japan, 24 percent. In the developing nations, however, young people make up a much larger part of the population: in Mexico, for example, 46 percent of the inhabitants are under fifteen; in Algeria, 48 percent.

Population growth therefore cannot be checked instantly, any more than a speeding car can be stopped as soon as one hits the brakes. Even if from this moment on parents had only enough children to replace their own generation, all the children who are not yet parents would still bear their own offspring before the momentum of growth would cease. Most of this growth would inevitably take place in the poorest and least developed nations. Even with the best efforts and most effective programs of population control, world population is virtually certain to reach at least 7 billion, and might easily go as high as 10 billion, before it can be brought to a halt.

[9]Rufus E. Miles, Jr., "Man's Population Predicament," *The Population Bulletin*, 26 (April 1971), 5; Ansley J. Coale, "The History of the Human Population," *Scientific American*, 231 (September 1974), 41–51; *1978 World Population Data Sheet*.

Recognizing the Danger:
Malthus and His Principle

It was an eighteenth-century English parson, Thomas Malthus, who first warned about the implications of population growth. Malthus lived at the height of the Industrial Revolution in England. It was an age of boundless optimism, founded on the idea of "the perfectibility of man"—the notion that human history is essentially an evolution, via industrialism, to a golden age of abundance, bliss, and human perfection. In his famous book, *Essay on the Principles of Population*, published in 1798, Malthus formulated a very simple principle that appeared to destroy utterly and forever the possibility of any future golden age: "Population, when unchecked, increases in geometric ratio. Subsistence only increases in arithmetic ratio."[10]

In other words, the natural tendency of unchecked population growth is to increase in powers of two: 1, 2, 4, 8, 16, 32, 64—a "geometric" ratio. But the food supply cannot possibly increase in the same ratio, because it depends on a fixed amount of land. At best, the food supply can be increased in a steady, additive fashion: 1, 2, 3, 4, 5, 6, 7—an "arithmetic" ratio. Inevitably, population tends to outrun the means of subsistence, only to be set back within the limits of the food supply by the intervention of certain unalterable facts of nature—"war, pestilence, and famine." To Malthus the logical conclusion was that misery, hunger, and poverty would therefore be the permanent and unavoidable fate of the bulk of the world's people.

The idea, obviously an unwelcome one, was widely attacked and ridiculed, and Malthus became known as the "gloomy parson." A critic called his theory "that black and terrible demon that is always ready to stifle the hopes of humanity."[11] One of Malthus' biographers notes that "for thirty years it rained refutations."[12] But the thesis was difficult to refute. There was the brutally simple logic of the principle; there was a

national census three years after publication of the *Essay* showing that the English population had increased 25 percent in thirty years; and there was the unquestionable fact of increasing poverty among the masses.

Malthus' theory quickly became associated with political conservatism, largely because of his attitude toward the poor. He was not hostile to the lower classes, but he did believe they were responsible for their own condition and for most of the population increase. If there was to be a check to population growth, it would have to occur primarily among the poor. Malthus recommended the abolition of poor relief and of state support of pauper children. To the privileged few who made the laws, this seemed a very sensible doctrine, and in fact, English poor laws were modified accordingly. For the rest of the population, Malthus recommended "moral restraint": postponement of marriage and prohibition of sexual intercourse until marriage. Artificial methods of birth control, however, were repugnant to Malthus—although, ironically, the principle of birth control became known as "neo-Malthusianism." And Malthus did not foresee a need to halt population growth entirely: it simply had to be slowed down so that the food supply could catch up.

Malthus' grim predictions were not fulfilled for the region with which he was concerned—Europe and, to a lesser extent, North America. He foresaw neither the rapid drop in birth rates that followed a few decades later as industrialization proceeded nor the improvement in agricultural methods that vastly increased crop yield from a fixed area of land. Both Europe and the United States grew in numbers and affluence, and it seemed that Malthus had been proved wrong. However, what was not realized until fairly recently was how much the continued prosperity and growing population of the developed countries depends on the exploitation of the resources of the less developed nations of the world.

THE DEVELOPING NATIONS:
A MALTHUSIAN TRAP?

Today it seems almost certain that humanity has

---

[10]Quoted in Judy K. Morris, "Professor Malthus and His Essay," *The Population Bulletin*, 22 (February 1966), 16–17.

[11]Robert Heilbroner, *The Worldly Philosphers*, 3rd ed. (New York: Simon and Schuster, 1967), p. 76.

[12]*Ibid.*, p. 76.

not escaped the "Malthusian trap." The problem is especially acute for the developing nations, although it has implications for the developed societies of the world as well.

Overpopulation and Global Malnutrition

Until quite recently there was a great deal of euphoria over the "green revolution" in agriculture—the use of chemical fertilizers and new hybrid strains of high-yield crops, which greatly increased agricultural production per acre. For a while it seemed that food supplies might keep pace with population growth, but these hopes now appear to have been unfounded. The fact is that more, not fewer, people are suffering from malnutrition every year. As Henry Borgstrom points out:

> If the entire world's food supply were parcelled out at the U.S. dietary level, it would feed only about one third of the human race. The world as a global household knows of no surpluses, merely enormous deficits. . . . Already short of food, the world is adding 70 million people to its feeding burden each year—the equivalent of the entire United States population every three years. The annual increase is itself growing at a rapid pace; it is outstripping the gains in world food production

Literally millions of people on the Indian subcontinent and elsewhere in the developing world are expected to die from the effects of malnutrition between now and the end of the century. Although India cannot feed her present population—only one citizen in fifty has an adequate diet—the total population of the country may exceed 1 billion by the year 2000 unless birth rates are reduced.

despite all the triumphs of agriculture and fisheries. . . . [13]

Nearly every other child born in the developing countries suffers from hunger or malnutrition; and, sometimes, from resulting brain damage. The brain of an infant grows to 80 percent of its adult size in the first three years of life. If supplies of protein are inadequate during this period, the brain stops growing—and the damage is irreversible. Undernourishment is rampant in the developing countries: in India, for instance, only one person in fifty has an adequate diet. Yet the fastest rates of population increases are usually in the poorest of the developing countries (Rwanda, for example, with an annual population growth rate of 2.8 percent, has an annual per capita gross national product of $110).[14] Merely to feed the present population of the earth adequately would involve doubling present agricultural production, but most cultivable land is already being farmed.

Overpopulation and Economic Development

Population growth can also undermine a developing country because a vicious circle may exist between demographic and economic factors. To reach the level of economic development that will bring about rising standards of living for all members of the population, massive industrialization is necessary, requiring capital investment in basic necessities such as factories, transportation systems, and technical education. In a society in which population remains constant, about 3 to 5 percent of the national income has to be invested each year to create a 1 percent increase in the per capita income. But if the population is growing at the rate of about 3 percent, as is the case with most developing nations, the investment must be between 12 to 20 percent. Such levels are quite impossible for poor countries, in which the lack of investment capital is often the main barrier to economic advance.

The poor countries are increasing their populations twice as fast as the rich ones, yet they have the least need of large populations and can least afford them. Any economic advances they do make are used to accommodate more people rather than to improve living standards. A country whose population is doubling every twenty years has to double its national income in that period—a staggering task—merely to remain where it was. Not only does increased population absorb economic gains, it also increases pressure on land already densely settled, thus retarding agricultural production. In urban areas the large numbers of younger children become heavy burdens on the working population, and older children are often obliged to work to support themselves, their parents, or their younger siblings. The result is mass illiteracy and critical shortages of trained workers.

The gap between the living standards of the developed and the developing worlds is wide and getting wider. In North America the annual per capita gross national product is $7,850, and in Western Europe it is $6,900. In Africa, in contrast, it is only $440; in Latin America, $1,100; and in Asia, $610.[15] In the late 1950s the developed nations, with only 30 percent of the global population, produced 82 percent of the world's goods and services. Today, with less than 30 percent of the world population, they produce nearly 90 percent of the goods and services. Despite foreign-aid efforts, this trend continues to grow, largely due to population increase. In fact, it is unlikely that many of the developing nations will ever be able to approach the standard of living that we take for granted in the United States. The planet may not have enough natural resources to support vast populations at anything resembling the American level.

Demographic Transition: A Way Out?

The population growth rate of the developed nations of the world increased while they were

---

[13]Henry Borgstrom, "The Dual Challenge of Health and Hunger," Washington, D.C.: Population Reference Bureau Selection no. 32, n.d.), pp. 1, 2. For a different and unusually optimistic view of the problem, see Roger Revelle, "Food and Population," *Scientific American*, 231 (September 1974), 161–170.

[14]1978 *World Population Data Sheet*.

[15]*Ibid*.

industrializing, but has since tended to level off,[16] encouraging demographers to speculate that the same pattern might repeat itself with other peoples. Research on the question has led to the theory of *demographic transition*, which holds that population growth rates tend to decrease and then stabilize once a certain level of economic development has been achieved.

Such a demographic transition takes place in three stages. In the first, which is typical of preindustrial agricultural societies, both birth rates and death rates are high, resulting in a fairly stable population size. The second stage, found in developing societies, is one in which birth rates remain constant and death rates drop, leading to a rapid increase in population growth rate. In the final stage, which occurs in developed industrial societies, both birth rates and death rates are low, resulting in a stable population size once more. The transition can be readily explained in functionalist terms. Because high death rates are inevitable in the first stage, high birth rates are necessary to maintain population at an equilibrium. As death rates drop and birth rates remain dysfunctionally high in the second stage, society becomes disorganized. In the third stage, with low birth rates balancing the low death rates, the social system moves back into equilibrium.

The theory of demographic transition is not a rigid "law" but, rather, an empirical generalization based on observations of how populations have tended to behave when faced with similar circumstances. Essentially, it appears that people will, on the whole, have as many children as they think they can adequately support, given existing and expected conditions. The theory provides us with a simple model that many societies seem to fit, one which suggests a fairly reliable ongoing process with a favorable outcome. But there are some difficulties.

One problem is that the concept of demographic transition is merely a theoretical model. Human events seldom conform to neat patterns, and the fact that some societies have a certain demographic history does not necessarily mean that all societies will repeat the same process. It is conceivable that other factors, such as religious or other cultural values, could "freeze" a society at its customary birth rate. Demographers cannot yet be sure what the key factors in the transition process are, or to what extent it depends on specific cultural institutions and values.

The Japanese demographic transition, for example, took place in a much shorter time and according to very different methods and values than did the Western transition. Before World War II the Japanese population was growing rapidly, but at the end of the war there was a general consensus that population control was necessary. In the ten years from 1947 to 1957 the Japanese birth rate dropped from 34 per thousand to 14 per thousand, one of the most rapid declines in birth rates on record. During this period, half of the conceptions in Japan were terminated by abortion, which had had a long tradition of being tolerated because it was not considered fundamentally immoral, as it was in Western societies. Irene Taeuber points out that the speed of the Japanese demographic transition and the means employed to bring it about were both intimately associated with Japanese culture. There is no reason to suppose that a similar transition could be achieved in a country with different cultural traditions.[17]

Although there is no certainty that other societies will follow the demographic patterns established in the industrialized nations, there is evidence, encouragingly, of some demographic transition in a few of the developing countries. Dudley Kirk points out that between World War II and the early 1960s virtually all nations fell into one of two categories—those with birth rates under 25 and those with birth rates over 35.[18] Since that time, however, a number of nations with high birth rates have been moving into an intermediate range. Kirk argues that

---

[16]Charles F. Westoff, "Marriage and Fertility in the Developed Countries," *Scientific American*, 239 (December 1978), 51–57.

[17]Irene B. Taeuber, "Japan's Demographic Transition Reexamined," *Population Studies*, 14 (July 1960), 39.

[18]Dudley Kirk, "A New Demographic Transition?" in *Rapid Population Growth: Consequences and Policy Implications*, prepared by a study committee of the National Academy of Sciences (Baltimore: Johns Hopkins Press, 1971), pp. 123–147.

once the birth rate in developing nations begins to fall, it drops at a much more rapid pace than it did historically in Europe and North America. In Asia, for example, the birth rate declined by only 2 percent between 1950 and 1965, but it fell by 17 percent between 1965 and 1975.[19] Although precise causes of the decline vary from one society to another, Kirk believes that there is always a definite connection to some "threshold" level of social and economic development, with education and per capita income as the major factors. On this basis, there is reason to hope that the demographic transition will be achieved in all countries—if the necessary level of development can be reached. However, most of the developing countries that have recently begun the transition have relatively small populations. The largest and poorest countries are still struggling with birth rates of 35 and up—in some cases as high as 50. Overpopulation drains their economic resources, and there seems no immediate prospect of their achieving the levels of industrial development that might reduce these rates.

Paul Ehrlich and John Holdren take a more pessimistic view of the demographic transition hypothesis.[20] They argue that even if all developing nations do industrialize, create better social and economic conditions, and begin a demographic transition within fifty years—a spectacular accomplishment—a rapid drop in birth rates would begin only around the year 2020, and world growth rates would not decline to the present United States level until about 2050. By that time the global population would already be four times as large as it is today. If the demographic transition takes place but leaves a huge part of the world's population living at a bare subsistence level, population growth will have been halted without solving the problem of overpopulation.

The question is not whether population will stabilize—it will. If the global population exceeds the carrying capacity of the earth, death rates will rise and halt population growth. The issues are whether stability will result from a decrease in birth rates or an increase in death rates, how long it will take before stability occurs, and how many people will be here when this finally happens. The prospect of a demographic transition offers the hope that if certain preconditions are met, population growth rates in the developing world will be reduced by a decline in birth rates rather than the grim alternative.

To gain a clearer understanding of some of the practical problems involved in reducing birth rates, let us look at two specific examples, India and China.

India

India's attempts to control population growth are of vital significance to the developing world. Within an area about one-third the size of the United States, India crowds a population nearly three times as large, 635 million people, making it one of the world's largest nations. It is also one of the poorest. If the current growth rate were to continue, India could have a population of over a billion by the end of the century, and the likelihood that such a nation could ever clothe and feed itself, let alone develop beyond a subsistence economy, is slender. An India of such proportions would more likely be constantly on the brink of famine.

The Indian birth rate has declined from 52.4 at the start of the century to about 34 today. But the death rate has fallen at an even faster pace, from 46.8 to 14, leaving the country with a growth rate of around 2 percent.[21] The effects of this population increase on living standards have been severe. The average Indian has a daily food intake of about 2,000 calories, although the minimum human requirement is about 2,300–2,500 (the average intake in the United States is 3,000–3,500). Per capita income in India is $150 dollars. The Indian government is certainly trying to combat poverty and undernourishment, but the population increase simply swallows up what might have been substantial progress.

[19]*New York Times*, February 15, 1978.

[20]Paul R. Ehrlich and John P. Holdren, "Avoiding the Problem," *Saturday Review*, March 6, 1971, p. 56.

[21]S. Chandrasekhar, "India's Population: Fact, Problem, and Policy," in S. Chandrasekhar (ed.), *Asia's Population Problems* (New York: Praeger, 1967), p. 80, Table 7; *1978 World Population Data Sheet*.

These are the words of Krittybas Dutta, aged forty years, a resident of Sonapalashi Village — about 60 miles north of Calcutta — West Bengal, India, in conversation with an American anthropologist, Nathaniel Wander, during the winter of 1976–77.

A Bengal "Life History"

"We are too poor here and this makes us weak. You remember when I had fever. I was in my bed for seventeen days, always with a temperature of 100 degrees or more. You tell me in United States, you fall sick like this and are recovered in four days or one week. And I am a young man. For children and old parents, what you call mild illness can end by dying.

"My family owns less than 5 *bighas* (about 1.6 acres) of land, which we give out to tenants. I have no oxen, no plough; if I hoped to farm myself, either I must sell land to buy these or to hire service from ploughman. For all this and seed and fertilizer too, there is no money. What I earn, we eat. If I could farm this land which is much scattered in small pieces, perhaps I could have just sufficient rice to feed my family. . . .

"We are poor now, but I have much concern for my sons. I try to make them study in school, but they are not always successful. They will have more difficulty to find employment when they are of age. Always there are more people wanting same number of works. They will each have only half the land, and it is already too little. Too many times, I am uneasy in my mind."

(*Source:* Nathaniel Wander. Copyright © 1979 Nathaniel Wander.)

In 1952 India became the first country to adopt an official family-planning program. At first the program was very poorly funded: in 1956, for example, total expenditures amounted to 1 cent per year for every twenty persons. By the early 1970s the figure had risen to 7.7 cents per person: 1 percent of the entire government budget and the highest percentage ever budgeted for family planning by any nation. In its early years, the program had little effect. The principal means of contraception promoted was the rhythm method, the inadequacy of which became clear by the early 1960s. In 1965 two new techniques were added: male sterilization (vasectomy) and the intrauterine device (IUD) for women. Oral contraceptives have since been added to the arsenal, but vasectomy and the IUD remain the preferred methods.

By the start of the 1970s some 13 percent of all couples in the reproductive ages (fifteen to forty-four) were using methods provided by the government program, and two million men were being sterilized each year.[22] The birth rate, however, declined hardly at all — perhaps because most of those using birth control were doing so only after they had already had a large family.

Until 1977 the Indian government under Mrs. Indira Gandhi followed a more aggressive strategy. Educational programs were used to persuade Indians that their problem is too many people, not too little food, and that a large family is an economic burden. Posters showing smiling two-child families appeared throughout the country. The federal government threatened to dismiss civil service employees who had more than three children, and bills calling for compulsory sterilization of parents after the birth of their third child were presented in some state legislatures. In 1977 the Indian government reported that about 20 percent of couples of child-bearing age were currently using some method of family planning and that over 7 million sterilization operations had been performed that year alone.[23] In that year, however, Mrs. Gandhi suffered a crushing electoral defeat — partly because of her government's record on civil liberties, but also partly because of the

[22]Dorothy Nortman, "Population and Family Planning Programs: A Factbook," *Reports on Population/Family Planning*, 2 (September 1972), 24, Table 4.

[23]*New York Times*, December 28, 1976, p. 2

China, a poor and overpopulated country, has significantly reduced its birth rate. The reduction has been made possible, however, only by the willingness of the Chinese masses to obey dutifully their leaders'

exhortations to abstain from premarital intercourse, to delay marriage, and to limit their families through contraception.

extreme unpopularity of her population-control programs. The present government favors reduced population growth but is not pursuing the activist campaigns of its predecessor. Yet at the current growth rate, India has about 35,000 more people every day than it had the day before.

China

It is often thought that the population growth rate of India is one of the highest in the world, but actually it is somewhat lower than those of many other developing countries. In 1978, in fact, over thirty countries had a growth rate of over 3 percent. Doubling time at that rate is a mere nineteen years. And there is one country whose population problem, in terms of sheer size alone, dwarfs that of India: China. Not even the

Chinese know exactly how large their population is, but present Western estimates place it at about 930 million. At the current rate of increase, 1.4, the Chinese population would double to a phenomenal 1.86 billion or so in fifty years.[24]

China's attitude to population size has varied over the years. Lacking sophisticated modern weapons, the Chinese have tended to regard their huge population as an important military resource in any potential conflict with the Soviet Union or the West, and they have frequently urged other developing nations to take the same view. Moreover, the Chinese version of commun-

[24]1978 *World Population Data Sheet*; Robert Reinhold, "China's Millions Are Still Hard to Count," *New York Times*, March 26, 1978, p. E. 7.

ism regards poverty as a result of defects in the international social order; it is caused not by overpopulation but by the greed of powerful and wealthy nations that exploit the developing countries. Nevertheless, the poor harvests and resulting food shortages of recent years appear to have convinced Chinese leaders that population control is essential. The country's campaign for family planning is officially based on the view that population control will improve the health and living conditions of young people, and in particular that it will liberate women from traditional restrictions. Propaganda posters remind women that a good career and education are easier to achieve with a small family.

Family planning in China is an integral part of a comprehensive national health-care service, available free of charge to all citizens. The Chinese have made extensive use of the "barefoot doctor," a member of the local community who after three months of intensive training becomes a family-planning propagandist and worker. These paraprofessionals distribute various contraceptive devices, give advice on birth control, and perform abortions. Because they are "insiders" in the community, they do not meet the resentment that is often directed against family-planning officials in India and elsewhere, who are often perceived as interfering intruders. There is also strong social pressure on couples to have no more than two children; to have a larger family is regarded as disrespectful to party and country. The Chinese government has asked men and women not to marry until the ages of twenty-six and twenty-three, respectively, and there is every indication that this injunction is being observed. Premarital sexual intercourse is illegal, and by all accounts young Chinese are exceptionally chaste before marriage (it is unusual for a boy and girl even to hold hands in public). The Chinese claim that in Peking, at least, the rate of natural population increase has been reduced to 0.1 percent. Although there has not been such a dramatic reduction in births in rural areas, where most of the population lives, the Chinese do claim that their overall birth rate has been dropping steadily. The rate is believed to have declined by as much as 25 percent since 1950, with most of this decline occurring in the

past decade.[25] In trying to limit its population, China has the advantage, in this respect at least, of a government that appears to enjoy the almost unquestioning loyalty of a rather conformist people. If China achieves a rapid demographic transition, the country's success will be based, like that of Japan, on unique cultural factors. Other developing nations, it seems, will have to find their own routes to a demographic transition.

THE AMERICAN POPULATION PROBLEM

What about the United States? By many standards we are the richest country in the world, and we have one of the lowest rates of population growth. Does the United States have anything that could honestly be labeled a population problem?

In 1970, Congress established the Commission on Population Growth and the American Future to inquire into this question. When the commission submitted its report in the spring of 1972, its answer was a considered yes. Obviously this problem is not as desperate or dramatic as that of India, but it is one that needs prompt, intelligent action nonetheless. The commission reported that the "quality of life" is central to the issue, claiming that "if this country is in a crisis of spirit—environmental deterioration, racial antagonisms, the plight of the cities, the international situation—then population is part of that crisis[26]

Growth and Its Problems

Population growth is nothing new to the United States. In the second half of the nineteenth century, population increased by 30 percent each decade as immigrants streamed across the Atlan-

[25]"China: Population in the People's Republic," *The Population Bulletin*, 27 (December 1971); *New York Times*, February 15, 1978.

[26]*Population and the American Future: The Report of the Commission on Population Growth and the American Future* (Washington, D.C.: U.S. Government Printing Office, 1972), p. 12.

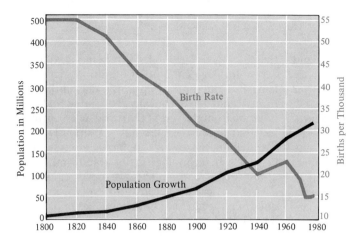

FIGURE 2.4 **U.S. population and birth rate, 1800–1977.** Although the U.S. birth rate has fallen steadily for 150 years, the size of the population has continued to increase. The main reason is that the death rate has been reduced by improvements in medical science, and public health standards.

(Adapted from Robin Elliott, Lynn C. Landman, Richard Lincoln, and Theodore Tsuoroka, *U.S. Population Growth and Family Planning: A Review of the Literature* [New York: Planned Parenthood—World Population, n.d.], p. vii; U.S. Bureau of the Census, *Statistical Abstract of the United States, 1978* [Washington, D.C.: U.S. Government Printing Office, 1978].)

tic to the New World. But as immigration slackened soon after the start of the twentieth century, the birth rate also declined, reaching a low in the depression years of the 1930s. At the end of World War II came the celebrated and unanticipated "baby boom" that peaked in 1955, when the birth rate reached 25. The birth rate then began to decline once more, until in the early 1970s the media began speaking of a "baby bust." Then, just when the children of the baby boom reached adulthood and the rate was expected to soar once more, it fell—from 18.4 in 1970 to a record low of 14.8 in 1975, before increasing slightly to 15.3 in 1977[27] (see Figure 2.4). One reason for the baby bust is that the present generation of young adults is postponing the age at which it begins child-rearing; as the childbearing age stabilizes, the rate will tend to rise again. A second reason is that young people today expect to have fewer children than people a few years their senior. To achieve an ultimate *zero population growth*—a situation in which population size remains stable—each set of parents would need to have about 2.1 children to allow for those offspring who die young or who for some other reason do not reproduce themselves. At present the average American woman is having only 1.8 children, a sharp decline from an average of 3.8 children two decades ago. The Bureau of the Census reported in 1978 that the average woman between the ages of eighteen

and thirty-four expects to have 2.11 births.[28] Unless the birth rate soars again, the prospects for zero population growth in the United States are now very favorable.

What kind of problems did the Commission on Population believe result from population growth in the United States? In an implicitly functionalist analysis, the commission traced the disruptive impact that growth in population size has on other areas of society. Among other things, pressure on schools and colleges, and ultimately on the job market, increases: youth unemployment has been at particularly high levels in recent years. Also, since crime rates are highest for persons aged fifteen to twenty-five, rising crime may be partly explained by the increase in the relative size of this age group. As young adults move out of their parents' homes and form families of their own, housing suffers pressure, and demands for all sorts of commodities and services grow. If the supply cannot easily be increased, inflation may follow. Metropolitan areas expand, along with the need for urban services—police and fire protection, sanitation, water supply, public transportation, recreational facilities. Government administration also becomes more complex and costly. None of these difficulties is insurmountable, but each exerts pressures on the society and the economy, and

---

[27]*Wall Street Journal*, October 16, 1978, p. 12.

[28]U.S. Bureau of the Census, *Statistical Abstract of the United States, 1978* (Washington D.C.: U.S. Government Printing Office, 1978), p. 59.

taken together they can become material and psychological strains on individuals.

The effects of population growth on resources and the environment must also be considered. Water is already in short supply in the Southwest, and the shortage will spread north and east in the coming decades. Americans have already felt the consequences of an energy shortage. Food production may also become a problem, especially if the nation's environmental policy restricts the use of pesticides and certain chemical fertilizers. Within the next thirty-five years the United States will need 30 million more acres of farmland to feed the population. An additional 300 million more acres of forest land must be found to satisfy demands for lumber and paper (the average American uses 450 pounds of wood and paper each year). The "great outdoors" in which Americans have long camped, hunted, fished, and played will continue to shrink. Admission to some national parks is already restricted, and during the hunting season many favored patches of forest are apt to contain more hunters than deer.

Increases in population cause increases in pollution, a more serious problem in a rich country like the United States than in a poor one like India. A high standard of living produces more waste products per person—more auto emissions, more industrial waste flowing into lakes and rivers, more smog, more plastic bottles and disposable beer cans littering the countryside, more of everything filling city dumps. Some of these pollution problems might be alleviated with present or foreseeable technology, but technology itself requires energy for its application, and energy is in short supply. Moreover, the production of energy usually causes thermal or atmospheric pollution. Americans are certainly in no imminent danger of starvation, but the quality of American life may deteriorate as the population increases.

Nonetheless, many people feel that the United States can afford to take a relatively leisured view of the situation. They argue that the land and its resources, if used sensibly and imaginatively, can support a larger population with little adverse effect on living standards. Sometimes this attitude stems from a suspicion

that the "population crisis" is being used as an excuse for neglecting other pressing social problems. But the spirit of optimism may also result from a tendency to consider the United States in isolation from the rest of the world. Many people feel that because we are not yet seriously overcrowded, because we can feed ourselves, and because our technology seems able to take care of our future requirements, we are all right.

One critical fact calls this optimism into question: the global interdependence of nations. The United States depends on other parts of the world for raw materials and those places, in turn, depend on the United States for food. The United States and Canada are the only countries that usually produce a large surplus of staple grains. When serious food shortages threaten elsewhere, it is mainly the North American surplus that can make the difference between starvation and survival for the threatened nations. If the population of the United States becomes so numerous that we ourselves need all the food we produce, the rest of the world may no longer have a safety margin.

To make matters worse, the world's cropland is being reduced by the combined effects of urban expansion, soil erosion, and the encroachment of deserts; within twenty-five years the available crop-growing land per person may be barely half what it is today.[29] According to the U.N. Food and Agriculture Organization, food production per person declined in forty-five developing nations between 1970 and 1976.[30] Among other consequences, the prospects for international conflict would increase as this trend intensifies.

In addition, the United States consumes so much of the world's resources that a single new American baby represents, in global terms, a greater ecological threat than thirty Asian babies. With only 6 percent of the world's population, Americans consume nearly 40 percent of the earth's energy and material resources. (Each American consumes during his or her

---

[29]Seth S. King, "Study Finds Decline in World Crop Soil," *New York Times*, November 27, 1978, p. 16.

[30]*New York Times*, March 15, 1978.

lifetime approximately 26 million gallons of water, 21,000 gallons of gasoline, 10,000 pounds of meat, and 28,000 pounds of milk and cream.) Even at the present low rate of population growth, the population of the United States will have increased to around 420 million in a hundred years. The impact on the rest of humanity will be enormous.

United States Population Policy

Birth control and family planning have been common in the United States for decades, but until 1971, federal law still classified contraceptives as "obscene or pornographic materials." Another law, dating back to 1873, outlawed the importation, mailing, and transporting by interstate commerce of "any article whatsoever for the promotion of contraception."[31] State laws reflected a similar attitude, and even as late as the 1960s there were prosecutions under these statutes. On the whole, however, these laws were widely disregarded, even though doctors who prescribed contraceptives, pharmacists who sold them, and people who bought them were technically liable to prosecution. Thanks to the strenuous efforts of the birth-control movement, government-sponsored family-planning pro-

grams are now operating in every state, and several federal agencies are specifically concerned with family planning and population research.[32]

The United States first became concerned about population growth in the early 1960s, but chiefly with regard to other countries. Beginning in 1963, assistance in family planning was offered to developing nations as part of general foreign aid for economic development. Soon after, however, legislators and officials realized that many people in the United States itself were nearly as disadvantaged as any Asian peasant when it came to the availability of contraception. Middle-class women could go to their private physicians for information and to their pharmacists for supplies, but poor women did not have private physicians, and the clinics they went to for medical care did not offer contraceptive information. When the "war on poverty" began in 1964, one of its strategies was to make family planning available to the poor. In 1967, Congress used one of the classic means by which social reforms have been urged on reluctant states and required that in order to qualify for federal funds for maternal and child health services, each state

---

[31]*Population and the American Future, op. cit.*, p. 98.

[32]James Reed, *From Private Vice to Public Virtue: The Birth-Control Movement and American Society Since 1830* (New York: Harper & Row, 1978).

Many American parents are able to provide for their large families and so tend to believe that they are not really contributing to the population problem. But this view neglects the global impact of more Americans: in terms of the resources they will consume and the pollution they will generate, these 8 American children represent a greater ecological threat to the planet than 240 Asian children.

must extend family-planning services to all its people by 1975. Even at this stage, however, no connection was made between private family planning and national population control. Birth control, at home as well as abroad, was simply one weapon in the war against poverty.

In 1969 the question of population size was finally made explicit. Congress conducted lengthy hearings on the subject, the media took up the issue, and President Nixon called population growth "one of the most serious challenges to the human destiny."[33] The next year Congress established the Commission on Population Growth and the American Future. Its report, published in 1972, unequivocally supported the goal of a stabilized American population and urged a number of measures to achieve it.

Family-planning services remain the core of population policy in the United States, but the Federal Center for Population Research has given some attention to other social factors, such as the role of women in American society and the assumption that their "career" will be in the home, raising children. There is little emphasis, however, on population education other than the provision of family-planning services. Legislators and appointed officials usually want to avoid controversy over sex education, and so there is typically no systematic attempt to educate young people in contraceptive techniques.

The predominantly poverty-related emphasis of government family-planning programs in the United States has also had some unfortunate side effects. Among the middle-class there has been a comfortable assumption that the poor are the largest contributors to population growth. But this is simply not so. In proportion to their numbers, those families with an income below the poverty level do have relatively more children. In absolute terms, however, it is the groups composing the remaining socioeconomic levels who contribute most to population growth.[34] A further unfortunate effect is that poor people and racial minorities have sometimes gained the impression that the purpose of the programs is not to help them but to eliminate them.[35] Even today, most white Americans remain unaware of the real fear of genocide that exists among some black Americans. As conflict theory would predict, some radical minority-group members have urged an increase in minority-group birth rates as a way of enhancing the political power of these groups.

The existing population structure of the United States also threatens to produce another unprecedented problem. Due to the post–World War II baby boom, our population is fairly young, with a median age of 29.4. Since the late 1950s, however, the birth rate has declined. This means that in a few decades, when the baby-boom children pass middle age, the average American will be much older than today, and our population structure will be top-heavy with the aged. By the year 2030, the median age will have risen to 37.3. This altered age structure will necessarily involve major changes in social policy and priorities. Providing adequate old-age homes and geriatric hospitals, for example, may become more important than building schools and colleges. Already, some elementary schools are standing empty for lack of pupils, baby-food manufacturers report declining sales, and the baby-service industry is now pitching new products to teen-agers and adults. (Some of the implications of this trend are discussed in Chapter 11, "Aging.")

CONFRONTING THE PROBLEM

What can be done about population growth? There are three basic methods that can be used, separately or in combination, to reduce birth rates. The first is family planning, with programs to educate people about birth control and provide them with contraceptive services. The sec-

---

[33]*Ibid.*, p. 3.

[34]Jack Rosenthal, "Birth Rates Found in a Sharp Decline Among Poor Women," *New York Times*, March 5, 1972.
[35]Sheila M. Rothman, "Sterilizing the Poor," *Society*, 14 (January–February 1977), 30–40.

ond method is the use of incentives to get people to voluntarily limit family size: in India, for example, the government gave transistor radios to men who had themselves sterilized. The third method is outright coercion of parents to limit the number of their children. All existing population-control programs are based primarily on family planning, although a few make use of incentives as well. Apart from some short-lived and unsuccessful attempts in India to force parents to have no more than three children, no systematic use has yet been made of coercion. Let's look at each method in more detail.

Family Planning

In Asia most of the larger nations and many of the smaller ones have family-planning programs explicitly aimed at reducing population growth. In Africa, where densities are lower and ethnic conflicts and rivalries often strong, neutrality or even permissiveness toward population growth is much more common. Several African countries actually fear underpopulation. In Latin America, family planning is becoming more common, but official programs are likely to emphasize health considerations rather than overpopulation. In North America, Europe, and Japan, family-planning advice and contraceptives are now widely available.

In a few developing countries family-planning programs have helped to significantly reduce the birth rate, notably in Taiwan, Singapore, South Korea, and Hong Kong. There is no country, however, in which family-planning programs alone have halted population growth. The main reason lies in a key principle of family planning: that couples should be encouraged to have the number of children they want—no more, and no less. But what parents want and what a country needs cannot necessarily be counted on to coincide. Many parents turn to family planning only after they have already raised a large family, not before. In many cases, too, the programs are inadequately funded, and neither the information nor the contraceptives are available to more than a fraction of the population. Many programs have also hesitated for political, moral, or religious reasons to use other methods such as

sterilization and abortion. Yet if unwanted births could be eliminated, population growth would be slowed considerably. A 1970 study of births in a representative sample of 5,000 American women found that one-fifth of all births and one-third of births to black women were reported to be unwanted at the time of conception.[36]

Incentives

If family planning alone is inadequate, what role can incentives play and what kind of incentives can be used? The most obvious incentives are financial ones, and several countries have experimented with cash rewards for sterilization or the acceptance of intrauterine devices. Another proposal is to allow tax deductions for only the first two children in a family, or even to impose an additional "child tax" on parents with more than a certain number of offspring. The chief argument against such penalties is that they would fall most heavily on the poor. The result would be that the children in large, poor families would suffer further as a result of the extra financial burdens placed on their parents.

Other incentive proposals are more far-reaching and would involve more basic changes in social values and attitudes. Kingsley Davis[37] has urged the adoption of social and economic policies that would work to change the prevailing probirth social norms of most societies so that large families would be considered undesirable. Couples would still be free to decide the size of their family, but social attitudes and values would make them reluctant to plan for families of more than two children. And if the existing sex roles of men and women were altered, women would become less dependent on home and children for personal fulfillment. Any measures that make the labor market more hospitable and attractive to women will tend, in the long run, to reduce birth rates.

---

[36]Larry Bumpass and Charles Westoff, "Unwanted Births and U.S. Population Control," *Family Planning Perspectives*, 2 (October 1970), 4.

[37]Kingsley Davis, "Population Policy: Will Current Programs Succeed?" *Science*, November 10, 1967, pp. 730–739.

Coercion

If family planning and incentives fail, governments may eventually be obliged to apply some form of compulsion to limit births. Any such effort, of course, would generate intense controversy and conflict. Most people believe that government interference in such a private matter would be tyranny. Moreover, a compulsory system of population control would be vulnerable to abuse and discrimination and would be very difficult to enforce. Nevertheless, various proposals along these lines have been put forward. One is that every woman of childbearing age could be issued a license entitling her to have however many children the zero-growth number happened to permit.[38] If she did not want to exercise these rights herself, she could transfer them to another woman, enabling a family that wanted a larger number of children to have them without affecting absolute numbers of births. The idea at least avoids some of the evils of uniform enforcement; but it might favor the affluent over the poor. Another proposal is to administer a chemical inhibitor to the entire population.[39] Such an agent would be designed to reduce fertility but not eliminate it; the dosage would be regulated so that no more than the desired number of children would be conceived each year. The usual suggestion is for some chemical that could be added to the water supply. A less subtle proposal would have all couples automatically sterilized after the birth of their second child.

The question of whether governments have the right, under any circumstances, to compel people to limit the number of their children is highly debatable. Do individuals have absolute rights, or are all personal rights ultimately subject to the good of society? A great deal of past legislation—such as laws against child labor, racial or sexual discrimination, environmental pollution, and the like—has been based on the principle that people's right to swing their fists ends where others' noses begin. Is the freedom to bear children subject to this principle too?

Paul Ehrlich, author of *The Population Bomb*, considers the whole question of "freedom" confused and irrelevant:

> People aren't sufficiently aware that their freedoms are rapidly disappearing *because* there are more and more people. As population grows, we find that there are more and more restrictive laws on where we can drive, whether we can own a gun, whether we can fly an airplane, where we can throw our garbage, whether we can burn leaves. And as conditions become more crowded, even stricter and more comprehensive Government controls and regulations will be implemented.[40]

If compulsory population control does ever become necessary, it may not take a particularly flexible and humane form. By that time the emergency may be so acute that personal rights will have to be subordinated to social survival. In any event, responding to the challenge of the population problem will surely involve major changes in social policy all over the world. Fortunately, human beings, unlike other animals, have the ability to manipulate their environment and plan their futures. But if we fail to use our opportunities, then, as Ehrlich points out, we could go the way of all other species that could not adapt to changing conditions: toward extinction.

SUMMARY

1. Overpopulation, particularly among the less developed nations, is a grave social problem in itself, and is directly or indirectly implicated in many other social problems. If growth continues unchecked, the global consequences could be catastrophic.

[38] Kenneth E. Boulding, *The Meaning of the Twentieth Century: The Great Transition* (New York: Harper & Row, 1964), pp. 135–136

[39] Melvin M. Ketchel, "Fertility Control Agents as a Possible Solution to the World Population Problem," *Perspectives in Biology and Medicine*, 11 (Summer 1968), 687–703.

[40] Paul R. Ehrlich, "Interview: Dr. Paul Ehrlich," *Playboy*, 17 (August 1970), 58.

2. From a functionalist perspective, the problem is one of social disorganization caused by rapid social change. Large families were functional for society in the preindustrial past, but are dysfunctional in the modern world. In many societies, however, people's attitudes toward large families have not yet caught up with the reality of their situation. From a conflict perspective, the problem is aggravated by the fact that many people and governments do not consider rapid population growth a problem or are opposed to population control.

3. Demography is the scientific study of population. Key elements of demography are the birth rate, the death rate, the growth rate, doubling time, and the age structure of populations. In most developing countries the birth rate has remained high while the death rate has dropped sharply, leading to a population explosion.

4. The danger of rapid population growth was noted in 1798 by Thomas Malthus, who pointed out that population would always tend to outrun the means of subsistence. Although it seemed for a while that his fears were groundless, the popu-

lous developing nations now seem to be caught in the "Malthusian trap."

5. According to demographic transition theory, population size tends to stabilize once a certain level of economic development is achieved. There is no guarantee, however, that this historical sequence will be repeated in the developing nations. Although Indian efforts have had only limited success, China appears to be making real progress in population control.

6. The United States has a population problem in that continued growth will place severe burdens on national resources. It will also threaten living standards elsewhere in the world because the United States consumes a disproportionate amount of the planet's resources and generates a disproportionate amount of its pollution. Official United States policy now favors zero population growth.

7. There are three basic methods for achieving population control: family planning, the use of incentives, and coercion. If the first two prove ineffective, some form of the third may become the lesser of the evils confronting us.

GLOSSARY

Age structure. The proportion of different age groups within a given population.

Birth rate. The number of births per year per thousand members of a population.

Death rate. The number of deaths per year per thousand members of a population.

Demographic transition. The tendency for the growth rate of a population to decrease and then stabilize once a certain level of economic development has been achieved.

Demography. The scientific study of the size, composition, growth rates, and distribution of human populations.

Developed country. A society that is fully industrialized, such as the United States, Japan, and the countries of Europe.

Developing country. A country that is in transition from a predominantly agricultural to a predomi-

nantly modern, industrial economy, such as most nations of Africa, Asia and Latin America.

Doubling time. The time it will take for a population to double in size.

Exponential growth. A type of growth in which the increase in a given period is based not on the original figure but on the figure for the previous period.

Growth rate. A measure of population growth obtained by subtracting the number of deaths from the number of births and expressing this figure as an annual percentage.

Life expectancy. The number of years of life that the average newborn will enjoy.

Migration rate. The number of people entering or leaving a population per year per thousand members of the population.

Zero population growth. A situation in which population size remains stable over time.

FURTHER READING

BERELSON, BERNARD (ed.). *Population Policy in Developed Countries,* New York: McGraw-Hill, 1974. A useful examination of the population policies of the industrialized nations. The contributors discuss social and economic policies that might affect demographic trends in their respective countries.

BROWN, LESTER R., PATRICIA L. MCGRATH, and BRUCE STOKES. *Twenty-two Dimensions of the Population Problem.* Washington, D.C.: Worldwatch Institute, 1976. A succinct and useful analysis of the effect of population growth on various aspects of social and economic life.

CALLAHAN, DANIEL. *Ethics and Population Limitation.* 1971. A discussion of the moral issues involved in the population debate. Callahan looks at population growth from the perspective of three main values, which are not necessarily compatible: individual freedom, justice, and survival.

EHRLICH, PAUL R. *The Population Bomb,* New York: Ballantine, 1971. A best seller written for the general public rather than an academic audience. Ehrlich traces the course of population growth and surveys its impact on food, energy, and other resources. He makes an urgent plea for drastic changes in public policy and private attitudes.

EHRLICH, PAUL R., and ANNE H. EHRLICH. *Population/Resources/Environment: Issues in Human Ecology.* San Francisco: Freeman, 1972. A readable and comprehensive account of the interrelationship between population growth, resources, and environmental pollution.

KAMMEYER, KENNETH C. W. *Population Studies: Selected Essays and Research.* 2nd ed. Chicago: Rand McNally, 1975. A useful collection of key articles on population issues, most of them by demographers.

MATRAS, JUDAH. *Introduction to Population: A Sociological Approach.* Englewood Cliffs, N.J.: Prentice-Hall, 1977. A useful text that provides a sound and up-to-date introduction to the principles and practice of demography.

MEADOWS, DONELLA H., *et al. The Limits to Growth: A Report on the Club of Rome's Project on the Predicament of Mankind.* New York: Signet, 1972. A summary of the controversial findings of a research team's computer projection on the future interaction of population, resources, and pollution.

Population and the American Future: The Report of the Commission on Population Growth and the American Future. Washington, D.C.: U.S. Government Printing Office, 1972. A report on recent population trends in the United States and their potential implications.

REED, JAMES. *From Private Vice to Public Virtue: The Birth Control Movement and American Society Since 1830.* New York: Harper & Row, 1978. An interesting account of efforts of the birth-control movement to overcome prejudice against contraception and to win public support for family-planning programs.

REID, SUE T., and DAVID R. LYON (eds.). *Population Crisis: An Interdisciplinary Perspective.* Glenview, Ill.: Scott-Foresman, 1972. A book of readings covering perspectives on the population problem from several disciplines in both the natural and social sciences.

WRONG, DENNIS H. *Population and Society.* Rev. ed. New York: Random House, 1976. A short introduction to demography, with a clear account of the dynamics of population growth.

3
Environment and Resources

THE PROBLEM

When fledgling social movements first brought the environmental issue to the public's attention a few years ago, their concerns were widely dismissed as little more than a passing fad. Yet within a remarkably short time, environmental pollution and the shortage of energy and resources have come to be regarded as one of the major social problems confronting the world. The affluent way of life that we enjoy in the United States, and that the less developed nations of the world also hope to enjoy one day, is made possible only by massive and rapid industrial growth. We now realize that this industrial growth has been achieved at a devastating environmental cost, for it has seriously depleted natural resources and has generated widespread pollution of land, sea, and air.

The problem of the environment derives, paradoxically enough, from a unique human characteristic that is largely responsible for our remarkable success as a species—our ability to alter the environment to suit ourselves and our needs. In recent decades we have been changing the environment at such a rate and on such a scale that our former asset threatens to become a liability. Our demands for a rising standard of living and for an increasing supply of natural resources seem infinite—but the earth is finite. We are running out of resources and energy, and we are running out of space to put ourselves and our waste products. It is highly doubtful whether, in the long run, the environment can sustain either our demands or the injuries we are inflicting on it.

The problem is compounded by the fact that its two components, environmental pollution and resource depletion, are so inextricably linked. The material life style that we value so highly relies on industrial production on a huge scale, but we cannot fuel this industry without depleting resources of energy and raw materials, nor manufacture and consume the products we want without causing some measure of pollution. As Irving Louis Horowitz suggests, "What people in this country want and feel entitled to is having their cake and eating it at the same time. . . . What the ecologists condemn, the economists celebrate."[1] Any and every attempt to solve the problem will therefore involve hard, unpleasant choices, for any solution will have its costs—in taxes, higher prices, shortages, or other inconveniences.

The problem is also complicated by the growing economic interdependence of the nations of the world. No country can rely entirely on its own resources for the materials it needs, and some scarce resources have become a crucial element in economic and political relationships among different nations. The advanced industrial societies have always relied heavily on cheap imports of raw materials from the less developed nations. Now, however, these poorer countries are determined to change the global imbalance of wealth—as Americans became painfully aware when the oil-producing nations sharply increased the price of oil, provoking massive inflation and

---

[1] Irving Louis Horowitz, *Ideology and Utopia in the United States, 1956–1976* (New York: Oxford University Press, 1977), p. 424.

57

encouraging economic recessions during the 1970s. As the poorer nations grow more insistent in their demands for a greater share of the world's wealth, and as they need more of their raw materials to fuel their own developing economies, many important resources are likely to grow even more scarce. Problems of pollution, too, cannot be confined to national boundaries. The pollutants pumped into the rivers, oceans, or skies of one country are often carried to others, contaminating air, agricultural products, and living creatures.

Although the problems of pollution and resource depletion are international, they involve the United States more than any other country. With only 6 percent of the planet's population, the United States consumes about 30 percent of its energy and nearly 40 percent of its natural resources and contributes about half of its industrial pollution. As one writer notes:

The average American uses more electric power than fifty-five Asians or Africans. The generation of electric power is a prime producer of pollution. A single American accounts for more detergents, pesticides, radioactive substances, fertilizers, fungicides, and defoliants in the rivers and oceans than are produced by a thousand people in Indonesia—a nation that is generally cited as a prime example of human overcrowding. One American is responsible for putting more carbon monoxide and benzopyrene in the air than 200 Pakistanis or Indians. One American consumes three times more food than the average person who comes from places that account for two-thirds of the world's population. The average American is responsible for 2,500 pounds of waste per year— many times the world average. If abandoned refrigerators, automobiles, and other bulky objects were included, the figure would be astronomically higher. The United States . . . accounts for almost 30 percent of the poisons being dumped into the sky and the seas. The notion, therefore, that Americans are less of a drain on the Earth than Chinese or Indians, because there are so many fewer of us, is an absurdity and a dangerous one.[2]

In many small, preindustrial communities, the inhabitants regard themselves as a part of the natural world, an element in an integrated system in which nature influences human beings as much as human beings influence nature. But in modern industrial societies, especially in those that share the Western cultural tradition, people tend to take a different view. The Book of Genesis teaches that we were made in the image of God, who gave us "dominion over all the earth, and over every creeping thing that creepeth upon the earth." The image of human beings struggling against nature is far more common in our literature and art than the image of a joint venture between the two. By acting on their cultural values, the industrialized nations have done immense damage to the environment.

Particularly in North America, the relationship between human beings and nature has been one of subjugation and exploitation. When the first settlers set foot on Plymouth Rock, they found "a hideous and desolate wilderness, full of wilde beasts and wilde men."[3] But this wilderness was also a land of seemingly unlimited abundance that would richly reward the efforts of any industrious man or woman.

Drawn by the promise of land and the opportunity to start a new life, great tides of immigrants came from the Old World, bringing with them the values and technology that would transform the New World. The pioneers acted on the conviction that the wilderness was to be remade (the image of the rugged, individualistic frontier settler that dominated that era persists to this day), and the new military and agricultural technology spelled the end of the Native American way of life. Woodcutters chopped down whole forests and moved on. Oilmen opened gushers that spewed oil at the rate of thousands of barrels a day from what seemed limitless wells. Cattle barons bred herds that stripped the plains of grass, creating wastelands. Farmers plowed up turf in the dry plains states, and the wind blew the topsoil away. Hunters wiped out millions of bison, often butchering the animals for the tongue—a delicacy—and leaving

[2]Norman Cousins, "Affluence and Effluence," *Saturday Review*, May 2, 1970, p. 53.

[3]Quoted in Stewart L. Udall, *The Quiet Crisis* (New York: Holt, Rinehart & Winston, 1963), p. 3.

The roadsides and highways of America have been made ugly through the unregulated profusion of garish advertising signs and billboards. Conservationists are now broadening their objectives to include an attack on this visual pollution of the landscape.

the rest of the carcass to rot. By the turn of the century, there were less than two dozen bison left. Alaskan seals were slaughtered down to 3 percent of their former numbers. Passenger pigeons, which represented a third of the entire bird population of the United States and which darkened the skies for several days during their annual migrations, were hunted to extinction.

Abundance encouraged waste: if the resources of one area were exhausted, there was plenty more elsewhere. Economic growth was considered a blessing: the man or woman who produced more was rewarded, not the person who preserved the surrounding natural beauty. Not all

Americans, of course, shared the myth of inexhaustible resources. People of conscience and foresight formed a social movement to conserve the environment. Their campaigns led to the creation of national and state parks and the legislation that, by the beginning of this century, had ended the most blatant and irresponsible examples of the plundering of natural resources. But the dominant American creed today still reflects many of our early values—rugged individualism, a striving for material goods, a frontier ethic that justifies the subjugation of nature to human wants.

ANALYZING THE PROBLEM

A sociological analysis of the environmental problem can draw on both the functionalist and the conflict approaches. Separately, each sheds a different light on the problem; together they provide a fuller understanding of the issues.

The Functionalist Approach

As seen from the functionalist approach, the problems of the environment stem from social disorganization brought about by rapid social change. The Industrial Revolution radically changed the way of life of peoples all over the world. In preindustrial agricultural societies most people were poor. The great majority of the population worked the land, living at little more

than a bare subsistence level. Any surplus produced was generally seized by a small upper class of aristocrats and landowners, who converted it into other forms of wealth and enjoyed an affluent life style. This social order was transformed by industrialism, which is a much more productive strategy (so productive that although in the modern United States the farm force is less than 5 percent of the population, it is able to feed the nation). Industrialism creates hundreds of thousands of new types of jobs, and makes possible a high standard of living for an unprecedentedly large part of a population. In this sense, industrialism is highly functional.

But the constant increase in the consumption of resources, in the generation of environmental pollution, and in the growth of the global population that has characterized industrialization is all too obviously dysfunctional. In addition, the rapidity with which industrialization has taken place has aggravated the problem further: most of the world's industrial capacity was created between 1950 and 1970, during which time the economic productivity of the human population trebled.[4] More and more people are demanding and creating ever greater quantities of material goods, but the pace of change has been so fast that we have developed few mechanisms to cushion the environmental impact of this headlong industrial advance. The delicate balance of nature is being upset to the point where population, industrialization, and pollution cannot continue to grow at their present rates without inviting possible disaster.

The Conflict Approach

According to the conflict approach, conflicts over values and interests are deeply involved in the problem of the environment. Many powerful elements in society, including political authorities and large corporations, have a stake in continued free exploitation of the environment. Federal, state, and local governments naturally favor an expanding economy and rising living standards, and corporations are dedicated to turning raw materials into marketable goods for profit. Pollution controls, whether they are paid for by the actual polluters or by the public through taxation, are expensive and often inconvenient. It is small wonder that intense conflicts often arise among the groups comprising the ecology movement, on the one hand, and economic interests and public authorities, on the other.[5]

The debate over the Alaskan oil pipeline illustrates the conflict between demands for resources and demands for environmental conservation. Environmentalists were able to delay construction of the pipeline for several years by pointing to the effects it might have on the wildlife and environment of Alaska. But as soon as an oil shortage developed in 1973, public opinion swung rapidly against the conservation movement, and legislation to permit construction was rushed through Congress. The nation opted for economic growth and exploitation of resources despite the environmental costs. Similarly, there are strong demands today that the requirements of the Clean Air Act be eased. State governments often deliberately overlook violations of the act, preferring that the guilty manufacturers continue to expand production instead of diverting their profits into antipollution controls. In fact, the Environmental Protection Agency has virtually given up the broad effort to enforce federal air-pollution standards strictly, concentrating instead on only the worst offenders. Even in California, the state with the most stringent antipollution regulations in the nation, officials see no prospect of meeting federally mandated clean-air standards by the 1980s deadlines.[6]

Government bureaucracies and profit-hungry corporations are not the only elements in society that oppose cleaning up the environment. At the other end of the political spectrum many radicals regard concern for the environment as a middle-class luxury—a largely aesthetic concern that distracts attention from more pressing social problems.[7] The various branches of the ecology movement—such as Friends of the Earth, Environmental Action, the League of Conservation Voters—are hardly filled with manual workers, racial minorities, or the poor and deprived. On the contrary, their ranks are composed mainly of white, middle-class suburbanites, who have the money and leisure to enjoy the unspoiled environment they are trying to preserve. But what of the blue-collar workers and the unemployed? It is often the case that to them "smoke means jobs"—in other words, resource depletion and environmental pollution can imply the economic development that offers their only chance of improved living standards. A forest may be

---

[4]RIO: Reshaping the International Order: A Report to the Club of Rome (New York: E. P. Dutton, 1976), p. 11.

[5]J. Clarence Davies, III, and Barbara S. Davies, The Politics of Pollution, 2nd ed. (Indianapolis: Bobbs-Merrill, 1975).

[6]New York Times, February 15, 1978.

[7]See "Ecological Movements vs. Economic Necessities," in Horowitz, op. cit., pp. 419–426.

saved by including it in a national or state park, but the jobs of lumberjacks may be lost; a factory may be closed because it is polluting a river, but the gates may close on hundreds of workers as well. Again, social priorities will have to emerge from this conflict of values and interests: do we want more industrial production and jobs despite the pollution they create, or less filth in the atmosphere and our lungs despite the economic costs?

There is even disagreement over the urgency of the problem. Some critics believe that the issue is phony or that conservational efforts are misguided. A few experts have argued that the prophecies of environmental doom are grossly exaggerated. The ecologist John Maddox, for example, takes the optimistic view that there is more energy available now than at any time in history. Maddox believes that there is relatively little pollution in the sense that the planet could probably tolerate a good deal more; and that the small quantities of insecticides found in Antarctic birds prove that the poison spreads very slowly, rather than that it threatens the world.[8] Others, such as the economist Harold Barnett, hope that future technological discoveries will provide a solution. Barnett recalls that there have been many gloomy predictions in the past, but that we have always triumphed through the use of new technologies: new fertilizers, new weed-killers, the power saw, long-distance pipelines, strip mining. Radical new methods, he suggests, will soon be found to solve our problems.[9]

All of us are involved in this conflict of values and interests, for all of us both suffer and benefit in different ways from the destruction of the natural environment. Robert Reinow and Leona Train Reinow suggest that American values contain little commitment to environmental conservation:

Americans have come to accept as a right an ignominious premise: that waste disposal is an essential use of surface water—that a basic function of a crystal stream or wholesome lake is to accept as much sewage and industrial filth as it can possibly handle without losing so much oxygen that it turns into a festering foul-smelling cesspool. On this premise we have built our whole national economy. . . .[10]

Thus, although environmental awareness has soared during the past decade, most Americans, including many who consider themselves environmentally conscious, carry on in the tradition of the early frontier settlers and resource raiders. They drive enormous cars that pollute the environment, they waste water and electricity, and they squander valuable resources in their consumption of, among other things, such niceties as tons of plastic and paper packaging. In pursuing our own life styles and interests, virtually all of us add to the problem.

In addition to having the insights of the functionalist and conflict approaches, sociologists are aided in their analysis of our environmental dilemma by data drawn from other disciplines—notably from the work of ecologists who study the biological aspects of the environment, and the work of futurologists who make projections of existing economic, demographic, and other relevant trends.

THE SCIENCE OF ECOLOGY

Life on earth exists only in the biosphere, a thin film of air, soil, and water at or near the surface of the planet. Within this biosphere, and particularly in the region immediately above and below sea level, countless species of organisms live in a delicately balanced and infinitely complex relationship with one another (Figure 3.1). The study of this interlocking web of life is only a few decades old. It is termed *ecology* (from the Greek word for "home"), and is the science of the mutual relationships between organisms and their environment. It studies all forms of life in their natural settings—from the worm to the tree

[8]John Maddox, *The Doomsday Syndrome*, New York: McGraw-Hill, 1972, pp. 4–5.
[9]Harold J. Barnett, "The Myth of Our Vanishing Resources," *Trans-action*, 4 (June 1967), 7–10.
[10]Robert Rienow and Leona Train Rienow, *Moment in the Sun* (New York: Ballantine Books, 1969), p. 131.

FIGURE 3.1 **The biosphere.** The biosphere is a thin film of life-sustaining air, soil, and water at or near the surface of the earth. The biosphere, with its countless interdependent organisms, is the largest of all ecosystems, but it is fragile and easily disrupted.
(John McHale, *World Facts and Trends* [New York: Macmillan, 1972], p. 9.)

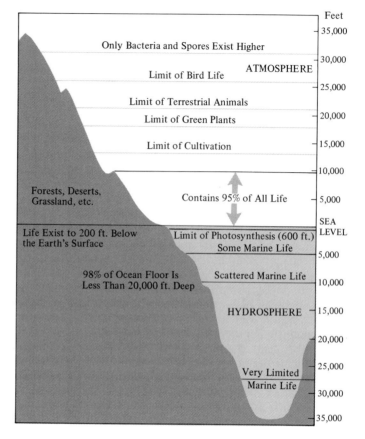

to human beings. More important, it attempts to trace how these organisms function in their distinctive environments, both alone and together. The ecological perspective has given us the notion of "Spaceship Earth"—the idea of our planet as a massive, life-sustaining vessel in the void of the universe, with finite, endlessly cycling resources.

The Concept of the Ecosystem. At the heart of the science of ecology is the concept of an *ecosystem,* a self-sustaining community of organisms within an inorganic (nonliving) environment. The ecosystem may be as large as the biosphere itself, or as small as a drop of pond water, teeming with microscopic yet interdependent inhabitants. There are four main elements in any ecosystem:

1. *Energy and inorganic matter.* Life can exist only in the presence of energy and inorganic matter. Energy is drawn mainly, though often indirectly, from the sun. Inorganic matter includes substances such as water, oxygen, carbon dioxide, nitrogen, and other nutrients. These sources of energy and nutrition provide the environment that sustains the processes of life.

2. *Plants (or producers).* These are the trees, shrubs, grasses, and other green plants that take energy from the sun and nutrients from the soil and atmosphere and convert them into organic (living) material. The producers range in size from microscopic algae to huge redwoods.

3. *Consumers.* These are the higher organisms that feed on the producers. Some—the primary consumers, or herbivores—feed directly on the plants, as in the case of deer and rabbits. Others—the secondary consumers, or carnivores, such as polar bears and lions—feed on other animals. Food chains can become very complex; for example, human beings are both primary and secondary consumers; a mosquito that feeds on a human being is a tertiary consumer.

4. *Decomposers.* These are tiny creatures—insects,

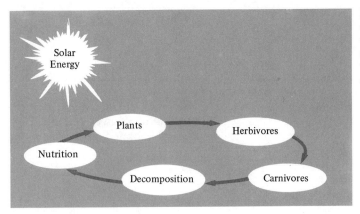

FIGURE 3.2 **The cycle of life.** Life on earth depends on a delicately balanced cycle involving energy, plants, animals, and nutrition sources. Disruption of the cycle at any point can have severe effects elsewhere in the process.

bacteria, fungi—that abound in the soil, the atmosphere, and the bodies of dead plants and animals. They break down the organic material of the dead organisms, releasing their nutrients back into the ecosystem. Even these lowly, invisible microorganisms, unmourned when they are exterminated, are essential to life on earth.

Each component in the ecosystem interacts with others in an astonishingly complex network of interlocking energy and chemical cycles. Although growth and decay are taking place continuously and simultaneously in an ecosystem, they balance each other in the long run: the ecosystem tends to equilibrium (Figure 3.2). All living things, including human beings, depend on the stability of this chain of life. As Alan Devoe points out:

> All creatures are in a common brotherhood . . . interconnected with everything else. . . . There is a bond between a man and a mouse, or a tree and a fox, or a frog and a raccoon. . . . We are one small ingredient in a whole of unimaginable vastness . . . a part of a general and embracing interdependence. . . . We are supported by starfish. An owl props us. Earthworms minister to hold us upright.[11]

Human Interference in the Ecosystem. Interference at any point in these cycles can have unforeseen and disruptive consequences. The first significant human interference with the ecosystem began to occur at the time of the Agricultural Revolution, when our hunting and

gathering ancestors learned to domesticate animals and plants, replacing the complex ecosystem with a simple one in which nearly all the energy and chemical cycles were directed at supporting the human species alone. Since that time, technological progress has been spectacular, and so has the accompanying rate of population increase. Within a relatively short period after the development of organized agriculture, the first urban societies were founded (and less than 6,000 years later, human beings were walking on the moon). Today, every month, we add to our numbers the equivalent of the entire human population at the time of the Agricultural Revolution, and we are capable of, and are achieving, large-scale interference in the global ecological balance. Again and again we disrupt the web of life by shutting out sunlight with smog, increasing the amount of atmospheric carbon dioxide by burning fuels, killing off decomposers with insecticides, polluting water sources with chemical effluents, or simply hunting species to extinction.

To biologist Paul Ehrlich, the main reason for the reckless human intervention in the planetary ecosystem is overpopulation.[12] Others, like ecologist Barry Commoner, believe that faulty technology is the major environmental threat. Commoner points out that pollution has increased more than 2,000 percent since World War II, a far greater increase than the growth in population. The real problem, he argues, is that "pro-

---

[11]Quoted in Rienow and Rienow, *op. cit.*, p. 45.

[12]Paul R. Ehrlich and Anne H. Ehrlich, *Population/Resources/Environment: Issues in Human Ecology*, 2d ed. (San Francisco: W. H. Freeman, 1972).

ductive technologies with intensive impacts on the environment have displaced less destructive ones."[13] For example, high-polluting detergents have largely replaced low-polluting soap; truck freight haulage, with high environmental impact, has replaced rail haulage, with its relatively low impact; synthetic, nondegradable fibers have replaced natural fibers; plastics have replaced wood. Commoner takes an implicitly conflict approach to the problem, arguing that the impetus for these technological developments has been the profit motive of powerful corporate industry, which now has a huge stake in manufacturing processes that are detrimental to the environment:

> This situation is an ecologist's nightmare, for in the four to five year period in which a new synthetic substance, such as a detergent or pesticide, is massively moved into the market—and into the environment—there is literally not enough time to work out its ecological effects. Inevitably, by the time the effects are known, the damage is done and the inertia of the heavy investment in a new productive technology makes a retreat extraordinarily difficult. The very system of enhancing profit in this industry is precisely the cause of its intense, detrimental impact on the environment.[14]

As a result, Commoner claims, we have created a counterecological pattern of growth: "Human beings have broken out of the cycle of life . . . to survive, we must close the circle."[15]

THE DETERIORATING ENVIRONMENT

From the time that our ancestors threw gnawed bones into the nearest gully, we have assumed that nature would swallow our wastes and render them innocuous. But now population and technology are overwhelming the capacity of nature to cope. We are fouling our own environmental nest and causing havoc elsewhere in the ecosys-

tem. Many smaller ecosystems that took millennia to evolve have been irreparably damaged. Entire species are no more than memories; and such familiar creatures as polar bears, tigers, and several species of whales are on the danger list.[16]

Let's look at some of the ways in which the multiplying industrial population is threatening the planetary ecosystem.

Air Pollution

Citizens on the streets of New York inhale the equivalent in toxic materials of thirty-eight cigarettes a day.[17] Atmospheric pollution cuts down on the amount of sunlight reaching New York by up to 25 percent. Other cities are worse off, however; pollution cuts out up to 40 percent of Chicago's sunlight.[18] Not only cities are affected; smog generated in urban and industrial areas has been sighted over the oceans and even over the North Pole. The United States dumps more than 200 million tons of wastes into the atmosphere every day—almost a ton per day per person.[19]

Air pollution comes from four main sources: transportation, power generation, industry, and waste incineration. By far the most serious contributor to air pollution is the private automobile. Each year more than 90 million cars spew forth hundreds of millions of tons of carbon monoxide, sulfur oxides, nitrogen oxides, hydrocarbons, particulate matter, and a variety of other poisonous substances.[20] Areas such as Los Angeles show a concentration of lead in the air that is fifty times greater than that in rural areas.[21] Asbestos particles from brake linings pollute city air and, in sufficient amounts, are

[13]Barry Commoner, *The Closing Circle* (New York: Knopf, 1971), p. 177.
[14]*Ibid.*
[15]*Ibid.*, p. 261.
[16]For a recent overview of the state of the American environment, see "The 1978 Environmental Quality Index: A Fresh Start," *National Wildlife*, 16 (February–March 1978), 17–32.
[17]Rienow and Rienow, *op. cit.*, p. 141.
[18]Ehrlich and Ehrlich, *op. cit.*, p. 147.
[19]Kenneth Auchincloss, "The Ravaged Environment," *Newsweek*, January 26, 1970, pp. 2–6.
[20]Ehrlich and Ehrlich, *op. cit.*, p. 146.
[21]John McHale, *World Facts and Trends*, 2d ed. (New York: Macmillan, 1972), p. 16.

An electricity generating plant pollutes air and water. The environmental impact of this plant illustrates a basic American dilemma: the more energy and re- sources we consume, the more pollution we create. Ultimately, we may have to choose between high consumption and a livable environment.

believed to be carcinogenic (cancer-causing). Despite government regulations and industry efforts, the situation is not getting any better. New automobiles are being added to our already clogged highways at such a rate that soon the gains made by antipollution devices in improving air quality may actually be reversed.

Power generation produces many noxious chemicals, particularly sulfur oxides derived from the burning of high-sulfur coal. Industry produces an almost infinite range of atmospheric pollutants.[22] Waste incineration, even when done properly, produces millions of tons of particulates and nitrogen oxides, and when done improperly, produces carbon monoxide as well.

Air pollution on this scale poses a grave threat to public health. Deaths due to lung cancer and bronchitis are doubling every ten years, and emphysema, a lung disease, is the fastest-growing cause of death in the United States. Air pollution has been directly implicated in these trends. In fact, under the particular climatic condition known as thermal inversion (a layer of warm air above a layer of cold air), smog becomes trapped near the earth's surface, in some cases so densely that it has directly killed numbers of people. The most notorious example was the 1952 smog in London, which killed 4,000 persons in the space of four days (the victims were mostly very old or very young people who already had respiratory problems). There have been several less dramatic instances in the United States. On Thanksgiving Day, 1966, an inversion trapped fumes in New York City and caused an estimated 168 deaths. Los Angeles, surrounded by mountains on three sides, lies in a basin that traps warm, polluted air.

---

[22]Ehrlich and Ehrlich, *op. cit.*, p. 147.

The following is an excerpt from a Sierra Club book.

. . .

The Pickwick Restaurant on Superior Street in downtown Duluth features fresh lake trout and a splendid view of the harbor and to get to either, or both, you go in through a door with a sign that reads: *FILTERED WATER*. The filter itself, one of those installed by the Army, is located under and attached to the water tap where the waitresses fill glasses on their way from the kitchen to the room with a view. The filter is a 12-inch jar packed tightly with thin shafts like pipe cleaners—your Maginot Line against a mouthful of amphibole fibers. To partake of water free of asbestiform fibers, of course, a resident of Duluth does not have to go out on the town every night. Ben Boo has made filtered water available at the city's

firehouses, and WDIO-TV, the local broadcasting station, generously shares its copious hilltop well with the populace, which carries away about 45,000 gallons each month. Not much, considering that Duluth's total consumption is 25 million gallons a day. Still, the WDIO water is there for anyone who wants it. And those who do, if you bother to ask their opinion, are more than happy to express themselves on the current distressing situation. "How come," said one elderly man emerging from the well shed with a plastic jug in each hand, "how come I have to pay for sewage disposal and everyone I know has to pay for sewage disposal and that outfit up the lake, that Reserve, gets it for nothing? How come . . .?"

And at the bar of the Pickwick sat a man who worked for twenty-eight years as a brakeman on trains hauling ore from Mesabi. He is retired. I found this out after I mentioned the filtered

The city declares occasional "smog days," on which conditions are so dangerous that schoolchildren are not allowed to engage in activities that might involve deep breathing.

The U.S. Public Health Service predicts that sulfur dioxide emission will increase from its 1960 level of 20 million tons to 35 million by the year 2000; nitrogen oxide emission will rise from 11 million to 30 million tons, and particulates, from 30 million to over 45 million tons. The number of automobiles is expected to quadruple in the same period.[23] The prospects for cleaner air, obviously, are not encouraging—especially when the auto manufacturers and gasoline producers constitute such powerful interests in American society and when American values place such emphasis on the virtues of the private car in preference to low-polluting mass-transit systems.

Water Pollution

The United States has the unique, if dubious, distinction of being the only country in the world to contain a river that has been declared a fire hazard. The river is the Cuyahoga in Ohio,

which has twice caught fire when the industrial chemicals, oils, and other combustible pollutants that it carries were accidentally ignited. Although few of our other rivers are likely to burst into flame, many of them are heavily polluted. Communities all over the United States depend for their domestic water supplies on the contaminated water flushed out of communities upstream from them. Immense sums are spent on making this water safe to drink, though not always successfully. Dozens of American cities are listed by the Public Health Service as having water supplies that are "unsatisfactory" or "a potential health hazard."

Many of our lakes, too, are in danger. Lake Erie is now almost dead, its bottom covered with a layer of effluent that is up to 125 feet thick in places. Other of the Great Lakes are also threatened by an acceleration of the aging process called eutrophication. Under natural conditions, eutrophication occurs slowly. A lake starts out cold and almost lifeless, but as streams carry in nutrients from the surrounding drainage basin, the fertility of the water increases, encouraging the growth of plants and animals. Organic material piles up on the lake bottom, and the water becomes shallower and warmer. The edges fill in,

---

[23]Ehrlich and Ehrlich, *op. cit.*, p. 152.

water. And then he began to speak of Lake Superior. "I love that lake," he said. "I fish it a lot, but mostly just look at it. In the war it was good to be from Minnesota because Minnesota was part of this lake. And you could be proud because all your buddies knew that this was where the fresh air and clean water was. But now these . . . in Cleveland and Dayton . . . ."

"Middletown," I said.

"And Middletown—all the way down in Ohio, can you believe it?—are pouring their crap in this lake. And they are killing it." Having said that, the man who loves Lake Superior slammed his fist on the bar and stalked out through the door, the one with the sign that reads: *FILTERED WATER.*

Me, I stalked out, too; and in the morning drove out along U.S. Highway 61, past the Lakewood Pumping Station. The pumphouse, I now understand, is finally to be retrofitted with a filtration system. The project may possibly be complete in time for a Bicentennial Year christening. Possibly but not probably, because Ben Boo is haggling with the United States of America, the State of Minnesota, and the Reserve Mining Company over the delicate question of who will help him pick up the six-million-dollar tab.

And then I was talking with Dr. Donald Mount, a biologist and director of the EPA's National Water Quality Laboratory, not far from the pumphouse off Highway 61. "Every liter of water coming into Duluth right now contains about 35 million asbestiform fibers," Mount was saying. "I can't understand how we can treat so many people as if they were laboratory animals."

. . .

Source: John G. Mitchell, *Losing Ground* (San Francisco: Sierra Club Books, 1975), pp. 157–158.

marsh intrudes, and swampy forests take over until the lake disappears completely. Created by a glacier a mere 20,000 years ago, the Great Lakes were very young when the first Europeans discovered them—cold, deep, extremely pure. But in the past fifty years the enormous amount of pollution has speeded up the eutrophication process—in the case of Lake Erie, by the equivalent of 15,000 years. The lake is probably unsalvageable and seems destined to appear on future maps as a gigantic swamp.[24]

Much of the pollution that falls out of the atmosphere or enters rivers finally ends up in the oceans (which contain four-fifths of the planet's animal life and the bulk of its vegetation). Even their vastness cannot absorb the mounting deluge of contaminants. A few years ago the explorer Thor Heyerdahl, crossing the Atlantic on a small raft, found the surface of the ocean littered like a city beach with plastic bottles and gobs of tar. Half a million tons of crude oil are leaked or dumped into the oceans every year, often finding their way to the shores.[25] Rivers now carry more than 6 million tons of phosphates to the sea each year, mostly in the form of agricultural fertilizers that disrupt the delicate ecosystems of the shoreline and beyond. Lead is being washed into the sea at a rate thirteen times higher than under natural conditions. The oceans are the ultimate accumulation site for as much as 25 percent of the DDT and other pesticides sprayed onto the land; as a result, large numbers of fish have been condemned for human consumption because of the high concentration of artificial poisons in their flesh.[26] It is often held that we can solve the problem of the world's food shortage by increased exploitation of the oceans, but this hope neglects the fact that about 90 percent of the ocean is essentially a biological desert. The open sea produces a negligible fraction of the world's fish catch at present and has little or no potential for yielding more in the future, since the nutrients that sustain oceanic life are concentrated in coastal waters.[27]

[24]Charles F. Powers and Andrew Robertson, "The Aging of the Great Lakes," *Scientific American*, 215 (November 1966), 95–104.

[25]McHale, *op. cit.*, p. 27.

[26]Goldsmith *et al.*, "Blueprint for Survival," *The Ecologist*, 2 (January 1972), p. 3.

[27]John H. Rhyther, "Photosynthesis and Fish Production in the Sea," *Science*, October 3, 1969, pp. 72–76.

Because the rivers that carry these nutrients to the sea are now laden with poisons, pollution may kill off much of this anticipated food resource and leave a good deal of the remainder inedible.

Again, the problems raised by water pollution require some hard choices. Can we maintain a high population and a high standard of living without producing billions of tons of pollutants? And if we do not dump them into the rivers and seas, where do we put them?

Despoiling the Land

Since the Agricultural Revolution, vast land expanses have been devastated by counterecological activities. The Sahara Desert, for example, is partly the result of human interference in the ecosystem; beneath the thick layers of sand are traces of luxuriant forests that existed less than 2,000 years ago. The dense woods that once covered Morocco have disappeared as a result of overgrazing by domesticated sheep and goats. Today, forests are being cut down throughout the tropics to make way for more economically rewarding activities such as cattle-raising. Again, the ecological consequences are unforeseeable—both for the regions concerned and for the global environment that depends on these forests to remove large quantities of carbon dioxide from the atmosphere.

Exploitation and despoliation of land resources occur all over the United States in such forms as the construction of highways, the development of massive engineering projects like the Alaskan pipeline, and dam building. Much of the dam construction that takes place in the United States is unnecessary, yields minimal benefits, and is environmentally destructive. In many cases, dam projects are examples of "pork barrel" politics at work: Congress votes funds for the projects to provide investment and jobs in members' home states, whether the dams are needed or not.[28] Environmental concerns are once more lost in a conflict of interests.

A major source of land despoliation is the strip mining of coal. Much of the coal in the United States—particularly in Western areas of outstanding natural beauty—lies just below the surface of the soil. This coal can be extracted more cheaply and safely than coal lying far below the surface, but only by stripping away the land that lies above it. In the process, forests and other plant life are destroyed, hilltops are leveled, water courses are altered, the fertile topsoil is destroyed, and the land is impregnated with sulfur released from the coal. Federal regulations now require mining companies to reclaim the land by returning it to its original condition, but full reclamation is costly and frequently impossible; moreover, these regulations are often half-heartedly enforced. Strip mining has already left ugly scars over more than 5 million acres of the United States.

Another way we despoil the land is by dumping our garbage on it. An urban population of 1 million needs dumping space for 5,000 cubic feet of refuse every day. Each year we junk over 3.5 billion tons of wastes, including 7 million automobiles, 20 million tons of paper, 55 billion cans, 26 billion bottles and jars, 65 billion metal and plastic bottle caps, and 10 million tons of iron and steel.[29] Solid wastes are unpleasant, odorous, and ugly. They pollute water that percolates through them, they pollute the atmosphere if they are incinerated, and they provide breeding grounds for many noxious pests. Yet these pollutants and wastes exist only because there is a demand, a market, and a profit for the original products. Our own values as a society have led inevitably to the despoliation of the land.

Chemicals and Pesticides

American women carry in their breasts up to ten times more of the toxic insecticide DDT than the maximum level permitted in dairy milk sold for human consumption in interstate commerce. Every morsel that we eat, even "organic" food, is tainted with pesticides. The soil and water of the planet have been contaminated with these chemicals, which are very stable and resist de-

[28]See Gene Marine, *America the Raped: The Engineering Mentality and the Devastation of a Continent* (New York: Simon and Schuster, 1969).

[29]McHale, *op. cit.*, p. 22; Ehrlich and Ehrlich, *op. cit.*, p. 159.

Our consumer society generates millions of tons of waste products every year. Some of the waste is burned, polluting the air; some is dumped at sea, polluting the ocean; but most is left to rust and rot on the land.

composition for decades after they are first used. DDT is found everywhere on earth, even in the tissues of Antarctic penguins, on a continent where the chemical has never been used. And there is growing evidence that many pesticides and synthetic chemicals are carcinogenic. Medical scientists now believe that about three-quarters of human cancers have environmental causes. The spread of DDT and other toxic chemicals shows how we have surrounded ourselves with hundreds of thousands of new compounds about whose potential effects we know virtually nothing. Neither we nor any other species on the planet has had any evolutionary experience with the new substances, and we have had no opportunity to evolve natural defenses against potential damage that they might do. Most of the chemicals may well prove innocuous to us, if not to other species; but many, such as chlorinated hydrocarbon insecticides or the tranquilizer thalidomide (which caused birth deformities when administered to pregnant women), can have unintended effects on the human population.

How have DDT and the other insecticides spread throughout the ecosystem, and why are they found in such high concentrations in consumers at the top of the food chain? The chemicals enter the ecosystem when they are sprayed on the land. Some of the substance remains in the soil, some is blown into the atmosphere, and some is washed into the rivers and seas. The chemical contaminates plant life, which is then eaten by animals which, in turn, are eaten by other animals, and so on, up the chain. DDT and many other pesticides are cumulative poisons; that is, they tend to be retained in the tissues of the organisms that consume them rather than being excreted back into the environment. The concentration of DDT increases

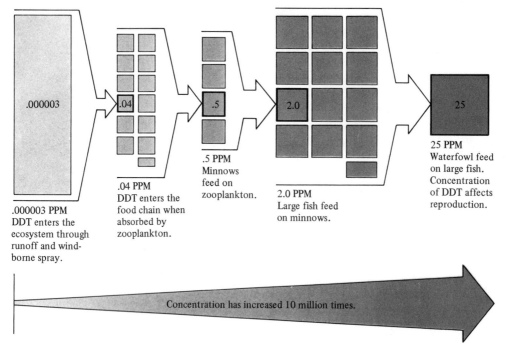

.000003 PPM
DDT enters the
ecosystem through
runoff and wind-
borne spray.

.04 PPM
DDT enters the
food chain when
absorbed by
zooplankton.

.5 PPM
Minnows
feed on
zooplankton.

2.0 PPM
Large fish feed
on minnows.

25 PPM
Waterfowl feed
on large fish.
Concentration
of DDT affects
reproduction.

Concentration has increased 10 million times.

FIGURE 3.3 **Magnification of DDT in parts per million (PPM).** Like many other pesticides, DDT is an extremely stable compound that does not decompose for many decades. It is readily absorbed into the tissues of plants and animals, and when these organisms consume each other, the concentration of the chemical is magnified at each step. Animals at the top of the food chain may absorb lethal quantities of a pesticide that was applied many years previously and hundreds of miles away.
(John McHale, *World Facts and Trends* [New York: Macmillan, 1972], p. 21.)

at each level in the food chain; concentrations in animals at the top of the chain are sometimes as much as ten million times higher than in animals lower down (Figure 3.3).

Pesticides have been effective against agricultural pests, but only to a limited and steadily diminishing extent. Some 250 pest species are resistant to one group of pesticides or another, and others require increasing applications of poison to keep their populations under control. Other previously rare or innocuous creatures— mites, for example—have actually become major pests because of the unintended eradication of their natural predators. The toxic substances spread everywhere, affecting animal life that was never the target of the exterminators. This has been the fate of the American bald eagle, our national emblem, which now faces extinction because the DDT in its eggs often prevents them

from hatching. The combined effects of pollution and habitat destruction now menace the survival of no less than 280 mammal, 350 bird, and 20,000 plant species.[30]

So far, the United States has released about 1 billion pounds of DDT into the environment, although its use has now been restricted. Annual world production of the chemical, which is only one of many similar pesticides, is 1.3 billion pounds.[31]

Radioactive Wastes

The United States now has nearly 70 nuclear power plants, and there are plans for over 200 more to be built within ten years. Although an

---

[30]Goldsmith *et al., op. cit.,* p. 6.
[31]McHale, *op. cit.,* p. 21.

explosion at any one of these plants would not be large, the nuclear fallout could be the equivalent of hundreds of Hiroshima-sized atomic bombs. In May 1974 the Atomic Energy Commission admitted that all plants operating in the previous year had suffered "abnormal occurrences," including 371 "potentially significant" incidents, of which 12 involved the release of radioactivity outside the power plants. Thirteen of the plants had to be shut down for extended periods.[32] Since then, virtually every nuclear plant in the country has been shut down at one time or another because of unanticipated but potentially hazardous accidents or other operating problems. The most serious of these events was the much-publicized 1979 accident at Three Mile Island, Pennsylvania, in which the danger of radioactive leakage from the crippled reactor caused over 200,000 people in neighboring areas to flee their homes. This single incident alerted the public to the dangers of nuclear power as never before.

Nuclear power plants generate radioactive nuclear wastes. These wastes emit radiation that in small doses can cause cancers or birth deformities, and in large doses, death. The wastes are particularly dangerous because many of them remain radioactive for tens, hundreds, or even thousands of years—in some cases, as long as 300,000 years. The problems posed by nuclear power plants are likely to increase if the United States eventually constructs new breeder reactors, each of which would hold one to three tons of plutonium 239 (if equally distributed among the human population, a grapefruit-size piece of this substance could supply a lethal dose to the entire human species). The breeder-reactor program has been strongly advocated by some experts since the energy shortage of the mid-1970s but has been at least temporarily shelved because of President Carter's opposition. One prototype breeder reactor was built outside Detroit in 1966; a few years later it closed down after a "near miss" that fell beyond the "maximum credible accident" that was considered possible in the official specifications for the installation.[33] That such a dangerous and experimental plant

could have been built so close to a densely populated industrial area is itself a cause for concern. A federal court declared that the "program presents unique and unprecedented environmental hazards to human health for hundreds of years."[34]

The disposal of nuclear wastes is a major problem. Some wastes are buried in covered trenches. Others—the most lethal, such as strontium 90 and plutonium—are buried in sealed concrete tanks, mostly in Richland, Washington. These tanks—which contain millions of gallons of concentrated radioactive waste that will remain lethal for thousands of years and is so hot that it boils by itself for years—have leaked at least sixteen times since 1968; in 1974 a leak continued for fifty-one days, flooded 115,000 gallons of the contents into the ground, and raised the radiation count high above the maximum measurable levels of the underground detectors. The tanks, which were built to last for decades, not thousands of years, are already showing signs of stress. The Nuclear Regulatory Commission has considered various proposals for the ultimate disposal of the wastes, ranging from firing them into space in rockets or burying them at sea to converting them into solids and storing them in the deepest abandoned mines that can be found.[35] The difficulty is not only technical but also political: as one energy department official commented, the problem is "deciding in which congressional district to put them." Meanwhile, the largest insurance companies in the Western Hemisphere have refused, even as a joint venture, to underwrite more than 1 percent of the potential liability for a major nuclear power plant accident.

Why has the Nuclear Regulatory Commission been allowed to pursue a program with acknowledged risks of catastrophic consequences over hundreds of years? Again, the issue is one of values and resulting priorities. If the United States is to achieve its goal of meeting all its

[32]*Village Voice*, July 4, 1974.

[33]Ehrlich and Ehrlich, *op. cit.*, p. 173. For an account of the Detroit incident, see John G. Fuller, *We Almost Lost Detroit* (New York: Readers Digest Press, 1975).

[34]*Village Voice*, July 4, 1974.

[35]*New York Times*, April 16, 1978, p. 34.

growing energy requirements without any reliance on foreign imports, then an expanded nuclear energy program seems necessary, regardless of its potential environmental impact.

Changing the Weather

The human population is altering the weather. Some of these alterations are relatively minor: cities, for example, are "heat islands," 10 to 20 degrees warmer than the surrounding countryside. The concrete and asphalt of an urban area absorb heat like a giant storage battery during the day, and continue to warm the air after sunset. Automobile engines and industrial production add to the heat. In addition, when the warm air covering the city comes into contact with a cold front, the result is fog, cloud, or rain, so cities have more wet weather than neighboring rural areas.[36]

We are also altering the global climate, with consequences that are not yet fully understood. We know that the main agent of this alteration is air pollution, but the ultimate impact is difficult to determine. On the one hand, we are increasing the amount of carbon dioxide in the atmosphere—partly by burning solid fuels and wastes, partly by destroying the forests and vegetation that convert carbon dioxide into oxygen. Since 1880 the carbon dioxide content of the atmosphere has increased by about 12 percent. Like the glass in a greenhouse, carbon dioxide is transparent to radiation in the form of light but not to radiation in the form of heat. As a result, the sun's rays pass through the carbon dioxide and warm up the earth, but the heat is trapped by the carbon dioxide on its way back into space—the so-called greenhouse effect. The result, at least up to 1945, was a progressive warming of the earth's atmosphere. But since the mid-1940s, and in spite of the increase in atmospheric carbon dioxide, there has been a slight decrease in global temperature. The reason seems to be that other pollutants—industrial emissions, particulates, dust from mechanized agriculture, and trails of high-flying jet aircraft— are blocking out some of the sun's rays and reflecting them back into space before they can warm up the earth.[37]

If the global temperature were to rise by as little as another 4 or 5 degrees, the polar icecaps would begin to melt, raising sea levels as much as 300 feet and flooding coastal cities all over the world. A drop of a few degrees in global temperature, on the other hand, would plunge the world into a new Ice Age, similar to the one that melted away about 12,000 years ago. Under these conditions ocean levels would drop by several hundred feet; and Chicago would be buried in ice up to a mile deep.[38] If we are lucky, these contradictory pressures—one toward the melting of the polar icecaps, the other toward the creation of a new Ice Age—will balance one another out. But we simply do not understand the full implications or possible effects of our interference with the weather.

ENERGY AND RESOURCES

Energy

In the mid-1970s the United States suddenly found itself in an "energy crisis," because political events in the Middle East had led to a shortage of oil and a sharp rise in the price of gasoline and heating fuels. For the first time the American public realized how vulnerable our industrial society is to energy shortages. Whereas most of the rest of the world survives on little more than 100 watts of energy per day, the average American lives on about 10,000 watts— and our consumption rate is increasing by 2.5 percent annually.

The current American energy crisis had been predicted for several years, but the problem was largely ignored. The lights were on, the bills were

[36]*U.S. News and World Report,* September 17, 1973, pp. 47–48.

[37]Peter V. Hobbs, Halstead Harrison, and E. Robinson, "Atmospheric Effects of Pollutants," *Science,* March 8, 1974, pp. 911–912.
[38]See R. A. Bryson, "A Perspective on Climate Change," *Science,* May 17, 1974, 753–760; G. J. Kukla and R. K. Matthews, "When Will the Present Interglacial End?" *Science,* October 13, 1972, 190–191.

low, and few people cared. Government energy policy was almost nonexistent; even though 10 percent of our national economic activity is devoted to extracting, refining, distributing, and consuming fuel, no separate government department oversaw energy problems until very recently. The natural-gas industry encouraged consumption of energy with advertisements declaring that "Gas heats best," but by 1972 natural gas was so scarce in twenty-one states that no new customers were accepted.[39] Electric companies promoted the all-electric American home, but in 1973 they were urging the consumer to "Save a watt!" Gasoline companies made the highways of America ugly with billboards advertising their product, but in 1974 they were advising the motorist to conserve fuel. Yet so great is the public's suspicion of the oil companies that a 1978 New York Times–CBS news poll found that only 43 percent of a national sample believed the energy shortage is "real"—while 47 percent believed "we are just being told there are shortages so oil and gas companies can charge higher prices."

The United States blundered into the energy crisis.[40] We have nearly half of the world's passenger cars and consume well over half of the world's gasoline. Throughout the world more oil has been consumed during the 1970s than was used during the entire hundred years from 1870 to 1970—and in the decade of the 1980s these demands will double again.[41] Supplies of oil and other fossil fuels—coal and natural gas—are finite and steadily decreasing. Sometime before the year 2000 the deposits still remaining will be so low-grade that it will no longer be technologically or economically feasible to extract them.[42]

We can continue to meet our growing energy requirements for a considerable time into the future, but only at the cost of further environmental deterioration.[43] The burning of fuel to

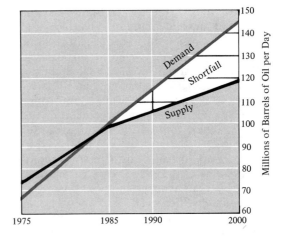

FIGURE 3.4 **Energy supply and demand in the industrial world.** Unless there are some unanticipated technological innovations, the world will enter a period of permanent and growing energy shortages during the mid-1980s. The projections in this graph are calculated in terms of millions of barrels of oil (or its equivalent) per day, and assume an average annual economic growth rate of 4.4 percent. (International Energy Agency, 1978.)

generate electricity pollutes the atmosphere. Geologists believe that there may be billions of gallons of oil beneath the waters of the Atlantic coast, but their exploitation will pose ecological risks. The United States has enough coal to last for several hundred years, but it would have to be strip-mined, laying waste vast surface areas and polluting water with sulfur washed from the exposed coal face by rain. The building of more nuclear breeder reactors would pose seemingly prohibitive hazards.

Resource Depletion

The energy crisis seems to herald the start of an era of shortages. Many key minerals and other raw materials are in short supply, both in the United States and in the rest of the world. Prior

[39]*New York Times*, February 10, 1974.

[40]Richard B. Manke, *Squeaking By: U.S. Energy Policy Since the Embargo* (New York: Columbia University Press, 1976).

[41]Stewart L. Udall, "The Last Traffic Jam," *Atlantic Monthly*, 320 (October 1972), 72.

[42]Andrew R. Flower, "World Oil Production," *Scientific American*, 238 (March 1978), 42–49.

[43]Barry Commoner, *The Poverty of Power: Energy and the Economic Crisis* (New York: Knopf, 1976).

to World War II, the United States was a net exporter of raw materials, but it has been a net importer ever since. In terms of global annual production, Americans use more than 60 percent of the world's natural gas; more than 40 percent of its aluminum and coal; more than 33 percent of its nickel, petroleum, platinum, and copper; and about 25 percent of its gold, iron, lead, mercury, silver, tin, zinc, and tungsten. One study suggests that current exponential growth patterns would exhaust existing known reserves of aluminum in thirty-one years, chromium in ninety-five years, copper in twenty-one years, iron in ninety-three years, lead in twenty-one years, nickel in fifty-three years, tin in fifteen years, and zinc in eighteen years.[44] These projections are probably too pessimistic, but there is no doubt that there will be critical shortages of many of these minerals over the coming few decades.

New mineral reserves will be discovered, of course, but it is worth noting that, despite intensified efforts, the rate of new discoveries and the development of reserves are declining for a wide range of minerals.[45] Advances in technology may also make it possible for low-grade deposits to be exploited. The extraction of minerals from very low-grade ores will have far greater environmental impact than existing processes, however, because of the much greater volume of material that will have to be mined, crushed, treated with chemicals, heated, cooled, and dumped.

There will be increasing shortages of many other raw materials—wood, paper, and foods of various types. World food production is currently inadequate to feed the present human population; famine is already widespread in several parts of the world. The United States, which has generally produced an annual agricultural surplus in the past, can no longer be confident of doing so. Most of the cultivable land on earth is already being used for agricultural production. Although mechanization and fertilizers might increase output up to a point, they would have other, undesirable effects on the environment. The United States will also face a severe water shortage later in the century. In 1900 Americans used 40 billion gallons of water annually; in 1970 they used 350 billion gallons; and by the end of the century they will require between 700 and 1,000 billion gallons. Yet even with optimum developments in water purification and engineering, not more than 650 million gallons will be available, and the actual figure is likely to be significantly lower.[46] In many parts of the western United States the dependable water flow is already too little. Of course the water shortage, like every other aspect of the social problem of environment and resources, is not simply a technical one: it also involves a conflict of interests. As one environmentalist points out:

> Water issues are not essentially engineering issues. Rather, they are political issues. Water is a form of wealth, and any time anyone tries to tinker with prevailing patterns of water management, a brigade of special interests rushes in to protect its respective bailiwicks: farmers, industry, communities, recreationists, real estate developers and Indian tribes pressing ancient claims.[47]

The growing shortage of resources has two significant implications. First, the United States is consuming and has already consumed so large a proportion of the world's nonrenewable resources that the extractable reserves that would be needed to raise the rest of the world to our present standard of living may not exist.[48] Second, even the United States may be unable to maintain its present style of living indefinitely in the face of dwindling resources, although technological developments might postpone the day of reckoning.

---

[44]Donella H. Meadows *et al., The Limits to Growth: A Report on the Club of Rome's Project on the Predicament of Mankind* (New York: Signet, 1972).

[45]Edmund Faltermayer, "Metals: The Warning Signals Are Up," *Fortune,* 86 (October 1972), p. 109.

[46]*Population Bulletin,* vol. 26, no. 2 (Washington, D.C.: Population Reference Bureau, 1970).

[47]Gladwin Hill, "What's Needed Is More Water Policy, Not More Water," *New York Times,* November 27, 1977, p. 5.

[48]Ehrlich and Ehrlich, *op. cit.,* p. 73.

The Limits to Growth

In 1970 the Club of Rome, a private international group of eminent business leaders and scientists, commissioned a research team at the Massachusetts Institute of Technology to make a detailed study of the likely effects of continued industrial and population growth. By using a complex computer model, the MIT team tried to project current trends well into the next century. The report, entitled *The Limits to Growth*,[49] was published in 1972 and immediately became an international best-seller. It also became a focal point in the debate on population growth, industrialization, resource depletion, and pollution. In clear language, and with the backing of statistical models and reams of computer printouts, the researchers concluded that humanity probably faces an uncontrollable collapse of society and economy within a hundred years—and possibly a good deal sooner—unless the nations of the world quickly establish a global equilibrium in which population growth and industrial output remain constant.

Projections for the World Ecosystem. The research team studied the dynamic interactions of five factors over time in a simulated computer model of the world ecosystem. They traced the effects that population increase, food production, depletion of natural resources, industrial output, and pollution have on one another. They found that in each of these factors, growth is not linear but exponential. Linear growth is a simple, additive type of growth—like putting away a penny every day for a month: at the end of thirty days, you will have thirty pennies. Exponential growth, however, is based on a fixed doubling time and involves increasingly rapid growth—like putting a penny away on the first day of the month, doubling it on the second, doubling that on the third, and so on. The exponential growth would result in a sum of over $10 million at the end of the month. The last day alone would yield more than $5 million, because at the moment of the last doubling time, growth leaps from half the limit to the ultimate limit. The MIT report implies that the human population stands on the brink of that last, fatal doubling.

At first the MIT team built a standard world model, in which they assumed that current trends would continue unchanged. In such a situation, they found, a shortage of natural resources would eventually destroy the world's industrial base, causing the collapse of the services and agricultural systems on which we depend. Food shortages and lack of health care would lead to a massive increase in the death rate.

The team tried to find a way out of this predicament by running several hypothetical variations through the computer. It was assumed, for example, that vast, hitherto undiscovered natural resources might be found and exploited. What would happen? The computer predicted that in such a case, industrialization would rapidly accelerate, and the resulting pollution would ravage public health, reduce agricultural production, and overwhelm the environment. What if technology provided new means of controlling the pollution? Even if that were the case, responded the computer, population would continue to soar and outstrip the capacity of the land to produce food. No matter how the factors were varied, growth would always cause a circular process in which human populations starved, raw materials became exhausted, or pollution exceeded livable limits. All growth projections led to severe social disorganization and ended, sooner or later, in the collapse of society. These projections took no account of the tensions and even wars that might result from overcrowding and social conflict over shortages of food and resources.

The researchers found only one possible solution: maintaining population and industrialization in a steady state of global equilibrium. This strategy would involve a deliberate antigrowth policy, no welcome prospect in a society in which "progress"—equated with economic and technological growth—is so highly valued.[50] In the new equilibrium, birth rate would equal death

---

[49]Meadows *et al., op. cit.*

[50]See Anthony J. Wiener, "Growth as Ideology," *Society*, 15 (January/February 1978), 49–53; also Sidney Polland, *The Idea of Progress* (New York: Basic Books, 1968).

rate, and investment in new industrial equipment would not exceed the retirement of old equipment. If exponential growth in population and industrialization could be brought to a halt, the exponential growth in pollution, resource depletion, and food requirements would automatically end. Even so, the poor countries of the world might have no realistic hope of matching the present living standards of the rich countries, whose pollution and natural resource load on the ecosystem is twenty to fifty times greater per person. Since there are far more people in the poor countries, a high standard of living for them would increase the planetary load at least tenfold, beyond the ability of the earth's systems to sustain it. In fact, observed the report, global equality is far more likely to be caused by a decline in the economic standards of the rich countries; wealthy industrial societies may be "self-extinguishing."

Major changes would be required in a no-growth society, such as a shift in emphasis from the acquisition of goods to the enjoyment of services. The MIT team acknowledged that radical changes in values and attitudes would be necessary before a no-growth proposal would be acceptable. The suggestion strikes at the very foundations of our most cherished beliefs about the inevitability of progress, the desirability of growth, and the virtues of free enterprise. But as Dennis Meadows, director of the study, pointed out:

> Our view is that we don't have an alternative—it's not as though we can choose to keep growing or not. We are certainly going to stop growing. The question is, do we do it in a way that is most consistent with our goals, or do we just let nature take its course?[51]

Reactions to the Report. The methods and findings of the MIT team's report have been heavily criticized. Predicting the future is never an easy task, with or without a computer. Many critics[52] have argued that the computer model was inevitably too simplistic, for it could not take into account unforeseen developments in the future, still less the interactions between any such developments. A historical case will make the problem clearer. In 1850 New York City was faced with a crisis: horse dung was accumulating on the streets in such quantities that it was impossible to keep them clean. A simple projection would have shown the streets of New York today piled with horse dung to the height of about fourteen stories. This projection would have been hopelessly wrong because it could not take into account later developments—such as efficient, mechanized street-cleaning equipment and, of course, the replacement of the horse with the automobile.

Several critics have also claimed that new technological breakthroughs will come to our aid, as they so often have in the past. Carl Kayson, for example, argues that advancing technology brings down the costs of using existing resources and literally creates new resources by making it possible to exploit supplies that could not be exploited through older technologies. Like the growth of population and industry, he points out, the growth of technology has also been taking place exponentially.[53] Technology is not necessarily the villain it is often portrayed to be. Many technologists are sensitive to environmental concerns and are making important contributions to tackling the problem.

However, the MIT report did win the support of thirty-three leading European scientists from various disciplines, who endorsed a statement, "Blueprint for Survival," published in the same year as *The Limits to Growth.*

> By now it should be clear that the main problems of the environment . . . are warning signs of a profound incompatibility between deeply rooted beliefs in continuous growth and the dawning recognition of the earth as a space ship, limited in its resources and vulnerable to thoughtless mishandling. . . . If a strategy for survival is to have any chance of success, the solutions must be formulated in the light of the prob-

[51]*New York Times,* February 27, 1972.

[52]E.g., Rudolf Klein, "Growth and Its Enemies," *Commentary,* 53 (June 1972), 27–44; H. S. D. Cole *et al.* (eds.), *Models of Doom: A Critique of "The Limits to Growth"* (New York: Universe Books, 1973).

[53]Carl Kayson, "The Computer That Printed W*O*L*F," *Foreign Affairs,* 50 (July 1972), 662–666.

lems. . . . If we plan remedial action with our eyes on political rather than ecological reality, then . . . very surely, we will muddle our way to extinction.[54]

Reshaping the International Order. Influenced, perhaps, by some of the sharp criticisms of the *Limits to Growth* report, the Club of Rome has since modified its position and no longer calls for a no-growth world. The club's more recent report, *RIO: Reshaping the International Order,*[55] draws on the insights of twenty-one specialists from various countries.

What the club now prescribes is "selective growth." The gap in living standards between the developed and the developing nations, the report argues, is growing intolerable and will become the source of major international tensions. Many of the poorer nations of the world face the prospect of massive famines in the next few decades, but they lack the investment capital to industrialize in order to create wealth. The main thrust of world industrial development in the future, therefore, must take place in the less developed countries. Conveniently, these countries have large reserves of unexploited resources, and because they are relatively unpolluted, they could more easily tolerate the environmental impact of careful industrialization. Most of this industrial development would have to be voluntarily financed by the wealthier nations, creating the added advantage of slowing their industrial growth.

The recommendations of the club are implicitly functionalist in that they aim at reorganizing a disorganized global system in such a way that it achieves equilibrium. Carefully planned selective industrialization would lead to a much more equal division of the world's riches and productive capacities. In this reshaped international order, global peace and prosperity would be achieved through greater economic interdependence. The economies of the developed nations would be allowed to grow further, but probably at a slower rate than at present. The club still accepts, however, the basic logic of the original MIT findings: that exponential growth in a world of limited resources must inexorably lead, sooner or later, to global disaster. And whatever the failings of the original MIT report, it did succeed in sparking public debate and scholarly research about the implications of a "steady-state" or, at least, a more slowly expanding world economy.[56]

CONFRONTING THE PROBLEM

What social action can be taken to confront the problem? Several immediate steps are possible.

Reduction of waste. Some of our staggering waste of energy and resources is due to technological problems; we waste in the form of useless heat a full five-sixths of the energy used in transportation, nearly three-quarters of the energy produced by nuclear power plants, two-thirds of the fossil fuel consumed to generate electricity, and nearly one-third of the fuel used for other purposes—all told, more than 50 percent of the energy used in the United States. This problem must be confronted by heavy investment in research aimed at refining our technology.

Other forms of waste are more easily curtailed, for example, by putting insulation in homes or by conserving domestic and industrial energy use. We also squander other resources in a highly

---

[54]Edward Goldsmith *et al.,* "Blueprint for Survival," *The Ecologist,* 2 (January 1972), 2–6.

[55]*RIO: Reshaping the International Order: A Report to the Club of Rome* (New York: E. P. Dutton), 1976.

[56]See, for example, Kenneth D. Wilson (ed.), *Prospects for Growth: Changing Expectations for the Future* (New York: Praeger, 1977); Fred Hirsch, *The Social Limits to Growth* (Cambridge, Mass.: Harvard University Press/Twentieth Century Fund, 1976); Herman E. Daley, *Steady State Economics* (San Francisco: W. H. Freeman, 1973); "Growth/NoGrowth: Next Steps," special issue of *Society,* 15 (January/February 1978).

Young people take part in community action to clean up the effects of an oil spill on a California beach. But the aim of community groups in the future must be to prevent pollution rather than fight the endless battle of clearing it up.

irresponsible manner. It is quite feasible to build cars that would last several times longer than they do at present; instead, they are deliberately built with a "planned obsolescence" that sends them to the junk heap in a few years, because social attitudes and values prize newer automobiles. We waste additional resources on a variety of useless or near-useless products and unnecessary packaging and wrapping materials. Pilot lights waste up to a third of the gas used annually on kitchen ranges. We use more energy for air conditioning alone than the Chinese, with a population about four times ours, use for all purposes. We squander energy largely because government, in response to public pressure, has kept it so cheap. In 1979, American motorists were outraged when the price of gasoline rose to $1 per gallon—yet motorists in most other industrial societies had been paying two or three times as much for several years past. Rising prices, however, are likely to provide a strong incentive for us to conserve energy and resources in the future.

Recycling resources. A shortage of resources could be remedied in part by the planned recycling of waste materials. The object would be to ensure that, as far as possible, the waste products from one process should become the raw materials for another. For example, urban sewage, instead of being dumped into rivers, can be used as fertilizer in agriculture. Water that is raised to high temperatures to cool one manufacturing process can be used as steam to drive another. City garbage, instead of being dumped on the land, can be cleanly burned to provide electricity. Discarded metal objects can be melted down and reused, instead of being left around to rust.

Many recycling programs are already in operation in the United States. Over a hundred cities now offer facilities for collecting used paper—a program so successful that over a fifth of the paper used in the United States is recycled, at a huge saving in timber. Nearly a fifth of the country's aluminum cans are recycled at over a thousand aluminum-reclamation centers. Many cities are developing plants for recovering glass, metals, and wood and paper products from municipal garbage. But the technological problems of separating these materials cheaply and efficiently have not yet been overcome. The most effective way of doing this, of course, would be for householders to put different types of garbage in different garbage pails, which would be collected separately. It is doubtful, however, if many people would take the trouble to cooperate in such a program unless forced to do so by law. Yet the savings from recycling could be huge. According to Environmental Protection Agency calculations, for every ton of steel recycled from municipal waste instead of being produced from ore, 200 pounds of the refining pollutants would not be poured into the atmosphere, about 6,700 gallons of fresh water would not be used, 102 pounds of water pollutants would not be produced, 2.7 tons of mining wastes would not be dumped on the landscape, and enough electricity would be saved to power the average American home for eight months.[57]

Development of New Energy. Energy has been so plentiful in the past that there has been little incentive for us to develop new sources. Several nonpolluting sources exist, if we can develop the technology to harness their potential. Some progress has been made in utilizing solar energy, which will heat 2.5 million American homes by 1985. Other potential sources are hydrogen gas derived from electrolysis; ocean tidal power; wind power; and geothermal energy from beneath the earth's crust.[58] The future of nuclear energy from conventional fission reactors (in

which atoms are split) is in some doubt, particularly since the near-disaster at the Three Mile Island plant in 1979. Although Americans are happy to use energy from this source, they tend to want the reactors to be "somewhere else" — that is, as far away as possible from their own communities. Also, energy from fission reactors is proving more costly than energy from other sources.[59] Research is in progress on the construction of fusion reactors (in which atoms are combined). Nuclear fusion is the process responsible for the sun's energy, and if it can be harnessed, it would provide energy in virtually unlimited amounts. The dangers and the technological difficulties involved are formidable, however. The fusion material has to be heated to the astonishing temperature of nearly 1 million degrees Centigrade, and some way has to be found to slow down and regulate the intense reaction that would follow. Future energy policies are unlikely to be based on any one or two major sources; instead, we will probably use a variety of technologies, depending on the resources that are most readily exploitable in particular areas. Fossil fuels would still be used, but more sparingly — both to conserve the fuels and to protect the atmosphere against pollution.

The Limitation of Population. As we have already noted, an expanding human population is a major threat to the environment, especially if the population is maintaining a high standard of living. Efforts must be made to keep the United States population stable and to help other countries around the world in campaigns to reduce their birth rates. Famine conditions are likely to provide global incentives to reduce birth rates, but developing nations will need economic, medical, and technical assistance in applying birth-control measures.

Legal Measures. Pollution and the squandering of scarce resources cannot be halted or even significantly reduced without tough federal and state legislation — and a willingness to enforce this legislation. A good deal of progress has already been made, particularly since 1970, when

---

[57]Boyce Rensberger, "Coining Trash: Gold Strike on the Disassembly Line," *New York Times Magazine*, December 7, 1975, p. 31; *Newsweek*, April 24, 1978, p. 38.

[58]See Amory B. Lovins, *Soft Energy Paths: Toward a Durable Peace* (Cambridge, Mass.: Ballinger, 1977); Lon C. Ruedisili and Morris W. Firebaugh (eds.), *Perspectives on Energy: Issues, Ideas, and Environmental Dilemmas,* 2nd ed. (New York: Oxford University Press, 1978).

---

[59]*RIO, op. cit.*

the Environmental Protection Agency was established to oversee environmental issues. The National Environmental Policy Act of 1970 requires that before a project requiring federal approval can be undertaken, there must be a public hearing and a study of the likely environmental impact. The Clean Air Act of 1970 empowers the EPA to set standards of air quality and to enforce these standards. The Water Pollution Control Act of 1972 prohibits the discharge of pollutants into a water supply without a permit.

In quite a few respects this legislation has been highly successful. The EPA has brought many industrial polluters before the courts. In some cases, fines totaling millions of dollars have been imposed, and the polluters have been required to eliminate or severely restrict the pollution. The EPA has been less successful, however, in its dealings with state and local authorities. Alarmed by the economic recession of the 1970s, many states have successfully argued that pollution controls should be suspended in the interests of economic development. In 1977 the EPA admitted that it had virtually abandoned attempts to reduce automobile-caused smog in many cities because of widespread violations of its directives. The EPA has also been hampered by the smallness of its staff, which makes effective monitoring of pollution impossible, and by the fact that it usually relies for its information about pollution on data supplied by the polluters themselves.

If we want a cleaner environment, stronger legal measures will be necessary. Among other possibilities, a "pollution tax" imposed on such items as "throwaway" containers, high-sulfur fuel, inefficient municipal incinerators, and gas-guzzling automobiles would encourage the development of nonpolluting alternatives. Also, federal and state regulatory agencies could be given wider powers to monitor and enforce environmental standards. Of course, these legal measures would be highly controversial. Apart from the inconvenience they would cause to the offenders, they would burden society with greater government regulation, more bureaucracies, increased paperwork, longer administrative delays, and higher taxes. Already industry and

government spend over $16 billion per year on pollution control.[60] Every solution to a social problem has its own costs and thus creates a potential for conflict.

Changes in Attitudes and Values. Most difficult of all, but perhaps most necessary to a solution of the problem, will be to change the attitudes and values that are largely responsible for the pollution and resource shortages. Probably nothing typifies the conflict between our traditional values and our environmental needs so much as the automobile. It poisons the air, devours gasoline, consumes mineral resources, kills and maims tens of thousands of citizens each year, requires the defacement of the country with concrete and gas stations, and ultimately becomes junk on the landscape. Yet to many people it seems to represent the heart and soul of the American way of life. Moreover, the highway-auto-petroleum complex employs one out of every five American workers. Many corporations and many citizens have a stake in the economic activities that generate pollution, and their private interests are reflected in their attitudes and values.

Attempts to change public attitudes and values may be expected to meet with strong opposition from the big corporate producers and polluters, who represent one of the largest power coalitions in the United States. Industry is naturally organized to resist any changes that will cost money or lower profits. Solving the problems of the environment will inevitably involve conflicts of interest, as President Carter found out whenever he submitted proposals for a national energy policy to Congress. Almost every item in his programs aroused controversy and stimulated lobbying from one organized interest or another. And in almost every case Congress either took no action, or produced a compromise that would satisfy the more powerful interests involved.

The issue of resources and environment is likely to remain a major social problem. It raises many profound questions about the relationship between rich and poor countries, about the effects of world population growth, about the

---

[60]*New York Times*, April 17, 1977.

virtues of economic growth and industrialism, and about the very values and destiny of our civilization. Yet the battle is by no means a hopeless one. Much of the problem stems from a state of social disorganization that need not be permanent. Our industrial system is having environmental effects we have not anticipated, and our attitudes, values, and capacity to control our technology have not yet caught up with this change.

The crucial step in solving the problem will be for all of us to recognize our personal responsibility in the matter. The problem cannot be reduced to a battle between the good guys who work for environmental preservation and the conservation of resources and the bad guys who ravage what remains of natural beauty and recklessly waste energy and other commodities. We are all "against pollution" and "in favor of protecting the environment"—but every one of us is guilty of countless practices that, taken together, may wreak havoc on our natural and social surroundings.

SUMMARY

1. Pollution and resource depletion have only recently been perceived as a major social problem, but the environmental issue is now recognized as one of the most serious facing the United States and an increasingly interdependent world.

2. From the functionalist perspective the problem is caused by social disorganization stemming from industrialism. Industrial production is functional in many respects, but it has the dysfunctions of encouraging population growth, polluting the environment, and depleting resources. The conflict perspective highlights the many conflicts of interest and values that are involved in the problem.

3. Ecology is the science of the relationship between organisms and their environment. An ecosystem is a self-sustaining ecological community; interference in any part of an ecosystem can cause a disruptive chain reaction throughout the system. Ehrlich sees human population growth as the main threat to the planetary ecosystem; Commoner sees the problem as one of faulty, high-polluting technology.

4. Some major threats to the environment are air pollution, water pollution, land despoliation, the spread of chemicals and insecticides, the disposal of radioactive wastes, and alteration of the weather.

5. The future may be one of grave shortages. Energy, once plentiful, is now a scarce resource, yet demands for it are rapidly increasing. Similarly, raw materials such as food and minerals are often in short supply, in a world that is industrializing rapidly and in which population is steadily growing.

6. An MIT research team commissioned by the Club of Rome projected current trends and predicted a collapse of industrial society unless pollution, resource depletion, and population growth are quickly halted. This conclusion has been much criticized, and the Club of Rome now calls for a slowing of industrial growth and a global redistribution of industry and wealth.

7. Ways of confronting environmental and resource problems include the reduction of waste, the recycling of resources, the development of new energy sources, the limiting of population growth, legal measures, and, perhaps most important, changes in traditional attitudes and values.

GLOSSARY

Ecology. The science of the mutual relationships between organisms and their environment.

Ecosystem. A self-sustaining community of organisms in its natural environment.

FURTHER READING

CAUDILL, HARRY M. *My Land is Dying.* New York: Dutton, 1973. A brief account of strip mining and the devastation of the land that it can cause.

COMMONER, BARRY. *The Closing Circle.* New York: Knopf, 1971. Commoner argues that population growth is not the main factor in the ravaging of our environment. The real culprit, he contends, is our "counterecological" technology. Changes in technology, he believes, could go a long way toward solving the problem.

GOLDSMITH, EDWARD, *et al.* "Blueprint for Survival," *The Ecologist,* 2 (January 1972). An important statement on the environmental crisis by a group of eminent European scientists. They contend that humanity must act now to halt economic and population growth—or we will "muddle our way to extinction."

LOVINS, AMORY B. *Soft Energy Paths: Toward a Durable Peace.* Cambridge, Mass.: Ballinger, 1977. An informed and detailed argument for the use of alternative sources of energy that would not have a destructive impact on the environment.

MADDOX, JOHN D. *The Doomsday Syndrome.* New York: McGraw-Hill, 1972. The author presents a strong argument that the environmental crisis is much exaggerated and suggests that concern over "ecology" is simply another fad.

MANKE, RICHARD B. *Squeaking By: U.S. Energy Policy Since the Embargo.* New York: Columbia University Press, 1976. An excellent overview of the problems and prospects of United States energy policy.

McHALE, JOHN. *World Facts and Trends.* New York: Macmillan, 1972. A collection of tables, graphs, and statistical information on international trends in population growth, resource depletion, and pollution. McHale provides a running commentary on the significance of these trends.

MEADOWS, DONELLA H., *et al. The Limits to Growth: A Report on the Club of Rome's Project on the Predicament of Mankind.* New York: Signet, 1972. A summary of the MIT research team's controversial findings on the potential consequences of continued population growth, pollution, and consumption of nonrenewable resources.

MILLER, G. TYLOR. *Living in the Environment: Concepts, Problems, and Alternatives.* Belmont, Calif.: Wadsworth, 1975. A wide-ranging text on environmental issues, containing a great deal of information in accessible and readable form.

RIENOW, ROBERT, and LEONA TRAIN RIENOW. *Moment in the Sun.* New York: Ballantine Books, 1969. A passionate and very readable account of the destruction of the American environment. The authors argue that the underlying problem is our value system, which favors technological advances over the preservation of natural beauty.

RIO: Reshaping the International Order: A Report to the Club of Rome. New York: E.P. Dutton, 1976. The book contains a strong argument for a slowing of industrial growth and a gradual redistribution of the world's wealth.

RUEDISILI, LON C., and MORRIS W. FIREBAUGH (eds.). *Perspectives on Energy: Issues, Ideas, and Environmental Dilemmas.* 2nd ed. New York: Oxford University Press, 1978. A useful and up-to-date collection of articles that illustrate the complexity of the energy problem and the environmental implications of the various solutions that might be explored.

WILSON, KENNETH D. (eds.). *Prospects for Growth: Changing Expectations of the Future.* New York: Praeger, 1977. An important collection of articles, by sixteen experts from various fields, on the prospects for economic growth (or no-growth) in the future.

4

Work: Unemployment and Alienation

THE PROBLEM

Work is a central focus of our adult lives, demanding a dominant part of our time and energies from the moment we enter the work force until the time, many decades later, when we retire. A very few people, such as the inheritors of large fortunes, are able to escape the obligation to work. But for most of us, work is a necessity—primarily because it meets economic needs, but also because it can provide social status, a sense of self-respect, a source of fulfillment, and a circle of friends and colleagues. If aspects of work become problematic, then the problems involved also become central to people's experience. This is the case in the United States today, where two work-related problems have preoccupied public attention over the past decade: lack of work, or unemployment, and the sense of dissatisfaction, meaninglessness, and powerlessness, or alienation, that many people find in the work place. This chapter will explore the social roots and effects of both problems.

In the mid-1970s, unemployment in the United States reached its highest levels since the Great Depression, with over 9 percent of the work force unemployed in the worst recession year, 1975. The unemployment rate has crept down since then, but jobs are still scarce, and even according to the most hopeful predictions, unemployment will remain a serious social problem at least until the early 1980s. To make matters worse, actual joblessness, or unemployment, is always accompanied by another problem, that of *underemployment*, a situation in which people are working for wages so low that they cannot adequately support themselves or are working at jobs below their level of skill. In a society long accustomed to steadily increasing affluence and material abundance, the economic recessions of the 1970s came as an unexpected and severe disruption to millions of Americans. It is hardly surprising that in the late 1970s the Gallup poll found economic concerns and unemployment ranked as the most serious social problems facing the nation.

The current focus on unemployment has partially obscured another and perhaps more persistent problem: the alienation that many people feel in their working lives. The word "alienation" has become a modern catch-all phrase to describe a variety of socially created psychological ills, but its sociological meaning is more precise. Essentially, *alienation* is the sense of powerlessness and meaninglessness that people experience when confronted by social institutions that they consider oppressive and outside their control. Alienation in the modern work force is demonstrated all over the country by workers insisting that their lives are their own, even when they are at work; that they are not simply commodities to be bought and sold on the labor market; that the authority of the firm must have strict limitations; and that employees deserve to be consulted on every aspect of the production process.[1]

---

[1] For discussions of the meaning of alienation and its relation to work, see Melvin Seeman, "On the Meaning of Alienation," *American Sociological Review*, 24 (1959), 783–789, and "On the Personal Consequences of Alienation at Work," *American Sociological Review*, (April 1967), 273–285; Richard Schact, *Alienation* (New York: Doubleday, 1970).

In 1973 a special task force prepared a report for the Secretary of Health, Education, and Welfare and made alienation its main theme. The report, *Work in America*, was widely publicized and had great impact. Its recounting of the phenomena of "blue-collar blues" and "white-collar woes" was immediately recognized by the American public as relating directly to their own work experience. The report outlined the nature of this problem:

> Significant numbers of American workers are dissatisfied with the quality of their working lives. Dull, repetitive, seemingly meaningless tasks, offering little challenge or autonomy, are causing discontent among workers at all occupational levels. This is not so much because work itself has greatly changed: indeed, one of the main problems is that work has not changed fast enough to keep up with the rapid and widescale changes in worker attitudes, aspirations, and values. A general increase in their educational and economic status has placed many American workers in a position where having an interesting job is as important as having a job that pays well. . . . Many workers at all occupational levels feel locked-in, their mobility blocked, the opportunity to grow lacking in their jobs, challenge missing from their tasks. Young workers appear to be as committed to the institution of work as their elders have been, but many are rebelling against the anachronistic authoritarianism of the workplace.[2]

Since the report was published, awareness of alienation as a work-related problem has receded somewhat: workers have tended to be more concerned about getting and keeping jobs than about the actual nature of their work. But if the United States achieves fuller employment in the future, then workers, feeling more secure in their jobs, are likely to become more resentful of the dehumanizing features of their work place.

THE MEANING OF WORK

To understand why unemployment is so devastating to individual workers and why so many

workers are experiencing alienation in their jobs, we must look more closely at the cultural meaning of work. Since the members of any society learn its values, norms, and beliefs and tend to act and feel in a way that is consistent with those cultural traits, they will evaluate their jobs (if they have them) or react to unemployment (if they lose their jobs) according to the meanings they have learned from their culture.

The Changing Meaning of Work

We tend to take our own attitudes toward work for granted, as though they were self-evident and inescapable. But social definitions of work—of its value, its dignity, its necessity—have varied a great deal through history and from one society to another.

Preindustrial society: Work as a Curse. In most traditional, preindustrial societies, labor was not highly valued. To the ancient Greeks, for example, work was a curse, a thoroughly burdensome and unpleasant way of life entirely incompatible with the dignity of the citizen. The highest and most distinctively human activity was the constructive use of leisure through the cultivation of the mind. The Greeks justified slavery on the grounds that it freed the citizens to spend their lives in cultural enrichment and philosophic contemplation. This attitude toward work may be a reason why the Greeks never produced a significant practical technology based on their highly developed scientific theories.

The ancient Hebrews accorded work rather more dignity than had the Greeks before them, but they regarded it as a grim necessity, a punishment imposed on humanity by a wrathful God for the disobedience of Adam and Eve. Early Christian doctrine generally accepted the Hebrew view of work as God's curse and associated it for the most part with purification and self-denial. In fact, many of the religious sects that arose during the early Middle Ages demanded incessant labor from their members on the grounds that it was a degrading but necessary scourge of the sinful flesh. The established Church, in contrast, saw so little value in labor that it was considered morally acceptable for

[2]*Work in America: Report of a Special Task Force to the Secretary of Health, Education, and Welfare* (Cambridge, Mass.: M.I.T. Press, 1973), pp. xv, xvii.

monks to go begging rather than work: the sole virtue to be seen in labor was that its products could be charitably shared with the poor and thus earn the giver the blessing of God. The idea that work was a virtue in itself, and that begging or idleness was a vice, triumphed only much later in the guise of the "Protestant ethic."

The Protestant Ethic: Work as a Duty. The great change in social values concerning work came with the Protestant Reformation. In one of the most provocative arguments in all sociology, the German sociologist Max Weber (1864–1920) asserted that the ideas of puritanism had provided an impulse for the transformation from traditional society to the modern industrial world, in which disciplined labor is seen as a fundamental basis of social and economic life. Puritanism, he argued, had elevated work from a painful necessity to a moral obligation, making it a valued activity and a source of self-respect. How did this change come about? In *The Protestant Ethic and the Spirit of Capitalism* (1904), Weber pointed out that Protestant thinkers such as Luther and Calvin had redefined the nature of work. They accepted the Old Testament view that work was a divinely imposed duty, but went further and claimed that labor was a form of service to God. Work was a "calling," and all who could work, should work.

This view of work as a matter of moral obligation was linked to another feature of puritan Protestantism: the belief that everyone was predestined, from the beginning of time, to salvation or damnation. Nobody could tell whether he or she was destined to be saved, but people were understandably anxious for signs of God's favor. Taking success at work as just such a sign, they naturally worked all the harder to be successful. And being successful, they accumulated considerable capital in the form of profits. However, since the puritan ethic regarded luxury and self-gratification as sinful, the profits could not be spent on idleness or pleasure—so they were simply reinvested to make even more profit. Thus, according to Weber, was the new economic form of capitalism born, and the modern industrial world created; and although the original psychological mechanism that drove these early capitalists to work and invest is now forgotten, its effect lingers on:

> The puritan wanted to work in a calling: we are forced to do so. For when asceticism was carried out of the monastic cells into everyday life, and began to dominate worldly morality, it did its part in building the tremendous cosmos of the modern economic order. This order is now bound to the technical and economic condition of machine production which today determines the lives of all individuals who are born into this mechanism.[3]

Whether Weber was correct in his belief that the Protestant ethic contributed to the birth of capitalism is a matter of longstanding controversy in sociology. There is no question, however, that the ethic of hard work as a moral duty and a means of achieving greater rewards in the future is a basic feature of modern industrial capitalism.

The Meaning of Work Today

The insistence of the old Protestant work ethic on labor as a moral duty has persisted almost unchallenged in the United States until quite recently. It has seemed almost heretical to suggest that work is either a burdensome nuisance or that it should be enjoyable in itself. The emphasis throughout our history has been on the virtues of a good, hard day's work, not just as a means toward achieving material ends but also as a beneficial experience for the individual. Former President Nixon voiced the feelings of many Americans when he declared in a speech on welfare reform that labor was good in itself, that it accorded with religious teachings, and that it was endorsed by the American tradition. He added: "Scrubbing floors and emptying bedpans have just as much dignity as there is in any work done in this country—including my own. . . . Most of us consider it immoral to be lazy or slothful."

But work in America is more than simply a culturally prescribed, morally valued activity. It is central to the lives of most adults, contributing

---

[3]Max Weber, *The Protestant Ethic and the Spirit of Capitalism* (New York: Scribner's, 1958; originally published 1904), p. 181.

Many Americans adhere to the traditional "work ethic"—a set of values that many sociologists believe is historically linked to the old Calvinist insistence on lifelong labor as a moral duty. Adherents of the work ethic generally take a poor view of welfare recipients and others who are believed to seek instant gratification in preference to dedicated labor.

to their identity and self-esteem, bringing order and meaning to their lives.[4] It is usually necessary to hold a job to gain approval from others; income from welfare brings low status. There is a strong link between pay and perceptions of personal worth, so that the more highly paid people are, the more highly they tend to regard themselves and to be regarded by others. The person at the bottom of the pay scale is frequently regarded as a nobody, and welfare recipients are sometimes almost regarded as "worthless" in society.

One of the first things we ask a stranger is "What do you do?" The answer to this question tells us a great deal about the person, because, in a very profound sense, people are what they do. A person's self-image is largely dependent on and continually reinforced by his or her work. Members of Congress make speeches, run in elections, give interviews—activities that constantly reinforce their self-image as influential public figures. Assembly-line workers perform routine mechanical tasks, day in and day out (essentially, attaching nuts to bolts)—activities that may make them think of themselves as personally insignificant, almost as interchangeable parts in the factory machinery. In fact, the *Work in America* report noted that people in low-status jobs find they can draw no satisfying identity from their occupations, and they resent the unflattering identities that society forces on them. Interviews with such people showed that the typical worker has "an overwhelming sense of inferiority: he cannot talk proudly to his children of his job, and feels he must apologize for his status."[5]

Work confers social status on the individual. Our occupation—housewife, janitor, corporation president—is often our most important social status, determining the kind of life we lead and the kind of roles we play in relation to other people. Work is thus a means by which people sense their personal usefulness and feel their integration into society (for this reason, retirees sometimes suffer a crucial and shattering loss of identity and purpose). Work is also a place to meet others and form friendships. For most people, work is also a matter of sheer economic necessity; other needs cannot be gratified without the income derived from labor. For some Americans, of course, work has yet another meaning: it can be inherently satisfying and deeply absorbing.

People interpret their work experience in the light of the cultural meanings their society offers. Thus, if they are unemployed, they experience not only a loss of income but also a loss of all the other sources of meaning that work provides. Similarly, if their work is not satisfying and absorbing, but, rather, is boring, degrading, and dehumanizing, they feel a sense of alienation from an important part of their lives.

---

[4]Curt Tausky, "Meanings of Work Among Blue-Collar Men," *Pacific Sociological Review*, 12 (Spring 1969), 49–55.

[5]*Work in America, op. cit.*, p. 45.

THE AMERICAN WORK FORCE

The nature of work in America and the occupational structure have changed radically over the course of the past century. In colonial times most people were farmers, working either on their own land or as laborers on the land of others. Even as late as 1850 the census recorded a grand total of only 323 distinct occupations in the entire country. From then on, however, industrialization took place at an increasingly rapid pace. New factories arose, employing hundreds, thousands, or even tens of thousands of workers. Huge corporations and government bureaucracies emerged, and both developed ever larger administrative staffs. Today there are over 35,000 official job titles in the United States (not to mention many more unofficial or even illegal ones, such as numbers runner, dope pusher, or pimp). The great majority of the work force is now employed by large government or corporate organizations, and individual workers have lost much of their autonomy. Work has tended to be fragmented into repetitive and specialized tasks, with each worker contributing only a tiny portion of the final product or service. Let's look more closely at this changing character of work and the work force.

Occupational Structure

Work in all industrial societies falls into one of three categories: primary, secondary, or tertiary industry. *Primary industry* is the gathering or extracting of undeveloped natural resources; examples are mining, fishing, or forestry. *Secondary industry* involves turning these raw materials into manufactured goods, such as steel, processed food, or furniture. *Tertiary industry* involves service activities of one kind or another, such as medicine, administration, automobile maintenance, or scientific research.

The proportion of the work force engaged in any of these sectors of industry depends on the degree of industrial development in the society. In the early stages of industrialization, most workers labor on the farms or in extractive industries; as the society develops, more and more workers are drawn into secondary industry; in a still more advanced industrial society, increasing numbers of workers are drawn into the generally cleaner and more pleasant jobs of tertiary industry. In the 1950s the United States became the first country in the world to have more than half of its labor force engaged in the predominantly "white collar" jobs of tertiary industry. In 1900 some 37.6 perent of workers were in primary industry, 35.8 percent were in secondary industry, and only 26.6 percent were in tertiary industry. Today some 4.5 percent are in primary industry, 33.4 are in secondary industry, and an astonishing 62.1 percent are in tertiary industry (see Figure 4.1).

The immense productivity of our advanced industrial system has made it possible for less than 5 percent of the work force to feed the rest of the population. In the most simple preindustrial societies, in contrast, it took the efforts of about seventy-five farmers to produce enough surplus to support one person in a nonagricultural role. The huge surplus wealth produced by our industrial system has created an apparently insatiable demand for new services, ranging from higher education to entertainment and leisure activities. An important advance in industrial technology has been *automation*, the use of self-regulating machines that monitor and control a production process. Automation has freed millions of workers from the hard manual labor more typical of early industrialism. The growth of new professional, technical, and managerial roles has radically transformed our occupational structure and the nature of countless jobs.

Composition of the Work Force

Various categories of workers face different work experiences, including the likelihood of becoming unemployed, underemployed, or alienated from their work.

Blue-Collar and White-Collar Workers. Blue-collar workers—most of whom are in primary or secondary industry—represent a steadily shrinking proportion of the nation's work force. Although they were the largest single category as late as the mid-1950s, they will probably represent less than one-third of the employed in

America by the early 1980s.[6] One reason for this development is the rapid growth of tertiary industry; another is the spread of automation. Although automation can dramatically improve productivity and efficiency, it also causes widespread unemployment, chiefly at the blue-collar level. The number of unskilled jobs is unlikely to shrink further in absolute terms, however; it will decline only as a proportion of all jobs. Even in an age of computers and automation, millions of Americans still earn a living by performing tasks that have not changed in centuries—making beds, sweeping floors, collecting garbage. Such

jobs tend to be held by disadvantaged sectors of the population, such as the poorly educated, minority groups, and illegal immigrants. Even so, the jobs are becoming harder and harder to fill, although they are now dignified by such titles as "dietary service aides" or "sanitation disposal personnel."

It is sometimes suggested that blue- and white-collar occupations are becoming increasingly similar. To some extent this is true. At the beginning of the century, white-collar workers tended to earn much more than manual workers. Today the range of earnings in each group is very wide, and incomes in office and factory jobs crisscross up and down the wage and salary scale. Blue-collar workers, however, start on full wages comparatively early in life, and must usually rely

---

[6]U.S. Bureau of Labor Statistics, *Bureau of Labor Statistics Bulletin*, no. 1673 (Washington, D.C.: U.S. Government Printing Office, 1970), p. 57.

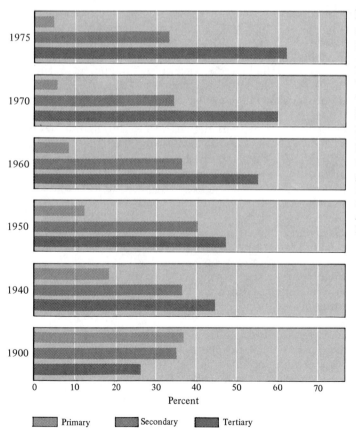

FIGURE 4.1 **Distribution of primary, secondary, and tertiary occupational groups as percent of total labor force: 1900–1975.** The distribution of primary, secondary, and tertiary workers within an economy depends on the degree of industrial development achieved by the nation in question. During the 1950s, the United States became the first country in the world to have more than half of its workers in tertiary industry. Work in this sector is generally cleaner and less strenuous than in primary or secondary industry. (Adapted from Daniel J. Rossides, *The American Class System.* Boston: Houghton Mifflin, 1976, p. 136.)

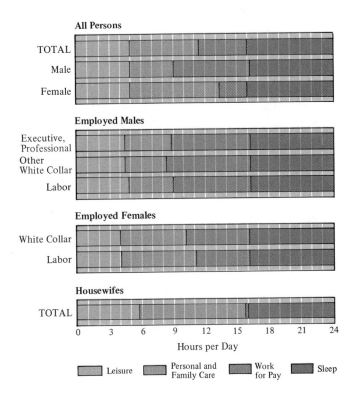

All Persons

TOTAL

Male

Female

Employed Males

Executive, Professional

Other White Collar

Labor

Employed Females

White Collar

Labor

Housewifes

TOTAL

0   3   6   9   12   15   18   21   24

Hours per Day

☐ Leisure   ☐ Personal and Family Care   ☐ Work for Pay   ☐ Sleep

FIGURE 4.2 **Daily use of time by sex and occupation.** This graph shows the relative amounts of time that people typically spend on such activities as work and sleep. The data were collected from a representative urban sample of adults who were asked to record their hourly activities in a diary. Interestingly, white-collar workers work a longer day than blue-collar workers, and housewives claim more leisure time than any other group. (SOURCE: John P. Robinson and Philip E. Converse, "66 Basic Tables of Time-Budget Data for the United States," Survey Research Center, Institute for Social Research, University of Michigan, Ann Arbor, Mich., June 1966. Executive Office of the President: Office of Management and Budget, *Social Indicators, 1973* [Washington, D.C.: U.S. Government Printing Office, 1973], p. 214.)

on union negotiations to win any further pay increases. These workers tend to reach an early plateau in their earning capacity, but their expenses may continue to rise as they become homeowners, as their children enter college, and as their parents grow older and require support. Yet the real earnings and working conditions of both blue- and white-collar workers have improved dramatically in recent decades. This is particularly true of conditions in the factory. Conditions in the office, where work is usually segmented and under authoritarian supervision, often still seem more like those of a factory, however.

Despite the improvement in working conditions brought about by the efforts of labor unions and governments, the work place can still be a dirty and dangerous environment. Every year more than 15,000 Americans are killed outright on their jobs, mostly in blue-collar occupations. Every year, too, an additional 90,000 workers are permanently injured. The toll from mental stress caused by working conditions and from latent diseases like occupationally induced cancers probably raises the figure much higher.

Exposure to industrial pollutants in the work place causes about a million new cases of occupational disease each year.[7]

Women Workers. Another significant distinction in the work force is that between men and women. Whereas in 1900 only 20 percent of all women were in paid employment, nearly 50 percent are today. Yet women are still largely confined to the lower-paid, less prestigious forms of labor in American society, the job of secretary being typical of their work status. There are 9 million secretaries in the United States, representing one-third of the female work force, and their work—especially for those in typing pools or operating keypunch machines—is hardly less monotonous than that of the assembly-line worker.

The division of labor along sex lines being part of the sexist heritage of our culture, there is often no particular rationale for the way work is

[7]*Work in America, op. cit.,* p. 26; see, also, a good overview in Kathy Slobogin, "Stress," *New York Times Magazine,* November 20, 1977, pp. 48–106.

divided between the sexes: work that is defined as appropriate for males in one era may easily be defined as appropriate for females in another, as has happened, for example, with such jobs as schoolteacher, telephone operator, and more recently, bank teller. In other societies, the sexual division of labor may be very different. In many preindustrial communities, for example, the carrying of heavy loads is primarily a woman's job. In the Soviet Union, to give another example, 79 percent of the doctors, 37 percent of the lawyers, 32 percent of the engineers, and 76 percent of the economists are women (it should be noted, however, that the prestige of these occupations has apparently been lowered as a result).[8]

The women's movement has so far had relatively little effect on the status of women in American work. In fact, the income of women workers is steadily declining in relation to that of men. In 1955, women earned 64 percent of the income of similarly employed men; in 1970 they earned only 59 percent; and in 1977, only 58 percent.[9] Women also have higher rates of unemployment. In 1960 the unemployment rate for women was 5.9 percent compared to 5.4 percent for men; in 1970 it was 5.9 percent compared to 4.4; in 1975, 9.3 percent compared to 7.9 percent; and in early 1978, 7.1 percent compared to 5.5 percent.[10] Women are still expected to concentrate on housework, which being unpaid, has low prestige. The contribution of women to the economy, and the rewards they receive for that contribution, are far below what could be expected in terms of their education, experience, and abilities.[11] (These problems are discussed more fully in Chapter 9, "Sex Roles.")

Minority-Group Workers. Minority groups, too, do not play a full role in the economy. The median income for white males in the United States in 1977 was $10,603; for black males it was $6,292. The median income for white women was $4,001; for minority women it was only $3,455.[12] (Minority women are particularly disadvantaged in the labor market because they suffer double discrimination on the grounds of race and sex. In early 1979, for instance, when the unemployment rate stood at 5.8 percent for the population as a whole, only 4 percent of white men were out of work—compared with 7.8 percent of black men and 10.6 percent of black women.)[13] In spite of the fact that federal equal-opportunity legislation has had some impact on the earnings of minority workers, causing their incomes to rise steadily for most of the past decade, the relative differences between minority workers' earnings and those of white workers have hardly changed at all. (The issue of discrimination against minority groups is discussed in more detail in Chapter 8, "Race and Ethnic Relations.")

Young Workers. The American work force is becoming younger and better educated. Two-thirds of the growth in the work force in the 1970s has come from those between the ages of sixteen and thirty-four. In the late 1950s some 19.3 million workers, representing over one-third of the adult civilian labor force, had completed only eight years or less of formal education. By the early 1970s this group had been reduced to about 12.5 million, or less than one-fifth of the entire labor force. Projections show that the proportion of poorly educated workers will continue to decline to about one-eighth of the labor force by 1980 and to about one-sixteenth by

[8]See Michael Swafford, "Sex Differences in Soviet Earnings," *American Sociological Review*, 43 (October 1978), 657–673; Michael Paul Sacks, *Women's Work in Soviet Russia: Continuity in the Midst of Change* (New York: Praeger, 1976), and "Sexual Equality and Soviet Women," *Society*, 14 (July–August 1977), 48–51.

[9]U.S. Bureau of the Census, *Statistical Abstract of the United States, 1978* (Washington, D.C.: U.S. Government Printing Office, 1978), p. 464.

[10]*Ibid.*, p. 399.

[11]See Martha Blaxall and Barbara Reagon (eds.), *Women and the Workplace: The Implications of Occupational*

Segregation (Chicago: University of Chicago Press, 1976); and David L. Featherman and Robert M. Hauser, "Sexual Inequalities and Socioeconomic Achievement in the U.S., 1962–1973," *American Sociological Review*, 41 (June 1976), 462–483.

[12]*Statistical Abstract of the United States, 1978, op. cit.*, p. 463.

[13]*New York Times*, February 3, 1979, p. 1.

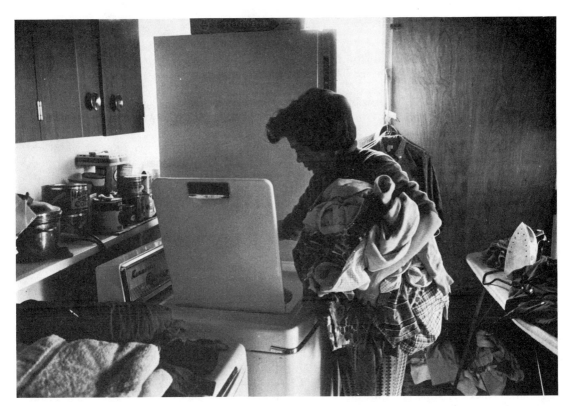

Housework is usually unpaid and, hence, not considered "real" work at all. The low status of housework is intimately linked to the relatively low status of women in American society. Even when workers are hired to perform household duties, wages are very low—domestic servants are among the most poorly paid employees in the nation.

1990.[14] Working-class children are increasingly attending college. The relative freedom of college life may influence these young people as they move into the labor force. As a result of their education and their experience of participation in campus decisions the young in general have high expectations and may come to the work place with an antipathy to hierarchy, authority, and alienating work conditions. Better-educated workers are likely to demand greater control over the entire production process—unless job scarcity forces them to conform.

Unemployment among teen-age workers is particularly high: it soared to nearly 20 percent in 1975; in 1978 it was still at almost 17 percent[15]—and this slight drop benefited only white youth. The job prospects for black youth are particularly gloomy, since even in times of economic prosperity black teen-age unemployment is far higher than that for whites. In 1977 the unemployment rate for young black workers was more than 40 percent, and in some urban areas it was well above 50 percent. When they do get work, young blacks are generally trapped in jobs that offer fewer hours, less pay, less permanence, and fewer prospects for advancement than those held by their white counterparts. The experience of continued unemployment and fruitless searches

[14]Denis F. Johnston, "Education of Workers: Projections to 1990," *Monthly Labor Review*, 96 (November 1973), 22–31.

[15]*Statistical Abstract of the United States, 1978, op. cit.*, p. 408.

for jobs understandably leads to a burning resentment among these young people.

Old Workers. One group whose problems have been very much neglected in contemporary America are the older workers, who are frequently victims of the myth that they have little to contribute after the age of forty. It is often difficult for older workers to switch from one career to another, and they may be unable to compete with younger people for jobs. Yet the workers over forty comprise nearly 40 percent of the American work force. There is an anti-age-discrimination clause in the Federal Employment Act, which stipulates that workers must be judged on merit rather than age for the purposes of hiring, promotion, or dismissal, but until recently the law has rarely been enforced. The economic recessions of the late 1960s and the 1970s have attracted more attention to the plight of older workers, however, and the Labor Department has brought suit against over 200 major companies on charges of bias. Many, if not most, firms still discriminate against older workers, however, especially in their hiring practices. (It is illegal to advertise a vacancy for someone who is "young" or a "recent college graduate," but in most states it is permissible to ask the age of the applicants.) Older workers, despite their greater maturity and experience, are often excluded even from job interviews because of their age. (These problems are discussed in more detail in Chapter 11, "Aging.")

Migrant Workers. Depending on whose estimates one accepts, there are between 3 and 9 million illegal immigrants in the United States. Statistics are obviously largely a matter of guesswork, but the U.S. Immigration and Naturalization Service estimates the total number at over 6 million.[16] These workers often have no welfare or unemployment benefits to fall back on, since application for assistance would make their presence known to the authorities. However, there is no shortage of employers to exploit their illegal status and hire them at grossly depressed wage levels. Migrant children are particularly susceptible. In the early 1970s the Department of Labor reported that more than a quarter of the country's seasonal farm work force—about 80,000 persons out of 3.1 million—were children under the age of sixteen. Half of them, in fact, were between ten and thirteen years old. Migrant workers and their children are among the most systematically underpaid and exploited workers in the nation.[17]

ANALYZING THE PROBLEM

The problems of unemployment and alienation can be usefully analyzed from both the functionalist and the conflict approaches. Each offers a way of understanding the issues, although they focus on different aspects of the problems.

The Functionalist Approach

From the functionalist approach, work-related problems can be seen as the result of social disorganization caused by rapid social and technological change. As applied to the problem of unemployment, the functionalist approach emphasizes that under ideal conditions the various components of the economy would be in equilibrium: specifically, the number and the skills of workers would be matched to the number and the kinds of jobs available for them. Economic growth would take place in a smooth, predictable way, without the disruptions caused by periodic booms and slumps. In practice, however, the economies of advanced industrial societies are highly vulnerable to the effects of sudden or unanticipated changes. The sharp rise in the price of oil, for example, dislocated the economies of the industrial world during the

[16]Leon F. Bouirer, Henry S. Shyrzock, and Harry W. Henderson, "International Migration: Yesterday, Today, and Tomorrow," *Population Bulletin* 32:4 (1977).

[17]See Alejandro Portes, "Labor Functions of Illegal Aliens," *Society,* (September–October 1977), 31–47.

1970s and contributed to world-wide recession, inflation, and unemployment. Similarly, technological innovations in the form of automation may improve the efficiency of the production process and create new categories of skilled workers who are responsible for the maintenance of the new machines. But automation may also be dysfunctional in that it can cause unemployment among the less skilled workers whose jobs have been taken over by computers and other machines. Another important social change, of great relevance to youth unemployment, is one in the age structure of American society (discussed in Chapter 2, "Population"). The unexpected "baby boom" of the post-World War II years has created a youth "bulge" in the population, with the result that there are now more young adults looking for jobs than there are jobs available for them. Similarly, the sharp decline in birth rates in recent years has created widespread unemployment in child-related service industries, particularly teaching. Unemployment can thus be seen as a result of the inability of the social system to adapt quickly enough to such social changes.

As applied to the problem of alienation, the functionalist approach focuses on the transformation that industrial development has caused in the nature and organization of work. Compared to modern-day workers, people in preindustrial societies often had more control over many aspects of their working lives. They worked primarily in small, intimate groups and had a more direct relationship to the product of their labor: carpenters, for example, made every part of a piece of furniture and had the satisfaction of creating a finished product that bore the stamp of their personal skills. Today, furniture is more likely to be made on an assembly line, with each worker contributing an endless series of the same small, standardized part. The underlying process behind industrialization is *rationalization*, a term used by Max Weber to refer to the way traditional, spontaneous methods of social organization are replaced by routine, systematic procedures. Through rationalization, the small craft shop gives way to the modern factory; the individual tutor, to the impersonal multiversity; distinctive architecture, to featureless office blocks; the stalls of the town market, to the supermarket and department store. Rationalized work is much more efficient than traditional procedures, and in this sense is functional. But it is also dysfunctional in that it reduces people to the role of mere cogs in a machine rather than allowing them to operate as autonomous, creative individuals. The problem is compounded by changes in cultural attitudes and values. Although the physical environment of work has improved beyond recognition in the course of this century, modern workers have been socialized to expect fulfillment from their labor. Often, therefore, a wide gap remains between their ideals and the reality of their work experience.

The Conflict Approach

The conflict approach to the problem emphasizes that work takes place in a context of social and economic inequality, in which different groups have very different interests to defend. Like all industrialized countries, the United States is a class-based society in which some people live to a greater or lesser extent off the labor of others. In the competition for scarce resources such as jobs and income, the more powerful groups in society are able to secure their interests at the expense of the weaker groups. For this reason it is no accident that the unemployment rate for minorities is far higher than for whites; that the rate for women is higher than for men; or that the rate for the less skilled blue-collar workers is higher than that for professional white-collar workers (see Figure 4.3). In times of recession, those who own or control the means of production will usually dismiss workers rather than see a decline in profits. The fact that unemployment hits certain categories of workers harder than others can often be fully understood only in terms of the conflict of interests among different groups.

Karl Marx regarded high unemployment as an inevitable feature of capitalism, a view shared by many social scientists who do not necessarily subscribe to other aspects of Marx's theories. It is certainly true that capitalist economies tend to go through cycles of booms and slumps, with

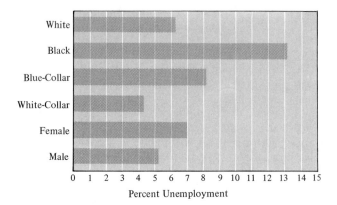

FIGURE 4.3 **Unemployment during a recession.** American workers do not shoulder the brunt of a recession equally: unemployment is significantly higher in some groups than in others. As conflict theory would predict, those groups that suffer the highest rates of unemployment comprise the less powerful members of society—blacks, blue-collar workers, and women.
(Department of Commerce, U.S. Bureau of the Census. *Statistical Abstract of the United States, 1977* [Washington, D.C.: U.S. Government Printing Office, 1977].)

high unemployment during the slump periods. Since the passage of the Employment Act of 1945 it has been official United States policy to encourage full employment—but except for the "boom" years of the 1960s, there has been significant unemployment in the United States throughout this period. Some conflict theorists explain this fact by pointing out that the corporate and other interests that have great influence over national economic policy favor some degree of unemployment, for it serves their own interests. The economist Robert Lekachman argues this viewpoint:

The brutal fact is that unemployment at "moderate" rates confers a good many benefits on the prosperous and the truly affluent. If everyone could be employed, extraordinarily high wages would have to be paid to toilers in restaurant kitchens, laundries, and other humble positions. . . . Unemployment calms the unions and moderates their wage demands. Business periodicals have been noting with unconcealed gratification that . . . contract settlements between major unions and large corporations [have become] considerably less expensive for employers. . . . When people are scared about losing their jobs, they work harder and gripe less. In more dignified language, absenteeism declines and productivity ascends. . . .

It goes without saying that it is scarcely respectable for the rich . . . to openly proclaim their affection for unemployment, although among their friends they tend to be more candid. . . . Full employment means diminishing longstanding inequalities of income, wealth, and power; inviting the black, brown, young, and female to

the American celebration; and controlling the rapacity of doctors, lawyers, giant corporations, and other reputable extortionists. . . . The fine . . . men whom the good Lord has placed in the seats of authority and the halls of the mighty know that there are far worse phenomena than unemployment. One of them is full employment.[18]

As applied to alienation, the conflict approach sees much of the problem as the result of a basic conflict of interest between the workers and the employers. The workers may be concerned about the fulfillment of their human potential on the job, but the employers' main concern is efficiency and profits. If employers believe that efficiency will be enhanced by assembly-line techniques, by a high degree of specialization, by keeping workers out of the decision-making process, or by the rigid enforcement of rules, then the psychological needs of the workers are likely to become a secondary consideration. As a result, there is an inevitable conflict between employers and workers in nearly every aspect of work. Conflict theorists argue, however, that this conflict can lead to beneficial social changes. When workers form social movements such as labor unions, they increase their collective power and are able to bring about improvements in their working conditions.

Let us now analyze the problems of unemployment and alienation in more detail, bearing these theoretical approaches in mind as we do so.

[18]Robert Lekachman, "The Specter of Full Employment," *Harper's*, (February 1977), 35–40.

The following comment is from a young man working at Great Lakes Steel in Detroit.

. . .

I work in track maintenance—the job used to be called a gandy dancer. When I came on the job, they told me the last time they went on strike was 1959. I thought, oh wow, this must be like a company shop. But when I saw what goes on, I came to the conclusion that they had been on strike for fourteen years.

The way we get the most free time is going to and from the jobs. We'll just go out to a shanty in a deserted part of the yard, do a couple of joints and hang out for an hour or two. If they challenge it, we just say we got held up by a train going to the job or there was a furnace we couldn't go by without a safety man. Nobody works too hard. I get in four hours of reading a night, myself.

I'm on the second shift. We used to do only emergency work. Then the company began sending us out to do routine maintenance as well. We used evasion tactics to stop it. We would shovel dirt, but only pick up a tiny bit in each shovelful—then, awhile later, someone else would shovel it back. We worked for hours, but lo and behold, nothing got done. When the foreman complained, we said, "What do you want, we've been working steady." Spike-hammer handles are supposed to be unbreakable. Well, when we go out on a job, we'll break three or four of them. Then we'll take turns using the one that's left while the other guys hang around and take it easy.

By contract we don't have to work if the safety man says a condition is unsafe. We have two safety men. One is an old union man; we can't do much about him. The other position we rotate among ourselves. The safety man doesn't have to do anything, so this gives everybody a chance to take it easy for a while.

. . .

Source: Jeremy Brecher & Tim Costello, *Common Sense for Hard Times* (New York: Two Continents, 1976), pp. 65–66. Copyright 1976 by Jeremy Brecher and Tim Costello.

UNEMPLOYMENT

A society with a high rate of unemployment is a society with a serious social problem, for unemployment has devastating effects on its members.

The most obvious of these effects is the lack of an adequate income, particularly when the unemployed person is a breadwinner on whom an entire family depends for support. In the United States, people who have lost their jobs but have worked for at least twenty-six weeks in the previous year may be entitled to unemployment compensation. The payments usually continue for fifty-two weeks, and then are cut off—even though some workers, such as people nearing retirement age who live in areas with chronic job shortages, may be unable to find work in this period, however hard they try. In most states the size of the payments is determined not by need but rather by how much the unemployed person earned in his or her last job; on average, the payments represent about 40 percent of the person's previous income. Although the position of the unemployed is better in this respect than it was in the Great Depression—when one worker in four was hopelessly unemployed and there were no unemployment compensation benefits to fall back on—the payments are hardly generous. In many cases the unemployed are forced to exhaust their savings or even sell their homes. Some of them, particularly those young and unskilled workers who are almost permanently unemployed, are tempted to turn to crime. Large numbers of the jobless are actually ineligible for unemployment compensation. These are self-employed workers who have not contributed to unemployment compensation, recent college graduates and others who have had no steady job in the previous year, people considered to have left their jobs without good cause, and those who have been unemployed for more than fifty-two weeks. In 1978 the National Commission on Employment and Unemployment Statistics estimated that there are anywhere from 20 to 60 percent more jobless persons than those receiving the benefits.[19]

The effects of unemployment are not only financial; they are also social and psychological. Unemployment severs workers from an important part of their daily lives and from the companionship of their fellow workers, often producing feelings of apathy, despair, hopelessness, boredom, ill temper, and even shame. If the period of unemployment is a prolonged one, these feelings may so intensify that they lead to such problems as alcoholism, voluntary isolation from former friends and colleagues, or discord and even violence within the family. Widespread unemployment also affects the working: the fear of losing their jobs becomes a gnawing preoccupation for a large part of the labor force. In addition, many of those who do have work become underemployed because they have to take whatever jobs are available to them: for example, factory workers may have reduced income because they are obliged to work shorter hours; college graduates may find themselves driving delivery trucks or working as secretaries. The whole society suffers when the productive capacity of many of its members is wasted.

At what point does the unemployment rate become "high"? No society ever has totally "full" employment, in the sense that every person capable of working has a job at any particular moment. Even under the most favorable conditions, there will always be some people who are unemployed—perhaps because of prolonged illness, or because they are changing jobs, or because they are recent graduates who have not yet found a job. In the countries of Western Europe, governments generally consider that they have full employment when the unemployment rate does not exceed about 2 percent of the work force. In the United States a rather higher level of unemployment—about 4 percent—is considered tolerable, and only when the rate goes higher is there much alarm. Yet American unemployment statistics are in many ways deceptive, and, as emphasized by a 1978 report of

the National Commission on Employment and Unemployment Statistics, which cited "glaring weaknesses" in the employment data,[20] the unemployment rate is probably even higher than it appears.

Official statistics on unemployment are compiled by the Bureau of Labor Statistics. The bureau's method is to make periodic surveys of households randomly selected from the total population. The respondents in the sample are classified as "employed," "unemployed," or "not in the work force," and the data from each survey are then extrapolated to the population as a whole. One problem with a survey of this kind is that it tends to omit workers who are transient, such as unemployed migrants and others who are drifting from place to place in search of a job. A more serious problem arises from the bureau's definition of "unemployed," which requires that a person must not have worked at all during the week prior to the survey and must also have taken specific action to find a job within the previous four weeks. The effect of this definition is that people who have become so discouraged that they have not looked for a job during the previous month are not counted among the unemployed, and those who have worked even for a few hours at a temporary job during the previous week are regarded as employed, even if they are no longer working. The official statistics thus underestimate unemployment and ignore underemployment. They provide little information about the category that is "not in the work force"—even though this category might include millions of people who would be willing to work if acceptable jobs were available.

Why is there extensive unemployment and underemployment in the most advanced industrial society of the world? There is no simple answer to this question, but it is helpful to break the problem into two components—the *general* level of unemployment, and the level of unemployment for *specific* groups. General unemployment in a society may be the product of one set of factors, whereas the fact that some groups suffer more than others may be the result of quite different factors.

[19]"U.S. Study Questions Accuracy of Job Data," *New York Times*, February 3, 1979, p. 1.

[20]*New York Times*, February 3, 1979, *op. cit.*

General Unemployment

In the classic economic theory that prevailed prior to the Great Depression, capitalist economies were believed to be self-regulating. There would be occasional booms and slumps, perhaps, but the "invisible hand" of free competition would soon bring the economy into balance once more: government intervention would merely disrupt the natural workings of economic forces and do more harm than good. The Great Depression of the 1930s was greatly worsened by adherence to this theory. Only when the entire capitalist system seemed threatened with destruction did Western governments accept full responsibility for managing and guiding the economy. Programs such as Roosevelt's New Deal were used to stimulate the economy by creating new jobs, and it seemed that the "crisis of capitalism" had been permanently averted.

Since the Great Depression, government regulation of the economy has been based primarily on the theories of the British economist John Maynard Keynes. In Keynesian theory, governments can regulate economic growth by a variety of means, such as raising or lowering taxes, subsidizing certain industries, or directly influencing prices and wage levels. If there are not enough jobs, for example, governments can create them by launching public-works programs, such as highway construction. If economic growth is too slow, governments can speed it up by tax cuts or investment incentives, which stimulate the demand for goods and services by encouraging people to spend more freely. Techniques of this kind have been used successfully in the past, as in the early 1960s, for example, when President Kennedy launched a boom in a sluggish American economy through a series of tax cuts. But these government measures have to be used with caution if they are to avoid the twin perils of unemployment and inflation, or rising prices. In Keynesian theory, unemployment and inflation have an inverse relationship: the more there is of one, the less there will be of the other. In times of full employment, people have plenty of money to spend and increase their demand for goods and services, driving up prices. In addition, labor unions, whose members do not fear unemployment when jobs are plentiful, are able to negotiate aggressively for large wage increases, which are then passed on to the consumer in the form of higher prices. In times of unemployment, on the other hand, people have less money to spend and there is less demand for goods and services; this, combined with the fact that when workers do not feel secure in their jobs, they are more inclined to accept lower wages, causes prices to remain more stable.

The problem since the mid-1970s is that, contrary to Keynesian theory, high rates of unemployment have been combined with high levels of inflation in almost every country of the industrialized world. Governments have consequently been reluctant to use traditional means of creating new jobs for fear of pushing the inflation level even higher. Yet because most Western European governments regard an unemployment rate of more than about 4 or 5 percent as far too high, in some cases they have had to face inflation rates exceeding 20 or even 30 percent a year in order to keep unemployment down. Inflation in the United States has been kept at a comparatively low rate, but only at the cost of very high unemployment.

Since the 1970s the economies of nearly all the capitalist industrial societies have been in a condition of *stagflation*—a combination of stagnation (low growth, low investment, high unemployment) and inflation. The reasons for this unprecedented situation are complex and are hotly debated by economists. A prime factor, however, seems to have been the sharp rise in the price of oil, a commodity so vital to modern industry that the price increase has had multiple effects throughout the international economy. The increased cost of oil has been accompanied, as we saw in Chapter 3 ("Environment and Resources"), by shortages and price increases in a wide range of vital minerals and other raw materials. These developments made a major contribution to world-wide inflation. As inflation increased, consumers could afford fewer purchases, and the demand for goods slackened. A vicious spiral followed, in which manufacturers cut production, laid off existing workers, and reduced investment in new plants and jobs. The unemployed workers had less purchasing power, so demand slackened further and the spiral continued. This process recurred in many countries, and was intensified by the global economic interdependence of nations. The economies of some of our weaker trading partners were hit even harder than our own, and the demands for American exports in these countries fell off sharply, increasing unemployment in the United States.

Unemployment in the United States has been compounded by several domestic factors. One is the fact that large corporate and governmental employers were readily willing to dismiss workers in times of economic recession, unlike their counterparts in many other societies. In Japan, for example, corporations assume an almost paternalistic responsibility for their employees, most of whom spend their entire working lives with the same organization. Governments in many other parts of the world accept a greater responsibility for creating jobs than do the federal, state, and local governments in the United States. The immediate government response to recession in the United States has been to cut back public programs and expenditures, throwing public employees out of work. In most Western European countries such action would be considered politically hazardous or even unacceptable. In the communist-ruled countries of Eastern Europe, governments have successfully combated unemployment by creating the necessary jobs within government bureaucracies—although at the cost of considerable overstaffing.

A second domestic factor accounting for high unemployment in the United States is technological development, such as the mechanization of agriculture, the automation of industry, and the use of computers for the processing of records and information. These developments have stripped the labor market of many jobs, particularly at the unskilled level. A third domestic factor is the tendency for many of our larger corporations to become multinational—that is, to extend their operations all over the world to take advantage of the cheaper labor, the markets, and the sources of raw materials that exist elsewhere. The effect has been to transfer abroad much of the capital and expertise that might otherwise have been applied to economic devel-

opment within the United States. A fourth domestic factor is the strong pressure on the labor market by two large groups that have only recently made their presence felt: the millions of young adults of the "baby boom" generation and the millions of women who, liberated from their earlier roles as housewives, are looking for part-time or full-time employment. The total effect of all these factors is that there are now too many people chasing too few jobs.

Unemployment in Specific Groups

The existence of an economic recession explains why there should be widespread unemployment, but why are unemployment and underemployment so prevalent in particular groups? The reasons vary somewhat from group to group. Consider the case of college graduates. In the economic boom of the 1960s, high-paying jobs for graduates were plentiful—so much so that thousands of college students were willing to "drop out" of college and the work force, confident that they could get jobs if they ever really wanted them. The economy was expanding rapidly, and the demand for the skills of the well-educated young was high. But when economic growth slowed down in the 1970s, colleges continued to produce ever greater numbers of graduates for a shrinking job market. In 1976 the number of college graduates was double that in 1966, but the number of professional, technical, managerial, and administrative jobs had increased by only one-third. In a classic example of social disorganization, the output of the educational system is badly out of balance with the demands of the economy. In fact, only about 20 percent of the jobs in America require more than a high-school diploma, but about half of all high-school graduates go on to some form of higher education—and the number of the young workers has been swollen by the post-World War II "baby boom." Of the 13 million people who have graduated or will graduate from college between 1975 and 1985, at least 1 million will remain unemployed or work at jobs that do not require college degrees.[21]

[21]"Slim Pickings for the Class of '76," *Time*, March 29, 1976, pp. 46–48; Jerry Flint, "Oversupply of Young Workers

Unemployment among racial and ethnic minorities is caused by quite different factors. Part of the problem is discrimination, which prevents minority-group members from enjoying equal opportunity in the labor market. Another factor is the relatively low average educational level of minority-group members, which leaves them unqualified for many of the job opportunities that do exist. Lack of qualifications and skills is, of course, largely a result of past discrimination and unequal opportunity. The problems faced by women workers are similar: there is extensive discrimination against them in employment, and they also have a lower average level of educational attainment than men. In addition, women have been socialized in the past to have low expectations of success outside the home, and many of them have failed to acquire the skills necessary for occupations that have been defined as "a man's job."

Blue-collar workers also suffer disadvantages, ones to which white-collar workers for the most part are not subject. Jobs on the production line are highly sensitive to slight changes in the demand for products—much more so than the jobs of executives, managers, and administrators. Blue-collar workers are often employed on an hourly or weekly basis and can be laid off with very little notice, whereas many white-collar workers have long-term contracts and may receive substantial sums in severance pay if they are fired. Employers are also more willing in many cases to dismiss unskilled or semiskilled blue-collar workers, who can be readily replaced if the need arises; they are more reluctant to dismiss highly skilled managerial employees who may prove difficult to replace when the economic climate changes. And, of course, blue-collar workers have borne the brunt of much of the unemployment caused by automation.

Unemployment and underemployment of migrant and other seasonal workers is linked to the very nature of their jobs as irregular laborers. The same is true of the employment problems of illegal aliens, who typically are employed in jobs that offer little long-term security. And older workers, particularly those nearing retirement age, face an almost insuperable problem. Companies are far more inclined to hire younger workers, whom they tend to regard as healthier, stronger, and more dynamic. Even highly skilled older professionals have great difficulty in finding jobs, especially when younger workers are available at salaries far below those that the older professional had earned in the past.

ALIENATION

Perhaps because the notion of worker alienation was originally developed by Karl Marx, the topic has always tended to be neglected in the United States, with other aspects of work holding center stage at one time or another. At the start of the century, attention focused on the often violent conflict between workers and management as the labor movement demanded better pay, better working conditions, and the right of workers to form unions. With the coming of the depression and its widespread poverty and lack of sufficient work, unemployment became the key issue. Some years later, automation was perceived as a major problem. In 1964 a presidential commission was established to study the impact of work automation on the American economy. The report of the commission offered stern warnings about how technological innovation might displace many workers from their jobs, but gave virtually no attention to the subject of alienation.[22]

Yet less than a decade after the report on automation, the focus shifted completely. In 1972 automobile workers at the new General Motors plant in Lordstown, Ohio, made industrial history by going on strike—not for higher pay but against the deadening conditions of the assembly line. The Lordstown plant had been regarded as a revolution in industrial design: it was to be the most efficient, most highly au-

Expected to Tighten Jobs Race," *New York Times*, June 25, 1978, pp. 1, 34; Walter Guzzardi, Jr., "The Uncertain Passage from College to Job," *Fortune*, (January 1976), 126–129, 168–172.

[22]*Report of the National Commission on Technology, Automation, and Economic Progress* (Washington, D.C.: U.S. Government Printing Office, 1965).

tomated, most trouble-free auto factory in the world, producing more than one hundred vehicles per hour. Every conceivable aspect of the production process had been meticulously planned—except, as it turned out, for one element, the human factor. The workers at the new plant were at first apathetic, then resentful. They began to sabotage the production line, and then, to the amazement of employers and even of the labor unions, they sat in at the plant, "occupied" the machines, and demanded radical changes in the very nature of their work. Since then, and particularly since the publication of the *Work in America* report in 1973, there has been wide recognition that many people who

have jobs—even secure, well-paying jobs—experience deep and persistent feelings of alienation at work. Because work is so central to our lives, these feelings can have a pervasive effect beyond the work place.

The Concept of Alienation

Karl Marx developed the concept of alienation as an account of the plight of people in modern industrial societies. Marx conceived of alienation as people's sense of their loss of control over their social world, which comes to confront them as a hostile, alien thing. Marx applied this perspective to virtually every social institution—govern-

Alienation is a pervasive but certainly not a universal feature of work in America. Millions of workers still find in their jobs a source of comradeship, creativity, and personal satisfaction.

ment, law, economics, religion. In the last instance, for example, the concept of alienation implies that people create various religions, then lose the sense that these religions are, in fact, social constructs and allow their lives to be controlled by the very institutions they have created. Industrial alienation follows a similar course. People establish systems of economic activity for their own benefit, but then find themselves the powerless victims of the very systems they have brought into being.

Alienated Labor.   Marx believed that constructive labor is one of the most distinctive aspects of human character. Through work we create our world, our culture, and our selves. Our labor enables us to experience ourselves as conscious, active beings rather than simply passive objects. The great tragedy of history, in Marx's view, is that people have become alienated from their work and thus separated from their products, from the natural world, from their fellow beings, and from their own essential nature. An important mechanism for this growth of alienation is the *division of labor,* the separation of economic activity into specialized tasks that are performed by specific people. The division of labor develops to its highest degree in the modern industrial state, where each person is forced to perform a particular, exclusive form of activity. People now use only a fraction of their talents, 'and the manual and intellectual aspects of their production tend to be separated. Work becomes an enforced activity, not a fulfillment of a creative urge: it is, according to Marx, "not the satisfaction of a need, but only a means for satisfying other needs. Its alien character is shown by the fact that as soon as there is no physical or other compulsion, it is avoided like the plague."[23] The advent of mechanized production compounds the problem; people create machines to help them, but instead become their slaves: "In the factory, we have a lifeless mechanism independent of the workman, who becomes its mere living appendage. . . . It is not the workman

that employs the instruments of labor, but instruments of labor that employ the workmen."[24]

Marx did not see the division of labor as the only source of worker alienation. He pointed out that there are always at least two classes in any society: a dominant class that owns the means of producing wealth, and a subordinate class or classes that work for the dominant class. Whether they are Roman slaves, feudal peasants, or modern industrial laborers, the workers are exploited by the dominant class: they produce more than they require to meet their basic needs, but do not enjoy the fruits of their labor because the dominant class seizes this surplus wealth and uses it for its own purposes. Work is central to their lives, but their work, and therefore much of their lives, belongs to someone else. They are deprived of the ownership and use of their product, and thus take part in an activity that has no inner meaning for them. Profound alienation is the result.

Class Conflict.   Marx had a solution. All history, he argued in *The Communist Manifesto,* has been the history of class conflict—between master and slave, lord and serf, capitalist and worker. Alienation and class antagonisms would develop to their greatest intensity in the capitalist state, leading to a final confrontation between the opposing classes. The impoverished workers, developing a common sense of their oppression as a class, would rise up in revolt. The result, after a temporary period of socialism under a "dictatorship of the proletariat," would be the communist, or classless, society. In such a society individual men and women would once again feel themselves in control of the social environment, and work would again become a creative, fulfilling activity. The future would be one of abundance in which

society regulates the general production and thus makes it possible for me to do one thing today and another tomorrow, to hunt in the morning, fish in the afternoon, rear cattle in the evening, criticize

---

[23]Karl Marx, *Economic and Philosophical Manuscripts of 1844* (New York: International Publishers, 1964), p. 111.

[24]Karl Marx, *Capital* (New York: Modern Library, n.d.), pp. 461–462.

after dinner, just as I have a mind, without ever becoming hunter, fisherman, shepherd or critic.[25]

Most American sociologists reject the contention that the abolition of classes would eliminate feelings of alienation. The same work might be equally alienating in a classless society. The countries of the Soviet bloc claim to have achieved socialism (communism is still in the distant future, and there is as yet no society in the world that describes itself as communist), but there is no reason to suppose that workers in those countries are immune to alienation. At the time that Marx wrote, all the industrial societies of the world were also capitalist societies. It may be that much of the alienation that Marx attributed to capitalism was really caused by industrialism, and that a large measure of alienation will be found in any industrial society, whether it be capitalist or socialist.

What about Marx's prophecy that alienation would end only with the general revolt of the workers? The fact is that the industrial working class has not yet staged a successful socialist revolution in any country in the world, let alone the United States. All the socialist revolutions of the past—in Russia, China, and Cuba, for example—occurred in preindustrial contexts, contrary to Marx's predictions. Was he hopelessly wrong, or might he yet be proved right?

It is important to remember that Marx wrote during an earlier phase of the Industrial Revolution, when a rural peasantry was being transformed into an urban work force under conditions of the most abject poverty and brutal exploitation. It seemed reasonable to Marx that the capitalists, in their ceaseless pursuit of profit, would tend to grow fewer and richer, the workers would become more numerous and poorer, and the middle class would gradually be squeezed out of the picture. What Marx could not foresee was the great adaptability that the capitalist system has shown since that time, and the way rising affluence has enlarged the middle class while shrinking the original working class.

The American working class today is hardly in the forefront of radical social change. On major issues of the 1960s and 1970s—the Vietnam war, changing sex roles, racial equality, sexual permissiveness, or ecological concerns—the blue-collar worker has, if anything, been in the rearguard of the forces for change. Growing affluence, a familiarity with middle-class life styles, a sense of the possibility of upward mobility—all these have brought about many changes in the values and attitudes of the American working class. Unlike their counterparts in many other countries, they show remarkably little evidence of class consciousness. Most of their labor unions are no longer a radical force in society, but have instead become a part of the establishment they originally set out to attack. By gaining concessions for the workers, the unions have reinforced the faith of their members in the system as a whole. Workers rarely feel themselves exploited by individual capitalists. It is now difficult for them to apportion blame for their economic woes with any precision; the lines between the classes are more blurred than ever, and the worker is likely to be employed not by one person but by a faceless corporation, owned by thousands or hundreds of thousands of shareholders.

American workers still seem to have a basic faith in American capitalist institutions. The workers in general have developed a stake in the system Marx expected them to overthrow, and their alienation would have to reach unforeseeable levels before there would be any real possibility of a revolutionary change in the system.

The Sources of Worker Alienation

What is the underlying source of worker alienation in America? A psychological model proposed by the late American psychologist Abraham Maslow may provide a basis for analysis.[26] Maslow suggested that human needs can be ranked in a hierarchy, with each successive step requiring fulfillment only when the previous need has been met. Our initial need is for the satisfaction of simple physical requirements—

[25]Karl Marx and Friedrich Engels, *The German Ideology* (New York: International Publishers, n.d.), p. 22.

[26]Abraham Maslow, *Motivation and Personality* (New York: Harper & Row, 1954).

A receptionist at a large business establishment in the Midwest speaks about her job. She is twenty-four. Her husband is a student.

I was out of college, an English Lit. major. I looked around for copywriting jobs. The people they wanted had majored in journalism. Okay, the first myth that blew up in my face is that a college education will get you a job.

I changed my opinion of receptionists because now I'm one. It wasn't the dumb broad at the front desk who took telephone messages. She had to be something else because I thought I was something else. I was fine until there was a press party. We were having a fairly intelligent conversation. Then they asked me what I did. When I told them, they turned around to find other people with name tags. I wasn't worth bothering with. I wasn't being rejected because of what I had said or the way I talked, but simply because of my function. After that, I tried to make up other names for what I did—communications control, servomechanism. [Laughs.]

You come in at nine, you open the door, you look at the piece of machinery, you plug in the headpiece. That's how my day begins. You trem-ble when you hear the first ring. After that, it's sort of downhill—unless there's somebody on the phone who is either kind or nasty. The rest of the people are just non, they don't exist. They're just voices. You answer calls, you connect them to others, and that's it. . . . Until recently I'd cry in the morning. I didn't want to get up. I'd dread Fridays because Monday was always looming over me. Another five days ahead of me. There never seemed to be any end to it. Why am I doing this? Yet I dread looking for jobs. I don't like filling out forms and taking typing tests. I remember on applications I'd put down, "I'd like to deal with the public." [Laughs.] Well, I don't want to deal with the public any more. . . .

I don't know what I'd like to do. That's what hurts the most. That's why I can't quit the job. I really don't think I'd mind going back and learning something, taking a piece of furniture and refinishing it. The type of thing where you know what you're doing and you can create and you can fix something to make it function.

. . .

Source: Excerpted from Studs Terkel, *Working* (New York: Pantheon Books, 1972, 1974).

such as food and a roof over our heads. When this need is satisfied, we become aware of the need for safety and security. Thereafter, the psychological need for companionship and affection presents itself. The next step in the hierarchy is the requirement for self-esteem and the esteem of others. Finally comes the need for self-actualization, the fulfillment of one's deepest potentials. Most people throughout history have led a hand-to-mouth existence, and the later needs in this hierarchy have never become dominant. In an affluent society such as the United States, however, the needs for self-esteem and self-actualization become pressing psychological requirements. Yet the organization of work systematically stunts the quest for the satisfaction of these higher human needs.

American industry has traditionally seen the worker merely as part of a process. This attitude is best exemplified in a statement at the turn of the century by Frederick Winslow Taylor, father of time and motion studies and scientific management:

> For success, then, let me give one simple piece of advice beyond all others. Every day, year in and year out, each man should ask himself, over and over again, two questions. First, "What is the name of the man I am now working for?", and having answered this definitely, then, "What does this man want me to do, right now?"[27]

Empirical research conducted as early as the 1930s challenged the assumption that the key to contented workers was simply good pay and pleasant physical conditions. In some experiments at the Hawthorne plant of the Western Electric Company, the researchers systematically changed aspects of both the workers' environment and incentives to find out which would increase productivity. They discovered that pro-

[27]Quoted in *Work in America, op. cit.*, p. 500.

ductivity increased no matter what changes were made: the workers were responding not to the content of the changes but to the fact that variety was being introduced into their lives and attention was being paid to them.[28] Later research has made it clear that a lack of sense of control over the work process has a direct effect on feelings of powerlessness and alienation.[29]

Nonetheless, changes in the nature and organization of work have continued to create jobs in which workers become little more than machine-tenders engaged in highly standardized tasks that might just as well be performed by anyone off the street. The result is that workers may find little significance in the activities that take up most of their adult lives and so are robbed of a vital source of meaning. As Peter Berger suggests, technological changes have produced countless new jobs whose content makes it almost impossible for people to derive a full sense of identity from their work:

> Work provided the individual with a firm profile. This is no longer the case with most workers in industrial society. To say "I am a railroad man" may be a source of pride, but the pride is as precarious as the occupational title. To say "I am an electroencephalograph technician" means nothing to most people to whom it is said. To say "I am an addressograph operator" means nothing for a different reason, not because people do not understand what kind of work it entails, but because it is next to impossible to derive any sort of self-identification from such an occupation, not even the self-identification with an oppressed proletariat that sustained many workers in earlier phases of industrialism.[30]

Largely for this reason, Berger claims, work is becoming, for many people, a "grey, neutral region that one puts up with more or less for the sake of other things supposed to be more important." People play roles as workers, reserving their true, authentic selves for the precious hours away from the work place.

The present trend is still toward large corporations and impersonal bureaucracies that typically organize work in such a way that the independence of workers is minimized and control and predictability are maximized. For example, office space is increasingly designed according to the "open plan" concept, in which there are no partitions between the work spaces of various employees (except, of course, the offices of high-level executives). A 1978 Harris survey found that most business executives believe that the open-plan system would improve productivity. But only 29 percent of office workers agreed, and 92 percent of them saw a link between their personal satisfaction, their office surroundings, and their job performance. Yet according to the survey, 87 percent of business executives and 97 percent of designers expect that future office buildings will have open-plan work space.

Management is thus sometimes insensitive to the needs of the workers. Yet as Maslow's model suggests, the more aware, democratic, educated, and self-affirmative a worker is, the less he or she will stand for boring, dehumanized, authoritarian work conditions. An earlier generation of workers may have found such conditions tolerable, but as an official of the American Telephone and Telegraph Company has lamented, "We have run out of dumb people to handle these dumb jobs."[31] The dumb jobs exist largely because work has been broken down into processes that are easy to learn but tedious to perform. This specialization reduces job satisfaction: where tasks are so minutely subdivided that the workers perform only a minor operation on their product, they have no interest in doing the job well for its own sake.

The automobile assembly line has always been the epitome of the rationalized production process, and the signs are that workers are increasingly resisting the discipline required by the industry. The reasons are not hard to find. As one foreman explains it:

---

[28]Fritz J. Roethlisberger and William J. Dickson, *Management and the Worker* (Cambridge, Mass.: Harvard University Press, 1939).

[29]E.g., Melvin L. Kohn, "Occupational Structure and Alienation," *American Journal of Sociology*, 82 (July 1976), 111–130.

[30]Peter L. Berger, "Some General Observations on the Problem of Work," in Peter L. Berger (ed.), *The Human Shape of Work* (New York: Macmillan, 1964), p. 215.

[31]*Washington Post*, January 1, 1973.

The line here, the moving line, controls the man and his speed. No matter how slow a man is, he has to keep moving. We're all human, we like to go as slow as we can unless we're pushed, and this line controls him perfectly.[32]

The workers themselves make such comments as these:

The work isn't hard, it's the never-ending pace. The guys yell "hurrah" whenever the line breaks down.

On the line you're geared to the line. You don't dare stop. If you get behind you have a hard time catching up.

The job gets so sickening—day in and day out plugging in ignition wires. I get through one motor, turn around and there's another motor staring me in the face. It's sickening.

The assembly line is no place to work, I can tell you. There is nothing more discouraging than having a barrel beside you with 10,000 bolts in it and using them all up. Then you get a barrel with another 10,000 bolts, and you know every one of those 10,000 bolts has to be picked up and put in exactly the same place as the last 10,000 bolts.[33]

The auto assembly line has come to epitomize the process of rationalization and automation in industry—a process that often involves the subordination of individual human capacities to the demands of mechanized production. Although auto workers are often well paid, the industry has a high labor turnover rate and a long history of labor disputes.

It is not surprising that absenteeism among the three leading auto manufacturers—General Motors, Ford, and Chrysler—has increased sharply in recent years. On Mondays and Fridays up to 15 percent of the workers in the industry simply fail to turn up. Annual labor turnover has also increased rapidly: in fact, in one recent year almost half of Chrysler's new employees did not last three months on the job.

Nevertheless, it remains true that many people do get pleasure out of work, even in a mass-production factory (only a minority of blue-collar jobs are on the production line, which is the extreme example of the subordination of

human being to machine). People have a great capacity to adapt themselves, to draw satisfaction from even limited effectiveness at work, to find companionship in their interactions with fellow workers. But throughout the labor force the symptoms and causes of alienation abound. As Robert Sherrill notes:

Regimentation and repetition may not have nearly as much to do with worker alienation as does the fact that much work just isn't worth doing at all or is basically corrupt. Even the dumbest worker hired to manufacture spray de-

[32]Charles R. Walker, Robert Guest, and Arthur N. Turner, *The Foreman on the Assembly Line* (Cambridge, Mass.: Harvard University Press, 1956), p. 11.

[33]Charles R. Walker and Robert Guest, *Man on the Assembly Line* (Cambridge, Mass.: Harvard University Press, 1952), pp. 54–55.

odorant containers, or plastic plates, or pressed sawdust furniture, or ersatz packaged food, must realize that it wouldn't really matter if his factory closed down forever. So why should he care about his work.[34]

Job Dissatisfaction

Dissatisfaction with one's job can be a useful indicator of alienation at work. Just how dissatisfied is the American work force? The question is not easily answered. Some studies seem to indicate a deep level of dissatisfaction with work, but others suggest the opposite. The sociologist therefore has to look more closely at the methodology of the various studies—what kinds of questions were asked and what did the respondents understand by the questions?

Surveys on Job Satisfaction. For years sociologists and public-opinion pollsters have been asking people if they are satisfied with their jobs, and the overwhelming majority (between 80 and 90 percent on Gallup and other polls) have consistently answered yes. Furthermore, when a representative sample of American men were asked "If by some chance you inherited enough money to live comfortably without working, do you think you would work anyway or not?" some 80 percent replied that they would.[35]

If we ask rather different questions, however, we get significantly different answers. For example, when the workers who said that they would continue working even if they did not have to were asked *why* they would stay at work, they were very unclear about the reasons. The main explanation they gave was that they wanted to "keep occupied." The implication of this response is that it was not the pleasures of work that influenced their original answer but rather an inability to conceive of any other way of spending their free time. Again, if we ask workers the question "Would you pick the same job over

again?" the answers suggest a high level of job dissatisfaction. Of white-collar workers, only 43 percent say they would choose the same jobs, and of blue-collar workers, only 24 percent reply that they would (see Table 4.1).[36]

Extensive studies of worker attitudes by the University of Michigan Survey Research Center also contradict findings of the less sophisticated opinion polls. When workers were asked to rank aspects of work in order of importance, they gave this order:

1. Interesting work.
2. Enough help and equipment to get the job done.
3. Enough information to get the job done.
4. Enough authority to get the job done.
5. Good pay.
6. Opportunity to develop special abilities.
7. Job security.
8. Seeing the results of one's work.[37]

This study and others like it suggest that money is not all-important to workers. They want to become masters of their immediate environment, and they resent constant supervision, lack of variety, and feelings of personal powerlessness.

Income is still very important, however. Early in the 1970s studies showed that about 20 percent of all workers earning less than $5,000 a year are dissatisfied; for those earning $5,000 to $10,000 the proportion drops to 10 percent; for those earning over $10,000 it drops to 8 percent. But dissatisfaction also varies from job to job, regardless of income. Among the self-employed in construction, only one in twenty is dissatisfied; in technical, managerial, and professional occupations, one in ten; and in manufacturing, service, and wholesale occupations, one in four.

There are also marked variations in dissatisfaction among different categories of workers. Blacks are dissatisfied more than any other group of workers in the nation, twice as much as whites: 37 percent of them express negative attitudes toward their jobs. The second most dissatisfied category are workers under thirty with some college education: about one in four expresses

---

[34]Robert Sherrill, "Review of *Job Power* and *Work in America*," *New York Times Book Review,* July 8, 1973, p. 3.

[35]Nancy C. Morse and Robert S. Weiss, "The Function and Meaning of Work and the Job," *American Sociological Review,* 20 (April 1955), 191–198; *Work in America, op. cit.,* p. 14.

[36]*Work in America, op. cit.,* p. 16.

[37]*Ibid.,* p. 13.

Table 4.1   Percent of People in Occupational Groups Who Would Choose Similar Work Again

Professional and Lower White-Collar Occupations		Working-Class Occupations	
Urban university professors	93	Skilled printers	52
Mathematicians	91	Paper workers	42
Physicists	89	Skilled autoworkers	41
Biologists	89	Skilled steelworkers	41
Chemists	86	Textile workers	31
Firm lawyers	85	BLUE-COLLAR WORKERS, CROSS SECTION	24
Lawyers	83	Unskilled steelworkers	21
Journalists (Washington correspondents)	82	Unskilled autoworkers	16
Church university professors	77		
Solo lawyers	75		
WHITE-COLLAR WORKERS, CROSS SECTION	43		

Source: Work in America: Report of a Special Task Force to the Secretary of Health, Education, and Welfare (Cambridge, Mass.: The M.I.T. Press, 1973), p. 16.

negative attitudes. Third most dissatisfied are women under thirty. Among different age groups, it seems that the younger workers are the most dissatisfied: of those over fifty-five, only 6 percent are dissatisfied; of those forty-five to fifty-four, 11 percent; of those thirty to forty-four, 13 percent; and of those twenty-nine and under, 25 percent.[38] The young are particularly and increasingly resentful of authority. Studies by Daniel Yankelovich show that whereas in 1968 some 56 percent of students said they would not mind being "bossed around on the job," by 1971 this figure had dropped sharply to 36 percent.[39] According to the University of Michigan Institute for Social Service surveys, there was a general decline in job satisfaction between 1973 and 1977—a decline particularly notable among college graduates.[40] Other studies cited in Work in America reveal burgeoning discontent among clerical employees and even among middle-management executives who apparently fear being trapped in large organizations where their talents will never be recognized or challenged.

Frederick Herzberg offers a solution to the apparent discrepancies among various research findings on the question of worker alienation. He suggests a novel way of looking at the needs of workers through two distinct factors: intrinsic and extrinsic satisfaction. In this model, job satisfaction and job dissatisfaction are not seen, as they usually are, as opposite ends of the same dimension. Rather, they are viewed as two separate phenomena caused by quite different forces. Dissatisfaction at work depends on extrinsic factors, such as low pay, poor supervision, or unpleasant working conditions. Satisfaction at work depends on intrinsic factors, such as a sense of achievement, responsibility, and challenge.[41] So when a worker is asked "Are you satisfied with your work?" he or she may tend to interpret the question as referring to the extrinsic factors and answer yes; but if the question were designed to tap the worker's attitude toward the intrinsic factors, the response might be entirely different.

Health and Job Satisfaction.   In addition to actual surveys of worker attitudes, there are other measures of worker alienation and its effects. Studies by the University of Michigan's Institute for Social Research have indicated that

[38]Neal W. Herrick, "Who's Unhappy at Work and Why," Manpower, 4 (January 1972), 2–7.

[39]Daniel Yankelovich, The Changing Values on Campus: Political and Personal Attitudes on Campus (New York: Washington Square Press, 1972), p. 28.

[40]New York Times, December 17, 1978, p. 34.

[41]Frederick Herzberg, Work and the Nature of Man (Cleveland: World, 1966).

A white woman from Somerville, a so-called "streetcar suburb" outside of Boston, has for a long time worked in the home of a prominent, quite well-off Cambridge family. Helen has cleaned for them, cooked for them. She has taken care of their two children. She knows them well—and herself, too; and knows the difference.

"I come over there every day. When they go away, I stay. They've given me a room. They say I can live with them. They mean to be nice, but I get upset. They don't stop and think that I have a family, too.

"I worry about my own children, while I take care of other people's children. That's the way it has to be, I know. I need the money. They have the money! I can't even leave this house when I go home. The place sticks in my mind. I'll think of what I did the day before, or what I'll be doing the next day. All those important people come here, and I serve them food. You get used to the way the rich live, and you go home at night, and suddenly you're poor again. I tell my husband he's lucky he works on a truck. He doesn't see what I do, so he doesn't miss what I do.

"I'll be working, and I'll hear them talk. The missus is a big talker. She goes gab, gab all the time, when she's home. She has a lot of money, but she works, too. She's in public relations, she tells me. She helps the museums. She writes articles. She calls a lot of people up and goes to see them. She has an office in Boston. She used to do volunteer work, a lot of it; but she said she should *work*, like men do.

"My husband thinks she's crazy, and so do I. If I had money, I'd quit this job, and go home and stay home for a thousand years. I'd be with my own kids and not someone else's. Does it make sense? The missus says that she has to get out and work, or else she'll 'stagnate'—her favorite word. She's always worrying about 'stagnating.' She says women are in danger of 'stagnating.' Maybe in her dictionary I'm not a woman!

"I don't envy the rich women I see over in that Cambridge house! A lot of them have husbands who are doctors or lawyers or professors, and they have more money than I'd know what to do with;

but I'll look at one of them, a pretty lucky woman. I'll think for a second or two, and she's not at peace with herself—that's how I'd put it. The missus I work for—she weighs herself twice a day. If she gains a pound—*one* pound!—she tells her husband she's 'depressed,' another of her words.

"I hear her and her husband talking about the colored people, and how they should have their rights, and the women, and they should have their rights. But when the missus wants me to do something, or the cleaning woman to do something, or the man who works on her plants and trees to do something, she doesn't worry about us; she worries about herself.

"She tells her children that they should feel sorry for the poor, and if they ever see a colored person, they should put themselves in that person's shoes. The way those kids order me around, I know they're not fighting over who gets to try out my shoes!

"Once the girl asked me if I liked the colored. She was eleven, and I didn't want to get into a long talk with her. I just told her yes, I thought some of them are good people, and some aren't so good. She didn't believe me! She said she knew I didn't like the colored. I asked her where she got *that* idea. She said her mother had told her that a lot of white people who don't have much money are afraid of the colored people, and are prejudiced against them. I told her I was going to tell her mother *a lot*, the next time I had a talk with her! But I didn't want to get into a fight. I'd lose my job. I need the money. She pays a good salary. The house is an easy one to take care of.

"I hear them talk at the table. The missus is always worrying about something happening far away. She calls people up and gets them to sign their names, to protest this and protest that. I've never heard of all those 'causes.' She calls them that. She says to me: 'I'm working on a cause; we've all got to help.' I'm glad she never asks me to sign. I'm not an important person, so she doesn't want me.

"If she ever did ask me, I'd probably do what she wanted. I wouldn't want to cross her. She calls people who disagree with her 'stupid.' Her husband is even worse when he hears that someone disagrees with him. He calls them Nazis or Fascists. I thought we beat them and got rid of them a long time ago! Or he'll talk about 'right-wingers.' I can't figure out who they are. Maybe, if they heard my husband talk, they'd call him one! But I never talk at home about what I hear those two bosses of mine say at work. I'm glad to say *good-bye* when I leave work.

"When the missus has an argument with her husband, she speaks and he speaks. Neither gives in. Then she changes. She starts crying. Then he collapses, and says yes to her. I heard her tell one of her women friends that she has her 'final weapon,' if nothing else works. I think she stays away from him until he surrenders! What's so smart about that! Is she really 'liberated'? I'd never do that! I'd rather scream and shout and throw dishes than hold out on my husband that way. It's being sneaky and dishonest.

"The trouble with those two is that they think they're so honest with each other, and she thinks she's equal with her husband. But she acts like a woman and he acts like a man, and that's how they get through their troubles. She told me that herself one night; she had a few drinks in her, and she laughed at herself and said she talks 'a big line,' but in her heart she's just like me. I thought to myself that she was talking a big line right then and there! But the more I thought about it, the more I began to believe her. She's a woman who thinks she's no different from men, she keeps saying; but she *is* a woman and she'll always act like a woman part of the day—and at night!—and I suppose we *are* alike, because we *are* both women.

"I hate to be so hard on her and her husband. I hate to say bad things about them. I'm grateful to them; they help me out, help me see a lot that's going on in the world. They're smart about other people, but they don't look at themselves and see as much as they do when they look at their friends. I think they're afraid they'll see what they see when they look at their friends. I think they're afraid of their friends. I sense it in the air when they're having friends over—the fright.

"The girl came home the other day, and was upset. She spoke up in class, and the teacher didn't agree with her. It's a fancy school she goes to—a private school. The mother gets angry with the teachers in front of her daughter, and tells the girl she's going to get the woman fired. I don't understand how a woman who is always talking about the way women are unfairly treated can speak of a schoolteacher, a woman, as if she's dirt to be brushed aside.

"Maybe that's the way they talk about me and the cleaning woman, too—behind our backs. She's a great one, that missus, for being sweet to people, then turning on them behind their backs later on, with her gossip and her 'stories.' She's home an hour before him, and does she go and help prepare supper? No, she takes another shower (two a day!) and changes from one fancy dress to another, and does herself up, and goes into her study to 'think.'

"My husband still won't believe me when I tell him what she does *then*. She sits and writes things down in her 'journal.' She's been writing her 'stories' to herself for years and years. She says it helps her to 'think'! I peeked once. I've never done it again. She went on and on about herself—what *she* thinks, and how *she* feels, and what someone said to *her*, and what *she* planned to do.

"I think the missus is right: everyone should be equal. She keeps on saying that. But then she has me working away in her house, and I'm not equal with her—and she doesn't want to be equal with me; and I don't blame her, because if I was her I'd hold on to my money just like she does. Maybe that's what the men are doing—they're holding on to their money. And the women are trying to get more money.

"She should know. She doesn't go throwing big fat checks at her 'help.' She's 'fair'; she keeps on reminding us—but she's not going to 'liberate' us, anymore than the men are going to 'liberate' their wives or their secretaries or the other women working in their companies. That's the world for you."

Source: Robert Coles and Jane Hallowell Coles, "The Grass Isn't Greener, Just the Money," in *The New York Times*, April 10, 1978, A19. Copyright 1978 Robert Coles and Jane Hallowell Coles.

a variety of health problems, especially psycho-somatic illnesses, are related to job dissatisfaction. In a major study of the mental health problems of industrial workers, Arthur Kornhauser found that

> poorer mental health occurs whenever conditions of work and life lead to continuing frustration . . . of strongly desired goals which have become indispensable elements of the individual's self-identity as a worthwhile person. Persistent failure and frustration bring lowered self-esteem and dissatisfaction with life, often accompanied by anxieties, social alienation and withdrawal . . . in short, poor mental health.[42]

Another surprising finding that emerged from an impressive fifteen-year-long study of aging is that work satisfaction was the strongest predictor of longevity. The second best predictor was overall "happiness." These two measures predicted longevity better than a rating by an examining physician, a measure of the use of tobacco, or a study of genetic inheritance.[43] A report on the Abkhasian people of the Soviet Union by the anthropologist Sula Benet provides another link between work and longevity. She found that 2.5 percent of Abhkasians were ninety years old or older, compared with 0.1 percent for all Russians and 0.4 percent for Americans. Abkhasian society has a social system in which increased prestige comes with age. But more important, work is literally a lifelong task. Even at the age of one hundred, Abkhasians gladly work in the fields for four hours a day.[44] In our society, in contrast, there is no respected work role for the old. Instead, we often offer them little more than a meaningless existence and a sick role that may encourage psychosomatic (and genuine) illness.

The Decline of the Work Ethic

A recurrent complaint from corporate employers and others in positions of political and economic power is that many workers are not merely dissatisfied with their jobs—they are dissatisfied with the whole idea of working. Is the work ethic as strong in the United States today as it has been in the past? The evidence is contradictory, but it does appear that many workers, particularly the better-educated younger members of the work force, are beginning to question the old ethic and to place an increasingly high value on leisure. Such a development seems almost unavoidable, for there is a deep and inherent tension in the modern industrial system: it demands self-denial and discipline from the individual as a worker, yet demands gratification and pleasure from the individual as a consumer. Under these circumstances the maintenance of the work ethic on which the whole system depends is inevitably a fragile enterprise. The critical tension in America between the requirements of work and the seductions of pleasure was prophetically expressed by Adriano Tilgher in the 1930s:

> In the very homeland of the religion of work a still later religion is growing up, the religion of large buying and of amusements, a religion of comfort, of well-being, of convenience. . . . This has the distinct tendency to relax the tautness of the will to work. . . . The divine madness of labor seems an unbearable chain, binding man to things outside his nature, locking his soul in a narrow prison where its energies are impoverished and weakened.[45]

During the 1960s a significant conflict of values emerged when adherents of the "hippie" counterculture seemed to reject the work ethic and its demands for apparently endless deferral of gratification. Part of the dismayed adult reaction at the time was surely based on the realistic perception that if the "hippie" values were adopted and maintained by the bulk of the younger generation, the industrial system as we know it would change dramatically. In practice, hard economic necessity forced most members of the youth counterculture to modify or abandon

---

[42]Quoted in *Work in America, op. cit.,* p. 84.

[43]*Ibid.,* p. 84.

[44]Sula Benet, "Why They Live to Be 100, or Even Older, in Abkhasia," *New York Times Magazine,* December 26, 1971, pp. 28, 29.

[45]Adriano Tilgher, *Work: What It Has Meant to Men Through the Ages* (New York: Harcourt, Brace, 1930), pp. 142, 147.

their new values, but Daniel Bell argues that the tension between the work ethic and the desire for pleasure and leisure is likely to become more severe in the future:

> American capitalism has lost its traditional legitimacy which was based on a moral system of reward, rooted in a Protestant sanctification of work. It has substituted a hedonism which promises a material ease and luxury. . . . The characteristic style of an industrial society is based on the principles of economics and economizing: on efficiency, least cost, maximization, optimization, and functional rationality. Yet it is at this point that it comes into sharpest conflict with the cultural trends of the day. The one emphasizes functional rationality, technocratic decision-making, and meritocratic rewards. The other, apocalyptic moods and antirational modes of behavior. It is this disjunction which is the historic crisis of Western society. This cultural contradiction, in the long run, is the deepest challenge to the society.[46]

The implication of Bell's argument is that if people should come to value leisure and pleasure more than hard work and the material goods that work enables them to acquire, they would be increasingly reluctant to submit themselves to the alienating discipline and routines of work. Lacking any sense of moral obligation to work, they would become unreliable, unproductive, and irregular employees. If the work ethic were to be abandoned on a wide scale, the basis of industrial capitalism would be undermined, throwing the entire economic system and the society it supports into increasing disarray and disorganization.

CONFRONTING THE PROBLEM

Many ideas have been suggested, and many put into practice, to deal with the problems of unemployment and worker alienation. The most radical proposals are those that assume these problems cannot be solved without major changes in the social, economic, and political structure of American society. Socialist critics have argued, for example, that unemployment cannot be combated within the framework of capitalism: what is necessary is a socialist economy, in which the government regulates the production and distribution of goods and services to meet social needs, not to provide profit. Other proposals call for "industrial democracy," in which the workers participate fully in all important decisions of their organization.[47] In Yugoslavia, for example, many factories are partly owned by their workers, and joint committees of workers and management are responsible for a variety of decisions, such as hiring and firing or future investment. The problem with these proposals, whatever their merits or weaknesses, is that they run counter to deeply held American values, and therefore have little prospect of being widely debated, let alone implemented, in the foreseeable future.

Most of the proposals that have been made are aimed primarily at alleviating rather than eliminating the problems of unemployment and alienation. Even so, many of these proposals are highly controversial, because government officials, labor unions, management, shareholders, employers, and taxpayers all have different interests and values to defend. As Ivar Berg comments:

> It may be America's curse or its genius that we wish to reform as many things as possible while changing things as little as possible. . . . We continually seek to study worker dissatisfactions while doing little to make changes that would

---

[46]Daniel Bell, "The Cultural Contradiction," *New York Times*, August 27, 1970. For a fuller statement, see Daniel Bell, *The Cultural Contradictions of Capitalism* (New York: Basic Books, 1976).

[47]See Paul Bernstein, *Workplace Democratization* (New Brunswick, N.J.: Transaction Books, 1980); Tom R. Burns, Lars Erik Karlsson, and Veljko Rus (eds.), *Work and Power: The Liberation of Work and the Control of Political Power* (Beverly Hills, Calif.: Sage, 1979).

affect a number of the initial conditions in which these dissatisfactions are rooted.[48]

Confronting Unemployment. The problem of unemployment can be confronted on two levels: general unemployment and unemployment among specific groups. The most illustrious economists of the Western world have wrestled with possible solutions to economic recession for several years, but are not even in agreement on its causes, let alone its solution. There is a general consensus that the cure for unemployment is rapid economic growth, but there is heated controversy over how to achieve this without unacceptably high inflation. Proposals have ranged from the cutting of taxes to the restriction of the money supply, but ultimately the most important factor may be a psychological one: optimism. If business leaders are optimistic about the future of the economy, they will invest in new plants and equipment, hire new workers, and increase production. However, even if the economy moves ahead at a rapid pace, unemployment is likely to remain a problem for several years to come because there will be a lag between new investment and the creation of new jobs. We might note in passing that although it may be a cure for unemployment, rapid economic growth will almost inevitably have a negative impact on the natural environment and on the supply of scarce resources. This situation is but one of many examples of the solution to one social problem having the effect of creating or aggravating another problem—or, in more sociological terms, of a social change having functional and dysfunctional effects.

The problem of disproportionate unemployment among specific groups is more amenable to an attempt at solution. Workers who have been displaced by automation can be retrained and given skills for other jobs. The status of illegal aliens is likely to improve markedly if Congress accepts proposals to grant at least some of them a more secure status. Unemployment among unqualified young workers, particularly in minority groups, can be combated by the creation of special federal or state job-training programs.

The impact of unemployment on older workers and others who may remain unemployed for very long periods can be lessened by reforms in unemployment compensation—specifically, by raising compensation levels and by making compensation available for longer periods to those who are genuinely seeking work but are unable to find it. Migrant and other seasonal workers can unionize and demand better wages and more job security. Women workers can be helped by equal-opportunity legislation to gain entry to jobs that have traditionally been denied to them, and which they have often considered it unrealistic to try to fill. None of these proposals would eliminate unemployment among these disadvantaged groups in times of general unemployment, but they would help to make its occurrence less disproportionate. Again, however, we should note that there is a serious potential for conflict among the various groups that hope to gain a greater share of employment opportunities: success for any one group will tend to diminish the opportunities for others.

Combating Alienation. Many employers have come to realize that alienation in the work force may actually reduce efficiency and productivity, and they are becoming more willing to implement proposals to redesign the nature of work. An example of the kind of changes that have been made so far is an experiment conducted at a General Foods plant that was built because many of the employees in an existing plant showed such extreme symptoms of alienation that production was seriously affected. At best, the workers were indifferent to the quality of the finished product; at worst, they resorted to minor industrial sabotage leading to waste, shutdowns, and poor labor-management relations. After extensive deliberations with academic consultants and the workers themselves, the firm decided on a new plant with several innovative features. Supervisors were abolished, and self-managing teams of workers were given full responsibility for important parts of the production process. Work was redesigned to make it more challenging: dull, routine jobs were eliminated if possible, and those that remained were shared among the team so that nobody was permanently stuck with

---

[48]Ivar Berg, "Employee Discontent in a Business Society," *Society,* 14 (March–April 1978), 56.

a tedious task. Different status symbols for different ranks of worker—separate parking lots, cafeterias, or types of office furniture—were abolished in order to develop feelings of equality among the workers.[49]

The results of the experiment were dramatic. The management had anticipated that 110 workers would be needed to run the plant, but the new system was so successful that only 70 were necessary. After eighteen months, the new plant's operating cost was 33 percent lower than the old plant's. Product rejects plummeted an astounding 92 percent, and absenteeism dropped to 9 percent below the industry average. Annual savings to the firm totaled more than half a million dollars. But, once again, we must note that although alienation declined and productivity increased, jobs were lost in the process.

Several other experiments have led to more positive worker attitudes.[50] At the Bankers Trust Company, typists had repetitive jobs that entailed recording stock-transfer data. Production was low, quality of work poor, and morale weak. When invited to redesign their jobs, the workers eliminated the work of a checker and of a special group that made corrections and took on these responsibilities themselves. The new system permitted annual savings of $360,000, with marked changes in the level of worker satisfaction. On a Corning Glass assembly line, workers had assembled hot plates, with each individual doing only a tiny part of the entire job. The routine was altered so that each worker assembled the entire hot plate, to which her initials were added. The workers were encouraged to design their work as a group, and to conduct their own quality checks. Within six months, rejects dropped from 23 percent to 1 percent of output, absenteeism fell from 8 percent to 1 percent, and productivity increased by 47 percent.

Other techniques that are being explored include participatory management, profit sharing, and the four-day week. Under participatory management, workers take part in decisions involving their own production methods, questions of recruitment, issues of internal leadership, and work schedules; they generally do not participate, however, in long-range economic decisions. Profit sharing may be in the form of either stock ownership or direct payment of an agreed proportion of company profits in addition to normal pay and fringe benefits. The four-day week involves the elimination of one working day and the lengthening of the remaining four. Often employees can choose which four days they wish to work. Between 700 and 1,000 American companies have so far adopted the four-day week, with about 100,000 employees being affected.[51] Early results are highly encouraging. A survey of a sample of organizations using the four-day week found that 62 percent reported improved production, whereas only 3 percent reported that output had been reduced; 51 percent had higher profits, whereas only 4 percent experienced lower earnings; and 66 percent considered that efficiency had been improved, whereas only 3 percent considered it had lessened.[52]

Not all experiments, of course, have worked. Some new approaches have led nowhere, others have merely led to trouble. In some cases, practical and economic restraints make major redesign of work extremely difficult. As the head of the Ford labor-relations department declared bluntly, "You can't stay in the auto assembly business by throwing parts on the floor and saying to the guy, 'Make an automobile out of it.'" But because many of the experiments have been highly rewarding, leading to greater productivity, better quality, lower absenteeism, and much more satisfied workers, the general trend in the future is likely to be in the direction of further experimentation and more widespread application of proven reforms. As Richard Walton of the Harvard Business School notes, "The roots of worker alienation go so deep that nothing less than comprehensive, radical, systematic redesign of the workplace can sever them."[53]

[49]Richard E. Walton, "How to Counter Alienation in the Plant," *Harvard Business Review*, 50 (November–December 1972), 70–82.

[50]For a detailed account of an experiment in a Swedish plant, see Lars E. Björk, "An Experiment in Work Satisfaction," *Scientific American*, 232 (March 1975), 17–23.

[51]*U.S. News and World Report*, March 20, 1972, p. 82.
[52]*Ibid.*, p. 82.
[53]Quoted in the *Washington Post*, January 1, 1973.

SUMMARY

1. The major social problems associated with work are unemployment, which has reached high levels in the recession of the 1970s, and alienation at work, the sense of powerlessness and meaninglessness that many people experience in their jobs.

2. Work means more than merely earning a living. Under the influence of the "Protestant ethic," work has become a moral obligation and a source of self-respect. Jobs also confer statuses on their holders and integrate them into society.

3. The nature of work in America is changing as the proportion of jobs in tertiary industry rises and that in primary and secondary industry declines. Different categories of workers, such as blue-collar, white-collar, women, minority-group, young, old, and migrant, have different likelihoods of being affected by unemployment or alienation.

4. From the functionalist approach, the problems associated with work are the result of social disorganization caused by rapid social change, such as automation, economic disruption resulting from increases in the prices of raw materials, demographic changes, and the rationalization of the work process. The conflict approach focuses on work in the context of social and economic inequality, and explains the problems as being largely the result of a conflict of interest among the different groups involved, with the outcome favoring the more powerful interests.

5. Official United States statistics underestimate the actual unemployment rate. The main cause of the generally high level of unemployment is the economic recession, although its impact has been worsened by specific domestic factors such as government and corporate attitudes to unemployment, technological development, corporate investment abroad, and the pressure of new female and "baby boom" youth workers on the market. The causes of disproportionate unemployment in specific groups are the product of different factors relevant to the particular groups concerned.

6. Karl Marx attributed alienation to the increased division of labor and the exploitation of the workers. He predicted class conflict and ultimately revolution, but his prophecies have not materialized. Maslow's model suggests that modern workers have psychological needs for self-actualization, which are stunted by the organization of work. Research findings point to extensive dissatisfaction in the work force, linked to a growing gap between worker ideals and actual conditions.

7. The general problem of high unemployment will be solved only when the international economy moves out of recession. Disproportionate unemployment in specific categories of workers can be confronted by job retraining, security for illegal aliens, government job-creation programs, unionization, and attacks on discriminatory barriers. Alienation in the work force can be alleviated by redesigning jobs to give workers greater control over their environment.

GLOSSARY

Alienation. The sense of powerlessness and meaninglessness that people experience when confronted by social institutions they consider oppressive and feel they cannot control.

Automation. The use of self-regulating machines that monitor and control a production process.

Division of labor. The division of economic activity into specialized tasks that are performed by specific people.

Primary industry. Economic activity involving the gathering or extracting of undeveloped natural resources.

Rationalization. The process by which traditional, spontaneous methods of social organization are replaced by routine, systematic procedures.

Secondary industry. Economic activity involving the transformation of raw materials into manufactured goods.

Stagflation. A combination of stagnation (low growth, low investment, high unemployment) and inflation.

Tertiary industry. Economic activity involving the provision of various services.

Underemployment. A situation in which people are working only for short or irregular periods, or for wages so low that they cannot adequately support themselves, or at jobs below their level of qualification.

FURTHER READING

BERGER, PETER L. (ed.). *The Human Shape of Work.* New York: Macmillan, 1964. A useful collection of essays dealing with the human aspects of work. The book includes an excellent essay by Berger on the meaning of work.

GARSON, BARBARA. *All the Livelong Day: The Meaning and Demeaning of Routine Work.* New York: Penguin, 1975. A critical account of work alienation. The book includes interviews with both workers and management, together with the author's own observations.

GERRY, HUNNIUS, G. DAVID GARSON, and JOHN CASE. *Workers' Control: A Reader on Labor and Social Change.* New York: Random House, 1973. A selection of articles on various aspects of the redesigning of jobs, focusing on changes that give workers greater participation in the decisions affecting their working lives.

MARCUSE, HERBERT. *Eros and Civilization.* Boston: Beacon Press, 1965. A radical philosopher's argument that industrial civilization is founded on the repression of the worker's "instinct" for pleasure, with profound effects for both the individual and society.

MARX, KARL. *Selected Writings in Sociology and Social Philosophy.* Ed. T. B. Bottomore and Maximilian Rubel. Baltimore: Penguin, 1964. A selection of Karl Marx's writings drawn from all his major works. The selections include many of Marx's comments on class conflict and his passionate denunciation of the alienation of labor.

RITZER, GEORGE. *Working: Conflict and Change.* 2nd ed. Englewood Cliffs, N.J.: Prentice-Hall, 1977. A useful, up-to-date sociological discussion of the problems of the work place.

ROSOW, JEROME M. *The Worker and the Job: Coping with Change.* Englewood Cliffs, N.J.: Prentice-Hall, 1974. An excellent selection of articles covering many aspects of work, including worker attitudes, redesigning of jobs, unionization, and changes in the occupational structure.

TERKEL, STUDS. *Working.* New York: Pantheon, 1972. A fascinating collection of tape-recorded interviews with workers of every kind. Terkel's book rapidly became a best seller as the general public realized the intense human interest in the working lives of these ordinary Americans. Some of the interviewees find fulfillment in their jobs; others, however, are deeply alienated.

WHYTE, WILLIAM H. *The Organization Man.* New York: Simon and Schuster, 1956. A perceptive and controversial account of the life of workers in large modern corporations. Whyte argues that the employees become so subordinated to the demands of these faceless organizations that all other areas of their experience suffer.

Work In America: Report of a Special Task Force to the Secretary of Health, Education, and Welfare. Cambridge, Mass.: M.I.T. Press, 1973. A government report that acknowledges the existence of worker alienation as a major social problem in America. Written in clear, nontechnical language, the report recounts the "blue-collar blues" and "white-collar woes" of many American workers.

5
The Cities

THE PROBLEM

America today is a predominantly urban nation, and the problems confronting most Americans are the problems of the city. According to Bureau of the Census data, over 70 percent of Americans live in urban areas, a proportion that may increase in the years ahead. In 1972 the national Commission on Population Growth and the American Future predicted that by the year 2000 some 60 percent of Americans will live in metropolitan areas of a million inhabitants or more.[1] Since then there has been a small but growing migration from densely populated areas to small towns and rural areas.[2] However, even if this trend continues, it will not affect the overwhelmingly urban nature of modern American society.

Americans have mixed feelings about the prospect of a primarily urban future, for many of our cities are in a state of decay, and the reality of "city life" falls far short of American ideals. Other societies have looked on their cities as the crowning achievement of their cultures. To the ancient Greeks, for example, urban living was almost synonymous with civilization itself; Aristotle described the city as "a common life to a noble end." In America today there are genuine doubts that our cities can survive as a habitable environment at all. In fact, a 1978 Gallup poll found that more than a third of city dwellers would move out of the city if they had their wish. The basic social problem of the city is a generalized urban decay, which is in turn a compound of multiple specific problems. The very word "city" can evoke images of bad housing, riots, congestion, poverty, and deteriorating public and social services. The reported incidence of nearly all forms of deviant social behavior is also much greater in urban areas than in rural ones: burglary rates are three times as high, rape rates are twice as high, robbery rates are six times as high. In addition, chronic alcoholism rates and suicide rates in cities of over 10,000 population are twice those of rural areas; and hard-drug addiction is primarily an urban problem.

The urban area is the locus of our more intractable social problems. In this chapter we shall see how the cities have been affected by complex social changes, particularly a population shift from city centers to suburbs. These changes have had devastating effects on urban housing, civic facilities, racial segregation patterns, employment opportunities, and tax revenues. It has been the interplay of these and other factors that has plunged urban areas into a state of crisis.

[1]*Population and the American Future: The Report of the Commission on Population Growth and the American Future* (Washington, D.C.: U.S. Government Printing Office, 1972), p. 34.

[2]Peter Morrison, "Rural Renaissance in America? The Revival of Population Growth in Remote Areas," *Population Bulletin*, 31:3 (1976).

URBANIZATION

A *city* is essentially a permanent concentration of large numbers of people who do not produce their own food. Large urban settlements were therefore an impossibility before organized agriculture, which made possible a surplus production of food, freeing some people from the land and allowing them to take up specialized nonagricultural roles. About 3000 B.C. distinctly urban settlements arose in the Indus River valley, in the Persian Gulf, and on the shores of the Mediterranean. By modern standards these settlements were very small—the walls of Babylon bounded an area of only 3.2 square miles, and the famous biblical city of Ur occupied only 220 acres. Nevertheless, the early cities rapidly became the center of political and religious influence, the natural crossroads for communication and ideas, and the source of technological innovation. The Greek city-state became the home of the democratic ideal, and the Roman Empire spread the planned, formally administered urban model throughout the known world. With the development of international trade hundreds of years later, new cities, such as Venice, arose at the mercantile centers of the world.

The modern city, however, is essentially a product of the Industrial Revolution, which made possible a vastly different ratio of urban workers to the agricultural laborers who fed them. Before 1800 little of the world was really urban, but thereafter urbanization took place at an increasing rate. By the beginning of the nineteenth century the population of London had reached 1 million; by the middle of the century 4 cities had passed the million mark; by the beginning of the twentieth century 19 cities had done so; and in the 1960s there were 141 cities of over 1 million inhabitants. At the end of this century there may be 500 cities with populations of more than 1 million, and several are expected to contain over 25 million people. By the year 2000 some four-fifths of the world's population will probably live in cities.[3]

The American City

The urbanization of the United States has been equally rapid. At the time of the first census in 1790, 95 percent of the American population lived on farms, and the country boasted a mere

twenty-four urban settlements, only two of which had populations of more than 25,000. But the cities expanded rapidly with the waves of immigrants arriving from rural areas and from abroad: a hundred years after the first census, 30 percent of the population was urban, and five cities had over a million inhabitants. In this century, internal migration, such as that of black Americans from the rural South to the urban North, has further increased the size of the cities. Nearly three-quarters of the national population now lives in urban areas, and less than 5 percent of the work force are engaged in farming. This unprecedented ratio of agricultural to urban workers—which can still periodically yield a substantial national food surplus—is largely the result of the highly industrialized and technological nature of American society. In comparison, for example, agricultural techniques in modern China are still so undeveloped that fully 75 percent of the Chinese population must laboriously work the land to produce food for themselves and for the minority who play nonagricultural roles.

Although most Americans today are urban dwellers, this does not mean that they live within the densely populated inner cities. As the population of the cities has expanded beyond their legal boundaries, there has been a rapid growth of *suburbs*—the less densely populated, primarily residential areas that surround the inner city. A city and its outlying suburbs together form a *metropolis*, which is in practice a socially and economically integrated unit, even though it may be geographically dispersed and divided for legal and administrative purposes into several different towns or counties. A majority of urban residents live in the suburbs rather than the inner cities, and many others live in relatively small towns (see Figure 5.1).

The Bureau of the Census defines any locality with over 2,500 inhabitants as an urban area, even if the residents themselves do not regard it as such. And the bureau, recognizing that city and suburb are inseparably linked, purposely ignores their political boundaries by the use of its concept of a *Standard Metropolitan Statistical Area*. An SMSA is any area that includes one city (or two or more close cities) with a population of

---

[3]Kingsley Davis, "The Urbanization of the Human Population," *Scientific American*, 213 (September 1965) 41–53.

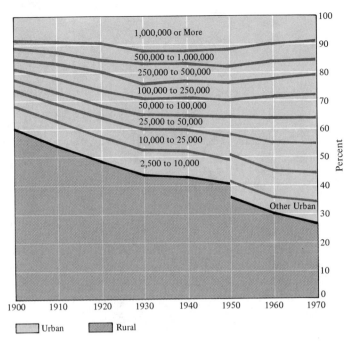

1,000,000 or More

500,000 to 1,000,000

250,000 to 500,000

100,000 to 250,000

50,000 to 100,000

25,000 to 50,000

10,000 to 25,000

2,500 to 10,000

Other Urban

Percent

1900 1910 1920 1930 1940 1950 1960 1970

☐ Urban   ▨ Rural

FIGURE 5.1 Population in urban and rural areas, 1900–1970. The United States has been transformed in the course of this century from a predominantly rural to a predominantly urban nation. Most urban dwellers, however, still reside in relatively small towns and suburbs.
(Bureau of the Census; Executive Office of the President: Office of Management and Budget, *Social Indicators, 1973* [Washington, D.C.: U.S. Government Printing Office, 1973], p. 242.)

over 50,000, plus the surrounding suburbs. There are now 277 SMASs, containing 73 percent of the American population.[4] The growth of the suburbs and the decline of the central city is one of the most significant developments in American society during this century.

Los Angeles, one of the few major cities to develop after the introduction of the automobile, is often cited as a possible prototype for the sprawling metropolitan area of the future. It contains a small central city, a county of nine other cities, and sixty-seven smaller self-governing communities. This great sprawl has often been termed a "group of suburbs in search of a city." Space is squandered, making public transport, when it exists, expensive. Automobile exhaust so pollutes the atmosphere that airline travelers may first glimpse the city as a gray pall intermittently pierced by mountaintops. Yet Los Angeles offers a distinctive life style to which millions of its citizens are devoted; they would not choose to live anywhere else.

Among social commentators, this modern me-

tropolis has excited widely varying reactions. The architect Frank Lloyd Wright recommended that urban renewal in Los Angeles should consist of the demolition and rebuilding of the entire city; the British town planner Fred Osborn termed the area "the hashish dream of a fanatical motorist"; the writer Aldous Huxley gave a more balanced view when he remarked that Los Angeles had the greatest potential of any place he had known—though whether it was a potential for horror or fulfillment, he could not tell.[5]

Another major urban development is the gradual linking of a series of metropolitan areas into what has been called the *megalopolis*—a vast unbroken area of cities and suburbs. The Bureau of the Census calls such an area a *Standard Consolidated Area* (SCA), and recognizes thirteen of these megalopolises (as shown in Figure 5.2). The most outstanding megalopolis is the great chain of cities and suburbs on the Eastern seaboard, from Boston to Virginia—an area containing 40 million people in an almost continuous urban tract. Other emerging examples of the megalopolis are to be found in

[4]*Population and the American Future, op. cit.*, p. 25; U.S. Bureau of the Census, *Statistical Abstract of the United States*, 1978 (Washington, D.C.: U.S. Government Printing Office, 1978), p. 17.

[5]Ralph Tomlinson, *Urban Structure* (New York: Random House, 1969), p. 305.

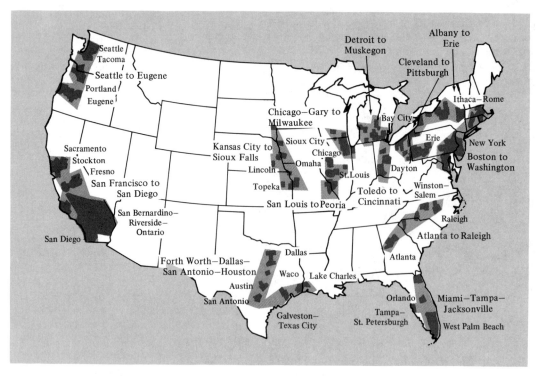

FIGURE 5.2 **Thirteen major megalopolises in the United States.** In several parts of the United States, spreading urban areas are merging with one another to form continuous, densely populated tracts. These megalopolises are expected to grow larger and more numerous in the future.

(Department of Commerce, U.S. Bureau of the Census.)

southern California, Texas, and the Great Lakes region. Ultimately, most Americans may live in areas such as these.

Life in the suburbs once provided an escape from the problems of big-city living, and to a considerable extent still does. During the 1950s and 1960s suburban living was much criticized as being socially homogeneous, deadly dull, and isolated from reality. The concerns of suburbanites were satirically portrayed as revolving around washing the car, mowing the lawn, attending cocktail parties and barbecues, driving to school and the supermarket, and generally gearing personal behavior and material consumption to the expectations of the neighbors. This picture was of course much overdrawn if not grossly exaggerated, and it is clear that many Americans found in the suburbs the ideal compromise between rural and urban living.

Now, although some idyllic suburban communities still exist, the residents of others are finding that the problems from which they escaped are inexorably following them as urbanization continues. Many suburbs are becoming more socially heterogeneous. Crime rates are rising rapidly, pollution and congestion are increasing, and tax rates have soared. A growing number of suburbanites are reluctant to commute to the central cities and now work in the suburbs, but the industries and other enterprises that provide their jobs are changing the nature of many suburban communities. No longer do these communities consist almost entirely of single-family homes: there are factories, corporate headquarters, hotels and apartment buildings, even emerging ghettos. As the suburbs expand and the boundaries of one merge with those of another, the sense of community may be lost in hundreds or thousands of square miles of suburban sprawl. In some suburbs whatever commercial centers they may have are already showing the telltale signs of urban decay—long-vacant shops, drug abuse and vandalism by bored and aimless juveniles, and deteriorating civic services. As the older suburbs gradually come to resemble the city centers, the wealthier subur-banites begin again the familiar exodus to the still unaffected suburbs that are opening up even farther afield.[6]

ANALYZING THE PROBLEM

Urban problems can be usefully analyzed from the vantage points of the functionalist, conflict, and deviance approaches.

The Functionalist Approach

From the functionalist approach, many of the current difficulties of the cities stem from social disorganization caused by rapid social change, the most important factor in the decay of the American central cities having been the flight of the middle class to the suburbs. The growth of the suburbs has been recent but rapid, gathering impetus after World War II. In 1920, 17 percent of the American people lived in the suburbs; in 1930, 19 percent; in 1940, 20 percent; and in 1950, 24 percent. Then came the great exodus from the cities; by 1960, 33 percent of the population lived in the suburbs and by 1970, 37 percent. The 1970 census showed that, for the first time, more Americans were living in the suburbs than in the cities. During the 1960s the suburban population increased by 15 million, while the population of the central cities remained virtually unchanged. In the 1970s, however, the population of nearly all the older central cities has actually declined. The Bureau of the Census reports that between 1970 and 1976 eighteen of the nation's twenty-five largest cities lost population. The only major cities to gain population were Houston, San Diego, San Antonio, Phoenix, Memphis, San Jose, and Jacksonville—all of them in the "sunbelt."

The escape to the suburbs seems to have been facilitated by several factors. One was mass ownership of the automobile, which has made it possible for workers to commute fairly long distances to their jobs. Federally subsidized highway programs, too, made commuting much easier for the suburban resident. Another factor was the postwar boom in the American economy, which made home ownership a possibility for millions of Americans, especially with the aid of low-cost mortgages facilitated through the Federal Housing Authority and the Veterans Administration. An additional factor has been the tendency of industry and commerce to relocate to the suburbs, where property and other local taxes are lower. Finally, the suburbs could accommodate the horizontal expansion that modern industrial production techniques demand, whereas the city allows for vertical expansion only. All these social changes were functional in some respects. But, as so often happens, the changes also had unforeseen dysfunctional effects: the older inner cities, once the thriving economic centers of the nation, have lost people and taxes and are becoming moribund.

Factories are moving from them to gain access to the suburban labor market. Many shops and professionals are following their customers and clients from the central cities. New highways cut through central city residential areas so that suburban commuters can travel more quickly to and from work. The town houses vacated by the middle class are quickly subdivided into apartments or rooming houses; overcrowding follows, and areas tend to degenerate into slums. White and middle-class children disappear from the city schools, and educational standards fall far below those in the suburbs. The suburban middle class pays no city property taxes yet makes daytime demands on the fire, police, transport, and other urban services for which the poor, the minorities, and the working class of the cities cannot pay.

[6]See Mark Gottdiener, *Planned Sprawl: Private and Public Interests in Suburbia* (Beverly Hills, Calif.: Sage, 1977).

The Conflict Approach

The conflict approach helps to explain why relatively little effort is made to "save the cities": quite simply, those groups that have the power to make a difference often have little interest in doing so. Since the earliest days of colonial America, a strong antiurban bias has existed in our society. The small community has been an American ideal, and, indeed, the population shift to the suburbs may be seen as people's attempt to re-create the smaller, more intimate community of rural areas and the historic past. Because the groups and individuals with the most power and influence in American society are unlikely to reside in the central cities, they are, obviously, less inclined than city dwellers to work for changes in urban policies and particularly in urban financing.

Major changes in the financing of the cities would inevitably mean a redistribution of resources from other areas, especially the suburbs; but suburban residents are unwilling to shoulder responsibility for the urban problems from which they have only recently fled. In most state legislatures, rural interests are represented disproportionately in comparison with urban interests. Typically, the representatives of rural and suburban districts tend to form antiurban coalitions on issues affecting the cities, a fact frequently revealed in the way the states allocate their resources to different areas. The problems of the cities are thus aggravated by a continuing conflict of values and interests between the city dwellers—who are often poor minority-group members, and relatively powerless—and the suburban, small-town, and rural residents who are

The suburban life style has been much criticized and even satirized for its alleged materialism, status-consciousness, homogeneity, and artificiality in social relationships. But millions of middle-class Americans have found in the suburbs the ideal compromise between urban and rural living.

reluctant to accept the financial burden of saving the American cities.

The Deviance Approach

The deviance approach can be usefully applied to one major problem of the cities: the high urban rates of suicide, crime, drug addiction, vandalism, and disapproved forms of sexual behavior. Deviant behavior on this scale may not only constitute a problem in itself; it may also aggravate the urban problem in general, by providing a further incentive for the middle-class exodus. According to a 1978 Gallup poll, residents who expressed a wish to leave cities—fully 36 percent of urban dwellers—were predominantly the younger, better educated, and more affluent workers. Crime and overcrowding, according to the poll, were the key factors that made them want to leave.

Population density correlates highly with a variety of forms of deviant behavior, but why? Some theorists, particularly in the biological sciences, have suggested that overcrowding itself contributes to deviant and antisocial activity, and have pointed to studies showing bizarre behavior among rats and other animals that are allowed to multiply under conditions of plentiful food but limited space.[7] Social scientists have generally rejected this view for the obvious reason that rats are not human beings. Evidence from animal studies provides only suggestive hypotheses—*never* proof—about human behavior. In fact, the many studies of overcrowding among human beings point overwhelmingly to the conclusion that crowding alone does not generate deviant behavior.[8] Rather, the behavior is encouraged by other factors that happen to correlate with population density.

Deviant behavior appears to be more common in urban areas than in rural areas primarily because mechanisms for social control are much weaker in densely populated cities. In a small,

[7]Notably, John B. Calhoun, "A Behavioral Sink," in E. L. Bliss (ed.), *Roots of Behavior* (New York: Harper & Row, 1962).
[8]Johnathan Freedman, *Crowding and Behavior* (San Francisco: W. H. Freeman, 1975).

traditional community, people tend to know one another personally, to share similar customs and values, to know about and care about each other's activities, and to apply strong control over individual behavior. In the city, with its diversity of subcultures and life styles, this social control breaks down. City dwellers are mostly strangers to one another, and because of this anonymity the group has less interest in and control over the behavior of the individual. People are confronted with a variety of options in the city, including deviant as well as conventional values and life styles, and inevitably some are tempted to deviate. The urban environment thus seems to encourage *anomie*, the situation that exists when social norms cease to be meaningful or effective, leaving the individual without conventional guidelines for behavior. In fact, it is highly probable that the anonymous and more tolerant environment of the city may actually attract deviants from other areas, where their behavior would be more readily noticed and where stronger pressures for conformity would be applied.

THE NATURE OF URBANISM

Before we analyze the problems of cities in detail, let us examine more closely the meaning of urban life. The growth of cities has radically transformed the nature of human social life. Human groups are essentially of two kinds, primary and secondary. A *primary group* consists of a small number of people who interact in personal, direct, and often intimate ways, usually over a long period of time. Typical examples of a primary group are the family, a peer group, a small village, or a rural community. A *secondary group* consists of a small or large number of people who have few if any emotional ties with one another, who do not know one another well, and who usually come together for a specific, practical purpose. Typical examples of a secondary group are committees, political parties, business corporations, or large urban populations. Throughout most of the history of our species, people have lived almost exclusively in the context of primary groups. But since the rise of large-scale urbanization, an ever greater amount of social life has taken place in the context of secondary groups.

The concepts of the primary and secondary groups are implied in an early but influential statement by the German sociologist Ferdinand Tönnies, who in 1887 made a classical distinction between the *Gemeinschaft* ("community") and the *Gesellschaft* ("association"). The *Gemeinschaft* is characterized by close interpersonal relationships. The solidarity of the community is based on traditional shared values and the communal feelings of the entire group. Such communities exist primarily in rural areas, traditional villages, or very small towns. In the *Gesellschaft*, on the other hand, relationships between people are distant and impersonal. Most individuals are strangers to one another, and such solidarity as they may have is based on the functional need that people have for each other. The large modern city is the typical example of this type of social organization.

Tönnies' theory strongly influenced sociologists at the University of Chicago during the earlier part of this century. These sociologists were particularly interested in urban problems and attempted to develop an *ecological approach* to the city. That is, they tried to analyze urban life as a pattern of relationships between human beings and their social and physical environment.

The classic statement of the "Chicago school" was contained in an essay by Louis Wirth,[9] who designated the essential features of the city as being *size, population density,* and *social diversity,* features that lead to a distinctive type of relationship among the inhabitants. In the large, complex mass of people in the city, individuals are reduced to virtual insignificance: they cannot personally know or be known by more than a tiny proportion of their "neighbors." The nature of their social relationships is thus profoundly different from that of people residing in a village. Urban residents may have more acquaintances than villagers have, but they know them much more superficially and impersonally, and interact with them only in specialized roles—as a bank clerk, perhaps, or a fellow commuter—rather than as complete individuals. Relationships are often predatory because they tend to be based on utility rather than affection, with the role people play in relation to others being a means toward achieving their own ends—usually economic. The city thus consists of a vast mass of people living in close proximity but without deep sentimental bonds with one another.

Wirth pointed out that diverse population groups tend to live in compact areas in the city and thus become segregated from one another, usually along class or ethnic lines. In addition, urban areas have a high degree of division of labor, which results in many areas of the city coming to have specific functions and distinctive characteristics (such as Broadway, Hollywood, or Nob Hill). The outcome is a juxtaposition of divergent personalities and ways of life, which tends to make the perspective of city dwellers more relativistic than that of members of small homogeneous communities, and therefore more accepting of the validity of other viewpoints and life styles.

A more recent analysis of urbanism by Herbert Gans[10] suggests that Wirth's formulation does not apply to the outlying metropolitan areas but may still have some relevance to the inner city. Gans analyzes the population of the inner city and distinguishes five categories of inhabitants. The *cosmopolites* are students, artists, writers, intellectuals, and professional people who live in the city for its cultural facilities. The *unmarried or childless* are mostly young people who come to the city and rent apartments to be close to job opportunities, but who tend to move to the outer suburbs when they get married. The *ethnic villagers* are ethnic groups who are isolated from significant contact with the rest of the city but maintain traditional ways of life (particularly kinship patterns) within their own areas. The *deprived* are the very poor, the handicapped, the emotionally disturbed, and the nonwhite popu-

[9]Louis Wirth, "Urbanism as a Way of Life," *American Journal of Sociology,* 44 (July 1938), 8–20.

[10]Herbert J. Gans, "Urbanism and Suburbanism as Ways of Life," in Arnold M. Rose (ed.), *Human Behavior and Social Processes.* (Boston: Houghton Mifflin, 1962), pp. 625–648.

Modern American cities contain very heterogeneous populations; unlike smaller, traditionalist communities, they include a variety of subcultures (including deviant ones) whose members are able to pursue their own interests in the anonymous urban environment.

lation. The *trapped* are people who are downwardly socially mobile, people who are old and living on fixed incomes, and people whose neighborhood is being invaded by commerce, industry, or other ethnic groups, but who cannot afford to move out. The first two categories are in the city by choice, and the third category by tradition and to some extent by necessity. The last two categories are in the inner city because they cannot leave it.

THE PROBLEMS OF THE CENTRAL CITIES

Although the city is a complex social organization, it is not a self-sustaining one. As the sociologist Senator Daniel Patrick Moynihan has forcefully argued, the cities are not "self-restorative" without outside aid; but assistance must be in accordance with an overall plan rather than

on the basis of piecemeal intervention. There are, Moynihan points out, four vital aspects of city organization—housing, transport, industry, and social services—and effective city planning must deal with them as a systematic whole. In the past, interventions in only one area have led to dysfunctional effects in the others—attempts to make industry assume a greater share of the city tax burden, for example, have simply encouraged industrial enterprises to move to outlying areas, resulting in further unemployment, a shrinking tax base, and increasing social disorganization.[11]

Finances

As the widely publicized plight of New York City has made clear, much of the decay of central

[11]Daniel P. Moynihan, "Toward a National Urban Policy," *The Public Interest*, 17 (Fall 1969), 3–20.

cities is a result of their financial strangulation. Cities derive about three-quarters of their income from property taxes. These taxes take an average of 7.6 percent of personal income in the cities, compared to about 5.6 percent in the suburbs, yet the suburbanites get more for their tax dollar. The reason is that the city has extra burdens—its crime rates are higher, so it needs more police; its population is poorer, so it needs more welfare services; its daytime population is far higher than the number of its residents, so it needs more transport; its buildings are more dilapidated, so it needs more fire protection. Yet taxes cannot be raised very much; most citizens of the central city are poor, and businesses will relocate to the cheaper suburbs without incentives for remaining.

As conflict theory would suggest, the suburbs use their power to look after their own interests. For example, suburban towns often manipulate zoning regulations to exclude the poor. Undeveloped land in the suburbs can be zoned for large residential lots of several acres each, thus earmarking it for large, expensive homes, which provide about as much tax revenue to the suburb as would a number of smaller, less expensive homes. Since this type of zoning gives the suburbs fewer and richer families, it also gives them fewer children to educate and fewer welfare recipients to look after. The same tax dollar therefore stretches a good deal farther.

Housing

Housing is one of the most serious problems of the central cities. Much of it is very old and decaying, and is left that way for financial reasons. Old property is usually more lightly taxed than new; but if it is renovated, the taxes will rise. Landlords are therefore inclined to allow their properties to deteriorate. This is particularly true in some cities, such as New York, in which the rents of certain categories of longstanding tenants—who are protected from arbitrary eviction—are controlled by law, often at uneconomically low levels.

The problem of housing has often been aggravated rather than helped by federal programs. The Federal Housing Association and the Veterans Administration facilitate single-family

home construction and mortgages for home ownership, but nearly all the homes built or bought under these programs have been in the suburbs. By the 1970s over 5 million private homes had been built under federal programs that benefited the suburban middle class, but only 600,000 units of low-income public housing had been constructed.[12] If federal housing programs have favored the affluent at the expense of the poor, programs for urban renewal have had an even more drastic effect. These programs were officially intended to eliminate the slums from the city centers, but little thought was given to what would replace them. Federal funds were used to buy up inner-city land, which was then sold to private developers, who naturally used the property for the most profitable forms of construction—office blocks and luxury apartment buildings. Little provision was made to rehouse the lower-income residents displaced by these programs; by the late 1960s, when most programs ground to a halt, urban renewal had demolished 404,000 units of housing, mostly in the central cities, but had constructed less than 40,000 replacement dwellings. The result has been further pressure on the remaining slum housing, forcing up rents. The National Commission on Urban Problems found that lower-income whites pay on average between a quarter and a third of their income for housing, whereas blacks pay an average of 35 percent.

Another effect of unplanned urban renewal has been to destroy the "ethnic villages," the local neighborhoods in which various ethnic groups maintain their traditions, speak their original languages, and develop close interpersonal ties. Herbert Gans studied in detail the urban renewal of Boston's West End, a process that shattered the traditional Italian community in the area, disrupting friendships and a whole way of life. The renewal did not seem to benefit the local inhabitants, who had opposed it; only the speculators and property developers rejoiced.[13]

[12]Nathan Glazer, "Housing Problems and Housing Policies," *The Public Interest*, 7 (Spring 1970), p. 30.
[13]Herbert J. Gans, *The Urban Villagers* (New York: Free Press, 1962).

Jane Jacobs, an ardent critic of poorly planned urban renewal programs, writes:

> There is a wistful myth that if only we had enough money to spend—the figure is usually put at a hundred billion dollars—we could wipe out all our slums in ten years, reverse decay in the great, dull, gray belts that were yesterday's and day-before-yesterday's suburbs, anchor the wandering middle class and its wandering tax money, and perhaps even solve the traffic problem.
>
> But look what we have built with the first several billions: Low-income projects that become worse centers of delinquency, vandalism and general social hopelessness than the slums they were supposed to replace. Middle-income housing projects which are truly marvels of dullness and regimentation. . . . Luxury housing projects that mitigate their inanity, or try to, with a vapid vulgarity. Cultural centers that are unable to support a good bookstore. Civic centers that are avoided by everyone but bums, who have fewer choices of loitering place than others. . . . Promenades that go from no place to nowhere and have no promenaders. Expressways that eviscerate great cities. This is not the rebuilding of cities. This is the sacking of cities.[14]

Urban Ghettos

Perhaps the most serious problem of the central cities today is the concentration within them of impoverished and isolated minority groups, such as Chicanos, Chinese, Puerto Ricans, and blacks. The 1970 census showed that 74 percent of the black population live in metropolitan areas. In fact, 40 percent of the black population are concentrated in twenty of these areas, with 4 million blacks located in the four cities of New York, Philadelphia, Chicago, and Detroit. The black population of New York—over 1.6 million, or more than a fifth of the city's total population—is the largest concentration of black people on earth.

Of the blacks who live in metropolitan areas, some 80 percent live in the central city, mostly in black ghettos.[15] These areas are often the locus of some of the city's worst problems. For one thing, the black population is increasing far faster than housing is becoming available. As a result, large, older properties are rapidly being converted to multiple-tenant occupancy, and the overcrowding tends to create slum conditions. The problem of ghetto housing is compounded by a conflict of interests between ghetto residents and financial institutions such as banks, many of which refuse to loan mortgage money for the purchase or improvement of housing in decaying urban areas, irrespective of the credit rating of the applicants. This practice—often illegal, but difficult to prove—is known as "redlining" (the bankers allegedly flag those neighborhoods they do not wish to invest in by drawing red lines around them on the map). A 1978 National Training and Information Center study of the activities of eighty-nine banks in eight major cities found that large urban tracts were virtually without mortgage credit or home-improvement loans. In the cities in question—Chicago, Cleveland, Columbus, Hartford, Oklahoma City, Salt Lake City, Waterloo, and Wilmington—the quarter of the neighborhoods most favored by the bankers received 61.6 percent of mortgage loans, whereas the least favored quarter received only 3.4 percent. The bottom quarter of neighborhoods was almost entirely within the central cities, and the report commented that low mortgage activity "appears to be more closely related to racial characteristics than income characteristics of neighborhoods.[16] Meanwhile, attempts to rehouse ghetto occupants elsewhere in the metropolitan area have consistently met with strong opposition from the local white communities.

Worse still are other aspects of the economic picture in the ghetto. Employment opportunities are scarce; most new jobs are opening up in the suburbs. In 1977 the median black family income was only $9,485, compared with $16,782 for whites; unemployment rates were 13.1 percent, compared with 6.2 percent for whites; and 33.9 percent of black families had a female head (which usually means a reduced family income),

[14]Jane Jacobs, *The Death and Life of Great American Cities* (New York: Random House, 1961), p. 4.
[15]E. J. Kahn, Jr., *The American People* (New York: Weybright & Talley, 1973), p. 111.

[16]*New York Post*, January 31, 1978, p. 76.

A parish priest in Chicago discusses some neighborhood problems and a community activism project (CAP) that arose to confront the problems.

. . .

We had a congregation of about twenty-four hundred families, two thousand attend regularly. We get about four thousand people at St. Daniel's every single weekend. It's a working-class, a lower-middle-class community. Most of the people are laborers. We have a high proportion of city workers, people who have migrated to the outer edge because of changing racial patterns. We're in the Twenty-third Ward. About twenty-four hundred policemen and their families live here. We have very few professional people.

The one high school here, John F. Kennedy, was built for fourteen hundred. Now thirty-six hundred kids go to this school. It's integrated because there's a public housing project nearby. Two white kids or two black kids can jostle and if they have a fight, it's just a fight. If a black kid and a white kid happen to jostle in the hall and a fight breaks out, it's a racial incident.

It's just one example of poor city planning of a community where taxes have doubled over the past ten years. People who were paying $350 are now paying $700. They're just about wild about that. They feel they're not getting the services they're paying for. They have been neglected by the city.

They couldn't do anything about their kid's poor education, the pollution caused by Commonwealth Edison and the Sanitary treatment plant that poured nine and a half tons of greasy aerosols on them every day. They couldn't do anything about the Crosstown Expressway when it was announced from on high. They wrote letters, they called the alderman, but nothing happened year after year. I was listening.

In January 1970 I got a call from a young Jesuit seminarian. He was working with a new organization known as CAP. I had lunch with him, and the next day I was off and running. It was like a roller coaster ride. It took off like wildfire. At St. Daniel's the women especially got active. I'm an advocate of the Women's Lib movment. I try to have as many women as possible participate in the church services. Many of the extraordinary ministers at St. Daniels are women. The women understand exactly the need for power. They became committed organizers for CAP.

There's a great difference between textbook civics and the actual civics of the streets. When people, fifty or a hundred, go to see the alderman or the mayor, they can't believe what they hear. They're resented by the men they put in power. For the first time in their lives they learn that

---

compared with 10.9 percent for white families.[17] Social problems such as crime, drug addiction, and poverty are rife in the ghettos, which the President's National Advisory Commission on Civil Disorders described as "an environmental jungle."[18] (Problems of racial segregation are discussed in more detail in Chapter 8, "Race and Ethnic Relations.")

Jobs

Unemployment is a persistent problem in the central cities, particularly the older cities of the Northeast and Midwest. Urban industries are moving to the outlying suburban areas, where their costs are lower. Naturally, they take jobs with them—jobs that become filled by suburbanites rather than their former employees. New industries do not take up the slack in employment; instead, they too are likely to establish themselves in the cheaper suburbs or the booming urban areas of the "sunbelt" states, where the economic as well as the natural climate is more favorable.[19] The plight of new entrants to the already overcrowded job market is particularly serious. The Department of Labor reports that

[17]*Statistical Abstract of the United States, 1978, op. cit.,* pp. 457, 408, xiii.

[18]*Report of the National Advisory Commission on Civil Disorders,* chap. 16 (New York: Bantam Books, 1968); abridged, pp. 390–408.

[19]See David C. Perry and Alfred J. Watkins (eds.), *The Rise of the Sunbelt Cities* (Beverly Hills, Calif.: Sage, 1978).

politics is power. People with the big money—the big institutions, corporations—have worked out deals in back rooms with politicians. They're not going to break these deals until they're forced to by the people.

We had five hundred down at Mayor's Daley's office during our battle with Commonwealth Edison. They were peaceful. Some of them for the first time in their lives had ever been to city hall. They were just digging it. They're really looking around and enjoying it. Out come two aldermen, Tom Keane and Paul Wigoda, and they yell at the people, "You should be home with your kids. Why do you have your kids down here?" "Who are you, sir?" said one lady. She couldn't believe an alderman would talk to her that way. The next thing, she's being shoved by a policeman. A middle-class woman who loves the system, who's a friend of the police because they're for law and order. All of a sudden she's pushed. She came up to me with tears in her eyes: "I didn't do anything. I would have moved if he'd asked me, but he just shoved me. I could understand what those kids went through in Lincoln Park in 1968." She hated these kids before.

Funny thing, a lot of the police are for CAP. Some of them are from our community. Their wives have actually participated. The people who delight me are the policemen and their wives. We have many of them involved. They can't take out-front roles, but they're silent supporters. They know the system needs an overhaul, that change must come.

Ours is a white community, except for the housing project. A strict racial balance was kept in the area adjacent to the project, fifty percent white, fifty percent black. During the civil rights decade, black organizations pressured for the removal of the quota system. Consequently, white people moved out and black people came in. Homes were built in this area, where you put five hundred dollars down and the rest of your life to pay. The community there is now ninety percent black. Youth gangs keep the black people of this area in fear.

This affects my parish nearby. "Where are we gonna go? We don't want to live in a black neighborhood." The blacks say, "We don't want to live in a white neighborhood." Both want to live where they can have good schools, good services, good transportation, and feel safe. I blame the CHA [Chicago Housing Authority], which couldn't care less about these blacks and whites.

. . .

Source: Studs Terkel, *Working* (New York: Pantheon Books, 1974), pp. 560–561.

between 1970 and 1976 the percentage of youths holding jobs rose nationally but declined in ten of eleven major cities (the only exception was Houston, Texas). In Philadelphia the employment rate for the young fell from 41 percent to 27.8 percent; in Detroit, from 37.6 to 25.8; in Washington, from 39.1 percent to 26.1 percent; in Baltimore, from 32.8 percent to 23.5 percent. The most severe drop was in New York City, where a staggering 74 percent of the white teen-agers and 86 percent of the minority-group teen-agers available for work were jobless. Part of the problem has been caused by the economic recession of the 1970s, but the main fact is that the central cities no longer have the economic base to provide full employment for their own residents.

Education
Education, too, suffers in the central cities. Racial segregation in the schools is one obvious result of the segregated residential patterns of the metropolitan area. Equally important is that education in the United States, unlike education in most of the world, is financed by local community taxes rather than by national resources. The result is a great disparity in per capita pupil expenditure, usually to the disadvantage of the central-city child. Even within states these discrepancies are striking. Some school districts spend over $10,000 per pupil per year; others spend less than $200. Per capita expenditures in the thirty-six largest metropolitan areas averages some 30 percent less than in the surrounding suburbs. (These problems are also discussed in

more detail in Chapter 8, "Race and Ethnic Relations.")

Government

One major obstacle to urban reform is the fragmented and obsolete system of urban government. Many cities have surprisingly little control over their destinies. They rely heavily on the federal government for grants, and they are often subject to state laws on such matters as their right to raise money—even by installing parking meters. More important, there is often an extensive overlap and duplication of effort among the various local authorities in any metropolitan region. A metropolitan area comprising several autonomous localities will have perhaps dozens of police chiefs, fire chiefs, health officers, and so on—a duplication that frequently means little more than a waste of public money. Most cities were originally established when they were merely clusters of people surrounded by the countryside, but the incipient megalopolis of today strains the original charters to the limit. A Bureau of the Census study showed that the SMASs contained an average of 87 governmental units each: St. Louis had 439 such units, New York, 555, Pittsburgh, 806, Philadelphia, 963, and Chicago, 1,060.[20]

The present political boundary lines of cities

[20]U.S. Bureau of the Census, "Governmental Organization," *U.S. Census of Governments, 1962* (Washington, D.C.: U.S. Government Printing Office, 1963), p. 11; see, also, Howard W. Hallman, *Small and Large Together: Governing the Metropolis* (Beverly Hills, Calif.: Sage, 1977).

The influx of immigrants from Puerto Rico and elsewhere, as well as the movement of the white middle class to the suburbs, has markedly altered the population of New York City in the decades following World War II.

and suburbs are largely irrelevant to services like public transport, freeways, water supplies, sanitation, food inspection, and pollution control — yet little progress has been made toward the reorganization of metropolitan governments. The wealthier suburbs find the situation to their liking, since many of their services are subsidized by the central city, and local communities are usually very reluctant to surrender their own spheres of authority. Although most countries treat education, housing, highways, and welfare services on a national basis, the United States has a tradition of state or local control in these areas. Demands for more uniform and centralized administration invite value conflicts concerning the virtues of local democracy. This is particularly true of such sensitive issues as "community control" of education by local neighborhoods. There are signs, however, that the federal government is increasingly concerned about the fragmentation of urban administration. It has already used its economic influence to force metropolitan-level planning in some services, such as mass transport.

The problems of city governments are compounded by the fact that due to the way electoral districts have been drawn, state legislatures have traditionally tended to represent rural rather than urban interests, so the former emerge victorious from many conflicts over the allocation of resources. In 1960 there were thirty-nine states in which the urban population constituted a majority, but there was not a single state in which the urban representatives controlled the state legislature. In 1965 about three-quarters of the state legislators were elected by little more than a quarter of the people. In the 1970s some states began to correct the situation, but others have not reapportioned their local boundaries for half a century. Several continue to delay in complying with federal and Supreme Court orders to redraw their precinct lines. As a result of the influence of rural areas in state legislatures, many state programs often show a marked bias against the cities.

Case Study: New York City

For well over a century, New York City has symbolized the pinnacle of American accom-

plishment. To people all over the world, the dominant image of the United States is provided by panoramic views of this vigorous city with its thrusting skyscrapers. Yet in the mid-1970s the city hovered for over a year on the brink of bankruptcy, and it remains in a continuing financial crisis while the services of which it was once so proud continue to deteriorate. Some of the problems of New York City are unique, but most are common to all the older cities of the Northeast and the Midwest. Like these cities, New York has been caught up in national trends over which it has no control: the exodus of the middle class, the general population shift from the Northeast and the Midwest to the states of the South and Southwest, and the cutback in federal and state funds resulting from the economic recessions of the 1970s.

The composition of New York's population changed drastically in the twenty years following World War II. Blacks displaced from their jobs in the South by the mechanization of the agriculture moved to the city in search of new opportunities. Immigrants from Puerto Rico also poured in, hoping to find better employment. At the same time, new suburbs arose beyond the city limits, and the white middle class began to move out. Within two decades there was a population exchange of over 2 million people, as poor, unskilled workers replaced the affluent and the skilled.

In response, the city tried to provide a full range of opportunities for the newcomers. New York has always taken pride in its treatment of the poor and the dispossessed. Its position as a port of entry, symbolized by the Statue of Liberty's welcoming of immigrants, has inescapably imposed this hospitality on the city. New York has taken in wave after wave of immigrants over the years, clothing, feeding, and housing them. No other city in the nation provides so wide a range of social services. New York offers the highest welfare payments in the nation. Its nineteen municipal hospitals have no parallel anywhere in the United States. The City University, larger than forty-three state universities, is unique; until the financial crunch came, it offered free tuition under an open-enrollment program to anybody with a high-school diploma.

All told, New York's spending on education, health, and welfare is eight times the per capita average for American cities. The range of other services is equally impressive, from the transit system—the nation's largest—to an unrivaled series of museums and other cultural institutions.

During the 1960s, New York had little difficulty maintaining these services: the national economy was thriving, and federal funds poured into the city. New day-care centers, drug-treatment facilities, youth services, and job-training programs proliferated. The number of city employees rose rapidly until the city employed one civil servant for every twenty members of the population and devoted 60 percent of its budget to municipal salaries. Police officers earned over $17,000 a year; sanitation workers, over $15,000. But the budget was growing 15 percent annually while local tax revenues were growing only 5 percent.

The crisis began as the national economy moved into recession at the beginning of this decade. Federal funds for city programs were reduced, businesses laid off staff, and newly unemployed workers looked elsewhere for jobs. Between 1970 and 1975 the city lost more than half a million people—and their local tax revenues. From 1969 to 1977, New York City lost over 680,000 jobs, enough to support 1.5 million people, or a city about the size of San Diego. The number of jobs remaining in the city in 1977 was the lowest since records first began to be kept in 1950. One New Yorker in six—most of them children—was on public assistance, at a cost to the city of over $200 million a year.

City housing, particularly that for lower-income groups, deteriorated rapidly; in 1977 alone, more than 30,000 apartments were abandoned. Unable to run their buildings profitably, many landlords allowed them to go to ruin. In some cases, in fact, they deliberately arranged for tenements to be set on fire so that they could collect the insurance money. In the South Bronx, for example, more than 30,000 buildings—most but not all of them abandoned—were burned between 1967 and 1977. In 1976 alone, arsonists caused more than 12,000 fires in the city, the majority of them in decaying neighborhoods.

City banks had "redlined" many of these neighborhoods, preventing owners from getting mortgages to improve buildings and preventing would-be owners from buying properties. A 1977 State Banking Department study found that only 13 percent of the money New Yorkers invest in city savings banks is reinvested in home mortgage loans in the city. Most of the remaining money goes instead to the suburbs, or even out of the state.

Attempts to increase city taxes often had a counterproductive effect. Taxes on real estate rocketed from 7.7 percent of personal income in 1971 to 11 percent in 1976, but the effect was frequently to encourage those who could to move elsewhere. The city relies on businesses for more than 40 percent of its taxes, yet manufacturers and other corporations left the city in increasing numbers to take advantage of lower costs elsewhere. Corporate departures from the city outnumber arrivals by more than three to one; over half the corporations arriving in the city between 1970 and 1976 have already left.

The problems of New York have been worsened by the federal government's formula for state aid. Over forty major federal programs allocate money on the basis of the per capita income of the states. This formula, however, does not take into account that local and state taxes are higher in some areas than others, or that there are great differences in the cost of living from one part of the country to another. To cite but one example, the cost of electricity in New York is by far the highest in the nation—83 percent higher than the national average. In terms of per capita income, New York State is the fourth richest in the nation. If the state's per capita income is adjusted for local taxes and living costs, however, it ranks twenty-second in the nation, lower even than such supposedly poor states as Alabama. It costs the average New York family at least $9,000 per year more than the average family in Austin, Texas, to maintain the same standard of living. Yet under the federal grant formula, the New York family is regarded as much better off and therefore less in need of assistance. Federal funds have therefore flowed to the newer and often more prosperous cities. New York, for example, receives a federal subsidy of three cents per transit rider, compared with twelve cents for Dallas, nineteen for Houston, and twenty cents for Los Angeles. To make matters worse, the city receives no federal funds for its huge (but officially unrecognized) population of more than a quarter million illegal immigrants.

Not surprisingly, New York City was faced in the mid-1970s with a budget deficit of over $800 million and a series of crushing debts that will take many years to repay. Much of the city's problem resulted from its refusal to cut back services before the crisis came; instead, it borrowed money as though tomorrow would never come. The city also suffered because, unlike most American cities, it has no overarching layer of county government to assume the costs of courts, hospitals, and other facilities. But if the residents of other cities believe that "it can't happen here," they may be in for a rude awakening if present urban policies persist unchanged.

CONFRONTING THE PROBLEM

In its final report the National Commission on the Causes and Prevention of Violence predicted a gloomy future for American cities if no urgent remedial action is taken. This is how the commission saw urban living a few years from now:

> Central business districts in the heart of the city, surrounded by mixed areas of accelerating deterioration, will be partially protected by large numbers of people shopping or working in commercial buildings during daytime hours, plus a substantial police presence, and will be largely deserted except for police patrols during nighttime hours.
>
> High-rise apartment buildings and residential compounds protected by private guards and security devices will be fortified cells for upper-middle and high-income populations living at prime locations in the city.
>
> Suburban neighborhoods, geographically far removed from the central city, will be protected mainly by economic homogeneity and by distance from population groups with the highest propensities to commit crimes. . . .
>
> Individually and to a considerable extent unintentionally, we are closing ourselves into fortresses when collectively we should be building the great, open, humane city-societies of which we are capable.[21]

------

[21]*Final Report of the National Commission on the Causes and Prevention of Violence.*

Such a situation is certainly not inevitable. How can we go about solving or at least alleviating the social problem posed by the crisis in our cities? There are no easy answers, but some strategies are available.

Nonresident Taxes. A basic requirement must be to place city finances on a more equitable basis. One possibility is for the central cities to extract revenues from suburbanites who use city facilities but often pay no city taxes. Some cities have attempted this by imposing a tax on all money earned in the central city, regardless of the place of residence for the worker. It also might be possible to impose higher employment taxes on nonresidents than on residents, but only at the risk of encouraging them and their employers to shift their operations to the suburbs. Cities could also extract taxes from the suburbs by charging higher rates for the various city services used primarily by suburbanites. Free or inexpensive access to bridges, tunnels, or highways leading to the central cities, for example, attracts traffic from the suburbs, leading to congestion, road-repair bills, decreased use of public transport, and extra traffic controllers—all costs that the inner-city resident has to pay.

Federal and State Aid. A second possibility is to obtain far more federal and state funds for the cities. Again, some progress has been made. Under the federal government's optimistically entitled Model Cities Program, cities are entitled to seek federal funds for a comprehensive attack on their problems. The money may be used for education, construction, antipoverty efforts, medical facilities, sanitation, day-care centers, and narcotics-addiction treatment. Yet the amount of federal funds available is strictly limited and inadequate.

One federal program that seemed promising at first is the revenue-sharing plan, under which a proportion of the tax revenues collected by the federal government is given back to state and local governments. Since 1972 this program has provided an average of $6 billion a year to the cities. However, the federal government views much of this money as a replacement for funds paid out under its other programs rather than as a supplement to existing ones, so the position of the cities has been only marginally improved.

Most important, the formula under which federal grant money is made available to states must be revised so that its basis is not the per capita income of states, but rather real per capita income after adjustments have been made for local taxes and cost of living. This change will not be accomplished without social conflict, however, because what the older cities stand to gain, the newer cities stand to lose. When congressional representation is reapportioned after the 1980 census, the "sunbelt" states, which are the main beneficiaries of the existing federal formula, will have significantly greater congressional representation. Attempts by the states of the Northeast and Midwest to increase their share of federal funds will therefore meet with stronger opposition than ever.

Annexation of Suburbs.   A third possibility is to extend urban boundaries through the annexation of the surrounding suburbs, bringing the entire metropolitan area under central control for some purposes at least. This would not only eliminate many duplications and inefficiencies, but would give poorer residents in the area a larger share of the revenues available for education and other vital services. Although a number of annexations of suburbs by central cities have, in fact, taken place during this century, it seems unlikely that under present conditions there will be many more. The reason is that annexation usually requires a referendum in the suburb to be annexed, and suburbanites see no benefits and many disadvantages in becoming part of the city from which many of them have only recently fled. More successful metropolitan governments have been established abroad, notably in Toronto and London. In both cases the central city was merged for some administrative and fiscal purposes with the entire surrounding region. But the suburbanites of Toronto and London had little to say in the matter; the amalgamations were carried out by acts of the respective provincial and national legislatures. Any such federal and state action in the United States would, of course, arouse intense conflict. However, one state, Texas, allows municipalities to annex adjacent land that has not been legally incorporated—which may be one reason why cities such as Houston have escaped some of the problems faced by cities of similar size elsewhere in the country. And there are a few modest examples of successful metropolitan government in the United States, such as those of Minneapolis and St. Paul, Miami and Dade County, and Nashville and Davidson City.

Luring Back the Middle Class.   Other proposals involve somehow bringing the middle class back to the city. That city life can be appealing for at least some members of the middle class is demonstrated by the remarkable persistence of such middle-class bohemian areas as Greenwich Village in New York, Beacon Hill in Boston, or Nob Hill in San Francisco. There are also signs that many young people reared in the suburbs find suburban living altogether too bland and are returning to the central cities. Whether they will remain to raise families is another question. One suggestion is that middle-class urban housing be subsidized in order to lure the middle class back to the cities, but this solution is unlikely to find favor with the urban poor, who understandably claim priority on funds for housing subsidies. Some cities, such as Philadelphia, are attempting to "give away" inner-city property: if the new owners will undertake to remodel old buildings, they can have the properties for a nominal cost. Herbert Gans takes the view, however, that attempts to lure back the middle class will be

Brasilia, the new capital of Brazil, presents a soaring spectacle of futuristic design. Most of the inhabitants are government bureaucracts whose jobs require them to live there, but they complain that the city has an artificial, formal atmosphere and lacks the "soul" of older, unplanned cities such as Rio de Janeiro.

futile. Instead, he argues, public policy should concentrate on the urban poor, with the goal of "elevating them to the middle class."[22]

New Cities. Another suggestion is to recognize that existing cities are obsolete and build new ones instead.[23] One country that has systematically built new towns from scratch is Britain, which has constructed several since 1948 with such success that it proposes to build many more. The objective is partly to keep the population of large cities down to manageable proportions and partly to rehouse low-income families in existing slum areas. The towns are intended to have about 100,000 inhabitants, and are carefully designed to have adequate areas of "green belt" (tracts of unspoiled countryside) and sufficient light industry to provide full employment opportunities.

Other countries such as Israel, Sweden, and Brazil have also constructed new towns, although for different reasons. Brazil, for example, has taken the unusual step of building its capital city, Brasilia, as a completely new urban settlement situated some 600 miles from Rio de Janeiro in the Brazilian interior. The intention

[22]Herbert Gans, "Why Exurbanites Won't Reurbanize Themselves," *New York Times*, February 12, 1977, p. 21.

[23]See Irving Lewis Allen (ed.,) *New Towns and the Suburban Dream: Ideology and Utopia in Planning and Development* (Port Washington, N.Y.: Kennikat Press, 1977); Carol Corden, *Planned Cities: New Towns in Britain and America* (Beverly Hills, Calif: Sage 1977).

in choosing this site was to help open up the resources of the Brazilian hinterland by forcing government and commerce to relocate from the coastal cities. The city is designed in the shape of an airplane, with housing on one axis and government, commerce, and recreational facilities on the other. Brasilia is a spectacle of futuristic design, but is generally considered a dull and unpopular place for living. Ironically, Brasilia already has slums—built and inhabited by the workers who were imported to erect the "model" city. There have been a few attempts at constructing new towns in the United States, of which the most successful have been Columbia in Maryland and Reston in Virginia. Although the idea does have some attractions, the costs could be prohibitive, and the proposal does not really solve the contemporary crisis of the existing central cities.

Changing Attitudes and Values.   There is one final obstacle to saving our cities. A deep antiurban bias has always existed in American life and still influences public policy today, for it makes taxpayers reluctant to support federal or state aid to the cities. The bias was present at the founding of the Republic: Thomas Jefferson felt that cities were "pestilential to the morals, the health, and the liberties of man." He wrote, "Our governments will remain virtuous for centuries, as long as they are chiefly agricultural."[24] The Jeffersonian vision was of a democracy based on yeomen farmers, sturdy, self-reliant folk who could make mature decisions uninfluenced by the frenzy and self-indulgence that seemed inseparable from city life.

As American cities grew larger, the hostility to them increased. Mark Twain wrote of New York in 1867:

> I have at last, after several months' experience, made up my mind that it is a splendid desert—a domed and steepled solitude, where a stranger is lonely in the midst of a million of his race. A man walks his tedious miles through the same interminable street every day, elbowing his way through a buzzing multitude. . . . Every man seems to feel that he has got the duties of two lifetimes

to accomplish in one, so he rushes, rushes, rushes. . . . All this has a tendency to make the city-bred man impatient of interruption, suspicious of strangers, and fearful of being bored, and his business interfered with.[25]

This antiurban bias, the feeling that the "authentic" America as captured by Norman Rockwell in his covers for the old *Saturday Evening Post* lies in the small community rather than in the unnatural excrescence of the great city, still exerts a powerful influence on American attitudes. Opinion polls in 1976 showed that the great majority of Americans were opposed to any federal assistance to New York City; in fact, the federal government gave limited aid to New York only when it became obvious that the city's bankruptcy would have devastating effects throughout the national economy. One survey of college seniors found that 43 percent agreed with the statement "I basically dislike large cities" and 54 percent agreed with the statement "I don't want my children to grow up in the city." In their classic study of a small town of 3,000 residents, Arthur Vidich and Joseph Bensman found that the townsfolk pitied the city people in their nerve-racking and vice-prone environment. They believed that the best traditions of America—democracy and individualism—were rooted in small towns and rural areas.[26]

Philip Hauser sees this antiurban bias and its effect on public policy as being largely responsible for our failure to solve, or even seriously confront, the urban crisis:

> The urban crisis which afflicts this nation is the product of the gap that exists between the 20th century technological and demographic world we have created and the 19th century and prior century ideologies, values and institutions we have inherited. . . . Our outmoded tenets, values and institutions are paralyzing us in our efforts to deal with our problems.[27]

---

[24]Murray S. Stedman, Jr., *Urban Politics* (Cambridge, Mass.: Winthrop, 1972), p. 21

[25]Franklin Walker and G. Ezra Lane (eds.), *Mark Twain's Travels with Mr. Brown* (New York: Knopf, 1940), pp. 259–278.

[26]Arthur Vidich and Joseph Bensman, *Small Town in Mass Society* (Princeton: Princeton University Press, 1958).

[27]Philip M. Hauser, *Cities in the 70's* (Washington, D.C.: National League of Cities, 1970) pp. 15–21.

Solutions to the problems of America's cities may well require a massive reassessment of national values and priorities and a reallocation of our economic and human resources. But our best efforts can be successful only if the will to save the cities is there.

SUMMARY

1. The United States is a predominantly urban nation, but the central cities are in a state of decay and are the locus of many serious social problems.

2. Urbanization was originally made possible by the development of agriculture, but the large modern city requires a substantial industrial and commercial base.

3. More Americans now live in the suburbs than in the central cities. A metropolis is a city (or cities) with surrounding suburbs; a megalopolis is a chain of metropolises. Suburbs differ in some respects from the inner cities, but some suburbs are now encountering problems similar to those of the urban centers.

4. From the functionalist approach, urban problems may be seen as a result of social disorganization caused by rapid social change, particularly the growth of the suburbs. The conflict approach helps explain why the problems of the cities are often neglected, in that central-city residents increasingly comprise the poor and the powerless. The deviance approach focuses on the high incidence of deviant behavior in cities, which can be seen as a result of the anomie that urban life generates.

5. The nature of urbanism is an important topic in sociology. In a distinction similar to that between primary and secondary groups, Tönnies outlined the concepts of the *Gemeinschaft* (community) and the *Gesellschaft* (association). The Chicago school took an ecological approach to urban analysis, with Wirth emphasizing the distinctive nature of urban life that results from size, population density, and social diversity. Gans distinguishes several categories of inner city residents: the cosmopolites, the unmarried or childless, the ethnic villagers, the deprived, and the trapped.

6. The principal problems affecting the central cities are financing, housing, urban ghettos, segregated and inadequate educational facilities, and fragmented urban government. The plight of New York City illustrates many of the typical problems of the older cities of the Northeast and Midwest.

7. Some proposals for confronting the problems of the cities include taxes on nonresidents, increased federal and state aid, annexation of suburbs, luring back the middle class, and building new cities. A change is also needed in the general antiurban bias of American society.

GLOSSARY

Anomie. A state in which social norms are no longer meaningful or effective, often causing deviant behavior.

City. A permanent concentration of large numbers of people who do not produce their own food.

Ecological approach. An approach to social phenomena that focuses on the relationships between human beings and their social and physical environment.

Gemeinschaft. A term describing a small community marked by intimate relationships, strong feelings of solidarity, and loyalty to traditional values.

Gesellschaft. A term used to describe a society marked by impersonal contacts, an emphasis on individualism rather than group loyalty, and solidarity based on utility rather than affection or shared traditions.

Megalopolis. A virtually unbroken urban tract consisting of two or more adjacent metropolises.

Metropolis. An urban area including a city and its surrounding suburbs.

Primary group. A group consisting of a small number of people who interact in direct, personal, and intimate ways, usually over a long period of time.

Secondary group. A group consisting of a small or large number of people who have few if any emotional ties with one another, who do not know one another well, and who usually come together for a specific, practical purpose.

Standard Consolidated Area. A term used by the Bureau of the Census to refer to a megalopolis, an urban tract consisting of two or more metropolises.

Standard Metropolitan Statistical Area. A term used by the Bureau of the Census to refer to a city or cities and their surrounding suburbs that have a population of over 50,000.

Suburb. A less densely populated, primarily residential area that lies beyond the boundary of a city.

FURTHER READING

ALCALY, ROGER E., and DAVID MERMELSTEIN (eds.). *The Fiscal Crisis of American Cities.* New York: Vintage, 1977. Useful articles on the financial plight of the cities, particularly New York.

BANFIELD, EDWARD. *The Unheavenly City Revisited.* Boston: Little Brown, 1974. A controversial assertion that our cities, with all their problems, are healthy, and offer unprecedented opportunities for human fulfillment. Banfield argues that we criticize the cities because we expect more of them now—not because urban conditions are worsening.

BUTLER, EDGAR. *Urban Sociology.* New York: Harper and Row, 1976. A comprehensive and up-to-date introductory text on urban sociology; the book includes useful material on the current crisis of the cities.

CLARK, KENNETH B. *Dark Ghetto: Dilemmas of Social Power.* New York: Harper & Row, 1965. A black social scientist describes the black ghettos of the central cities and shows how their conditions are maintained by neglect and by existing social policy.

DOWNS, ANTHONY. *Opening Up the Suburbs: An Urban Strategy for America.* New Haven: Yale University Press, 1973. Downs offers detailed and specific suggestions for solving urban problems, primarily through a greater fiscal and demographic integration of the cities and the suburbs.

FREEDMAN, JOHNATHAN. *Crowding and Behavior.* New York: Viking Press, 1975. An important summary of research findings on the effects of crowding and population density on human behavior. Freedman finds little evidence for the view that crowding is, in itself, a cause of pathological behavior.

GANS, HERBERT J. *The Levittowners: Ways of Life and Politics in a New Suburban Community.* New York: Random House, 1969. An account by a participant-observer of the first two years in the development of a new suburb. On the basis of his research, Gans strongly challenges the stereotype of suburbanites as bored conformists, although he sees that suburban living poses many problems.

————. *The Urban Villagers.* New York: Free Press, 1962. Gans provides a description of the tightly knit ethnic communities of our large cities. In this case study of how one such community was shattered by an urban-renewal program, no one seemed to benefit except the property speculators.

JACOBS, JANE. *The Death and Life of Great American Cities.* New York: Random House, 1961. Jacobs presents an indictment of the urban-renewal programs in America, which, the author contends, have been so badly planned that they have made the cities less habitable than before.

National Commission on Urban Problems. *Building the American City.* Washington, D.C.: U.S. Governmental Printing Office, 1968. The report of a federal commission on the problems of the American city. Contains a great deal of information, particularly on the plight of the poorer members of the urban community.

PERRY, DAVID C., and ALFRED J. WATKINS (eds.). *The Rise of the Sunbelt Cities.* Beverly Hills, Calif.: Sage, 1978. Useful articles dealing with a significant shift in the American demographic and economic structure: the rise of urban centers in the "sunbelt" states, challenging the long-established preeminence of the cities of the industrial Northeast.

SUTTLES, GERALD. *The Social Order of the Slum.* Chicago: University of Chicago Press, 1968. Rev. ed. An account of slum life in a large American city with an analysis of gang warfare as an example of territorial behavior in humans.

WIRTH, LOUIS. "Urbanism as a Way of Life," *American Journal of Sociology*, 44 (July 1938). Wirth's classic essay on the nature of the cities remains, to this day, a readable and relevant document.

3
INEQUALITY IN SOCIETY

Over two thousand years ago the Greek philosopher Aristotle observed that populations tend to be divided into three main groups: the very rich, the very poor, and those in between. His comment hardly comes as a revelation to us, for social inequality still exists in virtually every society, including our own. Inequality in America, moreover, goes beyond differences of economic class; it includes severe inequalities of power, race and ethnicity, and sex.

Social inequality is perceived as a social problem because it seems inherently unjust, particularly when it is passed on from generation to generation in such a way that the powerless, the poor, the nonwhite, or women are denied the chance to use their full talents because of the circumstances of their births. But, as we shall see, these inequalities are not "natural"—they are social arrangements that human beings have created and that they therefore can modify or abolish.

6
Government and Corporations: The Abuse of Power

THE PROBLEM

A crucial problem of government and corporations concerns power—and the abuse of it. Our lives are dominated by large public and private organizations. The public organizations, primarily government agencies, affect almost every area of our experience. They register our births, provide education and social services, record our marriages, regulate many of the conditions of our employment, collect our taxes, influence countless aspects of our lives through thousands of laws, and finally register our deaths. The private organizations, primarily business corporations, provide jobs for the bulk of the population and supply most of our consumer needs, from banking and television services to clothing and gasoline. Our lives and our entire complex civilization are inextricably dependent on large organizations. Yet these organizations, originally established to satisfy our needs and improve the quality of our lives, are often experienced as oppressive, unresponsive, impersonal, inefficient, arrogant, and even corrupt. Particularly since the Watergate scandal of the early 1970s, it has been apparent that the major organizations in American society sometimes work in concert to advance their own interests rather than those of the people. The lack of public answerability of these large organizations has become a major social problem.

Government and corporations are widely distrusted in the United States. The presidencies of Lyndon Johnson and Richard Nixon were marked by a well-founded public belief that their administrations were deliberately and systematically lying to the people.[1] Distrust of government reached its height during the Watergate affair, when the discovery of the abuse of power drove a president from office. Although Nixon himself was pardoned by his successor and escaped accountability for his acts in office, the Watergate affair led to the trials and convictions of many high public officials on such charges as extortion, perjury, conspiracy, subverting the course of justice, misuse of campaign funds, bribery, illegal wiretapping, and tax fraud.

The scandal provoked congressional investigations of the FBI and the CIA that turned up literally thousands of illegal acts in the executive branch of government. The FBI, for example, was responsible for hundreds of burglaries of presumed critics of the administration, and was guilty of widespread illegal wiretapping. It had also deliberately attempted to sabotage the civil rights movement in the 1960s. The CIA, whose charter specifically prohibits it from surveillance over the domestic population, had infiltrated the civil rights and antiwar movements, compiled dossiers on tens of thousands of Americans, and intercepted and read hundreds of thousands of private letters and telegrams. It had also, without any authorization from Congress, plotted the assassination of foreign heads of state, including leftists Fidel Castro of Cuba and Patrice Lumumba of the Congo and rightists Ngo Dinh Diem of South Vietnam and Rafael Trujillo of the Dominican Republic. The CIA had even enlisted Mafia "hit men" for one assassination attempt. The agency had also tested a variety of drugs, including LSD, on many people who were

---

[1]David Wise, *The Politics of Lying* (New York: Random House, 1973).

unaware that they were being used as guinea pigs, and had caused several deaths in the process.[2]

Fraud, embezzlement, and misappropriation of funds is also a major problem in government. The Department of Health, Education, and Welfare estimates that it loses as much as $7.4 billion each year through "fraud, abuse, and waste"—most of it stolen not by welfare cheaters but by the doctors, pharmacists, corporate executives, and others who contract with the department to supply goods or services and then systematically defraud it. The federal General Accounting Office estimates that outright fraud in federal assistance programs could run from $12 billion to $25 billion a year.[3] The sheer size of government makes these frauds difficult to detect or prosecute. Agencies and departments engaged in hundreds of programs and employing thousands or tens of thousands of people simply cannot keep a sufficiently tight control over their records, budgets, and expenditures.

As for corporations, they are widely believed to be more concerned with their own profits than with social responsibility, the quality or price of their products, or the truth of their advertising. To further their interests, large corporations maintain professional lobbyists in Washington to influence public officials behind the scenes. They argue for legislation to serve their own ends, influence the appointment of officials, block reforms they consider undesirable, and often seem to have more say in the councils of government than the ordinary voters.[4] There are now more than 15,000 professional lobbyists in Washington, representing a variety of economic and other special-interest groups.[5] One poll

showed that three out of five college students believe that "big business has taken the reins of government away from Congress and the Administration," and a national opinion poll found that nearly 60 percent of Americans think that "government is run by a few big interests looking after themselves."[6]

In looking after their interests, many corporations have resorted to illegal means, ranging from price-fixing to the bribery of public officials at home and abroad.[7] The Watergate investigations turned up seventeen cases of illegal corporate donations to President Nixon's reelection campaign. As a result of subsequent investigations, over 520 leading corporations confessed to bribery and similar corrupt practices. The most notorious case involved the Lockheed Aircraft Corporation, which distributed tens of millions of dollars in illegal bribes in several countries, including a bribe of $7 million to a single person in Japan in order to win sales over two of its American rivals. The Lockheed disclosures also implicated the prince of the Netherlands, the prime minister of Japan, and two Italian defense ministers, and provoked political crises in several countries.[8]

Corporate bribes have often induced poverty-stricken countries to purchase American equipment they did not really need. After a $200,000 bribe, two Colombian generals falsified their country's military requirements to persuade their government to buy Lockheed aircraft. Similarly, United Brands paid a bribe of $1.25 million to a Honduras cabinet member in return for a reduction in the Honduras export tax on

[2]See Jethro K. Leberman, *How the Government Breaks the Law* (Baltimore: Penguin, 1973); Morton H. Halperin *et al.*, *The Lawless State: The Crimes of the U.S. Intelligence Agencies* (New York: Penguin, 1976); David Wise, *The American Police State* (New York: Random House, 1976); Sanford J. Ungar, "The Intelligence Tangle: The CIA and the FBI Face the Moment of Truth," *Atlantic*, 237 (April 1976), 31–42.

[3]*New York Times*, April 16, 1978, p. 1.

[4]See Ralph Nader and Mark J. Green (eds.), *Corporate Power in America* (New York: Grossman, 1973).

[5]"The Swarming Lobbyists," *Time*, August 7, 1978, pp. 14–22.

[6]Richard J. Barnet, Ronald E. Müller, and Joseph Collins, "Global Corporations: Their Quest for Legitimacy," in Philip Brenner, Robert Borosage, and Bethany Weidner (eds.), *Exploring Contradictions: Political Economy in the Corporate State* (New York: McKay, 1974), p. 72.

[7]See M. David Erman and Richard J. Lundman (eds.), *Corporate and Governmental Deviance: Problems of Organizational Behavior in American Society* (New York: Oxford University Press, 1978); John E. Concklin, *"Illegal but Not Criminal": Business Crime in America* (Englewood Cliffs, N.J.: Prentice-Hall, 1977); John N. Johnson and Jack D. Douglas (eds.), *Crime at the Top* (Philadelphia: Lippincott, 1978).

[8]See Jim Hougan, "The Business of Buying Friends," *Harpers* (December 1976), 43–62.

bananas—a reduction very advantageous to the corporation, but not to a desperately poor country that needed the tax income. Dozens of other companies made questionable or illegal payments to public officials in the United States. Gulf Oil, for example, disbursed some $5 million to members of Congress and other officials, in places ranging from Senate offices to the men's room in a Holiday Inn. When the Senate Watergate committee questioned the Gulf official who distributed the money, the senators asked only brief and cautious questions. The reason, the official speculated afterward, was that every single member of the committee except its chairman had been a recipient of Gulf money.[9]

THE GROWTH OF BIG GOVERNMENT

"Big" government, characterized by a series of large interlocking departments and agencies, is inseparable from the modern state. In the most simple preindustrial societies, there is no government in the sense that we understand the term: decisions are typically made informally through group consensus. Big government appears only with the rise of large, complex societies based on organized agriculture and, later, industrialism. These large states need a centralized authority to maintain order, to collect taxes, and to administer social policies.

As the United States has industrialized, the size and complexity of its government have steadily increased. At the end of the eighteenth century, the federal government had a budget of about $4.3 million, compared with a budget of around $530 billion in 1978. A century and a half ago the federal government employed 5,000 people; today it employs nearly 3 million. The total of federal, state, and local government employees has more than doubled over the last two decades, to 15 million people, and may rise to 18 million by the early 1980s. Most of the increase is in state and local government. Contrary to popular belief, the number of people employed by the federal government has remained fairly constant for twenty years.[10]

Government has grown in size for two main reasons: because people have demanded more government services, and because a modern industrial society is so complex that it requires extensive regulation and supervision.[11] In the first federal administration there were only three departments (war, state, and treasury). For a century thereafter, growth was slow and was restricted to such basic services as the Post Office. During the rapid development of the economy after the Civil War, new departments, such as Agriculture and Labor, developed to meet the demands of special interests. At the end of the nineteenth century, public hostility to the uncontrolled profiteering of big business led to legislation aimed at restricting monopoly and similar practices, and new agencies arose to enforce these regulations. Roosevelt's New Deal involved social engineering on a massive scale, as the federal administration intervened in many new areas of social and economic life. By the time of the Kennedy administration, government was becoming involved in such issues as civil rights; and the succeeding Johnson administration created a wealth of new social programs in a strategy that has been called "throwing dollars at problems."

Big government has come under attack from both liberals and conservatives, although for different reasons. Conservatives tend to resent government bureaucracies because they consume tax dollars—often wastefully—and because their very existence seems to imply continuing efforts to meddle in society, to centralize control in state and federal authorities, and to interfere with the free enterprise system. Liberals tend to resent the bureaucracies because they believe that many of them have become self-perpetuating, uncontrolled juggernauts that are unduly influenced by private-interest groups and

[9]*The New York Times*, "Week in Review," May 20, 1977, p. 2.

[10]U.S. News & World Report, June 19, 1972, p. 78; *New York Times*, July 5, 1977, p. 1.

[11]Some implications of the growth of government are discussed in Barry D. Karl, "Philanthropy, Policy Planning, and the Bureaucratization of the Democratic Ideal," *Daedalus* (Fall 1976), 129–146.

BUYING CORPORATE INFLUENCE

Over five hundred twenty American corporations have admitted paying bribes or other "questionable" payments to public officials at home and abroad. These are some of the bigger spenders:

Ashland Oil, Inc. Admits paying more than $300,000 to foreign officials, including $150,000 to the President of Gabon. Admits paying $800,000 to senators, members of Congress, and other political figures in the U.S.

Boeing. Admits spending $50.4 million in "questionable payments" to foreign officials.

Burroughs Corp. Admits that $1.5 million may have been used in improper payments to foreign officials.

Exxon Corp. Admits paying $59.4 million to government officials and others in fifteen countries, including $27 million in secret contributions to seven Italian political parties. Admits these payments were illegal, and improper.

General Tire and Rubber. Admits spending $4.1 million in foreign bribes and other "questionable payments."

Gulf Oil Corp. Admits giving $4 million to South Korea's ruling party. Admits giving $110,000 helicopter to the President of Bolivia for oil rights. Admits giving $5 million in payments, mostly illegal, to U.S. public officials.

International Telephone and Telegraph Corp. Charged with making $8.7 million in "illegal, improper, corrupt and questionable payments" to foreign governments and officials, including at least $400,000 to subvert the government of Chile.

Lockheed Aircraft Corp. Admits giving $24 million in outright bribes, and about a further $180 million in "commissions and payoffs" to foreign agents and government officials in the Nether-lands, Italy, Japan, Turkey, Colombia, Greece, South Africa, and Nigeria.

McDonnell Douglas Corp. Admits paying $18 million in "commissions and consultant fees" and other "questionable payments" to foreign government officials.

Merck & Co., Inc. Admits giving $3 million, largely in "commission type payments" to officials of thirty-six foreign governments.

Northrop Corp. Admits in part to paying $34.3 million in commissions and bribes to government officials and agents in the Netherlands, Iran, France, West Germany, Brazil, Saudi Arabia, Malaysia, and Taiwan.

Phillips Petroleum Corp. Admits "laundering" $2.8 million through Swiss subsidiaries; approximately half was returned to the U. S. and spent mostly in illegal political donations; most of the rest went in overseas payoffs.

R. J. Reynolds. Admits paying $24.6 million to foreign officials in bribes and other "questionable payments."

Sanitas Service Corp. Admits giving $1.2 million to local Connecticut politicians.

Tenneco, Inc. Admits giving $12 million in "sensitive payments" to lawyers, consultants, and agents in twenty-four countries. Admits to illegal payments to public officials in U.S.

G. D. Searle & Co. Admits paying $1.3 million to officials of foreign governments to obtain sales.

United Brands Co. Admits paying $1.25 million to Honduran official for reduction in banana export tax, and $750,000 to European officials to head off proposed Italian restrictions on banana imports.

Source: *Newsweek*, December 8, 1975; *Time*, February 23, 1976; *The New York Times*, January 30, 1977; *Newsweek*, February 19, 1979.

squander resources better used elsewhere. In fact, a 1978 Gallup poll found that the public feels, on average, that nearly half of every tax dollar is wasted (see Figure 6.1).

The inefficiency and duplication of effort of the government is almost legendary.

It is virtually impossible to obtain an accurate count of just how many federal grant programs exist. Some estimates go as high as 1,500. Despite impressive attempts by individual legislators and by the Office of Economic Opportunity, there is still no agreement on a comprehensive list. . . .

Nine different Federal departments and 20 independent agencies are now involved in education matters. Seven departments and eight independent agencies are involved in health. In many major cities, there are at least 20 or 30 separate manpower programs, funded by a variety of Federal offices. Three departments help develop our water resources and four agencies in two departments are involved in the management of public lands. Federal recreation areas are administered by six different agencies in three departments of government. Seven agencies provide assistance for water and sewage systems. Six departments of the government collect similar economic information—often from the same sources—and at least seven departments are concerned with international trade. . . .[12]

FIGURE 6.1 **Attitudes toward government waste of tax money.** The number of Americans who believe that government wastes much of their tax money has grown sharply in recent years. This shift in attitude is only one symptom of an increasing public distaste for big government and what many regard as excessive taxation.
(Institute of Social Research, University of Michigan; *New York Times*, June 26, 1978.)

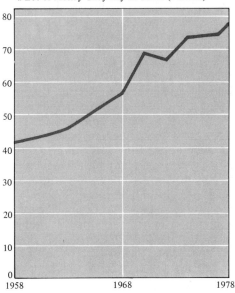

Respondents Who Think the Government Wastes a Lot of Money They Pay in Taxes (Percent)

An outstanding example of the growth of big government is the proliferation of federal regulatory agencies and the rules they issue. In 1977 the *Federal Register*, a compilation of these regulations, ran to 65,603 pages. The costs of enforcing the 75,000 regulations involved is immense: the actual spending of the regulatory agencies was $4.8 billion in 1978; the costs to employers and others of complying with the regulations totaled an estimated $63 billion.[13] These statistics seem almost preposterous. Are these regulations and the agencies that issue them really needed?

The answer is that regulatory agencies exist only because the public or some powerful interest demands them; in fact, the great majority of the regulations are designed to protect the public. For instance, the first regulatory agency of the United States government was the Interstate Commerce Commission, established in 1887 to control the railroads, which were exploiting their monopoly position by raising freight charges during the harvest season. Major among the many other agencies that have since been created is the Securities and Exchange Commission, which brought order to Wall Street after the Great Crash and now acts as a watchdog against financial impropriety in the world of finance and industry. The Food and Drug Administration tests all new drugs and other chemicals to ensure that they are fit for human consumption. Thanks to the efforts of the FDA, the United States was the only country in the world that prevented the distribution of the tranquilizer thalidomide during the 1960s. The drug, hastily prescribed in other countries, caused monstrous birth deformities in thousands of children whose mothers had used it during pregnancy. The Occupational Safety and Health Administration issues regulations to ensure safe working conditions in offices, factories, and construction sites. The Consumer Product Safety Commission issues regulations to ensure that products sold to the public are safe to use. For

[12]Richard M. Nixon, "State of the Union Address, January 22, 1971," quoted in the *New York Times*, March 25, 1971.
[13]Jay Palmer, "The Rising Risks of Regulation," *Time*, November 27, 1978, pp. 85–87.

VOICES

Larry Ross, a business consultant and former corporation president, reveals some of his impressions about life in the corporate power structure.

. . .

When the individual reaches the vice presidency or he's general manager, you know he's an ambitious, dedicated guy who wants to get to the top. He isn't one of the gray people. He's one of the black-and-white vicious people—the leaders, the ones who stick out in the crowd.

As he struggles in this jungle, every position he's in, he's terribly lonely. He can't confide and talk with the guy working under him. He can't confide and talk to the man he's working for. To give vent to his feelings, his fears, and his insecurities, he'd expose himself. This goes all the way up the line until he gets to be president. The president *really* doesn't have anybody to talk to, because the vice presidents are waiting for him to die or make a mistake and get knocked off so they can get his job.

He can't talk to the board of directors, because to them he has to appear as a tower of strength, knowledge, and wisdom, and have the ability to walk on water. The board of directors, they're cold, they're hard. They don't have any direct-line responsibilities. They sit in a staff capacity and they really play God. They're interested in profits. They're interested in progress. They're interested in keeping a good face in the community—if it's profitable. You have the tremendous infighting of man against man for survival and clawing to the top. Progress.

We always saw signs of physical afflictions because of the stress and strain. Ulcers, violent headaches. I remember one of the giant corporations I was in, the chief executive officer ate Gelusil by the minute. That's for ulcers. Had a private dining room with his private chef. All he ever ate was well-done steak and well-done hamburgers.

There's one corporation chief I had who worked, conservatively, nineteen, twenty hours a day. His whole life was his business. And he demanded the same of his executives. There was nothing sacred in life except the business. Meetings might be called on Christmas Eve or New Year's Eve, Saturdays, Sundays. He was lonesome

---

example, the commission reported in 1979 that some 77,000 Americans are injured by power-mower blades each year—injuries that result in about 10,000 amputations of fingers, toes, hands, and feet. Most of these accidents occur while people are attempting to clear grass out of the mower with the motor running. The commission accordingly proposed new regulations requiring that mowers automatically shut off within three seconds after the operator lets go of the handle.[14]

Americans in theory may dislike the idea of so many regulations, but in practice they insist on them. If there is a midair collision of commercial jetliners, the public demands better regulations from the Civil Aeronautics Board. If a steel suspension bridge gives way during construction, the public demands better supervision from the Occupational Safety and Health Administration. If drinking water looks and tastes polluted, the public demands stricter controls by the

Environmental Protection Agency. And although many people would agree that federal regulation of economic and social life is excessive, few would agree on which regulations or agencies should be abolished.

Besides, once a department or agency is established, it is difficult to abolish, even if it has outlived its usefulness. Members of its staff develop a vested interest in keeping its programs and thus their jobs going, and in increasing the range of their activities and the size of their budgets. If a social problem emerges, such as drug addiction or the energy shortage, the immediate response is to establish federal and state programs to confront it. But the resulting bureaucracies seem to become self-perpetuating, and continue to grow and extend their areas of jurisdiction even if the original problem is checked or disappears. As one critic of government bureaucracy observes: "It is a vast, indestructible mollusk that absorbs kicks and taunts and seductions and does nothing but grow.[15]

[14]*New York Times*, January 21, 1979, p. E8.

148

when he wasn't involved with his business. He was always creating situations where he could be surrounded by his flunkies, regardless of what level they were, presidential, vice presidential. . . . It was his life.

In the corporate structure, the buck keeps passing up until it comes to the chief executive. Then there ain't nobody to pass the buck to. You sit there in your lonely office and finally you have to make a decision. It could involve a million dollars or hundreds of jobs or moving people from Los Angeles, which they love, to Detroit or Winnipeg. So you're sitting at the desk, playing God.

You say, "Money isn't important. You can make some bad decisions about money, that's not important. What is important is the decisions you make about people working for you, their livelihood, their livelihood, their lives." It isn't true.

To the board of directors, the dollars are as important as human lives. There's only yourself sitting there making the decision, and you hope it's right. You're always on guard. Did you ever see a jungle animal that wasn't on guard? You're always looking over your shoulder. You don't know who's following you.

The most stupid phrase anybody can use in business is loyalty. If a person is working for a corporation, he's supposed to be loyal. This corporation is paying him less than he could get somewhere else at a comparable job. It's stupid of him to hang around and say he's loyal. The only loyal people are the people who can't get a job anyplace else. Working in a corporation, in a business, isn't a game. It isn't a collegiate event. It's a question of living or dying. It's a question of eating or not eating. Who is he loyal to? It isn't his country. It isn't his religion. It isn't his political party. He's working for some company that's paying him a salary for what he's doing. The corporation is out to make money. The ambitious guy will say, "I'm doing my job. I'm not embarrassed taking my money. I've got to progress and when I won't progress, I won't be here." The shnook is the loyal guy, because he can't get a job anyplace else.

Source: Studs Terkel, *Working* (New York: Pantheon Books, 1974). Copyright 1972, 1974, by Studs Terkel.

For reasons that we shall explore shortly, large bureaucracies are intrinsically likely to lose touch with the people they are supposed to serve. Power becomes concentrated in the hands of their senior officials rather than in those, such as the voters or Congress, to whom the organizations are theoretically responsible. As a result, Americans have definitely come to view big government with distaste: in an annual Gallup poll designed to find out which problems the people regard as the most significant, "big government" regularly appears among the top three.

THE RISE OF THE CORPORATION

The American economy is today dominated, perhaps even controlled, by another kind of organization, the giant corporation. The corporation is a relatively new type of commercial organization that first became widespread in the late nineteenth century. Unlike business enterprises owned by an individual or a partnership, the corporation is owned by stockholders, who may number in the hundreds of thousands and even include other corporations.

A corporation is run by a professional management appointed by a board of directors who are elected by the stockholders. In theory the stockholders control the corporation, but in practice the board usually becomes a self-perpetuating body whose recommendations, including nominations for new board members, are ratified as a matter of course by the stockholders.[16]

The basic goals of corporate enterprises are profit and growth, objectives achieved by ever more efficient means of production, heavy in-

[15]Matthew P. Dumont, "Down the Bureaucracy!" *Transaction* (October 1970).

[16]Ralph Nader, Mark Green, and Joel Seligman, "Who Rules the Giant Corporation?" *Business and Society Review* (Summer 1976), 40–48.

vestment in technological innovation and advertising, and a quest for expanding markets and fresh sources of cheap raw materials. The larger corporations have also tended to consume one another through mergers and takeovers. As competition among the survivors declines, their products grow more and more similar and are distinguished by advertising gimmicks rather than qualitative differences—consider, for instance, the similarity between the products of General Motors and Ford, or the services of the major airlines.

The economic (and therefore political) power of the largest corporations is immense. A major corporation such as General Motors has a budget larger than that of any government in the world other than the United States and the Soviet Union. The hundred largest corporations (less than 0.01 percent of all corporations in the country) account for more than half of the nation's manufacturing assets, and the top 1 percent of corporations for more than 80 percent of these assets. But who owns the corporations themselves? The question is difficult to answer, partly because ownership of corporate stock is often concealed through trust funds and other guises, and partly because of the complex layers in which corporations own stock in other corporations, which in turn own stock in other corporations, and so on. A 1978 study by the Senate Subcommittee on Reports, Accounting, and Finances found that fewer than two dozen corporate investors—most of them banks—held enough stock-voting power to control 122 of the nation's largest corporations, whose stock in turn represents 41 percent of the value of all stock in the United States. These corporate investors, however, are investing most of the money on behalf of private individuals, and the indications are that the ultimate ownership of stock is highly concentrated among a very few wealthy people. The richest 1 percent of individuals and families own more than half of the total market value of all stock in the United States and receive nearly half of the dividend income from stocks. A tiny group of wealthy people thus has an economic influence out of all proportion to its numbers.[17]

Many economists have argued that this concentration of the ownership of wealth and man-

ufacturing capacity undermines the free enterprise system that is so highly valued in the United States. In the traditional model of free enterprise, each individual freely pursues his or her own economic self-interest. Ideally, these competing interests produce an overall balance, maximizing the economic benefits to society as a whole and preventing domination of the economy by any one interest. A system of informal checks and balances is thus essential for the effective operation of the free enterprise system. But if more and more power is concentrated in the hands of a few interlocking corporations, the balance is upset. Economic competition is reduced, monopolies are able to artificially distort market forces, and the corporate sector of society dominates the noncorporate sector.

One of the most important developments in the world of these giant private organizations is the emergence of *multinational corporations:* vast business enterprises that are based in one country but own subsidiary corporations in many other countries. The global impact of such corporations is immense; they now account for nearly a quarter of total world production, and their share will rise to over a half by the end of the century.[18] Many of the corporations are far more wealthy than the countries in which they operate, and their direct investment of capital in foreign countries has replaced trade as the single most significant element in international economics.[19] Most of the multinational corporations are based in the United States. Industry abroad that is controlled from the United States comprises the third largest economy in the world after that of the United States itself and the

[17]See Gabriel Kolko, *Wealth and Power in America* (New York: Praeger, 1962); Charles H. Anderson, *The Political Economy of Social Class* (Englewood Cliffs, N.J.: Prentice-Hall, 1974); Marshall E. Blume *et al.*, "Stock Ownership in the United States: Characteristics and Trends," *Survey of Current Business* (Washington, D.C.: U.S. Department of Commerce) 54 (1974), 16–40; Morton Mintz and Jerry S. Cohen, *America, Inc.: Who Owns and Operates the United States* (New York: Dell, 1973).

[18]Ronald Segal, "Everyone at Home, Home Nowhere," *Center Magazine* (May–June 1973), 8–9.

[19]Frank Church, "Will They Usher in a New World Order?" *Center Magazine*, 6 (May–June 1973), 15.

Multinational corporations conduct their business in several countries, and are one of the most important factors in the international economy. Because they can escape the laws of many of the countries in which they operate, much of their activity is unscrutinized and unregulated.

Soviet Union[20] About 200 of the big multinationals maintain full-time offices in Washington, primarily for the purpose of influencing government decisions.[21]

These huge, powerful organizations are subject to the authority of no single nation; they are responsible only in a fictional sense to the stockholders; they are dedicated to the pursuit of profit and are little concerned with social goals; and they exercise an influence that is largely unscrutinized. For these reasons, their activities are increasingly recognized throughout the world as a major social problem. As Richard Barnet,

Ronald Müller, and Joseph Collins point out:

The rise of the planetary enterprise is producing an organizational revolution as profound in its implications for modern man as the industrial revolution and the rise of the nation-state itself. . . . The rise of the global corporation . . . has put the world economy under the substantial control of fewer than five hundred business enterprises which do not compete with one another according to the traditional rules of the market. . . . Power to influence the direction of national economies is now being concentrated in what are, legally and politically speaking, private hands. . . .

The rise of the global corporation is producing new sets of loyalties which transcend and often conflict with national loyalties. . . . Because of their incentive and their ability to shift jobs and profits from one country to another, global cor-

[20]Neil H. Jacoby, "The Multinational Corporation," *Center Magazine*, 3 (May 1970), 37–55.
[21]Richard L. Barovick, "The Washington Struggle over Multinationals," *Business and Society Review*, (Summer 1976), 12–19.

Table 6.1 The 25 Largest Industrial Corporations (Ranked by Sales)

Rank '78	'77	Company	Sales ($000)	Assets ($000)	Rank	Net Income ($000)	Rank
1	1	General Motors (Detroit)	63,221,100	30,598,300	2	3,508,000	1
2	2	Exxon (New York)	60,334,527	41,530,804	1	2,763,000	3
3	3	Ford Motor (Dearborn, Mich.)	42,784,100	22,101,400	4	1,588,900	4
4	4	Mobil (New York)	34,736,045	22,611,479	3	1,125,638	6
5	5	Texaco (Harrison, N.Y.)	28,607,521	20,249,143	6	852,461	10
6	6	Standard Oil of California (San Francisco)	23,232,413	16,761,021	7	1,105,881	7
7	7	International Business Machines (Armonk, N.Y.)	21,076,089	20,771,374	5	3,110,568	2
8	9	General Electric (Fairfield, Conn.)	19,653,800	15,036,000	8	1,229,700	5
9	8	Gulf Oil (Pittsburgh)	18,069,000	15,036,000	9	791,000	13
10	10	Chrysler (Highland Park, Mich.)	16,340,700	6,981,200	21	(204,600)	491
11	11	International Tel. & Tel. (New York)	15,261,178	14,034,866	11	661,807	16
12	12	Standard Oil (Ind.) (Chicago)	14,961,489	14,109,264	10	1,076,412	8
13	13	Atlantic Richfield (Los Angeles)	12,298,403	12,060,210	12	804,325	12
14	14	Shell Oil (Houston)	11,062,883	10,453,358	14	813,623	11
15	15	U.S. Steel (Pittsburgh)	11,049,500	10,536,300	13	242,000	49
16	16	E. I. du Pont de Nemours (Wilmington, Del.)	10,584,200	8,070,300	18	787,000	14
17	18	Western Electric (New York)	9,521,835	6,133,617	25	561,200	20
18	17	Continental Oil (Stamford, Conn.)	9,455,241	7,445,165	20	451,340	24
19	19	Tenneco (Houston)	8,762,000	10,134,000	15	466,000	23
20	20	Procter & Gamble (Cincinnati)	8,099,687	4,983,817	33	511,668	21
21	21	Union Carbide (New York)	7,869,700	7,866,200	19	394,300	28
22	22	Goodyear Tire & Rubber (Akron, Ohio)	7,489,102	5,231,103	30	226,127	53
23	23	Sun (Radnor, Pa.)	7,428,238	5,497,826	29	365,393	32
24	32	Caterpillar Tractor (Peoria, Ill.)	7,219,200	5,031,100	32	566,300	18
25	29	Eastman Kodak (Rochester, N.Y.)	7,012,923	6,801,067	23	902,284	9

Source: From Fortune magazine's list of the 500 largest corporations. Fortune, May 7, 1979.

porations are exacerbating some fundamental conflicts. Tax-avoidance practices, currency transactions, pricing arrangements, and job-relocation policies that are optimal from the corporation's viewpoint have highly unfavorable effects on the majority of people who, unlike the corporations, cannot escape the territory in which they live. . .

The most revolutionary aspect of the planetary enterprise is its political pretension. The managers of the global corporations are seeking a role in shaping the contemporary world. . . . What they are demanding in essence is the right to transcend the nation-state, and in the process to transform it.[22]

ANALYZING THE PROBLEM

Both the functionalist and the conflict approaches illuminate the problem, although they do so in different ways.

The Functionalist Approach

According to the functionalist approach, the problem of abuse of concentrated power by government and corporations can be seen as the result of social disorganization brought on by rapid social change, particularly over the past century. As American society has become more complex and as people have demanded an increasing range of government services, government bureaucracies have flourished and multiplied. This tendency has been functional in some ways, for it has met many important social needs. But it has also been dysfunctional in that private individuals have exerted less control over the decisions that regulate their lives. Similarly, the massive economic development of the past century has been inseparable from the growth of huge corporations, which can muster far more expertise and investment capital than individual entrepreneurs could hope to offer. In this sense, the growth of corporations has been functional for economy and society; but it has been dysfunctional in that the world economy is now dominated by a handful of firms with little formal responsibility to society.

Social disorganization exists to the extent that the means of exercising social control over government and corporations have not kept pace with the growth of these formal organizations. Government has become so big and complex that it can no longer be effectively scrutinized by the representatives of the people: members of Congress often lack the time or the technical expertise for the task, and often remain ignorant of the activities (including flagrantly illegal ones) of government departments. Similarly, large corporations have become centers of economic and political power in a way that was never originally foreseen. In their pursuit of profit, corporations may threaten the democratic process by their behind-the-scenes attempts to influence public policy. The concentration of corporate economic power may also subvert free enterprise.

The Conflict Approach

The conflict approach is particularly appropriate for the problem of government and corporations, focusing as it does on the conflict of interests that is the very essence of American political and economic life. It views the problem of the abuse of power by government and corporations as the outcome of a continuing struggle for advantage among various interests in American society, with the victorious interests at any time being those having the most powerful resources (such as money, influence, or organization).

The United States is a class society, in which there are major inequalities in wealth and income. As Karl Marx pointed out, the economically dominant class in any society is always the politically dominant class as well, for it is able to translate its wealth into political power and influence. For this reason, those who have a

[22]Barnet, Müller, and Collins, "Global Corporations." *op. cit.*, pp. 56–57.

disproportionate share of the nation's economic assets—that is, wealthy individuals and corporations—also have a disproportionate influence in government, which they often use to further their own interests and to maintain the inequality from which they so richly benefit. Because less powerful and less organized groups with different interests, such as ordinary consumers or voters, do not enjoy the same access to the higher levels of power, they become in some respects the victims of the collaboration between government and corporations. Conflict theory predicts, however, that this tension may have beneficial effects in the long run, for disadvantaged groups are likely to form social movements to redress their grievances. When these groups organize themselves, their collective power is enhanced, and they may be able to bring about needed social changes.

THE NATURE OF BUREAUCRACY

To understand why power becomes as concentrated as it does in such large organizations as government departments and industrial corporations, we must examine the nature of these organizations more closely.

Sociologists call large organizations of this kind formal organizations, to distinguish them from informal social groupings. Unlike an informal group, a *formal organization* is one that is deliberately and rationally structured to achieve specific goals. In any large formal organization, such a structure takes the form of a *bureaucracy*, in which officials have specific tasks and work under a formal system of rules to maximize the efficiency of the organization as a whole. To the individual who deals with bureaucracies, they often seem exasperatingly slow and inefficient, hidebound by red tape and petty regulations. But bureaucracies are more effective than any other form of social organization in coordinating large numbers of people to achieve particular objectives. Taxes, for example, could hardly be collected by informal methods: it is only through a system of complex rules and a hierarchy of officials, each with a specialized role, that the task is possible at all. Similarly, a large modern factory or insurance company could not possibly be run informally, with people switching roles and making up rules as they pleased. Formal organizations such as government departments and large corporations are therefore an essential part of the modern world, and it is impossible to imagine society without them.

The general tendency of bureaucracies, however, is to grow, and in growing, to become still more bureaucratic. They tend to be impersonal, resistant to change, and in many individual cases, infuriatingly inefficient. Any bureaucracy also tends to become an *oligarchy*—that is, its power tends to be concentrated in the hands of a few, even if the power is theoretically vested in many. Why should this be the case? A closer look at some of the characteristics of bureaucracies will suggest the answer.

Weber's Analysis

In a highly influential analysis of bureaucracy written at the beginning of this century, the German sociologist Max Weber pointed to bureaucractic structure as a specific example of what he called *rationalization*—the process by which traditional, spontaneous methods of social organization are replaced by routine, systematic procedures.[23] Weber regarded rationalization as the dominant process in the modern industrial world, but he viewed it without enthusiasm. The world, he felt, was being "disenchanted," and in the process the finest human values were being submerged in a quest for technical efficiency. Weber saw bureaucracy as a particularly disturbing form of rationalization. Unlike the rationalization of, say, industrial production, which is based on the calculated arrangement and organization of mere machinery, bureaucracy involves the rationalization of human beings, who are systematically subordinated to the technical requirements of running formal organizations.

According to Weber, a bureaucracy is usually the most efficient possible means of coordinating

---

[23]See *From Max Weber: Essay in Sociology*, trans. Hans H. Gerth and C. Wright Mills (New York: Oxford University Press, 1946).

a large number of people to achieve a given objective. The typical bureaucracy has the following basic characteristics:

1. There is a division of labor among the various officials. Each individual has limited, specialized duties to perform.
2. There is a hierarchy of authority, pyramidal in shape. Each official takes orders from above and then supervises and is responsible for immediate subordinates.
3. An elaborate system of rules, regulations, and procedures guides the day-to-day functioning of the organization. All decisions are based on these rules and on established precedents.
4. Officials treat people as "cases," not as individuals, remaining emotionally detached so that their rational judgment is not distorted by sympathy for particular people.
5. Employees tend to make a lifelong career of service in the organization. Promotion is supposedly based on merit or seniority or both, but not on favoritism, kinship, or other criteria that might be used in an informal group.
6. Bureaucracies have a specialized administrative staff, whose duties are to keep the organization functioning by maintaining files, records, accounts, and internal communications.

Weber saw the growth of modern bureaucracy as inevitable. Indeed, he saw it as essential for the existence of democracy. Without a system of rules, regulations, and procedures to limit them, officials would have a free rein to exercise their authority at whim. Favoritism and despotism can be checked only by laws and bureaucratic procedures that apply equally to everyone. Yet Weber noted an inescapable paradox: although bureaucracy is necessary for democracy in some ways, it tends to subvert democracy in other ways. The very existence of bureaucracy means that individual citizens have less control over their lives; they are subject to more and more regulations and interference by organizations that are less and less accountable to the public. The pursuit of equality in society inevitably means the rise of great bureaucracies to regulate the economy and social services, but the freedom of individuals to do as they please often suffers as a result.

Dysfunctions of Bureaucracy

If bureaucracies are such an efficient means of organizing people to achieve particular goals, why are they so inefficient and even irrational in particular cases? The reason is that although a bureaucracy (such as a college administration) is functional for the efficient handling of general cases, it can be dysfunctional when dealing with particular cases (like the student who wants to take an unusual combination of courses). Officials tend to think in terms of rules and regulations and precedents, which are appropriate for standard situations but not for exceptional ones. When they encounter an unusual case, they are often unable to take any initiative other than passing the buck. Thorstein Veblen described this tendency as "trained incapacity"—the result of bureaucratic training, which makes officials unable to handle any situations that do not fit the rule book. A striking example of the ineptitude of the formal organization in the face of unexpected situations occurred in American colleges in the 1960s, when administrations were suddenly confronted by militant student movements. The response of the college bureaucracies was predictable and typical: to set up committees and subcommittees, draft memos and prepare reports, and propose vague, long-term modifications of existing institutions—when what was needed were rapid, flexible, and sensitive responses. The reactions of the college administrations, although often made in good faith, were widely interpreted as stalling devices or attempts to deceive the militants, and thus served to increase rather than relieve tensions.

Workers in bureaucracies may also be subject to feelings of alienation in their jobs. Because they have so little opportunity for taking initiatives or making innovations, and because their field of authority is so specialized and limited, they are apt to perceive themselves as cogs in a machine. Victor Thompson found that bureaucrats suffer from lack of recognition of their talents and resent the apparent meaninglessness of work routines, such as filling in and filing endless triplicated forms.[24] (The alienating effect of this kind of work on those who perform it is discussed in more detail in Chapter 4, "Work.")

A large organization always has a bureaucratic structure, with officials working at carefully defined tasks and with an extensive system of rules, procedures, and records. Bureaucracies achieve overall efficiency, but can be slow and inefficient in handling individual cases.

Bureaucracies, too, tend to become concerned with their own preservation and to lose sight of their original goals. Several writers have made half-satirical references to the internal inefficiencies of bureaucracies. C. Northcote Parkinson, for example, has outlined "Parkinson's law"—that in any formal organization, "work expands to fill the amount of time available for its completion."[25] A surprisingly high number of officials, he claims, perform redundant tasks; for example, checking each other's work, or producing trivial memos "for the record." Laurence Peter has outlined the "Peter principle"—that in any formal organization all employees tend to rise in the hierarchy "to their own level of incompetence."[26] Employees who are performing their duties well, argues Peter, tend to be promoted steadily until they finally find themselves in a job that is beyond their capacities—where they remain. As a result, any official who is

[24]Victor Thompson, *Modern Organization* (New York: Knopf, 1961).

[25]C. Northcote Parkinson, *Parkinson's Law* (Boston: Houghton Mifflin, 1957).

[26]Laurence J. Peter and Raymund Hull, *The Peter Principle: Why Things Always Go Wrong* (New York: Morrow, 1969).

doing a job well tends to be promoted out of it, and officials who are performing badly tend to remain where they are. The entire organization would be in a permanent state of inefficiency except that some people who are doing their jobs well have not yet been promoted out of them.

The Iron Law of Oligarchy

Why, then, do formal organizations of every kind tend to be ruled by the few at the top of the bureaucratic hierarchy? The answer was provided by the sociologist Robert Michels, a contemporary and a friend of Max Weber. Writing soon after World War I, Michels came to the conclusion that any organization would inevitably become an oligarchy. His analysis applied primarily to political parties, but it has such wide implications that it has come to be known as the iron law of oligarchy.

Michels was a socialist and had been deeply disturbed to find that the new socialist parties in Europe, which had elaborate rules and procedures designed to give the mass membership control over party affairs, seemed to be dominated by their leaders no less than the older, aristocratic parties. In both cases, it seemed, authority was exercised almost exclusively by the leaders, and the socialist parties' rules for participation by the mass membership did not make the slightest difference. Michels concluded that democracy and large-scale organization are always incompatible: "It is organization that gives birth to the domination of the elected over the electors, of the mandatories over the mandators, of the delegates over the delegators. Who says organization says oligarchy."[27]

Why should this necessarily be so? Michels points out that if a large social group is to have any realistic hope of achieving its objectives over any length of time, it must be formally organized: the problems of the group and the range of its activities alone require some kind of bureaucracy. Then, because immediate, day-to-day decisions cannot be made by large numbers of

people, some power must be delegated to the officials at the top of the hierarchy. Hence the dilemma: the very organizations on which our society depends can work effectively only if power is mostly in the hands of the few people who head them.

Michels suggests several reasons why the mass membership cannot exercise effective control over the organization. He points out that the leaders achieve their position precisely because they have superior talents for persuasion, organization, public speaking, and manipulating opinion. They are people who are adept at getting their own way and winning support for their views. Once they are in leadership positions, their ability to influence others is increased: they now have prestige, information, and facilities unavailable to people lower down in the hierarchy. The leaders also prefer promoting junior officials who share their views, so the oligarchy tends to become a self-perpetuating one. The leaders are strongly motivated to retain their positions and promote the policies they believe in, and they use all their power and influence for these purposes.

The masses, on the other hand, tend to revere and and trust the leaders, placing far more credence in what they say than in statements from lesser officials. The mass membership is much less sophisticated and is prepared to allow the leaders to exercise their own judgment on most matters. Moreover, in contrast to the dedicated full-time leaders, the ordinary members have only a partial commitment to the organization and lack the time and the knowledge to keep a close check on the leadership. Michels did not see the leaders as necessarily evil, power-hungry, or dishonest. They might be people of the very highest ideals, shaping the organization and its policies in a selfless way for what they believe to be the best interests of the people. But the very structure of bureaucratic organizations implies that, whether the leaders are right or wrong, the masses can have little influence on their decisions.

Michels' thesis has disturbed many social scientists for decades. His iron law should not be too uncritically accepted, however, for he overlooked certain checks on the abuse of author-

[27]Robert Michels, *Political Parties* (New York: Free Press, 1962), p. 365.

ity.[28] For example, in most organizations there are competing oligarchies, such as the different factions in American political parties. If the dominant oligarchy gets out of touch with popular sentiment, another may take advantage of the situation and displace the established leadership, as happened when the McGovern forces seized the Democratic presidential nomination from the party establishment in 1972, or when the Carter forces repeated the feat in 1976. Furthermore, if the leaders depart too far from the wishes of their subordinates, there may be mass defections from the organization as members switch their allegiance to some other competing organization or interest.

It must also be remembered that organization has its positive aspects. Without organization many desired social goals could not possibly be achieved. In particular, many social problems could not be effectively confronted without the collective action of organized social movements. It does seem clear, however, that the very structure of organizations limits the possibility of popular control over their affairs, whether it is control of corporations by stockholders or of government bureaucracies by voters.

IS THERE A "POWER ELITE"?

To what extent are major decisions in America made by a small elite of government and corporate officials? The issue was raised by the conflict theorist C. Wright Mills in his book *The Power Elite*, published in 1956, and has been debated by sociologists ever since. Mills argues that corporate capitalism requires long-range, highly coordinated decision-making. To this end it cooperates with other institutions, primarily governmental, that can guarantee the conditions in which corporate interests will be maximized. The "power elite" is not really a conspiracy, and the people within it have not necessarily tried to attain political power and influence; they simply

happen to be at the top of the great organizations that dominate society:

> The power elite is composed of men whose positions enable them to transcend the ordinary environments of ordinary men and women; they are in a position to make decisions having major consequences. . . . They are in command of the major hierarchies and organizations of modern society. They rule the big organizations. They run the machinery of the state and claim its prerogatives. They direct the military establishment. They occupy the strategic command posts of the social structure, in which are now centered the effective means of the power and the wealth and the celebrity which they enjoy.[29]

This power elite, according to Mills, is composed of people of very similar background. They are mostly native-born male Americans of American parents; they are from urban areas; and except for the politicians, they are mostly from the East. The majority are Protestant, and a high proportion have attended Ivy League colleges. The members of the power elite tend to share the same attitudes and values and to know one another on a personal basis. They sit together on corporation boards and government commissions, forming an informal "interlocking directorate." At this level, decisions made in one area are likely to affect interests in other areas, so the power elite tend to coordinate their activities and policies to reflect this community of interest.

Mills contends that there are three distinct levels of power and influence in American society. At the top is the power elite, which operates invisibly but makes informal decisions on the most vital matters of public policy. The second level consists of various interest groups that operate visibly but make decisions of lesser importance, primarily through the lobbying and legislative process in Congress. At the third level is the mass society, consisting of almost powerless individual citizens who have little direct influence over decisions and who often are unaware that decisions are being made at all.

[28]A classic study of the failure of the iron law is Seymour M. Lipset, Martin A. Trow, and James L. Coleman, *Union Democracy: The Internal Politics of the International Typographical Union* (Glencoe; Ill.: Free Press, 1956).

[29]C. Wright Mills, *The Power Elite* (New York: Oxford University Press, 1956), pp. 3–4.

Other sociologists have challenged Mills' thesis. David Riesman, for example, accepts that power is unequally shared in American society but strongly denies the existence of any coordinated power elite.[30] He suggests instead that there are two levels of power in the United States. The upper consists of a balanced series of "veto groups"—strong interest groups that protect themselves by blocking efforts of other groups encroaching on their interests. No one group determines policy; in fact, the locus of influence shifts from issue to issue, and in the long run no one group is favored over the others. At the second level is the unorganized public, which Riesman believes is not so much dominated by the groups as it is sought by them as an ally in their campaigns. The difference between the two views, then, lies in Riesman's denial of the existence of a coordinated elite that uses power to serve its own interests.

It is difficult to prove or disprove either of these views, because the processes they describe are often informal and secret. But there is useful evidence from other sources. Numerous studies of patterns of power and influence in local communities have all come to the conclusion that important decisions are made by powerful local interests, often without the community's knowledge. In some cases these interests seem to conform to the power-elite model, while in others, the officials merely act under pressure from powerful groups as the more pluralist veto-group model would predict.[31]

The ordinary American voter displays little enthusiasm for voting. In the democracies of Western Europe, anywhere from 70 percent to 90 percent of the voters turn out at election time. American voters, in contrast, have by far the lowest turnout rate among the world's democratic nations. In the 1976 presidential election only 54 percent of eligible voters actually voted—the lowest turnout in a presidential election year since 1948. In off-year elections the figures are even lower: in the 1978 elections less than 35 percent of voters cast their ballots, the lowest turnout since 1942 (see Figure 6.2). Since the poor suffer the most from existing social arrangements, we might expect them to be particularly eager to change them. Yet studies of voting behavior have shown that the lower the person's income, the less likely that person is to vote or otherwise participate in politics. The failure of the poor to vote implies that they see no connection between voting and political influence; and, indeed, in a Hart Research Associates study of nonvoters in the 1976 presidential election, four out of five of them cited feelings of political alienation as the reason for their apathy.[32] Other studies have indicated the existence of a "ruling class" consisting of a small number of high corporate and government officials and wealthy individuals who fill an astonishing number of the seats on corporate boards and in government commissions and agencies,[33] but the precise use to which they put their power is still in dispute.

Whichever view one accepts, it does seem that major decisions are in the hands not of the ordinary citizen but of organized groups. Many of these groups have been highly successful in achieving their aims, which they press in Congress through the use of professional lobbyists who deluge politicians with propaganda, favors, proposed legislation, or organized letter campaigns. One interest group whose congressional lobbying has been markedly successful is the American Rifle Association. This organization has thwarted several attempts at gun-control legislation, which it has fought with funds derived largely from weapons manufacturers. The American Medical Association, representing most of the country's physicians, has pre-

---

[30]David Riesman, *The Lonely Crowd* (New Haven, Conn.: Yale University Press, 1969).

[31]See particularly Floyd Hunter, *Community Power Structure* (Chapel Hill, N.C.: University of North Carolina Press, 1953); and Robert Dahl, *Who Governs?* (New Haven, Conn.: Yale University Press, 1961).

[32]For discussions of political alienation and voter apathy, see the special issue of *Society*, 13 (July–August 1976); Everett Carl Ladd, Jr., *Where Have All the Voters Gone?* (New York: Norton, 1978); Arthur T. Hudley, *The Empty Polling Booth* (Englewood Cliffs, N.J.: Prentice-Hall, 1978).

[33]Charles H. Anderson, *The Political Economy of Social Class* (Englewood Cliffs, N.J.: Prentice-Hall, 1974); G. William Domhoff, *Who Rules America?* (Englewood Cliffs, N.J.: Prentice-Hall, 1967).

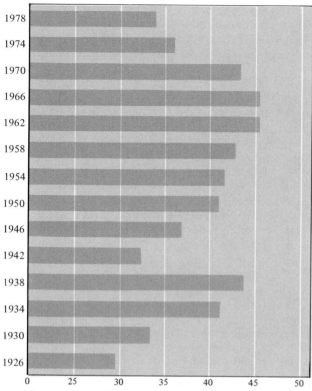

TURNOUT
Off-Year Elections—1926-1978

Percentage of the Electorate Who Voted for U.S. Representatives

FIGURE 6.2 **Turnout in off-year elections.** Voter turnout at American elections—particularly in non-Presidential election years—has always been very low compared to all the other Western democracies. Since the early 1960s, the proportion of the electorate participating in these elections has declined to less than a third of the eligible voters. These data seem to indicate a pervasive political apathy—a widespread feeling that voting is simply not worth the trouble.

(Adapted from data supplied by the Department of Commerce, U.S. Bureau of the Census, and the Committee for the Study of the American Electorate, 1978.)

vented the introduction of a national health-insurance system through strenuous campaigns that have included successful efforts to unseat legislators who favored the proposal (see Chapter 12, "Health").

There can be little doubt that the oligarchies of major interest groups exercise a disproportionate power in American society, and that this power is used primarily in the interests of those who wield it. Yet it should not be forgotten that, in the long run, the electorate in a democracy passes the final judgment on the acts of its rulers. The mere awareness of the potential force of public opinion—an awareness reinforced by the example of Watergate—must inhibit the gross abuse of power by privileged groups.

THE MILITARY-INDUSTRIAL COMPLEX

One of the areas in which the interrelationship

between government and corporations has been most closely studied is that of the *military-industrial complex*—the interlocking network of politicians, Pentagon bureaucrats, military chiefs, and executives of corporations that supply military equipment. The military-industrial complex has been severely criticized both by liberals who believe that funds are often wastefully channeled into corporate coffers by officials shielded from public accountability, and by conservatives who charge that the complex is undermining the free enterprise system in the United States.

The term "military-industrial complex" was not coined by any radical critic of the American system. It was first used by President Dwight Eisenhower, a conservative and former general of the U.S. Army. In his farewell presidential address to the nation, Eisenhower issued a grave warning to the American people:

Until the latest world conflicts, the United States

had no armaments industry. American makers of ploughshares could, with time and as required, make swords as well. But now we can no longer risk emergency improvisation of national defense; we have been compelled to create a permanent armaments industry of vast proportions. . . .
The conjunction of an immense Military Establishment and a large arms industry is new to the American experience. The total influence—economic, political, even spiritual—is felt in every statehouse, every office of the Federal Government. We recognize the imperative need for this development. Yet we must not fail to comprehend its grave implications. Our toil, resources, and livelihood are all involved; so is the very structure of our society. In the councils of government we must guard against the unwarranted influence, whether sought or unsought, by the military-industrial complex. The potential for a disastrous rise of misplaced power exists and will persist.[34]

Eisenhower's admonition has been widely quoted, but his advice has been largely neglected. Nearly a quarter of the federal budget goes to defense expenditures, with more than half of the sum being devoted to the Defense Department's huge payroll. The department is located in the Pentagon, the largest office building in the world, and employs a million civilians, over a third of all federal civilian employees. The Pentagon owns more property than any other organization in the world and has assets worth well over $200 billion. The influence of the Pentagon extends throughout the economy: about 3.8 million industrial workers owe their jobs directly to defense contracts, and one of every nine jobs in America is dependent on the military establishment. Some 350 American communities have at least one defense plant or factory, and in many it is the dominant industry or largest employer. Defense money flows into more than three-quarters of the nation's congressional districts.[35]

The military-industrial complex described by Eisenhower is an informal system of organizations, interests, and officials acting to further common objectives. In recent years industries have emerged that depend for their very existence on winning contracts for sophisticated defense equipment. The top one hundred corporations in the United States monopolize three-quarters of these contracts, more than 80 percent of which are awarded without competition. Defense contracts are especially appealing to large corporations because not only are they lucrative to begin with, but the Pentagon permits massive cost "overruns" beyond the price originally agreed upon. Even when projects are abandoned, often because the products fail to meet design specifications, the Pentagon still pays the manufacturers handsomely.

The nuclear ANP aircraft was scrapped after $511.6 million had been invested in its development; the Seamaster aircraft, after an investment of $330.4 million; the Navaho missile, after an investment of $679.8 million; and the Dyna-soar ordnance, after an investment of $405 million.[36] The F-111, a plane proposed by General Dynamics, was unanimously rejected on several grounds by a panel of Pentagon experts, but after the intervention of Navy Secretary Fred Korth—former president of a bank that had loaned General Dynamics large amounts of money to keep the company solvent—the Pentagon ordered 1,700 of the planes at $2.4 million each. The final product did not meet design specifications: among other defects, it was too heavy to fly with some of the sophisticated equipment specially manufactured for it. It also displayed an alarming propensity to crash (though not so alarming as the Starfighter plane, known as the "widowmaker" because more than 170 of them have crashed so far), and it proved unfit for combat service in Vietnam. Meanwhile, the cost had escalated to $8 million apiece, at which point the Pentagon canceled the original contract, paid General Dynamics compensation of over $215 million, and proceeded to order a modified version of the plane (which still did not

[34]Quoted in Seymour Melman, *Pentagon Capitalism: The Political Economy of War* (New York: McGraw-Hill, 1970), p. 235.
[35]See Stephen Cobb, "Defense Spending and Defense Voting in the House: An Empirical Study of an Aspect of the Military-Industrial Complex Thesis," *American Journal of Sociology*, 82 (July 1976), 163–182.

[36]Melman, *op cit.*, pp. 177–179.

A. Ernest Fitzgerald was Deputy for Management Systems in the Air Force. In 1969 he found his job eliminated after his congressional testimony revealed a $2-billion cost overrun in Lockheed's contract for the C-5A transport plane.

. . .

Our secret patriots told us the Air Force was prepared to fund Lockheed's expenditures through most of the *following* fiscal year under the existing contract, provided Congress ponied up the money as usual. Lockheed's other military customers were no less solicitous.

What had panicked Lockheed into threatening bankruptcy just then? Lockheed's performance on contracts was dismal, but they were generally considered to be the best cash managers in the aerospace business. Getting money from the government was a focus of Lockheed's managers, and they were good at it.

The notion that these superb manipulators could be in *cash* trouble on military contracts seemed inconceivable to me. Yet Packard had testified, "I have asked the company for additional data which will support, by specific periods and programs, *their short-term cash needs.*" (Emphasis mine.)

After considerable study of the scanty facts available to us, the Joint Economic staff and I concluded that Lockheed's immediate cash problems could not be due to their military contract troubles, and unless the Pentagon made a complete turnabout and became strict constructionists on contract enforcement, Lockheed faced no serious future threat from that quarter. By elimination, Lockheed's cash problem, which appeared

---

meet original specifications) at more than $14 million each.[37]

The reason for the Pentagon's tolerance of incompetence among the corporate suppliers of its weaponry is that it has become a captive customer of these industries—if they should collapse into bankruptcy, the Pentagon would have no suppliers at all, since only a few companies have the capacity to produce sophisticated defense equipment. Admiral Hyman Rickover, a Pentagon official who is critical of the incompetence of the corporations, declares:

Large defense contractors can let costs come out where they will, and count on getting relief from the Department of Defense. . . . Wasteful subcontracting practices, inadequate cost controls, shop loafing, and production errors mean little to these contractors, since they will make their money whether their product is good or bad; whether the price is fair or higher than it should be; whether delivery is on time or late. Such matters are inconsequential to the management of most large defense contractors, since, as with other regulated industries, they are able to conceal the real facts concerning their management ineptitude from the public and from their stockholders, until they stumble finally into the arms of the government for their salvation.[38]

Because major corporations in the defense industry, such as Lockheed and General Dynamics, obtain nearly all their income from federal defense contracts, they have a strong interest in persuading the Pentagon and Congress to spend ever larger sums on defense. These corporations maintain numbers of lobbyists in Washington who try to convince both the Pentagon and Congress of the need for new weapons, and they make great efforts to keep close ties with the Pentagon establishment. By the end of the 1960s the top one hundred military contractors employed some 2,072 retired military officers with the rank of colonel or above. The ten largest contractors employed 1,100 ex-officers, many of whom presumably retained influence with their former colleagues at the Pentagon. In 1975 it was estimated that more than 5,000 former Pentagon officials were currently employed in the defense

---

[37]A useful summary of the F-111 case is I. F. Stone, "Nixon and the Arms Race: The Bomber Boondoggle," *New York Review of Books,* January 2, 1969, pp. 5–12.

[38]Quoted in Ernest Fitzgerald, "The Pentagon as the Enemy of Capitalism," *World,* February 27, 1973, p. 21.

real enough, had to have its origins in nonmilitary projects. Lockheed's only major civilian project at the time was the L-1011 trijet airbus. Therefore, the unidentified sinkhole for cash at Lockheed had to be the L-1011.

From my viewpoint, all this was in the nature of suspicions confirmed. Since my first visits to Lockheed's C-5A operations in early 1966, I had suspected that Lockheed was deliberately overrunning the C-5A project, partly in order to help finance their upcoming commercial projects through shared indirect expenses. Just as Max Ajax could have used his vastly increased government contract overhead allowances to expand and improve his coat-hanger business instead of hiring his girlfriend, so could Lockheed (or any other big contractor in a similar situation) use its increased overhead allowances to finance at least part of a new commercial venture.

I should point out that playing the allocation game in order to have the government pay for "company funded" private ventures is not only widespread but also legitimate under the Pentagon's convoluted procurement and contract financing rules. More direct methods of financing commercial work through government contract payments, such as mischarging (politely called "migration") of direct labor costs and diversion of materials were not legitimate but were also widespread, though seldom reported by the audit agencies.

. . .

Source: A. Ernest Fitzgerald, *The High Priests of Waste* (New York: W. W. Norton, 1972). pp. 290–91. Copyright 1972 by A. Ernest Fitzgerald.

industry.[39] The revolving door between the large corporations and the Pentagon sometimes turns the other way. President Eisenhower's secretary of defense, for example, was Charles E. Wilson, former president of General Motors (noted for his observation that "what's good for General Motors is good for the United States"). President Kennedy's and President Johnson's secretary of defense was Robert McNamara, former president of Ford Motors. President Nixon's undersecretary of defense was David Packard, founder of the Hewlett-Packard Company, a major defense-contracting firm in which Packard owned $3.4 million of stock and to which he returned after his time at the Pentagon.

Critics have claimed that the major impetus behind the arms race comes from the pressures of contract-seeking corporations rather than genuine strategic needs. Ralph Lapp argues that much of our weapons production is

> due to the self-interest of the military-industrial complex. Once the defense plants were built they could be abandoned only at great political risk . . . the Congress was not equipped to do battle with the Pentagon. Furthermore, the economic impact of defense expenditures on the various states grew greater with each passing year. . . .
> When a state has a considerable fraction of its manufacturing labor force working on defense or other federal contracts, the danger exists that a temporary contractual arrangement will harden into a permanent feature of its economy. Here we find the cruelest expression of the weapons culture—its perpetuation for reasons other than national security.[40]

Yet this seems to be what has happened; the economy is so geared to military production that it would be severely dislocated if weapons manufacture were significantly reduced. When Lockheed found itself on the brink of bankruptcy in 1971 after an ill-advised investment in a civilian aircraft, the federal government came to its aid with a loan of $250 million—a remarkable step in a society priding itself on a free enterprise system in which government supposedly does not aid or interfere with the free operation of the marketplace.

---

[39]Michael D. Edwards, "Golden Threads to the Pentagon," *Nation*, March 15, 1975, pp. 306–308.

[40]Ralph Lapp, *The Weapons Culture* (New York: W. W. Norton, 1968), pp. 11–30.

At the time it was granted the federal loan, Lockheed employed over 200 high-ranking ex-military officers. In their efforts to persuade Congress to approve the measure, Lockheed's representatives received the full support of the Pentagon lobby, the largest professional lobby in Washington—about one lobbyist for every two members of Congress. (In all, the Pentagon spends over $30 million each year on public relations—in effect, using public tax money to persuade the public to spend more tax money on Pentagon programs.)

The implications of the Pentagon's massive support of failing or incompetent corporations is a serious one, for it undermines the free enterprise system at the very highest levels of government. Ernest Fitzgerald contends that

> the principal threat to American capitalism as we have known it comes not from anticapitalism ideologists but from government support of inefficient and incompetent practices that are the antithesis of a free economy. . . . How ironic that the one institution most intimately identified with the preservation of the American business system—the Pentagon—should turn out to be its enemy . . . [41]

In fact, the relationship between the Pentagon and the leading corporate suppliers of military equipment is barely distinguishable from the relationship between government and industry under socialism—except that in the American case, corporations can make fat profits.

Since the Vietnam war, congressional criticism of the Pentagon has mounted. But the Pentagon has unique characteristics that make it resistant to reform: much of its activity is classified; few outsiders have the technical knowledge to make informed judgments of its plans; and opposition to the Pentagon's programs has been easily misinterpreted as lack of patriotism. As a result, the Pentagon is relatively immune from scrutiny as it—and indirectly the corporate suppliers of military equipment—consumes the lion's share of taxes from the American people.

THE ABUSE OF POWER: THE ITT CASE

To see the abuse of the concentrated, interlocking power of government and corporations in action, let us look at a case study involving the International Telephone and Telegraph Company (ITT), a vast multinational conglomerate owning hundreds of companies in diversified industries all over the world. It has been alleged that ITT not only attempted to corrupt the United States government but also tried to bring down the democratically elected government of another country, Chile, in order to preserve its own supposed economic interests.[42]

In 1968 Harold Geneen, the president of ITT, attempted to bring about the greatest merger in American history by taking over the Hartford Insurance Group, one of the largest insurance companies in the world. The proposed merger was vigorously resisted by Richard McLaren, the chief of the Justice Department's antitrust division, on the grounds that such a merger would reduce the economic competition necessary for effective free enterprise and would, therefore, not be in the public interest. A court case resulted, which the Justice Department was determined to take to the Supreme Court if necessary.

Suddenly, however, the Justice Department decided to drop the case against ITT. Coincidentally, Sheraton Hotels, an ITT subsidiary, made a $400,000 pledge to the Republican National Convention in San Diego—the largest sum ever given by any corporation for such purposes. A clearer indication of the relationship between the two events emerged when muckraking Washington columnist Jack Anderson obtained and published a secret internal ITT memo written by the corporation's congressional lobbyist. The memo stated:

> I am convinced . . . that our noble commitment has gone a long way toward our negotiations on the mergers coming out as [Geneen] wants them. Certainly the President has told Mitchell [then attorney-general] to see that things are working

---

[41]Fitzgerald, *op cit.*, p. 18.

[42]Anthony Sampson, *The Sovereign State of ITT* (Greenwich, Conn.: Fawcett Books, 1973).

According to the "power elite" thesis, the major decisions in American society are made by a small group of white, middle-aged, wealthy holders of high political and economic offices, while the ordinary people are often unaware that these decisions are even being made.

out fairly. It is still only McLaren's mickey-mouse we are suffering. . . . Please destroy this, huh?[43]

In the face of growing public concern, both ITT and the administration denied any collusion in the matter. When Richard Kleindienst, who as acting attorney general had finally ordered the court case dropped, was asked at his Senate confirmation hearings whether any pressure had been applied on him from the White House, he emphatically denied that it had. This was an outright lie, as was later discovered when, under court subpoena, President Nixon surrendered White House tape recordings in which he specifically instructed Kleindienst to drop the case.

Meanwhile, columnist Jack Anderson obtained further copies of internal ITT memos indicating that corporate executives were trying to prevent the re-election of the left-wing Salvador Allende as president of Chile, and if necessary to bring down his democratically elected government. One internal ITT memo to Harold Geneen suggested these tactics against Chile:

(1) Banks should not renew credits or should delay doing so.
(2) Companies should drag their feet in sending money, in making deliveries, on shipping spare parts, etc.
(3) Savings and loan companies there are in trouble. If pressure were applied, they would have to shut their doors.[44]

Another memo, addressed to an ITT director who had previously headed the CIA, recounted preliminary steps to bring about a military coup in Chile:

Today I had lunch with our contact . . . and I summarize for you the results of our conversation. Approaches continue to be made to select members of the Armed Forces in an attempt to have them lead some sort of uprising—no success to date.[45]

Another paper recorded a telephone message from a high ITT official to the Nixon administration:

Mr. Geneen is willing to come to Washington to discuss ITT's interest and we are prepared to assist financially in sums up to seven figures.[46]

A final paper stated:

Late Tuesday night [the U.S. ambassador to Chile] finally received a message from the State Department giving him the green light to move in the name of President Nixon. The message gave him maximum authority to do all possible . . . to keep Allende from taking power.[47]

Salvadore Allende's government was eventually overthrown by a military coup in which Allende himself was murdered. The new Chilean regime quickly attracted international notoriety for its brutal suppression of civil liberties and systematic torture of political opponents. In 1974 a Senate investigation discovered that the CIA had spent at least $8 million in an effort to bring down Allende; the money had been used for such purposes as financing opposition groups and bribing legislators to vote against Allende's programs. The facts of this sordid alliance between American government and corporations have done the United States immense damage throughout Latin America.

Between 1972, when ITT's involvement in Chile was first revealed, and 1976 the corporation continued to deny the charges. Finally, Harold Geneen (still president of ITT, and being paid $700,000 a year for his job) admitted that the corporation had received "recent information tending to show that some $350,000 of ITT funds may have been sent to Chile" to support anti-Allende forces in 1970. In response to the wave of criticism and bad publicity generated by the facts of the Chilean intervention, ITT spent $6.4 million in public-relations advertising designed to improve its image, so successfully that a poll commissioned by the

[43]Ibid.
[44]Quoted in "The Square Scourge of Washington," Time, April 3, 1972, p.42.
[45]Ibid.
[46]Ibid.
[47]Ibid.

company showed that the number of persons who believed "ITT cares about people" jumped from 20 percent to 43 percent within a year.[48]

Anthony Sampson considers that the ITT case highlights the need for new forms of controls over the activities of the multinational corporations, which are not inherently good or evil but have emerged so rapidly that there has been no time for the development of appropriate social regulation:

> Without need of much plotting, the multinationals have achieved over the last twenty years, with the opening up of world communications, a position of sudden dominance: they have found a vacuum and filled it. Their skills and technology have brought new benefits, and paved the way for others to follow; but they have also produced a serious imbalance between their centralized drive and the fragmented and confused state of the countries and communities with which they deal. This imbalance should be gradually rectified, as the nations catch up with the new state of the world, and begin to come together to form their own communications and controls. But in the meantime the multinationals must open themselves up, and allow themselves to be inspected and questioned, if they are not to find themselves in a bitter conflict with their hosts.[49]

Of course, such abuse of power should not be seen as typical of the practices of domestic American corporations or of multinationals based in the United States. There is no reason to suppose that the great majority of these corporations do not adhere to the law and to acceptable standards of business ethics. In fact, many American corporations are internationally known for their scruples and tact in dealing with foreign host countries. The problem is that the relationship between government and corporations is so exempt from critical public scrutiny that the potential and the temptation to abuse power are always present.

CONFRONTING THE PROBLEM

With the steady trend toward increased concentration of economic power in giant domestic and multinational corporations, and with continued growth in the size and number of government bureaucracies, the prospects for preventing the abuse of power by government and corporations might seem gloomy. Yet there are some hopeful signs—resulting, paradoxically enough, from the Watergate scandal, which riveted public attention on this problem as never before. The Watergate abuses were investigated by Senate and House committees before TV cameras; the Supreme Court made several important rulings on the case; headlines in the press documented President Nixon's slow but inevitable downfall; cabinet members and other high officials of government and corporations were convicted of crimes; corporations fired many executives who had admitted to corrupt practices.

The result of that period of social conflict and tension has been a marked change in the social atmosphere in which government and corporations operate, and this change is of vital importance. As Watergate proved, laws alone will not prevent the abuse of power. They must be complemented by social values and informal norms that set effective limits to the way power is used. The standards of professional and personal conduct required of public officials have perhaps never been higher in the United States than today; any blemish in a person's past career may be enough to deny him or her an elective or appointed office in public life. Jimmy Carter's own rapid rise from relative political obscurity to the presidency in 1976 occurred largely because he, of all the candidates, had the fewest links to Washington and projected an image of greater honesty. Hundreds of corporations have volun-

---

[48]Michael H. Crosby, "ITT's Chile Confession: A Definite 'Maybe'," *Business and Society Review*, 18 (Summer 1976), 66–67.

[49]Sampson, *op. cit.*, pp. 312–313.

tarily admitted to malpractices in the past and have pledged that there will be no repetition of them in the future. Provided these new standards in political and corporate life can be maintained, the nation may benefit in some sense from the turmoil of Watergate. There are several steps that can be taken to ensure that these standards will actually be maintained.

Citizen groups. One of the most promising developments in recent years has been the emergence of citizen groups that act as watchdogs over government and corporations.[50] The best known of these are the various bodies established by the consumer advocate Ralph Nader—the Center for Auto Safety, the Center for the Study of Responsive Law, Nader's Raiders, and the Public Interest Research Groups, among others. Nader's work provides an outstanding example of the impact that even a single dedicated citizen can make. His success in forcing corporations to respond to public interest has lent enormous prestige and confidence to the consumer movement.

Nader first came to public attention in the 1960s with his book *Unsafe at Any Speed,* in which he accused General Motors of putting profits before auto safety. General Motors responded by setting private investigators after Nader in the hope of uncovering information that could be used to discredit him. In turn, Nader sued GM for invasion of privacy and was granted damages of $280,000, all of which he used for his work. Many of his investigations have resulted in legislation to correct abuses that he uncovered. His findings that our meat supply is "often diseased or putrescent, contaminated by rodent hairs and other assorted debris," resulted in the Wholesome Meat Act of 1967. After his report on slackness at the Federal Trade Commission—where some officials spent hours "working" in bars and others never came to work at all—the federal government thoroughly reorganized the agency. When Nader's re-

searchers compiled damning evidence about the Food and Drug Administration's continued approval of cyclamates as artificial sweeteners, despite having known for some years that the chemical might cause cancer and genetic mutations, the FDA rapidly banned cyclamates and rejected protests from the corporate manufacturers. Other Nader-inspired legislation includes the Gas Pipeline Safety Act of 1968, the Radiation Control for Health and Safety Act of 1968, the Coal Mine Health and Safety Act of 1969, and the Comprehensive Occupational Safety and Health Act of 1970. More recently he has charged that the mid-1970s oil shortage was partly an artificial creation of the major oil companies, designed to force up the price of gasoline.

Nader does not consider himself a radical: he is not trying to bring down the capitalist system, but is merely trying to make it function better by eliminating deceit, corruption, and inefficiency.[51] In fact, he charges that the corporations are the real radicals, in the sense that they threaten the established social order:

> Corporate fraud and other economic crimes . . . escape the normative perception that would be applied, for example, to a pickpocket by most people. From educational to media systems, people are not afforded adequate opportunities to learn about and ethically evaluate price-fixing, adulterated citrus juices, hams and poultry, deliberately fragile bumpers, unperformed but billed-for services, suppression of life-giving innovations and many other crimes which bilk the consumer of some $200 billion yearly. . . . These depredations are part of a raging corporate radicalism which generates technological violence, undermines the integrity of government, breaks laws, blocks needed reforms and repudiates a quality-competitive system with substantial consumer sovereignty. If radicalism is defined as a force against basic value systems of a society, then the corporate state is the chief protagonist.[52]

Another important citizen group is Common Cause. This movement also has as its aim chang-

---

[50]Jeffrey M. Berry, *Lobbying for the People* (Princeton, N.J.: Princeton University Press, 1977); David Vogel, *Lobbying the Corporation: Citizen Challenges to Business Authority* (New York: Basic Books, 1978).

[51]See Ralph Nader, Mark Green, and Joel Seligman, *Taming the Great Corporation* (New York: W. W. Norton, 1976).
[52]Quoted in Mintz and Cohen, *op. cit.*

ing the system from within, by attempting to confront corruption in government and waste of public money by federal bureaucracies. The group has attracted a large membership and has already been credited with some legislative changes, such as the federal election law requiring full disclosure of major political campaign contributions. Common Cause intends to force the federal administration, through the courts if necessary, to abide by its own laws and regulations on such matters as antitrust policy. Many other smaller citizen groups have scored notable successes, particularly environmental-protection groups that have brought cases against big corporate polluters.

Reorganizing Government. The prospects for cutting down the size of big government are slim. Although virtually everyone agrees that federal and state bureaucracies are excessively large, there is little agreement on where best to wield the ax. Americans who are against big government in principle are quick to raise howls of protest if a service benefiting them is cut. Reducing the size of budgets and staff in such areas as welfare, defense, environmental protection, law enforcement, or education might be considered a solution by some groups but a problem by others.

Furthermore, the need to regulate government agencies and corporations more closely will inevitably mean creating even more agencies with regulatory and investigatory powers. (This is yet another example of the paradox pointed out by Weber: although bureaucracy threatens our freedom in some respects, it is necessary to preserve our freedom in others. It is also an example of how an attempt at solving a social problem can create further problems.)

There is, however, a strong need for the reorganization of government, and, indeed, President Carter made this challenge one of his main priorities. Many federal and state programs need to be consolidated to eliminate the overlap in their functions and fields of jurisdiction. The very existence of some departments and programs needs to be questioned anew, and careful safeguards must be created to prevent bureaucracies from becoming self-perpetuating jugger-

nauts of little proven social value. For example, new federal programs could include a well-defined performance standard for measuring their success, so that the public would know whether or not they were being effective and thus justifying their existence. And Congress could write expiration dates into legislation creating new programs, so that the programs would lapse unless a need to renew them could be shown.

Scrutinizing the Large Organizations. It will be necessary in the future to develop more effective means of scrutinizing large private and public organizations. Multinational corporations, for example, have become so significant in the international economy that their continuing freedom from regulation and from enforced social responsibility can no longer be tolerated. Individual nation-states will have to coordinate policies that take account of the advantages the multinational corporation offers by way of economic development, but prevent these organizations from pursuing their own interests to the exclusion of those of their host countries or to the detriment of international relations.

The inefficiencies of government bureaucracies also need closer scrutiny. At present one federal agency, the General Accounting Office (GAO), acts as a watchdog on the affairs of other government departments; it claims to save the taxpayer some $300 million a year by reducing waste and inefficiency elsewhere in the federal bureaucracy. The GAO has also extended its activities into other fields. It found, for example, that in 1972 wheat sales to the Soviet Union by the Department of Agriculture were mismanaged; that military equipment held by United States troops in Europe for emergency use was not even combat-ready; and that the Justice Department failed to carry through investigations into campaign-law infractions. The GAO scrutinizes only a tiny fraction of federal bureaucratic activity, however, and most wastage and abuses probably go unchallenged. Unlike many other federal regulatory bodies, the GAO has retained some independence and has not become a mere adjunct of the organizations it is supposed to be investigating—as some critics charge happened with the Federal Communications Commission, the Food and Drug Administration, and many other regulatory agencies.

One fortunate effect of Watergate is that Congress has become more assertive in its relations with the executive branch of government. President Carter's nominees for high public office have been subjected to searching and grueling investigation by Congress. The CIA has been the subject of a highly critical congressional inquiry, although many of the facts uncovered—described as "horror stories" by members of Congress who learned of them—have been suppressed in the interest of "national security."

Until the death of FBI Director J. Edgar Hoover in 1975, after a tenure of no less than forty-eight years, the FBI was almost immune from congressional scrutiny; in fact, Congress passed nineteen of Hoover's last twenty-two budgets exactly as he had submitted them. Hoover's power was so great that even senators and presidents feared him, for it was known that he maintained files on the private lives and past indiscretions of thousands of political figures. Several successive presidents, including Richard Nixon, dearly wished to fire Hoover, but none could find the courage. (Nixon once summoned Hoover to the White House with the intention of dismissing him, but, according to the then White House Chief of Staff Bob Haldeman, the president "chickened out.")[53] The FBI has now come under close congressional questioning, and its future directors will probably always have a strictly limited term of tenure to prevent them from building an independent power base in the executive branch of government.

One of the most difficult areas to scrutinize is the military-industrial complex, because much of its activity is conducted in secret for national security reasons. But the declining prestige of the military, due to the Vietnam war and the détente in East-West relations in the 1970s, has created a climate in which it may be possible for Congress to oversee the Pentagon and its corporate weapons suppliers more aggressively than before. The Pentagon itself is now examining contracts much more carefully, and has discovered several cases of huge profit markups concealed by tricks of accountancy (such as subcontracting work to another division of the same company and thus doubling the profit margin). In 1974, when the Pentagon signed a contract with General Dynamics for the single most expensive item it has ever purchased, a submarine costing $285.4 million, special safeguards against cost overruns were written into the agreement at the Pentagon's insistence.

Congress, too, is becoming less willing to hand out public money to the armaments manufacturers. In 1974 the Senate voted down by 53 votes to 35 an appeal from Grumman, a major weapons supplier, for a loan of $100 million to ensure the continuing solvency of the company. Senators were particularly irritated to learn that Grumman had already received a massive loan from the Navy to meet operating expenses, but had instead invested the money in short-term, high-dividend securities which yielded a net profit of $3 million for the company.[54] In 1977 President Carter decided, in the face of intense pressure from the Pentagon, not to proceed with a colossally expensive B-1 bomber program on the grounds that the aircraft was not really needed. His act was a marked contrast to the responses of previous presidents, who were inclined to support virtually any Pentagon demand for major new weapons systems.

Corporations, too, are coming under much closer examination, particularly from the Securities and Exchange Commission. Prompting by the SEC has encouraged many corporations to admit past corrupt practices, but the corporations did so on the understanding that the SEC would take a more lenient view if they confessed to abuses rather than waited for them to be discovered. In the future the SEC and the courts will have to apply heavier sanctions on corporations and corporate officials found guilty of malpractices. The few corporations or corporate executives who were brought before the courts in Watergate-related cases generally received light fines—hardly a strong deterrent for the officials (the chief executives of the hundred largest

[53]For a summary of Hoover's activities during his tenure, see Time, December 22, 1975, pp.14–22; Halperin et al., op. cit.

[54]Time, August 26, 1974, p. 69.

corporations earn an average of well over $200,000 a year) or for multimillion-dollar enterprises. The 1977 Foreign Corrupt Practices Act makes provision for very heavy corporate and personal penalties for the bribing of foreign officials, but it remains to be seen whether the courts will impose stiffer sentences in the future.

Gross corporate malpractice cannot be checked if the guilty parties are treated less severely than a person who steals an automobile or smuggles marijuana across the border. Ultimately, even the richest corporation or the mightiest government must be made aware of its full responsibility to the society it should serve.

SUMMARY

1. A serious social problem is the abuse of concentrated power by government and corporations working in concert to further their own interests. Government agencies and corporations have both tended to grow larger and more powerful.

2. From the functionalist approach, the problem is one of social disorganization resulting from rapid change: government and corporations have grown faster than the means of social control over them. From the conflict approach, the problem is one of inequality: economic power translates into political power, and powerful groups use their position to further their own interests.

3. Weber's analysis showed that bureaucracy is highly efficient for handling general cases. It may be dysfunctional, however, in other respects. Michels argued that any bureaucratic organization tends to become an oligarchy.

4. According to C. Wright Mills, the United States is ruled by a "power elite" of corporate and government officials. This view is disputed by those who believe the power structure is more pluralistic. But it is clear that powerful interests do have a disproportionate influence in government.

5. The military-industrial complex centers on the Pentagon and its corporate weapons suppliers. The complex is criticized for inefficiency, waste, unnecessary arms production, and improper influence by corporations.

6. The ITT case provides a specific example of the attempts of a multinational corporation to influence domestic and international political events in its own private interests.

7. Watergate has strengthened social values requiring higher ethical standards in government and corporations. Means of confronting the problem include the efforts of citizens' groups and other social movements; reorganizing government; and better scrutiny of our large organizations.

GLOSSARY

Bureaucracy. An organizational structure in which officials have specific tasks and work under a formal system of rules to maximize the efficiency of the organization as a whole.

Formal organization. A group that is deliberately and rationally structured in order to achieve specific goals.

Military-industrial complex. An interlocking network of politicians, Pentagon bureaucrats, military chiefs, and executives of corporations that supply military equipment.

Multinational corporation. A large business enterprise that is based in one country but owns subsidiary corporations in many other countries.

Oligarchy. The concentration of power in the hands of a few officials of an organization or group.

Rationalization. The process by which traditional, spontaneous methods of social organization are replaced by routine, systematic procedures.

——— FURTHER READING ———

BARNET, RICHARD, and RONALD MÜLLER. *Global Reach: The Power of the Multinational Corporations.* New York: Simon and Schuster, 1974. An important discussion of multinational corporations and their implications for the international political and economic scene.

BLAU, PETER, and MARSHALL W. MEYER. *Bureaucracy in Modern Society.* 2nd ed. New York: Random House, 1971. A short but comprehensive account of bureaucracy, including a discussion of its functions, dysfunctions, and social impact.

DOMHOFF, G. WILLIAM. *Who Rules America?* Englewood Cliffs, N.J.: Prentice-Hall, 1967. An important study of the American "governing class" and its influence over national policy.

DOUGLAS, JACK D., and JOHN M. JOHNSON (eds.). *Official Deviance: Readings in Malfeasance, Misfeasance, and Other Forms of Corruption.* Philadelphia: Lippincott, 1977. A collection of articles on various forms of governmental and corporate corruption and abuse of power.

ERMAN, M. DAVID, AND RICHARD J. LUNDMAN (eds.). *Corporate and Governmental Deviance: Problems of Organizational Behavior in American Society.* New York: Oxford University Press, 1978. A selection of articles on lawbreaking at the highest levels of government and corporate bureaucracies. The book includes some suggestions for curbing corruption in high places.

ETZIONI, AMITAI. *A Sociological Reader on Complex Organizations.* New York: Holt, Rinehart and Winston, 1969. A useful collection of important articles on various aspects of formal organizations and bureaucracy.

HAPGOOD, DAVID. *The Screwing of the Average Man: How the Rich Get Richer and You Get Poorer.* New York: Bantam, 1974. A racy book, as its title implies; it offers an eye-opening investigation of how the American political and economic system heavily favors the big organizations over the ordinary consumer.

MELMAN, SEYMOUR. *Pentagon Capitalism.* New York: McGraw-Hill, 1970. A perceptive study of the military-industrial complex and its use of public money.

MICHELS, ROBERT. *Political Parties.* New York: Free Press, 1967. Although first published after World War I, this book remains a classic and still relevant to the problem—the difficulty of regaining democratic control over large organizations. The book contains a clear account of Michel's famous "iron law of oligarchy."

MINTZ, MORTON, and JERRY COHEN. *America, Inc.: Who Owns and Operates the United States.* New York: Dell, 1973. A well-documented account of the immense economic and political power of 200 leading corporations in the United States. The book exposes the interrelationship between economic and political power in America.

NADER, RALPH, MARK GREEN, and JOEL SELIGMAN. *Taming the Giant Corporation.* New York: W. W. Norton, 1976. Ralph Nader and his associates give an account of the workings of large corporations, including their abuses of power, and offer some suggestions for applying social control to these organizations.

ORUM, ANTHONY M. *Introduction to Political Sociology.* Englewood Cliffs, N.J.: Prentice-Hall, 1978. A useful short introduction to the study of politics and political institutions from a sociological perspective.

SAMPSON, ANTHONY. *The Sovereign State of ITT.* Greenwich, Conn: Fawcett Books, 1973. A carefully documented and highly readable account of the abuse of power by the International Telephone and Telegraph Company. Sampson provides a critical analysis of the potential for good and evil that such huge multinational corporations possess.

7
Poverty

THE PROBLEM

By many standards the United States is the most fabulously wealthy society in history. Yet over 24 million people—more than 1 American in 10—are living at or below the official poverty line, on incomes that the federal government considers insufficient to meet basic requirements of food, clothing, and shelter.[1] These people are not the only poor in the United States; there are millions more, living slightly above the poverty line, whose plight is not much better. Despite our celebrated affluence, social services in the United States compare unfavorably with those in most industrialized societies. Furthermore, the affluent majority sometimes seems indifferent to the problems of the poorest section of the population. As we shall see, this attitude is reinforced by widely believed myths about the poor—myths the facts prove to be grossly inaccurate.

POVERTY IN THE UNITED STATES

Poverty in the United States does not simply mean that the poor do not live quite as well as other citizens. It means many old people eating dog and cat food to supplement their diets. It means malnutrition and deprivation for hundreds of thousands of children. It means greater susceptibility to disease, to alcoholism, to victimization by criminals, and to mental disorders. It often means unstable marriages, slum housing, illiteracy, ignorance, inadequate medical facilities, and shortened life expectancy. Poverty can

mean low self-esteem, despair, and stunting of human potential.

To make matters worse, a large part of the poor population finds that despite their best efforts, their poverty is almost "escape proof." The employment opportunities available to the poor typically offer none of the stability and fringe benefits of the jobs available to the more affluent and better educated. Migrant workers, for example, are locked into a cycle of seasonal work; the urban poor can usually hope for only low-paying jobs that offer no security against sudden periods of unemployment; the rural poor can often find no jobs at all. And the children of the poor are exposed to the rigors of a job market without the protection and advantages that the rich can provide their own offspring.

Although the number of poor declined fairly steadily for several decades until the recessions of the 1970s, there is no evidence that the plight of the remaining poor is improving. In testimony before the Senate Select Committee on Nutrition and Human Needs, physician Robert Coles reported:

> We had seen . . . not only extreme poverty, but gross, clinical evidence of chronic hunger and malnutrition—evidence that we as doctors found it hard to deal with ourselves, let alone talk about, because we had been unprepared by our own medical training for what we saw. Today's American physicians are simply not prepared by their education to find in this nation severe vitamin deficiency diseases, widespread parasitism, and among infants, a mortality rate that is comparable, say, to the underdeveloped nations of Asia or Africa. . . .

---

[1]U.S. Bureau of the Census, *Statistical Abstract of the United States, 1978* (Washington, D.C.: U.S. Government Printing Office, 1978), p. 465.

I saw . . . malnourished children, children who are not getting the right amount and kinds of food, who suffer from several diseases and see no physician, who indeed were born in shacks without the help of a doctor and under conditions that are primitive, to say the least. . . . Why . . . must these children go hungry, still be sick? . . . Why do American children get born without the help of a doctor, and never, never see a doctor in their lives? It is awful, it is humiliating for all of us that these questions still have to be asked in a nation like this, the strongest and richest nation that ever was. . . .

I do not understand why these things have to persist and why we have to talk about this again and again and again, and people like me have to come and repeat all these findings.[2]

That statement was made in 1969. In 1974 the same Senate committee heard evidence, based on studies of over a hundred specialists, that the poor in the United States were hungrier and needier than they had been at the end of the 1960s.[3]

The Emergence of Poverty as a Social Problem

Even though the United States has always had an impoverished "underclass," poverty has not always been regarded as a significant social problem. Unemployment and the poverty it caused were certainly seen as a major social problem during the depression years of the 1930s, but World War II diverted public attention to other issues. In the relatively prosperous postwar years new issues aroused public concern—anxieties about the cold war, communism, and America's new global involvement. The topic of poverty was almost nonexistent in sociological literature. Of the eleven most widely used social–problems textbooks published in the United States between 1956 and 1964, eight did not mention poverty at all, and only one—published in 1964—gave the topic serious treatment.[4] It was only in the 1960s that poverty reemerged as a

major social problem, perceived once more as a condition that represented a glaring gap between American ideals and American reality.

Why did the problem of poverty recede from public consciousness for so long? John Kenneth Galbraith has argued that the poverty that afflicted millions in the 1930s was regarded primarily as a problem of unemployment.[5] Once the New Deal and the post–World War II economic recovery provided new job opportunities, and a very large section of the population that had previously experienced poverty began to enjoy a more secure and affluent life style, it came to be widely assumed that poverty as a major problem had been eliminated.

But some people were left behind and forgotten. The newly prosperous middle classes moved away from the city centers and insulated themselves from the poor in the expanding suburbs. The poor gradually became invisible to the rest of society—confined to city ghettos, trapped in the more remote rural areas, living in isolation in rented rooms and old-age homes. No social movements or powerful lobbies pressed their case, and it went unheard.

In 1960, presidential candidate John Kennedy was appalled to discover firsthand the extent of poverty in West Virginia and other states during his primary campaigns. He made poverty an issue in the presidential election, and the problem began to reemerge once more. Then, in 1962, a single, powerful book riveted attention on the existence of poverty in the midst of an affluent society. Michael Harrington declared in *The Other America* that as many as a quarter of the American people lived in poverty, and provided startling evidence of severe deprivation and malnutrition in America.[6] His work stimulated a large number of studies of poverty, the media took up the issue, and public interest in the problem increased rapidly. The book and its reception reinforced President Kennedy's deter-

---

[2]Robert Coles, Testimony Before the Select Committee on Nutrition and Human Needs of the United States Senate, February 1969.

[3]*New York Times*, June 20, 1974.

[4]Jack L. Roach and Janet K. Roach (eds.), *Poverty: Selected Readings* (Baltimore: Penguin, 1972) p. 9.

[5]John K. Galbraith, *The Affluent Society* (New York: Houghton Mifflin, 1958), pp. 100–102.

[6]Michael Harrington, *The Other America* (New York: Macmillan, 1962), p. 9.

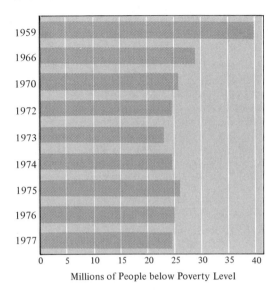

Millions of People below Poverty Level

FIGURE 7.1 **Persons living in poverty.** Over the past two decades, the number of Americans living in poverty has been significantly reduced—partly as a result of anti-poverty programs, partly as a result of the general expansion of the American economy during most of this period. During the economic recession of the mid-seventies, however, the number living in poverty actually rose once more.
(Adapted from the U.S. Bureau of the Census, *Statistical Abstract, 1978*, p. 466.)

mination to confront the problem. In 1964 the late president's resolve was perpetuated by President Johnson in a special message to Congress in which he announced the War on Poverty—a major, wide-ranging campaign that made the elimination of poverty one of the highest priorities of the nation and generated such programs as VISTA, Head Start, Neighborhood Youth Corps, Job Corps, Title I Educational Funding, Neighborhood Legal Services, and the Community Action Program.

The problem of poverty was publicly recognized and government intervention was accepted as an appropriate way to solve it. Johnson was determined to make the eradication of poverty the great achievement of his administration—comparable to Roosevelt's New Deal in the 1930s. Instead, the United States became

embroiled in a long, costly, unwinnable war in Southeast Asia, which distracted public and congressional attention, diverted national resources from the poverty programs, and finally drove Johnson from office. Public awareness of the problem had increased, the poor had benefited measurably from some of the new programs, but the basic problem of widespread poverty remained.

Johnson's successor, President Nixon, proposed to Congress a Family Assistance Plan (FAP) that would guarantee a minimum income to all Americans, but the principles and details of the plan aroused so much opposition from different interest groups that it was defeated in a Senate subcommittee in 1970. By 1978 President Carter was trying to win public and congressional support for a reform of the welfare system. His plan called for a classification of welfare recipients into those who are able to work and those who are not and also included provision for a guaranteed minimum income. Again, however, the proposals encountered strong resistance from several quarters, and Congress shelved the issue. The problem of poverty is still with us.

Poverty in the Midst of Wealth

The problem of poverty in the United States is aggravated because it occurs in a society in which the overall distribution of wealth (property and other capital) and income (wages, salaries, and other earnings) is very unequal. Like all but the most simple societies, the United States is characterized by *social stratification*—that is, it is divided into social classes that have varying degrees of access to the rewards the society offers. It was estimated in 1974 that if the wealth in the United States were evenly distributed, every adult would have a net worth of around $25,000. But, as Figure 7.2 shows, the distribution of wealth is highly unequal. The richest fifth of American individuals and families owns more than three-quarters of the wealth in the United States, whereas the lowest fifth owns only 0.2 percent of the wealth. There are over 210,000 millionaires in the United States, about 155 families that are worth $100 million, and about 60 families that are worth between $100 million

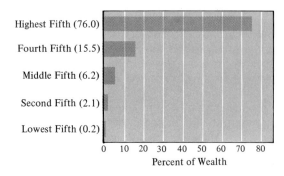

Percent of Wealth

FIGURE 7.2 **Distribution of wealth in the United States.** The distribution of wealth in the United States is strikingly unequal, with the richest fifth of the population owning more than three quarters of the nation's wealth.
(Executive Office of the President, Office of Management and the Budget, *Social Indicators,* 1973, Washington, D.C.: U.S. Government Printing Office, 1973 Chart 5/15.)

and $500 million.[7] The richest 1 percent of individuals and families owns more than half of all stock and receives nearly half of the dividend income from stocks.[8] Most of this wealth, of course, has not been accumulated through the hard work or imaginative skills of those who now enjoy it; it has been inherited. Just as the children of the poor are born into poverty and tend to remain there, so the children of the rich tend to enjoy a lifetime of affluence.

The distribution of income in the United States follows a similar pattern. As Figure 7.3 shows, the richest fifth of American families receives over 40 percent of the national income, whereas the poorest fifth receives only 5.2 per-

cent. This pattern has remained virtually unchanged at least since World War II. About 3,000 families receive, in addition to whatever wealth they may possess, an annual income of over $1 million, most of it from investments.[9] The highest executives of major corporations enjoy staggering salaries; a 1979 Industrial Conference Board report showed that the heads of the nation's major manufacturing corporations earned an average of $241,000 a year. Corporate executives enjoy many other tax-free benefits

Percent Distribution of Aggregate Income

Year	Lowest Fifth	Second Fifth	Middle Fifth	Fourth Fifth	Highest Fifth	Top 5 Percent
1977	5.2	11.6	17.5	24.2	41.5	15.7
1976	5.4	11.8	17.6	24 1	41.1	15.6
1975	5.4	11.8	17.6	24.1	41.1	15.5
1974	5.4	12.0	17.6	24.1	41.0	15.3
1973	5.5	11.9	17.5	24.0	41.1	15.5
1972	5.4	11.9	17.5	23.9	41.4	15.9
1971	5.5	12.0	17.6	23.8	41.1	15.7
1970	5.4	12.2	17.6	23.8	40.9	15.6
1969	5.6	12.4	17.7	23.7	40.6	15.6
1968	5.6	12.4	17.7	23.7	40.5	15.6
1967	5.5	12.4	17.9	23.9	40.4	15.2
1966	5.6	12.4	17.8	23.8	40.5	15.6
1965	5.2	12.2	17.8	23.9	40.9	15.5
1964	5.1	12.0	17.7	24.0	41.2	15.9
1963	5.0	12.1	17.7	24.0	41.2	15.8
1962	5.0	12.1	17.6	24.0	41.3	15.7
1961	4.7	11.9	17.5	23.8	42.2	16.6
1960	4.8	12.2	17.8	24.0	41.3	15.9
1959	4.9	12.3	17.9	23.8	41.1	15.9
1958	5.0	12.5	18.0	23.9	40.6	15.4
1957	5.0	12.6	18.1	23.7	40.5	15.8

FIGURE 7.3 **Percentage share of total income received by each fifth and top 5% of families: 1957–1977.** The distribution of income in the United States is highly unequal, and shows little change over the years—with the highest fifth of the population, for example, consistently earning around 40 percent of the nation's income, and the lowest fifth, around 5 percent.
(U.S. Bureau of the Census, *Statistical Abstract,* 1978.)

[7]See Arthur Lewis, "The New Rich of the Seventies," *Fortune,* September, 1973; and "The Super-Rich," *The Progressive,* August, 1974.

[8]Marshall E. Blume, Jean Crockett, and Irwin Friend, "Stock-ownership in the United States: Characteristics and Trends," *Survey of Current Business,* 54 (November 1974), 16–40. See, also, Daniel W. Rossides, *The American Class System* (Boston: Houghton Mifflin, 1976); Robert A. Rothman, *Inequality and Stratification in the United States* (Englewood Cliffs, N.J.: Prentice-Hall, 1978).

[9]Philip M. Stern, "Uncle Sam's Welfare Program—for the Rich," *New York Times Magazine,* April 16, 1972, p. 28.

from their companies, such as the use of cars and private jets, expense accounts, medical care, and vacations disguised as business trips. These untaxed benefits can easily represent the equivalent of hundreds or even thousands of dollars of income every month. Gabriel Kolko found that 80 percent of the checks at the most expensive restaurants and over a third of Broadway theater tickets were covered by expense accounts.[10]

In an impoverished country of Africa, Asia, or Latin America, poverty is often seen as simply a fact of life, a misfortune that these countries just do not have the resources to eradicate or even alleviate. The continued existence of poverty in a generally affluent society, however, raises serious moral questions—and inevitably creates fierce conflicts of interest and many political controversies.

ANALYZING THE PROBLEM

In any stratified society some people will be poorer than others. To understand the problem of poverty in America, therefore, we must ask why societies should be stratified into social classes in the first place. Both functionalist and conflict theorists have addressed this problem, but they have arrived at radically different conclusions.

The Functionalist Approach

In a classic statement, Kingsley Davis and Wilbert E. Moore[11] analyzed social stratification from the functionalist approach, which sees social inequality as functional for the maintenance of society. In any society, they pointed out, some roles—such as those of physician, corporation president, nuclear physicist, or military commander—require scarce talents or long training. People will not perform these demanding roles unless they are commensurately rewarded for doing so; therefore society offers them such compensation—usually in the form of wealth or income—to ensure that scarce talents are matched with the jobs that demand them. Similarly, jobs that do not require scarce talents—such as those of sanitation worker, secretary, fruit picker, or cab driver—receive lower

rewards. Society functions more efficiently as a result, but social stratification is the inevitable outcome.

Even if stratification is inevitable, however, there seems to be no functional reason why it should take such an extreme form as it does in the United States, where some people have annual incomes of millions of dollars and others are without the basic necessities of life. Clearly, some people earn far more than their roles require and others earn far less than their society can afford to pay them. To explain this anomaly, functionalists would argue that social disorganization is present to the extent that a society is more stratified than it needs to be. Thus, in the United States, there is social disorganization to the extent that wealth and income are very unequally distributed and to the extent that some people, such as racial minorities and the children of the poor, are arbitrarily denied equal access to social rewards. If a society is "overstratified" in this way, inequalities can become dysfunctional.

The Conflict Approach

Sociologists who take a conflict approach have been highly critical—even contemptuous—of the functionalist explanation.[12] Far from dis-

[10]Gabriel Kolko, *Wealth and Power in America: An Analysis of Social Class and Income Distribution* (New York: Praeger, 1962), p. 19.

[11]Kingsley Davis and Wilbert E. Moore, "Some Principles of Stratification," *American Sociological Review*, 10 (1945), 242–249.

[12]Especially Melvin Tumin, "Some Principles of Stratification: A Critical Analysis," *American Sociological Review*, 18 (1953), 378–394, and "On Inequality," *American Sociological Review*, 28 (1963), 19–26; see, also, Denis H. Wrong, "The Functional Theory of Stratification: Some Neglected

tributing social rewards on the basis of merit, they argue, social stratification tends to have the opposite effect. The reason is that there can be no equality of opportunity in a class system, because the parents of each generation tend to pass their social status on to their children. Movement from one social status to another is called *social mobility*. Extensive research has shown that the rate of upward social mobility—that is, movement from a lower social status to a higher one—is rather low in all societies, and the United States differs surprisingly little from other countries in this respect.[13] Most people have much the same social status as their parents had, and social stratification, far from ensuring that the fittest people train for and fill the most important roles, merely ensures that they tend to stay where they are. Some of the most rewarded people, such as jet-setting inheritors of family fortunes, perform roles that have no obvious social value; others, born in less fortunate circumstances, are denied the opportunity to make full use of their talents.

Conflict theorists offer a very different explanation of social stratification. Their analysis derives directly or indirectly from the work of Karl Marx, who saw social inequality as the outcome of a conflict over scarce resources. Social classes, Marx argued, exist because one group is able to gain control of the means of producing wealth—means such as slaves, land, or capital. This group becomes the dominant class, and is able to use its economic power to influence the political process by which social inequality is maintained. The class or classes that do not own the means of production work for the dominant class, but are not paid the full value of the goods or services they produce. Instead, this surplus wealth is seized by the dominant class as "profit" for its own use. All history, Marx claimed, is the

history of class conflict—a conflict that will end only with the establishment of a communist society, in which the means of production are owned communally, not privately.[14]

Few Western sociologists accept Marx's view that all societies will evolve toward communism, but modern conflict theorists do make use of his basic insight that social inequality arises because of a conflict over the possession and enjoyment of scarce resources. Once one group achieves economic advantages for itself, it tends to pass these advantages down through the generations, and it uses its political power to preserve the class system. Essentially, poverty boils down to this: some people are poor because others are rich. Since the rich have greater political power than the poor, government policy tends to favor them. The rich therefore tend to remain rich, and the poor tend to remain poor. According to conflict theory, this situation will change significantly only if the balance of power shifts, so that the poor have greater political influence.

DEFINING POVERTY

When is someone poor? The question is not easy to answer, because there is no obvious dividing line between the poor and the nonpoor. Sociologists have tackled the problem by using one of two methods of defining poverty. The first is to establish it in terms of *absolute deprivation*, that is, a lack of basic necessities. The second is to establish it in terms of *relative deprivation*, that is, a lack of the living standards that are customary in the society. Each of these methods yields a rather different picture of poverty.

Absolute Deprivation

A definition of poverty in terms of absolute deprivation centers on the inability of a person or a household to provide even the basic necessities of life—that is, to "maintain minimum stan-

Considerations," *American Sociological Review,* 24 (1959), 772–782; and William Buckley, "Social Stratification and the Functional Theory of Social Differentiation," *American Sociological Review,* 23 (1958), 369–375.

[13]Peter M. Blau and Otis Dudley Duncan, *The American Occupational Structure* (New York: Wiley, 1967); Seymour Martin Lipset and Reinhard Bendix, *Social Mobility in Industrial Society* (Berkeley, Calif.: University of California Press, 1959).

[14]A useful selection of Marx's writings on class and related topics is T. B. Bottomore and Maximilian Rubel (eds.), *Karl Marx: Selected Writings in Sociology and Social Philosophy* (Baltimore: Penguin, 1964).

This Texas oil millionaire is one of the few super-rich Americans. Despite tax reforms of recent years, many of the wealthy are still able to use legal loopholes to escape much of their tax liability, with the result that they frequently pay a lower percentage of their income in taxes than middle- and even lower-income workers do.

dards of medical care, nourishment, housing, and clothing."[15] The poor, then, are those who are lacking these necessities. The "necessities of life" vary from time to time and place to place; in some parts of the world, a change of clothes is a luxury, not a necessity. In the United States, conceptions of what constitutes a "necessity" have been greatly enlarged through cultural change and economic growth.

Poverty in the United States is usually defined in terms of absolute deprivation. Most analysts simply set an annual income below which they believe an individual or family will inevitably be deprived of what are considered basic necessities of modern life. The point on the income scale that is selected as the poverty line naturally determines what proportion of the total popula-

tion is in poverty. In 1958, for example, John Kenneth Galbraith arbitrarily set the figure at $1,000 per year and on that basis considered that a tenth of the population was poor. In 1962 Leon Keyserling set the limit at $4,000 for an urban family of four and concluded that some 23 percent of the population were at a poverty level.[16] A more ingenious and less arbitrary method is used by the Social Security Administration to determine the official poverty line.

This method is based on a fact revealed by past surveys: that the average American family spends approximately a third of its income on food. The SSA devises an economy budget for the food needed to maintain adequate nutrition

[15]Kolko, *op. cit.*, p. 70.

[16]Leon Keyserling, *The Prevalent Monetary Policy and Its Consequences* (Washington, D.C.: U.S. Government Printing Office, 1964), pp. 6, 39.

under emergency or temporary conditions, and then trebles this cost to allow for all other expenditures. The amount is adjusted for differences in family size, sex of family head, place of residence, and other factors, and is revised annually to take account of inflation.

The cutoff point for a nonfarm family of four has risen from $2,937 in 1959 to $6,191 in 1977. The sum is scarcely a princely one, particularly for a family living under "emergency or temporary conditions" for months or years on end. There is, in fact, no guarantee that families living at the poverty line will actually achieve adequate nutrition. Not all households are as skilled at shopping as the federal experts might like to believe. There is strong evidence that the poor tend to pay more for inferior goods; often, for example, they cannot afford the larger "bargain-size" food packages, and have to make do with smaller and more expensive ones. As David Caplovitz notes, the poor

> tend to lack the information and training needed to be effective consumers in a bureaucratic society. Partly because of their limited education and partly because they are unfamiliar with urban culture, they are not apt to follow the announcements of sales in newspapers, to engage in comparative shopping, to know their way around the major department stores and bargain centers, to know how to evaluate the advice of salesmen.[17]

The poor, too, are sometimes inclined to buy items that might be considered frivolous by federal budget analysts, such as used cars or TV sets. Caplovitz calls these purchases "compensatory consumption"—an attempt to share some small part of the American dream, even at the cost of increasing real deprivation by diverting scarce budgetary resources. The federal calculations also take no account of sudden, unexpected emergency expenditures that may wreak havoc with a poor family's finances.

Just how marginal the SSA's poverty line of $6,191 is can be judged by comparing it with the U.S. Department of Labor's estimate of the minimum income necessary to maintain a decent standard of living. In 1977 the department reported that the minimum income necessary to support the average nonfarm family of four was about $9,700. And in comparison with the median family income in 1977—$16,009—the federal poverty line hardly seems a generous one.

In some respects, then, the federal government's method of measuring poverty provides an unrealistically low minimum income. The method does have the advantage, however, of determining with some precision the number of Americans who are unquestionably without the means to enjoy the basic necessities of life.

Relative Deprivation

A serious problem with an absolute definition of poverty is that it does not take into account that people are poor not only in relation to their needs but also in relation to other people who are not poor. This fact is most apparent at the international level, as economist Kenneth Boulding notes:

> In the twentieth century, the per capita income of the richest country is at least forty times that of the poorest . . . and the gulf widens between them all the time. It is this gulf which constitutes the main problem of poverty today. Persons regarded by a rich society as very poor would be regarded as relatively rich in a poor society. We see this illustrated in the fact that to the American, the migrant laborer is the poorest of the poor and constitutes in his mind a serious problem. To the Mexican villager, joining the ranks of our migrant workers is seen as a road to riches and as a way to lift the grinding burden of the poverty under which he labors. And yet Mexico is one of the richer of the poor countries. To hundreds of millions of Asians and Africans, the standard of life of the Mexican laborer would seem almost luxurious.[18]

The same principle applies at the national level. The poor in America can see the affluent

[17]David Caplovitz, *The Poor Pay More* (New York: Free Press, 1963), p. 14.

[18]Kenneth E. Boulding, "Reflections on Poverty," in *The Social Welfare Forum: 1961* (New York: Columbia University Press, 1961), pp. 45–58.

all around them, and they evaluate their poverty not only in relation to their basic needs but also in relation to the surfeit of wealth in the surrounding society.[19]

A definition of poverty in terms of relative deprivation centers on the economic inability of people to maintain the standards of living that are considered normal in the society in which they live. Under this concept of poverty, the poor are arbitrarily defined as some proportion of the lowest income earners in the society, say, the bottom tenth or the bottom fifth. Improvement in the status of the poor is then measured by how much their income rises in relation to the rest of the population. As we have seen, the data for the United States show no such trend: the proportion of income received by the lowest fifth has remained fairly stable since the end of World War II; and the very richest group has maintained almost the same share of the national income since the turn of the century.[20] Under a relative definition, poverty can never be completely eliminated while there is significant inequality in society.

The choice of whether to use absolute or relative criteria in defining poverty is largely a matter of personal judgment. Definitions of poverty are not simply a technical matter; they are influenced by the values of the analyst concerned.

WHO ARE THE POOR?

Who are the millions of Americans that the federal government defines as poor? Census Bureau data indicate that the poor are not randomly distributed throughout the population; instead, poverty is concentrated in certain population categories and geographic regions.

Fatherless Families. Poverty is particularly common among fatherless families. Of the more

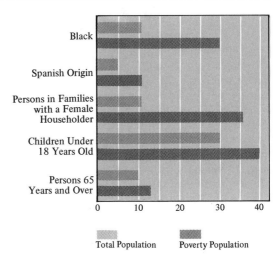

Total Population   Poverty Population

FIGURE 7.4 Groups overrepresented among the poverty population in 1976. Poverty does not occur randomly among the population: it is disproportionately likely to affect racial minorities, families with a female householder, children, and the aged. Clearly, most of these people are poor because of circumstances over which they have little or no control. (Bureau of the Census, *Current Population Reports*, Series P-60, no. 115, "Characteristics of the Population Below the Poverty Level: 1976" Washington, D.C.: U.S. Government Printing Office 1978.)

than 5 million American families that live in poverty, 2.5 million have a female householder, with no husband present. The proportion of poor persons living in these families is increasing, from 18 percent in 1959 to 36 percent in 1976.[21] The lack of, or the cost of, day-care facilities means that many of these mothers must stay at home to take care of their children. Unable to work, they have to rely on public assistance in the form of Aid to Families with Dependent Children (AFDC). In a great many cases they have no other source of income, and existence on welfare is the only way of life they know. Those mothers who are able to work are often poorly educated

[19]Herman Miller, "Changes in the Number and Composition of the Poor," in Edward C. Budd (ed.), *Inequality and Poverty* (New York: Norton, 1968), p. 165.

[20]*Ibid.*, p. 163; *Statistical Abstract of the United States, 1978, op. cit.,* p. 411.

[21]U.S. Bureau of the Census, *Current Population Reports*, series P-60, no. 115, "Characteristics of the Population Below the Poverty Level: 1976" (Washington, D.C.: U.S. Government Printing Office, 1978), pp. 1–4.

and can obtain only low-paying jobs; even better-educated women are generally paid less than men with equivalent qualifications. Nationwide, 37 percent of female-headed households live in poverty, compared with 6 percent of male-headed households. Black mothers, subjected to double discrimination in the job market on the grounds of both race and sex, are particularly vulnerable: almost three-fifths of the black poor live in families with a female householder, compared with about a quarter of poor whites.[22] (Sex discrimination is discussed in more detail in Chapter 9, "Sex Roles.")

Children. A high proportion of the poor— some 40 percent—are children under the age of eighteen. More than 10 million of America's children live in poverty, more than half of them in fatherless homes.[23] Children are particularly prone to poverty if they are members of large families: over 40 percent of all poor children are in families with five children or more. Some 8 million American children rely almost entirely on AFDC welfare payments for their basic necessities.

Minorities. Most poor people—about two-thirds of them—are white. But minority groups are disproportionately likely to suffer poverty. Although blacks constitute only 11.7 percent of the American population, they represent nearly a third of the poor: fewer than one white in ten is poor, compared with nearly one black in three.[24] The reasons for the extent of poverty among blacks are complex, but racial discrimination is at the root of the problem. Blacks have long been denied equality of opportunity in education and employment, and they tend to be concentrated in areas, such as the ghettos of decaying cities, where job prospects are poor. American Indians, too, suffer disproportionate poverty. About two-thirds of them live on or near some 300 tribal reservations, where most of the dwellings are substandard. About a third of Indian families live below the official poverty line. Another

minority that suffers a high incidence of poverty—24.7 percent—is the Mexican Americans, or Chicanos—particularly those who work as migrant laborers at seasonal jobs in agriculture.[25] (The problems of minorities are discussed in more detail in Chapter 8, "Race and Ethnic Relations.")

The Elderly. People aged sixty-five and older constitute about 13 percent of the poor.[26] The median income for old people is around $5,000, and more than half of them are living in poverty or in conditions bordering on poverty. The aged poor, too, often suffer isolation and loneliness: more than 40 percent of them are living alone or with unrelated individuals. Over 80 percent of these isolated poor people are women. The elderly poor have few resources, although their position has improved since 1972, when the government began to link increases in their Social Security pensions to rises in the cost of living. Even so, these pensions remain largely inadequate. Many depend primarily on Social Security or other public assistance, or else rely on their savings, which can easily be wiped out by medical or other unanticipated expenses. Older workers are discriminated against in the job market, and are sometimes obliged to retire even if they are physically healthy and mentally alert. The sudden transformation from being a responsible breadwinner to a dependent on public assistance can be traumatic, and the plight of the aged is made worse by the fact that our society, unlike other more traditional societies, offers no honored or useful role for the old. (These problems are discussed more fully in Chapter 11, "Aging.")

The Regional Poor. Poor families and individuals are concentrated in certain regions of the country, about 40 percent of them living outside metropolitan areas. There are pockets of rural poverty throughout the United States, in areas such as the Ozarks or Appalachia. The South, which has a relatively high proportion of rural

---

[22]*Ibid.,* pp. 4–5.

[23]*Ibid.*

[24]*Ibid.,* p. 5.

[25]*Ibid.,* p. 1.

[26]*Ibid.,* p. TK

This welfare mother of six children lives in a home without water or electricity. Yet her welfare payments are dismally low—largely because of the American attitude that incentives must be provided for the poor to go out to work.

residents, also has a disproportionate concentration of the poor—41 percent.[27] Many of the rural poor are living on small farms, where they are unable to compete with large-scale mechanized agriculture. Others are seasonal workers, employed only at certain times of the year. Others can find only low-paying jobs, or no jobs at all, for unemployment is higher in rural areas than in most urban areas. In many urban areas, however, there are also pockets of severe unemployment; this is particularly true of the decaying cities of the Northeast and Midwest, where the poor watch helplessly as jobs are lost to the more affluent suburbs that they cannot afford to enter. Some 38 percent of the poor now live in the central cities, compared to 27 percent two decades ago.[28]

The uneven distribution of poverty makes it clear that personal characteristics or failings cannot alone account for the fact of being poor. Many if not most of the poor are in poverty because they were born to the wrong parents, or in the wrong part of the country, or in the wrong racial or ethnic group.

THE SOURCES OF POVERTY

If lack of resources is not the origin of poverty in the United States, what is? There can be no

---

[27]*Ibid.*, p. 5.

[28]*Ibid.*, p. 7.

simple answer to such a question. The poor are not a homogeneous group, and there are many factors that can push a person or a family into poverty, such as unwise management of credit, illness, or unemployment. But while these factors may be satisfactory explanations for particular cases of poverty, they do not account for the persistence of poverty as a general feature of the society.[29] The sources of poverty lie much deeper—in imbalances of the economy, in cultural values and attitudes, and in the political realities of contemporary America.

Economic Factors

We have seen that poverty is not spread more or less at random throughout the population. It is concentrated in certain geographical areas of the country, especially in the central cities of older metropolitan areas and in the South and adjacent states. Closer examination of these and other "pockets" of poverty indicates that high unemployment rates and low average incomes usually go hand-in-hand. Persistent, localized unemployment of this kind is known as *structural unemployment*, because unlike other forms of unemployment (such as that occurring in a temporary recession), it is built into the very structure of the economy and is extremely difficult to correct.

Structural unemployment is usually the result of dislocations caused by economic change. The history of the mining industry in Appalachia, still one of the most impoverished areas of the country, illustrates this process. When the extraction of coal from the region started in earnest at the beginning of the century, much of the labor was done by hand. Thousands of agricultural workers, black and white, were lured off the cotton plantations and the farms by the relatively attractive wages offered by the mines. The industry grew rapidly and became the dominant employer in the area. The workers formed unions and gained significant wage increases. But after World War II, the industry began to install new and efficient machinery. This change caused

economic and social disorganization in the region. Large-scale automation threw thousands of miners out of work. By the early 1960s about 140,000 miners dug more coal than 700,000 were able to dig at the turn of the century.[30] Although the energy crisis of the 1970s has now created a greater demand for coal and thus improved the outlook for the region, there are still large pockets with a persistent high rate of structural unemployment and low average incomes.

Structural unemployment caused by social disorganization of this kind has followed in the wake of automation in many parts of the economy. Small farmers and agricultural laborers have been displaced by the introduction of tractors, threshers, mechanical pickers, and other technological devices that make it possible for food to move from field to supermarket virtually untouched by the human hand. One result of these innovations is that American agriculture has become the most productive in the world. Another result is that the farm labor force has declined rapidly, from 12 percent of the nation's workers in 1950 to less than 5 percent today. Automation in these and other parts of the economy not only throws people out of work; it also tends to reduce the number of unskilled jobs available, and there are many workers who are not equipped for any other jobs. The days of self-made people who start as unskilled laborers and work their way to the top are almost over. Education is the route for advancement, and the poorly educated are employable only in the dwindling number of unskilled or semiskilled jobs that remain. Automation, of course, opens up new jobs, but they typically require a higher level of skill than the tasks the machine has replaced, so retraining is often necessary. In some cases, displaced workers can migrate to another part of the country where employment opportunities are better. But people may be understandably reluctant to make the move, which is often to more expensive and inferior urban housing, away from their relatives and the community that they know.

Automation has not taken place so rapidly in

[29]See Robert Holman, *Poverty: Explanations of Social Deprivation* (New York: St. Martin's Press, 1978).

[30]Harry Caudill, "The Permanent Poor: The Lesson of Eastern Kentucky," *Atlantic Monthly*, 213 (June 1964), 50.

the less skilled service occupations, such as domestic cleaners, hospital attendants, dishwashers, or janitors, and the prospect of these jobs has lured many displaced rural workers to the cities. But unskilled service jobs usually pay very low wages and provide little security and no fringe benefits. Employment opportunities of this kind offer no solution to the problem of poverty; indeed, the last national census showed that over half of the heads of the families officially defined as poor were employed. Some 20 percent of all poor families were headed by a person who worked all year round but still failed to bring home enough wages to raise the family living standard above the poverty line. Another 33 percent of the poor-family breadwinners were able to find work only in part-time occupations or in seasonal jobs such as fruit-picking. Many of the poor are not so much unemployed as underemployed.

The cumulative effect of these changes in the structure of the economy is to trap an "underclass" of unemployed or unemployable people at the bottom of American society. S. M. Miller has argued that the United States is moving into a "dual economy," with a main economy characterized by high standards of living and stable employment, and a marginal economy characterized by low standards of living and unstable employment. The marginal economy is centered on low-level service trades and occupations, many of them offering only part-time or temporary work. The workers in the marginal economy are often drawn from minority groups and remain unemployed for long periods. The children of these workers tend to receive inferior educations, making it difficult for them to break out of the marginal economy into the more affluent main economy.[31]

Cultural Factors

Do the cultural values of the poor differ significantly from those of the rest of society, and if so,

is this a reason for the persistence of poverty? Many observers have noted a tendency for poverty to be passed down from one generation to the next. City welfare rolls all over the United States are registering the adult sons and daughters of welfare parents, which indicates that many of the poor are in some sense passing on their dependent status to their offspring. Some social scientists have argued that it is not only welfare status that is passed on, but also a wide range of other values that make it more difficult for the poor to enter the mainstream economy. These writers suggest that the poor are members of a distinctive subculture in society—a subculture, which, like all cultures, has its own values, norms, and roles. Children born into this subculture, they argue, are socialized into an acceptance of the subculture and its limited expectations, and are therefore very unlikely to break out of poverty.

The anthropologist Oscar Lewis is the most widely known advocate of this notion of a *culture of poverty*.[32] Drawing on his field studies of poor neighborhoods in different parts of the world, he asserts that there is a distinct culture or life style that transcends ethnic divisions, national boundaries, or regional differences. Those who live in the culture of poverty, Lewis holds, tend to be socially isolated. They have few organized ties to a group larger than their own family and are hostile to those institutions they perceive as belonging to the dominant classes. The general outlook of the poor is provincial and narrow. They have little sense of their own history and know only their own way of life and their neighbors'. They lack the knowledge and the political ideas that might enable them to recognize similarities between their own problems and those of their counterparts elsewhere. Their very isolation prevents them from seeing their private troubles as a part of a social problem that might be solved by collective social action.

Lewis argues that this culture, like any other, fosters the development of a distinctive set of psychological and personality traits:

[31]S. M. Miller, "Poverty, Race, and Politics," in Irving L. Horowitz (ed.), *The New Sociology: Essays in Social Science Theory in Honor of C. Wright Mills* (New York: Oxford University Press, 1964), pp. 298–299.

[32]Oscar Lewis, "The Culture of Poverty," *Scientific American*, 215 (October 1966), 19–25.

From an interview with Irene Martin, a welfare mother in Atlanta, Georgia.

. . .

We didn't hardly have enough to live on. My husband was trying to make some extra money when they caught him with 75 gallons of corn whiskey, and he went to prison. What they say is that colored people don't stay together, but I was determined I was going to keep my marriage, and when he was released, I got pregnant. With that baby I like to have a nervous breakdown. Baby weighed three pounds two ounces, had to go in an incubator for two months. We didn't have no money at all. Finance company took back all our furniture. No place to stay. Nothing to eat. I left my husband and went home to my mama.

Then I come to the project, went on welfare. I had this young baby, and I didn't know how I was going to feed him because he was in a cast with a broken foot and I couldn't get nobody to take care of him if I went out and worked. Only furniture I had at the start was two old chairs my grandmother give me, so I had to buy things. When a guy saw me about selling furniture, I explained I only had a little money, told him I could pay him something on the fifteenth of the month because the check on the first went toward the rent. He gave me this long business about not turning the account over to no finance company—but that is what he did. First time I was in a bind and missed a payment the man from a loan outfit said to come and renew the account with him. While I was there, he said I could borrow money to pay off all my other bills, so I wouldn't owe nobody but him. I didn't understand how these things work, and I signed up. I got $400 and used it to pay off everything I owed to everybody except him.

Next, I got the flu and pneumonia, and I missed a payment with the finance company. Here comes two big detectives. I am not sure they was detectives; they could have been from the company. They have a routine. One talks real nice; the other

talks to you like you are a dog. This gentleman called me a bitch, and he and I got to fighting. Everything my husband had ever done to me, everything every man had ever done, come up, and I took it all out on this man. When the police showed up, the only thing that kept me from going to jail was that I didn't have anybody to take care of the little boy. "She wasn't drinking, and she was in her own home," a policemen said. I still had to go to court, and that put something on my record.

Whites don't understand why colored feel they are defeated at every turn. I put in for a job at the post office and passed the examination. Then they said I couldn't be hired because I had this record. Everything goes in a bind. It was like I was losing my mind. When I got to hearing voices, I asked the county hospital for help, but a desk clerk explained to me that colored people don't get nervous breakdowns. That settled that. Made me feel real good. I even told it to whoever it was that I heard talking to me. Can't tell you how the voices stopped. They just did.

Can you see how all this starts? People don't have enough to live on. That's why a man don't represent anything but money to a colored woman. Nobody believes it, but this is actually what happen in the poor neighborhoods. Say, like you owe $80 and you only got $65. You know what a man is? He is a $15 deal. Take a case where you got $10 and the grocery bill is $9.95. You know good and well you have to have money for your light bill. Somebody come by and say, "I got $5," and you say, "My light bill is $5.35." You don't have time to be a lady; you have to grasp the money because you don't have enough to make ends meet.

. . .

Source: Earl and Miriam Selby, *Odyssey: Journey Through Black America* (New York: G. P. Putnam's Sons, 1971), pp. 119–120. Copyright 1971 by Earl and Miriam Selby.

The individual who grows up in this culture has a strong feeling of fatalism, helplessness, dependence and inferiority; a strong present-time orientation with relatively little disposition to defer gratification and plan for the future, and a high tolerance for psychological pathology of all kinds.[33]

---

[33]*Ibid.*, p. 23.

Lewis believes that the culture of poverty is not simply the result of low incomes: many so-called primitive peoples have low incomes but do not display these cultural characteristics. Rather, the culture of poverty emerges only after long periods of deprivation in highly stratified capitalist societies, where the poor are trapped into attitudes of despair. They evolve a culture that continues to have an existence independent of the economic situation that created it, and their own norms, values, and expectations serve to limit their options and prevent their escape.

Several social scientists have strongly criticized Lewis' theory. Charles Valentine, for example, suggests an alternative interpretation of Lewis' data.[34] It may be that the poor do not participate in major social institutions as fully as the better-off—but this is because they are effectively barred from full participation, not because of any culturally perpetuated life style. In fact, he points out, the poor participate far more than the affluent in some social institutions, such as the law courts or the welfare system. Any differences between the social participation of the poor and the rest of society are the result not of cultural characteristics but of the different opportunities that the social structure offers to different groups.

From the point of view of some other writers, any distinctive culture of the poor is the result, not the cause, of their continuing poverty, and their characteristics and attitudes are a realistic and understandable response to their situation.[35] The poor have to abandon the attitudes, values, and expectations of the predominantly middle-class society around them, because middle-class culture is irrelevant to their circumstances. For example, middle-class culture emphasizes "deferred gratification"—saving income and postponing pleasures today in order to reap greater benefits tomorrow. The culture of the poor, however, tends to emphasize "instant gratification"—spending one's money and enjoying what

one has while it lasts. Clearly, the value of deferred gratification makes no sense to someone who does not have money to save and is pessimistic about the future. Instant gratification is a rational response to this situation, but it is the result, not the cause of poverty. Indeed, empirical studies of impoverished ghetto residents show that if they do manage to get jobs that offer a stable income, they become "mainstreamers," concerned about such middle-class values as deferred gratification and respectability.[36]

In a powerful critique, William Ryan charges that the culture-of-poverty theory is simply a classic case of "blaming the victim." Instead of attributing poverty to the social system that allows poverty to persist, he claims, the theory encourages us to focus instead on the faults of the poor. As a result, we can conveniently escape any responsibility for changing the system. The problem of the impoverished, Ryan states bluntly, is not that there is something wrong with their culture. It is that they do not have enough money.[37]

The importance of cultural factors in the persistence of poverty is still an unsettled issue. Cultural factors alone, however, cannot account for poverty, because the poor population is actually a fairly fluid one, with as many as 10 million people moving above or below the poverty line each year.[38] This means that at least some people living in the alleged culture of poverty do manage to escape it, and that many others who have not experienced this culture nevertheless become poor.

Political Factors

One reason for the persistence of poverty in the United States is the acquiescence of Congress

---

[34]Charles A. Valentine, *Culture and Poverty: A Critique and Counter-Proposals* (Chicago: University of Chicago Press, 1968).

[35]See Eleanor Leacock (ed.), *The Culture of Poverty: A Critique* (New York: Simon and Schuster, 1971).

[36]See Elliot Liebow, *Tally's Corner: A Study of Negro Street-corner Men* (Boston: Little, Brown, 1967); Ulf Hannertz, *Soulside: An Inquiry into Ghetto Culture and Community* (New York: Columbia University Press, 1969); Eleanor Leacock (ed.), *op. cit.*

[37]William Ryan, *Blaming the Victim*, rev. ed. (New York: Vintage, 1976).

[38]David E. Rosenbaum, "Officials Are Up Against the Myths of Welfare," *New York Times*, May 22, 1977, p. E.3.

Is this child being reared in a "culture" of poverty? Some social scientists believe that the children of the chronically poor internalize attitudes of resignation and hopelessness which make it even more difficult for them to escape from poverty. Others regard this argument as a form of "blaming the victim" for faults that lie not in the individual, but in the society at large.

and other political institutions, which are under constant pressure from many interest groups to resist changes that might lead to a redistribution of wealth and income in favor of the poor. As Herbert Gans points out, poverty is useful and functional to society in several respects. The existence of an underprivileged, impoverished section of the community serves to maintain the stability of the rest of society and the privileges of the other classes. According to Gans, some of these functions include the following:

1. *Poverty ensures that "dirty" work will get done.* If there were no poor people willing to scrub floors and clean bedpans, "dirty" work would have to be rewarded with incomes superior to that of "clean" work before anyone would touch it.
2. *Poverty creates jobs for some of the nonpoor.* A substantial part of the population holds jobs that involve "servicing" the poor—police, social work-

ers, welfare investigators, pawnbrokers, and the like.
3. *Poverty facilitates the life style of the affluent.* The existence of poverty guarantees a supply of gardeners, cooks, domestic cleaners, and similar workers who perform various chores and thus free the upper classes to pursue other activities, including frivolous ones.
4. *Poverty provides a market for inferior goods and services.* Poor people buy the goods and services that others do not want: day-old bread, secondhand autos, deteriorating housing, or the advice of incompetent doctors and lawyers.
5. *Poverty guarantees the status of the nonpoor.* In a hierarchical society someone has to be at the bottom, and the existence of an underprivileged class confirms the superior status of those above. Just as poverty makes the poor feel relatively deprived, so it makes the nonpoor feel relatively advantaged.
6. *Poverty legitimizes American values.* The poor, by their very existence, confirm the desirability of the

qualities they are supposed to lack. As Gans points out, "to justify the desirability of hard work, thrift, honesty, and monogamy, for example, the defenders of these norms must be able to find people who can be accused of being lazy, spendthrift, dishonest, and promiscuous."

7. *Poverty provides a group that can be made to absorb the political and economic costs of change.* The poor, for example, bear the brunt of the unemployment that results from automation; or when new highways have to be constructed, these highways are routed through and devastate the neighborhoods of the poor rather than the wealthy.[39]

The very existence of poverty thus lends stability to the norms and institutional arrangements of the entire society. If poverty were to be eliminated, various other interest groups would suffer. Gans stresses, however, that many of the functions of poverty are not socially necessary, even if they are socially convenient in some respects, and many could be fulfilled in ways that would not require the existence of poverty. He also points out that poverty is dysfunctional as well. It has obvious dysfunctions for the poor, it creates a potential conflict in society, and it causes a drain on social resources that could be productively used in other ways.

Many political and economic interests oppose measures that might improve the position of the poor through income redistribution. As we saw in Chapter 6 ("Government and Corporations"), the more affluent corporate and private interest groups have a disproportionate influence in government policy-making. Combining a conflict approach with his functionalist analysis to give a fuller view of the problem, Gans emphasizes that

legislation in America tends to favor the interests of the businessman, not the consumers, even though the latter are a vast majority; of landlords, not tenants; of doctors, not patients. Only organized interest groups have the specific concerns and the time, staff, and money to bring their demands before government officials. . . .

The poor are powerless because they are a minority of the population, are not organized politically, are often difficult to organize, and are not even a homogeneous group with similar interests that could be organized into a single pressure group. . . . Given the antagonism toward them on the part of many Americans, any programs that would provide them with significant gains are likely to be voted down by a majority. Legislative proposals for a massive anti-poverty effort . . . have always run into concerted and united opposition in Washington.[40]

Given the facts of the distribution of power in the United States and the nature of our economic system, the persistence of poverty becomes understandable. But let us look more closely at another factor that Gans mentions in the quotation above—the "antagonism" that many Americans have toward the poor.

POVERTY AND AMERICAN VALUES

It has been calculated that it would require about $16.7 billion a year to raise the income of all American families and unrelated individuals above the poverty line.[41] That sum represents less than a seventh of our annual expenditure on defense and less than 2 percent of our gross national product. An attempt to eradicate poverty would have many social costs—including, perhaps, higher taxes and a great deal of controversy and conflict—but the elimination of poverty is well within our means. Nevertheless, we make little attempt to achieve this goal; in fact, the United States spends about half as much of its national income on welfare as the generally less affluent countries of Western Europe.[42] Why do Americans deplore the very existence of poverty, yet do so little to improve the living standards of the poor?

The answer lies in the traditional values of American culture, which have always encouraged a negative attitude to the poor. In colonial

---

[39]Herbert J. Gans, "The Uses of Poverty: The Poor Pay All," *Social Policy*, 2 (July–August 1971), 21–23.

[40]Herbert J. Gans, *More Equality* (New York: Pantheon, 1968), pp. 133–135.

[41]*Current Population Reports, op. cit.*, p. 8.

[42]Robert L. Heilbroner, "Benign Neglect in the United States," *Trans-action*, 7 (October 1970), 15–22.

Ben Frazier, a miner all his life in the hills of Kentucky, describes his world, his job and his family.

. . .

You hear people say we should all be grateful for the progress we've made—*some* of us have made. My mother and father never expected anything especially good to happen. They were born up a creek, and they died up there. They never went to a doctor, and they never went over to Pineville to ask for welfare or help of any kind. They never had food stamps, and no one gave us lunches paid for by the government. The teacher would bring us a box of crackers, and we'd bring a little something, or if there was nothing, we'd just not go to school at all. In the winter it's the worst time—the weather, and the food starts running out—so we'd stay away from school then. Come to think of it, we'd hibernate, just like the animals do. We'd go into the cabin and stay there. My daddy would have the wood stored up, and we'd use it, log after log. I recall once there was a warm spell, near Christmastime, and my brother and me, we went out and walked down the creek, and all we could see was a cabin and the smoke coming out, rising up to the trees and the sky, and then another cabin, and the same smoke—but not a person was there, no one in sight. We came back and told our mother that, and she said something I've never forgotten, nor will I. She said, 'Yes, it's wintertime, and everyone in the creek is hiding, and it took you kids to stop and figure out that the weather is warm and good for going outside.'

Then I asked her why we were all hiding, and that's what she said that sticks in my mind: 'Son,

we're hiding because if we don't we'll die. We'll freeze to death, or we'll starve to death, because we only have enough food to fuel a quiet body, and no more, and maybe not even that much.' She wasn't being too sad, and she wasn't feeling sorry for herself; she never cried, and that's what you should know about people around here—no matter how bad off they are, they don't start feeling sorry for themselves. That goes for miners, and it goes for people up the creeks or the hollows. I don't mean we don't have our faults here; we do. Instead of weeping over life, we go and drink, a lot of us do, and we take to fighting and feuding. Sometimes a man will get real silent, or he won't have anything to say for so long that it worries you, or he'll start talking strange, about how his legs won't work, or his arms, and there's something crawling up his spine. But it's hard to figure out what's wrong with people here; there's no doctor for most of them, and they don't get the right food, and where they live, it's either too cold or else it gets too hot and the flies and mosquitoes practically feed off your skin. So, it's natural that you'd find people getting themselves upset and not feeling right some of the time. But even so, we don't like to cry over ourselves, not around here, and we don't like to go begging—that's the worst thing in the world to do, worse than anything.

"My children have all left here, left the county—and I'm as happy as can be about that, too. My son Ben, he's up in Dayton, learning to be an engineer. I have a boy who's a teacher over near Asheville. I have a girl married to a teacher over in Knoxville. She learned to be a teacher, too. I told my sons never even to think about going down to

America, with its strong Puritan ethic, the poor were believed to be responsible for their own plight. Poverty was seen almost as a sign of disgrace; to be unemployed was proof of one's laziness. American values have historically extolled the ethic of hard work, self-reliance, and financial independence, and those who seek public assistance have been regarded as shiftless, idle, even immoral.

When a group of people have interests to defend, they tend to develop an *ideology*—a set of ideas and beliefs that justifies the perceived interests of those who hold it. Because the most powerful group in a society is able to impose its ideology on the society as a whole, the dominant ideology in any society will be one that justifies the interests of the dominant group. Thus, in any unequal society, there is always a dominant ideology that legitimizes the inequality by making it seem right, proper, and morally acceptable. If there is racial inequality, for example, there will be a racist ideology that defines the domi-

those mines. I told them if they once even came near the entrance, I'd be standing there, and they should expect me. They'd have to fight me and knock me out, kill me I said, before they could get in. I guess they heard me! If I was to tell you the truth, it would be that I would have been killed at the sight of them going down, even if they never put a hand on me. It's Hell being a miner, that's what. People will never know, because they never see. And us, the ones who *do* know, we won't admit the truth, except to each other, and even then we usually don't. What's the point? The more you talk, the worse you feel, and the harder it is to keep going, day after day. They near die down there, our men, but they try to live; and that's all they want out of life, actually: a chance to stay alive and have a little money in their pockets. If you ask me, a lot of the way miners act can be explained when you stop and think that they are people who are walking on thin ice every second, and they could drown. When you're almost drowning, you don't have time to feel sorry for yourself and you don't talk too much and you go about your business. And if you *like* it here, besides—not in the mine, but in the county, where you've grown up—then you feel even more that it's best to keep your mouth shut and keep from drowning, and then you won't have to go and leave here, because *that's* like drowning, too. You see?

. . .

Source: Robert Coles. *Migrants, Sharecroppers, Mountaineers*, vol. II of *Children of Crisis* (Boston: Atlantic Monthly Press, 1971), pp. 336–339. Copyright 1967, 1968, 1969, 1971 by Robert Coles.

that people are born into a particular caste and must remain in it all their lives.

Somewhat surprisingly, perhaps, members of subordinate groups tend to accept the ideology of the dominant group. Marx called their acceptance of an ideology that runs counter to their interests "false consciousness," or a subjective view of one's situation that does not accord with the objective facts. Thus, slaves often seem to have believed that they were fit only to be slaves; women have tended throughout history to believe that they are indeed inferior; feudal peasants seem to have accepted unquestioningly the right of the nobility to rule them; low-caste Indians left the caste system unchallenged for thousands of years.

The ideology that legitimizes social inequality in the United States holds that everybody has an equal chance to get rich by working hard, and that those who do not succeed have only themselves to blame.[43] Inequality is justified as a means of providing incentives for people to work and rewards for those who do, and our folklore is rich in legends of those who made it from rags to riches or from the log cabin to the White House. In fact, these cases are exceptional. In the United States as in other countries, most peoples' chances in life are largely determined by the class into which they are born. A person born into the American working class, for example, has only about one chance in ten of entering the professional elite,[44] whereas the children of professional fathers are nearly five times as likely to become professionals as would be expected with completely open competition.[45] Despite these facts, most Americans—including even many of

nant group as superior to any others, and therefore better suited to receive social rewards. If there is inequality between the sexes, there will be a sexist ideology that defines one gender as superior to the other, and therefore entitled to superior status. In the late feudal system of Europe, the power and wealth of the nobility were justified by the belief that people were, through God's will, born into a particular "station in life." Similarly, the caste system in India was justified by the Hindu religion, which holds

[43]See Joan Huber and William Form, *Income and Ideology* (New York: Free Press, 1973); Lee Rainwater, *What Money Buys: Inequality and the Social Meanings of Income* (New York: Basic Books, 1974).

[44]Peter Blau and Otis Dudley Duncan, *The American Occupational Structure* (New York: Wiley, 1967); Thomas G. Fox and S. M. Miller, "Inter-Country Variations: Occupational Stratification and Mobility," *Studies in Comparative International Development*, 1 (1965), 3–10.

[45]Elton F. Jackson and Harry J. Crockett, "Occupational Mobility in the United States: A Point Estimate and a Trend Comparison," *American Sociological Review*, 24 (1964), 5–15.

the poor—seem to accept the ideology that justifies economic inequality.

The effect of this ideology has been to make American society extremely reluctant to aid the impoverished. Until 1935, private charities and some local and state governments assumed the responsibility for welfare. In the depression years these haphazard arrangements broke down completely under the burden of some 40 million poor people, and in the face of bitter opposition, the Social Security system was established. But the system was and is based on one overriding principle: financial relief is intentionally designed to fall short of adequate assistance in order to provide the cherished motive to work. Apart from the food-stamp program and income supplements to the old, the blind, and the disabled, little attempt is made to place an income floor under those who are unable to earn enough—that is, to supplement low wages so that they meet some minimum income. Instead, those who work but do not earn enough to make a decent living are left in poverty; those who for various reasons do not work are treated as if they were lazy but would work if given the proper incentives. President Nixon expressed the dominant attitude well when, speaking of welfare, he declared:

> I advocate a system that will encourage people to take work, and that means whatever work is available. If a job puts bread on the table, if it gives you the satisfaction of providing for your children and lets you look everyone else in the eye, I don't think that it is menial.[46]

So strong are the traditional attitudes against welfare "handouts" to the poor that those who receive them suffer an immediate loss of social status and often of personal pride. Americans tend to esteem the rich because of their wealth (even if they have not earned it) but to look down on the poor (even if they are not responsible for their poverty). Attempts to provide adequate federal assistance to the poor always

run into opposition on the ground that increased benefits will undermine the work ethic (one proposed federal family-assistance plan was entitled "workfare" by its advocates in an attempt to make it more acceptable to the public). Opposition comes not only from the middle and upper middle classes in American society but also from working-class citizens who are managing, often with great effort, to remain a few income dollars away from the welfare rolls and who deeply resent the use of their taxes to support supposed chiselers who choose not to work.

Let us examine how the American work ideology affects public assistance for the poor—and for the rich.

Public Assistance for the Poor

Since the 1930s the American public assistance system has simply just grown; new programs have been added to existing ones without any overall plan. Between 1968 and 1977, welfare payments rose from $4.2 billion to $38 billion. At present there are more than fifty major federal programs that provide cash or services to people with low incomes, and states and local authorities offer many other programs. These various programs are administered by some 4,000 federal and 342,000 state and local officials.[47] The system is cumbersome and often irrational. A person might be eligible for some form of public assistance in one state but ineligible in another. Some states will make AFDC payments to mothers only if the father is absent; others will do so even if he is a member of the household. The amount of the payments under various programs varies greatly from state to state. In some states people living on welfare may have incomes marginally above the poverty line; in others they will be far below it.

The various public assistance programs can be divided into three main categories. First, there are the insurance programs, such as Social Security and unemployment compensation, which benefit certain categories of Americans like the

---

[46]Remarks of the President at the Republican Governors' Conference, Office of the White House Press Secretary, Washington, D.C., April 19, 1971.

[47]*U.S. News and World Report*, August 8, 1977.

Many of the poor are locked into poverty because they are old, handicapped, live in depressed rural areas, or are members of minority groups that suffer job discrimination.

retired or those who have lost their jobs after a period of steady employment. Second, there are programs that offer assistance to low-income people (working or unemployed) in the form of services and other nonmonetary aid, such as housing, Medicaid, and food stamps. Third, there are outright cash benefits such as AFDC or Supplemental Security Income (SSI) for the aged, the blind, and the totally disabled.

It is the latter two categories, and particularly the AFDC program, that arouse the greatest controversy. Because the recipients of these programs have made no contribution to the funds from which they are paid, their claims tend to be regarded as less legitimate than claims under the first category. Ironically, the considerable stigma

often attached to being a welfare recipient (many Americans think of a person living on welfare as being virtually a deviant) works against the effectiveness of these programs. A high proportion of those entitled to benefits under welfare programs fail to claim them, in some cases because they are unaware that the programs exist, but in many cases because they are too proud to receive income from these sources. About a third of those entitled to food stamps, for example, do not claim them. One survey in 1974 found that some 275,000 aged people in New York City were eligible for Supplementary Security Income, but only 70,000 received it—although more than 100,000 of these old people lived on less than $1,000 a year, half of which was spent on rent.[48]

The degree to which Americans regard welfare recipients as chiselers and freeloaders—as people who, too lazy to work, prefer to spend their time lounging about, drinking beer, and breeding children—has been reflected in a number of polls. In 1964, when the War on Poverty was declared and when public awareness of the problem was at its height, a Gallup poll asked, "In your opinion, which is more often to blame if a person is poor—lack of effort on his own part, or circumstances beyond his control?" In all, 33 percent of the respondents felt that lack of effort was responsible, 29 percent felt that circumstances were responsible, 32 percent felt that both factors had equal influence, and 6 percent voiced no opinion. A 1972 Harris poll found that nearly nine out of ten Americans favored the idea of "making people on welfare go to work."[49] In 1978 a New York Times–CBS News poll found that a substantial part of the adult population—41 percent—was willing to "cut welfare and social services a lot." Yet these attitudes bear no relation to the reality of the American welfare system: the welfare rolls are overwhelmingly composed of children, retired and disabled people, and others who cannot work for a living at

[48]*New York Post* (May 29, 1974).

[49]Attitudes to the poor are fully discussed in Joe Feagin, *Subordinating the Poor: Welfare and American Beliefs* (Englewood Cliffs, N.J.: Prentice-Hall, 1975).

all. The Department of Health, Education, and Welfare has estimated that only 2 percent of welfare recipients are able-bodied unemployed males—and most of them are between the ages of 60 and 64 and must sign up for work or training in order to retain welfare payments.[50] Yet—such are our values as a nation—the welfare system remains based on the notion that the poor must have an incentive to work and thus penalizes all the poor, irrespective of their circumstances. As the accompanying boxed insert shows, the belief that most welfare recipients could work if they wanted to is only one of several unfounded myths.

"Public Assistance" for the Rich

Conflict theory would predict that the rich, being more powerful than the poor, would benefit more from public assistance—and this is precisely what we find.

The United States pays out vastly greater sums in welfare to the nonpoor than to the poor. This fact escapes notice because these payments are not called "welfare," although their effect— to increase income—is identical. As Dale Tussing points out, the United States has a "dual welfare system":

Two welfare systems exist simultaneously in this country. One is well known. It is explicit, poorly funded, stigmatized and stigmatizing, and is directed at the poor. The other, practically unknown, is implicit, literally invisible, is nonstigmatized and nonstigmatizing, and provides vast but unacknowledged benefits for the nonpoor. . . . Our welfare systems do not distribute benefits on the basis of need. Rather, they distribute benefits on the basis of legitimacy. Poor people are viewed as less legitimate than non-poor people. . . . By and large, welfare programs for the poor are obvious, open and clearly labeled, and those for the non-poor are either concealed (as in tax laws, for instance) and ill understood, or are clothed in protective language. . . . Whether or

not a person is poor can often be determined by the names of his welfare programs. If his programs are called "relief," "welfare," "assistance," "charity" or the like, he is surely poor; but if they are called "parity," "insurance," "compensation" or "compulsory saving," he is surely a member of the large majority of non-poor persons who do not even think of themselves as receiving welfare payments.[51]

The most obvious of these income supplements to the nonpoor are the various loopholes in a tax system that President Carter has called "a disgrace to the human race." In theory the American tax system is progressive—that is, it takes away progressively more in tax as income increases. In fact, however, the poor have at least as heavy a tax burden as the rich.[52] One reason is that indirect taxes, such as a sales tax, hit the poor proportionately harder than the rich. Both pay the same amount of tax on the same purchase, but the tax represents a much greater percentage of the poor person's income. The second reason is that the wealthy are able to take advantage of a system that Philip Stern has called "Uncle Sam's welfare program for the rich."

Stern investigated tax data over several years and found, for example, that in 1968 some 381 people with incomes of over $100,000 a year (21 of whom had incomes of over $1 million a year) paid no taxes whatever—quite legally.[53] In 1970 he found that 112 persons with incomes in excess of $200,000 a year managed to pay no taxes at all. In 1976 nearly 250 people with incomes above $200,000, and 5 with incomes above $1 million, did not contribute a cent in taxes.[54] Stern points out that if the tax relief obtained by those with incomes of over $1 million a year were renamed "welfare," there would be a public outcry, for the

---

[50]U.S. Department of Health, Education, and Welfare, *Welfare: Myths vs. Facts* (Washington, D.C.: U.S. Government Printing Office, 1972); Walter R. Mears, "Ending the Welfare Myths," *New York Post*, May 27, 1977, p. 36.

[51]A. Dale Tussing, "The Dual Welfare System," *Society*, 11 (January–February 1974), 50–57.
[52]Herbert J. Gans, "The New Egalitarianism," *Saturday Review*, May 6, 1972, p. 43.
[53]Philip M. Stern, "How 381 Super-Rich Americans Managed Not to Pay a Cent in Taxes Last Year," *New York Times Magazine*, April 13, 1969, p. 30.
[54]*New York Times*, May 6, 1976, p. 19.

WELFARE: MYTHS VS. FACTS

MYTH: Welfare families are loaded with kids, and have more children just to get more money.

FACT: More than half of welfare families have either one or two children. The payment for an additional child is insufficient to cover the costs of rearing it.

MYTH: Most welfare families are black.

FACT: There are far more white than black welfare families: over two-thirds of poor people are white.

MYTH: Why work, when you can live it up on welfare?

FACT: Welfare payments in nearly all states are below the poverty line—in other words, less than the minimum necessary under "emergency or temporary conditions."

MYTH: Most welfare children are illegitimate.

FACT: Nearly 70 percent of welfare children are legitimate.

MYTH: Once on welfare, always on welfare.

FACT: Half the families on welfare have been receiving it for less than 21 months. About ten million people move above the poverty line each year, while a roughly equivalent number sink below it.

MYTH: Welfare people are cheats.

FACT: All welfare claims are checked for possible fraud, but less than half of 1 percent are referred for prosecution for fraud. Most overpayments result from errors by the agency making the payment, not from false claims by the applicants. Tax fraud, on the other hand, costs the nation vastly greater sums, but only one tax return in 50 is checked for possible fraud.

MYTH: The welfare rolls are full of able-bodied loafers.

FACT: Only 2 percent of welfare recipients are able-bodied unemployed males. Many of these are old, poorly educated, or live in areas where jobs are scarce. They are required to sign up for work or job training in order to get benefits.

MYTH: If people were willing to work, they wouldn't be poor.

FACT: More than half of the heads of poor families are working. Millions of people work full-time year-round and still earn incomes below the poverty line. Others cannot find jobs because no jobs are available. At some periods in the seventies, as many as 9 percent of people actively looking for jobs remained unemployed—among minority teenagers actively looking for jobs in some cities, more than 50 percent.

Source: Adapted from *Welfare: Myths vs. Facts* [pamphlet], (U.S. Department of Health, Education, and Welfare. Washington, D.C.: U.S. Government Printing Office, 1972.); Walter R. Mears, "Ending the Welfare Myths," *New York Post*, May 27, 1977, p. 36; David E. Rosenbaum, "Officials Are Up Against the Myths of Welfare," *New York Times*, May 22, 1977, p. E.3.

savings amounted to an average of $720,000 for each of these super-rich citizens, or a total of $2.2 billion a year. It makes little difference whether these sums are called "welfare" or "tax relief"; in either case, the U.S. Treasury was $2.2 billion poorer, and the rest of the taxpayers had to pay an additional $2.2 billion to make up the difference. In contrast, the average tax relief for the poorest section of the community—those earning less than $3,000 a year—was $16. In 1976 Congress finally enacted legislation to plug some of the more notorious tax loopholes, but many still remain. The passage of the tax-reform law has been followed by a flurry of conferences of accountants and tax lawyers who scrutinize the new laws for loopholes for their wealthy clients.

The same pattern of concealed preferential payments to the nonpoor is repeated in many other areas. For example, homeowners can deduct from their taxable income the costs of mortgage interest and local property taxes. In effect, these deductions are a "rent supplement" to those who are rich enough to own their homes.

According to U.S. Treasury figures, some 85 percent of the benefits of this government "handout" goes to taxpayers with incomes above $10,000, while less than .01 percent goes to those with incomes below $3,000. The Treasury calls these and other forms of government handouts "tax expenditures"—that is, tax money that is "spent" before it is even collected. In 1976, groups with incomes below $10,000 received 19 percent of the tax expenditures; those with incomes between $10,000 and $50,000 received 40 percent; and those with incomes in excess of $50,000 received 41 percent of the benefits.[55] The political system favors those with economic power rather than those without it.

CONFRONTING THE PROBLEM

There is no single cause of poverty in the United States, and similarly there is no single solution to the problem. Efforts to alleviate and perhaps ultimately eliminate poverty can therefore be made on a number of different fronts.

Eliminating Discrimination. Discrimination against ethnic minorities, women, and older people underlies much of the poverty in America today. Because discriminatory practices are pervasive in our society, they will be fully eradicated only with great difficulty and over a long period of time. Nevertheless, there is an "equality revolution" abroad in the United States, with blacks, women, consumers, students, Native Americans, Chicanos, and others demanding an end to established hierarchies, old prejudices, and artificially limited opportunities. Government cannot legislate directly for changes in attitudes, but it can prevent people from translating these attitudes into practice. Public attitudes tend to follow changes in the law, however, so the legal initiatives may indirectly influence attitudes as well as practices. Already, federal and state governments have enacted many statutes to protect the interests of groups that have suffered discrimination in the past, but in every case it has taken strong pressure from organized social movements to bring about government action.

Creating Job Opportunities. The relationship between poverty and economic change is complex, but properly directed economic growth can bring about an expansion of jobs and a reduction in poverty. A situation of full employment, in which there is a high demand for labor, is a powerful solvent of discriminatory barriers. Groups that are impoverished largely as a result of discrimination, such as women or blacks, are especially benefited in an expanding economy, just as they are particularly penalized in times of recession. Job opportunities can be expanded in various ways. One method is to cut taxes, which gives people more money to spend, raises demand, and so stimulates production. Another method is to cut interest rates, which encourages borrowing and thus allows people to spend more on goods and services. Measures such as these can be highly effective, as illustrated by President Kennedy's tax cuts which stimulated a period of great prosperity in the early 1960s. But these measures can also be dangerous because increased demand for goods and services can generate inflation. Economic change therefore has to be very carefully guided if it is to avoid the twin perils of unemployment and inflation.

There are a number of other complexities involved, as well. For one thing, stimulating an economy does not necessarily create more jobs. If business invests its money in more sophisticated equipment rather than in a large work force, economic advance might not lead to a corresponding increase in jobs. Moreover, economic change may bypass some rural and inner-city areas that are permanently depressed. For these impoverished areas, more specific programs are needed. One such measure was the Area Redevelopment Administration (ARA). Founded in 1961, this federal agency was supposed to supply long-term loans to attract private industry to

---

[55]Murry L. Weidenbaum, "In Defense of Tax Loopholes," *New York Times,* June 26, 1977.

depressed areas and thereby create jobs. But the ARA's useful years were few; in the conflict over how the funds were to be spent it quickly became a "pork barrel," raided by many members of Congress to aid their own not-so-depressed areas and thus win favor with local voters. Many other countries deal with depressed areas by offering tax incentives to industries to locate in them and by establishing government-supported enterprises in persistent pockets of poverty.

Training and Education. In an industrial society in which jobs are increasingly specialized, there is less and less opportunity for the unskilled laborer, and lack of education and training severely restricts occupational mobility. In the United States the poorly educated citizen who lacks specific job training is at a severe disadvantage and is likely to join the ranks of the impoverished. One strategy that can be used to combat poverty, therefore, is intensive training designed to upgrade the skills of people who might otherwise be unemployable. Congress has already enacted a number of programs to provide financial support for training of this kind, notably the Manpower Retraining and Development Act, the Economic Oportunity Act, and the Work Incentive Program. There has been much criticism of these programs, however, on the grounds that they are poorly funded, do not offer training in a sufficiently wide range of skills, and fail to reach many of those who would most benefit from them.

It is vitally important, too, that jobs be available for those who have trained or retrained for them. Many unemployed workers retrained for new jobs during the 1970s, only to find their efforts wasted: the recessions had stripped so many job opportunities from the economy that there was still no work for them. In times of economic boom the newly skilled worker is at an advantage. In times of recession, job training without deliberate attempts to create jobs can lead to frustration and bitterness.

Reform of the Welfare System. The American welfare system is cumbersome, inefficient, and often unfair. Its reform is essential if the United

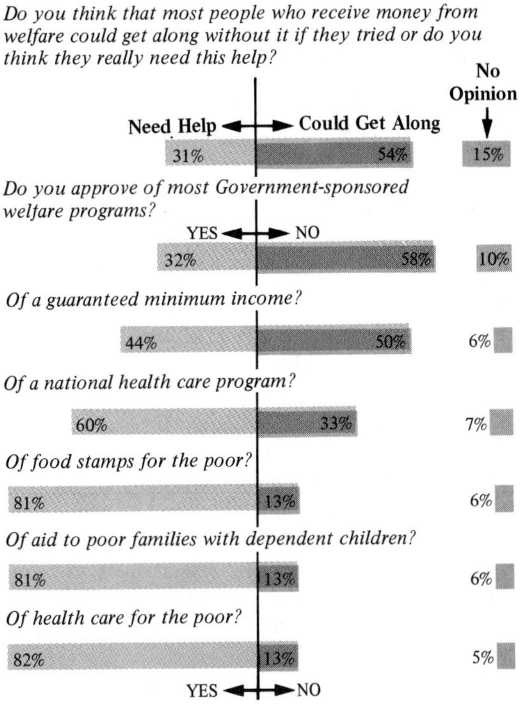

FIGURE 7.5 **Attitudes toward welfare programs.** The findings of this opinion poll reveal a curious inconsistency in public attitudes toward welfare: although most Americans believe that the poor can get along without welfare and claim to oppose government welfare programs, they are overwhelmingly in favor of specific programs such as food stamps or AFDC. (There is less enthusiasm for the untried guaranteed minimum income, however.) It seems that Americans disapprove of welfare in the abstract, but are reluctant to see individuals suffer through the abolition of specific programs. (New York Times/CBS News Poll, *New York Times*, 3 August, 1977.)

States is to mount an effective campaign against poverty. President Carter had made reform one of the major goals of his administration, but the task is likely to take years. Almost everyone agrees that the existing system must be scrapped, but there is little agreement on what should replace it.

Some general goals can be outlined, however. The new welfare system should provide an adequate income for those who, for one reason or another, are unable to earn it themselves. It should provide incentives for those who are able to work, and for whom jobs are available, to join the labor force. It should prevent fraud and abuse, not only by welfare recipients but also by the providers of services, such as the private nursing homes and physicians who have defrauded Medicaid of millions of dollars in the past. It should encourage families to stay together rather than penalize households with a father present. It should provide the same benefits to people in the same circumstances. Finally, it should be as efficient and inexpensive to operate as possible.

Redistribution of Wealth and Income. Poverty cannot be eliminated simply by the use of programs designed to alleviate its symptoms. It is an inevitable result of the inequality in American society and is likely to persist until there is some significant redistribution of wealth and income. The more radical socialist proposals for the takeover of large corporations and large personal fortunes are unlikely to find much favor because of our deeply ingrained belief in the virtues of free enterprise.[56] But there are a number of intermediate measures that could reduce some of the poverty stemming from our institutionalized inequality. Further tax reform could plug many of the remaining loopholes by which the wealthy escape the payment of millions of dollars each year. Another possibility would be to increase the amount of direct welfare payments and to allocate more tax money to services for the poor: low-cost housing, job retraining, medical clinics, education, school lunches, food stamps, and the like. Another possibility, practiced in virtually all the other industrialized countries of the West, is to provide a family with cash benefits for each child. In most countries these benefits are available to rich and poor families alike, but, of course, they represent a greater proportion of a poor family's income. But whatever methods are employed,

some redistribution of wealth and income seems necessary. The continuing existence of poverty in the midst of material abundance seems morally unjustifiable and is a poor international advertisement for the American system.

Negative Income Tax. An idea that has been widely debated in recent years is that of the "negative income tax." The proposal is a simple one: persons earning above a certain amount would pay income tax; persons earning below that amount would receive a grant—the negative tax—to bring their income up to the fixed level. The level would be reviewed from time to time, but would always be enough to sustain an individual or family at a level somewhat above the poverty line. The main advantage of the system is that it directly aids all of the poor, irrespective of the occupational, regional, age, or other category they belong to. The system could replace virtually all existing programs and would also apply to those of the poor who are not covered by any of these programs.

Naturally, such a system would involve many administrative problems (including a major revision of the existing tax structure), but it would probably be more efficient and less expensive to operate than the variety of measures now in existence. The main obstacle to a guaranteed minimum income of this kind is, of course, the public's view that such sweeping reform would amount to handouts of "something for nothing." A 1977 New York Times–CBS News poll found that the public opposed the idea of a guaranteed minimum income by 50 percent to 44 percent. (Interestingly, those earning less than $8,000 a year favored the proposal by 60 percent to 35 percent, but those earning over $20,000 opposed it by 62 percent to 34 percent.) There are also fears that a guaranteed minimum income would have undesirable effects on those who received it. A long-term study, the Seattle and Denver Income Maintenance Experiments, tested the effects of several variations of a guaranteed minimum income program on some 4,800 low-income families. Two principal effects were found: a rate of marital dissolution 60 percent higher than among families in ordinary welfare programs, and a noticeable decline in the

---

[56]For a strong argument in favor of a socialist economy, see Michael Harrington, *Socialism* (New York: Saturday Review Press, 1972). The same author offers a sophisticated critique of capitalism from a Marxist viewpoint in *The Twilight of Capitalism* (New York: Simon and Schuster, 1976).

number of hours worked by both male and female householders.[57] The experimental plans lacked both work incentives and job opportunities, however—elements that would have to be a vital part of any guaranteed-minimum-income program.

Some idea of the difficulties involved in providing a guaranteed minimum income can be gleaned from the fate of President Nixon's Family Assistance Plan, which was based on a concept not unlike that of a negative income tax. The intention was to replace various public assistance programs by providing a minimum annual income of $1,600 for a nonfarm family of four, plus food stamps that would bring their total income to $2,400. These benefits would cover not only the families of the unemployed but also families whose income from work fell below a minimum level. In addition, the plan included incentives to ensure as far as possible that the unemployed found jobs.

The FAP proposal ran into opposition from both liberals and conservatives and became embroiled in conflicts of interests and values. Liberals objected to the stringent work incentives, which would have forced unemployed people to take almost any kind of job before they became eligible for payments. They also argued that the level of payments was too low, for it would not move families above the poverty line. Conservatives either objected to the whole plan in principle or claimed that it would be far too costly. Opposition also came from government bureaucracies and officials in various existing poverty programs, who feared they would lose their jobs if their departments were abolished to make way for a simpler system. Although the FAP proposal was passed twice by the House of Representatives, it was "killed" in a Senate subcommittee before the full Senate even had a chance to consider it.[58] President Carter's 1978 proposals for welfare reform (a federal payment of $4,200 to a family of four, with the payment reduced by 50 cents for each dollar of family earnings and

eliminated when outside income reached $8,400) seemed destined to a similar fate for similar reasons.

Organizing for Change. A potentially significant development in the battle against poverty has been the creation of the National Welfare Rights Organization (NWRO), which was founded in 1966 with an objective that seemed hardly radical: to make welfare agencies abide by their own rules and regulations. Many of the eligible poor are not on the welfare rolls at all, and many are getting fewer benefits than they are entitled to. As Frances Piven and Richard Cloward point out:

> Welfare practice has everywhere become more restrictive than welfare statute; much of the time it verges on lawlessness. Thus, public welfare systems try to keep their budgets down and their rolls low by failing to inform people of the rights available to them; by intimidating and shaming them to the degree that they are reluctant either to apply or to press claims, and by arbitrarily denying benefits to those who are eligible.[59]

With the rules, regulations, and law on its side, the NWRO has won many court cases, including a Supreme Court ruling upholding the privacy of welfare recipients against arbitrary inspection of their homes by officials. For the first time the poor are being represented by a social movement devoted to their interests—a prerequisite for any measure of political influence. The assumption behind the NWRO's work is that improvements in the living conditions of the poor will not happen automatically; they must be made to happen. So far, however, NWRO has failed to organize the poor for collective action on any significant scale. It seems that most of the poor still perceive little relationship between political participation and the achievement of their goals; and, of course, they lack the financial resources to support a well-organized nationwide social movement. The NWRO has only about 100,000 members, a

---

[57]*New York Times,* November 16, 1978, p. 23.

[58]For a full discussion of the FAP and its fate, see Daniel P. Moynihan, *The Politics of a Guaranteed Income* (New York: Vintage, 1973).

[59]Frances Fox Piven and Richard A. Cloward, "A Strategy to End Poverty," *The Nation,* May 2, 1966, p. 510.

minute number in comparison with the total of the poor population. To a large extent the interests of the poor are represented instead by other special-interest organizations, particularly those formed to further the interests of racial minorities. Conflict theory would predict that the poor will have to challenge the existing order much more effectively in the future if they are to gain the power necessary to have real influence in the American decision-making process.[60]

Of all the countries of the world, the United States has the best chance to utterly eradicate absolute poverty. The resources exist; only the will and the effort are lacking.

SUMMARY

1. Although the United States is a generally affluent society, it is also a highly unequal one and contains extensive poverty involving severe deprivation for millions of people. The problem has been a particular focus of concern since the 1960s, when the War on Poverty was launched.

2. Functionalists explain social inequality by pointing out that societies must reward people unequally because people have different talents; American society is disorganized to the extent that it is more unequal than is functionally necessary. Conflict theorists explain social inequality as the result of a conflict between classes over scarce resources; some people are poor because others are rich and can use their influence to maintain the status quo.

3. Poverty may be defined in terms of absolute deprivation (the lack of basic necessities) or relative deprivation (the lack of customary living standards). The federal poverty line is calculated in terms of absolute deprivation.

4. The poor are concentrated in particular population categories: fatherless families, children, minorities, the elderly, and certain regions.

5. Poverty has several sources. One set of factors are economic, particularly structural unemployment. Another possible set of factors are cultural; an alleged culture of poverty may hinder the attempts of the poor to break out of poverty. A third set of factors are political; poverty is functional in some ways for the nonpoor, and there are strong political pressures to maintain the inequalities that result in poverty for a minority.

6. According to the American ideology, inequality is justified as a means of providing incentives. For this reason there is great reluctance to give the poor more than the barest minimum in welfare. Those who receive public assistance suffer stigma and a loss of status, and there are many unfounded myths about them. On the other hand, the United States offers much greater "public assistance" to the nonpoor, although in disguised form such as tax relief.

7. Some strategies for confronting the problem of poverty are the elimination of discrimination; the creation of job opportunities; training and education of the poor; reform of the welfare system; some redistribution of wealth; the negative income tax; and political organization for change.

GLOSSARY

Absolute deprivation. A lack of the basic necessities of life.

Culture of poverty. A set of values, norms, and other cultural characteristics alleged to exist among the poor in industrialized societies.

Ideology. A set of ideas and beliefs that justifies the perceived interests of those who hold it; the ideology of the dominant group in any unequal society therefore justifies the inequality.

---

[60]See Frances Fox Piven and Richard A. Cloward, *Poor Peoples' Movements: Why They Succeed, How They Fail* (New York: Pantheon, 1977).

Relative deprivation. A lack of the living standards considered customary in the society.

Social mobility. Movement from one social status to another.

Social stratification. The division of a society into social classes that enjoy varying degrees of access to the rewards the society offers.

Structural unemployment. Persistent unemployment that is built into the structure of the economy.

FURTHER READING

ANDERSON, CHARLES H. *The Political Economy of Social Class.* Englewood Cliffs, N.J.: Prentice-Hall, 1974. A short text that analyzes social stratification from a radical conflict perspective.

GALBRAITH, JOHN KENNETH. *The Affluent Society.* Boston: Beacon, 1958. A classic work in which a well-known economist explains the workings of the American economy in nontechnical language. Galbraith argues that the United States is marked by "private affluence" and "public squalor"—that is, expenditures of national resources are devoted disproportionately to private consumption rather than public need.

GANS, HERBERT J. *More Equality.* New York: Pantheon, 1973. Gans takes a hard look at the American belief that all citizens are given equal opportunity to advance in our society. His examination of the many difficulties that stand in the way of more equality helps distinguish practical possibility from more utopian goals.

GRONBJERG, KIRSTEN, DAVID STREET and GERALD SUTTLES. *Poverty and Social Change.* Chicago: University of Chicago Press, 1978. A valuable analysis of the American welfare system, with particular emphasis on the obstacles standing in the way of a solution to the problem of poverty.

HAMALIAN, LEO, and FREDERICK R. KARL (eds.). *The Fourth World: The Imprisoned, the Poor, the Sick, the Elderly, and the Underaged in America.* New York: Dell, 1976. A collection of articles by and about those who are denied entry to the mainstream of affluent America.

HARRINGTON, MICHAEL. *The Other America.* New York: Macmillan, 1962. A powerful book that first drew attention to continuing poverty in America; it still remains readable and relevant today.

LEACOCK, ELEANOR B. (ed.). *The Culture of Poverty: A Critique.* New York: Simon and Schuster, 1971. A collection of essays on the concept of the culture of poverty. Most of the contributors reject the concept and find other explanations for the persistence of poverty.

LEWIS, OSCAR. *La Vida.* New York: Random House, 1966. The anthropologist outlines his controversial "culture of poverty" theory, using evidence drawn from the Puerto Rican communities of San Juan and New York City. The use of ethnographic materials enlivens his discussion.

LUNDBERG, FERDINAND. *The Rich and the Super-Rich.* New York: Bantam, 1968. A fascinating account of the lives and fortunes of that tiny minority of Americans who enjoy immense wealth.

MEISSNER, HANNA H. (ed.). *Poverty in the Affluent Society.* New York: Harper & Row, 1973. A useful collection of articles on the nature, extent, and effects of poverty in the United States.

PIVEN, FRANCES FOX, and RICHARD A. CLOWARD. *Regulating the Poor: The Functions of Public Relief.* New York: Pantheon, 1971. The book presents a provocative argument that the public welfare system in the United States functions not so much to help the poor as to regulate them—by preventing them from resorting to violence and by labeling them as nonparticipants in normal social life.

ROSSIDES, DANIEL W. *The American Class System.* Boston: Houghton Mifflin, 1976. An excellent text on social stratification in the United States. Recommended to the student who wants a detailed overview of the field.

RYAN, WILLIAM. *Blaming the Victim.* Rev. ed. New York: Vintage, 1976. A forceful argument that the blame for poverty is placed on the poor rather than on the social institutions that create poverty. Ryan systematically dissects and debunks many of the popular myths concerning the poor.

STERN, PHILIP. *The Rape of the Taxpayer.* New York: Random House, 1973. A detailed, racy, and indignant account of how super-rich Americans manage to dodge taxes by the use of legal loopholes.

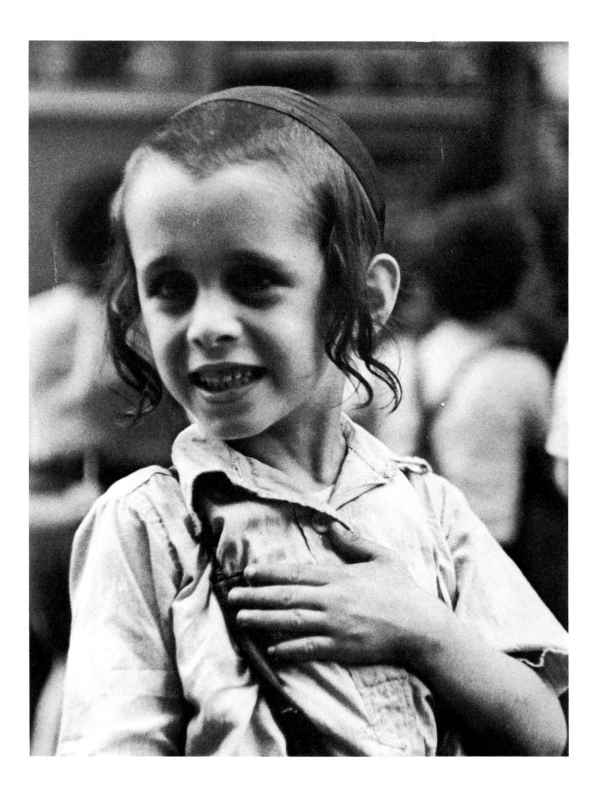

8
Race and Ethnic Relations

THE PROBLEM

Unlike most other peoples, Americans are primarily a nation of immigrants. Our citizens or their ancestors immigrated from many parts of the globe—some as refugees from religious and political persecution, some as adventurers from the Old World seeking a better life, some as captives brought to our shores against their will to be sold into slavery. Though we all share a common American culture, the nation contains many racial and ethnic subcultures with their own distinctive characteristics. These differences might seem trivial or irrelevant to outside observers, but they have contributed to intergroup conflicts that have been a persistent social problem to American society.

The United States was explicitly founded on the principle of human equality, but in practice the nation has fallen far short of that ideal. American society is a stratified one, in which power, wealth, and prestige are unequally distributed among the population. This inequality is not simply a matter of distinctions between social classes: it tends to follow racial and ethnic lines as well, with the result that class divisions often parallel racial divisions. The first settlers from "Anglo-Saxon" northern Europe quickly took control of economic assets and political power in the United States, and they have maintained this control, to a greater or lesser degree, ever since. Successive waves of immigrants from other parts of Europe and elsewhere in the world have had to struggle long and hard to become assimilated into the mainstream of American life. Some have succeeded and have shared in the "American dream"; others—notably those whose ethnic or racial characteristics

differ most markedly from those of the dominant group—have been excluded by formal and informal barriers from full participation in American life. The result of this discrimination has been a severe and continuing racial tension in the United States that has periodically erupted into outright violence. Particularly since the civil rights demonstrations, ghetto riots, and other unrest in the 1960s, race and ethnic relations have been a major preoccupation of social scientists, politicians, and the general public.

Race and Ethnicity

Before we discuss the problem of intergroup hostilities and inequalities, we must clarify the terms "race" and "ethnicity." The more than 4 billion people who populate the world today display an almost bewildering variety of distinctive physical features, such as skin color, hair type, lung capacity, or limb-to-trunk ratio. Complementing this range of physical types is an astonishing variety of ways of life. People who share similar physical features are socially defined as a race; those who share cultural patterns are socially defined as an ethnic group.

A *race* consists of a large number of people who have interbred over a long period of time; as a result, they share distinctive physical features and regard themselves, and are regarded by others, as a biological unity. All human beings, of course, belong to the same species—that is, they can interbreed with one another—but over the last 50,000 years or so, population groups in different parts of the world have adapted to their environments by evolving specific physical characteristics. Peoples living at high altitudes, for example, have developed large lung capacity to maximize their oxygen intake; peoples living in tropical climates have developed dark skins to protect them from the rays of sun. There is no convincing evidence that different groups have inherited different psychological characteristics, such as intelligence or musical ability; distinctions of race affect only physical features.

Confronted with this great range of human physical characteristics, anthropologists tried for decades to classify the human population into broad racial categories. Some anthropologists found three races; others, dozens; still others, over a hundred. The reason for the confusion was that the concept of race is a social rather than a scientific one: "racial" categories are a creation of the observer, not of nature. Different populations have been interbreeding for so long that there is no such thing as a "pure" race; rather, there is a continuum of physical types. For this reason most modern anthropologists have abandoned the attempt to classify people into races and regard the term "race" as scientifically useless.[1] The physical differences between people are simply a biological fact. The sociologist is interested in these differences as *social* facts, because people attribute meanings to the differences and act on those meanings. The difference between people with long noses and people with short noses is also a biological fact, but because society attaches no particular significance to this difference, it has few if any social consequences and is of no interest to the sociologist. When people regard themselves as a race, and are so regarded by others, however, important social consequences may result. For instance, one group may distinguish itself from others by attributing virtues to itself and undesirable characteristics to the others—and problems of race relations result.

An *ethnic group* consists of a large number of people who have had a high level of mutual interaction over a long period and who therefore share distinctive cultural traits; as a result they regard themselves, and are regarded by others, as a cultural unity. These cultural traits can be of many different kinds—characteristics such as religion, language, historical traditions, dietary practices, and so on. In many cases there are no racial differences between ethnic groups in the same society. A Polish American, for example, may be physically indistinguishable from an Irish American, but each may participate to some extent in a distinctive ethnic subculture of the group in question. Because ethnic differences are not as immediately apparent as racial differences, it is more difficult to use them as a basis for discrimination, so antagonism between ethnic groups is usually much less intense than that between racial groups. In other cases, however, groups living in the same society may be both racially and ethnically different. Black and white Americans, for example, are racially distinct, and they also tend to belong to different subcultures of American society. In such cases each group may view the other as doubly different, and the barriers to mutual understanding and cooperation may be greater.

ANALYZING THE PROBLEM

The problem of hostile race and ethnic relations is common to many societies that contain heterogeneous populations. Both the functionalist and conflict approaches are helpful in analyzing the problem.

The Functionalist Approach

A functionalist analysis suggests that problems of race and ethnic relations result from social disorganization. Ideally a society would be organized in such a way that any racial or ethnic groups it might contain would live together under conditions of harmony and equality. But this ideal situation is seldom met; instead, the social system fails to adjust to the arrival or

[1]See Michael Banton and Jonathan Harwood, *The Race Concept* (New York: Praeger, 1975); and Ashley Montagu (ed.), *Statement on Race* (London: Oxford University Press, 1975).

continued presence of minority groups, with dysfunctional consequences for the groups involved and often for the society as a whole.

When a society is disorganized in this way, inequalities between racial and ethnic groups become deeply structured into the social system, causing some groups to be arbitrarily denied full opportunity to achieve social, economic, political, and personal goals. In the United States a long tradition of formal and informal discrimination against certain minorities has restricted their participation and opportunities in the society, as evidenced by the statistics on these minorities' average incomes, unemployment rates, life expectancies, housing standards, educational attainments, and so on. In terms of our society as a whole, this discrimination is dysfunctional in two basic ways: it generates continuing social tensions and antagonisms and it prevents a large part of the population from contributing to the economy and society to the full extent of its talents.

A functionalist analysis implies that the problem can be solved through adjustments that would bring the social system back into equilibrium once more. Barriers to racial and ethnic equality would have to be eliminated, and some new relationship would have to be developed among the groups concerned—perhaps full assimilation of the minorities by the majority, or perhaps full respect by the majority for the rights and culture of the minorities as separate and distinctive groups.

The Conflict Approach

A conflict analysis focuses more on the problem of why racial and ethnic antagonisms arise in the first place, and why they tend to persist. Conflict theorists view these antagonisms as the result of inequalities between groups, and argue that the inequalities themselves are caused by a conflict over access to scarce resources.

For racial or ethnic conflict to arise and persist, three conditions must be present. First, there must be two or more social groups that are identifiable by their physical or cultural characteristics. Second, there must be competition among these groups for scarce resources, such as

land, food, housing, or jobs. In the ensuing struggle, each group tries to secure its own interests by denying the other groups equal access to these resources. Third, one group must attain sufficient power to make good its claim over the resources. At this point, the inequality becomes structured into society and tends to be maintained over time through custom, law, or even outright force.[2]

From the conflict approach, then, disputes among racial and ethnic groups are not really about physical or cultural differences. They are basically disputes about access to economic, social, and political rewards, in which group differences are used to justify the "right" of the dominant group to its superior claim. Conflict theorists emphasize that change is likely to come about only when there is a shift in the power relations between the dominant and minority groups.[3] In other words, the subordinate groups must attempt, through social movements or other means, to apply an irresistible pressure for reform on the dominant group. Conflict theorists point to the successes of the civil rights movement as an example of this process, and argue that further reforms will be achieved only through continuing pressure from the subordinate groups.

RACISM

A characteristic feature of any hostile relationship between racial or ethnic groups is racism, which translates into prejudice and discrimination against the subordinate group.

The Nature of Racism

Any group that regards itself as a racial or ethnic unity tends to be *ethnocentric:* that is, it automatically assumes that its own values, attitudes, and norms are right and proper, while those of

[2]Donald L. Noel, "A Theory of the Origin of Ethnic Stratification," *Social Problems*, 16 (Fall 1968), 157–172.
[3]See Lewis M. Killian, *The Impossible Revolution, Phase 2: Black Power and the American Dream* (New York: Random House, 1972).

other peoples are quaint, bizarre, immoral, or even savage. This phenomenon is found throughout social life. For example, members of one religious group assume that their faith is true and that the faith of other groups is false; nations at war regard the battles they win as glorious victories and the battles they lose as bloodthirsty massacres. In its milder forms, ethnocentrism can have useful social functions: it gives people pride in their group and enhances their social solidarity. In extreme cases, however, ethnocentric views form the basis for oppressive treatment of other groups. As we saw in Chapter 7 ("Poverty"), any group that dominates another always develops a set of beliefs, or *ideology*, that justifies its domination and exploitation of the subordinate group. The ideology that justifies the domination of one racial or ethnic group by another is called *racism*.[4]

For centuries racist attitudes were respectable in the Western world. The European colonial powers believed that their technological civilization was a sign of their own racial superiority over the "primitive" peoples whose lands and labor they exploited. It was even argued that God had divided the human species into different races in order to distinguish the superior from the inferior. Similarly, the institution of slavery in the United States and elsewhere came to be justified by racist beliefs: if the slaves were defined as innately inferior or even subhuman, it was possible for the slaveowners to treat them in ways that would otherwise have seemed morally wrong.

Racist beliefs, however, are by no means restricted to the whites of Europe and North America: they are to be found all over the world. In many parts of the Sahara, where the desert is expanding and encroaching on what were once lush pastures, Arabs and black Africans are slaughtering one another over the cultivable land—and using racist beliefs to justify their acts. In parts of East Africa, black Africans have displayed racist attitudes toward Asian minorities and have systematically expelled them from countries in which they have lived for generations. These Asians are primarily middle-class merchants and technicians and as they have been displaced, Africans have taken over their jobs. In many parts of South America the dominant Spanish-speaking population adopts racist attitudes toward the indigenous tribes. Even in the 1970s the Brazilian government has been accused of tolerating and even encouraging the slaughter of indigenous peoples whose land is wanted for agricultural development. Elsewhere, the dominant group in the Soviet Union discriminates against Jews; Catholics and Protestants maim and kill one another in Northern Ireland; Greeks and Turks have fought pitched battles in Cyprus; Christians and Muslims have butchered one another in Lebanon; and the Indian subcontinent was partitioned into separate states because of the inability of Hindus and Muslims to live together peaceably.

It is by no means inevitable that different racial or ethnic groups should live in conflict. There are many plural societies around the world in which such groups live in great harmony. Tanzania, for example, has excellent race relations among its black, white, Arab, and Asian populations. The German, French, and Italian populations in Switzerland coexist peacefully, as do the white, Chinese, Japanese, and native inhabitants of Hawaii. There is nothing innate in the nature of humanity that makes us react favorably or unfavorably toward other groups: race relations, be they good or bad, are a purely social product, and can be worsened or improved by social forces.

Prejudice and Discrimination

Racism is commonly expressed in the forms of prejudice and discrimination. *Prejudice* refers to "prejudged" negative *attitudes* toward members of other groups; *discrimination* refers to *actions* directed against others on the grounds of their group membership and supposed group characteristics. Prejudice and discrimination are the

[4]Robert Blauner, "Internal Colonialism and Ghetto Revolt," *Social Problems* (Spring 1969), 393–408; Manning Nash, "Race and the Ideology of Race," *Current Anthropology*, 3 (1962), 285–288; Donald L. Noel, "Slavery and the Rise of Racism," in Donald L. Noel (ed.), *The Origins of American Slavery and Racism* (Columbus, Ohio: Merrill, 1972); William J. Wilson, *Power, Racism and Privilege* (New York: Free Press, 1973).

two sides of the same coin, but they should not be confused.

The distinction between the two concepts was first made evident in a classic study conducted by Richard LaPiere in 1934. He accompanied a Chinese couple on an extended tour of the United States, during which they stopped at some 250 hotels and restaurants. In only one case were they discriminated against by being refused service. LaPiere then sent letters to each of the 250 establishments inquiring whether they would serve "members of the Chinese race." Half of the hotels and restaurants ignored the query, but over 90 percent of those that replied indicated that they would not accept Chinese: that is, they were prejudiced against them. When presented with real-life Chinese, however, they had failed to translate their prejudice into discrimination.[5] Robert Merton suggests that there are four different "types" of persons, each with a characteristic response to other groups:

1. The *unprejudiced nondiscriminator*, in both belief and practice, upholds American ideals of freedom and equality. This person is not prejudiced against other groups and, on principle, will not discriminate against them.
2. The *unprejudiced discriminator* is not personally prejudiced but may sometimes, reluctantly, discriminate against other groups because it seems socially or financially convenient to do so.
3. The *prejudiced nondiscriminator* feels hostile to other groups but recognizes that law and social pressures are opposed to overt discrimination. Reluctantly, this person does not translate prejudice into action.
4. The *prejudiced discriminator* does not believe in the values of freedom and equality and consistently discriminates against other groups in both word and deed.[6]

The Nature of Prejudice.   The prejudiced person is essentially someone who maintains a rigid mental image, or *stereotype*, of a group and applies it indiscriminately to all its members. A prejudiced person may, for example, harbor a stereotype of the "inscrutable" Chinese, or of the "miserly" Jews, or of the "lazy" blacks. Such a stereotype is not easily altered by evidence that contradicts it. If the prejudiced person believes that some group has a particular characteristic and meets a member of the group who obviously does not share the characteristic, the discrepancy is simply dismissed as "the exception that proves the rule." Stereotyped thinking, combined with a consistent refusal to test the stereotype against fact, is basic to racial or ethnic prejudice.[7]

Many studies have shown that prejudiced people make little attempt to check stereotypes against social reality.[8] In one of the most dramatic experiments illustrating this tendency, Eugene Hartley gave his subjects a long list of races and nationalities for comment. There were prejudiced responses not only to Jews and blacks but also to the Danireans, the Wallonians, and the Pireneans: in the case of the last three peoples some subjects recommended such discriminatory acts as refusing them admission to the United States or even expelling all those presently living there. In actuality, of course, the Danireans, the Wallonians, and Pireneans do not even exist; Hartley had dreamed them up to see if people prejudiced against existing groups would also be prejudiced against nonexisting ones. His experiment showed that over three-quarters of the people prejudiced against Jews and blacks were also prejudiced against people whom, obviously, they could never have met or heard anything about. Clearly, then, prejudiced attitudes are learned through contact with prejudiced people rather than through contact with the people toward whom prejudice is directed.[9]

Other studies have indicated that the thinking of prejudiced people is often confused and

[5]Richard T. LaPiere, "Attitudes Versus Action," *Social Forces*, 13 (December 1934), 230–237.

[6]Robert Merton, "Discrimination and the American Creed," in Robert M. MacIver (ed.), *Discrimination and National Welfare* (New York: Harper, 1949).

[7]Gordon W. Allport, *The Nature of Prejudice* (Garden City, N.Y.: Anchor, 1958).

[8]See John Brigham and Theodore Weissback (eds.), *Racial Attitudes in America: Analysis and Findings of Social Psychology* (New York: Harper & Row, 1972); and Irwin Deutscher, *What We Say/What We Do: Sentiments and Acts* (Glenview, Ill.: Scott, Foresman, 1973).

[9]Eugene Hartley, *Problems in Prejudice* (New York: King's Crown Press, 1946).

inconsistent: they tend to believe any statements that feed their prejudice, even if several of these statements contradict each other. In a test designed to measure attitudes toward Jews, Theodore Adorno and his associates deliberately inserted unfavorable propositions that were mutually inconsistent. They included, for example, pairs of items that dealt with the "seclusiveness" and "intrusiveness" of Jews:

— Much resentment against Jews stems from their tending to keep apart and exclude gentiles from Jewish social life.

— The Jews should not pry too much into Christian activities and organizations nor seek so much recognition and prestige from Christians.

and:

— Jews tend to remain a foreign element in American society, to preserve their old social standards and resist the American way of life.

— Jews go too far in hiding their Jewishness, especially such extremes as changing their names, straightening their noses, and imitating Christian manners and customs.

Adorno found that nearly three-quarters of those who dislike Jews for being "intrusive" also dislike them for being "seclusive." Similarly, those who dislike them for being capitalistic and controlling business also dislike them for being communistic and subversive; those who dislike them for being miserly also dislike them for giving money to charities to curry favor, and so on. It seems that genuine group characteristics are not at issue; prejudiced people are simply seeking any justification for their attitudes.[10]

The Nature of Discrimination. Discrimination may take many forms, but discriminatory practices can be conveniently divided into two main types: legal, or de jure, discrimination and institutionalized, or de facto, discrimination.

Legal discrimination refers to discriminatory acts and policies that are encoded in the law of

the land. Throughout most of American history, racial discrimination was written into our statutes. In addition to legalizing existing patterns of discrimination, these laws had the further effect of reinforcing prejudicial attitudes by restricting intergroup contact and making segregation seem natural and respectable. Laws that discriminate among the various racial groups in the United States have been repealed or struck down by the Supreme Court since the middle of the present century, and are now considered unconstitutional.

Institutionalized discrimination refers to discriminatory acts and policies that are not necessarily encoded in law but nevertheless pervade the major institutions of society such as the economy, political life, education, or the legal system. As Stokely Carmichael and Charles Hamilton express it:

> When white terrorists bomb a black church and kill five black children, that is an act of individual racism, widely deplored by most segments of society. But when in the same city . . . five hundred black babies die each year because of the lack of proper food, shelter, and medical facilities, and thousands more are destroyed and maimed physically, emotionally, and intellectually because of conditions of poverty and discrimination in the black community, that is a function of institutional racism.[11]

This institutionalized discrimination is rarely the result of deliberate policies intended to place the subordinate groups at a disadvantage. Rather, it is built into the very structure of society. For example, long years of informal discrimination have prevented blacks from earning incomes similar to those of whites. Largely as a result, most urban blacks can afford to live only in inner-city ghettos, whereas the more affluent urban whites are able to live in the surrounding suburbs. As a further result a variety of neighborhood facilities ranging from churches to schools have become segregated almost as effectively as if they were segregated by law. These factors and others interact with one another in a

[10]Theodore W. Adorno *et al., The Authoritarian Personality* (New York: Norton, 1950).

[11]Stokely Carmichael and Charles V. Hamilton, *Black Power: The Politics of Liberation in America* (New York: Vintage, 1967), p. 4.

The ideal of cultural assimilation has a long history in the United States—but the reality is very different. Those groups that shared the racial, cultural, and religious characteristics of the dominant group were readily assimilated; but those groups that differed in significant respects have never been fully accepted.

vicious cycle that compounds the disadvantage of the subordinate group: an infant mortality rate for blacks and other nonwhites of 24.2 per thousand, compared with 14.2 per thousand for whites; a median family income for blacks and other nonwhites that is less than two-thirds that of whites; an unemployment rate for blacks and other minorities that is over twice that of whites.[12] It is conditions such as these that signal the presence of institutionalized discrimination.

Institutionalized discrimination is difficult to eradicate, since, obviously, it cannot be repealed, and in most cases is not susceptible to remedial legislation. Many whites fail to appreciate this fact, for they are often inclined to believe that civil rights acts and similar legislation have eliminated barriers to equal opportunity. (Now that laws discriminating against them are being repealed, American women, too, are discovering the hard facts of institutionalized discrimination, particularly in the work place.)

MINORITIES IN CONTEMPORARY AMERICA

It is a long-cherished American belief that the United States serves as a "melting pot" in which diverse races and cultures are blended; its essence was captured in the play *The Melting Pot*, a popular Broadway success in 1908. As expressed by one of the characters, the "melting pot" credo holds that:

> America is God's crucible, the great Melting Pot, where all the races of Europe are melting and re-forming! Here you stand, good folk, think I, when I see them at Ellis Island, here you stand in your fifty groups, with your fifty languages and histories, and your fifty blood hatreds and rivalries. But you won't long be like that, brothers, for these are the fires of God you've come to— these are the fires of God. A fig for your feuds and vendettas! Germans and Frenchmen, Irishmen and Englishmen, Jews and Russians—into the crucible with you all! God is making the American.[13]

[12]Bureau of the Census, *U.S.A. Statistics in Brief, 1978* Washington, D.C.: Government Printing Office, 1978).

[13]Israel Zangwill, *The Melting Pot* (New York: Macmillan 1930), p. 33.

The truth, however, is that the United States is and always has been a very heterogeneous society. Although there has been a good deal of assimilation of new immigrants into the American mainstream, the process has been a long and arduous one, largely restricted to those groups—such as Germans and Scandinavians—who were racially and ethnically akin to the dominant Anglo-Saxon group. Other immigrant groups, such as blacks or Chinese, have proved an unassimilable element in the melting pot.

In the broadest sense, there is an almost infinite number of minorities in the United States, ranging from red-haired people to vegetarians. Sociologists, however, use the word "minority" in a special sense to refer to a group that is considered "different" and suffers in consequence. In a classic definition, Louis Wirth described a minority as

> a group of people who, because of their physical or cultural characteristics, are singled out from the others in the society in which they live for differential and unequal treatment, and who therefore regard themselves as objects of collective discrimination. The existence of a minority in a society implies the existence of a corresponding dominant group with higher social status and greater privileges. Minority status carries with it the exclusion from full participation in the life of the society.[14]

In effect, therefore, any group other than the dominant, white Anglo-Saxon Protestant ("WASP") majority is a "minority" group in American society. Let us look more closely at those minorities whose problems have attracted the most public attention in recent years: blacks, Indians, Hispanics, Asian Americans, and the "white ethnics."

Blacks

The largest of the racial and ethnic minorities in the United States is the blacks, who number over 25.2 million, or 11.7 percent of the population. Their history in the United States has been one of sustained oppression, discrimination, and denial of basic civil rights and liberties.[15]

The first blacks were brought to North America in 1619. Within a few decades the demand for their cheap labor led to a massive slave trade that ultimately transported some 400,000 Africans to this continent. Captured by neighboring tribes in their native villages and then sold to white traders, the slaves were shipped in wretchedly crowded conditions to the Caribbean and then to the United States, where they were sold like cattle at auctions. The myth of their racial inferiority—their irresponsibility, promiscuity, laziness, and lower intelligence—was assiduously propagated as a justification for their continued subjugation. The whip or the lynch mob served to assert social control over slaves who challenged the established order.

The Northern states had all outlawed slavery by 1830, but the Southern states, in which slaves had become the backbone of the economy, maintained the institution until it was finally ended by the Civil War, Lincoln's emancipation of slaves in 1863, and the Thirteenth Amendment to the Constitution in 1865. But even after the abolition of slavery, wholesale discrimination was practiced against black Americans. Many states passed segregation laws to keep the races apart in schools, housing, restaurants, and other public facilities, and institutionalized discrimination kept blacks in the lowest-paid jobs. A variety of methods, such as rigged "literacy" tests, were used to keep blacks off the voters' rolls and thus prevent them from exercising their political rights. Segregation laws continued to be enforced in Southern states until the 1950s; in the North informal methods were used—often just as effectively.

Throughout most of their history in America, blacks were concentrated in the South and served as agricultural laborers or menial domestic servants. During the course of this century,

---

[14]Quoted in George Eaton Simpson and J. Milton Yinger, *Racial and Cultural Minorities: An Analysis of Prejudice and Discrimination*, 3rd ed. (New York: Harper & Row, 1965), p. 16.

[15]Robert Blauner, *Racial Oppression in America* (New York: Harper & Row, 1972); August Meier and Elliot M. Rudwich, *From Plantation to Ghetto*, 3rd ed. (New York: Hill and Wang, 1976).

however, there has been a massive migration of blacks to the cities of the North and a corresponding urbanization of blacks in the South. Today, half of the black population lives in the North (although there are now signs that a reverse migration to the South has begun) and more than 80 percent of all blacks live in urban areas. The movement from the traditional rural environment to the more heterogeneous and sophisticated urban context has enhanced black consciousness of inequality and discrimination and has contributed to the increasing militancy that blacks have shown throughout most of this century.

As the Swedish sociologist Gunnar Myrdal pointed out in 1944 in his classic work *An American Dilemma*,[16] the treatment of black Americans utterly contradicted the American creed of human equality and civil rights. Myrdal predicted that the tension between egalitarian values and discriminatory practices would ultimately grow intolerable. He was eventually proved right.

Changes were at first slow. Earlier in this century black organizations such as the National Association for the Advancement of Colored People (NAACP) were remarkably moderate in their approach: they presented petitions, tried to negotiate improvements in the economic and social status of blacks, and used legal channels to challenge the validity of existing discriminatory statutes. In fact, the most significant advances were made by the Supreme Court, which after World War II began to whittle away at the structure of racial segregation in America. In its most important decision, in the case of *Brown versus Board of Education* (1954), the court ruled that "separate educational facilities are inherently unequal."[17] A year later the court ordered schools to be desegregated "with all deliberate speed,"[18] although for another fifteen years little was done to implement the ruling. The doctrine that separate facilities are necessarily unequal was gradually extended by the

court to a number of other public facilities, ranging from golf courses to beaches. The court progressively struck down various segregation laws, such as those banning interracial marriage, as well as a series of legal pretexts that had been used to deny blacks their voting rights. But a great deal of legal discrimination remained on the statute books, and institutionalized discrimination continued as the American norm.

By the late 1950s many black Americans would no longer tolerate discrimination. Young blacks, often aided by radical white students, began to "sit in" at segregated restaurants, demanding sevice. Protestors went on "freedom rides" to desegregate buses and terminals. Massive campaigns for voter registration were mounted in a climate of growing violence; dozens of young volunteer campaigners were murdered and hundreds were injured. But the mood for change was irresistible, and by the start of the 1960s a major social movement for civil rights was under way. The federal government responded. President John F. Kennedy ordered school desegregation in the South, and Attorney General Robert F. Kennedy sent federal marshals to Southern schools to enforce the order. Congress passed a sweeping civil rights bill, which empowered federal agencies to deny funds to localities and organizations that practiced discrimination in accommodations, employment, and other areas.

The changes, however, came too late to prevent violence. In 1964 riots erupted in the streets of New York, Chicago, and Philadelphia. The following year there was a major riot in the Watts area of Los Angeles. In 1966 there were some 43 outbreaks of rioting, with particularly serious episodes in Chicago and Cleveland. In 1967 there were 8 major riots, plus more than 250 disorders in over 170 cities. The following year Dr. Martin Luther King, Jr., the leader of the civil rights movement, was shot down by a white assassin, touching off a coast-to-coast wave of the most violent rioting yet seen. As conflict theory would predict, the heightened tension stimulated further social change. Within a week Congress enacted a new civil rights bill—one which had been pending for the previous two years—to end discrimination in housing.

[16]Gunnar Myrdal, *An American Dilemma* (New York: Harper, 1944).

[17]*Brown versus Board of Education*, 347 U.S. 483 (1954).

[18]*Brown versus Board of Education*, 389 U.S. 294 (1955).

Since the civil rights movement of the 1960s, some blacks—perhaps as many as a third—have gained entry to the middle class. But their achievement should not obscure the fact that a large part of the black population remains in an "underclass" of poverty and despair.

The rioting finally subsided, but it left a new mood among many black Americans. Feelings of pride replaced feelings of inferiority; slogans declared that "black is beautiful"; and the black community showed signs of unprecedented self-confidence. Equally important, many black leaders began to disclaim full integration into the American mainstream as the goal of the black minority. Instead, they argued, blacks ought to coexist with other groups in a plural society containing heterogeneous and distinctive communities living in mutual respect.

The current status of black Americans presents a mixed picture. The elimination of legal barriers to their advancement has been a major gain, but institutionalized discrimination is still rife. Housing, in particular, remains highly segregated: the great majority of blacks continue to live in neighborhoods that are overwhelmingly black, and most whites live in neighborhoods that are overwhelmingly white. Busing and other programs aimed at integrating the schools have had some impact in inner-city areas but have made virtually no difference to the segregation that exists between predominantly black urban centers and the predominantly white suburbs and small towns that surround them. Blacks have achieved considerable educational gains: black enrollment in colleges rose spectacularly between 1966, when 4.6 percent of college students were black, and 1976, when 10.7 percent were black.[19] Median family income of blacks rose from $3,230 in 1960 to $10,142 in 1977, but the

[19]William Brashler, "The Black Middle Class: Making It," *New York Times Magazine,* December 3, 1978, p. 36.

median income of white families rose at least as fast, and the income gap between the two groups has widened in recent years: the black-white income ratio was .57 in 1977, compared with .61 in 1970[20] (see Figure 8.1). A major source of this differential is the fact that blacks tend to be barred from positions of authority over other workers, and are restricted instead to lower-paying jobs further down the work-place hierarchy. This factor alone accounts for about a third of the total black-white income gap.[21] The political influence of blacks is increasing, both in the South, where they are voting in unprecedented numbers, and in the major cities of the North, Midwest, and West, where they are a major voting bloc and, in some cases, a majority. In recent years blacks have won the mayorships of several large cities, including Los Angeles, Atlanta, New Orleans, Cleveland, Newark, Cincinnati, and Washington. But there is no black in the Senate, and no state has a black governor.

Race relations between black and white still leave much to be desired, although there is unmistakable evidence of some improvements in attitudes. Harris polls between 1963 and 1978, for example, have shown a steady decline in racial stereotyping on the part of whites (see

[20]U.S. Bureau of the Census, *Statistical Abstract of the United States, 1978* (Washington, D.C.: U.S. Government Printing Office), pp. 436, 457.
[21]James R. Kluegel, "The Causes and Costs of Racial Exclusion from Job Authority," *American Sociological Review*, 43 (June 1978), 285–301.

Figure 8.2). Similarly, a 1978 *New York Times*–CBS News poll of blacks and whites in twenty-five large Northeastern and Midwestern cities showed an increased white tolerance for racial integration. Some 66 percent of the whites said they would "not mind at all" if a black family of similar social class moved in next door, compared with only 46 percent who had felt this way when a similar sample was polled in these cities ten years earlier. In that poll a third of the whites had asserted that whites have "a right to keep blacks out of their neighborhoods if they want to"; by 1978 only one white in twenty admitted such feelings. The 1978 poll also found that only 39 percent of the blacks felt that whites in their city "disliked" them, compared to 57 percent of the blacks in the 1968 sample.

More ominously, however, there was a sharp divergence between the races in 1978 on the question of how much progress had been made in ending discrimination. Two-thirds of whites believed that there has been "a lot of progress" in getting rid of discrimination, but more than half of the blacks felt that there has not been "much real change." Only 17 percent of the whites believed that many blacks miss out on jobs and promotion in their city because of discrimination, whereas 47 percent of the blacks felt this to be the case. In fact, blacks in 1978 were more pessimistic about progress in race relations than they had been ten years previously.

One reason for the difference in the perceptions of the two groups may be that blacks are more acutely aware that a great many of their

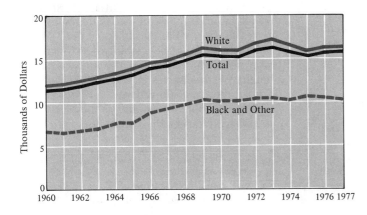

FIGURE 8.1 **Median annual money income of families, by race: 1960–1977.** Although the median black family income has increased since 1960, median white family income has increased also, so that the relative status of the races is little changed. In fact, the gap has grown slightly in recent years.
(Bureau of the Census, *Statistical Abstract of the United States*, 1978, p. 436.)

Here are some statements people sometimes make about black people. For each statement please tell me whether you personally tend to agree or disagree with that statement.

	Percent of Whites who Agreed					
	1963	1966	1967	1971	1976	**1978**
Blacks tend to have less ambition than whites	66	65	70	52	50	**49**
Blacks want to live off the handout	41	43	52	39	37	**36**
Blacks breed crime	35	33	32	27	31	**29**
Blacks have less native intelligence than whites	39	36	46	37	28	**25**
Blacks care less for the family than whites	31	33	34	26	22	**18**
Blacks are inferior to white people	31	26	29	22	15	**15**

FIGURE 8.2 **What whites think of blacks.** Opinion polls show a steady decline in prejudiced attitudes of whites toward blacks.
(National Conference of Christians and Jews. *A Study of Attitudes Toward Racial and Religious Minorities and Toward Women*. Conducted by Louis Harris and Associates, Inc., November 1978.)

number have failed to share in the more general gains made by blacks since the 1960s. Over the past decade many blacks, perhaps as many as a third, have worked their way into the middle class, in the process often moving from the ghetto to the suburbs or to better housing within the cities. But, as William Junius Wilson has emphasized, other blacks have been left behind, and the urban ghettos now contain a permanently impoverished "underclass" of habitually unemployed or underemployed black people. Many members of this "underclass" are young and unskilled. They live in cities where the unemployment rate for teen-age black workers runs as high as 50 percent, or about eight times the rate for the American work force as a whole. Wilson points out that this "underclass" could continue to persist, even in the absence of racial discrimination, in much the same way as other pockets of poverty persist—that is, for reasons of social-class inequality.[22] In any event, such progress as has been made in the past decade has

[22]William Junius Wilson, *The Declining Significance of*

brought no benefit whatever to the black "underclass." Living in an environment of poverty, decay, crime, drug addiction, joblessness, and hopelessness, this ghetto underclass offers an explosive potential for the future.

Indians

When the first European settlers arrived in America, there were at least 1.5 million Native Americans, or Indians, in the country. By 1800 the Indian population had been reduced to around 600,000, and by 1850, to a mere 250,000. Today the Indian population consists of just under a million people, most of whom live on or near the 300 reservations that are all that is left to them of the territory that was once their own. Few minority groups have been as consistently denigrated or treated in terms of such absurdly false stereotypes as the Indians. Indeed, they have been so effectively segregated from the national life that their problems remained virtually unknown to most other Americans until a social movement for "Red Power" emerged in the late 1960s.

When the early colonists and pioneers found the Native American tribes standing in the way of their westward advance, they adopted a policy that in many cases amounted to deliberate extermination. "The only good Indian," it was said, "is a dead one." The whites stripped the Native Americans of their lands, almost wiped out the buffalo on which many tribes depended for existence, and caused the deaths of tens of thousands of the native inhabitants, either directly through outright slaughter or indirectly through famine, disease, forced marches in freezing weather, and other hardships.[23]

The advancing settlers rapidly developed ethnocentric attitudes toward the Indians. They thought of themselves, for example, as "pioneers" rather than "invaders," and viewed the indigenous people's resistance as the product of cruel savagery rather than stubborn patriotism.

Race: Blacks and Changing American Institutions (Chicago: University of Chicago Press, 1978).
[23]See Dee Brown, *Bury My Heart at Wounded Knee* (New York: Holt, Rinehart and Winston, 1971).

These early stereotypes have become deeply embedded in our historical consciousness. Alvin Josephy points out:

> The relating of American history by white historians has reflected their own Western-civilization-based point of view, as well might have been expected, but what they wrote has also been self-serving. The frontier Indian, resisting white expansion and exploitation, *had* to be a skulking savage. To the seeker of his land, he *had* to be an aimless nomad. To the civilizer, he *had* to be lazy. Even the romantic, the poet, and the philosopher had to give the Indian a false image: to them he was the noble child of nature. To almost no one could he be real.[24]

Once the culture of the Native Americans had been almost destroyed and the bulk of their lands taken from them, the federal government was left with the problem of how to deal with the shattered tribes that remained. After the Civil War, government reservations were established for the Indians, and in 1871 Congress decided that no tribe would ever be recognized as an independent political entity again and made all Indians wards of the federal government, without any rights of citizenship. (The legal status of "ward" is normally applied to a child under the care of a guardian.) A government report of 1890 reveals the contemporary attitude toward Indians and their future. The indigenous inhabitants, the report noted, are "cowards in warfare," "treacherous," "the embodiment of cruelty," "filled with insatiable greed," "low in instincts," and lacking in "reasoning powers." The report pointed out:

> Being the original occupant and owner of the lands, the Indian can not see why he should give way, go to the wall, or move to parts unknown. He cannot understand the profit to him and his by being despoiled first and absorbed afterward. . . . In all future dealings with the reservation Indians . . . teach the Indian that it pays to be clean, to be industrious, to have but one wife . . . and teach him to follow the best habits

of the white people. Show him that it is to his interest to be like other men.[25]

Not until 1924 was the right of American citizenship extended to the original inhabitants of the land.

The social and economic conditions of Indians are probably worse than those of any other minority group. A third of the families live below the poverty level. The unemployment rate in recent years has been as high as a staggering 45 percent.[26] The alcoholism and suicide rates are far above the national averages. The average life expectancy is around fifty years—about twenty years below that for the nation as a whole. Indians have the highest infant mortality rate of any minority group in the United States. In 1976 the American Indian Policy Review Commission commented that the health "standards of Indians today are comparable to those of the general population twenty to twenty-five years ago."[27] On the reservations many Indians live in unheated log houses, tarpaper shacks, old tents, caves, and even old automobile bodies.[28] Their problems are compounded by the stereotyped images that most other Americans—reared on Western movies—continue to apply to them. Pierre van den Berghe has caustically charged that the reservations have been reduced "to the status of human zoos for the amusement of tourists and the delight of anthropologists."[29]

Since the 1960s a militant Indian social movement has arisen, inspired by the success of the

[24] Alvin M. Josephy, Jr., "Indians in History," *Atlantic Monthly*, 225 (June 1970), p. 69.

[25] *Indians Taxed and Indians Not Taxed in the United States at the 11th Census: 1890* (Washington, D.C.: n.p., 1894), p. 63.

[26] Peter I. Rose, *They and We: Racial and Ethnic Relations in the United States*, 2nd ed. (New York: Random House, 1974), p. 25; Richard T. Schaefer, *Racial and Ethnic Groups* (Boston: Little, Brown, 1979), pp. 250–261; Howard M. Bahr, Bruce A. Chadwich, and Robert C. Day (eds.), *Native Americans Today: Sociological Perspectives* (New York: Harper & Row, 1972).

[27] American Indian Policy Review Commission, *Indian Health*, Task Force #6 (Washington, D.C.: U.S. Government Printing Office, 1976).

[28] Robert Burnette, *The Tortured Americans* (Englewood Cliffs, N.J.: Prentice-Hall, 1971), p. 22.

[29] Quoted in Rose, *op. cit.*, p. 22.

The social and economic conditions of American Indians are worse than those of any other minority group in the nation: no other group has such high rates of poverty or unemployment.

movement for black civil rights. Indians have founded intertribal organizations and demanded "Red Power." The American Indian Movement (AIM) attracted international publicity by "capturing" the South Dakota town of Wounded Knee, scene of the historic defeat of the Plains tribes.[30]

More significant, Indians are now taking legal steps to recover land that was illegally wrested from them in the past. The long-forgotten Indian Non-intercourse Act of 1870 provided that all land transactions between Indians and others must be ratified by Congress or become null and void. Many such transactions never received the required ratification, and more than half of the

[30]Robert Burnette and John Koster, The Road to Wounded Knee (New York: Bantam, 1974).

266 federally recognized tribes are now bringing legal claims for land and associated rights over minerals and rivers. The most dramatic demand to date is that of two tribes in Maine, whose claim to half of the land in the state has already been declared valid, forcing the state to attempt to negotiate a financial settlement with the tribes. In Alaska, Indians have gained $1 billion and 40 million acres of land in compensation for illegal seizures of their territory in the past. Other major claims for hundreds of thousands of acres are pending in Massachusetts, Rhode Island, Connecticut, and South Carolina, and there are lesser claims in a number of Western states. Many of these claims involve densely populated white neighborhoods and commercially valuable land rich in fossil fuels.

The most controversial claims, however, are likely to be those involving control over rivers in the Southwest, where there is an acute water shortage. Several tribes are making a collective claim on the water rights of the Arkansas River, and similar lawsuits in Arizona and New Mexico could give local tribes control over parts of the Colorado, San Juan, and Rio Grande rivers. Ironically, the suing tribes enjoy the full support and resources of the U.S. Justice Department, because the federal government is obliged by law to act as "guardian" for its legal "wards." Like many black Americans, many Indians are now demanding not assimilation but respect for their own culture; not full integration but the right to control their own affairs.

Hispanics

The Spanish-speaking population of the United States is a large, diverse, and rapidly growing one. It contains at least 7.2 million Mexican Americans, or Chicanos, 1.8 million Puerto Ricans, 700,000 Cubans, and 2.4 million other people from various Spanish-speaking nations of Central and South America. This official total of around 12 million people is definitely an underestimate, because a substantial part of the Hispanic population is not represented in Census Bureau data—partly because language difficulties discourage many Hispanics from completing and returning census forms, but primarily because a huge population of illegal Hispanic immigrants tries to avoid all contact with government agencies. In any event, the official statistics show that the Hispanic population is growing much faster than the rest of the population: between 1970 and 1978 it increased by a third, while the overall population increased by only 6.1 percent. The Hispanic population is growing so rapidly because of three factors: its relative youth (the median age is only twenty-two, meaning that a high proportion of the women are in the child-bearing years); its cultural reluctance, as a conservative, traditionalist, Catholic group, to practice family planning; and the constant inflow of new immigrants, legal and illegal, mostly over the Mexican border. Some demographers expect that Hispanics will overtake blacks as the nation's largest minority some time in the mid-1980s.[31]

The diverse groups within the Hispanic population share a common predicament as a primarily poor, Catholic, Spanish-speaking people in a predominantly affluent, Protestant, English-speaking country. Most Hispanics have relatively low levels of education and income: in 1976 they had completed a median of 10.3 years of education, compared with 12.3 for the general population;[32] in 1978 the median income for Hispanic men was $7,797, compared with $10,261 for other workers; and 21 percent of Hispanics live below the poverty line, compared with 9 percent of the remaining population.[33] The significant exception to this pattern is the Cuban population, which consists mostly of middle-class refugees who emigrated from their country in the 1960s and who have since used their skills to build a relatively prosperous community, centered in Miami. The Hispanics are an over-whelmingly urban population: 79.5 percent of the Chicanos and 96.1 percent of the Puerto Ricans live in metropolitan areas, an even higher percentage than that of the American population as a whole.[34] Nearly three-quarters of the Hispanic population lives in six states—New York, Texas, California, Arizona, Colorado, and New Mexico—but there are now substantial Hispanic enclaves in such urban centers as Chicago, St. Paul, Newark, New Orleans, Hartford, and Kansas City.

Chicanos have occupied the territories of the Southwest for over four centuries; ancestors of some of the present inhabitants became United States citizens involuntarily in 1848 when parts of the Southwest were ceded to the United States after the Mexican War. Yet for most of the period since then, other Americans have tended to regard Chicanos almost as aliens on American soil or, at best, what one writer refers to as "Americans on parole."[35] It is only in recent years that the Chicanos have come to be generally recognized as a genuinely American minority. Their ambiguous status has resulted from the fact that, unlike most other immigrant groups, they did not have to desert a homeland and cross an ocean in order to immigrate to the United States; and because Chicanos can and do travel easily and frequently between the United States and Mexico, constantly renewing their personal and cultural ties with their country of origin, there has been a tendency to think of them as being Mexican rather than American—as sojourners in the United States who can "go back home" if they are dissatisfied.[36] (Adding considerably to this image is the fact that an unknown but certainly substantial proportion of the Chicanos in the United States are illegal aliens.)

[31]Robert Lindsey, "U.S. Hispanic Populace Growing Faster Than Any Other Minority," *New York Times*, February 18, 1979, pp. 1, 16.

[32]Bureau of the Census, *Educational Attainment in the United States: March 1977 and 1976, Current Population Reports*, series p-60, no. 105 (Washington, D.C.: U.S. Government Printing Office, 1977), p. 13; and *Persons of Spanish Origin in the United States: March 1976, Current Population Reports*, series p-20, no. 310 (Washington, D.C.: U.S. Government Printing Office, 1977), pp. 23–25.

[33]Lindsey, *op. cit.*

[34]*Statistical Abstract of the United States, 1978, op. cit.*, p. 32.

[35]John Womack, Jr., "The Chicanos," *New York Review of Books*, August 31, 1972, p. 13.

[36]For good surveys of the Chicanos, see Joan W. Moore and Harry Pachon, *Mexican Americans*, 2nd ed. (Englewood Cliffs, N.J.: Prentice-Hall, 1976); and Carol A. Hernandez, Marsha J. Haug, and Nathaniel N. Wagner (eds.), *Chicanos: Social and Psychological Perspectives*, 2nd ed. (St. Louis: Mosby, 1976).

A Chicano mother in Texas describes her children's encounter with local bigotry.

. . .

"The worst time is when the children start asking me *why*. I discourage them. I tell them please, stop coming at me with questions. I don't know why the Anglos are on top and we are on the bottom. I don't know why we are so many in this country and they are so few, and they control everything. I don't know why we all don't get together and start marching down the road. One child tells me that we could win, if we only fought. Another child says we wouldn't have to fight, just stand up and shake our fists, and teach them that we are going to be our own bosses. That is fine—the talk of someone who is not old enough to work, not a man or a woman, but instead drunk on a dream.

"Let them have their hope, though. I do not want to crush my children with too much of the knowledge I have picked up over the years. There is a nun I know who has helped me a lot; she has made me a better mother. She will tell me what to say, how to answer questions. I used to argue with her. I used to say that I shouldn't say anything. But she won me over. She made me see that I can't ignore my children and hope that they stay out of trouble. After all, my mother always took me aside when I was a small girl and told me things. I recall her lowering her voice, almost to a whisper; and I would go away and think about what she said. Now I do the same; I call Carlos over to me, and I tell him that he is a strong boy, and he will be a strong man, but he must not say bad things to the Anglo foreman when he walks near, and he must not wave his toy gun around and promise to kill people—the sheriff. There is a good chance that the sheriff would laugh, if he heard Carlos threaten him, but there is just as good a chance that the sheriff would begin to wonder what is going on. He and his police come through here once or twice a year; they go from house to house, 'just checking,' they tell us.

"I remember a year ago, the sheriff saw a toy pistol, and picked it up, and pretended it was real. He asked the children to put their hands up. They saw he had the toy in his hand, so they laughed. He repeated his order. They still laughed. Then he got angry. He threw the toy on the floor and shouted at the children to get against the wall and put their hands up. They did too—right away; even Carlos, only two then, knew that he had better do exactly as told. I was afraid the sheriff would pull his guns, but he didn't. He just kept his hands on them and gave us a lecture: don't we know who's boss, and don't we know how to obey the law, and don't we know how to stay out of trouble, and from now on he's going to keep a special eye out for us, and we'd better be ready at any moment for him to come around, or one of his deputies, and when they do, we'd better not get fresh, or we'd all spend the night in jail, and he'd put us in one cell, and we could stay on the floor and have bread and water, and nothing else, because he doesn't believe in spoiling prisoners. Then he told the children that he was 'only kidding!'"

. . .

Source: Eskimos, Chicanos, Indians: vol. IV of *Children of Crisis*, by Robert Coles, M.D. (Boston: Little, Brown and Company, 1977). pp. 322–24. Copyright 1977 by Robert Coles.

The United States has long regarded workers on the other side of the Mexican border as a potential labor pool, whose members may be drawn on when needed and expelled when no longer required. Around the turn of the century, tens of thousands of Mexicans were brought into the United States to build the railroads and other facilities that would develop the Southwest. Still more were imported to help in the industrialization of the region during and immediately after World War I. In the depression years, however, work was scarce, and white Americans found competition from Mexican laborers highly unwelcome. During the 1930s, half a million people were deported to Mexico—many of them, perhaps a majority, being United States citizens who were unable to prove their citizenship and who were therefore assumed to be illegal aliens. During the 1940s, and especially during the years of World War II, cheap Mexican labor again became attractive, and contracted laborers, or *braceros*, were imported each year, with some interruptions, until 1964. In the early 1950s, however, illegal immigration began to increase noticeably, and there have been continual campaigns since then to stem the flow and to deport those immigrants who do gain entry to the United States.[37] But because Mexico has a 20 percent unemployment rate with nearly a fifth of the population earning less than $75 a year, the prospect of jobs in the United States, however menial, has become a magnet that increasingly draws work-seekers. In 1978, United States immigration officials caught some 860,000 illegal would-be immigrants, but it is likely that a far larger number escaped detection.

Urban Chicanos are concentrated in *barrios*, or ethnic neighborhoods, while many of the small rural population work as migrant farm laborers. The Chicano population is a relatively poor one: in 1978, 19 percent lived below the poverty line, a figure that was far greater than the national average. Educational achievement is also relatively low; a fifth of the population has less than five years of schooling.[38] Poor education and an often limited facility in English tend to restrict job opportunities. Many Chicano families use Spanish exclusively at home, and the children have little chance to learn English before going to school. Resentment at past attempts to "Anglicize" the Chicanos in school—for example, by forbidding the use of Spanish—has led to renewed and sometimes successful demands for Spanish or bilingual education. The extensive use of Spanish in schools will doubtless increase ethnic pride and solidarity, but it may also lessen the command of English that is necessary for real social mobility in what is an overwhelmingly English-speaking country.[39]

Much of the low income of the Chicano population, however, results from institutionalized discrimination and outright exploitation. A 1979 *New York Times*–CBS News poll showed that 66 percent of the inhabitants of the West believe that illegal Mexican immigrants do jobs that Americans will not. This opinion, it seems, is an accurate assessment of the illegal immigrants' economic function. Employers consistently hire Chicano workers at or below minimum wage rates: for example, when the California Division of Labor Enforcement recently surveyed nearly 1,000 companies in the garment industry, which relies heavily on Chicano migrants, it found that only 8 percent were paying as much as the minimum wage, and it also issued 616 citations for child-labor-law violations.[40]

The economic exploitation of Chicano farm workers has been an explosive issue in California and parts of the Southwest ever since Cesar Chavez unionized migrant workers, brought them out on strike, and organized nationwide boycotts of fruit picked by underpaid workers. Powerful economic interests have deeply resented the work of Chavez, and there have been several violent attempts to break strikes that he has organized. Inevitably, Chavez's campaign has provided an example and incentive for other collective action by Chicanos. They have taken an increasing part in electoral politics in the Southwest, but still wield far less power and influence than their numbers might suggest. In the long run, however, the Chicano population will be a political force to be reckoned with. Like the black leaders before them, Chicano leaders are demanding entry into mainstream America without assimilation into the "Anglo" culture.[41]

The other major Hispanic group, Puerto Ricans, are a people of Spanish, Indian, and negroid descent. The island of Puerto Rico has been an American possession since the Spanish-American War, and Puerto Ricans have been citizens of the United States since 1917. Over the past few decades migration from the island

[37]See Matt S. Meier and Feliciano Rivera, *The Chicanos: A History of Mexican Americans* (New York: Hill and Wang, 1972).

[38]*Statistical Abstract of the United States, 1978, op. cit.*, p. 32.

[39]Ellwyn R. Stoddard, *Mexican Americans*, 2nd ed. (New York: Random House, 1974).

[40]Lindsey, *op. cit.*

[41]Manuel P. Servin (ed.), *An Awakened Minority: The Mexican Americans*, 2nd ed. (Beverly Hills: Glencoe Press, 1974).

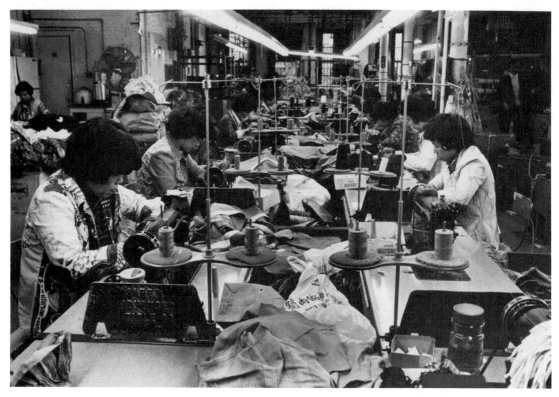

The "sweatshop" is still not a thing of the past. Throughout American history, recently-arrived minority groups have been economically exploited by groups that have already established themselves. Hispanic Americans are the main victims of this exploitation today; many of them are illegal immigrants or are unable to speak English, and they often have to work under conditions that violate federal and state laws on employment and earnings.

to the relatively better job opportunities available here raised the Puerto Rican population in the United States to more than 1.8 million, better than half of it being located in New York. Yet employment prospects, wages, and other conditions here are actually so bleak that a staggering 39 percent of Puerto Rican families live below the poverty line.[42]

Perhaps because of disappointment over these conditions, the Puerto Ricans are doing something no immigrant group has ever done before: they are returning to their homeland at a greater rate than they are immigrating here.[43]

Asian Americans

The Asian minority in the United States is a small but diverse one. At the time of the 1970 United States census there were rather more than 2 million people of Asian descent, repre-

[42]Lindsey, *op. cit.*

[43]Some useful sources on Puerto Rican Americans are Commission on Civil Rights, *Puerto Ricans in the Continental United States: An Uncertain Future* (Washington, D.C.: U.S. Government Printing Office, 1976); Kall Wagenheim, *Puerto Rico: A Profile*, 2nd ed. (New York: Praeger, 1975); Joseph P. Fitzpatrick, *Puerto Rican Americans: The Meaning of Migration to the Mainland* (Englewood Cliffs, N.J.: Prentice-Hall, 1971); and Stan Steiner, *The Islands: The Worlds of the Puerto Ricans* (New York: Harper & Row, 1974).

senting 1 percent of the population. Although no precise later statistics are available, their numbers have doubtless increased substantially since then, both through natural population growth and through continued immigration. The Asian Americans share certain social characteristics: in particular, they are concentrated in two states, Hawaii and California; they are very highly urbanized; and they include a greater proportion of foreign-born persons than other minorities in the United States. Yet there are considerable social and cultural differences among them. The largest Asian American groups are the Chinese and Japanese, followed by the Filipinos, Hawaiians, Koreans, and—the most recent arrivals—Vietnamese. In addition, there are even smaller minorities from a number of other Asian nations. Thus far, only the Chinese and the Japanese have been thoroughly studied by sociologists.

Most Chinese immigration to the United States took place between 1850 and 1880, when over 300,000 Chinese settled in America—chiefly in California, where they provided cheap labor for the construction of railroads and for the mining industry. The threat of their economic competition soon aroused violent anti-Chinese feelings among white workers, and beatings and lynchings of Chinese were not uncommon in California and other Western states (in Wyoming twenty-nine Chinese were massacred in a single incident in 1885). Fears of the so-called Yellow Peril reached almost hysterical levels, and Congress responded with the Chinese Exclusion Act of 1892, which severely restricted the number of Chinese entrants to the United States. The anti-Chinese movement remained unsatisfied, however, so from 1902 until 1943 the immigration of Chinese laborers was completely prohibited.

The Chinese in the United States have retained a great deal of their cultural heritage—including, for example, language, ideographic writing, cuisine, and organizations such as clans and secret societies. Perhaps as much by their own choice as by discrimination against them, they have kept to their own urban communities—the Chinatowns that exist in the major American cities. Despite their thriving appearance, the Chinatowns contain an array of social problems—most notably overcrowding (the population density of San Francisco's Chinatown is ten times that of the rest of the city) and extensive poverty (a 1974 study found that more than two-thirds of the families in New York's Chinatown had incomes below the poverty level).[44] The Chinese population is unusual in that it is significantly overrepresented in both the high-paying professional and technical jobs and in the very low-paying service jobs. Statistics for the average family income therefore tend to balance out, obscuring the fact that such a large proportion lives in poverty.[45]

The Japanese began immigrating to the United States—mainly to Hawaii—somewhat later than the Chinese, but they received a similar welcome: several anti-Japanese organizations were soon campaigning to prevent their continued entry. The state of California passed an Alien Land Act in 1913, which effectively prevented Japanese from owning land, and the Supreme Court held, until 1952, that persons born in Japan could not become United States citizens. The most extraordinary act of discrimination against the Japanese occurred during World War II, when, by presidential order, the entire Japanese population (including citizens born in this country) was removed from the cities of the West Coast and interned in "security camps" in the desert and the Rocky Mountains, allegedly because its members might be disloyal to the United States (no similar action was taken against German or Italian Americans, however). Many of those who were interned lost their jobs and businesses as a result of this arbitrary invasion of civil liberties.[46]

---

[44]Schaefer, *op. cit.*, pp. 329–330.

[45]Wen Lang Li, "Chinese Americans: Exclusion from the Melting Pot," in Anthony Gary Dworkin and Rosalind J. Dworkin (eds.), *The Minority Report* (New York: Praeger, 1976). For an excellent sociological portrait of the Chinese Americans, see Stanford M. Lyman, *Chinese Americans* (New York: Random House, 1974).

[46]Roger Daniels, *Concentration Camps U.S.A.: Japanese Americans and World War II* (New York: Holt, Rinehart and Winston, 1972).

In the extent to which it is assimilated, the contemporary Japanese American population contrasts not only with the Chinese Americans but also with virtually all other minority groups. Each succeeding generation has been more successfully assimilated than the preceding one. The Japanese even have words to describe these generations: *Issei*, Japanese-born; *Nisei*, second-generation, American-born; *Sansei*; third generation; and *Yonsei*, fourth generation. Culturally the latter generations are virtually indistinguishable from white Americans. They make little or no effort to maintain ties with Japan or its culture; they may know no Japanese; and their achievements in the professions and such fields as education are as high as, and sometimes higher than, those for the population as a whole.[47]

Yet, as Richard Schaefer points out:

> Today they have achieved success according to virtually any standard. There are some qualifications, however. . . . It is easy to forget that the achievements made by several generations of Japanese Americans were accomplished by overcoming barriers created by American society, not because they were welcomed. Many acculturated, successful Japanese Americans, if not most, are still not wholeheartedly accepted into the dominant group's inner circle . . .[48]

White Ethnics

At the time of the 1820 census virtually all the white inhabitants of the United States were of Anglo-Saxon Protestant background. From that point on, however, successive waves of immigrants of different European nationalities came to the United States. The first group, arriving soon after 1840, was the Irish. Other immigrants from Catholic areas of northern Europe followed soon after. A large section of the established population deeply resented the new arrivals, whom they saw as competition for jobs, housing, and other resources. Intense conflict followed,

and there were virulent anti-Irish and anti-Catholic riots in several major American cities during the mid-nineteenth century. Between 1860 and 1890 there was another major influx of immigrants, this time from Scandinavia and Germany; in fact, the Germans were the largest immigrant group ever to come to America. The final waves of European immigration took place between 1880 and 1914, this time from two main areas, Italy and eastern Europe. Over 4 million Italians left their native land to come to the United States, and millions of other immigrants, many of them Jewish, arrived from such countries as Hungary, Poland, the Balkan states, and Russia.

All these groups tended to be resented at first by those that had preceded them. Some groups, however, were eventually assimilated fairly readily into American society, particularly Protestant Germans and Scandinavians, who tended to disperse relatively soon after their arrival. Other ethnic groups, such as the Catholic Poles, Irish, and Italians, were less acceptable and from the time of their arrival tended to form large, closely knit communities in urban centers.[49] In the large Eastern cities these ethnic groups developed an informal alliance with the local Democratic party machines, which effectively traded jobs and other economic benefits for the votes of the newcomers. Even to this day these "white ethnic" groups remain overwhelmingly Democratic in their political allegiance.

The conventional assumption in the United States had always been that all the white ethnic groups would eventually be fully assimilated, gradually losing their distinctive identities as they merged into the American mainstream. Yet the early 1970s saw an entirely unexpected revival of ethnic sentiment in the United States—an event that seems closely related to the militancy among racial minorities during the previous decade.[50]

---

[47]Harry L. Kitano, *Japanese Americans: The Evolution of a Subculture*, 2nd ed. (Englewood Cliffs, N.J.: Prentice-Hall, 1976).

[48]Schaefer, *op. cit.*, p. 343.

[49]See William L. Yancey, Eugene P. Ericksen, and Richard N. Juliani, "Emergent Ethnicity: A Review and Reformulation," *American Sociological Review*, 41 (June 1976), 391–403.

[50]See Andrew M. Greeley, *Ethnicity: A Preliminary Reconnaissance* (New York: Wiley, 1974); and Leonard Dinner-

Many white ethnics, particularly among the working and lower middle class, have developed a resentment of the WASP (white, Anglo-Saxon Protestant) culture, whose members seem to have much easier access to the heights of social, political, and economic power. Michael Novak, an American of Slavic ancestry, writes of the experience of growing up in America as a member of an ethnic minority:

I am born of PIGS—those Poles, Italians, Greeks, and Slavs, non-English-speaking immigrants, numbered so heavily among the workingmen of this nation. Not particularly liberal, nor radical, born into a history not white Anglo-Saxon and not Jewish—born outside what in America is considered the intellectual mainstream. And thus privy to neither power nor status nor intellectual voice. Growing up in America has been an assault upon my sense of worthiness. . . . All my life, I have been made to feel a slight uneasiness when I must say my name. Under challenge in grammar school concerning my nationality, I had been instructed by my father to announce proudly, "American." When my family moved from the Slovak ghetto . . . to the WASP suburb on the hill, my mother impressed upon us how well we must be dressed, and show good manners, and behave—people think of us as "different" and we mustn't give them any cause. . . .

Nowhere in my schooling do I recall an attempt to put me in touch with my own history. The strategy was clearly to make an American of me. English literature, American literature; and even the history books, as I recall them, were peopled mainly by Anglo-Saxons. . . . I don't remember feeling envy or regret: a feeling, perhaps, of unimportance, of remoteness, of not having enough to count.

We did not feel this country belonged to us. We felt fierce pride in it, more loyalty than anyone could know. But we felt blocked at every turn.[51]

Like all other minority groups, the ethnic minorities have been made to feel "different," and in the past accepted to some extent the image that the dominant culture had of them.

The new racial pride of black Americans had a profound impact on white ethnic groups in that it legitimated cultural pluralism in America: for the first time a minority group had asserted its right to be different instead of attempting to minimize its differences, and white ethnics, too, have now come to regard their ethnicity as a source of potential pride.

Many analysts have suggested, however, that there is a deeper reason for the surge of white ethnic sentiment—a reason rooted in a perceived conflict of interest between the white ethnics and the nonwhite minorities. Peter Rose, for example, claims that many white ethnics resent the WASP majority for appearing to favor black Americans over other minorities, and resent the blacks themselves for not "waiting in line" for their turn to rise in the social hierarchy as other groups did before them. Rose argues that white ethnic feeling grew in the 1970s as a backlash reaction to the supposed success of the blacks in extorting benefits—such as affirmative-action programs, which apply to racial but not ethnic minorities—from guilt-ridden WASP policymakers.[52]

There may be some truth in this picture, but recent research suggests that the stereotype of the white ethnics as veritable Archie Bunkers—working-class, politically conservative, anti-intellectual, and racially prejudiced—needs substantial revision. Research by Andrew Greeley has shown that the ethnic Catholics are now the most financially and educationally mobile group in the United States. While it remains the case that the white ethnics are underrepresented in certain high-prestige positions, particularly those in foundations, private universities, and major business corporations, white Catholics now have the same number of years of education as the national average, and their average income slightly exceeds the average for the nation as a whole. Most of this progress, however, has been made by the Irish and the Italians—the two

stein and David M. Reimers, *Ethnic Americans: A History of Immigration and Assimilation* (New York: Harper & Row, 1975). For a more critical view of the issue, see Orlando Patterson, *Ethnic Chauvinism: The Reactionary Impulse* (Stein & Day: New York, 1977); and Howard F. Stein and Robert F. Hill, *The Ethnic Imperative: Examining the New White Ethnic Movement* (University Park, Penn.: Pennsylvania University Press, 1977).

[51]Michael Novak, "White Ethnic," *Harper's*, 243 (September 1971), 4–5.

[52]Rose, *op. cit.*, p. 103.

White ethnic Americans have found their voice and are insisting on respect for their own religious, linguistic, and other cultural traditions. Lapel buttons with such slogans as "Irish Power," "Polish and Proud," or "Kiss me, I'm Italian" all symbolize a new pride in ethnic diversity.

white ethnic groups that originated in western Europe and also the two that have been in the United States the longest. Irish Catholics, in fact, have more education and higher family incomes than any other Christian denomination. The ethnic groups from eastern Europe, however, still tend to lag behind. Moreover, there is no evidence that the white ethnics are more prejudiced than other whites against racial minorities.[53]

Ironically, after many decades in which assimilation has been unquestionably accepted as the proper and inevitable fate of American minorities, pluralism has become more respectable and legitimate than at any time in American history. Many Americans no longer criticize the society for its failure to serve as a "melting pot"; instead they question the desirability of a bland, homogeneous, "melted" nation. Good race relations, it is argued, are quite compatible with a plural society—provided the various groups interact together on the basis of equality and respect.

The Costs of Prejudice and Discrimination

Prejudice and discrimination against racial and ethnic minorities have many dysfunctional social costs for contemporary America.

Economic Costs. Any society that erects artificial barriers against full participation by a substantial number of its citizens invites economic losses. In the United States institutional discrimination denies minority-group members the opportunity to contribute to their society and to exploit their talents to the full;[54] and the entire nation suffers in consequence.[55] Moreover, vast sums of federal and local revenue must be spent in attempting to combat the many social problems—such as poverty, riots, crime, unemployment, and alcoholism—that result in part from discrimination.

Political Costs. Discrimination and prejudice result in poor race relations and lead to tension and antagonism that poison interpersonal rela-

---

[53]Andrew M. Greeley, *Ethnicity, Domination, and Inequality* (Beverly Hills: Sage, 1976), and *The American Catholic: A Social Portrait* (New York: Basic Books, 1977).

[54]For several more detailed examples, see H. Roy Kaplan (ed.), *American Minorities and Economic Opportunity* (Itasca, Ill.: Peacock, 1977).

[55]There is some dispute as to whether the white working class benefits economically from racial discrimination or whether racism tends to depress the incomes of white workers as well as nonwhites. Arguments for the former viewpoint are offered by Gary S. Becker, *The Economics of Discrimination* (Chicago: University of Chicago Press, 1971); and Robert Blauner, *Racial Oppression in America* (New York: Harper & Row, 1972). Arguments for the latter viewpoint are offered by Michael Reich, "The Economics of Racism," in David M. Gordon (ed.), *Problems in Political Economy* (Lexington, Mass.: Heath, 1971); and Albert Szymanski, "Racial Discrimination and White Gain," *American Sociological Review*, 41 (June 1976), 403–414.

tions among the groups in question and sometimes culminate in open conflict, including rioting and other forms of civil strife. The attention of government and administrative agencies is diverted from other pressing national problems to the persistent threat of political instability posed by poor race relations.

Psychological Costs. Discrimination and prejudice can have severe psychological effects on minority-group members—particularly if they internalize and partially accept the derogatory stereotypes that others apply to them. Studies conducted in the 1960s, for example, indicated that black children had a clear preference for white dolls or playmates over black, a preference strongly suggesting that the black children had low self-esteem.[56]

Personal Costs. For minority-group members the personal costs of prejudice and discrimination are multiple. As we have seen, there is a strong relationship between membership in a minority group, educational attainment, and income level. Minority-group members are likely to be poorly educated and therefore tend to earn less and to rear their children in a depressed neighborhood with low-quality schools—and so the cycle repeats itself in the next generation. Institutionalized discrimination makes it difficult to break out of the cycle. Lack of job opportunities traps minority-group members in the lower stratum of society, where life expectancy is shorter, crime rates higher, drug addiction more common, and marital breakdown much more frequent.

International Costs. Few Americans realize the extent to which continuing intergroup tensions and institutionalized discrimination damage America's international reputation. The United States tries to win support around the globe for values of liberty, equality, and human rights, yet continues to tolerate a system of stratification in which the boundaries of racial or ethnic groups are tied to those of social class. Indeed, foreign diplomats in the United States frequently complain of being mistaken for, and hence treated like, members of American minority groups. Understandably, the nations of the world—most of which are nonwhite—look askance at our domestic race relations. American prestige and influence suffer as a result.

CONFRONTING THE PROBLEM

The problem of poor race and ethnic relations and discrimination against minority groups is one that will not be easily solved. The object of public policy, however, must be to eliminate the barriers to equality that result from institutionalized discrimination. Legislation alone cannot solve the problem, although laws are a vital element in the process of improving race relations. Martin Luther King, Jr., once commented: "The law may not make a man love me, but it can restrain him from lynching me, and I think

[56]Judith Porter, *Black Child, White Child: The Development of Racial Attitudes* (Cambridge, Mass.: Harvard University Press, 1971). See also Kenneth J. Moreland, "Race Awareness Among American and Hong Kong, Chinese Children," *American Journal of Sociology*, 2 (November 1969), 360–374.

that's pretty important." In addition, laws have an impact that goes beyond the immediate practical effects they might have, for even if they lack strong public support at the time they are passed, laws tend to shape social values and attitudes in the long run.

There are some indications that American race and ethnic relations are improving—paradoxically, largely because of the turmoil caused by the civil rights movement and the ghetto riots of the 1960s. Conflict theory implies that tension over race and ethnic relations, like many other forms of conflict, can be beneficial because it provides an impetus to change; the events of the last two decades seem to bear out the validity of this approach. Black Americans, for example, were successfully oppressed for perhaps thirteen or fourteen generations, and for the most part accepted their plight with relative passivity. But as soon as a social movement for civil rights challenged the existing order, national attention was focused on the problems, a series of civil rights acts was passed, legal segregation was abolished, and overt discrimination declined abruptly. Similar gains are likely to be made by other groups as they launch social movements to bring about change, as the Indians and Chicanos are doing.

The history of earlier immigrant groups has shown that they are treated on a basis of equality when they have "made it" into the mainstream of American economic life. When this happens, the minority-group members are no longer socially isolated and concentrated in the most impoverished sections of the community, but instead are more or less randomly distributed among the social classes. Their different occupations and life styles make it much more difficult for others to maintain group stereotypes about them, and a variety of common political and economic interests emerge that crosscut racial or ethnic distinctions. This has been the case, as we have seen, with Japanese, Irish, or Italian Americans—all groups that were once held in contempt by the dominant majority. As minority-group members gain middle- and even upper-class status, their economic and hence political power becomes a force to be reckoned with, and social norms, values, and institutions are modified accordingly. For this reason, the elimination of economic discrimination against minority-group members is a prerequisite for good race relations and genuine equality.[57]

Although discrimination in employment is now illegal, the practice is still widespread and difficult to confront, because it is usually impossible to prove that an applicant has been denied a job on the grounds of minority-group membership. Largely as a result of this problem, the federal government and the courts have insisted on "affirmative action" to open up job opportunities and admission to educational institutions for racial minorities (and for women). The lack of minority-group employees or students is itself held as an indication that such discrimination is taking place, and to avoid this charge, employers and colleges have in the past often established quotas, or specific targets, for the numbers of minority persons they would admit, hire, or promote.

In yet another example of an intended solution to a social problem tending to create further problems, these affirmative action programs became highly controversial. What is "affirmative action" to one group is "negative discrimination" to another, and many majority-group members bitterly resent the experience of being discriminated against on the grounds of their group membership. They argue that jobs or college places should go to the most qualified applicants, regardless of race or sex, and that affirmative action is unjust. Supporters of the programs retort that the majority had shown little concern about such discrimination in the past, when they were the beneficiaries rather than the victims of discrimination. They also argue that there is no other way to make up rapidly for past discrimination against minorities, or to ensure that this discrimination does not continue into the future.

In 1978 the Supreme Court considered a landmark case on affirmative action in education, *Regents of the University of California versus Bakke*. Allan Bakke, a white man, had been refused admission to University of California Medical School, although his qualifications were better than those of some blacks and Chicanos who had been admitted. The school, it turned out, had a specific quota of sixteen places for minority admissions, and Bakke claimed that he had been illegally discriminated against because of his race. In a narrow 5 to 4 decision, the Supreme Court upheld Bakke, and ordered that he must be admitted to the medical school. The court's objection, however, was not to affirmative action as such but only to rigid quotas: it held that other college admission programs that give preference to minority applicants, but without specific quotas, are acceptable.

[57]For a useful analysis of some trends in patterns of socioeconomic inequalities, see David L. Featherman and Robert M. Hauser, "Changes in the Socioeconomic Stratification of the Races, 1962–73." *American Journal of Sociology*, 82 (November 1976), 621–651.

In 1979, the Supreme Court considered the important case of *United Steelworkers of America versus Weber,* which dealt with affirmative action in employment. Brian Weber, a white man, worked at a Kaiser Aluminum plant where 39 percent of the area's work force was black, yet blacks made up only 2 percent of the plant's skilled workers. To correct the imbalance, the company started a new training program, open to blacks and whites on a 50/50 basis, which would remain in operation until blacks were proportionately represented in skilled jobs. Weber did not have sufficient seniority to get one of the places reserved for whites in the training programs, and claimed that he was the victim of illegal discrimination. In a 5 to 2 majority decision, the Court ruled that private employers can legally give special preferences to minority workers, if the purpose is to eliminate "manifest racial imbalance" in their work force. In such cases, the court held, numerical quotas are acceptable.

What is public opinion on the issue? In 1977, before the rulings, the Gallup poll found that 83 percent of the public opposed affirmative action. Indeed, the programs were supported by fairly few even among the minority-group members that they were supposed to benefit—by only 11 percent of women and only 27 percent of nonwhites. But in 1979 the Harris poll reported that by a majority of 70 percent to 21 percent, whites support affirmative action as long as there are no rigid quotas. In other words, there seems to be wide support for the concept of equal opportunity in employment and college admissions, but little for systematic reverse discrimination. Even without rigid quotas, however, affirmative action programs will inevitably tend in many instances to favor minority-group members over whites. The issue of affirmative action raises delicate and complex issues of both principle and practice,[58] but no other means has yet been found to prevent subtle discrimination against minorities in hiring and admissions policies.

Even more controversial, perhaps, are attempts to desegregate the schools through the busing of children from one school district to another. This policy has two goals: to improve the standard of minority childrens' education and to encourage the more tolerant racial attitudes that are known to develop if different groups are integrated rather than isolated from one another. The policy is considered necessary because de facto segregation of neighborhood schools (especially in the North) has been little affected by de jure school desegregation, and there is strong evidence that school segregation contributes to the academic underachievement of racial minority groups. The relatively depressed educational attainments of these groups translates, in turn, into poorer jobs, lower incomes, and the perpetuation of racial inequalities from one generation to the next. Both the majority and the minority groups know that education is the key to social mobility and economic advantage in the United States, and it is hardly surprising that the issue has generated conflict between them.

What do we know about the effects of segregated schooling? In the early 1960s the federal government asked James Coleman to survey the subject. His findings, published in 1966 as *Equality of Educational Opportunity,*[59] are an important source of information on race and education in America. Coleman's data confirmed that blacks consistently scored lower than whites throughout the school years, but also indicated that the quality of school facilities was a relatively unimportant factor behind this difference in achievement. The most significant influences on the individual, he found, were the family background of the child, the cultural influence of the child's neighborhood, and the social-class "atmosphere" of the school, as determined by its ratio of lower-class to middle-class pupils. Thus, middle-class black children did better in school than lower-class white children, and lower-class blacks in schools with middle-class atmospheres did better than similar blacks in schools with lower-class atmospheres. Cole-

[58]Two useful sources for this complex issue are Nathan Glazer, *Affirmative Discrimination: Ethnic Inequality and Public Policy* (New York: Basic Books, 1975); and Barry R. Gross (ed.), *Reverse Discrimination* (Buffalo, N.Y.: Prometheus Books, 1977).

[59]James Coleman et al., *Equality of Educational Opportunity* (Washington, D.C.: U.S. Government Printing Office, 1966).

man's study indicated that school integration would have positive advantages for the lower achievers, but no effect on the academic attainment of the higher achievers.

Busing to desegregate the schools has proved highly unpopular in many quarters. Although more than 80 percent of all school systems that have desegregated in this way have done so without disruption, many have used busing only under court order; and in some districts there have been ugly incidents of racial violence. Some of the opposition comes from parents, black as well as white, who want their children to attend a neighborhood school; but much is clearly the result of racial prejudice. Yet once schools are desegregated in this way, local opposition tends to evaporate. A 1979 Harris poll found that only 8 percent of whites and only 16 percent of blacks considered the experience of busing their children to desegregated schools "unsatisfactory."

Two further concerns about busing have been voiced among sociologists: whether school integration in an atmosphere of hostility and even violence really does improve black pupils' achievements,[60] and whether school integration is hastening the "white flight" to the suburbs—and thus making the schools even more segregated as a result of the effort to integrate them.[61] Although more research will be needed before these questions can be fully answered, it does seem clear that there cannot be equal educational opportunity in schools that are segregated by class and race; and that as long as residential segregation persists in the United States, busing will be the only way to integrate the schools.

What will be the pattern of our race and ethnic relations in the years ahead? Milton Gordon has suggested that there are three possible patterns of intergroup relations for the future: Anglo-conformity, melting pot, and cultural pluralism.[62]

Anglo-conformity assumes the desirability of maintaining modified English institutions, language, and culture as the dominant standard in American life. In practice, "assimilation" in America has always meant Anglo-conformity, and the groups that have been most readily assimilated have been those that are ethnically and culturally most similar to the Anglo-Saxon group.

The *melting pot* is, strictly speaking, a rather different concept, which views the future American society not as a modified England but rather as a totally new blend, both culturally and biologically, of all the various groups that inhabit the United States. In practice, the melting pot has been of only limited significance in the American experience.

Cultural pluralism implies a series of coexisting groups, each preserving its own tradition and culture, but each loyal to an overarching American nation. Although the cultural enclaves of some immigrant groups, such as the Germans, have declined in importance in the past, many other groups, such as the Italians, have retained a strong sense of ethnic identity and have resisted both Anglo-conformity and inclusion in the melting pot.

Current trends indicate that, for the foreseeable future at least, cultural pluralism is likely to be the dominant pattern in the United States. In the long run, the society may become a true "melting pot," or it may eventually tend toward Anglo-conformity. At present, however, most minorities are finding a source of pride and

[60]See Frederick Mosteller and Daniel Patrick Moynihan, *On Equality of Educational Opportunity* (New York: Random House, 1972); Nancy H. St. John, *School Desegregation: Outcomes for Children* (New York: Wiley, 1975); Thomas F. Pettigrew et al., "Busing: A Review of the Evidence," *Public Interest* 20 (Winter 1973), 86–118; Howard B. Gerard and Norman Miller, *School Desegregation: A Long-Term Study* (New York: Plenum, 1975); and Ray C. Rist, *The Invisible Children: School Integration in American Society* (Cambridge, Mass.: Harvard University Press, 1978).

[61]See James S. Coleman, Sara D. Kelly, and John A. Moore, *Trends in School Segregation, 1968–1973* (Washington, D.C.: Urban Institute, 1975); Thomas F. Pettigrew and Robert F. Green, "School Desegregation in Large Cities: A Critique of the Coleman White-Flight Thesis," *Harvard Educational Review*, 46 (February 1976), 1–53; Christine H. Rossell, "School Desegregation and White Flight," *Political Science Quarterly*, 90 (Winter 1976), 675–695; and Michael W. Giles, "White Enrollment Stability and School Desegregation: A Two-Level Analysis," *American Sociological Review*, 43 (December 1978), 848–864.

[62]Milton M. Gordon, "Assimilation in America: Theory and Reality," *Daedalus*, 90 (Spring 1961), 363–365; and *Human Nature, Class, and Ethnicity* (New York: Oxford University Press, 1978).

identity in their own histories and cultural backgrounds. But it should be remembered that the three possible patterns are not mutually exclusive. A group like the Jews, for example, may be Anglo-conformist in dress, may be assimilated into the economy, and yet may be pluralist in its religious or marital preferences. It is likely that members of various groups will experience many problems of role conflict as they attempt to determine their identities and sort out their lives into Anglo-conformist, assimilated, and pluralist elements. The general trend, however, seems to be toward pluralism. But whether an openly pluralist society will enjoy better race relations than our present society remains to be seen.

SUMMARY

1. Poor race and ethnic relations have been an enduring problem for American society. A race consists of people who share distinctive physical features and are regarded as a biological unity; an ethnic group consists of people who share distinctive cultural features and are regarded as a cultural unity. The United States is often regarded as a "melting pot," but in fact those groups that differ both physically and culturally from the dominant majority have been excluded from full participation in American life.

2. From the functionalist approach the problem results from social disorganization: there is a dysfunctional discrimination against certain groups, which has negative effects for both these groups and for the society. From the conflict approach, racial and ethnic antagonisms are caused by competition among groups for scarce social, economic, and political resources.

3. Racism is the ideology that is used to justify the domination of one group over another. Racism translates into prejudice (attitudes) and discrimination (acts). Prejudiced thinking involves a refusal to test negative stereotypes against reality, and is often irrational and inconsistent. Discrimination may be legal (de jure) or institutionalized (de facto); the latter form is pervasive in the United States and is difficult to eradicate.

4. Some important minorities in contemporary America are blacks, Indians, Hispanics, Asian Americans, and "white ethnics." All suffer in some measure from prejudice and discrimination, and members of each group are now asserting their group's right to be different rather than to be assimilated.

5. Prejudice and discrimination result in economic, political, psychological, and personal costs and seriously damage American prestige abroad.

6. Minority groups have made some progress in recent years, largely because social movements have organized to press their case. Opinion polls show that the majority group is becoming less prejudiced but that much racial antagonism remains. A major goal must be to eliminate economic discrimination against minority groups, since this is the source of much of the problem. Programs to achieve this objective, such as affirmative action and school integration through busing, are highly controversial. The options open to the United States in the future appear to be Anglo-conformity, the melting pot, and cultural pluralism; current trends are toward the last.

GLOSSARY

Discrimination. Action against others on the grounds of their group membership and supposed group characteristics.

Ethnic group. A large number of people who have had a high level of mutual interaction over a long period of time and who therefore share distinctive cultural traits; as a result they regard themselves, and are regarded by others, as a cultural unity.

Ethnocentrism. The tendency for members of one group to assume that their own values, attitudes, and norms are superior to those of other groups and to judge other groups by their own standards.

Ideology. A set of ideas and beliefs that justifies the interests of those who hold it; the dominant ideology in any unequal society therefore justifies the inequality.

Institutionalized discrimination. Discriminatory acts and policies that, although not necessarily encoded

in law, are nonetheless pervasive in the major institutions of the society.

Legal discrimination. Discriminatory acts and policies that are encoded in the law of the land.

Prejudice. A "prejudged" negative attitude toward members of other groups.

Race. A large number of people who have interbred over a long period of time; as a result, they share distinctive physical features and regard themselves, and are regarded by others, as a biological unity.

Stereotype. A rigid mental image of a group that is applied indiscriminately to all its members.

FURTHER READING

BAHR, HOWARD M., *et al.* (eds.). *Native Americans Today: Sociological Perspectives.* New York: Harper & Row, 1972. A useful collection of articles on the Native Americans, covering a series of topics such as assimilation, militancy, discrimination, and problems of urban life.

GREELEY, ANDREW, M. *The American Catholic: A Social Portrait.* New York: Basic Books, 1977. An important study of the Catholic "white ethnics," in which many established stereotypes are challenged.

HERNANDEZ, CAROL A. *et al.* (eds.). *Chicanos: Social and Psychological Perspectives.* 2nd ed. St. Louis: Mosby, 1976. A comprehensive series of articles on various aspects of Chicano life in the United States.

JENCKS, CHRISTOPHER, *et al. Inequality: A Reassessment of the Effect of Family and Schooling in America.* New York: Harper & Row, 1973. A controversial and important book in which the authors contend that educational inequality is the result, not the cause, of social and racial inequality.

JONES, JAMES M. *Prejudice and Racism.* Reading, Mass.: Addison-Wesley, 1972. A useful summary of theories and research findings on prejudice. The book draws on the disciplines of sociology, psychology, and social psychology.

KITANO, HARRY L. *Japanese Americans: The Evolution of a Subculture.* 2nd ed. Englewood Cliffs, N.J.: Prentice-Hall, 1976. A good sociological profile of both immigrant and native-born Japanese Americans.

MOORE, JOAN W., and HARRY PACHON. *Mexican Americans.* 2nd ed. Englewood Cliffs, N.J.: Prentice-Hall,

1976. An excellent sociological study of the Chicanos, with special emphasis on the problems they face in the United States and their responses to those problems.

NOVAK, MICHAEL. *The Rise of the Unmeltable Ethnics.* New York: Collier, 1973. A provocative discussion of the "white ethnics," by a writer who himself feels a sense of alienation from the American mainstream because of his Slavic background.

PINKEY, ALPHONSO. *Black Americans.* 2nd ed. Englewood Cliffs, N.J.: Prentice-Hall, 1975. A useful survey of the black minority in the United States; the book includes material on black history, current problems, and recent social movements.

ROSE, PETER I. *They and We: Racial and Ethnic Relations in the United States.* 2nd ed. New York: Random House, 1974. A brief and readable review of intergroup relations in the United States. The book includes material on the history, life style, and problems of each group.

SCHAEFER, RICHARD T. *Racial and Ethnic Groups.* Boston: Little, Brown, 1979. A comprehensive and up-to-date survey of race and ethnic relations in the United States, with useful chapters on each of the country's minority groups.

WILSON, WILLIAM J. *The Declining Significance of Race: Blacks and Changing American Institutions.* Chicago: University of Chicago Press, 1978. A controversial argument that differences of social class are becoming more important than differences of race as an influence on the social status of black Americans.

9
Sex Roles

THE PROBLEM

In the early 1960s a new social movement began to capture American public attention: a women's movement that demanded liberation from the traditional restraints placed upon the female sex in American society. Since that time the issue of sex roles has come to be regarded as a serious social problem—so much so that an amendment to the Constitution prohibiting sex discrimination has already been passed by Congress and awaits ratification by the states. And although attention has been focused primarily on the traditional roles of women, the traditional role of men is increasingly being seen as problematic also.

This is not the first time that a social movement has demanded the equality of the sexes in the United States. In the early part of the nineteenth century, women working for the abolition of slavery became aware that they, too, were denied such elementary rights as the vote. (Women were even refused seats at a major antislavery conference in 1840 on the grounds of their sex, while the male delegates delivered impassioned speeches about the oppression of slaves.) By the latter part of the nineteenth century some feminist leaders had become very radical indeed: a few of them even demanded the abolition of the family, which they considered an oppressive institution. In the early twentieth century, however, the movement began to focus all its energies on winning the franchise. After a long campaign marked by fierce controversy and jailings of feminist militants, women finally won the right to vote in 1919. Almost immediately the movement lost its im-petus, and the issue of womens' rights receded into the background.[1]

In the latter half of the twentieth century new social forces precipitated the present women's movement. The American birth rate was steadily declining and women were spending less time in their traditional childrearing activities. The number of women in the labor force rose rapidly after 1950, and although they were relegated mostly to low-paying jobs, more and more of them were enjoying some measure of financial independence. Yet women found many career avenues closed to them, and at all levels they were paid less than men for equal work. The gap between social ideals and social realities was widening: traditional sexual inequalities had changed little, but the expectations of women were rising. For centuries a sex-based division of labor and hierarchy of power had been regarded as part of the natural order, biologically and perhaps even divinely ordained. In the space of a few years these social arrangements came to be widely seen as artificial, cultural products—created by society, and therefore, in principle, capable of being modified by society as well.

Betty Friedan, one of the earliest leaders of the women's liberation movement, writes of the dawning perception among middle-class women of sex roles as a social problem:

[1]See William L. O'Neill, *Everyone Was Brave: The Rise and Fall of Feminism in America* (New York: Quadrangle Books, 1969); and Judith Papachristou, *Women Together: A History in Documents of the Women's Movement in the United States* (New York: Knopf, 1976).

The problem lay buried, unspoken, for many years in the minds of American women. It was a strange stirring, a sense of dissatisfaction, a yearning that women suffered in the middle of the twentieth century in the United States. Each suburban wife struggled with it alone. As she made the beds, shopped for groceries, matched slipcover material, ate peanut butter sandwiches with her children, chauffeured Cub Scouts and Brownies, lay beside her husband at night—she was afraid to ask even of herself the silent question—"Is this all?" . . . If a woman had a problem . . . she knew that something must be wrong with her marriage, or with herself. Other women were satisfied with their lives, she thought. What kind of woman was she if she did not feel this mysterious fulfillment waxing the kitchen floor? She was so ashamed to admit her dissatisfaction that she never knew how many other women shared it. If she tried to tell her husband, he didn't understand what she was talking about. She did not really understand it herself. . . .

But on an April morning in 1959, I heard a mother of four, having coffee with four other mothers . . . . say in a tone of quiet desperation, "the problem." And the others knew, without words, that she was not talking about a problem with her husband, or her children, or her home. Suddenly they realized they all shared the same problem.[2]

Today millions of people have changed their ideas about the "natural" basis of established sex roles. What was once unthinkingly accepted as an unalterable fact of life is now seen as an irrational, wasteful system that threatens one half of the population with permanent inferiority and frustration of potential and the other half with demands for lifelong competitiveness, aggressiveness, and emotional insensitivity.

SEX ROLES IN AMERICA

What exactly is a sex role? The sociological concept of a role is analogous to the role of the actor in the theater: that is, a role is a set of behaviors and attitudes taken on by someone in a given social position in accordance with the social expectations of how a person in that particular postion should behave and be treated by others. *Sex roles* are the learned patterns of behavior expected of the sexes in a given society. During the socialization process, each person learns the content of these roles and plays his or her part accordingly.

At birth every person in every society is classified on the basis of physical characteristics into one of two categories, male or female. But each society also elaborates these basic biological differences between male and female into secondary, nonbiological differences—cultural notions of "masculinity" and "femininity," which refer to social and psychological differences, as reflected, for instance, in clothing, prestige, occupational role, and temperament. The distinction between male and female is based on the biological fact of *sex*; the distinction between masculine and feminine is based on cultural notions of *gender*. Each society, however, tends to regard its own conceptions of gender as being as natural and inevitable as the physical differences of sex.

Largely as a result of the challenge to traditional American assumptions concerning gender, sex roles in the United States have changed rapidly in recent years and are certainly among the most flexible in the modern world. Unlike women in many societies, the American wife is no longer treated, in practice and indeed in law, as the property of her husband; and it is possible, though difficult, for a woman to achieve independence and even eminence in what is essentially a man's world. But this flexibility in sex roles is only relative. Clearly defined roles still exist, and are reflected in the personality characteristics of the sexes and in the occupational roles that men and women play.

Sex-Linked Personality Characteristics. The American woman is traditionally supposed to be conformist, passive, affectionate, sensitive, intuitive, dependent, self-sacrificing for her family, and primarily concerned with domestic life. She is supposed to be ignorant of sports, politics, and economics, but deeply concerned about her personal appearance and her routine domestic

[2]Betty Friedan, *The Feminine Mystique* (New York: Dell, 1963), pp. 11–15.

duties. She should not appear ambitious or obviously intelligent, or she risks being regarded as "unfeminine." In her relationships with men she should not take the initiative, but should be expressive, emotional, tender, and appreciative.

The American man, on the other hand, is traditionally supposed to be fearless, tough, self-reliant, logical, competent, independent, and aggressive. He should display little emotion, and in particular must never cry. The American male should have definite opinions on the major issues of the day, should be capable of making authoritative decisions in the home and on the job, and should be the breadwinner for the family. He takes the initiative in the relationships with women, and expects to dominate them in virtually every sphere of life.

Paradoxically, however, the masculinity of the American boy seems to be regarded as potentially fragile, and far more care is taken to maintain it than the femininity of the girl. The boy has a terror of appearing in any way "effeminate," and parents are far more disturbed by indications that their son is a "sissy" than that their daughter is a "tomboy." The social reaction against boys who violate "masculine" norms is very strong. The fashion of long hair on males had to be imported to America from Europe, and was met with an intensely negative reaction: the very right of a boy to choose his own hair length in school or at work has had to be won piecemeal in court battles across the nation. Yet a girl who chooses to wear her hair short is hardly likely to encounter the same outraged response. This feature of the socialization process stems from the fundamental inequality of the sexes in our society. The little girl who aspires to the higher status by acting in a boyish way is behaving in a manner considered understandable; the little boy who behaves in a girlish way is regarded as seriously maladjusted.

Sex-Based Division of Labor. The division of labor in America reflects a belief in the superior abilities of the male. Traditionally the woman's place is in the home, and housework is considered a very menial job indeed; when domestic servants are paid to do it, their wages are among the lowest in the nation. Men work outside the

Young American males are socialized into roles that demand aggression, competitiveness, toughness, and control of the emotions. Boys who deviate from these norms may arouse anxiety in parents, teachers, and even psychiatrists.

home, usually in more highly paid jobs than women, and they tend to be promoted to much higher positions. Interestingly, the personality characteristics attributed to each sex are very selectively interpreted in the division of labor. Women are supposed to have deft fingers—but only for sewing, not for brain surgery. Women are supposed to be understanding and intuitive—but only as mothers, not as clergy or psychiatrists. Women are supposed to be caring and nurturing—but only as nurses, not as doctors. Thus it is that women represent only 35.5 percent of American writers, artists, and entertainers, 31.7 percent of college teachers, 27.5

percent of accountants, 11.2 percent of physicians, 9.5 percent of lawyers, and 2.7 percent of engineers. On the other hand, they represent 71 percent of teachers (mostly in elementary schools), 79.8 percent of librarians, 87 percent of cashiers, 96.3 percent of typists, 96.7 percent of nurses, and unsurprisingly, 99 percent of all secretaries.[3]

As noted, women earn far less than men, partly because they are paid less for doing similar work and partly because they are concentrated in the lower-paying jobs.[4] The average working white woman earns less than the average working black man, and the black woman, subject to double discrimination, earns least of all. Of the 7.7 million families in America that have a female householder with no husband present, 2.5 million live below the poverty line.[5] The median income of women is actually shrinking in relation

to that of men. In 1955 it was 63.9 percent of the male income; in 1970 it was 59.4 percent; and in 1977, 58.5 percent.[6]

This sex-based division of labor and income is basic to the maintenance of existing sex roles in America because it institutionalizes the role of the male as family breadwinner and thus ensures the economic dependency of the female. Major changes in American sex roles are unlikely to come about unless there are significant changes in the distribution of jobs and incomes between men and women. At present the man who is supported by his wife, or who earns less than she does, is likely to experience feelings of inadequacy and even shame. There are still some social sanctions, too, against the wife who makes a success of her career outside the home, as though there were something "wrong" with the professional woman.

ANALYZING THE PROBLEM

Both the functionalist and the conflict perspectives throw light on the problem of sexual inequalities. A functionalist analysis is particularly useful in explaining why these inequalities arose in the first place; a conflict analysis helps us to understand why they continue to persist.

The Functionalist Approach

The functionalist approach starts from the fact that some differences in the roles of men and women appear to have existed throughout history in every society. The functionalist explanation of this phenomenon is that traditional sex roles must play some function in maintaining the stability of the social system—at least in the simple, preindustrial societies in which these sex roles first arose.

Every society establishes some division of labor among its members, with people specializing in particular tasks. Such division ensures that people train for and become expert in particular occupational roles, and thus increases efficiency. There are many possible criteria for assigning various roles among the members of a population, such as intelligence, race, educational achievement, physical strength, or good looks. Two criteria, however, are universal in every society: age and sex. In all human societies the old play different roles than the young, and women play different roles than men—sometimes slightly different, sometimes very different. Like role differences based on age, the division of certain forms of labor by sex is in some

[3]U.S. Bureau of the Census, *Statistical Abstract of the United States, 1978* (Washington, D.C.: U.S. Government Printing Office, 1978), pp. 419–421.

[4]See David L. Featherman and Robert M. Hauser, "Sexual Inequalities and Socioeconomic Achievement in the U.S., 1962–1973," *American Sociological Review* (June 1976), 462–483.

[5]U.S. Bureau of the Census, *Current Population Reports*, series P-60, no. 115, "Characteristics of the Population Below the Poverty Level: 1976," (Washington, D.C.: U.S. Government Printing Office, 1978), p. 1.

[6]*Statistical Abstract of the United States, 1978, op. cit.*, p. 464.

ways useful and has a sound biological basis. The human infant is helpless for a longer period after birth than any other animal and must be cared for. It would be quite possible, of course, for the social role of "mother" to be played by someone other than the biological mother—including the father or some other male. It is more convenient, however, if the role is played by the biological mother, who has already borne and nursed the child. In simple, preindustrial societies, therefore, women stay home to play their child-raising role and, consequently, tend to take on those tasks that can be performed in and near the home. Men, on the other hand, take on tasks that lie beyond the home (such as the care of wandering livestock), or play roles that make optimum use of their greater short-term physical endurance (such as those of warrior or hunter).

This analysis explains why men and women have tended in the past to fill different roles, but why is the role of the male considered superior? Part of the reason is that the male is physically stronger than the female and can therefore control her by force if necessary,[7] and part of the reason is that she is dependent on him for protection and food. The man therefore becomes the dominant partner in the arrangement, and his activities and personality patterns tend to be more highly regarded and rewarded. Over time these sex roles gradually become institutionalized and are passed on from generation to generation. The social origins of the gender differences between the sexes are forgotten, and the differences come to be regarded as part of the natural order. Some functionalists have argued that the sex-based division of labor is effective even in modern societies: they claim that the modern family functions better if it has one member (the husband) who plays an instrumental, active role in relation to the outside world, and one member (the wife) who plays a nurturing, passive role in relation to the other family members.[8]

The Conflict Approach

Conflict theorists do not dispute this explanation of why traditional sex roles first arose, but they claim that the traditional roles are not functional in modern society. We no longer live in simple, preindustrial communities: we are living in a vast, highly diversified modern economy, where the daily activities of men and women are far removed from these primitive origins. American women, for example, no longer spend virtually the whole of their reproductive period bearing one child after another. In fact, the average American woman spends only 3 percent of her entire lifetime in pregnancy and nursing. Apart from the activities related to childbirth, gender characteristics in modern societies are simply relics from the past. Traditional sex roles may actually be dysfunctional in a modern society, for they create artificial barriers that prevent people from achieving their full potential.

Conflicts theorists draw parallels between inequalities based on sex and those based on class or race.[9] An early statement of this view was made by Friedrich Engels.[10] Engels wrote:

> The first class antagonism which appears in history coincides with the development of antagonism between man and woman . . . and the first class oppression with that of the female sex by the male. . . . The wellbeing and development of the one group are attained by the misery and repression of the other.[11]

According to this analysis, the inequalities of the sexes are based on a conflict of interest between

[7]This idea is explored in Susan Brownmiller, *Against Our Will: Men, Women, and Rape* (New York: Simon and Schuster, 1975).

[8]See Talcott Parsons and Robert F. Bales, *Family, Socialization, and Interaction Process* (Glencoe, Ill.: Free Press, 1953).

[9]For example, Helen Hacker, "Women as a Minority Group," *Social Forces*, 30 (1951), 60–69; Randall Collins, "A Conflict Theory of Sexual Stratification," *Social Problems*, 19 (1971), 3–12; William Henry Chafe, *Women and Equality: Changing Patterns in American Culture* (New York: Oxford University Press, 1977).

[10]Friedrich Engels, *The Origin of the Family, Private Property, and the State* (New York: International Publishers, 1942).

[11]Quoted in Arlene S. Skolnick and Jerome H. Skolnick (eds.), *Family in Transition* (Boston: Little, Brown, 1971), p. 280; see, also, Floyd Dotson, "Marx and Engels on the Family," *American Sociologist*, 9 (November 1974), 181–186.

the dominant and the subordinate group. Men can enjoy superior status only by keeping women in an inferior status, preventing them from making full use of their talents and thereby providing themselves with greater opportunities to do so. There is no doubt a good deal of truth to this analysis, yet it remains a crude one. In particular, it overlooks the fact that sexual stratification differs from class stratification because it crosscuts the other inequalities in society: for example, a woman may be upper class because she is white and married to a wealthy man, and may thus enjoy superior status in relation to many black or lower-class males and other females as well.

Modern theorists take a more subtle approach to the issue, but still maintain, as Michael Gordon puts it, that "the economic position of women is the key determinant of the relations between husbands and wives, as it is the key determinant of relations between men and women in society at large."[12] In other words, to quote an old folk saying, "He who pays the piper, calls the tune." To the extent that men make the greater contribution to the economy of both the society and the family, they will have greater power and influence than women. Conversely, to the extent that women make gains toward full economic equality with men, they will have greater social and political equality also.

The empirical evidence lends strong support to this analysis.[13] In the most simple preindustrial societies–those that subsist by hunting and gathering whatever food they need–there is some sexual division of labor but very little inequality between the sexes. The men tend to the hunting, primarily because it can take them many hours or possibly days to track down even a wounded animal–a task that is more readily done by someone who is not pregnant, suckling, or carrying infants. The women, on the other hand, do the bulk of the more leisurely gathering

of vegetables, fruits, nuts, and insect delicacies. Hunting with primitive weapons, however, is only rarely successful: the men may hunt for days and catch nothing. The women thus produce the bulk of the society's food, and this major economic contribution is reflected in the high degree of equality between the sexes in these societies. In more advanced agricultural societies, however, men tend to make a greater economic contribution: they are typically responsible for the heavy agriculture, the masonry, carpentry, and similar craft work, and the military plundering of neighbors that together generate most of the wealth of their societies. As a result, the inequality of the sexes becomes much more marked. This situation continues in early industrial societies, in which the bulk of the labor force is male, with those few women who work outside the home being paid very low wages. Since most women in these societies generate little or no income themselves, they are entirely dependent on their breadwinning men. In more advanced industrial societies like the United States, however, women begin to play an ever increasing part in the economy. In 1890 only 4.6 percent of married American women were in the work force; in 1940 it was 16.7 percent; by 1977 it had risen to 47.1 percent.[14] More than 40 percent of American workers are now female (See Figure 9.1).[15] Conflict theory would predict that as more women entered the work force, they would demand and gain greater social, economic, and political equality–and that is precisely what is happening.

Conflict theory does not imply, of course, that men take part in a deliberate, conscious conspiracy to subjugate or oppress women. It simply means that men benefit from the existing sex-role patterns and have little motive to change them. Since it is still men, not women, who hold political, economic, and social power, the prevailing arrangements continue to reflect their interests. According to conflict theory, changes are likely to result when a social movement of

[12]Michael Gordon, *The American Family: Past, Present, and Future* (New York: Random House, 1978), p. 199.

[13]See Alice Schlegel (ed.), *Sexual Stratification: A Cross Cultural View* (New York: Columbia University Press, 1977); and M. Kay Martin and Barbara Voorhies, *Female of the Species* (New York: Columbia University Press, 1975).

[14]*Statistical Abstract of the United States, 1978, op. cit.*, p. 404.

[15]*Ibid.*, p. 398.

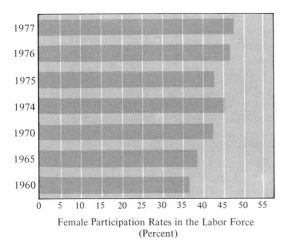

Female Participation Rates in the Labor Force
(Percent)

FIGURE 9.1 **Female participation in the labor force: 1960–1977.** Female participation in the American labor force has increased so rapidly since the early 1960s that nearly half of the nation's women are now engaged in or seeking work outside the home. This trend implies both a release from the traditional homemaker role and an enhanced financial independence for women, and American sex roles have inevitably been changing as a result.

the subordinate group challenges the existing order, as the women's movement has been doing.

SEXISM

The traditional sexual inequalities are rooted in the division of labor, and are maintained not by force but by the power of ideas. For centuries it seems to have been generally assumed that men are inherently superior to women, just as it has often been assumed that aristocrats are inherently superior to peasants or that one race is inherently superior to another. As we saw in Chapter 7 ("Poverty") and Chapter 8 ("Race and Ethnic Relations"), the domination of one social group by another is always justified by an *ideology,* a set of ideas and beliefs that justifies the perceived interests of those who hold it; the ideology of the dominant group in any unequal society therefore justifies the inequality. Typically, the ideology becomes so pervasive that

even the subordinate group tends to accept it: peasants may believe in the right of aristocrats to rule them; colonized peoples may believe in the superiority of the colonizers; or women themselves may believe in the superiority of men.

The ideology that justifies racial inequalities is called racism; in recent years a parallel term, *sexism,* has been coined to refer to the beliefs and values that justify the domination of women by men. According to sexist ideology, the gender differences that we find between men and women are rooted in their biological differences: "anatomy is destiny," and men are equipped for an active role in the world, women for a passive one.[16]

Vivian Gornick and Barbara Moran explain the concept of sexism:

Woman's condition, here and now, is the result of a slowly formed, deeply entrenched, extraordinarily pervasive cultural (and therefore political) decision that—even in a generation when man has landed on the moon—woman shall remain a person defined not by the struggling development of her brain or her will or her spirit, but rather by her childbearing properties and her status as companion to men who make, and do, and rule the earth. Though she is a cherished object in her society, she shall remain as an object rather than becoming a subject. . . . She may use wealth but cannot make it; she may learn about independence only so that she can instill it in her male children, urge it forward in her husband. . . . Her sense of these characteristics of adult life is sharply and distinctly *once removed.* . . . Everything in her existence, from early childhood on, is bent on convincing her that the reality of her being lies in bearing children and creating an atmosphere of support and nurturance for those who aggress upon the world with the intent of asserting the self, grasping power, taking responsibility—in other words, those who are living life as it has always been defined by human principle.
This is the substance of sexism. This is the creation of thousands of years of thought and

[16]See Sheila M. Rothman, *Woman's Proper Place: A History of Changing Ideals and Practices, 1870 to the Present* (New York: Basic Books, 1978); Viola Klein, *The Feminine Character: History of an Ideology* (Urbana, Ill.: University of Illinois Press, 1975).

reinforced patterns of behavior so deeply imprinted, so utterly subscribed to by the great body of Western conviction, that they are taken for "natural" or "instinctive." Sexism has made of women a race of children, a class of human beings utterly deprived of self-hood, of autonomy, of confidence—worst of all, it has *made the false come true.* Women have so long shared acquiescently in society's patriarchal definition of them . . . that they have become the very thing itself.[17]

Let us examine more closely the differences between the sexes, to determine what basis—if any—there is for the sexist assumption that nature has adapted men and women for their traditional social roles.

HOW DIFFERENT ARE THE SEXES?

The changes that can take place in American sex roles will obviously be limited by any inborn differences between the sexes that are relevant to the roles of men and women in society. The question of which differences between the sexes are innate and which are learned—and which differences are even relevant—has therefore been a major focus of research. We shall look first at the evidence from biological and psychological studies, and then at the cross-cultural evidence of sex roles in other parts of the world.

Innate Sex Differences: Biological and Psychological Evidence

Few social or biological scientists would dispute that there are certain innate, unlearned differences between the sexes. The problem that confronts researchers is to determine which differences are innate and which are learned through the socialization process.

There are obvious anatomic sexual and reproductive differences between males and females, and these differences are inevitably reflected in some of the cultural arrangements

concerning sexual behavior and kinship structure. In addition, men and women have different levels of some hormones in their bodies. A hormone is a chemical substance that can influence physical development and some forms of behavior. Each sex has both "male" and "female" hormones, but the proportion of male hormones is greater in men and that of female hormones greater in women. Experiments have shown that if male hormones are injected into the females of some animal species, the females become more aggressive and have heightened sex drive. This evidence cannot be uncritically applied to human beings, however, since the behavior of lower animals is much more subject to hormonal influences than our own, which is almost entirely learned. Hormonal differences may have some effect on the behavior of the sexes, but the current consensus among scientists is that this influence is a minor one.[18]

Apart from these basic differences, there is clear evidence that women are in most respects physically healthier than men in all societies. The male fetus inherits a greater number of sex-linked weaknesses resulting from characteristics of the male chromosomes. Over thirty disorders, such as hemophilia, webbing of the toes, and certain forms of color blindness, are found exclusively in the male for this reason. The rate of fetal and infant mortality is significantly higher for males than for females, and women are less susceptible to most diseases and tend to live substantially longer than men. Women's rate of physical maturation is also faster than that of men in every respect except muscular development. Women can tolerate pain better than men and have greater physical endurance, except in short-term feats of strength.[19]

Some psychological differences between the

---

[17]Vivian Gornick and Barbara K. Moran (eds.), *Women in Sexist Society: Studies in Power and Powerlessness* (New York: Basic Books, 1971), pp. ix–xx.

[18]See Richard C. Friedman, Ralph M. Richart, and Raymond L. Vande Wiehe (eds.), *Sex Differences in Behavior* (New York: Wiley 1974).

[19]See Shirley Weitz, *Sex Roles: Biological, Psychological, and Social Foundations* (New York: Oxford University Press, 1977); Betty Yorburg, *Sexual Identity: Sex Roles and Social Change* (New York: Wiley, 1974); Michael Teitelbaum (ed.), *Sex Roles: Social and Biological Perspectives* (New York: Doubleday Anchor Books, 1976).

sexes can be observed soon after birth.[20] Female babies, for example, tend to be more content and less physically active than boys and are also more sensitive to a number of physical stimuli—warmth, cold, touch, and sound. Greater differences between the sexes emerge as the children grow older, but it is almost impossible to determine the origins, learned or innate, of many of these differences. Frequently, girls become more docile and eventually more dependent than boys. They also learn to talk and read at an earlier age and seem more intellectually mature: remedial education classes in elementary and junior high schools are filled with boys, not girls. Girls are superior to boys at numerical computation and tasks involving verbal facility, whereas boys are better than girls at tasks based on mechanical, spatial, and analytic ability; but the relative skills of the sexes vary to some extent according to age. These differences might be innate, but they might also be the product of cultural conditioning. Girls may be better at language and reading than boys, for example, simply because they are encouraged to spend more time in the company of adults; and they may escape remedial classes simply because they are socialized to be more attentive and docile in school and therefore learn more readily.

Some of the most significant research on sex-linked behavior concerns children who have been deliberately or mistakenly assigned to the wrong sex at birth. (This may happen when psychologically impaired parents, wanting their child to be of the opposite sex, raise a boy as a girl or vice versa. It may also occur when various genital deformities cause confusion about an infant's sex and result in the child's being assigned, on the basis of apparent genital characteristics, to a sex at variance with its hormonal and chromosomal sex; or when a male infant is born without, or through some accident loses, his penis, leading physicians and psychologists to recommend that he be raised as a transsexual female.) If a child is biologically male but reared as a female, what happens? If anatomy were destiny, we would expect the child to resist socialization as a female, and to grow up with "masculine" characteristics as a result of his innate genetic predispositions. In fact, however, children can be readily socialized into the "wrong" sex role. John Money and his associates studied clinical evidence from a number of cases in which a baby's sex had been incorrectly classified. They found that the misassigned children fully and easily adopted the sex roles into which they had been socialized, and that unless the assignment was corrected before the age of three or four, the children strongly resisted attempts to change them and had great difficulty identifying with the new role. Money concluded that sex role is quite independent of physiological sex, and that the human species is "psychosexually neuter at birth."[21]

Other Cultures: Anthropological Evidence

Humans are reared by other humans, and it is therefore very difficult to separate the learned from the unlearned components of behavior. Historical and cross-cultural evidence can be helpful in this respect, however. If all cultures reveal much the same pattern in their sex roles, then the case for an absolute, biological basis for these roles is strengthened; but if there are wide cultural variations in the sex roles, the biological basis must be much less important.

In fact, sex roles vary a great deal across cultures and through history. Even within Western culture there have been many historical variations. Today we consider a concern with cosmetics and finery to be a primarily feminine characteristic, but not so long ago it was the European male who wore silks, wigs, stockings, and perfume. Long hair on males has been

[20]The outstanding source for the psychological similarities and differences of the sexes is Eleanor Maccoby and Carol Jacklin, *The Psychology of Sex Differences* (Palo Alto, Calif.: Stanford University Press, 1974.)

[21]John Money, Joan Hampson, and John Hampson, "Imprinting and the Establishment of Gender Role," *Archives of Neurology and Psychiatry*, 77 (March 1967), 333–336; See, also, John Money and Anke A. Ehrhardt, *Man and Woman, Boy and Girl* (New York: New American Library, 1974); and Richard Green, *Sexual Identity Conflict in Children and Adults* (Baltimore: Penguin, 1975).

In many other countries, women perform work that Americans have traditionally regarded as appropriate only for men. American attitudes are changing, however, and it is now possible for women to do "men's jobs"—although stigma still attaches to the man who does a "woman's work."

normal throughout most of western European history, yet it has been considered "effeminate" for most of this century. In several parts of Europe men have worn skirts; the Scottish kilt and the monk's frock are among the few surviving examples.

Studies by social scientists of cultures around the world have consistently shown a fairly clearly defined division of labor between the sexes. In an analysis of the division of labor by sex in some 224 societies, George Murdock found that although there are some sharp differences in the activities assigned to members of each sex, the allocation of duties does not necessarily correspond to our own notions of what constitutes man's or woman's work. Until recently there were many local laws in the United States restricting the weights that a working woman

could lift, but in most cultures the carrying of heavy burdens is considered a woman's job.[22]

In another survey of 565 societies, Murdock found that about three-quarters of them transmitted rights and property patrilineally (through the father) and only a quarter matrilineally. He also found polygamous marriage to be permitted in some 431 societies, only 4 of which allow the wife to have more than one spouse.[23] Other cross-cultural studies have shown that in most societies men have greater formal power in the family than women. Wives are usually expected to show

[22]George P. Murdock, "Comparative Data on the Divison of Labor by Sex," *Social Forces*, 15 (May 1935), 551–553.
[23]George P. Murdock, "World Ethnographic Sample," *American Anthropologist*, 59 (August 1957), 664–687.

Table 9.1   Division of Labor in 224 Societies by Sex

ACTIVITY	NUMBER OF SOCIETIES IN WHICH ACTIVITY IS PERFORMED BY				
	Males Always	Males Usually	Either Sex Equally	Females Usually	Females Always
Pursuit of sea mammals	34	1	0	0	0
Hunting	166	13	0	0	0
Trapping small animals	128	13	4	1	2
Herding	38	8	4	0	5
Fishing	98	34	19	3	4
Clearing land for agriculture	73	22	17	5	13
Dairy operations	17	4	3	1	13
Preparing and planting soil	31	23	33	20	37
Erecting and dismantling shelter	14	2	5	6	22
Tending fowl and small animals	21	4	8	1	39
Tending and harvesting crops	10	15	35	39	44
Gathering shellfish	9	4	8	7	35
Making and tending fires	18	6	25	22	62
Bearing burdens	12	6	35	20	57
Preparing drinks and narcotics	20	1	13	8	57
Gathering fruits, berries, nuts	12	3	15	13	63
Gathering fuel	22	1	10	19	89
Preservation of meat and fish	8	2	10	14	74
Gathering herbs, roots, seeds	8	1	11	7	74
Cooking	5	1	9	28	158
Carrying water	7	0	5	7	119
Grinding grain	2	4	5	13	114

Source: Adapted from George P. Murdock, "Comparative Data on the Division of Labor by Sex," *Social Forces* (May 1935).

deference to their husbands; a rare exception to this general rule was medieval chivalry, which required a very elaborate courtesy by the upper-class male to the upper-class female. (Traces of this chivalry still remain today: it is considered polite for a man to open a door for a woman or to rise when a woman enters a room.) Although there are a few societies, such as the Berber in North Africa, in which the females appears to exercise more authority in the family than the male, there are no societies in which men are not politically dominant.

In an extensive cross-cultural survey of human sexual behavior, Clellan Ford and Frank Beach found a consistent pattern of male sexual dominance and privilege. In most societies, people believe that men should take the initiative in sexual matters, although there are some societies, such as the Maoris and the Trobrianders, in which the women are expected to do so. Also, in nearly all societies the sexual behavior of unmarried girls is much more rigidly controlled than is that of unmarried boys, and married women are usually subject to much stricter sanctions for extramarital sex than married men.[24]

Are there recurrent similarities in the temperament and personality of the sexes in different cultures? After a study of the available evidence, anthropologist Roy D'Andrade concludes:

The cross-cultural mode is that males are sexually more active, more deferred to, more aggressive,

[24]Clellan S. Ford and Frank Beach, *Patterns of Sexual Behavior* (New York: Harper & Row, 1951).

less responsible, less nurturant, and less emotionally expressive than females. The extent of these differences varies by culture. And in some cultures some of these differences do not exist (and occasionally the trend is actually reversed).[25]

That some societies succeed in reversing the "normal" personality characteristics associated with each sex is significant, because it shows how the content of sex roles can be radically altered by an appropriate cultural environment. The anthropologist Margaret Mead conducted one of the most influential studies of societies whose roles differed from our own. She studied three tribes in New Guinea and found that the first required both males and females to behave in a way we would consider "feminine"; the second required both sexes to behave in a way we would consider "masculine"; and the third reversed the personality types we would consider "normal" for the two sexes. Mead concluded: "We no longer have any basis for regarding such aspects of behavior as sex-linked. . . . Standardized personality differences between the sexes are . . . cultural creations to which each generation, male or female, is trained to conform."[26]

SEX-ROLE SOCIALIZATION

Human beings can survive under an extraordinary variety of conditions precisely because, unlike other animals, we lack complex, inborn, rigidly patterned responses: we are highly adaptable because almost all our behavior is learned. Through the learning process of socialization, people in every society internalize social norms, accepting them as defining the "natural" or "right" way to behave.

Acquiring Sex Roles

By what process of socialization do people acquire the sex roles that their society expects them to play? Three main theories have been pro-

posed: the Freudian, the social-learning, and the cognitive-developmental. Although the Freudian theory of sex-role acquisition has few supporters among modern psychologists, it has had and continues to have such immense influence among the public that we will consider it here. The social-learning and the cognitive-developmental theories are more plausible modern approaches to the question.

Freudian theory. Sigmund Freud (1856–1939) was the founder of psychoanalysis. He was an original, profound, and imaginative thinker, and his forthright discussion of sex has had a liberalizing influence on the sexual attitudes of the twentieth century. His analysis of sex-role acquisition, however, has had an unfortunate effect, for it has reinforced the "anatomy is destiny" view.[27] The problem is that Freud, tending like most people to be ethnocentric, had difficulty seeing beyond the confines of his own society. That society was the highly puritanical environment of late-nineteenth-century middle-class Vienna, where children were supposed to be seen but not heard; where fathers were supposed to be remote, stern, and aloof, and mothers, passive and docile; and where sex was a forbidden topic.

Freud believed that both male and female infants identify at first with the mother, because they are reared by her and because they perceive the father as more remote and less nurturing. This situation poses a particular problem for the growing boy, who has to break his identification with the mother and identify instead with his father if he is to develop into a normal male adult. Freud believed that the male child develops a strong sexual love for the mother and deeply resents the father, who has prior sexual

[25]Roy G. D'Andrade, "Sex Differences and Cultural Institutions," in Eleanor Maccoby (ed.), *The Development of Sex Differences* (Stanford: Stanford University Press, 1966), p. 201. See, also, Martin and Voorhies, op. cit.; and Ernestine

Friedl, *Women and Men: An Anthropologist's View* (New York: Holt, Rinehart and Winston, 1975).

[26]Margaret Mead, *Sex and Temperament in Three Primitive Societies* (New York: Morrow, 1935), pp. 190–191.

[27]See Sigmund Freud, "Some Psychical Consequences of the Anatomical Distinction Between the Sexes" (originally published 1925) in Jean Strouse (ed.), *Women and Analysis* (New York: Viking, 1974). See, also, Jean B. Miller (ed.), *Psychoanalysis and Women* (Baltimore: Penguin, 1973); and Juliet Mitchell, *Psychoanalysis and Feminism* (New York: Random House, 1974).

rights over the mother. Freud called this phenomenon the "Oedipus complex," after the mythical Greek hero who unwittingly killed his father and married his mother. The boy experiences intense conflict, realizing that his love for his mother is inappropriate and sometimes even fearing that the father will castrate him. This conflict is finally resolved when the boy represses his love of the mother and identifies instead with the father, and is thus able to internalize masculine norms of behavior. Freud also suggested a parallel process for the girl. Although her sex role is already established through her identification with the mother, she still needs to loosen this bond to some extent in order to develop an independent sense of self. Freud therefore hypothesized a "penis envy" on the part of the small girl, which leads her to identify to some extent with her father. Once she realizes the futility of the envy, she is free to develop her own independent female sex role.

Most modern psychologists dismiss this theory as fanciful speculation, especially since the processes involved are supposed to be unconscious and therefore cannot be tested. Further, the theory assumes that anatomy is destiny because it sees the basic nature of woman as being determined by her discovery that she lacks a penis, which causes her to feel deprived and envious and to assume a passive, subservient role—a role Freud regarded as a natural, normal part of female personality. The male, on the other hand, identifies with the hostile, castrating father in order to preserve his valued appendage, and develops feelings of superiority over the female, who lacks this organ. But however outside the mainstream this analysis may seem today, Freud did make one valuable contribution: the notion that sex-role acquisition is a complex process depending very much on early experiences in both the familial and social environment.

Social Learning Theory. Psychologists of the social-learning school are influenced by the "behaviorist" theory that all human behavior is learned through a process of rewards and punishments. According to behaviorism, the child who touches a hot stove is punished by the experience of pain, so the act is not repeated; the child who conforms to the "right" sex role is rewarded, so the behavior is repeated and extended. Deviance from the appropriate sex-role behavior (for example, a little boy's playing with girls' dolls) is punished, if only by ridicule, so the behavior is discouraged. Social-learning theorists accept this basic behaviorist approach, but believe it is a simplistic analysis of a very complex process. They argue that additional but somewhat different types of social learning are also at work. Specifically, they hold that children will learn behaviors simply through observing them in others, even though they are not rewarded or punished themselves. Social learning is particularly likely to take place, these theorists argue, if children identify with models—such as the mother or father—and observe these models being rewarded for specific sex-role behavior.[28]

Some of these social-learning experiences are selectively offered by parents and others. They provide opportunities for the girl, but not the boy, to learn to sew; they provide the boy, but not the girl, with a baseball. Other conditioning occurs more randomly as children attempt various behaviors for themselves, and find that some of their acts are rewarded while others draw a negative social response. In this manner boys and girls are gradually conditioned into an acceptance of whatever sex-role behaviors are considered appropriate in their society, and they regard any deviation from these roles, in themselves or in others, as being somehow "wrong."

Cognitive-Developmental Theory. This newer approach, as outlined by Lawrence Kohlberg, differs from behaviorist theory in an important respect. Kohlberg acknowledges the importance of social learning, but places much more emphasis on the individual. Children, Kohlberg believes, actively construct their own sex roles instead of being passively conditioned into them. Kohlberg regards sex-role acquisition as a result of cognitive—that is, intellectual—development. The child makes a basic intellectual judgment early in life that he or she is a boy or

---

[28]Walter Mischel, "A Social Learning View of Sex Differences in Behavior," in Maccoby (ed.), *op. cit.*, pp. 56–81.

girl, and then actively selects those activities and values that conform to this self-image. Children define themselves as belonging to one category or another; they develop a strong preference for the category that includes themselves, and they then construct their experience to conform to this preference.

Kohlberg succinctly explains the difference between the social-learning approach and his own theory. In the former, the child says, "I want rewards; I am rewarded for doing boy things, therefore I am a boy." In the latter, the child says, "I am a boy, therefore I want to do boy things, therefore the opportunity to do boy things is rewarding to me." The difference between the two approaches lies in the role of the individual. In social-learning theory the child is passively conditioned by society; in cognitive-developmental theory the child takes cues from the surrounding society but actively constructs his or her own sex role. Both theories acknowledge, however, the importance of socialization as the main source of sex-role identification.[29]

Sex Role Socialization in the United States

The learning of sex roles in America takes place largely through several important agencies of socialization, notably the family, the schools, and the media. During this process, which begins at birth and continues in various forms throughout the life cycle, the peer group plays an important role in monitoring and reinforcing sex-appropriate behavior.

The Family.   Socialization into appropriate sex roles starts early in the United States, almost at the time of birth. Frequently, babies are dressed in sex-related colors and given sex-related toys; girls are cooed over and boys are bounced on the parental knee. By the time they are eighteen months old, children are already behaving according to expectations; the few who attempt to deviate from these expectations thereafter are subject to strong family and peer-group pressure to conform.

In fact, children are so effectively socialized into "appropriate" sex roles by their parents that they attain a clear sense of their own sex identity long before they are aware of the physical basis of sex differences. Allan Katcher found that when children up to the age of four or five are asked to assemble segments of dolls in such a way that the segment containing the genitals matches other parts of the body and clothing style, most children reveal themselves to be confused or entirely ignorant of the genital basis of sex differences.[30] Yet they are quite satisfied that the categories of "boy" and "girl" exist, and identify strongly with their own personal category.

Throughout the childhood years, parents take great care to induce sex-appropriate behavior in their children. As Ruth Hartley notes:

> There is little in the girl's training to emphasize instrumental competence or achievement in the mastery of the impersonal aspects of the environment. From infancy, small females are valued in terms of the attractiveness of their persons and the appropriateness of their interpersonal responses. They are directed toward the manipulation of persons as a means of obtaining gratification. Little is demanded of them in the way of competitive or autonomous achievement. The stress is not on proving one's prowess, but rather on avoiding the objectionable. Girls gain approval . . . by doing the rather undemanding things that are expected of them. . . . A girl need not be bright as long as she is docile and attractive. . . . This kind of treatment is likely to produce rather timid, unventuresome, unoriginal, conformist types.[31]

The early socialization of boys, however, is entirely different:

> Almost from birth the boy has more problems to solve autonomously. In addition, he is required

---

[29]Lawrence Kohlberg, "A Cognitive-Developmental Analysis of Children's Sex-Role Concepts and Attitudes," in Maccoby (ed.), *op.cit.*, pp. 82–173.

[30]Allan Katcher, "The Discrimination of Sex Differences by Young Children," *Journal of Genetic Psychology*, 87 (September 1955), 131–143.

[31]Ruth E. Hartley, "American Core Culture: Changes and Continuities," in Georgene H. Seward and Robert C. Williamson (eds.), *Sex Roles in Changing Society* (New York: Random House, 1970), pp. 140–141.

Boys and girls are socialized into separate attitudes and interests. Parents contribute to this differential socialization in many ways—for example, by giving children sex-related toys and encouraging sex-specific activities.

to limit his interest at a very early age to sex-appropriate objects and activities, while girls are permitted to amble their way to a similar status at a more gradual and natural pace. . . . He is challenged to discover what he should do by being told what he should *not* do, as in the most frequently employed negative sanction, "Don't be a sissy!" . . . Interest in girlish things is generally forbidden and anxiety-provoking in American boyhood. . . . The boy is constantly open to a challenge to prove his masculinity. He must perform, adequately and publicly, a variety of physical feats that will have very little utility in most cases in adulthood. He is constantly under pressure to demonstrate mastery over the environ-

ment, and, concomitantly, to suppress expression of emotion.[32]

By encouraging or discouraging various behaviors, the parents ensure that the early experience of their children will equip them with particular sex-role orientations.

The School. The school reinforces sex roles in many ways, chiefly through sex-based segregation of many curricular activities: girls, for instance, are often channeled into sewing and cooking classes; boys, into woodworking and printing classes. The girl who tries to enter a mechanics class may still face ridicule and even a tough battle to register for the course, and so may the boy who tries to register for a sewing or ballet class. The school discourages boys in particular from pursuing "feminine" interests: teachers and counsellors may find deviance from the female role in the direction of the male role tolerable, but reverse deviance is regarded as shameful and incomprehensible. Although girls are academically more advanced than boys of the same age during the early school years, they gradually lose this advantage. They do progressively less well compared with boys: fewer girls go on to college, and fewer still to graduate school. A number of factors underlie this waste of female talent, one of them being that many schools do not encourage academic success in girls to the same extent as in boys. Girls, perhaps lacking confidence in their ability to achieve in such subjects as science, or perhaps fearing that they will be labeled "unfeminine," are reluctant to tackle "masculine" courses.

Children's schoolbooks also encourage sex-typed attitudes.[33] Several studies have shown how children's literature, in both its stories and illustrations, presents sex-typed images of adult behavior. A study by Lenore Weitzman and her associates focused on those children's picture books regarded by the American Library Association as the best books of the year. In close to a third of the sample there was no female character

---

[32]*Ibid.*, p. 141.
[33]Nancy Frazier and Myra Sadker, *Sexism in School and Society* (New York: Harper & Row, 1973).

at all; when females were present, they usually had an insignificant or inconspicuous role. Since women represent 51 percent of the population, it might have been expected that about half the characters would be female, but, in fact, males outnumbered females in the books by a ratio of 11 to 1. In the case of the other animals with obvious sex identities, the ratio of males to females was even higher: 95 to 1. The ratio of titles featuring males and females was 8 to 3.[34]

School textbooks follow a similar pattern. A study of textbooks by Marjorie U'Ren found that they devoted only 15 percent of their illustrations to women. She comments: "The significance of this imbalance is obvious. We tend to forget the simple fact that the female sex is half the species, that women are not merely a ladies' auxiliary to the human race."[35] Florence Howe points out that in an annotated catalog of books distributed to teachers through the National Council of Teachers of English, titles are listed separately under "especially for boys" and "especially for girls." Howe's own analysis of school readers that are intended for both sexes concluded:

> Primers used in the first three grades offer children a view of a "typical" American family: a mother who does not work, a father who does, two children—a brother who is always older than a sister—and two pets—a dog and sometimes a cat—whose ages and sexes mirror those of the brother and sister. In these books, boys build or paint things; they also pull girls in wagons and push merry-go-rounds. Girls carry purses when they go shopping; they help mother cook or pretend they are cooking; and they play with their dolls. . . . Plots in which girls are involved usually depend on their inability to do something—to manage their own roller skates or to ride a pony.[36]

These images, Howe points out, may contribute significantly to children's sense of their own identity and potential.

The Media. The media, and particularly media advertisements, are an important influence on sex-role socialization. Lucy Komisar draws attention to this function of advertising:

> Advertising . . . legitimizes the ideal, stereotyped roles of woman as temptress, wife, mother and sex object, and portrays women as less intelligent and more dependent than men. . . . Advertising also reinforces men's concepts about women's place and women's role—and about their own roles. . . . Why is it masculine for men to wash cars, but a sign of "henpecking" for them to wash dishes?[37]

Critics allege that media advertisements, particularly TV commercials, not only reflect false stereotypes but also exploit the sexuality of women and demean their intelligence. Germaine Greer makes this point with considerable force:

> Every survey ever held has shown that the image of an attractive woman is the most effective advertising gimmick. She may sit astride the mudguard of a new car, or step into it ablaze with jewels; she may lie at a man's feet stroking his new socks; she . . . may dance through woodland glades in slow motion in all the glory of a new shampoo; whatever she does her image sells. . . . Her glossy lips and mat complexion, her unfocused eyes and flawless fingers, her extraordinary hair all floating and shining, curling and gleaming, reveal the inhuman triumph of cosmetics, lighting, focusing and printing, cropping and composition. She sleeps unruffled, her lips red and juicy and closed, her eyes as crisp and black as if new painted, and her false lashes immaculately curled. Even when she washes her face with a new and creamy toilet soap her expression is as tranquil and vacant and her paint as flawless as ever. If ever she should appear tousled and troubled, her features are miraculously smoothed to their proper veneer by a new washing powder or a bouillon cube. For she is a doll: weeping, pouting or smiling, running or reclining, she is a doll. . . .

---

[34]Leonore J. Weitzman *et al.*, "Sex Role Socialization in Picture Books for Preschool Children," *American Journal of Sociology*, 77 (May 1972), 1125–1149.

[35]Marjorie B. U'Ren, "The Image of Women in Textbooks," in Gornick and Moran (eds.), *op cit.*, p. 326.

[36]Florence Howe, "Sexual Stereotypes Start Early," *Saturday Review*, October 16, 1971, p. 82.

[37]Lucy Komisar, "The Image of Women in Advertising," in Gornick and Moran (eds.), *op. cit.* pp. 304–311.

Christian Dior's 'Sculptured Body' collection. Sleek new bodywear worn with Christian Dior's silky smooth support pantyhose. Both made with Lycra® so they can hug and caress your every move. A sensuous body conscious way of dressing for day or nights out.

Christian Dior

American women learn to place great value on their physical attractiveness and their youth. Mass media advertising encourages these attitudes, and a multibillion dollar cosmetics industry exploits them.

So the image of woman appears plastered on every surface imaginable, smiling interminably. An apple pie evokes a glance of tender beatitude, a washing machine causes hilarity, a cheap box of chocolates brings forth melting joyous gratitude. . . even a new stick-on bandage is saluted by a smirk of satisfaction.[38]

Advertising copywriters do not seem to have a high regard for the intelligence of their female audience. As a result, TV ads show women rapturously caressing newly polished tables, or going into ecstasies over the dazzling whiteness of their wash. Advertising directed to a male audience also exploits the stereotype of the unintelligent woman. Parker pens used this advertisement: "You might as well give her a gorgeous pen to keep her checkbook unbalanced with. A sleek and shining pen will make her feel prettier. Which is more important to any girl than solving mathematical mysteries."[39] IBM had a telling advertisement for a typewriter: "If she makes a mistake, she types right over it. If her boss makes a revision, she types just the revision." Secretaries, it seems, make "mistakes," but bosses make only "revisions."[40] We might note, too, that it is not only women who are absurdly stereotyped by advertising. Men always appear handsome, assertive, well-built, cleanly shaved

[38]Germaine Greer, *The Female Eunuch* (New York: Bantam, 1971), p. 57.

[39]Komisar, *op. cit.*, p. 306.
[40]*Ibid.*, p. 308.

VOICES

The following recollection is by the artist, Miriam Schapiro:

. . .

My mother was also a splendid housekeeper. About her domestic gifts I was, and am, ambivalent. When I talk of work, I mean "outside" work. My own attitude toward householding is to do as little of it as possible. My mother's floors were always shined, her linens always clean. Even as I describe this, I realize that in the development of my own attitudes toward nesting, her kind of caring was important. Yet, like everyone else in this society, I still have difficulty assigning reality or meaning to the work-at-home to which many women have devoted their entire lives. Although my mother gave me many important examples of caring and working, it was only when I joined the women's movement, only when I provided a context of femaleness for myself, that I could absorb and appreciate my mother's experience. Yet, I have lived out an experience parallel to hers all through the years; I too have been a homemaker, a nester, and a mother.

During the depression, my mother took a job in a department store. Once she had "real" work— "worldly" work—I began to assign her a space I had previously reserved for my father; however, I still believed that to be out in the world, making your mark on it, you had to be a man. Once my mother took that job she appeared more forceful, more concentrated, more economical in her use of time—as we would say now, "more together." But even this didn't prove to me that a woman, my mother, could do real work in the world. Somehow my conditioning rigidly reinforced a perverse sense of the world as being a place where only a man could work.

As a child, as an adolescent, as a college student, I was remarkably single-minded. I cared most about being an artist, about making my art. The first complication in my life was marriage to another artist.

. . .

Only once did marriage and work seem at odds—when Paul took a job at the University of Missouri and, jobless, I went with him. I was not happy. The transition between graduate school and the world hadn't worked for me. When we married, we had made an unspoken pact to preserve *his* ego and career. I didn't realize what it would cost me. Nor did he. After two years, I prevailed upon him to move to New York.

New York was a small art world then and we plunged immediately into it. We found companionship among artists for the first time. Abstract expressionism was the prevailing, vigorous style of the period—I began making abstract expressionist paintings. I was also conducting my own postgraduate education in painting. I was tapped for the work I did and invited to show my paintings. I became "visible."

As I neared the age of thirty-two, I wanted to

and smoothly groomed, bristling with the symbols of success such as a new car, seductive tobacco, an elegant sports jacket, or odor-destroying chewing gum—all to win the favors of the inevitable fawning female.

What happens to the portrayal of the sexes in advertising happens throughout the mass media. As a useful exercise, you might take a look at "human interest" articles and reports in any newspaper or magazine. You will notice that men are always described in terms of their occupations or activities; women, almost always in terms of their physical appearance. If a man is murdered, the headlines will read "Prominent lawyer slain in city apartment"; but if it is a woman, we are more likely to be told "Attractive blonde slain in city apartment." The social column will tell you that "Mr. Kevin Williams, a successful record producer, was accompanied by his lovely auburn-haired wife, Debbie," not that "Mrs. Debbie Williams, an employment agency supervisor, was accompanied by her slim, blond husband, Kevin." If you change the names and sexes in the articles and the news printed by the mass media, you will gain a sharp insight into the way they trivialize the female sex.

All these images are part of our culture, both reflecting and reinforcing existing sex roles.[41]

have a child. I felt as if it were "now or never." Paul was doubtful about combining art with parenthood, but felt it was my *right* to have a child. I was living in the realm of WISH and fantasized that I could do *everything*—take care of my child, do my art, enjoy my friends.

From the time I was pregnant, I entered the world of mothers. I belatedly realized that inside I had suffered from the gossip and gaze of people who maligned women who stepped out into the world to make a place for themselves in it. Now I felt womanly, I was womanly, and the whole world could see it. I painted paintings of pregnant women. I wanted to glorify my condition. I felt the glory. I lived it out.

When the baby was born, people congratulated me as if I had done something very special. The other women artists we knew did not have children, and they cast me in a heroic light. The dramatic side of me lived it to the hilt, but the painter was suddenly confronted with the problem of TIME. Although my husband "helped" with the baby, he limited the time he would spend and put professional needs first. I was left with total responsibility.

. . .

Fortunately, I had two unbelievable mothers on call—my own, Fannie Schapiro, and my husband's, Molly Brach. They gave me the impression that they had waited all their lives to take care of my baby. Both of them accepted my ambitions and my art completely. Of course their old-fashioned ways produced no small amount of guilt in me. (My mother had a certain way of looking in the refrigerator and saying, "My *God*, there's no milk," as if the holocaust had come.) But this effect was so unintended, so unrecognized by them, that the guilt became my problem.

Despite their help, I still felt that I never had enough time. I seemed to be forever making *arrangements* for the baby and the household, even when I wasn't caring for them. I insisted to my husband that we must have help. But we were very poor, my husband and I. I did not have a job that brought in a weekly paycheck. Sales were as sales are. They come when they come. You can't count on them. Paul said, "If you want help, *pay* for it. I can only pay for what we have now." The income from his paintings and teaching was supporting all three of us, and he felt that if I required more money it was my responsibility to earn it. I have always been grateful to my husband for taking a very specific and clear stand on this. He was not against me, not my enemy, at any level; at the same time he knew his own mind.

. . .

Source: Miriam Schapiro, "Notes from a Conversation on Art, Feminism, and Work," *Working It Out* (Jan Ruddick and Pamela Daniels, eds.), New York: Pantheon, 1977. pp. 284–286.

Nobody reared in our society is entirely immune from them, and most of us are unconsciously but profoundly affected by them.

THE SOCIAL COSTS OF CONTEMPORARY SEX ROLES

Our existing sex-role arrangements have considerable personal and social costs—partly through

the economic and cultural loss to society resulting from the failure to use fully the talents of the population, and partly through the psychological stresses that adherence to rigid sex roles can cause in both males and females.

The United States makes poor use of the potential talents of women. Since the defining aspects of success in America—dominance, aggressiveness, competitiveness—are all ascribed to the male in our society, women tend to be relegated to a subordinate status, and valued for their personal appearance and nurturing support rather than for their talents and abilities. Women are not expected to become writers,

---

[41] See Gayle Tuchman, Arlene Kaplan Daniels, and James Benet (eds.), *Hearth and Home: Images of Women in the Mass Media* (New York: Oxford University Press, 1978).

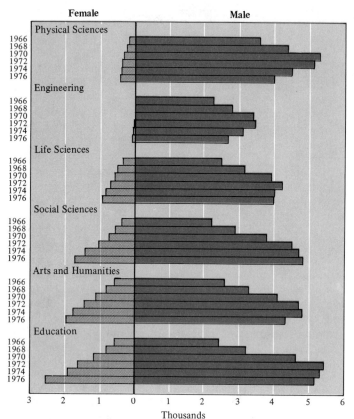

	Female	Male

Physical Sciences
1966
1968
1970
1972
1974
1976

Engineering
1966
1968
1970
1972
1974
1976

Life Sciences
1966
1968
1970
1972
1974
1976

Social Sciences
1966
1968
1970
1972
1974
1976

Arts and Humanities
1966
1968
1970
1972
1974
1976

Education
1966
1968
1970
1972
1974
1976

3 2 1 0 1 2 3 4 5 6

Thousands

FIGURE 9.2 **Doctoral degree recipients by sex and selected fields of study: 1966–1976.** Women are taking a steadily greater proportion of graduate degrees, yet they are far outnumbered by men at this stage in their educational careers. Women graduate students are still concentrated, too, in such traditional fields as education, while men continue to dominate such disciplines as engineering.
(*Social Indicators*, 1976.)

rock guitarists, engineers, or nuclear physicists, and this expectation becomes a self-fulfilling prophecy. Many women internalize the low image that society has of them and do not seriously consider a "male" career. The socialization process prepares women to aspire primarily to menial, low-paid positions—eternally the organization's secretary, never its president.

Women have little influence in public life; they make up 53 percent of the nation's voters but hold only 5 percent of the elective positions. In 1978 they held only 18 out of 435 seats in the House of Representatives, 1 out of 100 seats in the Senate, only 2 state governorships, 6 lieutenant governorships, and 6 mayorships of large cities.[42] They headed no large corporations or major universities. The educational attainment of women, relatively low at the college level as

compared to that of men, compounds their difficulties in achieving eminence in other areas of life. Women represent 42 percent of those taking a bachelor's degree, 37 percent of those taking a master's degree, and only 13 percent of those taking a Ph.D. or its equivalent.[43]

In addition to the economic, cultural, and educational barriers that women face, they also have had to contend with legislation based on the premise that women are incapable of handling their own affairs. Although many of these laws are being repealed, and all will become unconstitutional if the Equal Rights Amendment is ratified, formal or informal restrictions sometimes bar married women from owning property, acquiring credit cards, or entering contracts without their husband's signed consent. Many banks, for example, are reluctant to pro-

[42]*Statistical Abstract of the United States, 1978, op. cit.,* p. 169.

[43]*Ibid.,* p. 516.

254

vide mortgages for women, even if their incomes are sufficiently high.

Traditional sex roles pose difficult psychological problems for many women. Germaine Greer argues that these role requirements turn women into "female eunuchs" rather than females: "the characteristics that are praised and rewarded are those of the castrate—timidity, plumpness, languor, delicacy, preciosity." Modern women, she maintains, are not so much women as "female impersonators," mimicking, with the encouragement of a thriving cosmetics industry, an impossible and absurd notion of femininity. If they accept this stereotype, women must surrender all possibility of fully exploring their human potential and talents; if they reject it, they face problems of role conflict and questioned personal identity, and risk being regarded as "unfeminine." The psychological costs are particularly severe when a woman approaches middle age. Socialized into believing that her main asset is her physical attractiveness and her main function the rearing of a family, she often watches with feelings of desolation as both her children and her youth leave her.

Although much has been written of the psychological costs to women of contemporary roles, the psychological costs to men have been largely neglected. The American male is often unable to show emotion; in particular, he is prohibited from exhibiting signs of distress or from expressing the same degree of affection to other males that American females may express to one another. Although we are now an urbanized, sophisticated society, the image of the tough, self-reliant frontiersman still lingers. Ruth Hartley argues that the sex-role socialization process for males inevitably destines them to personal conflicts in later years:

> The boy is not adequately socialized for adulthood. . . . . The boy is conditioned to live in an all-masculine society, defining his own self-image by rejecting whatever smacks of femininity. In adulthood he will have to adjust to a heterosexual work world, perhaps even take orders from a female, a species he has been taught to despise as inferior. Finally, the emphasis on repression of the emotions, the high value of stoicism, leaves the boy wholly unprepared for the emotional closeness and intimate personal interaction now more and more expected of a lover and a spouse.[44]

American men are also subject to some legal restrictions or obligations that do not apply to women: they must fight in time of war, for example. A husband is legally obliged to provide financial support for his family, and failure to do so can constitute grounds for desertion or divorce by the wife. A separated husband who wishes to rear his own children may also find himself facing a divorce court that tends to view women as being uniquely equipped, regardless of their personal characteristics, to bring up children. In disputes over custody of children, legal agencies look much more favorably on the claims of the mother.

The passivity expected of women thus has its counterpart in the lifelong competitiveness demanded of men. The traditional male role in our society can be highly stressful. Men are five times more likely than women to commit suicide, and it is noteworthy that the suicide rate among husbands rises much more sharply than among wives after the breakup of a marriage. Men suffering from severe mental disorders outnumber women by three to one. Alcoholics and narcotics addicts are overwhelmingly male. Men are also far more prone to violence, criminal activity, and other deviant behavior of almost every kind. They also have a disproportionately high rate of stress-related illnesses, such as ulcers, hypertension, and heart disease. It is hardly surprising that a growing number of men are wondering whether they really do benefit from the traditional roles—or whether they would be better off sharing more of the burden of breadwinning, and more of the satisfaction of parenthood, with women.

Each sex role has its advantages and disadvantages. Because they permit men and women to feel superior to one another in some ways and inferior in others, they encourage a feeling of mutual dependence. The problem is that many of our sex-role attributes are relics of a past age, serve no useful function, and exact unnecessary social and personal costs.

---

[44]Hartley, op. cit., p. 142.

CONFRONTING THE PROBLEM

American sex roles are changing rapidly, primarily under the impact of the women's liberation movement: women who demand equal rights with men are no longer considered neurotics or deviants. The double standard of sexual morality, which tolerated a degree of sexual promiscuity on the part of males but required females to be virginal before marriage and faithful thereafter, is fast disappearing. The rights of women to achieve high occupational status are at least formally recognized, and many corporations, colleges, and other organizations claim to be making deliberate efforts to hire women in preference to similarly qualified men. Several states have enacted legislation to make abortions easier to obtain, and this legislation has been held constitutional by the Supreme Court. (It should be noted that many people reject the view that abortion is a "women's lib" issue and see it as a purely moral one.) The need for extended day-care facilities that might release women from the home is recognized, and these facilities are being provided to an unprecedented, if still inadequate, extent. Yet in spite of significant advances, there still remain major barriers to further changes in sex roles.

One of these barriers is the attitudes of women themselves, who have been somewhat conservative and slow to assert their rights. This phenomenon is found in all subordinate groups in the early stages of their awakening to their disadvantaged situation: it happened, for example, in the first years of the civil rights movement, and still remains a problem for the gay liberation movement. In a 1970 Gallup poll some 65 percent of American women agreed that "women get as good a break in this country as men." In 1971 a Harris poll showed that a plurality of women (42 percent to 40 percent, with the rest undecided) were opposed to "efforts to strengthen and change women's place in society." The following year views had changed somewhat: such efforts were supported by a small plurality of women (42 percent to 38 percent). Most women still remained unsympathetic to radical liberationist efforts to improve their position, however, and opposed the women's liberation movement by

49 percent to 35 percent. A 1977 New York Times–CBS News poll found that only 23 percent of women favored "affirmative action" programs designed to enhance their employment prospects.

Some women's groups have been in the forefront of the opposition to the federal Equal Rights Amendment (ERA), which guarantees equality of the sexes. The amendment requires ratification by thirty-eight states if it is to be passed, but so far only thirty-five have ratified it—and some of these states have tried to rescind their ratification. Most of the remaining states are considered unlikely to ratify the amendment, which was due to lapse in 1979 unless fully ratified. In 1978 Congress, recognizing that the amendment would never be passed in the time remaining, extended the deadline for ratification to 1982. Yet, significantly, the prospects for ratification still seem doubtful: in referenda in such diverse states as New York, New Jersey, Florida, and Nevada, voters have rejected one proposal or another that was designed to guarantee the equal rights of the sexes. In each case anti-ERA women's groups spearheaded the opposition to the proposals, and observers credited female voters wth sealing the doom of measures designed to protect and enhance their own rights. Nevertheless, and whether or not the ERA is passed in the immediate future, it is almost inevitable that women's support for changes in the female sex role will increase in the long run. Cultural change always tends to be slow, but an idea of equality that once seemed far-fetched and unnatural is gradually becoming an accepted part of common-sense reality, and American society will eventually adjust to this fact.

A second barrier, however, is likely to be the bulk of the male population. A 1975 Harris poll found that only 59 percent of men favored greater opportunities for women. Already discomfited to some extent by the new demands of women, men are likely to have to face a campaign for "men's liberation" at some point in the future, and since male sex roles are both more advantageous and more deeply entrenched, change is likely to be slow. But if women are enabled to occupy the more highly paid jobs, the basis for the male's domination of the family will be substantially eroded as he is deprived of his sex-linked economic importance. Some adjustment in the patterns of authority and deference between husband and wife will inevitably follow.[45]

Full sexual equality will involve extensive structural changes in American society. The sexes will have to be offered equal educational and economic opportunities. According to a 1978 study by the Scientific Manpower Commission, a white male high-school dropout earns, on average, $2,203 per annum more than a white woman with a college degree.[46] Equal wages will have to be paid for equal work, and the sex-based segregation of jobs (women as typists, men as janitors, and so on) will have to be eroded. Socialization patterns as mediated through the schools, movies, TV, radio, and newspapers will have to be altered. Many powerful interests, such as the advertising industry or the giant $3-billion-per-year cosmetics industry, will not readily sacrifice the profits to be gleaned from

stressing traditional sex-role stereotypes. Many of these structural changes may come about if the Equal Rights Amendment is passed. The amendment states unambiguously: "Equality of rights under the law shall not be denied or abridged by the United States or by any State on account of sex."

At the moment it is not clear exactly what the sex roles of a future American society will be like. Sexual equality does not necessarily mean sexual similarity, and there is no reason to suppose that a "unisex" society will ultimately emerge. Similarly, sexual equality does not necessarily mean that women will have to adopt the present characteristics of men, or that men and women will have to converge on some happy medium between the two present roles. What is important is that we realize that human beings can, in principle, be socialized into whatever kind of sex role is desired: what is to be hoped for is that the new roles will be sufficiently flexible to allow everyone to explore all possible options and thus to achieve their human potential without the encumbrance of artificial and irrational barriers.

SUMMARY

1. As a result of several social forces, women are again demanding changes in American sex roles. Sex roles are the learned patterns of behavior expected of the sexes in a given society. Each society elaborates the physical differences of sex into cultural distinctions of gender. Through the ideology of sexism, which asserts the superiority of men, these differences are viewed as "natural" and the inequality therefore seems legitimate.

2. Although American sex roles are changing rapidly, many traditional sex-linked personality characteristics prevail: women are supposed to be passive and primarily concerned with the home; men are supposed to be active and primarily

concerned with the outside world. There is also a sex-based division of labor, in which the most highly rewarded occupational roles are filled predominantly by men.

3. Traditional sex roles seem to have arisen in the past because it was functional for women to do work required in or near the home and for men to do the work beyond, but the traditional roles may be dysfunctional in modern society. From a conflict approach, inequalities of sex persist because they favor the interests of the economically and therefore socially and politically dominant sex, men.

4. There are obvious biological differences between the sexes that affect their roles, and there is some evidence of minor psychological differences that may be present from birth. The anthropological evidence shows that although there is a general tendency for men to dominate

---

[45]See Juanita M. Kreps (ed.), *Women and the American Economy: A Look to the 1980s* (Englewood Cliffs, N.J.: Prentice-Hall, 1976).

[46]*New York Times*, November 20, 1978, p. D11.

women, many societies have sex roles that are very unlike our own.

5. Three theories of sex-role acquisition have been proposed: the Freudian, the social-learning, and the cognitive-developmental. The main agencies of sex-role socialization in the United States are the family, the school and the mass media, all of which are reinforced by the peer group. These agencies encourage conformity to traditional stereotypes.

6. Traditional sex roles exact many social and psychological costs: the potential talents of the population are not exploited, and stresses are placed on both men and women.

7. Confronting the problem of sexual inequality will require further changes in the attitudes of both men and women. Changes in sex roles may also be achieved through legislation and through the growing economic independence of women, which will undermine the economic inequality on which male superiority is based.

GLOSSARY

Gender. Refers to cultural concepts of masculinity and femininity, as distinct from the biological fact of maleness and femaleness.

Ideology. A set of ideas and beliefs that justifies the interests of those who hold it; the dominant ideology in any unequal society therefore justifies the inequality in such a society.

Sex. Refers to the biological fact of maleness and femaleness, as distinct from cultural concepts of gender.

Sexism. An ideology or set of values and beliefs that justifies the domination of women by men on the grounds that the inequality results from inborn differences.

Sex roles. The learned patterns of behavior expected of the sexes in a given society.

FURTHER READING

CHAFETZ, JANET SALTZMAN. *Masculine/Feminine or Human?* New York: Peacock, 1978. A short introductory text on sex roles. Chafetz strongly argues the need to develop new sex roles and not simply to make women more like men.

FORD, CLELLAN S., and FRANK BEACH. *Patterns of Sexual Behavior.* New York: Harper & Row, 1951. A modern classic on sex roles and sexual behavior, drawing together and comparing data from many cultures around the world. The book is essential reading for anyone who wishes to see American sex roles in broader perspective.

FRIEDAN, BETTY. *The Feminine Mystique.* New York: Dell, 1963. The book that launched the women's liberation movement. A movingly written account of the subordinate role of women in America.

GORNICK, VIVIAN, and BARBARA K. MORAN (eds.). *Women in Sexist Society: Studies in Power and Powerlessness.* New York: Basic Books, 1971. An outstanding collection of contributions covering a variety of topics, including the sex-role socialization provided by the school and the media.

GREER, GERMAINE. *The Female Eunuch.* New York: Bantam, 1971. A best seller, probably the most widely read book of its kind in recent years. Greer writes in a warm, humorous, and pungent style that provides penetrating insights into the way women are socialized into adopting certain attitudes toward their bodies, themselves, and men.

KANTER, ROSABETH MOSS. *Men and Women of the Corporation.* New York: Basic Books, 1977. An important study of the career patterns and the social interaction of the sexes within the modern corporation.

MACCOBY, ELEANOR, and CAROL JACKLIN. *The Psychology of Sex Differences.* Palo Alto, Calif.: Stanford University Press, 1974. The book offers a valuable survey and evaluation of the existing evidence on psychological differences between the sexes.

MEAD, MARGARET. *Male and Female.* New York: Morrow, 1975. A distinguished anthropologist who studied sex roles in the United States and elsewhere analyzes our notions of masculinity and feminity in a cross-cultural context.

PETRAS, JOHN W. (ed.). *Sex: Male/Gender: Masculine*. Port Washington, N.Y.: Alfred, 1975. A useful collection of articles on the much-neglected subject of masculinity and the male sex role.

ROTHMAN, SHEILA M. *Woman's Proper Place: A History of Changing Ideals and Practices, 1870 to the Present*. New York: Basic Books, 1978. An interesting, well-documented social history of sex roles in the United States over the past century.

SCHLEGEL, ALICE (ed.). *Sexual Stratification: a Cross-Cultural View*. New York: Columbia University Press, 1977. An important collection of case studies of sex roles in various societies, including some that exemplify male domination, some that have qualified male domination, and some with a high degree of sexual equality.

WEITZ, SHIRLEY. *Sex Roles: Biological, Psychological, and Social Foundations*. New York: Oxford University Press, 1977. An excellent and comprehensive study of sex roles that integrates a wide range of relevant facts and theories from several disciplines.

YORBURG, BETTY. *Sexual Identity: Sex Roles and Social Change*. New York: Wiley, 1974. A short introduction to the problem of sex roles; the book is primarily sociological in focus but includes psychological and biological information.

4

PRIVATE TROUBLES
AND
PUBLIC ISSUES

One of the most important sociological insights is that an intimate link exists between the problems of the individual and the nature of the social environment. However private a person's troubles may seem to be, their source can often be traced ultimately to the features of the society in which he or she lives. C. Wright Mills believed that the ability to see the connection between "private troubles" and "public issues" is the essence of the sociological imagination.

In this unit we examine several social problems that may appear at first sight to originate with the individual—problems such as marital breakdown, the isolation of the aged, poor health, mental disorder, crime and violence, variant sexual behavior, and drug abuse. Yet we will find that in each instance a full understanding of the problem requires that we look not only at individual behavior, but also at the social forces that so profoundly influence our lives.

10
The Family

THE PROBLEM

About one American marriage in every three is likely to end in the divorce courts.[1] Many of the marriages that survive are merely "empty shell" arrangements, in which the unloving partners remain together through sheer habit, economic necessity, or "for the sake of the children." There is no shortage of critics who assert that the family as we know it is in grave danger; throughout the past decade, a stream of books and articles has lamented—and sometimes welcomed—the doom of the American family.[2]

There is certainly a good deal of evidence to support the view that there is something seriously amiss with our family system. The divorce rate has doubled since the early 1960s and is still rising. A sixth of all school-age children are living in one-parent families. Illegitimacy rates among teen-age and preteen girls are rising rapidly, and would be far higher if contraception

and abortions were not so readily available to a large part of the population. One out of five live births, and one in three abortions, involve a teen-age mother. About a million adolescents, most of them from the middle class, run away from home each year (usually temporarily). The aged are being cast adrift from the family, and are increasingly left to live alone or in old age homes with other unrelated people.

The "sexual revolution," with its sanctioning of premarital and extramarital intercourse, seems to be undermining a traditional basis of marriage, monogamous fidelity. The women's liberation movement has put new strains on established family patterns by asserting the right of the wife to full equality (some feminists have even condemned the entire institution of marriage as inherently oppressive). Experimental alternatives to traditional marriage abound: group "marriage," "open" marriage, "free love" communes, and semipermanent cohabitation between partners who do not intend to marry. Homosexuality and bisexuality are being openly advocated as life styles, and a number of churches have performed homosexual marriages. The family is also the scene of a great deal of interpersonal and intergenerational conflict. Nearly a fifth of murder victims are related to their killers.[3] According to a study by Murray Straus, Richard Gelles, and Suzanne Steinmetz, about 7.5 million couples go through a "violent episode" each year, and 2.3 million children

[1]Paul C. Glick and Arthur J. Norton, "Perspectives on the Recent Upturn in Divorce and Remarriage," *Demography*, 10 (August 1973), 301–314; Arthur J. Norton and Paul C. Glick, "Marital Instability: Past, Present, and Future," *Journal of Social Issues*, 32 (Winter 1976), 5–20.

[2]See, for example, Gordon F. Streib (ed.), *The Changing Family: Adaptation and Diversity* (Reading, Mass.: Addison-Wesley, 1973); Gwen B. Carr, *Marriage and Family in a Decade of Change* (Reading, Mass.: Addison-Wesley, 1972); Frank D. Cox (ed.), *American Marriage* (Dubuque, Iowa: William C. Brown, 1972); John F. Crosby, *Illusion and Disillusion: The Self in Love and Marriage* (Belmont, Calif.: Wadsworth, 1973); Michael Novak, "The Family Out of Favor," *Harpers*, (April 1976), 37–46; Carolyn Shaw Bell, "Let's Get Rid of Families," *Newsweek*, May 9, 1977, p. 19; Christopher Lasch, *Haven in a Heartless World: The Family Besieged* (New York: Basic Books, 1977); and David Reiss and Howard Hoffman, *The American Family: Dying or Developing?* (New York: Plenum, 1979).

[3]Federal Bureau of Investigation, *Uniform Crime Reports for the United States, 1977* (Washington, D.C.: U.S. Government Printing Office, 1978), p. 9.

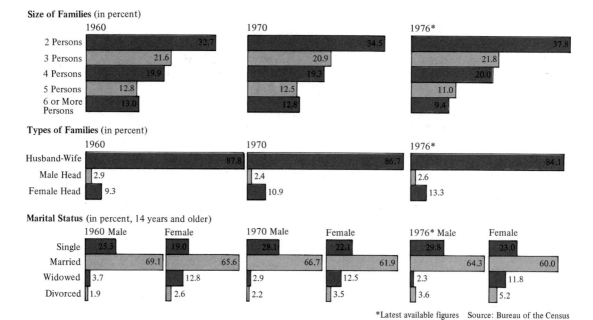

Size of Families (in percent)

	1960	1970	1976*
2 Persons	32.7	34.5	37.8
3 Persons	21.6	20.9	21.8
4 Persons	19.9	19.3	20.0
5 Persons	12.8	12.5	11.0
6 or More Persons	13.0	12.8	9.4

Types of Families (in percent)

	1960	1970	1976*
Husband-Wife	87.8	86.7	84.1
Male Head	2.9	2.4	2.6
Female Head	9.3	10.9	13.3

Marital Status (in percent, 14 years and older)

	1960 Male	Female	1970 Male	Female	1976* Male	Female
Single	25.3	19.0	28.1	22.1	29.8	23.0
Married	69.1	65.6	66.7	61.9	64.3	60.0
Widowed	3.7	12.8	2.9	12.5	2.3	11.8
Divorced	1.9	2.6	2.2	3.5	3.6	5.2

*Latest available figures   Source: Bureau of the Census

FIGURE 10.1 The changing American family. As these data on the American family show, the institution is still thriving. At the same time, however, it is changing: families are becoming smaller, the number of female-headed families is increasing, and the proportion of unmarried people is growing. (U.S. Bureau of the Census.)

wield a gun or knife against a brother or sister.[4] The modern family, too, often seems ill adapted to handle the many personal problems—such as mental disorders, alcoholism, or juvenile delinquency—that may affect the home.

Although sociologists recognize that the family institution is currently in a state of some disorganization, they rarely share in these gloomy predictions. Fears about the disintegration of the family and a resulting disruption of society are as old as history; ancient manuscripts from many cultures contain long catalogs of complaints that might be very familiar to modern Americans. Although the United States has had the highest divorce rate in the Western world for over twenty years, there are other societies—notably in the Middle East—that have experienced much higher rates without a collapse of their family or social systems. The

family, it is true, has contributed to a good deal of human grief over the centuries, but it has also had such positive personal and social value that it remains the basic social institution in every culture. Sociologists therefore take the view that the family is not so much dying as changing in response to altered social conditions.[5] The changes may be drastic, they may take forms that we cannot yet foresee, and the future family may fulfill functions rather different from those of our present institution, but there will still be families of some kind.

Before we consider family problems in more detail, we should look at the basic nature of the family. What exactly is a "family"? Why is the family so fundamentally important to society? And what is the broad character of the changes that are taking place in the family institution?

[4]Murray A. Straus, Richard Gelles, and Suzanne Steinmetz, *Behind Closed Doors: A Survey of Family Violence in America* (Garden City: N.Y.: Doubleday, 1979).

[5]See, for example, Michael Gordon, *The American Family: Past, Present, and Future* (New York: Random House, 1978); and Mary Jo Bane, *Here to Stay: American Families in the Twentieth Century* (New York: Basic Books, 1976).

THE NATURE OF THE FAMILY

A *family* is essentially a group of people who live together and who are related by ancestry, marriage, or adoption. In all societies, a new family is expected to be formed through marriage or some equivalent ceremony. *Marriage* is a socially approved sexual union of some permanence between two or more people. The fact that the union is socially approved gives any offspring legitimate status, because society is able to assign the social role of father to a specific person. If children are born out of marriage, on the other hand, there may be no male on whom society can formally place the responsibility of fatherhood.

Our definition of the family is a rather broad one, whereas the popular conception of the family tends to be rather narrower—that of a household consisting of a husband who works, a wife who stays at home, and two dependent children. Yet this family, so relentlessly depicted in TV commercials and other flights of the imagination, is very much the exception rather than the rule. A mere 6 percent of American families, or 3.3 million out of 56 million families, fit this stereotype. Millions of families, of course, have more or less than the "standard" two children. In most families both father and mother work. Only 12 million husbands are the sole breadwinners for their families, and 1.5 million wives support their husbands and children. Nearly 8 million families have no father in the home.[6]

Yet social attitudes to family problems are strongly influenced by the popular conception of the family. People tend to regard this particular form as the "ideal" family, and to believe that it is natural and good, if not God-given and immutable. As a result, changes in the family are automatically branded as bad. Potential alternative forms are belittled because they seem to violate the natural order. Those who defy the marital conventions are apt to be regarded as escapist, immoral, neurotic, immature, or irresponsible. Family units that differ from the

"ideal" form are often treated as deviant and undesirable, rather than as viable alternatives in their own right.

All families are embedded in a wide network of relatives, or *kin*. In traditional, preindustrial societies, kinship groups usually form the basis of social organization, serving as the fundamental social, economic, and political building blocks of the society. In such societies people identify strongly with, and owe great loyalty to, their kinship group. Conversely, they think of nonkin not merely as individuals but also as members of another kinship group, so a grudge against a single person can become a grudge, or even a vendetta, against all that other person's kin. In modern societies, on the other hand, the importance of kinship has declined drastically. Although people in modern urban communities do tend to keep in touch with their closer kin, they may never see and may not even know their more distant relatives. Kinship groups rarely live together or act as cohesive social units. The idea of a vendetta between kinship groups is thus absurd in a modern society.

The Functions of the Family

One of the reasons sociologists are so confident that the family is unlikely to disappear is that no society has ever existed without the institution. As William Goode observes:

> The family still looms large as a major kind of social arrangement in all societies, not just in our own. Many societies do not have formal organizations for making war. A goodly number of societies do not have markets as we know them; many have economic systems that are not at all separated from the family patterns. But all societies, however primitive or industrialized, have family patterns.[7]

As functionalist theorists have pointed out, the family is a universal social institution because it performs a number of irreplaceable functions

---

[6]Bell, *op. cit.*, p. 19; see, also, Charles H. Mindel and Robert W. Habenstein (eds.), *Ethnic Families in America: Patterns and Variations* (New York: Elsevier, 1976).

[7]William J. Goode, *The Contemporary American Family* (Chicago: Quadrangle Books, 1971) p. 5.

The modern American family is typically a nuclear one, consisting of a married couple and their dependent children. The absence of other relatives in the home and in daily activities emphasizes the personal bonds between family members, but it also means that stresses and strains are concentrated on a very few individuals.

that help to maintain the stability and continuity of society.[8]

Replacement of Members. No society can survive unless it has some system for replacing its members. The family provides a convenient, institutionalized means for this replacement to take place in a regularized and predictable way. The biological capacity to reproduce is thus placed in a stable social context, in which the mutual rights and obligations of the reproductive partners are clearly defined and protected.

Regulation of Sexual Behavior. Every society must somehow regulate the sexual behavior of its members. Failure to provide this regulation would result, among other things, in the birth of large numbers of illegitimate infants for whom no fathers could be held responsible. A totally permissive society would tend to be a society with numerous unwanted children, and there would be no social unit to which they could be specifically attached.

Care of the Young. Unlike the young of most other animals, human offspring are virtually helpless for several years after birth, and require care and protection until at least the age of puberty. The family is an institution that can take full responsibility for the care and upbringing of the young. This function cannot easily be fulfilled by the mother alone, because preg-

[8]See George Peter Murdock, *Social Structure* (New York: Free Press, 1949); William J. Goode, "The Sociology of the Family," in Robert K. Merton, Leonard Broom, and Leonard J. Cottrell (eds.), *Sociology Today* (New York: Basic Books, 1959); and Talcott Parsons and Robert F. Bales, *Family, Socialization and Interaction Process* (Glencoe, Ill.: Free Press, 1955).

nancy, childbirth, and the need to tend new infants may periodically restrict her economic activity.

Socialization of New Members. To become a full member of society, infants have to be socialized into their culture. The child is expected to acquire language, to internalize social values, and to dress, behave, and otherwise perform like any normal member of the society. In traditional societies the family serves as the main agent of socialization at least until adolescence, and often beyond. In modern societies the family is still responsible for the primary socialization of new members of society, although other institutions play their part in a further socialization process. The schools, which teach technical skills and impart the intellectual heritage of the culture, the mass media, and peer groups all provide other influences—many of them clashing with those offered in the family environment.

These functions of the family are basic to the maintenance of society. That is why the problems and future of the family arouse such intense concern. Sociologists are well aware, however, that these functions can be fulfilled by family systems that differ from the traditional American ideal.

FAMILY PATTERNS IN OTHER CULTURES

Although the family is a universal social institution, it takes a great variety of forms around the world, many of them quite unlike our own. Generally speaking, the greatest differences from our own family patterns are found in small, preindustrial societies.

There are many societies, for example, in which husbands can have more than one wife, and a few in which wives may have more than one husband. There are many societies that do not forbid premarital or extramarital intercourse, and there are even some that encourage it. There are societies in which children are sent to live permanently in other households. In some societies husband and wife are expected to live in

separate dwellings, and in others they are required to separate for several years after the birth of a child. A few societies make provision for homosexual as well as heterosexual marriage. There are some societies in which the biological father has no responsibility for his children, since the social role of father is always assigned instead to the mother's eldest brother.

In some societies a man cannot marry a woman without making a substantial gift to her father, and in others the father must make a substantial gift to the intended husband. Some societies expect or even require a man to marry his father's brother's daughter, whereas others consider such a union incestuous and insist instead that he marry his mother's sister's daughter. There are societies that do not make any distinction between siblings (brothers and sisters) and cousins—separate words for "brother" and "cousin" do not even exist in their languages. In many parts of the world the "arranged" marriage is the norm, and parents often select prospective partners for their children without consulting them. Many societies do not recognize such a thing as romantic love, and others consider the very idea ridiculous. There are societies where old men are expected to marry young girls, where older women are expected to marry young boys, and even where infants are married before they are born (the marriage being dissolved if the babies turn out to be the wrong sex). People in all these societies, of course, are apt to regard their own family patterns as perfectly normal, as an inevitable product of " human nature," and probably as divinely ordained as well; and like ourselves, they are prone to regard any changes in their family systems with suspicion and dismay.[9]

Extended and Nuclear Family Systems

In the midst of all this variety, one crucial distinction seems relevant to the modern American family. All family systems can be divided into two basic types: the extended family and the

[9]Two useful and classic sources for information about family and sexual patterns in other cultures are Clellan S. Ford and Frank A. Beach, *Patterns of Sexual Behavior* (New York: Harper & Row, 1951); and Murdock, *op. cit.*

nuclear family. The most significant historical change in family patterns is from the extended to the nuclear type.

In the *extended family*, several generations of the same kinship line live close together, so the parent-child relationship is embedded in a wider context of aunts, uncles, grandparents, and perhaps in-laws and cousins. The extended family has been the dominant form in most societies throughout history, and remains to this day the typical pattern in nearly all preindustrial societies, where it provides many advantages. It functions as a self-contained economic unit, with the family members dividing various agricultural, domestic, and other duties among themselves, and it offers a reservoir of material and emotional support to any individual member who needs it.

The *nuclear family* consists of a single married couple and their dependent children, living away from other relatives. The widespread emergence of this independent family unit is a relatively recent historical phenomenon, but the nuclear family has rapidly become the norm in virtually every industrialized society of the world. (There were always some nuclear families in preindustrial Europe, however, even when the dominant pattern was the extended family.[10]) In the United States the nuclear family pattern has always been the most common one. Since early colonial times few American newlyweds have expected to spend their entire lives in the same neighborhood as the parents of one of the spouses, let alone to live with them. The nuclear family is better suited to the demands of complex modern societies than the extended family is: its smaller size and potential mobility enable it to adapt more easily to changing conditions, such as the need to relocate the home in search of better job prospects.

ANALYZING THE PROBLEM

The functionalist, conflict, and deviance approaches can all be applied to family problems.

The Functionalist Approach

From the functionalist view, the problems stem from rapid social changes that have placed unprecedented stresses on the family system. Social disorganization thus exists to the extent that the family has failed to adjust.

We have seen that the rise of the large modern industrial society has irrevocably shattered the stable extended family system of the past, for that system would be dysfunctional in societies that prize individualism and mobility rather than kinship groups and tradition. Yet the nuclear family, better adapted as it is to the demands of modern societies, suffers some novel defects that make it dysfunctional in certain ways. For example, the death, desertion, unemployment, illness, or imprisonment of the breadwinner in a nuclear family can mean hardship or even poverty for the remaining spouse and children, whereas in the extended-family system other kin would take up the slack. Another example is the isolation and loneliness experienced by many elderly people, particularly among the widowed. The modern nuclear family often has no place or role to offer the aged, whereas in the extended-family system the old would remain as respected members of a large and caring kinship group.

Other relevant changes are those in demographic patterns of fertility and life expectancy. Because life expectancy in the past was much shorter than it is today, and the average wife bore many more children, a couple might spend the greater part of their married lives playing parental roles. Today, with the average couple having about two children and with an average life expectancy of sixty-nine for men and seventy-

---

[10]See Peter Laslett and Richard Wall (eds.), *Household and Family in Past Time* (Cambridge, Mass.: Harvard University Press, 1972); and Lawrence Stone, *The Family, Sex and Marriage in England, 1500–1800* (New York: Harper & Row, 1977).

seven for women, a couple might spend two-thirds of their married life free of the responsibility for young children, and a third without any children living at home. The nature of the relationship between the partners is thus very different than it might have been in the shorter marriages of the past.

Changes in social values have also had a disruptive effect on the modern family. Established patterns of marriage and family have been undermined by such developments as increased sexual permissiveness, the widespread tolerance of divorce, the greater personal freedom demanded by adolescents, and the new social and economic independence of wives. The American family was never designed to accommodate these new trends. Thus, in the functionalist view, social changes have generated some imbalances in the family institution, which has been unable to adapt rapidly enough to respond to altered circumstances.

The Conflict Approach

An early conflict approach to the family was that of Karl Marx's cowriter, Friedrich Engels, who argued that the family was by its very nature an oppressive institution. Engels drew parallels between the oppression of workers by capitalists, on the one hand, and of women by men, on the other—a theme that has since been taken up by some of the more radical feminists today.[11] In its crude form, however, this view is not widely accepted by modern conflict theorists, because it seems to confuse a particular family pattern—the traditional, male-dominated one—with the family institution in general. That wives have always tended to be dominated by their husbands in the past does not necessarily mean that this must be the case in the family of the future, and, in fact, American wives are achieving greater equality with their husbands in many respects. Modern conflict theorists emphasize, however,

[11]Friedrich Engels, *The Origin of the Family, Private Property, and the State* (New York: International Publishers, 1942); see, also, Floyd Dotson, "Marx and Engels on the Family," *American Sociologist*, 9 (November 1974), 181–186; and Al Syzmanski, "The Socialization of Women's Oppression," *Insurgent Sociologist*, 6 (Winter 1976), 31–58.

VOICES

This American working-class couple have been married eight years and have three children.

. . .

(The wife)
It takes quite a bit of managing to run the house with so little money, and with taxes and prices going up all the time, and his wages not going up. Every time we fix up the house a little bit, they call it an improvement and increase the property tax. But it's really just that we're trying to keep the place together so it shouldn't fall down on our heads.

It's really a problem because I never know how much the new taxes are going to be. I save a little every week to put away for taxes and then, all of a sudden the new tax bill comes and it's higher than I expected. So we have to go into debt to pay the taxes again. And he gets mad because he says if I managed better, it wouldn't happen.

(The husband)
She spends too much. I don't know why she can't manage better. We always seem to be behind; she just can't save anything. As soon as she's got a couple of bucks in her hands, she finds something to spend it on. It makes me mad as hell sometimes when I work so hard and there's not enough money for me to spend on something I want.

You know, I'm dying to get away on vacation, to see some of the country. But there's never any money. Can you believe it, I've been to Vietnam but I've never seen the Grand Canyon. Hell, I've never even been to Lake Tahoe.

. . .

Source: Lillian Breslow Rubin, *Worlds of Pain/Life in the Working-Class Family* (New York: Basic Books, 1976), p. 109. Copyright 1976 by Lillian Breslow Rubin.

that the demands of the women's movement are placing a strain on established family patterns, for these demands imply a significant change in the relationship between husband and wife. They also argue that this conflict will be beneficial in the long run, for it will result in a family structure that is better adapted to modern conditions (see Chapter 9, "Sex Roles").

Conflict theorists also focus on the conflict of values that is central to some family problems. There are many competing ideas in American society about the desirability of the nuclear system and its alternatives. Some people believe passionately that the present institution should be maintained and strengthened; others believe that the family is outmoded, restrictive, and should be modified or even radically changed. There are also value conflicts over many other issues associated with the family: for example, over the professional and domestic status of wives, over how society should react to illegitimacy, over premarital and extramarital sexuality, and even over the right of women to expect alimony payments from their divorced husbands. The conflict approach sensitizes us to the fact that what may be seen as a solution by one group is likely to be regarded as a problem by another group that holds different values.

The Deviance Approach

Although widely used by sociologists in the past, the deviance approach to family problems is regarded as less fruitful today. From this approach, many of the problems of the family arise because people have failed to learn or have rejected the social norms governing appropriate marital and family behavior. If the traditional norms were adhered to, such problems as infidelity, divorce, or children's disrespect toward parents would be much reduced. The difficulty with this approach is that deviance from many traditional norms is now so widespread that the behavior can hardly be regarded as deviant any longer. Premarital sexual experience, for example, was once regarded as deviant, but today it seems to have become a norm for the majority of the population (see Chapter 15, "Sexual Variance"). Similarly, a divorced person was stigmatized in American society until fairly recently, but in most circles today a divorcee is no longer regarded as disreputable. Certain other family problems, however, such as wife-beating or child abuse, can still be usefully analyzed as deviance from important social norms.

LOVE AND MARRIAGE IN AMERICA

Most American families begin with marriage, and most American marriages follow from romantic love and a personal choice of spouse by the partners concerned. In order to aid our understanding of why so many marriages fail, let us examine in more detail the role of romantic love in mate selection.

Americans look with horror on marriages based on anything other than love, yet there are many societies that do not regard romance as the best, or even a normal, foundation for a marriage. In most of the preindustrial and newly industrializing societies of the world, far more pragmatic considerations determine marriage partners—and there are some societies in which the concept of romantic love is apparently unknown and others in which it occurs rarely and is regarded with amusement or dismay. In those societies where marriage is not viewed as a love match between individuals, it is seen, rather, as a means of sealing a practical economic, social, or political alliance between kinship groups. In such circumstances, romantic love may become an inconvenience that interferes with the parents' rational selection of mates for their offspring.

This attitude was widespread among the middle and upper classes of the Western world until fairly recently: parents were eager for their daughters to marry "well"—that is, to a male who was eligible by reason of his social status and economic assets. A standard dramatic theme of the novels of the last century concerns the havoc wrought by the daughter who falls in love with someone beneath her "station in life." Even today middle- and upper-class parents are likely to look askance at their daughter's dating a lower-class male.

From a very early age Americans learn of the

Most Americans regard romantic love as a necessary basis for a successful marriage. Although two people rarely live "happily ever after," romantic love may serve to perpetuate a relationship. Certainly our society places a higher value on "falling in love" than most other societies.

glories of romantic love. Children's stories are filled with tales of breathtaking romance. Magazines provide countless "happy ending" romantic adventures. Books, movies, and TV programs all serve to convince us that every normal person eventually falls in love and gets married. Accordingly, much of our emotional energy, particularly in our teens and twenties, is devoted to finding somebody to love—that special person with whom we will want to spend the rest of our lives.

Sidney Greenfield sums up the "culture trait" of American romantic love in five steps:

1. Two . . . rational adolescents of the opposite sex meet, most probably by accident, and find each other to be personally and physically attractive.
2. They soon come to realize that they are "right for each other."
3. They fall victims to forces beyond their control, and fall in love.
4. They then begin—at least for a short time—to behave in a flighty, irrational manner that is at variance with the way they normally conduct themselves.
5. Finally, believing that love is a panacea and that the future holds only goodness for them, they marry and form a new nuclear family.[12]

The implication is that, once married, the couple will "live happily ever after," and that love will solve whatever problems may arise in the course of their future lives together.

It is perhaps significant that we use one set of terms—bride and groom—to describe people at the climactic moment of the romantic-love relationship, and another set of terms—husband and

---

[12]Sidney M. Greenfield, "Love and Marriage in Modern America: A Functional Analysis," *The Sociological Quarterly*, 6 (Autumn 1965), 361–377; see, also, Ira L. Reiss, *Family Systems in America* (New York: Holt, Rinehart, and Winston, 1971), p. 90.

wife—to describe their subsequent life together. The change in terminology almost seems to be a tacit recognition of the fact that romantic love does not, after all, solve all difficulties, and that more prosaic and rational considerations must enter into the lifelong mutual commitment of two people.

The American married-life ideal is somewhat different from the romantic-love ideal. The married-life ideal focuses more on familial and social roles, and contains a definite economic element. There is usually a fairly clear sex-role distinction, despite the changes wrought by the women's liberation movement: the husband is usually the main breadwinner and the wife, even if she works, has primary responsibility for the home. The couple are expected to raise children, and the greater part of the wife's time and interest is supposed to be devoted to their care. The economic position of the family is expected to improve over the years as a result of the husband's steady advancement in his job. The family hopes ultimately to acquire ownership of its own home. The children should do well at school and ideally should go to college. Over the years the couple's enjoyment and appreciation of each other's company is expected to remain deep and secure.

Clearly, this ideal is not always fulfilled in practice. But unrealistic as it may be in many cases, there is a certain beauty about the concept: it suggests harmony, peace, and fulfillment—values well worth seeking. Yet this married-life ideal does not really require romantic love for its foundation. One can imagine such a family being built—as stable and fulfilling families were often built in the past and as they are still built in many parts of the world today—on the basis of a rational, cool-headed choice of partners by both sides. There is even some reason to suppose that nonromantic considerations do, in fact, carry more weight in the mate-selection process than we usually like to admit. Why, then, do Americans place such value on romantic love?

The answer, William Goode suggests, is that romantic love is highly functional in maintaining the institution of the nuclear family.[13] For one thing, it helps young couples to sever the bonds to their original families, a necessary step if a new nuclear family is to be successfully established. Conversely, romantic love would be dysfunctional in an extended-family system—distracting the couple from their heavy obligations to the rest of their kin and disrupting the rational use of marriage to form alliances between kinship groups—so it is often discouraged by societies practicing the system. A second function of romantic love is that it helps to tide the young couple over in hard times and to maintain their mutual loyalty. In the extended-family system this mutual love would not be so vital, because many other relatives would be available to lend emotional support. A third possible function of romantic love is suggested by Sidney Greenfield, who points out that nuclear marriage holds many disadvantages for the partners, such as the requirement of sexual fidelity, support obligations for the husband, and overdependence on the part of the wife. Since people in modern societies, unlike members of traditional societies, are able to decide for themselves whether or not they will marry, romantic love may serve as emotional bait to lure them into marriage.[14] Romantic love may seem to emerge entirely from the breast, but its presence (or absence) in both individual and society is really the product of much wider social forces.

DIVORCE

One of the most obvious signs of the mounting pressures on the American family is the incidence of divorce. Although intact families may suffer from painful conflicts, tensions, and dissatisfactions, the official declaration that the unit is dissolved represents a final admission of failure by the marital partners.

Divorce presents a series of problems to those involved. In a couple-oriented society, the divorced person is to some extent excluded from the normal patterns of social life, although this is

---

[13] William J. Goode, "The Theoretical Importance of Love," *American Sociological Review*, 24 (February 1959), 38–47.

[14] Greenfield, *op. cit.*

The writer of this article, a journalist, talks to single parents who are raising their children alone.

. . .

Next to the motel where I stopped for the night was a diner crowded with refugees from the storm. And weaving his way determinedly through the confusion was a toddler—the 15-month-old son of one of the waitresses.

"How do you manage him?" I asked.

"Oh, the customers take care of him when I'm busy," she said. "And if I'm not busy, I take care of him. This is the best place I could work; we get all our meals here free." The child appeared robust for one fed mostly on waffles and french fries, traces of which still stuck to his face.

"The manager doesn't mind if you bring him to work?"

"No; he knows I have to. The rest of the time we live in a room at the motel."

"Your husband?" I asked.

"Haven't got one. This trucker and me—we stayed together a couple of years. But he's not the settlin'-down type. I had to quit riding around with him when the baby was coming. He just doesn't want kids. Twice he gave me money for Mike—but he's not interested in being with him."

"Do your parents help you any?"

She shook her head no.

"They live a piece from here. We never did get along too good. Me and Mike get along real good just the way we are." While she poured coffee for customers at the counter, someone entering the diner pulled Mike away from a revolving door.

Where does he sleep when he gets tired?" I asked.

"In a booth, if there's one vacant. Usually we're not so crowded. Depends the shift I'm working."

Before I'd finished my supper, the crowd had thinned a bit. Mike climbed up onto the seat opposite me, curled up comfortably, and drifted off to sleep. His mother grabbed a mug of coffee, seated herself on the same bench, and seemed eager to resume our conversation.

"Did you ever debate about keeping him?" I asked. "Did you consider offering him for adoption?"

"Sure," she admitted, "I thought about every-thing—abortion, everything. But I live for him. Without him, no me. I want him to grow up, get somewhere, do something. And I think we can make it. . . ."

The child slept peacefully, undisturbed by the clatter of dishes, the swirl of cigarette smoke, our conversation.

Adaptable. That's one word that fits Mike.

And his mother? Improvising and maternal.

Across the continent, in Los Angeles, a musician (a "victim of women's lib," he says) relies on school and neighbors to watch over his two daughters, ages 7 and 9. He puts the girls on the school bus in the morning, and the older one wears a key on a string around her neck to let them both back into the house when they get home. Supper is a succession of carryouts: fried chicken on Monday, hamburgers on Tuesday, fish on Wednesday, pizza on Thursday.

"Adie [the children's mother] just got tired of being a mother," this father explains. "She thought she'd like to get into acting, and she left to try her luck." He shrugged his shoulders. "We're managing."

In St. Louis, an insurance salesman I know is a part-time single parent—a weekend father. His children live with their mother and her second husband during the week.

"We know the zoo better than the animal caretakers," he laughs. "And every hamburger joint near here knows us."

"My son likes to go out to Valley Park [a suburb southwest of St. Louis] on Sunday afternoons to watch the model plane people fly their airplanes remote control. If Suzy doesn't want to go, I let her stay in the apartment and watch TV. Suzy never gets tired of TV—I think she watches too much of it at her mother's place and at my place, too. I suppose TV is her missing parent . . . but lots of families let their kids watch too much TV, even when there are two parents there."

. . .

Source: "Raising a Child Alone," by Eloise Taylor Lee. *The Christian Science Monitor*, Monday, August 14, 1978. Copyright 1978 The Christian Science Publishing Society.

less true today than it was a few decades ago. The emotional effects can also be severe, for divorce can disrupt the individual's personal universe. Research has shown that men are more likely to be fired from their jobs, or to perform their jobs less well, during or shortly after a divorce.[15] Even the death rates for divorced persons are higher than for other people, at nearly all age levels.[16] This is particularly true for suicide rates among divorced men. The one-parent family faces many difficulties: the functions that the nuclear family performs assume a two-parent family structure, and if that structure is fractured, it is harder for the family to carry out its social and personal functions.[17] If, as is usually the case, the children remain with the mother, the family may face real hardship as a result of the lower earning capacity of women in our society. If the mother is also black, and thus subject to double discrimination, the economic problem is compounded (see Chapter 7, "Poverty").

But divorce may be a partial solution as well as a problem. In the past, divorce was seen as a personal catastrophe to be avoided at any cost; but today there is a growing recognition that some marriages are better ended than continued. Divorce may sometimes be more constructive than an attempt to preserve a conflict-ridden marriage, and many couples are now prepared to make a break and start again, for their children's sake as well as their own. The issue thus involves considerable value conflict, with some people opposing divorce on religious or other grounds and others arguing just as conscientiously that divorce is a practical rather than a moral issue.

The Incidence of Divorce

According to the Bureau of the Census, more than a million American married couples wind up in the divorce courts each year. What, then, is

the likelihood that a marriage will end in divorce?

One way of calculating the divorce rate is to compare the number of marriages in a given year with the number of divorces in the same year. This method shows that in 1920 there was about one divorce for every seven marriages; in 1940, one for every six; in 1960, one for every four; in 1970, one for every three; and in 1977, one for every two.[18] A difficulty with these figures is that the population that is eligible for divorce is far larger than the population that is eligible for marriage. Anyone who is currently married is a potential candidate for divorce, but most of the potential candidates for marriage come from a much smaller group—primarily the unmarried population aged eighteen to thirty. It is hardly surprising, therefore, that the divorce rate looks high compared with the marriage rate in any one year. Moreover, the factors that influence the decision to marry or to divorce vary over time. Divorce rates, for example, may be influenced by changes in the law that make it easier to get a divorce, or by the current employment opportunities for single women. Marriage rates, on the other hand, may be influenced by such factors as the number of people in the country who are aged eighteen to thirty, or by contemporary attitudes toward "living together" in other alternatives to legal marriage.

Another means of establishing the divorce rate is to calculate the number of divorces per thousand members of the population. This method also shows a steady increase in divorce; in 1960 there were 2.2 divorces per thousand people; in 1965 there were 2.5; in 1970, 3.5; in 1975, 4.9, and in 1977, 5.1.[19] A third method is to trace the fortunes of a representative sample of married couples over the years, to record their divorce rates, and to generalize from these statistics to the overall population. The broad conclusion drawn from all these methods is that about one

[15]William J. Goode, *After Divorce* (New York: Free Press, 1956).

[16]Alexander A. Plateris, *Increases in Divorces: United States—1967* (Washington, D.C.: U.S. Department of Health, Education, and Welfare, 1970), Table 5, p. 14.

[17]Paul Glasser and Elizabeth Navarre, "Structural Problems of the One-Parent Family," *Journal of Social Issues*, 21 (January 1965), 98–109.

[18]U.S. Bureau of the Census, *Population of the United States*, series p-23, no. 49 (Washington, D.C.: U.S. Department of Commerce, 1974), p. 70; *Statistical Abstract of the United States, 1978, op. cit.*, p. 79.

[19]*Statistical Abstract of the United States, 1978, op. cit.*, p. 74.

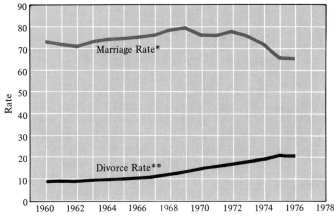

90
80
70
60
50
40
30
20
10
0

Rate

Marriage Rate*

Divorce Rate**

1960 1962 1964 1966 1968 1970 1972 1974 1976 1978

* Rate per 1,000 unmarried women, 15 years old or older.
** Rate per 1,000 married women, 15 years old or older.

FIGURE 10.2 **Marriage and divorce rates: 1960–1976.** As this graph shows, the divorce rate has been rising steadily in recent years, while the marriage rate has dropped.
(U.S. Bureau of the Census. Data from U.S. National Center for Health Statistics.)

American marriage in three is likely to end in divorce.

However, the statistics undoubtedly underestimate the extent of marital breakdown, because they include only partners who are formally divorced, and leave out partners who have separated because their marriages have become hopeless. Nor do the divorce statistics take account of the many couples who live together for long periods as "man and wife" without the benefit of formal marriage, but who later separate. Divorce statistics must be treated with caution. They tell us only about the rate of formal dissolution of marriages—not about the rate at which marriages are souring or falling apart. A rise in the divorce rate does not necessarily mean that more marriages are breaking down than before; it may simply mean that more of those couples whose marriages have broken down are taking the formal step of dissolving their union, a step they would have been less likely to take in the past.

Mary Jo Bane suggests a rise in the divorce rate need not be a cause for undue alarm:

It is distressing in and of itself . . . only if staying together at all costs is considered an indicator of healthy marriages or healthy societies. . . . Some things are fairly clear. The majority of marriages do not end in divorce. The vast majority of divorced people remarry. Only a tiny proportion of people marry more than twice. We are thus a long way from a society in which marriage is rejected or replaced by a series of short-term

liaisons. . . . Society may be changing its attitudes toward the permanence of marriage and its notions of the roles of husbands and wives. It may simply be recognizing that there is no particular benefit to requiring permanence in unhappy marriages.[20]

Divorce-Prone Marriages

Which marriages are more likely to end in divorce? Sociological research reveals certain patterns in those marriages that break up, and it is possible to identify several characteristics that may predict the likelihood of success or failure of a marriage.[21]

Age at marriage. Partners who are married at a very young age are especially prone to divorce.
Duration of engagement. Divorce rates tend to be high for those who get married after only a brief acquaintance or engagement.
Age of partners. A marriage is most likely to break up while the partners are in their twenties. The divorce rate declines as couples grow older.

[20]Bane, *op. cit.*, pp. 31–33.

[21]William J. Goode, "Family Disorganization," in Robert K. Merton and Robert Nisbet (eds.), *Contemporary Social Problems,* 4th ed. (New York: Harcourt Brace Jovanovich, 1976); Goode, *After Divorce, op. cit.*; Paul C. Glick, *American Families* (New York: Wiley, 1957); J. Richard Udry, *The Social Context of Marriage,* 2nd ed. (Philadelphia: Lippincott, 1971).

Duration of marriage. Most divorces take place within two years after marriage. The longer a couple is married, the less the likelihood of their being divorced.

Marriage order. People who have been previously married are considerably more likely to be divorced in their second marriage than are partners in a first marriage. The more often they have been divorced, the more likely they are to get divorced again.

Social class. Divorce is more common at the lower socioeconomic levels, probably because unemployment and other economic problems put an additional strain on these marriages.

Education. The chances for a lasting marriage are better for those with more years of schooling. Divorce is more likely if the husband's educational level is below that of the wife.

Religion. Divorce rates are higher for interfaith marriages and for Protestant marriages than for Catholic or Jewish marriages. The less religious the partners, the more likely they are to become divorced.

Disapproval of friends and relatives. Partners whose friends and relatives disapproved of the marriage from the outset are disproportionately likely to get divorced—perhaps because the disapproval places a strain on their marriage, perhaps because the parents and friends correctly perceived the partners' incompatibility in the first place.

Urban residence. Divorce rates are higher in urban areas than in rural areas.

Richard Udry spells out the general conclusion of sociological research on divorce-prone couples:

> The larger the social differences between two people, the more social differences, and the more significant the social differences, the more likely their marriage is to be a source of conflict between them and other social groups (relatives, neighbors, friends, and social institutions). . . . *Those who are least likely to marry are, therefore, most likely to have trouble if they do.*[22]

Divorce and the Law

Divorce represents the formal dissolution of an important social unit, and it can take place only with society's approval, in a manner prescribed by law.

Because society has always discouraged the breakup of the family, the divorce laws have historically been designed to make divorce difficult. The divorce court typically followed the standard "adversary" judicial procedure, in which an aggrieved party attempted to prove the "guilt" of an offending party. The case was heard on the legal assumption that one party was innocent, whereas the other was guilty of "cruelty," desertion, or some other offense. In many if not most instances, of course, both partners contributed to the breakdown of the marriage, but divorce under the adversary system was obtainable only if they were prepared to maintain the fiction that one of them was at fault. The great majority of these divorces were uncontested: one partner agreed beforehand to accept the "blame" for some offense against the other. Consequently, there was very little correlation between the actual causes of marital breakdown and the legal grounds on which the court allowed a divorce.

The adversary system had one very undesirable effect: it pitted the two partners against each other, making expensive and psychologically damaging battles very likely. Often one partner would agree to an uncontested divorce only as part of a bargain involving alimony payments or visitation privileges. For these reasons most states have now passed "no fault" divorce laws, which eliminate the need to lay blame on one of the partners; the couple merely declare to the court that their marriage has broken down irreparably. The old adversary process is usually still available to those who wish to make use of it, however.

The legal responsibility for alimony payments and for support payments to the partner who retains custody of the children remains controversial. In most cases custody of the children is awarded to the mother, and the father is often ordered to pay both alimony and child-support payments. Former husbands, however, default on child-support payments more often than not. One federal survey found that 46.9 percent of all families that should have been receiving court-ordered support payments were not receiving

[22]Udry, *op. cit.*, p. 301.

any money at all, and from other studies it appears that only 13 percent of orders are complied with by the tenth year after the divorce.[23]

Changes in sex roles have also led to the emergence of new problems. Many fathers now wish to retain custody of their children and resent the sexist bias of courts that assume that only women can adequately perform child-rearing tasks. And whereas until recently alimony could be awarded only to the wife, most states now make provision for the wife to be required to pay alimony to the husband—although few courts have yet issued such orders.

Divorce can be a traumatic experience with multiple problematic consequences—but the experience of divorce does not seem to destroy the appetite for marriage. The marriage rate for divorcees is higher than that for widowed or single persons at all ages. The old adage "Once burned, twice shy" does not seem to hold: the divorced seem still committed to the idea of marriage.[24]

Sources of Marital Breakdown

The factors that precipitate a breakdown of a particular marriage can range from alcoholism to infidelity, from personal incompatibility to sheer boredom. Specific factors like these, however, cannot account for the soaring divorce rate in the United States: the divorce rate is a social fact, not an individual one, and it must be explained in social terms. The social factors that contribute to marital breakdown ending in divorce are complex and interrelated, but several of them can be identified.

The Aftermath of Romantic Love. The American culture trait of romantic love, so important in mate selection, contributes, indirectly, to marital breakdown. Because Americans are thoroughly socialized into an almost impossible ideal of lifelong romantic love with their chosen

partners, they are often severely disappointed when their married life falls short of their hopes. Romantic love is built on fantasy, mystery, spontaneity, bursting emotion, and surprise. It is meant to "sweep you off your feet," to make you "lose your senses," to leave you "blind to all else." When these expectations are confronted with the garbage can, the diapers, and the weariness after a day's work at office or factory, they tend to shrivel. And when they do, millions of Americans assume that because the "thrill is gone" from their relationship with their spouses, the partnership must have failed. This is not necessarily true, for love takes many forms. Married love can grow and change as the partners grow and change; it is a love that may be mature, reasonable, realistic, and deeply fulfilling—but Americans are not socialized to expect it, to recognize it, or to appreciate it.

Thus, as long as the passions of romantic love continue to be extolled as the only viable grounds for a successful marriage, and as long as the fading of romance is believed to herald the

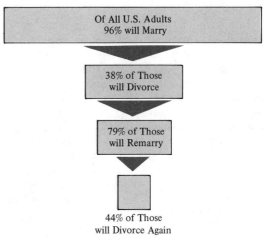

Of All U.S. Adults
96% will Marry

38% of Those
will Divorce

79% of Those
will Remarry

44% of Those
will Divorce Again

FIGURE 10.3 **The marriage odds.** Marriage remains immensely popular in the United States, as does remarriage after divorce. Second and subsequent marriages are more likely than first marriages to end in divorce.
(*Newsweek,* May 15, 1978, p. 67.)

---

[23]*New York Times,* January 5, 1974; *New York Times,* April 2, 1974.

[24]But see André Cherlin, "Remarriage as an Incomplete Institution," *American Journal of Sociology,* 84 (November 1978), 634–650.

fading of a marriage, the American family will have problems as millions of disillusioned couples discover that their dreams about their "one true love" are slowly disappearing in a pile of laundry, work and financial pressures, and routines.

Sexual Permissiveness.   The formal morality of American society has always restricted sexual intercourse to marital partners. But we are an increasingly permissive and eroticized culture, and marriage—which is theoretically grounded firmly in strict, monogamous fidelity—is inevitably affected by this development.[25]

In the past, nonmarital sexuality was limited by religious scruples, feelings of guilt, lack of opportunity, the immense value placed on virginity in women, and especially by fear of pregnancy. Before the advent of modern contraceptives it was necessary for society to inhibit nonmarital sex in order to prevent the birth of large numbers of dependent, illegitimate children. Now that sexual relations need not imply the prospect of pregnancy, the old prohibition on nonmarital sexuality has lost much of its logic and force, and the more permissive attitudes and values of the modern United States reflect that fact.

In a permissive society in which sexual satisfaction is culturally valued, it is scarcely surprising that many people look outside their marriages for sexual pleasure, or, if unmarried, see no reason why they should be deprived of sexual experience.[26] Most adult Americans have had premarital intercourse, and most of those who are married have had extramarital sexual experience (see Chapter 15, "Sexual Variance"). Many otherwise respectable (and usually politically conservative) middle-class Americans engage periodically in "swinging," or consensual exchange of marital partners; it has been estimated that hundreds of thousands of Americans have par-

ticipated in these activities.[27] All these trends serve to some extent to challenge the traditional institution of marriage.

Women's Status.   The changing status of women in the United States has inevitably unbalanced a family system that has traditionally assigned to the wife a subordinate role as housekeeper, child-rearer, and nurturing supporter of her economically active husband. As Andrew Hacker observes:

> The major change in the family in recent years, and in the problems of the future, are both summed up in one word: women. In the past and until very recently, wives were simply supplementary to their husbands, and not expected to be full human beings. . . . The trouble comes from the fact that the institution we call marriage can't hold two full human beings—it was only designed for one and a half.[28]

The changes in the attitudes and expectations of women have been accompanied by a gradual increase in female economic independence. Nearly half of American women are now in the work force, and although on the average they still earn substantially less than men, they are no longer as heavily reliant on their husbands for economic support as they were a few decades ago. It is now possible for a wife to have her own career—and even to earn more than her husband, whom, if it were not for the likely social reaction, she might reasonably expect to stay at home and do the housework. Influenced by the women's movement, many wives feel confined by their traditional roles, but their attempts to find new ones may disrupt established relationships with their husbands.[29] Women who are newly confident of being able to support themselves are also much more likely to consider abandoning a

[25]See Thomas M. Kando, *Sexual Behavior and Family Life in Transition* (New York: Elsevier, 1978).

[26]See B. Krishna Singh, Bonnie L. Walton, and J. Sherwood Williams, "Extramarital Sexual Permissiveness: Conditions and Contingencies," *Journal of Marriage and the Family*, 38 (November 1976), 701–712.

[27]Gilbert Bartell, "Group Sex Among the Middle Americans," in James R. Smith and Lynn G. Smith (eds.), *Beyond Monogamy* (Baltimore: Johns Hopkins Press, 1974), pp. 185–201; Charles Palson and Rebecca Palson, "Swinging in Wedlock," *Society*, 9 (February 1972), 28–37.

[28]Quoted in "The American Family: Future Uncertain," *Time*, December 28, 1970.

Although they are usually founded on romantic love, American marriages are frequently marred by discord between the spouses. Personal incompatibilities may develop over time and threaten the stability of the marriage.

soured marriage than they might have been in the past.

The Growth of Individualism. Americans are inclined to regard marriages that are arranged without consulting the partners as heartless and humiliating. But the partners in societies where marriages are so arranged rarely see it that way; they are content to abide by the wishes of their kinship group. The fact points again to a major cultural difference between traditionalist and modern societies: in the former, people tend to regard themselves as members of a group first and as individuals second, whereas people in the latter tend to place greater emphasis on the rights of the individual than on loyalty to the group.

The growth of individualism is one of the most significant features of modern industrial society. We are far more aware than our ancestors of the individual person—of his or her wants, needs, rights, and potential. This individualist attitude is expressed in many ways, some of them perhaps difficult to reconcile with the traditional family system. The women's liberation movement, for example, draws much of its inspiration from a concern for the dignity of the individual woman rather than any concern for the family as a traditional institution. William Goode comments on some implications of the growth of individualism:

> It is not possible to state the basic "causes" of this change in attitude. It is merely one facet of a broader set of changes in Western society called

[29]See Janet G. Hunt and Larry L. Hunt, "Dilemmas and Contradictions of Status: The Case of the Dual Career Family," *Social Problems*, 24 (April 1977), 407–416; and Rosabeth M. Kantner, *Work and Family in the United States* (New York: Russell Sage Foundation, 1977).

"secularization": patterns that were once weighted by strong moral norms have come to be evaluated by instrumental norms. Instead of asking, "Is this moral?" the individual is more likely to ask, "Is this a more useful or better procedure for my needs?" . . . Instead of asking whether his church or his community approves of divorce, the individual asks, "Is it the right thing for *me* to do?"[30]

Modern individualism has far-reaching implications throughout society, and the family has inevitably been affected.

ILLEGITIMACY

An illegitimate child is variously defined as one born out of wedlock; as one conceived out of wedlock, even if born after marriage; or as one born to any woman, whether married or not, if fathered by someone other than her husband. The whole issue of illegitimacy raises an important conflict of values. Some people see illegitimacy as a problem because it appears to be a symptom of the breakdown of the family and of moral decay; others see it as a problem because illegitimate children and their mothers may suffer considerable stigma and sometimes economic hardship as a result of prejudiced social attitudes.

The Incidence of Illegitimacy

The statistics on illegitimacy have to be treated with caution because, as in the case of all other forms of deviant behavior, reporting is uneven and probably inaccurate. Moreover, the illegitimacy statistics are affected by changes in other social factors, such as the size of the total population and the number of marriages and legitimate births.

The illegitimacy rate—the number of births per thousand unmarried women of childbearing age—rose very rapidly until the early 1970s. In 1940 the rate was 7.1 per thousand; in 1960, 21.8

per thousand; in 1965, 23.5 per thousand; and in 1970, 25.7 per thousand. But in 1971 legal abortions became available, and the illegitimacy rate dropped noticeably.[31] There are signs, however, that this trend may be checked, largely because many unwed mothers are now rejecting abortion and choosing to have their babies—and to keep them. As Leslie Westoff notes:

Less than five years ago, when a single, middle-class white teen-ager became pregnant, she had no choice. Her parents dragged themselves up out of the shock, shame and anger she had plunged them into, and covertly shipped her off to the abortion factories of less restrictive countries, or got an underground abortionist's number from a friend at the hairdresser's, or whisked her away to a maternity home where she secretly had her baby. The newborn infant was left there for adoption, sometimes being sold to pay the expenses, and the girl returned home from her "trip" abroad or her "visit" with a distant relative whom no one could recall ever meeting.

Today, this girl is no longer in disgrace, except perhaps in scattered areas where people still cling to more rigid moralistic judgments. Usually now, the girl can be seen at home, shopping in the supermarket, going about her daily chores, her belly gradually rising like a warm bread dough. Her friends, her family, her neighbors, are all aware that she is still in her teens, still unmarried, still a dependent child, and very much about to become a mother.[32]

In the mid-1960s about 65 percent of illegitimate white babies were given away for adoption. By the early 1970s only 18 percent of illegitimate white babies were adopted. In 1977 the Planned Parenthood Federation estimated that over 90 percent of all illegitimate babies were being kept by their mothers. More than a million unmarried teen-age girls become pregnant every year. About 72 percent of them have abortions, about 14 percent miscarry, and the rest give birth. Some

[30]William J. Goode, in Robert Merton and Robert Nisbet (eds.), *Contemporary Social Problems* (New York: Harcourt, Brace & World, 1966), p. 488.

[31]Alice J. Clague and Stephanie J. Ventura, *Trends in Illegitimacy: United States—1940–1965* (Washington, D.C.: U.S. Department of Health, Education, and Welfare, 1968); Shirley F. Hartley, *Illegitimacy* (Berkeley, Calif.: University of California Press, 1975).

[32]Leslie Aldridge Westoff, "Kids with Kids," *New York Times Magazine*, February 22, 1976, p. 14.

two-thirds of the pregnancies are unintended, and usually result from misinformation or ignorance about birth control.

The illegitimacy rate is higher for nonwhite than for white women. This does not necessarily mean, however, that nonwhites are more likely to conceive illegitimate children; it may simply mean that they are less likely to have abortions or to marry the father before the birth of the child. Although the illegitimacy rate for older women is declining, the rate for teen-age and particularly preteen women is rising rapidly. A 1976 survey found that 12 percent of teen-age girls have had a premarital pregnancy—an increase of one-third since 1971. Six out of seven of these unwed mothers had never used contraceptives.[33]

Social Attitudes Toward Illegitimacy

Why does American society still take an unfavorable attitude toward the illegitimate child and its mother? At first glance, there would seem to be no rational reason why children born outside a family should be treated any differently than other children, and the stigmatization of thousands of guiltless individuals seems to be a result of little more than middle-class self-righteousness. But, in fact, there are some sound social reasons for the dominant negative attitude toward illegitimacy. The legitimately constituted family provides a structure for the economic support and socialization of children, functions not easily fulfilled outside that structure in our society. The stigmatization of illegitimacy is thus functional, for it helps to ensure that most births will take place within the context of the family. There are certainly some social groups in the United States in which illegitimate births are not stigmatized and in which an unwed woman may have a child through choice rather than by accident—but these are precisely the groups that display the least loyalty to the traditional family system. If illegitimacy produced no social stigma whatever, marriage would tend to have fewer attractions

and the institution of the nuclear family might be endangered.

VIOLENCE IN THE FAMILY

One of the most serious of all family problems is violence—a seeming paradox, for it is family members, of all people, who should love and protect one another. Yet about a fifth of all murders in the United States are perpetrated by a relative of the victim—in half the cases, the spouse. So-called "disturbance calls"—principally family fights—are also the largest single category of police calls. For good reason, the police heartily dislike intervening in these disputes: more police fatalities arise from these situations than from any other.[34] As Suzanne Steinmetz and Murray Straus observe, "it would be hard to find a group or an institution in American society in which violence is more of an everyday occurrence than it is within the family."[35] Whenever one family member willfully inflicts pain and suffering on another, some measure of trust, loyalty, and affection is destroyed. Since these qualities are basic to the functioning of the family, violence is profoundly disruptive of the institution.

Explanations of Family Violence

Why should violence be so common in a social institution that is supposedly founded on love?

Force is a personal resource that can be applied to gain advantage. In the family it can be used for many purposes—either directly, as when a brother pushes his sister from the room or when a parent physically punishes a child, or indirectly, as when a husband implicitly threatens violence to make his wife obey him. The critical question for sociologists is: under what conditions does force, rather than respect and love, become the dominant resource for control and power in the family? The plausible answer, suggested by John

[33]Melvin Zelnick and John F. Kantner, "First Pregnancies to Women Age 15–19: 1976 and 1971," *Family Planning Perspectives*, 10 (January/February 1978), 11–20.

[34]*Uniform Crime Reports for the United States, 1977, op. cit.*, p. 292.

[35]Suzanne K. Steinmetz and Murray A. Straus, *Violence in the Family* (New York: Dodd, Mead, 1974), p. 3.

O'Brien and others,[36] is that people resort to force when their other resources are exhausted, diminished, or nonexistent. Thus a man who feels he has lost the respect and affection of his family, perhaps because he is an alcoholic or because he cannot support them, may fall back on physical abuse as a final resource to assert his authority.

Another explanation of family violence may lie in the link that psychologists have observed between frustration and aggression. Steinmetz and Straus point out that "in a society such as ours, in which aggression is defined as a normal response to frustration, we can expect that the more frustrating the familial and occupational roles, the greater the amount of violence."[37]

As a response to frustration, violence is by no means confined to the father. A mother who has tended a houseful of children all day is almost expected to "blow her stack" by early evening; a child who fails again and again to successfully complete a particular task is almost expected to "throw a tantrum"; and an adolescent son who cannot make his parents understand his view of things is almost expected to "storm out of the house" in a fury. In lower-class culture, violence is often valued as an appropriate response to frustration, perhaps because its members have less access to other resources than do middle-class people. (See also Chapter 14, "Crime and Violence.")

Child Abuse

One aspect of family violence that has attracted a great deal of attention in recent years is child abuse. This practice does not refer to the spankings and other physical punishments typically meted out to American children by their parents: it means much more serious acts, such as subjecting children to vicious beatings, sometimes severe enough to break their bones; tying them up, or locking them in closets, for hours or days on end; burning them with cigarettes or forcing

them to put their hands on a hot stove; and even — in extreme cases — killing them. David Gil defines child abuse as "the intentional, nonaccidental use of physical force, or intentional, nonaccidental acts of omission on the part of a parent or other caretaker, aimed at hurting, injuring, or destroying that child."[38] On the basis of his research, Gil estimated at the end of the last decade that between 250,000 and 4 million children in America experience real abuse each year.[39] A 1979 report estimated that parents kick, punch, or bite as many as 1.7 million children each year, beat up as many as 750,000 more, and attack 46,000 with knives and guns.[40]

Research on the characteristics of child abusers indicates that a disproportionately large number of them are poor. Many of the families involved have females as the head of the household; many others contain an adult male who is not the child's biological father; and most have fairly large numbers of children. The parents are usually under thirty and tend to be poorly educated. The abusers frequently have a history of mental disorder, criminal conviction, or mental retardation. Significantly, abusive parents frequently have histories of abuse in their own childhoods. They often set unrealistically high standards of conduct for their children and respond in an angry and uncontrolled way to behavior they perceive as misconduct. They frequently consider their disciplinary measures justified; and, indeed, they are merely taking to deviant extremes the socially sanctioned right of parents to physically punish their children.[41]

[36]John O'Brien, "Violence in Divorce Prone Families," *Journal of Marriage and the Family,* 33 (November 1971), 692–698.

[37]Steinmetz and Straus, *op cit.,* p. 9.

[38]David G. Gil, *Violence Against Children: Physical Child Abuse in the United States* (Cambridge, Mass.: Harvard University Press, 1970), p. 6.

[39]David G. Gil, "Incidence of Child Abuse and Demographic Characteristics of Persons Involved," in Ray E. Helfer and C. Henry Kempe (eds.), *The Battered Child* (Chicago: University of Chicago Press, 1968), pp. 19–40.

[40]Straus, Gelles, Steinmetz, *op. cit.*

[41]Brandt F. Steele and Carl B. Pollock, "A Psychiatric Study of Parents Who Abuse Infants and Small Children," in Helfer and Kempe (eds.), *op cit.*; see, also, Saad Z. Nagi, *Child Maltreatment in the United States* (New York: Columbia University Press, 1978).

Wife-Beating

Assaults by husbands on their wives are a serious problem in the United States, but one that has been very much overlooked. A reason for this neglect, disturbingly enough, is that many husbands and wives seem to regard this form of violence as acceptable, even normal, behavior. A survey conducted for the National Commission on the Causes and Prevention of Violence found that one man in four, and one woman in six, approved of a husband slapping his wife under certain conditions. Several other studies have confirmed that a significant minority of both men and women believe that it is appropriate for a husband to beat his wife "every once in a while."[42]

The study by Murray Straus and his associates, which was based on interviews with a representative cross section of over 2,000 American families, estimated that each year 7.5 million couples go through a violent episode in which one spouse tries to cause the other physical pain or injury.[43] Wives assault their husbands as often as husbands assault their wives. Because on the average they are physically weaker, wives do considerably less damage than husbands in fights that do not involve weapons. However, wives use knives or similar weapons more often than husbands do, with the end result that they are as likely to murder their spouses as husbands are.

The violence takes place in apparently normal homes, and occurs as often among the well educated as among the less educated. Since many couples may have been reluctant to admit the full extent of their violent behavior to the interviewers, it is probable that the amount of violence in the family is even greater than these estimates suggest. Many, if not most, marital homicides committed by husbands can be considered as wife-beating: whether the violence takes the form of aggravated assault or actual homicide probably depends less on the husband's intentions than on such more fortuitous circumstances as the nature of the blows or the presence of a weapon.

Most wives who are seriously beaten by their husbands do not abandon the marriage, and many—even some who are repeatedly stabbed—seek no outside help at all. Three major factors seem to influence their decision to stay. The wives are more likely to remain in the home if the violence is fairly infrequent or not considered very severe; if they were abused by their parents when they were children; or if they have few resources of their own, such as the educational qualifications or job experience that might enable them to achieve economic independence. Many wives also persist in believing, despite continual evidence to the contrary, that their husbands will reform.[44]

CONFRONTING THE PROBLEM

As our survey of the American family suggests, there is not really one family problem so much as a series of interrelated problems, rooted ultimately in certain defects of the otherwise functional nuclear family. Some of these problems can be confronted with specific social action, whereas others will probably require the slow evolution of modifications or alternatives to the existing nuclear system. Let us look first at specific responses to the problems of illegitimacy and family violence and then at the more general problem of marital breakdown and similar pressures on the nuclear family.

Reducing Illegitimacy. Illegitimacy is a social problem in two respects: the mother and child

[42]Richard J. Gelles, *The Violent Home: A Study of Physical Aggression Between Husbands and Wives* (Beverly Hills, Calif.: Sage, 1974); Murray A. Straus, "Leveling, Civility, and Violence in the Family," *Journal of Marriage and the Family,* 36 (February 1974), 13–30.

[43]Straus, Gelles, and Steinmetz, *op. cit.*

[44]Richard J. Gelles, "Abused Wives: Why Do They Stay?," *Journal of Marriage and the Family* (November 1976), 659–668.

suffer a certain amount of social stigma; and the one-parent family is far from ideal as a social or economic unit. The rapid growth in the illegitimacy rate among teen-age girls is particularly disturbing, especially now that most of them are choosing to keep their babies. The unwed teen-age mother faces intense economic, social, and psychological pressures that she may not have the resources or emotional maturity to bear. Although the lessening of the stigma attached to illegitimacy may remove an important social discouragement to illegitimate births, it does seem desirable on other grounds. In particular, it will make unhappy "shotgun marriages" a less likely outcome of pregnancy among unmarried women, and it will ensure that illegitimate children do not suffer because of the marital status of their parents. The Supreme Court has now ruled that laws discriminating against the illegitimate are unconstitutional, because they amount to punishing one person for another's behavior. Some states have abolished the legal concept of illegitimacy altogether, and many no longer note a child's illegitimacy on birth certificates.

The illegitimacy rate could be reduced if the incidence of premarital intercourse were reduced, but this is unlikely to happen in a permissive society. Two alternatives remain: abortion and effective use of contraception. Abortion can have damaging psychological effects on the mothers, and for this and several other reasons is regarded by many people as a social problem in itself. Ideally, unwanted babies ought not to be conceived in the first place, and there are therefore strong arguments for making both information about contraception and contraceptive devices more freely available to the young. Several studies have shown widespread ignorance about sexuality among teen-age mothers: many believed, for example, that they would not get pregnant because they did not have intercourse very often, or because they were too young; others used totally ineffective methods of "contraception" or were ignorant of the

female reproductive cycle.[45] The problem of illegitimacy is largely a problem of adjustment to social change: if attitudes and practices related to contraception adjust to the reality of widespread premarital intercourse, the rate of illegitimacy will shrink.[46]

Reducing Family Violence. In one respect there is a hopeful improvement in this area: the problems of child abuse and wife-beating are now receiving social recognition, a necessary step if something is to be done about them. The federal government has established a National Center on Child Abuse and Neglect to coordinate research into the problem of battered children, and the Child Abuse Prevention and Treatment Act of 1974 offers aid to communities to help abusive parents. The emphasis of social policy has shifted from punishing to treating parents who abuse their children, and these parents (or others who know about them) are encouraged to contact treatment agencies for help. Early results are promising: it seems that if the children are temporarily withdrawn from the home and the parents given intensive help at that time, with follow-up support later, the majority of children can be returned home without further risk.

An immediate step to confront the problem of wife-beating is the establishment, at least in large urban centers, of refuges for battered wives. Wives who remain at home even when they are frequently and severely beaten are likely to have few outside resources to turn to and nowhere else to go. Several European countries have opened refuges of this kind, and a few have now begun to appear in the United States. The refuges give the wife a temporary place to stay, offer advice, and, if necessary, make arrangements for medical or psychiatric assistance. They also try to put the husband in touch with counselors or others who might be able to help. Many husbands are

[45]Frank Furstenberg, Jr., Leon Gordis, and Milton Markowitz, "Birth Control Knowledge and Attitudes Among Unmarried Pregnant Adolescents: A Preliminary Report," *Journal of Marriage and the Family*, 31 (February 1969),

34–43; Sadja Goldsmith *et al.*, "Teenagers, Sex, and Contraception," *Family Planning Perspectives*, 4 (January 1972), 33, 37.

[46]See Melvin Zelnick and John F. Kantner, "Sexual and Contraceptive Experience of Young Unmarried Women in the United States, 1976 and 1971," *Family Planning Perspectives*, 9 (March–April 1977), 55–73.

sufficiently jolted by their spouse's unexpected departure that when she returns, they refrain from further violence—sometimes for long periods, sometimes permanently. These centers are merely a stopgap measure, however. The problem of the battered wife will be effectively confronted only if there is an end to the widespread social attitude that some measure of physical violence is acceptable between marriage partners and that such violence is, in any case, a strictly private matter for the family concerned.

Alternatives to Traditional Marriage. Religious leaders and others argue forcefully that a return to the traditional norms and values would slash the divorce rate and solve many of the problems of the nuclear family. Whether this view is correct or not is perhaps less significant than the fact that such a return to older standards is unlikely to happen, least of all as a result of moral exhortations. The family is changing and will continue to change because society is changing. We expect change in all our other major institutions—such as education, government, the economy, science, or law—and there is no reason to suppose that the family can be exempt.

It is hardly surprising that many Americans are now experimenting with a variety of new kinds of sexual relationship and family organization. To some people these experiments represent sincere and needed efforts to create more satisfying ways of meeting basic human needs; to others they are utopian and unrealistic; to still others they are merely so many excuses for irresponsibility and immorality. Although there may be some truth in all these views, it is clear that the alternative forms represent something more profound than a mere carnival of fornication.[47]

The experimental alternatives to traditional marriage today are so various and fluid that only the main ones can be outlined here.

Remaining single. A small minority of Americans apparently prefer to remain single, perhaps engaging in casual or even long-term sexual relationships.[48] This is true of both men and women, including unwed mothers who refuse to enter forced marriages. Young Americans are generally tending to delay their first marriage. Since 1960 the incidence of never-married women aged twenty to twenty-four has jumped from 28 percent to 40 percent. Among men aged twenty-three—the average age for first marriage by males—the never-marrieds rose from 42 to 52 percent between 1970 and 1977.

Communal and group marriages. These arrangements involve several men and women who share economic and child-raising responsibilities and sometimes sexual relationships as well.[49] Communes range from highly organized establishments with strict membership requirements to amorphous, relaxed groups with shifting membership. Sexual practices vary: the true group marriage, in which all adults participate in sexual relations with one another, is quite rare; the complications involved in these multilateral arrangements are so great that they rarely last more than a few months.[50] In most cases couples pair off to some extent, although without claiming exclusive right to each other. After infancy, children are generally regarded as being as much the responsibility of the group as of the parents.

"Serial" marriage. The practice of entering and leaving several formal marriages is becoming increasingly common. One in every four marriages in the United States today involves someone who has been previously married. Divorced people usually marry again within a few years, and the more often they are divorced, the more likely they are to marry yet again. The partners in these marriages clearly have a strong commitment to the institution of marriage, but only a temporary commitment to particular spouses.

[47]James W. Ramey, *Intimate Friendships* (Englewood Cliffs, N.J.: Prentice-Hall, 1976); Bernard I. Murstein, *Current and Future Intimate Lifestyles* (New York: Springer, 1977).

[48]See Peter Stein, *Single* (Englewood Cliffs, N.J.: Prentice-Hall, 1976).

[49]See Larry L. Constantine and Joan M. Constantine, *Group Marriage* (New York: Macmillan, 1974).

[50]Albert Ellis, "Group Marriage: A Possible Alternative?" in Herbert A. Otto (ed.), *The Family in Search of a Future* (New York: Appleton-Century-Crofts, 1970), pp. 85–97.

Rather than try to make a failing marriage work, they simply move on to another one.

"Open" marriage. The open marriage is one in which the spouses agree (sometimes through a formal contract) to flexible marital arrangements, often including the right of the partners to extramarital intercourse. Participants in these arrangements are committed to marriage because it offers them security and the opportunity to make some mutual commitments, but they wish to avoid those aspects of traditional marriage they find overly restrictive.[51]

Cohabitation. "Living together," or cohabitation, is probably the most common alternative to marriage.[52] Census Bureau data show that the number of unmarried people sharing a household doubled between 1970 and 1977, from 645,000 to 1.3 million people. The partners choose to live together for many reasons, but wariness about the prospects of formal marriage failing seems to be the main one. Most of the partners appear to practice sexual fidelity, and a great number live together for long periods. Cohabitation seems to be especially popular among college students. One survey of students at a northeastern university found that nearly 80 percent said they would be willing to live together with a member of the opposite sex without marriage. In fact, about a fifth of the sample were already doing so, although most had not informed their parents of the arrangement. Males and females approved of cohabitation about equally, although for different reasons. The most common reason offered by the men was the sexual convenience of cohabitation, whereas the most common reason given by the women was that cohabitation was a first step toward marriage. The second most common reason given by both sexes was that living together was cheaper than living alone.[53]

Cohabitation has been strongly discouraged in the past, not only by social values and norms but even by law. In fact, the practice is still illegal in twenty states, with penalties ranging up to three years' imprisonment, but the law is rarely enforced. Since 1977, courts in several states have ruled that an agreement by unmarried partners to share their property while living together is valid and binding; if the arrangement breaks up, one partner can sue the other for part of the property in exactly the same way as a divorced person can.

The Future of the Family. What form is the typical American family likely to take in the future? It would be foolhardy to attempt any precise forecasts, but it is safe to predict continuing change. The divorce rate, the number of unsatisfied couples, and the number of people looking for alternatives may well increase. This does not mean that the family, or even the nuclear family, is in any danger of disappearing. Many, if not most, people are still committed to the traditional patterns and find deep satisfaction through them. However, we may find ourselves in the unique position of supporting, for the first time in history, more than one generally recognized form of family within the same society. Although no society has yet existed that has sanctioned multiple family forms, it is also true that no society has ever before offered the opportunities for alternative life styles that are available in modern America.

The fact remains, however, that at present over 90 percent of Americans enter into a traditional marriage at some time during their lives. The family is in a state of profound change, but it will remain a central institution in our society. As the anthropologist Margaret Mead once remarked, the family "is the only institution we have that doesn't have a hope of disappearing."

[51]Nena O'Neil and George O'Neil, *Open Marriage* (New York: Avon, 1973); Jacqueline Knapp, "An Exploratory Study of Seventeen Sexually Open Marriages," *Journal of Sex Research,* 12 (August 1976), 206–219.
[52]For a useful summary of the cohabitation issue, see "Living Together," *Newsweek,* August 1, 1977, pp. 46–50.
[53]Ibithaj Arafat and Betty Yorburg, "On Living Together Without Marriage," *Journal of Sex Research,* 9 (May 1973), 97–106.

SUMMARY

1. The American family system faces a number of severe problems, but sociologists see these as symptoms of change rather than breakdown.

2. The family is a universal social institution because it performs several vital social functions. Marriage and family patterns vary a great deal from one society to another. The extended family was functional in preindustrial societies, but the nuclear family is more functional in modern industrial societies.

3. The functionalist approach sees family problems as resulting from social disorganization caused by rapid social change, some of which has made the nuclear family dysfunctional in certain respects. The conflict approach focuses more on the competing values involved in family issues: one group's solution may be another's problem. The deviance approach sees some family problems as the result of deviance from social norms; but much behavior that was considered deviant in the past is now regarded as normal.

4. Romantic love is found primarily in industrialized societies, where it is functional in maintaining the nuclear family. Americans tend to fall in love with and to marry people who share their social characteristics.

5. The American divorce rate is very high. Divorce usually involves young partners with children, and has many adverse legal, emotional, and economic consequences. The sources of marital breakdown lie in the fading of romantic love, sexual permissiveness, changes in women's status, and the growth of individualism.

6. The illegitimacy rate has leveled off as a result of the legalization of abortions, but is still rising among teen-age and preteen girls.

7. Family violence is a serious though neglected problem. It involves child abuse and violence between spouses, particularly the beating of wives.

8. Illegitimacy can be confronted to some extent through better availability of contraceptive devices and information; the stigma attached to illegitimacy could also be eliminated. Family violence can be confronted by helping rather than punishing those who commit the violence, and by providing places of refuge for their victims. Some alternatives to traditional marriage and family patterns include remaining single; communal and group marriages; serial marriage; open marriage; and cohabitation. The basic nuclear family, however, is in no danger of disappearing.

GLOSSARY

Extended family. A family system in which several generations of the same kinship line live together or near each other.

Family. A group of people who live together and who are related by ancestry, marriage, or adoption.

Kin. A network of people related by ancestry, marriage, or adoption.

Marriage. A socially approved sexual union of some permanence between two people.

Nuclear family. A family system in which a single married couple and their dependent children live apart from their other relatives.

FURTHER READING

BANE, MARY JO. *Here to Stay: American Families in the Twentieth Century.* New York: Basic Books, 1976. A useful and readable analysis of the problems and prospects of the American family.

BARTELL, GILBERT. *Group Sex: A Scientist's Eyewitness Report on Swinging in the Suburbs.* New York: Peter Wyden, 1971. An anthropologist's study of "swinging" in Middle America.

BERNARD, JESSIE. *The Future of Marriage.* New York: Bantam, 1973. A readable and realistic analysis of modern marriage and its future prospects.

CONSTANTINE, LARRY L., and JOAN M. CONSTANTINE. *Group Marriage.* New York: Macmillan, 1974. The best book on group marriage and its many problems.

DELORA, JOANN S., and JACK R. DELORA (eds.). *Intimate Life Styles: Marriage and Its Alternatives.* 2nd ed. Pacific Palisades, Calif.: Goodyear, 1975. An extensive compilation of articles and data on the American family and various alternative sexual and family patterns.

GORDON, MICHAEL. *The American Family: Past, Present, and Future.* New York: Random House, 1978. An excellent discussion of the American family, analyzed in a richly informed historical and modern context.

HARTLEY, SHIRLEY F. *Illegitimacy.* Berkeley, Calif.: University of California Press, 1975. A useful discussion of the various issues raised by illegitimate births, with an analysis of some trends in the illegitimacy rate.

HELFER, RAY E., and C. HENRY KEMPE (eds.). *The Battered Child.* 2nd ed. Berkeley, Calif.: University of California Press, 1978. An important collection of articles on child abuse; it contains particularly valuable information on the background of parents who abuse their children.

MELVILLE, KEITH. *Marriage and Family Today.* New York: Random House, 1977. A clearly written and interesting college text that provides a good introduction to the current American family and its problems.

SKOLNICK, ARLENE. *The Intimate Environment: Exploring Marriage and Family.* 2nd ed. Boston: Little, Brown, 1978. A popular and comprehensive text on marriage and family, useful for the student who wants an overview of the sociological approach to the field.

STRAUS, MURRAY A., RICHARD GELLES, and SUZANNE K. STEINMETZ. *Behind Closed Doors: A Survey of Family Violence in America.* Garden City, N.Y.: Doubleday, 1979. The findings of an important survey of family violence in the United States. The book includes evidence on both child abuse and violence between spouses and siblings.

11
Aging

THE PROBLEM

The plight of the aged, for so long neglected, has recently come to be regarded as a major social problem in the United States. In a sense the elderly (conventionally, those aged sixty-five and over) are a "newly discovered" minority group. Like other minority groups, the old are subjected to job discrimination; they suffer high rates of poverty; they face prejudice founded on inaccurate stereotypes; they are excluded from the mainstream of American life on the basis of supposed group characteristics; and they are offered few meaningful roles in their society. In addition, the aged may face such problems as high rates of victimization by criminals, a heavy burden of chronic illness and medical expenses, and psychological problems that result from their loss of independence and their sense of being unwanted.

The problems of the elderly are attracting greater attention largely because the American population is growing steadily older as the proportion of its aged members increases. At the time of the first United States census in 1790, half of the people in the country were 16 or younger. By the turn of the present century the median age of the population had risen to 22.9 years; by 1970, it was 27.7; and by 1977 it had reached 28.9. The median age will pass 30 in 1981, reach 35 by the year 2000, and will approach 40 by the year 2030 (see Figure 11.1). At present there are 23 million aged Americans, or about 1 person in every 10. By the year 2030 their number will have doubled to some 52 million people, or 1 in every 6.

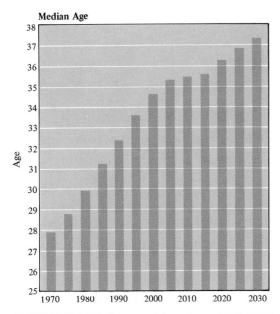

Median Age

FIGURE 11.1 **Median age of Americans: 1970–2030.** The median age of the American population is increasing as the population grows older. The long-term implications of this trend will be enormous, for the United States will no longer be such a youth-oriented society and a variety of social and economic changes will result.
(U.S. Bureau of the Census.)

AGE AND SOCIAL STRUCTURE

Gerontology is the scientific study of aging. The discipline relies heavily on sociological principles

In nearly all traditional preindustrial societies, the old have an honored role; they are respected by the young because of the wisdom that their long years of experience have given them. But in a rapidly changing modern industrial society, the knowledge of the elderly is soon outdated, and they have no roles that might command the respect of the young.

and data, particularly the sociological insight into the relationship between the aging process and social forces.

Sociologists point out that all human societies differentiate among their members on the basis of age, distributing different rights and obligations to people at various stages of life. Different societies have definite norms specifying, for example, at what age a female may have sexual intercourse, at what age a boy should undergo initiation rights, how old a youth should be before his first lion hunt, or when an adult may become a member of a tribal council. In the United States we make many such distinctions on the basis of age. We let people vote if they are eighteen, but not if they are seventeen. We arrest them for appearing naked in public if they

are twenty, but not if they are two. We allow them to run for the Senate at thirty, but not at twenty-one, and we let them collect Social Security retirement benefits at sixty-five, but usually not before.

As we grow up and grow old, our society offers us a sequence of possible age-related roles, such as schoolchild, apprentice, college student, graduate, spouse, corporation executive, and retiree.

[1]Matilda White Riley, "Age Strata in Social Systems," in James E. Birren (ed.), *Handbook of Aging and the Social Sciences* (New York: Van Nostrand Reinhold, 1976); see, also, the lucid discussion in Matilda White Riley and Joan Waring, "Age and Aging," in Robert K. Merton and Robert Nisbet (eds.), *Contemporary Social Problems*, 4th ed. (New York: Harcourt Brace Jovanovich, 1976).

Various role opportunities thus open or close to us at different points in our passage from the cradle to the grave. In this connection it is useful to think of society as containing two fluid structures: a structure of ages, and a structure of roles.[1] The *age structure* refers to the number and proportion of people in different age categories, such as infants, the middle-aged, or the old. The *role structure* refers to the number and type of roles that society makes available, such as those of warrior, airline captain, or grandparent. Both the age structure and the role structure of a society are constantly changing.

Every society has to try to provide appropriate roles for its members, including the aged. In a small number of societies where resources are very limited, there are few roles for the old to play, and they may even be driven from the community to die. The Eskimo, for example, sometimes left unproductive older members to perish in the snow, and even today the Ik of Uganda leave the old and infirm to starve to death.[2] In most traditional societies, however, the aged are accorded an honored role, so much so that people may look forward to old age. The old typically live out their lives in a large extended family containing children, grandchildren, and even great-grandchildren. Their lifelong experience makes them the repository of wisdom in the community, on subjects ranging from folklore to religion to medicine. Old men typically wield great political power as heads of families, and the aged of both sexes are usually expected to remain active in the community and to perform some forms of light labor until advanced old age.[3]

We offer no such role to the elderly in modern America; in fact, we offer them hardly any role at all. Although at the turn of the century nearly three-quarters of men aged sixty-five or older were active in the labor force, the proportion has dropped to less then a third today and will

decline to less than a fifth by 1985. This steady disappearance of economic roles is compounded by the virtual absence of meaningful roles within the family. As we saw in Chapter 10 ("Family Problems"), the extended family has almost disappeared from modern industrial society, having been replaced by a nuclear family system containing a married couple and their dependent offspring living apart from other relatives— a system in which the grandparents have at best only a limited role to play.

This tension between the age structure and the role structure of American society is likely to become more strained in the future as a result of major changes in the birth rate over the past quarter century. The post-World War II "baby boom" (discussed in Chapter 2, "Population") saw the most rapid rise in birth rates ever recorded. During the period of the boom, roughly from 1947 to 1960, some 45 million babies were born, representing about a fifth of the present population. This generation flooded

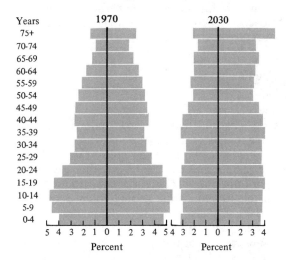

FIGURE 11.2 **Population structure of the United States: 1970 and 2030.** The population structure of the United States is undergoing a slow but radical change. As this chart shows, the population was disproportionately young in 1970; by the year 2030, however, it will be "top-heavy" with the elderly. (Bureau of the Census, National Center for Health Statistics.)

[2]See Colin M. Turnbull, *The Mountain People* (New York: Simon and Schuster, 1972.)

[3]See Barbara Myerhoff and Andrei Simic (eds.), *Life's Career—Aging: Cultural Variations on Growing Old* (Beverly Hills, Calif.: Sage, 1977).

the schools in the 1950s and 1960s. Today it is crowding the job market. By the 1980s it will cause a middle-aged bulge in the American age structure, swelling the present group of those of between thirty-five and forty by no less than 80 percent. By the time the baby-boom generation reaches retirement early next century, the United States will be dominated by the elderly, and the days in which American society was youth-oriented will be past (see Figure 11.2 on page 293). The progress of this generation is, as Philip Hauser aptly puts it, "like a goat passing through a boa constrictor."[4] The demographic shift toward an elderly population will be further reinforced by two other factors. One is the "baby bust"—the sharp decline in birth rates that brought the average number of children per woman down from a postwar high of 3.8 in 1957 to an unprecedented low of 1.8 in 1976. The second factor is the marked increase in life expectancy caused by nutritional, sanitary, and medical advances. A century ago the average life expectancy in the United States was about forty years; today it is over seventy. American society contains more than a million people aged eighty-five or over, and more than 100,000 who have lived for a century. We have more old people living for longer than ever before, but we have made few social arrangements for adjusting to this fact.

You may be fortunate enough, by reason of your race, sex, class, or other personal characteristics, to escape the effects of some of the social problems described in this book. But however distant that time may seem, you will inexorably grow old—and if the social problem faced by the aged is not effectively confronted, it will one day be your personal problem as well.

ANALYZING THE PROBLEM

Both the functionalist and the conflict approaches can help in understanding the problems faced by the aged.

The Functionalist Approach

The functionalist approach sees the problem as one of social disorganization caused by rapid social change: there are now more old people living for longer than ever before, but they have fewer roles to play in the economy, the family, or elsewhere in society. To put it another way, there is an imbalance between the age structure and the role structure of the society, to the detriment of the old.

Ideally, a society should be able to offer fulfilling roles for the members of every generation. As we have seen, social changes have shattered the meaningful and rewarding role that the elderly once had. The breakdown of the extended-family system has deprived the old of their honored domestic role, and the rise of industrialism has deprived them of their former economic roles. Jobs in agriculture and in various forms of self-employment have been rapidly disappearing, to be replaced largely by governmental, corporate, and other bureaucratic jobs. These jobs discriminate against the elderly because they require higher levels of education than the aged can offer and, as a matter of administrative convenience, they usually have an arbitrary retirement age. These changes in the American role structure have been compounded by the shift in the age structure that is making the society an increasingly older one. The problems of the aged, in the functionalist view, can thus be traced back to the social disorganization implied in the imbalance between role structure and age structure.

The Conflict Approach

The conflict approach to the problem highlights a different aspect of the issue: discrimination against the old. In analyzing the problem, conflict theorists ask their usual question, who benefits? The answer is that the beneficiaries of

---

[4]"The Graying of America," *Newsweek*, February 28, 1977, p. 50.

Table 11.1   Old People's Perceptions of Themselves Compared with
Public Perceptions of "Most People over 65"

Characteristics of people over 65	Self perceptions of people 65 and over (percent)	Public perceptions of "most people over 65" (percent)	Net Difference
Very friendly and warm	72	74	+ 2
Very wise from experience	69	64	− 5
Very bright and alert	68	29	−39
Very open-minded and adaptable	63	21	−42
Very good at getting things done	55	35	−20
Very physically active	48	41	− 7
Very sexually active	11	5	− 6
How people over 65 spend "a lot of time"			
Socializing with friends	47	52	+ 5
Gardening or raising plants	39	45	+ 6
Reading	36	43	+ 7
Watching television	36	67	+31
Sitting and thinking	31	62	+31
Caring for younger or older members of the family	27	23	+ 4
Sleeping	16	39	+23
Just doing nothing	15	35	+20
Working part time or full time	10	5	− 5
Doing volunteer work	8	15	+ 7

Source: Adapted from National Council on the Aging, "The Myth and Reality of Aging in America," Washington, D.C. (mimeographed), 1975, pp. 53, 59.

discrimination against the aged are those who are not old. For example, when older workers are forced to retire, even against their will, jobs are created for younger people. The conflict approach thus focuses on the competition between different generations—a conflict in which the elderly, being numerically and usually economically weaker, have tended to be the losers.

Conflict theorists point to parallels in the conflict between the aged and nonaged and the conflicts between rich and poor, black and white, male and female.[5] In each case the dominant group enjoys superior access to social rewards at the expense of the subordinate group, and in each case it uses an *ideology*, or belief system, to justify its position. Analogous to "sexism" and "racism," *ageism* is a new word sociologists now use to refer to the set of beliefs that justifies systematic discrimination against the elderly.[6] According to the ideology of ageism, the continued inequality between the aged and the nonaged is rooted in the facts of life—that is, in the mental and/or physical inability of the old

[5]Anne Foner, "Age in Society: Structure and Change," *American Behavioral Scientist*, 19 (November–December, 1975), 144–165; and "Age Stratification and Age Conflict in Political Life," *American Sociological Review*, 39 (April 1974), 187–196.

[6]The word was coined by Robert N. Butler in "Ageism: Another Form of Bigotry," *Gerontologist*, 9 (Winter 1969), 243–246. See, also, Erdman Palmore and Kenneth Manton, "Ageism Compared to Racism and Sexism," in Mildred Seltzer, Sherry Corbett, and Robert Atchley (eds.), *Social Problems of Aging: Readings* (Belmont, Calif.: Wadsworth, 1978).

to play significant and rewarding social and economic roles. Like sexism and racism, which make similar claims about women or minority-group members, the ideology of ageism takes no account of individual differences, nor of the social rather than biological roots of some of the characteristics (real or imagined) of the subordinate group (see Table 11.1 on page 295). Conflict theorists emphasize, however, that tension and controversy over the rights of the aged may ultimately be beneficial. As the aged and their sympathizers form social movements to campaign for change, the issue will increasingly be brought to public attention; and only when there is widespread social awareness of the problem will any significant changes be made.

THE LIFE CYCLE

At first sight, aging seems to be a purely biological process. Barring premature death, every human being proceeds through a predictable course of biological development—leading from infancy to childhood, on to adolescence and young adulthood, and then to middle age, old age, and, finally, extinction. Although we may view the latter part of this biological process with dismay, it is not a social problem, for there is nothing we can do about it. But aging is also a social process. The nature of the life cycle—its length, its stages, its opportunities, challenges, and rewards—varies according to the historical and social location of each generation and each individual.[7]

One obvious illustration of this social influence is the quality of medical services, nutrition, and public sanitation in any society. Our average life expectancy in the United States today is twice that of our ancestors a few generations ago. At the turn of the century the infant mortality rate was over 160 per thousand live births; today it has been reduced to about 14 deaths per thousand. The ailments that once claimed most human life were communicable diseases such as smallpox, cholera, or diphtheria, which usually

struck in the early stages of the life cycle. Today the main causes of death are degenerative diseases such as heart and lung ailments, strokes, and cancer, which usually affect people much later in the life cycle. Thus social factors—modern medicine, improved nutrition, and higher standards of public sanitation—have had a profound effect on the average life expectancy of human beings: for the first time in the history of our species, most people can expect to grow old. Let us look at the life cycle in more detail to see other ways in which it is affected by social as well as biological factors.

Childhood and Adolescence

The United States is a very child-centered society. Parents derive great gratification from their children, and focus much of their energies on the physical, social, emotional, and intellectual development of their offspring. We romanticize childhood, looking back on it as a particularly carefree period. We mark it out as a distinct stage of life, with specific childhood games, children's clothes, and a distinct set of childhood privileges and responsibilities. We protect children, too, from the harsher facts of life, conspiring to prevent them from learning "too early" about such potentially embarrassing subjects as sex and death.[8]

It may come as a surprise, therefore, to learn that many preindustrial societies had scarcely any concept at all of childhood as a separate stage of life. In these societies people simply passed from a prolonged infancy, in which they had no adult responsibilities, to full adulthood. In the Europe of the Middle Ages, for example, there were no distinct children's clothes or children's games, and paintings of the period always show children as nothing more than dwarfish adults, with fully mature faces.[9] The reason was, of course, that in these agricultural societies children began to work in the fields and to play

[7]See Denis P. Hogan, "The Variable Order of Events in the Life Course," *American Sociological Review*, 43 (August 1978), 573–586.

[8]See Marvin R. Koller and Oscar W. Ritchie, *Sociology of Childhood*, 2nd ed. (Englewood Cliffs, N.J.: Prentice-Hall, 1978).

[9]J.H. Plumb, "The Great Change in Children," *Horizon*, 13 (Winter 1971), 4–13; Philippe Aries, *Centuries of Childhood: A Social History of Childhood* (New York: Knopf, 1962).

other adult economic roles as soon as they were physically capable of doing so. The young often married in their early teens, although they typically continued to live with their parents and grandparents as part of a large extended family. In early industrial societies children continued to perform adult economic roles, often working long shifts under appalling conditions in factories and mines. This practice continued even in the United States until early in this century: in 1900, in fact, a quarter of the boys aged ten to fifteen were in the labor force. On the whole, child labor simply had not been considered a social problem. It was only when a new concept of childhood and children's rights developed that the practice was widely perceived as a scandal. Even today there are still a few simple hunting-and-gathering societies, such as the Aranda of Australia and the San of the Kalahari desert, that make a rigid distinction between only two main stages of life, immaturity and adulthood. In such societies the change from one status to another is usually an abrupt one. It typically takes place at the time of puberty and, especially in the case of males, it may be marked by a painful initiation ceremony.[10] (Interestingly, we still retain vestiges of initiation ceremonies in our own society, in such events as the high-school graduation, the twenty-first birthday party, or the Jewish bar mitzvah: each of these ceremonies signifies a changed social status for those who undergo it.)

In the modern world we no longer pass immediately from an immature to a mature social status at the time of puberty: industrial societies have added a new stage to the life cycle—adolescence. Although this stage of the life cycle was unknown in preindustrial societies, we today take adolescence, with all its turmoil and confusion, as a "natural" and inevitable part of growing up. As a matter of fact, the word came into common usage only in 1904, when the psychologist Stanley Hall used it to refer to a new age category that was emerging at the time—a category of

young people who had reached puberty but who were denied adult sexual, social, and economic responsibilities.[11]

This new age category emerged because industrial societies, unlike the agricultural societies that preceded them, need workers with relatively developed and specialized skills. At a minimum, an industrial worker must be able to read and write, and some of the members of the industrial work force must have highly refined technical knowledge and expertise. As a result, prolonged formal education became a necessity. Since 1900 the amount of education received by the average American has increased by more than six years; at the turn of the century only 6.4 percent of Americans completed high school, compared with over 80 percent today. Instead of moving fairly abruptly from childhood to adulthood, teen-agers in industrial societies are relegated to marginal, ambiguous, and often confusing roles. They are capable of reproduction, but sexual experience and marriage are forbidden them. They are physically capable of working full time, but they are largely excluded from the labor force. Because they are segregated from other age groups in schools and elsewhere, they tend to form their own subcultures, with norms, values, and attitudes that may differ markedly from those predominating in the society as a whole—a situation that leads, understandably enough, to a "generation gap."

As Talcott Parsons pointed out, the period of adolescence is functional for modern industrial society: it provides a transitional period of adjustment between the very different roles that children and adults are expected to play in American society.[12] Childhood can be experienced as a veritable paradise of play, pleasure, and instant gratification, but in adulthood we face inescapable demands for responsibility, a rigid separation of work and leisure, and deferred gratification. The psychiatrist Erik Erikson argues that adolescence is essentially a period of

---

[10]See Anne Foner and David Kertzer, "Transitions over the Life Course: Lessons from Age-Set Societies," *American Journal of Sociology*, 83 (March 1978), p. 1103; see, also, Joseph Kett, *Rites of Passage* (New York: Basic Books, 1977).

[11]Stanley Hall, *Adolescence: Its Psychology and Its Relations to Physiology, Anthropology, Sociology, Sex, Crime, Religion and Education* (New York: Appleton, 1904).

[12]Talcott Parsons, "Age and Sex in the Social Structure of the United States," in Talcott Parsons, (ed.), *Essays in Sociological Theory* (New York: Glencoe, 1949).

"moratorium," a psychosocial interlude between childhood and adulthood during which emerging identities can be explored and consolidated. Yet because the role of adolescent is a transitional one, its rights and obligations are poorly defined: hence the tendency for adolescence in modern society to be marked by rebellion, confusion, and emotional trauma.[13]

When does adolescence end? A few decades ago, when most young people entered the work force as soon as they had graduated from high school, this stage of life effectively ended in the late teens. Today, with so many young people going on to college and to graduate school, and with others "dropping out," on at least a temporary basis, from many social responsibilities, it seems that adolescence is being prolonged even further. One observer, Kenneth Keniston, sees a "new" stage of life emerging between adolescence and adulthood: "Millions of young people are in a stage of life that lacks even a name." Keniston suggests that this new stage, which he calls "youth," is still an optional one, in that people may choose whether to enter it or skip it. The stage of youth, he claims, runs from roughly eighteen to thirty, and comprises many young people who refuse to "settle down" into an acceptance of those attitudes, life styles, and responsibilities that our society regards as the defining characteristics of mature adulthood—a steady job, a marriage, a mortgage, and the rest.[14]

Mature Adulthood

Most people marry in their twenties or early thirties, and husband and wife begin the process of establishing a home, raising a family, and developing the life style that will give meaning and satisfaction to the years ahead. As we saw in Chapter 9 ("Sex Roles"), the roles of husband and wife are becoming increasingly fluid. But the husband still typically plays the role of major breadwinner; the wife commonly works until she has children, and may then withdraw from the full-time labor force until the children reach

adolescence. These are years in which people consolidate their entry into mature adulthood; and they are also years of aspiration and ambition for what the future holds.

By the time people reach their forties, however, they can usually have no more illusions about the future course of their lives; the pattern of their existence is becoming settled and predictable. Both partners face the inevitable signs of aging; they lose the sense of growing up and realize they are beginning to grow old. The change in orientation from time-since-birth to time-left-to-live can be traumatic, although the age at which people experience these feelings and the degree to which they are disturbed by them varies a great deal. As John Clausen points out:

> Some men and women are acutely aware of aging at a period of life when others feel they are at their prime. Chronic poor health and loss of youthful looks are obvious cues that vigor and beauty are on the decline, but there may be more subtle cues as well. Declining response from members of the opposite sex can be devastating to the erstwhile Don Juan or his female counterpart. . . . The athletic individual who took great pride in his ability to perform physical feats may experience a measure of despair when his manifest strength and endurance begin to drop off noticeably, even though he may surpass most people in their prime. One man takes pleasure in seeing his son's powers surpass his own; another strongly contests his son because the son's ascendance can only mean his own decline.[15]

It is only recently that researchers have focused attention on the "mid-life crisis" faced by many people, usually in their forties. The mid-life period is marked by relatively high rates of depression, alcoholism, suicide, and divorce. Many social scientists believe that these problems are related to the personal crises that men and women experience, in somewhat different ways, as they come to the realization that their lives are more than half over. Gradually, the individual begins the process of coming to terms

---

[13]Erik H. Erikson, *Childhood and Society*, rev. ed. (New York: Norton, 1964).

[14]Kenneth Keniston, "Youth: A New Stage of Life," *American Scholar*, 39 (Autumn 1970), 631–654.

[15]John A. Clausen, "The Life Course of Individuals," in Matilda W. Riley and Anne Foner (eds.), *Aging and Society: A Sociology of Age Stratification*, vol. 3 (New York: Russell Sage Foundation, 1969), p. 493.

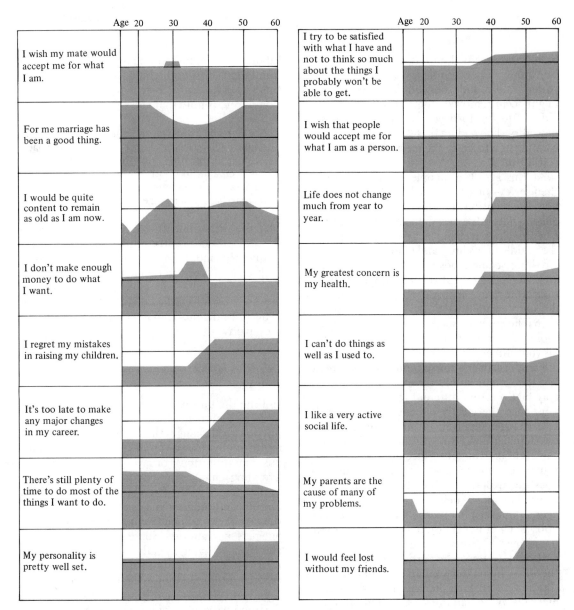

FIGURE 11.3 **Changing attitudes throughout the life cycle.** People's attitudes to themselves, their lives, and other people shift markedly at different points in the life cycle. These charts show the average responses of people of different ages to various questions about their attitudes.

(Adapted from Roger Gould, "Adult Life Stages: Growth Toward Self-Tolerance." *Psychology Today* [February 1975], 74–78.)

with the inevitability of his or her own death, an event that earlier had seemed impossibly distant. Gail Sheehy, who has made an extensive study of the mid-life crisis, comments that this is the time when people begin to feel perishable. Suddenly headaches are believed to be the first sign of a brain tumor; any lump is suspected of being cancerous. The middle-aged watch as their parents and friends die; and these deaths, which might seem removed from the twenty-five-year-old, are to the forty-year-old a sign of personal mortality. The feeling that "I'm next" becomes a warning sign to make the most of life while there is still time.[16]

At this age, too, people must take stock of themselves—of what they have become, and of how their options in life are slowly closing off. Sheehy notes that as a man approaches forty, he faces the disconcerting fact that he has arrived at the middle of his life—and of his career. At thirty anything seemed possible; his ultimate career and success were still open to hopeful speculation. At forty he realizes "where he has placed in life's professional battles,"[17] and he senses that even if he has been successful, he must now try to avoid stagnation. But if he has failed to achieve his youthful expectations of himself, he faces the difficult task of coming to terms with that reality. For the woman in our society the mid-life crisis may take a rather different form. Every woman must face the clearly demarcated and predictable changes involved in menopause, although the actual timing and psychological impact of the event are variable. Since most women today usually do not have a professional career, she does not experience directly some of the concerns that affect her husband; but if she has devoted most of her married life to the care and upbringing of her children, their departure from home may be equally traumatic. This "empty nest" situation may be particularly disturbing to the wife who has focused much of her life on her children to distract herself from an unhappy marriage. A woman in this situation often experiences feelings of loneliness, isolation, and futility. Deprived of what had become almost the main reason for her existence and realizing that much of her life has been devoted to her family rather than to any enhancement of personal talents and abilities, she may come to resent her

subordinate status and may start to look for fulfillment outside the home—to the consternation of her husband. Sheehy describes this situation in one couple that she studied:

> She is ready to strike out, get a job, go back to school, kick up her heels; just as he is drawing back, gasping for breath, feeling futile about where he has been and uncertain about simply keeping his balance on the job and in bed. How is he likely to react to her sudden surge toward independence?[18]

Many marital difficulties ensue at this stage of the life cycle as the husband and wife—frequently under no romantic illusions about each other—face the remainder of life without the company of their children and with the prospect of a significantly lower standard of living once the husband has retired. Increasingly, they worry about the experience of old age in America.

Old Age

In time the burden of the years affects even the healthiest individual. Aging is accompanied by physiological changes that are not necessarily the result of any disease: apart from the more obvious manifestations of age—such as baldness, wrinkling, changes in body form, and stiffness of limbs—there is a general process of cellular atrophy and progressive degeneration. However, the rate of physiological aging varies greatly from one person to another. Some people show noticeable signs of aging as early as fifty. Others seem relatively young and vital at seventy, and may even continue to enjoy a vigorous sex life.

In general, however, ill health becomes more common with advancing age. More than three-quarters of those over sixty-five suffer from some chronic health condition. But ill health need not have only physiological causes; it can have social and psychological causes as well. People tend to follow social expectations, to fill the roles that are offered to them. In a sense, all we offer the aged is a sick role—the role of the infirm person

[16]Gail Sheehy, "Catch-30 and Other Predictable Crises of Growing Up Adult," *New York Magazine*, February 18, 1974, p. 36.
[17]Sheehy, *op. cit.*, p. 44.

[18]Gail Sheehy, "Why Mid-Life is a Crisis Time for Couples," *New York Magazine*, April 29, 1974, p.33.

who has outlived his or her usefulness to society. An urbanized, industrialized society such as the United States is oriented toward youth, mobility, and activity. It does little to integrate the old into the social structure. Unlike the elders in traditional society, the American aged can no longer lay automatic claim on their kin for support and social participation; on the contrary, they are more likely to have to try not to be a "nuisance" to their now independent adult offspring. Nor are they regarded as the wisest members of the community as the elders in a traditional society would be; instead, any advice they give is likely to be considered irrelevant in a changing world about which their descendants consider themselves much better informed.

Compulsory retirement and the loss of an economic role can have a devastating effect. For all the euphemisms about "senior citizens" and their "golden age," the fact is that retirement often signifies little more than a swift transition from a meaningful role to a meaningless one. The transition is not simply from work to leisure. It can also be a transition from relative affluence to economic hardship; and if the old person is still living with mature children, he or she becomes, overnight, a dependent in the household.

It is often observed that the aged spend much time thinking and talking about their past lives, rather than about the future or even the present. These reminiscences are not simply random or futile memories, nor is their purpose merely to make conversation. The old person's recollections of the past help to preserve an identity that is becoming increasingly fragile: lacking any role that brings respect or any goal that might provide orientation to the future, the individual invokes the past as self-assurance, and a reminder to listeners, that here was a life worth living.[19] In addition, the memories form part of a continuing life review, in which the old person integrates the events and experiences of the years gone by and reflects on the overall meaning of his or her own almost completed life.[20]

As the life cycle draws to its close, the aged must also learn to accept the reality of their own impending death.[21] Yet this task is made difficult by the fact that death is almost a taboo subject in the United States. The mere discussion of death is often regarded as morbid, even indecent. As children we are protected from full knowledge of death; as adults many of us find the topic frightening and are reluctant to think about it—and certainly to talk about it in the presence of someone who is dying. All too often the interaction between the living and the dying is one of mutual embarrassment, often compounded by resentment and guilt. Apart from the pity and grief that the dying arouse, their plight provides others with a vivid and unwelcome reminder that they too are mortal.

Death has achieved this taboo status only in the course of the present century and only in modern industrial societies. There seem to be two reasons for our reluctance to confront the idea of death. One is the very fact that death, almost alone of natural processes, remains beyond our control. The rational, scientific methods and technologies that have enabled us to alter or master the rest of the natural environment have had no impact on the inevitability of death. In fact, although medical science has extended life expectancy (the length of life the average newborn will enjoy), it has had little or no effect on our life span (the maximum length of life possible in our species). Thus this final moment of the life cycle, involving the annihilation of the self and the ultimate confrontation with the unknown, mocks our claim to mastery of the world. We therefore try to deny the mystery and power of death by pushing it from our thoughts.

The second reason for the taboo on death is that it has been effectively removed from the ongoing life of the community. In traditional societies, as Margaret Mead has observed, people died as they had been born and had lived: in the home, in the care of the family:

In peasant communities where things didn't

[19]Clausen, op. cit., p. 498.
[20]Robert N. Butler, "The Life Review: An Interpretation of Reminiscence in the Aged," Psychiatry, 26 (February 1963), 65–76.
[21]For the classic analysis of the societal significance of death, see Robert Blauner, "Death and Social Structure," Psychiatry 29 (1966), 378–394.

change and where people died in the beds they were born in, grandparents taught the young what the end of life was going to be. So you looked at your mother, if you were a girl, and you learned what it was like to be a bride, a young mother. Then you looked at your grandmother and knew what it was like to be old. Children learned what it was to age and die while they were very small. They were prepared for the end of life at the beginning.[22]

In the modern United States, in contrast, more than two-thirds of all deaths occur in hospitals or geriatric institutions. The dying—most of whom, in industrial societies, are aged—face their end in a bureaucratic institution surrounded by professional staff rather than in the intimacy of the home with loved ones. Yet there is serious doubt over whether such a death— often in the context of a general conspiracy of friends, relatives, and doctors to deny its existence—really does provide the most dignified and painless passing. Although the hospital provides all the advantages of modern facilities, it also creates an environment that may be deeply stressful to the dying and to their loved ones.

Our understanding of the social and psychological process of dying has been vastly increased since the 1960s, when Elisabeth Kübler-Ross conducted pioneering research that included many interviews with dying people. She identified five stages through which the terminally ill patient typically proceeds after being told the truth. The first stage is *denial,* usually expressed in disbelief—"It can't happen to me." The second stage is *anger* and resentment—"Why me?" The third stage is *bargaining*—an implicit agreement with God or fate to go quietly if one can just live long enough to enjoy some important event, such as the arrival of spring or a family wedding. The fourth stage is *depression,* which is marked by anxiety over the loss of self and the loss to one's family. The final stage is *acceptance,* in which the dying individual approaches death with true peace of mind.[23]

Kübler-Ross stressed the importance to the dying patient of open and honest interaction with others:

> After the first shock, numbness, and need to deny the reality of the situation, the patient begins to send out cues that he is ready to "talk about it." If *we,* at that point, need to deny the reality of the situation, the patient will often feel deserted, isolated, and lonely and unable to communicate with another human being what he needs so desperately to share. . . .
>
> To such patients, we should never say, "Come on now, cheer up." We should allow them to grieve. . . . Only through this kind of behavior on our part are our patients able to reach the stage of acceptance. . . . The patient now shows no more fear, bitterness, anguish, or concern over unfinished business. People who have been able to sit through this stage with patients and who have experienced the beautiful feeling of inner and outer peace that they show will soon appreciate that working with terminally ill patients is not a morbid, depressing job but can be an inspiring experience.
>
> The tragedy is that in our death-defying society, people grow uncomfortable in the presence of a dying patient, unable to talk to the terminally ill and at a loss for words when they face a grieving person.[24]

Hospital staff and relatives, however, frequently conspire to prevent patients from finding out that they are dying. Barney Glaser and Anselm Strauss have done extensive research on terminally ill patients and find that they are usually kept in a *closed awareness* context; that is, they are prevented from learning of impending death. In the beginning, at least, this attempt to hide the facts is successful; patients are medically incompetent to interpret their own symptoms, the hospital is able to hide the medical diagnosis from the patient, and medical personnel and family maintain the illusion that the patient will get well. When patients finally do begin to suspect the truth, some of them join in the pretense, whereas others confront doctors

---

[22]Margaret Mead, "Dealing with the Aged: A New Style of Aging," *Current,* no. 136 (January 1972), p. 44.

[23]Elisabeth Kübler-Ross, *On Dying and Society* (New York: Macmillan, 1969).

[24]Elisabeth Kübler-Ross, "Facing Up to Death," *Today's Education* (January 1972), 30–32.

and family and demand the opportunity to talk about their fate. Glaser and Strauss strongly support the view that patients should be told the truth: in an *open awareness* context patients become able to act toward themselves and others in a more honest and realistic way, which markedly eases the acceptance of death.[25]

A great deal of later research has likewise shown that although a small minority of patients prefer to be kept in ignorance and to deny the reality of death almost to the end, a large majority prefer an open-awareness context and are greatly helped by it. Yet, although public attitudes toward death are now beginning to show noticeable signs of change, hospital staffs and family members may still find it difficult to shake off inhibitions about death that have been deeply ingrained since childhood. In fact, some of the most healthy and accepting attitudes toward death appear to be in retirement communities, old-age homes, and other places where the elderly live together.[26] The inhabitants are constantly confronted with the deaths of their friends and other fellow residents. They tend to react in a way that is both realistic and mutually supportive; they learn to accept without fear (and sometimes to welcome) the fact of death, and they socialize new entrants into these attitudes. And, in preparing their final wills in anticipation of death, old people in these institutions often disinherit the families from which they have become isolated, leaving their estates instead to fellow residents and other friends.[27]

[25]Barney G. Glaser and Anselm L. Strauss, *Awareness of Dying* (Chicago: Aldine, 1965); *Time for Dying* (Chicago: Aldine, 1968); and "Patterns of Dying," in Orville G. Brim *et al.* (eds.) *The Dying Patient* (New York: Russell Sage Foundation, 1970), pp. 129–155. See, also, Robert Kastenbaum, "The Kingdom Where Nobody Dies," *Saturday Review of Science*, 55 (January 1973), 33–38; Thomas Powers, "Learning to Die," *Harper's*, 242 (June 1971), 72–80; Jeanne C. Quinn, *The Nurse and the Dying Patient* (New York: Macmillan, 1967); Elisabeth Kübler-Ross, *Death: The Final Stage of Growth* (Englewood Cliffs, N.J.: Prentice-Hall, 1975); and E. Mansell Pattison (ed.), *The Experience of Dying* (Englewood Cliffs, N.J.: Prentice-Hall, 1979).

[26]See Victor W. Marshall, "Socialization for Impending Death in a Retirement Village," *American Journal of Sociology*, 80 (1975), 1124–1144.

[27]Jeffrey P. Rosenfield, *The Legacy of Aging: A Sociology of*

Some elderly, perhaps a sizeable minority, have the physical, economic, social, or personal resources to enjoy a fulfilling old age, from the time of retirement to the time of death. But a great many of the elderly face the plight described by Robert Butler:

Old age in America is often a tragedy. Few of us like to consider it because it reminds us of our own mortality. It demands our energy and resources, it frightens us with illness and deformity, it is an affront to a culture with a passion for youth and productive capacity. We are so preoccupied with defending ourselves from the reality of death that we ignore the fact that human beings are alive before they are actually dead. At best, the living old are treated as if they were already half dead. . . . In America, childhood is romanticized, youth is idolized, middle age does the work, wields the power and pays the bills, and old age, its days empty of purpose, gets little or nothing for what it has already done. . . . For many elderly Americans old age is a tragedy, a period of quiet despair, deprivation, desolation and muted rage. . . . The tragedy of old age is not that each of us must grow old and die but that the process of doing so has been made unnecessarily and at times excruciatingly painful, humiliating, debilitating and isolating through insensitivity, ignorance, and poverty. . . . For the most part the elderly struggle to exist in an inhospitable world.[28]

Let us look at some of the problems of the aged in more detail.

PROBLEMS OF THE AGED

Mandatory Retirement

By late middle age many workers are looking forward to retirement, and millions of those who have retired are only too glad to exchange the routines of work for the satisfactions that a more leisured life style may bring. Many other workers,

Inheritance and Disinheritance (Norwood, N.J.: Ablex, 1978).

[28]Robert N. Butler, *Why Survive? Being Old in America* (New York: Harper & Row, 1975), pp. xi–xii, 2–3.

Older workers, contrary to popular myth, are productive members of the labor force—more so, in fact, than young workers. Until industrial societies introduced mandatory retirement policies, people worked until they were no longer physically able to do so. Today, many physically and mentally alert old people are forced into premature retirement.

however, are reluctant to give up their jobs—a 1974 Harris poll found that nearly a third of retired people aged sixty-five or over would prefer to work. The desire to continue working often stems from harsh economic reality, for retirement usually brings a sharp drop in income. Some workers, too, fear the loss of social identity that can result from not having a job. They may be left with "nothing to do," and may find that their lives are robbed of a significant source of meaning and fulfillment. Those old people who would like to continue working are all too often the victims of what is perhaps the most striking example of age discrimination: the practice of mandatory retirement, under which people are forced to give up their jobs once they reach a certain age. Until recently the precise age for mandatory retirement varied from job to job—fifty-six for air-traffic controllers, fifty-five for New York City fire fighters, seventy for Harvard professors. The usual mandatory retirement age, however, was sixty-five; in 1978 more than half of the workers in the United States held jobs that they would automatically lose in their sixty-fifth year. In 1978, however, Congress passed new legislation that raised the legal mandatory retirement age to seventy for most employees. Under the new law, employers cannot require a worker to retire before the age of seventy, although workers of course may still retire before that age if they wish. The only exceptions are bona fide executives with annual retirement benefits of $27,000 or more, who may be forced to retire at sixty-five; tenured college professors, who may still be required to retire at sixty-five until the year 1982; and workers in high-risk jobs, such as police officers and fire fighters, who may be forced to retire at any age. In addition, the new law completely eliminates any upper age limit for federal workers.

Pressure groups lobbying for the elderly strongly supported the bill, but as conflict theory would predict, business organizations, colleges, and others lobbied against it on the grounds that the old would benefit at the cost of other workers eager for jobs—minorities, women, and the young. Whether the improved job prospects for the elderly will adversely affect the chances of other groups will depend largely on how many aged workers choose to continue after the age of sixty-five. They still face many pressures and inducements to retire voluntarily at this age, and most of those who remain at work will again face a demand for mandatory retirement five years later.

The objection to mandatory retirement is that it throws people out of their jobs at a purely arbitrary age, without any regard for their individual abilities. There is no evidence to suggest that most people over the age of sixty-five or seventy are incapable of working; at the turn of the century, in fact, 70 percent of men over sixty-five were active in the labor force. Mandatory retirement absurdly implies that people are capable of productive labor until the day before their seventieth birthday, then abruptly become physically or mentally incapable of performing their jobs. Mandatory retirement also implies that we treat all members of the same age group as though they had identical competence or incompetence at their jobs—when, in fact, the mental and physical abilities of any group of people born at the same time become more dissimilar, not more similar, as they grow older.

Why does enforced retirement exist, and why do employers try to persuade their employees to retire at the age of sixty-five? The reason is that mandatory retirement or induced voluntary retirement is an administrative convenience for employers. In the past, when most workers produced their own goods or were their own bosses, they worked until they either died or chose to stop work. This is still the case today with self-employed workers, such as artists, owners of businesses, or lawyers. But fully 80 percent of Americans today are employed by other people or organizations—primarily large corporations and federal, state, or local government agencies. Because the toll of advancing years must eventually make everyone unfit for work, these organizations face the problem of finding some orderly way of phasing out their older employees who might have become unproductive. It is far more convenient for the employers to achieve this by an arbitrary retirement age rather than by the fairer but more cumbersome alternative of periodically reviewing the productivity of each individual worker.

The original choice of sixty-five as the usual age for mandatory retirement had no particular rational basis. Employers tended to select this age because Social Security legislation permits workers to draw their Social Security benefits at the age of sixty-five, but not before. But why was this age chosen? When the relevant legislation was being prepared several decades ago, the drafters simply followed the precedent set by Germany, which introduced the first social-security legislation in 1889. The German choice of age sixty-five was based on an arbitrary personal decision by the German chancellor, Bismarck. Our own discrimination against those aged sixty-five or older was thus founded on an accident of history rather than on any dispassionate analysis of the facts. Yet the age of sixty-five will almost certainly become the voluntary norm for retirement, because the Social Security system is still based on the assumption that people will stop working at that age.

Other population categories such as women or minority groups have been denied job opportunities in the past on the grounds of supposed group characteristics. Americans have come to regard such discrimination as intolerable, as a violation of the deep-rooted value of equality of opportunity. The aged, however, still face job discrimination based on false stereotypes about their ability to perform productive work. Yet the fact is that older workers compare favorably with younger workers in many aspects of job performance. They are not as physically suited to hard manual labor, and they often lack the more sophisticated skills of the generally better educated younger workers. But older workers have better job attendance than younger workers, are less likely to change jobs, and have a generally higher productivity than younger workers in both blue-collar and white-collar occupations.

Economic Problems

One of the most common and serious problems faced by the aged is that of making ends meet from one day to the next. In 1977 the aged had a median family income of around $6,292, compared with $12,702 for those aged eighteen to sixty-four. This figure is even lower than that for blacks and other racial minorities. As recently as 1970 some 25 percent of the aged were living below the poverty line. Public awareness of this shameful fact led to improvements in Social Security benefits, which have reduced the proportion of the elderly living in poverty to 16 percent. Many other aged people live just above the poverty line; the number who can be said to be living in real affluence is small indeed.

The economic problems of the elderly often begin before they reach retirement age, for there is considerable discrimination against workers some time before they reach sixty-five. Older workers generally receive higher wages and more benefits than younger workers performing the same job, and employers are often tempted to oust them. Unemployed workers in this age bracket have great difficulty finding new jobs and remain unemployed for much longer than younger unemployed workers. One reason is that employers may perceive younger applicants as more dynamic or adaptable; another is that older workers lack the educational qualifications of the young; another is that job-training or retraining programs cater primarily to younger workers. Workers aged forty to sixty-five are protected to some extent by the 1967 Age Discrimination in Employment Act, which makes it illegal for an employer to advertise for job applicants of a specific age or to refuse employment on the grounds of age alone. This legislation is easily circumvented, however. Employers can advertise, for example, for someone with "1–5 years experience," thus automatically disqualifying older workers. They can also reject older applicants on spurious grounds, such as being "overqualified" (if they have too much experience) or "underqualified" (if they have little education).

Retirement almost always brings a sharp drop in income. More than half of families aged sixty-five or over have less than half of the annual income they enjoyed during the previous ten years. For some the drop in income is even more precipitous, thrusting them into or near poverty. The only real asset that most of the elderly have is a home that they own free and clear. The number of elderly who have substantial savings or investments constitute a small minority; of those aged people who live alone, more than a third have assets of less than $2,000. A minority of the aged have pensions from private employers, but for 80 percent of retired Americans Social Security is the only source of income.

Originally intended as an income supplement, not a sole means of support, Social Security pensions have hardly been generous in the past. Despite important improvements, they remain at an inadequate level today. In 1972, thanks largely to the efforts of the American Association of Retired Persons and other interest groups, the level of benefits was significantly increased, and payments rose to a maximum benefit per individual of around $3,500 a year in 1975. Since then the level of benefits has been tied to the cost of living—an arrangement that has the advantage of protecting the old from the inflation that would reduce the value of fixed-level payments. Unfortunately, it also has the disadvantage of maintaining the benefits indefinitely at a level that is low in relation to national average income.

The fact that the elderly live on much less than the young is often taken, by a form of perverse logic, as proof that they need less money to get by. The truth of the matter is that the elderly live cheaply because they cannot afford to live any other way. They may often have to meet many expenses that younger workers do not encounter. The elderly, for example, lose their complete medical coverage at the time when they are most likely to have need of it, and many are faced with a heavy burden of medical expenses. The homes of the elderly tend to be much older than those of the general population—about 10 percent of their houses are substandard—so they must spend more on maintenance. The elderly are more susceptible than the young to cold, and must spend more on heating. The elderly who are unable to get about on their own may have to use taxis for shopping and other necessities of life. The elderly person also finds it particularly hard to get loans or credit. And even the classic American retort to the person who pleads poverty—"get a job!"—has no meaning to the aged.

Health Problems

One of the severest problems faced by the aged is that of declining health—and of how to pay for the medical treatment needed to combat it. Although the aged represent only 10 percent of the total population, they represent a third of hospital populations and consume a quarter of the drugs prescribed each year. Their medical expenses are far greater than those of the non-aged—six times more than those faced by young adults, and three times more than the costs for the middle-aged. Changes in the Medicaid and Medicare programs have dramatically reduced some of the costs to elderly patients, but the old must still meet many medical expenses out of their savings or pensions. These programs, for example, do not cover the costs of medical checkups, drugs prescribed outside hospitals, eyeglasses, or hearing aids.

The medical costs of the elderly are particularly high because they suffer primarily from chronic illnesses—conditions that cannot be cured, although they can often be treated to alleviate symptoms or to retard the process of the disease. Over 80 percent of the aged population have at least one chronic illness, such as arthritis, diabetes, heart disease, glaucoma, and cancer, and many of them suffer several chronic illnesses simultaneously. The elderly are less likely than the young to contract acute illnesses, such as viral infections, but when they do, they take much longer than the young to recover.

The aged have always had short shrift from the American medical profession, for physicians tend to regard their health problems as uninteresting and unrewarding to treat. Younger doctors are far more interested in acute diseases, where there is a possibility of dramatic cure, than in treating conditions that will inevitably grow worse, in people who will inevitably die within a few years. In the early 1960s Robert Butler found that of 20,000 medical-school teachers in the United

States, only 15 specialized in *geriatrics*, the science of the medical problems of the aged.[29] The situation has presumably improved since then, but in 1970 a survey of ninety-nine medical schools found that fifty of them did not offer courses in geriatrics in any form—a remarkable fact when one considers that one hospital patient in every three is over sixty-five.[30]

Many of the medical problems of the aged are strongly influenced by factors other than the aging process. This is particularly true of mental illness among the old. Despite the prevalent stereotype of the aged as tending to be senile, only about 5 to 10 percent of people aged sixty-five to seventy-five suffer from senility, although the proportion increases markedly after seventy-five. Senility, which is incurable, is caused by loss of brain cells and affects various mental functions, such as memory and the ability to perform simple tasks. Many old people, however, are labeled as senile when, in fact, they are suffering from the side effects of medication or from undiagnosed heart or lung ailments that impede the flow of blood and oxygen to the brain.[31]

Others are thought to be senile when actually they are suffering from severe depression that has social and psychological origins. A common source of this depression is loneliness caused by social isolation. A quarter of the elderly, most of them women, live alone. Because women tend to live longer than men, there are over 140 aged women to every 100 aged men. Most aged men remain married or remarried until death, but the proportion of widowed women rises sharply with advancing age; two-thirds of women age seventy-five or over are widowed. Those who live alone tend to be the poorest of the old, and they typically rent apartments or small rooms in decaying urban neighborhoods, where they are a prime target for criminals, particularly street muggers. As a result, their social isolation is compounded by their fear of leaving their

[29] Butler, *Why Survive?*, op. cit., p. 181.
[30] Joseph T. Freeman, "A Survey of Geriatric Education: Catalogues of United States Medical Schools," *Journal of the American Geriatrics Society*, 19 (1971), 746–762.
[31] Butler, *Why Survive?* op. cit., 225–259.

homes: a 1974 Harris poll found that fear of crime was the problem that bothered old people the most. Then, too, whereas many old people show improved mental health after retirement, there are some who lapse into apathy, ill temper, or alcoholism. Although this reaction to unemployment exactly parallels that found among younger workers who are unemployed for prolonged periods (see Chapter 4, "Work"), the aged are likely to be labeled as senile rather than as temporarily depressed. People live up to the role expectations that society has of them, and to a considerable extent we make old people sick by offering them the role of a sick person.

Contrary to popular belief, only about 5 percent of the aged are confined in institutions, usually nursing homes. Many of the nation's 20,000 nursing homes are excellent, and others provide at least competent health care. The worst homes, however, are a national scandal. Inspectors have found patients abused, robbed, defrauded, underfed on as little as 54 cents a day, wallowing in their own filth, beaten by attendants, and given the wrong medication by unqualified staff. Courts all over the nation have dealt with case after case of bribery, corruption, and Medicaid fraud on the part of the nursing-home operators. The conditions in these nursing homes are an excellent example of how an ill-conceived attempt to solve a social problem can create a new one. Under the Medicaid program, the federal government agreed to pay the nursing-home bills of aged patients. Speculators and entrepreneurs who previously had never

---

VOICES

A foreign nurse at a home for the elderly gives her impressions of the treatment of old people in this country.

. . .

In America, people doesn't keep their old people at home. At a certain age they put them away in America. In my country, the old people stay in the home until they die. But here, not like that. It's surprising to me. They put them away. The first thing they think of is a nursing home. Some of these people don't need a nursing home. If they have their own bedroom at home, look at television or listen to the radio or they have themselves busy knitting . . . We all, us foreigners, think about it.

Right now there's a lady here, nothing wrong with her, but they put her away. They don't come to see her. The only time they see her is when she say "I can't breathe." She wants some attention. And that way she's just aging. When I come here, she was a beautiful woman. She was looking very nice. Now she is going down. If they would come and take her out sometimes . . .

We had one lady here about two years ago, she has two sons. She fell and had a broken hip. They called the eldest son. He said "Why call on me?

Call the little one. She gave all the money to that little one." That was bad. I was right there.

All these people here are not helpless. But just the family get rid of them. There is a lady here, her children took her for a ride one day and push her out of the car. Let her walk and wander. She couldn't find her way home. They come and brought her here. And they try to take away all that she has. They're tryin' to make her sign papers and things like those. There's nothing wrong with her. She can dress herself, comb her hair, take a walk . . . They sign her in here, made the lawyers sign her in. They're just in for the money. She will tell you, "There's nothin' wrong with me."

Things that go on here. I've seen many of these patients, they need help, but they don't have enough help. Sometimes they eat and sometimes they don't. Sometimes there's eight hours' wait. Those that can have private nurse, fine. Those that can't suffer. And this is a high-class place. Where *poor* old people . . . (She shakes her head.)

Source: Studs Terkel, *Working* (New York: Pantheon, 1974), pp. 502–503. Copyright 1972, 1974 by Studs Terkel.

shown any interest in the aged saw an immediate opportunity to cash in on the federal funds, and a rash of new nursing homes appeared. Some of these homes produced profits of over 40 percent a year on the initial investment, and by the mid-1970s, nursing-home stocks were among the hottest prospects on Wall Street. The profits came from the difference between the amount provided by Medicaid and the amount actually spent on patient care. (These nursing homes are discussed more fully in Chapter 12, "Health".)

CONFRONTING THE PROBLEM

Until the 1970s the plight of elderly Americans had gone so unacknowledged that not one social problems textbook contained a chapter on the problems of the aged. Now the situation of the aged is widely recognized as an important social problem—and that is the first step to finding a solution. In fact, the aged have made several significant gains since the early 1970s, but a great deal more remains to be done.

Political Pressure. As the conflict approach would predict, the success of the aged in changing their situation will depend largely on the amount of power and influence they are able to wield.[32] In this respect at least, the outlook for the aged is favorable, because they will be an increasingly large proportion of the American electorate in the years ahead. Their political clout will be even further enhanced by an additional factor: they will be supported by another vast section of the population—those people between the ages of approximately fifty and sixty-five, who will become increasingly worried about what the future holds for them when

---

[32]See *Society*, 15 (July–August 1978), special issue, "The Politics of Aging."

they grow older. Still another factor will favor the elderly: they are far more likely to vote than the young. Past studies of voting behavior have shown consistently poor turnouts by the young at elections. In the 1976 presidential election, for example, only half of the eligible voters aged eighteen to thirty had bothered to register, and of these, less than half bothered to vote. The aged take a much keener interest in politics than the young, and have mounted some formidable campaigns to persuade Congress of the rightness of their claims.

The appearance of powerful social movements promoting the rights of the aged has also had a marked impact. The main organization representing the aged is the American Association of Retired Persons, with a membership of 9 million. A more radical organization is the Grey Panthers, which keeps no membership lists but draws support from some concerned Americans under thirty as well as those over sixty-five—a new version of the traditional conspiracy between grandchildren and grandparents against the authority of the middle-aged. The fate of programs that might benefit the elderly will depend largely on the political pressure that such organizations can muster, for the aged will often find themselves in competition with other organized interests for scarce social and economic resources.

Abolishing Mandatory Retirement. Opposition to mandatory retirement has already inspired Congress to raise the mandatory retirement age for most workers to seventy. But will the practice ever be completely eliminated? Many powerful interests have supported demands for its abolition. The AFL-CIO executive council has declared that it opposes mandatory retirement except where unions favor it. The American Medical Association, although usually on hostile terms with organizations representing the aged, has declared that mandatory retirement is a "direct threat to health and life expectancy." However, the Supreme Court (whose members are not subject to mandatory retirement at any age) has so far refused to rule that the practice is unconstitutional, and Congress (whose members legislate mandatory retirement for others but have never considered it

for themselves) has shown little eagerness to abolish the practice.

Nevertheless, there is one very potent factor that will eventually undermine the mandatory retirement system: the Social Security pensions of the retired population are paid for by a Social Security tax on the population that works. Changes in the age structure of American society have tilted the balance between workers and retirees to an increasingly perilous degree.[33] In 1945 there were thirty-five workers to one Social Security recipient, but by 1955 the ratio was seven to one; in 1960, four to one; and in 1977, about three to one. Within the foreseeable future it will take two workers to support one retiree—and the burden on the workers will be even heavier if, as is likely, the retired person draws a more generous pension. An obvious solution to the problem will be to increase the number of workers and decrease the number of retired people by extending the mandatory retirement age, perhaps to seventy-five, and by encouraging rather than discouraging workers of sixty-five to remain at their jobs. The goal, however, must be to allow the minority who wish to continue working to do so for as long as they can perform their jobs effectively.

Economic Improvements. There has been a considerable improvement in the Social Security income of aged Americans during the past decade. As we have seen, the level of benefits has been increased and in the future will keep pace with the cost of living. Yet the benefits are barely adequate at best: the average monthly payment to an elderly individual in 1978 was $245, and for couples, $407. Since 1974 the Supplemental Security Income (SSI) program has guaranteed a minimum income of $130 per month to every aged American, regardless of his or her previous work history. This means that the small minority of workers who are not covered by Social Security are not left penniless, but the SSI payments still fall significantly below the poverty line.

---

[33]See Robert J. Lampman, "Who Pays for Social Security?" *Society* 14 (May–June 1977), 54–56; Harold L. Sheppard and Sara E. Rix, *The Greying of Working America: The Coming Crisis of Retirement-Age Policy* (New York: Free Press, 1978).

In a supportive social environment, old age can be a time of satisfaction and fulfillment. All too often, however, our society accords no useful role to its older citizens.

All told, improvements thus far are not enough. At a bare minimum, no aged person should live below the poverty line. Beyond that, the United States has the resources to ensure that all the aged enjoy at least a decent standard of living, and this should be a goal of public policy in the future.

Death Education and Research. Because of the taboo that surrounds death, countless people in decades past have died in some degree of emotional isolation, unable to fully share mutual feelings and support with those they loved. The work of Kübler-Ross and later researchers on death and dying is at last having a significant and growing effect—on the discipline of sociology, on hospital practices, and on public attitudes toward death. Within less than a decade after the first research in the field, *thanatology*—the scientific study of death and dying— has become a major subdiscipline of sociology. The results of thanatological research are now percolating through to hospitals, where they are gradually reshaping medical practice, and a new generation of nurses and medical students is being taught fresh attitudes toward dying patients. Perhaps more important, the major findings of research on death have been widely reported in the mass media and have attracted strong public interest. Courses on death and dying are proliferating in colleges and high schools, where they are often among the more popular offerings in the curriculum. The momentum behind death research and death education should be maintained, for greater public knowledge of, and franker discussion about, death and dying can only be to the good. In this way the final episode of the life cycle will be made more acceptable; the taboo on death will be eroded; and death will be brought back where it belongs—in the ongoing life of the society and its members.

Health Care. Several changes may be necessary in the health care of the aged. One important change would be a shift in emphasis from a concern for acute disorders among the young to one for chronic disorders among the elderly; the latter illnesses, after all, are the nation's major health problem. This change of focus will probably occur as a matter of course as the proportion of older people grows steadily greater. American physicians will tend to concentrate on the growing pool of older patients rather than compete for the diminishing pool of younger patients. We may therefore expect geriatrics to become a major focus of American medicine over the next two decades.

The coverage of medical expenses offered by Medicare and Medicaid will have to be further extended to relieve the aged of the heavy inroads that medical expenses make on their limited incomes. Changes along these lines are probable, for it is inevitable that the United States will eventually follow all the other industrialized countries of the world in establishing a national system of medical insurance that will provide free or heavily subsidized medical treatment for all, regardless of their income or illness (see Chapter 12, "Health"). An urgent interim measure would be to take nursing homes out of the hands of private speculators and to place them under the control of public authorities, where their prime purpose would be to provide nursing care for the sick rather than extravagant profit for private investors.

Efforts could also be made to end the sense of uselessness and social isolation that affects the mental health of many aged Americans. Several experimental programs designed to integrate the aged into society by offering them meaningful roles are already under way. Under the federal Older Americans Act and projects such as the Foster Grandparent program, aged people are working part-time as teachers' aides, business consultants, supervisors of youngsters, or helpers of other old people who are confined to their homes.

Changing Attitudes. Finally, it is fundamentally important that social attitudes toward the elderly change to reflect the realities and not the myths of aging. Ageism has deeply pervaded American life, and discrimination against the aged can never be effectively combated until the stereotypes on which it is based are abandoned. We need to gain an accurate picture of aging, and a full understanding of the social as well as biological forces that determine the nature of this closing stage of the life cycle. Only then can we direct social change to ensure that the final years of people in this society are fulfilling and rewarding ones, providing for the elderly of today the kind of life that we will want for ourselves tomorrow when we too have grown old.

SUMMARY

1. The plight of the elderly is now recognized as a serious social problem, in part because the United States population is growing much older. Society contains an age structure and a role structure; changes in both have left the aged with little role to play in American society.

2. From the functionalist approach the problem is one of social disorganization caused by an imbalance between age structure and role structure, particularly the increase in the proportion of the elderly and the disappearance of economic and family roles that were formerly available to the old. From the conflict approach the problem is one of discrimination against the aged by the nonaged; this discrimination is justified by the ideology of ageism.

3. The life cycle is both a biological and social process. The length of the life cycle and the character of such "stages" as childhood, adolescence, young adulthood, mature adulthood, and old age to the point of death are deeply affected by social factors.

4. Major problems of the aged are mandatory retirement, which deprives many workers of income and social identity even though they wish to work and are capable of doing so; inadequate income, which can result from job discrimination and the low level of Social Security payments on which most of the elderly depend; and health problems, primarily chronic physical and mental ailments that are expensive to treat and that American medicine is poorly equipped to deal with.

5. Some means of confronting the problem include political pressure by the increasingly large elderly electorate and social movements representing its interests; the abolition of mandatory retirement; improvements in Social Security payment levels; research and education on death to remove its alien, taboo character; a shift in emphasis in medicine to geriatrics and an extension of medical insurance coverage to all health problems of the aged; and a general change in the ageist attitudes that permit discrimination against the elderly to persist.

GLOSSARY

Ageism. A set of beliefs that justifies systematic discrimination against the elderly by supposing that inequalities between the young and the old are the natural outcome of biological and not social factors.

Age structure. The relative number and proportion of people in different age categories within a population.

Geriatrics. The scientific study of the medical problems of the elderly.

Gerontology. The scientific study of aging.

Ideology. A set of ideas and beliefs that justifies the interests of those who hold it; the dominant ideology in any unequal society therefore justifies the inequality.

Role structure. The relative numbers and the types of roles that a society makes available to its members.

Thanatology. The scientific study of death and dying.

FURTHER READING

ARIES, PHILIPPE. *Centuries of Childhood: A Social History of Childhood*. New York: Knopf, 1962. A lively classic that throws interesting light on conceptions of childhood through history.

ATCHLEY, ROBERT C. *The Social Forces in Later Life: An Introduction to Social Gerontology*. 2nd ed. Belmont, Calif.: Wadsworth, 1976. An excellent introductory text on gerontology.

BUTLER, ROBERT N. *Why Survive? Being Old in America*. New York: Harper & Row, 1975. A major survey of the plight of the elderly in the United States, written in a clear and often compelling style. Strongly recommended for an overview of the problem.

FISHER, DAVID HACKETT. *Growing Old in America*. New York: Oxford University Press, 1977. An important analysis of the aging process as it occurs in the context of modern American society.

KÜBLER-ROSS, ELISABETH. *On Death and Dying*. New York: Macmillan, 1969. An important study of the meaning of dying; the focus is on the ways that terminally ill people face up to the fact of their impending death.

LOFLAND, LYNN H. *The Craft of Dying: The Modern Face of Death*. Beverly Hills, Calif.: Sage, 1978. A study of death and dying and of the current social and individual responses to these events.

MEAD, MARGARET. *Culture and Commitment*. New York: Doubleday, 1970. An analysis of the problem that rapid social change can produce in the life cycle and the relations between the generations—written by a distinguished anthropologist when she was in her seventies.

RILEY, MATILDA W., *et al*. *Aging and Society: A Sociology of Age Stratification*. Vol. 3. New York: Russell Sage Foundation, 1972. An important and comprehensive analysis of aging from a sociological perspective. The authors use the concept of social stratification to illuminate the inequalities of different age groups.

SELTZER, MILDRED, SHERRY CORBETT, and ROBERT ATCHLEY (eds.). *Social Problems of the Aging: Readings*. Belmont, Calif.: Wadsworth, 1978. An excellent collection of articles on the problems of the aged in the United States.

SHEEHY, GAIL. *Passages*. New York: Dutton, 1976. An absorbing study of the typical characteristics and crises that mark the life cycle in modern America. The book was a national best seller.

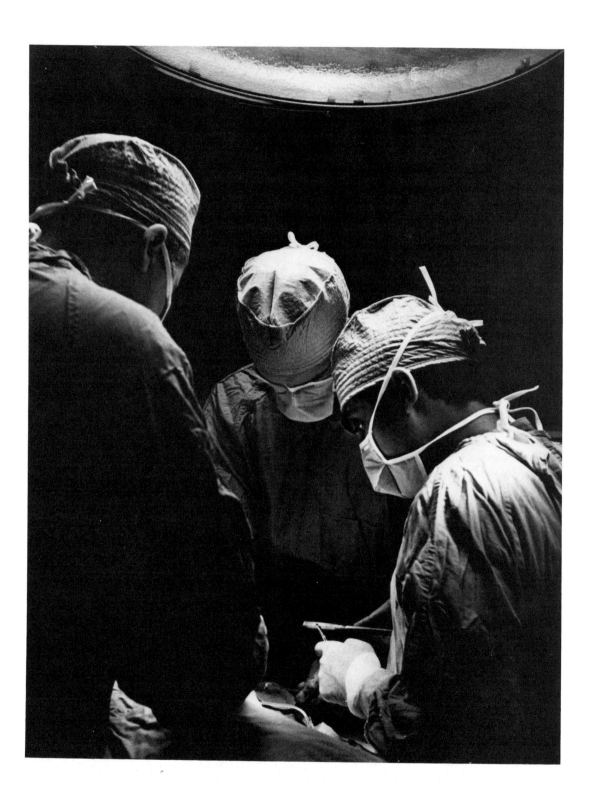

12
Health Care

THE PROBLEM

The social problem presented by health care in the United States can be simply stated: for most people, health care costs far too much, and for many people, prompt and adequate care is too difficult to obtain. The United States has the dubious distinction of being the only industrialized society in the modern world that does not have a national health-insurance program or some similar means of making health care freely available to all who need it. Instead, consumers must buy their health care in much the same way they buy other goods and services such as automobiles or TV repairs. The present health-care system has come under such widespread and sustained criticism over the past few years that there is now a general acceptance that some reforms are necessary—but there is little agreement over what shape those reforms should take or how far they should go.

The costs of medical treatment, always high, have skyrocketed during the past decade. The United States today spends more money on health care, in both absolute and proportionate terms, than any other nation. Medical costs represent over 9 percent of the country's total production of goods and services; only agriculture and construction generate more spending. The price of the nation's total health bill, including doctors, dentists, hospitals, drugs, and other expenditures, was about $3.8 billion in 1940, $12 billion in 1950, and $69 billion in 1970. Since then the rate of increase has been staggering, far exceeding the general rate of inflation: by 1979 the total cost exceeded $200 billion, and it is continuing to rise rapidly.[1] The risk of serious illness is a constant threat to the security and living standards of the typical American family,

for a stay of a few weeks in the hospital can cost many thousands of dollars, with a good possibility that much of the bill will not be covered by insurance. In fact, the medical bills associated with serious illness account for about half of the bankruptcies in the United States each year.

Many people find health care difficult to obtain. The delivery of medical services in the United States is uneven, resulting in gross shortages of health-care facilities for certain parts of the population and certain areas of the country.[2] Affluent urban and suburban neighborhoods have an oversupply of doctors; urban ghettos and other low-income neighborhoods have relatively few physicians; and many smaller rural communities have no doctors at all. The affluent are able to buy quicker and better treatment than the poor: they can afford visits to private practitioners; they can schedule appointments at their convenience; they can get to know their doctor personally; and if they are hospitalized, they may occupy private rooms and enjoy the services of highly paid specialists. Those who cannot afford it may have to attend municipal clinics and hospitals, often waiting for hours or days for an appointment; they are likely to be seen by

---

[1]U.S. Bureau of the Census, *Statistical Abstract of the United States, 1978* (Washington, D.C.: U.S. Government Printing Office, 1978); *New York Times*, May 7, 1978, p. 69; "Health Costs: What Limit?" *Time*, May 28, 1979, pp. 60–68.

[2]Charles E. Lewis, Rashi Fein, and David Mechanic, *A Right to Health* (New York: Wiley, 1976); Diana B. Sutton, "Explaining the Low Use of Health Services by the Poor: Costs, Attitudes, or Delivery Systems?" *American Sociological Review*, 43 (June 1978), 348–368.

Per Capita

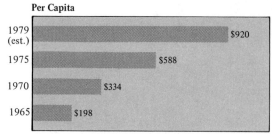

Nationwide Total (public and private) in billions of dollars

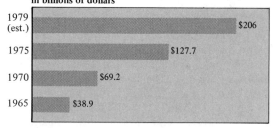

Percentage Of G.N.P.

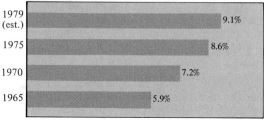

FIGURE 12.1 **Medical care expenditures.** The costs of medical care—whether measured as a percentage of gross national product, as expenditures per capita, or as a national total—have soared spectacularly since the mid-1960's. This rapid rise in costs, far exceeding the general rate of inflation, is a major component of the social problem of health care.
(Adapted from *Time*, May 28, 1979, p. 61.)

These problems of high medical costs and uneven delivery of medical services prove, on closer diagnosis, to be the symptoms of a deep malaise. The underlying source of the problem is that the American health-care system is not in business only for people's health; it is also in business to make profits. As Barbara and John Ehrenreich suggest, "health is no more a priority of the American health industry than safe, cheap, efficient, pollution-free transportation is a priority of the American automobile industry."[4] The health-care system that seems chaotic, costly, and unfair from the point of view of the consumer seeking quick, efficient, inexpensive care is, in fact, a highly successful one if judged by its own primary goal, that of making money. The most profitable small business in the United States today is a private medical practice; physicians earn five times as much as the average male wage-earner, and their earnings are rising more steeply than those of any other occupational group. One of the most profitable enterprises of intermediate size is the nursing-home business, whose stocks have for some years been among the hottest items on Wall Street. And one of the most profitable large businesses in the United States is the drug industry; in recent years the manufacture and sale of drugs has consistently ranked as the first, second, or third most profitable industry in the country.[5]

Every other modern industrial nation regards medical care as a social service, to be based on a simple principle: the kind of care you receive should depend on the kind of illness you have. The United States alone regards medical care as a private business, based on the principle that the kind of care you receive depends on how much money you are willing or able to spend.

different doctors on each visit; and if they are hospitalized, they are likely to be placed in public wards under the care of interns, residents, and medical students. Largely as a result of the unequal delivery of health-care services, the United States has an infant death rate that exceeds those of fourteen other nations, and a male life expectancy that is shorter than nine other countries.[3]

[3]Population Reference Bureau, *World Population Data Sheet, 1978* (Washington, D.C.: Population Reference Bureau, 1978).

[4]Barbara Ehrenreich and John Ehrenreich, *The American Health Empire: Power, Profits, and Politics.* (New York: Vintage, 1971), p. vi.

[5]See David Kotelchuck (ed.), *Prognosis Negative: Crisis in the Health Care System* (New York: Vintage, 1976); and Mary Adelaide Mendelson, *Tender Loving Greed* (New York: Vintage, 1975).

The introduction of modern medicine to the less-developed nations of the world has had a dramatic effect on patterns of illness and death in these countries. Systematic childhood vaccination, for example, has virtually eliminated smallpox, which was once a leading cause of childhood mortality.

That, in the view of most critics of the existing system, is the root cause of our health-care crisis.

Sickness and Society

Sickness may seem at first sight to be merely a personal physical problem, but it is a social problem as well, because social factors profoundly influence our state of health, the likelihood of our becoming ill, the kind of illness we are likely to suffer, the type and quality of treatment we receive, and the chances we have of recovery.[6]

This basic principle of medical sociology is most dramatically revealed in the differences between the patterns of disease and mortality in preindustrial, developing societies and those in the developed, industrial societies. In preindustrial societies, most disease and death is caused by nutritional disorders, parasites, and infections. The highest mortality rates occur among young children, who suffer and often die from such diseases as protein deficiency, smallpox, tetanus, diphtheria, whooping cough, and polio. Industrialization, however, is generally accompanied by radically improved standards in medical practice, public sanitation, and childhood nutrition. In modern societies most serious ailments are chronic and noninfectious: the highest mortality rates are among the old, who after middle age suffer increasingly from various degenerative diseases such as cancer, heart ailments, or emphysema.

[6]For an overview of medical sociology, see Andrew C. Twaddle and Richard M. Hessler, *A Sociology of Health* (St. Louis: Mosby, 1977).

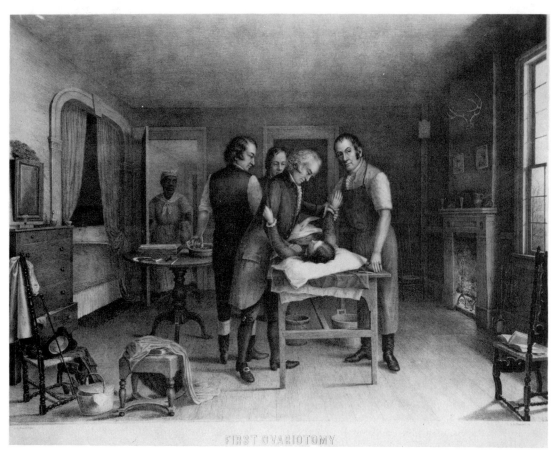

FIRST OVARIOTOMY

It is only in the course of the past century or so that physicians have become true professionals, basing their practices on systematic empirical and theoretical knowledge about the human body and its workings. In earlier times, the practice of medicine was founded on a mix of rule-of-thumb methods, superstition, ignorance, and folk cures (a few of which were actually effective).

The kinds of health problems that we have in the United States are intimately linked to certain aspects of American life styles. Tens of millions of Americans smoke, drink to excess, and abuse drugs. Our diet is generally high in starches, sugar, and animal fats. We take such little exercise that a 1979 Harris poll found that only 15 percent of American adults are active enough to be considered fit. The fast, competitive pace of urban life causes widespread stress. The environment is filled with thousands of noxious chemicals, from auto emissions to factory effluents, which pose many health hazards, both known and perhaps unknown also. And the fatality rate from accidents is staggeringly high, largely because of the carnage caused by automobile collisions.

In any society, as Talcott Parsons has pointed out, those who fall ill usually play a *sick role*— that is, they enact the behavior their society expects of a person who is ill.[7] Because the sick cannot fulfill their normal social obligations, they cause some measure of social disruption. Others must provide care for them and also

[7]Talcott Parsons, *The Social System* (Glencoe, Ill.: The Free Press, 1951), pp. 428–473. See, also, Eliot Friedson, *The Profession of Medicine: A Study of the Sociology of Applied Knowledge* (New York: Dodd, Mead, 1970).

perform the tasks they can no longer handle. By playing the sick role, the ill person is excused from this failure to meet normal role obligations. But a crucial requirement in the sick role is that the person concerned must attempt to get better, usually by seeking expert help. The sick person's cooperation in this process indicates that he or she is not merely lazy or malingering and ensures others' continued toleration of that person's abandonment of his or her normal role.

Every society has experts in healing to whom those who play the sick role are expected to go for help. Healers always have a high social status, although their healing powers may be more imaginary than real. In most simple, preindustrial societies, the healer also played the role of priest—or, as we commonly describe it, that of shaman or witch doctor. The healer was supposed to have contact with the gods or spirits, to know magical spells and incantations, and to have esoteric knowledge of herbal and other folk remedies (some of which worked, and some of which did not). Before the seventeenth century the medical knowledge of European doctors was likewise based on superstition, ignorance, and, fortunately, some folk wisdom; indeed, the roles of surgeon and barber were commonly played by the same person, for the skills involved were judged roughly equal! In the seventeenth and eighteenth centuries, however, doctors began to observe patients and their symptoms in a more orderly fashion and to gain a better understanding of anatomy and physiology. By the nineteenth century the experimental method was being systematically applied to the field of medicine. The discipline was becoming truly scientific, and physicians were becoming professionals.

Unlike an ordinary job, a *profession* is an occupation requiring extensive knowledge or training in an art or a science. A profession differs from other occupations in several respects. The skill of professionals is based on systematic, theoretical knowledge, not just on training in particular techniques. Professionals have great autonomy in their work, and are proud of this professional independence. Professionals form associations that regulate the conduct of their members, often through a code of ethics. Admission to certain professions is carefully controlled by the existing members: anyone can claim to be a furniture mover or carpenter, but to become a doctor or lawyer a person must pass examinations and receive a license, usually after an educational process that is controlled by practitioners of the profession.

The significance of this development is that in the United States the practice of health care is centered around a powerful, prestigious, close-knit medical profession. As we shall see, the social organization of health care is strongly influenced by the goals and priorities of the profession itself, even when, as sometimes happens, these conflict with the needs of the public.

ANALYZING THE PROBLEM

The social problem of highly priced and unevenly delivered health care can be usefully analyzed from both the functionalist and conflict approaches.

The Functionalist Approach

From the functionalist approach the problem is that the health-care system fails to fulfill its function properly in the social system as a whole.

Under ideal conditions a society would be so organized that its medical system would fully meet the population's needs for health care. To the extent that the health-care system fails to meet these demands, social disorganization exists.

In the functionalist view, much of this social disorganization results from rapid social changes over the past few decades. One important change has been the shift of focus in medical

VOICES

An occupational therapist at a medical-surgery unit in a Midwestern university's medical center describes the circumstances of her work.

. . .

A hospital is a dehumanizing institution. People get in and they become arms or legs or kidneys or bladders or something besides Joe Smith the human being. If a hospital was a good place for people to work, it would meet the patient's needs. There would be no need for me.

The nurses, the doctors, the medical students, are set up on a rigid status kind of system. If you buy into this kind of system, you buy the idea that "I'm not quite as good as the guy above me." The resident doesn't strike back at the attending man when he has a bad day. He strikes out at the nurse. The nurse strikes out at the hospital aide or the cleaning lady.

Many patients tell me the best person for them has been the cleaning lady. Yet the doctors and nurses, everybody is saying that the cleaning lady just does a rotten job—"That dirt's been on the floor three days!" The cleaning lady deals with the patient on a human level. She's scrubbing the floor in the room and the patient says, "My son didn't come to visit me today." The cleaning lady smiles and says, "I know how you feel. I know how I'd feel if my son didn't come to visit me if I was sick." The cleaning lady doesn't see the patient as a renal failure or an ileostomy. She just sees a poor lady who's sick.

Until recently, I wasn't sure how meaningful my work was. I had doubts. A surgeon does a really beautiful job. That's meaningful to him *immediately*. But it's not the kind of sustaining thing that makes a job meaningful. It must concern the relationship you have with the people you work with. We get hung up in the competition: "Who's responsible for saving this life?" "Who's responsible for the change in this dying patient?" Rather than saying, "Isn't it beautiful that we all together helped make this person's life better?"

I worked in the leading rehab hospital in the country. The schedule was very rigid. Everybody punches time clocks when they come to work and when they leave. You get so many minutes for coffee break. The patient's day was regimented as my day was regimented. You have a quadriplegic who at eight o'clock goes to occupational therapy—nine o'clock goes to physical therapy—ten o'clock sees the social worker—twelve o'clock goes back to occupational therapy. We see him as a quadriplegic rather than as a person. We're, both of us, things.

That's what happens in hospitals—not because

practice from the family doctor to the large urban hospital. In some respects this change has been functional for society: for example, it is only very large hospitals that can afford to support advanced medical research, teams of specialists, and highly expensive equipment. But the change has been dysfunctional in other respects: in particular, it has made health care much more impersonal, much more urban, and much more concerned with the exotic diseases of interest to researchers than with routine preventive medicine. Another important change has been in the financing of medical expenses, which increasingly are paid by some third party, such as insurance companies or the government, rather than by the patient directly. The growth in third-party payments, particularly those by the federal and state governments, has been a major factor behind the increase in medical costs. The effect of these payments has been to vastly increase the amount of money flowing into the system without producing a corresponding increase in the quality or quantity of services flowing out of it. Instead, much of the money has been either wasted on nonessentials, stolen through fraud, or absorbed as excess profit.

Simultaneously, another significant social change has been taking place, this time in social values. Attitudes toward health care have altered radically in the course of this century. There was a time when many people might have been willing to regard medical care as a privilege; today more and more are inclined to regard it as a right. Moreover, the practical worth of health-care services has increased steadily as new discoveries and technological advances have made it

320

people are unfeeling or don't care, but because they feel put-down. You have to protect yourself in some way. Many things in the institution frustrate me. The doctor who refuses to deal with the patient who knows he's dying. He says, "He doesn't want to know anything." Or the alcoholic with cirrhosis. What's the use of putting him in this hospital bed, prolonging his life, to send him back to the lonely, isolated world where he'll sit in his room and drink and nobody to cook for him? You know there's no place to send him. Or the old lady who's had a stroke, who lives alone. She's been very dear to all the staff and you know you can't keep her in that hundred-dollar-a-day bed, and she's shipped to some rotten nursing home that welfare put her into. She can't live alone. And the bastards you have to deal with—sarcastic doctors. They're not really bastards—it's the way the institution makes them. You think, "What's the use?"

For several months I worked with hemiplegics, elderly people who've had a stroke. Half their body is paralyzed. First thing in the morning I'd get to the old men's ward and I'd teach them dressing. They didn't think they could do anything, but they could dress themselves. If people can take care of themselves, they have more self-esteem.

They were in long wards and they had curtains around the bed. I'd start out with just the shirt, work on getting the affected arm into the sleeve. Some people, it would take ten days to learn. Some could do it in one day—getting their shirt on, their pants on, how to wash themselves with one hand. . . . The patients taught me a lot. They have better ways they've learned on their own. They'd say, "Wouldn't it be better if I did it this way?" I learned a lot about self-care from them. I try to tell my students to listen to the patients.

Being sick can be like going through early developmental stages all over again. It can have profound growth potential for people. It's like being a child again, to be sick. The doctor is like the parent. I've seen it happen with kidney transplant patients. People who've been seriously ill may come out much stronger, happier. . . . Some kind of learning. Something can happen in the sick role. It's one of the areas where we say it's okay to be dependent, as an adult, in our society. It's not intellectual learning.

. . .

Source: Studs Terkel, *Working* (New York: Pantheon 1974), pp. 494–495. Copyright 1972, 1974 by Studs Terkel.

---

possible to control or cure many diseases that were once beyond the power of medicine to influence. Thus the demand for freely available health care has rapidly expanded, increasing the gap between social ideal and social reality in American medicine.

The Conflict Approach

The conflict approach emphasizes the conflict of interests among the various parties involved, such as that between doctors and patients or between rich and poor.[8] For example, conflict

[8]See Robert R. Alford, *Health Care Politics: Ideological and Interest Group Barriers to Reform* (Chicago: University of Chicago Press, 1975); Elliot A. Krause, *Power and Illness: The Political Sociology of Health and Medical Care* (New York: Elsevier, 1977).

theorists explain much of the inequity in the delivery of medical services as the inevitable result of social and economic inequalities. Since the most powerful and wealthy people in the United States live in urban and suburban areas, it is hardly surprising that the availability of superior medical facilities is much greater in these areas than in ghettos or rural areas. Similarly, the incidence of infant mortality and low life expectancy vary, predictably, along the lines of race and social class. For example, the average life expectancy for whites in the United States is 72.2 years, whereas the average expectancy for minority-group members is only 65.9 years. Similarly, the incidence of most diseases is significantly higher in the lower social classes than in the upper ones. The high cost of, and unavailability of, medical services to the poor—many millions of whom are not covered by any form of health insurance—must be a prime factor behind these differences.[9]

Conflict theorists emphasize that American medicine has become a matter of big money, big organizations, and big politics. They argue that much of the spiraling cost of medical care can be traced back to the pursuit of self-interest by physicians, nursing-home operators, drug companies, insurance companies, and hospitals, as represented by such powerfully organized lobbies as the American Hospitals Association, the American Association of Medical Schools, the Pharmaceutical Manufacturers Association, and the American Medical Association.

A classic example of the use of this political and economic power is the sustained attempt by the American Medical Association (AMA), which represents the majority of the nation's physicians, to prevent the introduction of a national health-insurance system.[10] Doctors have always tended to oppose proposals for such a system, fearing that it would undermine their professional independence and, in particular, their right to determine fees. For decades the AMA has successfully fought off all attempts to introduce national health insurance, branding proposals for such change "socialized medicine." As early as 1935 the AMA headed off an attempt by President Roosevelt to combine health insurance with Social Security; the AMA warned Roosevelt that such a system would be unworkable because the nation's doctors would never cooperate with it. Soon after World War II, President Truman tried to introduce a new national health-insurance program, but the powerful AMA lobby in Washington, declaring that the proposal was "Marxist medicine," prevented it from even reaching the floor of Congress. During the 1950s, the AMA set up the Political Action Committee, which systematically attempted to unseat members of Congress who favored reform. The AMA was credited with causing the defeat of several leading advocates of national medical insurance through handsome campaign donations to their election opponents. In the late 1950s and early 1960s congressional fear of the AMA lobby was so great that national medical insurance became almost a dead issue.[11] Since then the public demand for change has grown so intense that dozens of bills to reform the system have been introduced, though none has ever reached a vote on the floor of Congress.

The AMA gives more money to members of Congress than does any other single organization. Its 1976 political contributions totaled $1.79 million; in that year 382 House candidates and 42 Senate candidates received donations from the AMA. The average gift to House candidates was $3,500, to Senate candidates, $5,800. When Congress assembled the next year, 299 of the House candidates who had received AMA handouts were House members.[12] According to conflict theorists, we must take account of such pressures by powerful interest groups if we are to understand why the health-care system continues to reflect the interests of the providers rather than the consumers.

A COMPARISON: THE BRITISH SYSTEM

Before we look at the American health-care system in more detail, it might be useful to

---

[9]See Victor Fuchs, *Who Shall Live? Health, Economics, and Social Choice* (New York: Basic Books, 1974); Aaron Anatovsky, "Class and the Chance for Life," in Lee Rainwater (ed.), *Inequality and Justice* (Chicago: Aldine, 1974); Lu Ann Aday, "Economic and Noneconomic Barriers to the Use of Needed Medical Services," *Medical Care*, 13 (June 1975), 447–456; and Vicente Navarro, "The Underdevelopment of Health of Working America: Causes, Consequences, and Possible Solutions," *American Journal of Public Health*, 66 (June 1976), 538–547.

[10]Theodore R. Marmor, "Origins of the Government Health Insurance Issue," in Kotelchuck (ed.), *op. cit.*, Richard J. Margolis, "National Health Insurance: The Dream Whose Time Has Come?" *New York Times Magazine*, January 9, 1979, pp. 12–43.

[11]Elton Rayack, *Professional Power and American Medicine*, 4th ed. (Cleveland: World, 1967); Roul Tunley, *The American Health Scandal* (New York: Harper & Row, 1966.)

[12]Common Cause, *How Money Talks in Congress: A Study of the Impact of Money on Congressional Decision-making* (Washington, D.C.: Common Cause, 1978).

[13]For a more detailed analysis, see David Mechanic, "The English National Health Service: Some Comparisons with the United States," *Journal of Health and Social Behavior*, 12 (March 1971), 18–29.

briefly examine a very different system, that of Britain.[13] More than three decades ago the British created a system of "socialized medicine" that served as a model for the health-care reforms which have since been introduced into the other industrial societies of the world. A study of the British system can thus provide a reference point for our analysis of health care in America, allowing us to highlight unique features of our own system that we might otherwise take for granted.

Under the British system, medicine is regarded as a public service, in much the same way as elementary and high-school education are regarded as a public service in the United States. The government owns and operates the hospitals, clinics, and other facilities, and most doctors are salaried employees of the government or its agencies.

The British National Health Service is financed through taxes and offers free medical treatment to any person in the country (including even temporary visitors who face medical emergencies). There is no charge for visits to or by a doctor, no charge for surgery or other medical treatment, and no charge for a hospital bed or even for such services as hospital meals or ambulances. A sick person can spend months in intensive care, receive the services of teams of specialists, undergo batteries of tests and complicated surgery, and not pay a penny. Essential medical supplies, such as crutches, eyeglasses, false teeth, wheelchairs, even home dialysis machines, are available free. The only charges that are levied are a flat rate of about 35 cents for any drug prescription—the price is always the same, whether the drug in question has an actual cost of 10 cents or hundreds of dollars—and a charge of around $10 for any dental checkup and subsequent course of preventive or restorative treatment. The aged over sixty-five, the young under sixteen, and any persons with low incomes are excused even these payments. Purely cosmetic medical services, however—such as gold fillings or face-lifts—must be paid for in full.

Under the British system every individual signs up with a family doctor of his or her own choosing; these doctors are general practitioners who will see patients in their offices or, if necessary, will make house calls. The general

practitioners receive a basic salary from the government, plus a small annual fee for every patient on their registers. This annual fee is the same whether the patient sees the doctor once a year, a hundred times a year, or never at all in twenty years. Doctors' incomes are thus related to the number of patients they can attract and enroll on the register, and not to the amount or kind of treatment the patients receive. In the case of serious illness the family doctor will make arrangements for the patient to consult specialists or perhaps enter a hospital, and will coordinate the care the patient receives. The income of British doctors is much lower than in the United States: a British general practitioner earns about $18,000 a year, and a specialist, about $36,000, far less than their American counterparts.

There is nothing in the British system to prevent doctors from taking private, fee-paying patients if they wish, and a small minority of physicians and patients do choose to remain partly or wholly in the private rather than the public sector. Hospitals also maintain private wards for those who wish to pay fees. The quality of the medical treatment in the private wards does not differ from that in public wards, but accommodations are more spacious, and nonessential ailments may receive quicker treatment than they would in the public sector.

The main complaint against the National Health Service, in fact, is that there are often long waiting lists for treatment of nonessential medical problems. A heart attack, cancer, or broken leg will receive immediate attention, but the demand for services is so great that less serious illnesses may sometimes have to wait for days, weeks, or in some cases even months before they are treated. When they introduced the National Health Service, the British had hoped that they would be able to satisfy the demand for health care fully; they have since found that this demand appears insatiable, consistently expanding as more services are made available. Despite this criticism, British opinion polls consistently show that over 80 percent of the public approves the National Health Service, making it by far the most popular government service in Britain. The system is supported by all political parties and, indeed, by the British medical profession, and there are no significant pressures to alter it. Although the British spend only about 6 percent of their gross national product on health care, compared with over 9 percent in the United States, their health seems better. The British live longer than Americans, spend less time in hospitals, have a lower infant and maternal death rate, and in 1976 achieved this at a per-person health-care cost of $189, compared with $638 in the United States.[14]

The fact that the British system works so well does not necessarily mean, of course, that it can or should be transplanted to the United States. The National Health Service succeeds in Britain because it fits well with important strands in British culture—including a long tradition of service-oriented rather than profit-oriented medicine, an absence of a powerful medical lobby, and a general belief that part of the responsibility of the welfare state is to guarantee the health of the population. Different conditions prevail in American culture, and it may be that different reforms will be necessary to take account of them. The British system is merely one model that we might bear in mind in considering the future shape of our own health-care system.

THE AMERICAN SYSTEM

The American health-care system has given us one of the highest standards of health in the world, a fact that should not be overlooked. Yet there is still room for much improvement. Let us look now at some of the problematic elements of our system in more detail—at medical insurance, at Medicare and Medicaid, at the hospitals, at the doctors, and at the nursing homes.

Medical Insurance

Until the late 1920s about 90 percent of all medical bills were paid directly to the doctor by the patient. Today direct payments cover less than a third of medical bills; the rest are settled in the form of third-party payments by private insurers or by federal and state governments. Private medical insurance now pays for about 35 percent of the nation's medical fees.

Historically, the purpose of these third-party payments has been not so much to protect the sick person from the burden of medical expenses as to protect the income of the hospitals and doctors. During the Great Depression, many people were simply unable to pay their hospital bills. To guarantee against any such loss of income in the future, the hospitals decided to create a third party that would pay patients' bills for them—Blue Cross. The idea behind Blue Cross was a simple one: an individual would pay regular insurance premiums to a nonprofit agency, which would then pay at least part of the costs of any hospitalization that person might require. Later on, a parallel insurance program, Blue Shield, was added to cover doctor's fees for medical and surgical expenses inside hospitals. The "Blues" have always maintained an intimate relationship with the hospitals, and their regional boards are still typically dominated by hospital doctors and other members of the medical establishment. The primary purpose of the "Blues" is not to save money by keeping bills down; rather, it is what it has always been—to ensure that hospital bills, however high they may be, get paid.[15]

In the 1940s and 1950s, fringe benefits such as health insurance were recognized as a legitimate area for bargaining between unions and employers. The result was a massive new health-insurance market, which was quickly exploited by commercial insurance companies. More than a thousand firms are now active in the health-insurance business, with eight major companies dominating the field. These commercial insurers differ from the "Blues" in that their goal is profits for themselves—profits derived largely from the margin between their payments to doctors and hospitals and their income from the premiums paid by their clients. Profit margins can be preserved only if increases in health-care

---

[14]Judith Randa, "Health Service Is 30 and British Still Love It," *Daily News* (New York), July 5, 1978, p. 36.

[15]See Sylvia A. Law, *Blue Cross: What Went Wrong?* (New Haven, Conn.: Yale University Press, 1974).

prices are passed on in full to the public in the form of higher premiums.

Thanks to Blue Cross, Blue Shield, and the commercial insurance companies, about four-fifths of the American population is now covered by some kind of health insurance. But much of this coverage is inadequate and expensive. Blue Cross does not cover outpatient care, nor did Blue Shield until very recently, so most of the population is not covered for doctor's house calls or for visits to doctor's offices. Only a minority is covered by insurance for dental care. Nearly all the insurance programs have a high deductible— that is, the patient must assume a substantial part of the cost of medical bills before the insurer takes over. Nearly all the programs have a ceiling—that is, there is a limit to the amount the insurer will pay, and if the bills exceed that limit, the burden of payment reverts to the patient. Moreover, millions of workers enjoy medical insurance only as a job-connected fringe benefit: if they lose their jobs, they lose their medical insurance as well. During 1976 an estimated 27 million workers and their families were temporarily deprived of medical coverage because of layoffs.

In addition, about 24 million people are not covered by health insurance of any kind.[16] As conflict theory would predict, this group is disproportionately made up of the poor. Hospital insurance is held by more than 90 percent of families with incomes above $10,000, but by fewer than 54 percent of poor families. In fact, there are 9 million people living below the poverty line who have no private health insurance but who are not quite poor enough to receive assistance from public funds in meeting their medical bills.

Medicare and Medicaid

In 1965 Congress finally made an attempt to withstand the AMA lobby and passed legislation creating two new programs, Medicare and Medicaid, both designed to make medical care more freely available to certain categories of the popu-

lation. *Medicare* is a public health-insurance program financed from federal and Social Security taxes and designed to cover some—but by no means all—of the medical expenses of people over the age of sixty-five. *Medicaid* is an assistance program financed from federal and state taxes and designed to cover the medical expenses of people with very low incomes.

In a classic case of an attempted solution to a social problem turning into a problem in itself, these programs have become a major cause of runaway costs in the medical system; this is especially true of Medicaid, which has been an utter disaster in this respect. Recognizing that Congress was determined to introduce Medicare and Medicaid, the AMA and the American Hospitals Association concentrated their lobbying energies and influence on ensuring that the level of fees in these programs would be set by the receivers of the money—the hospitals and doctors—and not by the providers—the federal and state governments. By insisting on the right of the medical profession to make the final decisions on matters of treatment and costs, and by raising the cry of "socialized medicine" and the specter of bureaucratic regulation, the medical lobby won a significant victory.[17] Provided the expenditures fall under the programs, Medicaid and Medicare will pay whatever fees a doctor charges and will supply virtually any equipment a hospital wants. There is thus no incentive to save money, no reason to be efficient, no cause to buy only essential equipment.

With the passage of Medicaid and Medicare, inflation in the health-care industry took quantum leaps. In just two years the programs boosted the income of the average physician by some $7,000, yet the amount of health care dispensed hardly increased at all.[18] The changing attitude of doctors toward the programs speaks eloquently enough: before the legislation was passed, only 38 percent were in favor; by 1967 the number of doctors supporting the programs had risen to 81 percent; and by 1970, as funds

---

[16]*New York Times*, May 7, 1978, p. 69.

[17]Theodore R. Marmor, *The Politics of Medicare* (Chicago: Aldine/Atherton, 1973).

[18]A. F. Ehrbar, "A Radical Prescription," *Fortune* (February 1977), 165–172.

continued to gush into the medical profession, 92 percent of physicians favored them.[19]

Medicare and Medicaid have also given rise to a new industry, dubbed "Medifraud"—the business, valued at anything between $1 billion and $5 billion a year, of defrauding the programs.[20] Much of this fraud takes place in what are known as "Medicaid mills"—storefront clinics, usually in impoverished ghetto areas, where unscrupulous doctors perform phony examinations and tests on poor patients, relying on Medicaid to foot the bills. A new vocabulary of swindling has emerged from these clinics:

"Ping-ponging": the practice of referring patients back and forth to other doctors in the clinics in order that Medicaid can be billed for several consultations instead of just one.

"Upgrading": billing for services and tests that are not actually provided.

"Family-ganging": the practice of making parents bring their entire families in for unneeded examinations and phoney treatments.

"Steering": referring patients with prescriptions to a particular drug store, one that is either associated with the clinic or gives kickbacks to the clinic operators.

"Shorting": delivering fewer pills to patients than Medicaid is billed for.

Many doctors in these clinics earn incomes in excess of $100,000 a year from Medicaid.

In 1976, Senate investigators made visits to more than one hundred of these clinics in New Jersey, California, New York, and Michigan. In each case they dressed as poor people, complained of something simple, such as a cold, and then allowed themselves to be processed through the "mill" to see what happened. One investigator, a senator from Utah, disguised himself as a

derelict and presented himself and his "cold" at a New York clinic; he was given a blood test, a urine test, an x-ray, and then issued prescriptions for three drugs to be filled "at the pharmacy next door." Another investigator with excellent vision received three different prescriptions for eyeglasses; others in perfect health were diagnosed as suffering from everything from bronchitis to urinary-tract infections. Perhaps worse than the fraud is the fact that the treatment in these clinics, which provide the only available medical help to millions of the poor, is incompetent. One Senate investigator, for example, was x-rayed on a machine that had no film; another submitted a concoction of soap and cleanser as a urine sample, only to find that it was duly tested as "normal."[21]

"Medifraud" continues rampant in the United States (the Senate investigators estimated that fraud absorbs about 10 percent of Medicaid funds). Prosecutors shun these cases because they are hard to win, requiring expert knowledge of both medical practice and sophisticated white-collar crime. The federal government has attempted to monitor cases of fraud, but in one year, 1976, only half of the states even bothered to file federal reports on the subject. The states that did report had found a total of only 854 cases—surely the tip of the iceberg—of which a mere 47 had been referred for prosecution.[22]

The Hospitals

Until World War II the American medical system was structured around the solo general practitioner, who served as family doctor and often as personal adviser as well. Hospitals had only a subsidiary role; essentially they offered a hotel service for the sick, together with trained assistants for the doctor and some equipment unavailable in the doctor's office. Since World War II this picture has changed radically: the solo general practitioner has become hard to find, and a large part of the population no longer

[19]John Colombotos, Corinne Kirchner, and Michael Millman, "Physicians View National Health Insurance: A National Study," *Medical Care*, 13 (May 1975), 369–396.

[20]Subcommittee on Long-Term Care, Special Committee on Aging, United States Senate; *Fraud and Abuse Among Clinical Laboratories* (Washington, D.C.: U.S. Government Printing Office, 1976); see, also, *Newsweek*, "Medifraud," May 9, 1977, p. 92.

[21]"Inside the Medicaid Mills," *Newsweek*, September 6, 1976, p. 18.

[22]*New York Times*, September 5, 1976, p. 4.

has a permanent family doctor. Instead, medicine now centers around large, impersonal, urban hospitals. The major university-based teaching hospitals have themselves become the hubs of great "medical empires" containing satellite hospitals and affiliated nursing homes and clinics.[23]

Three factors have brought this important change about. The first is the rapid development of modern medical knowledge and technology. Since World War II, medical knowledge has increased at an unprecedented rate, requiring greater and greater specialization. And the more specialized doctors become, the more they must rely on the presence of many other specialists to

advise them in areas beyond their own field. Meanwhile, the equipment for diagnosis and treatment of disease has become steadily more complex and more expensive: some items, such as a CAT scanner, can cost $500,000 or more, and in addition must be operated by trained technicians. Such equipment is far beyond the reach of the solo practitioner. As a result of these trends, more than half the nation's doctors now work in hospitals or in group practices.

The second factor stimulating the growth of the hospitals has been the increasing predominance of third-party payment of medical bills. As we have seen, Medicare, Medicaid, and many private insurance plans virtually give hospitals and hospital doctors a blank check. The hospitals, not the solo general practitioner, have been the main beneficiaries of this vast inflow of

---

[23]Ehrenreich and Ehrenreich, *op. cit.*; see, also, John Duffy, *The Healers: The Rise of the Medical Establishment* (New York: McGraw Hill, 1976).

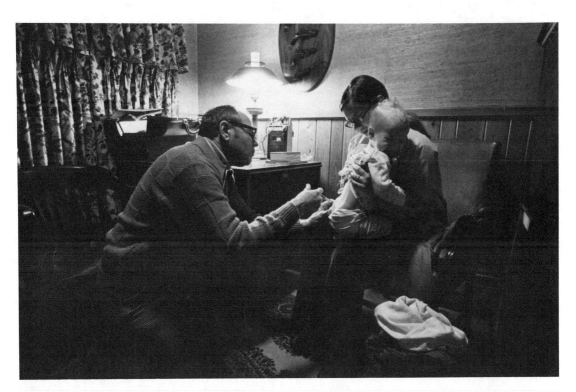

The family doctor who makes house calls and maintains close personal and professional contact with the patient is rapidly becoming a phenomenon of the past. The "Marcus Welby" of old is being replaced by the modern urban hospital, where relationships between physicians and patients are typically impersonal.

VOICES

Julia Cook, wife of the author, died as a result of negligence and error in her postoperative treatment after successful open heart surgery.

. . .

"Get well, dear," I told her as I gave her the pills, "and we'll go on a vacation up to New Hampshire in the fall."

Julia smiled at me faintly and began to doze in the large reclining chair we had moved into the dining room to make space for her hospital bed. I prepared my own supper and was eating it at the table, not far from where she slumbered, when she suddenly roused and called out, "I've got a splitting headache."

She put both hands to her head. I jumped up from the table and reached her in three strides; but in that instant her whole body seemed to go flaccid. I urged her to help herself by pushing down on the arm of the chair with one hand while I lifted her on the other side. She managed to do this, just barely, and I staggered with her to the hospital bed. Into this she collapsed, murmuring over and over: "Help me, help me. I'm going to die, I'm going to die."

In a panic, I telephoned Barbara. She summoned the first-aid service. While we were waiting, Julia's hands twitched and she murmured over and over, "Gotta get up, gotta get up." Then she lost consciousness. The first-aid men dashed in, administered oxygen, lifted her onto a stretcher, and sped off to the hospital.

There The Great Doctor's residents and nurses in the emergency ward did their best to save her; and there the great man himself finally put in an appearance. He came up to me, greatly worried, and asked if Julia had been getting any extra Coumadin.

"No," I told him, "I've been giving her all her medications, and she's been getting just the one five-milligram tablet a night the hospital prescribed."

"You're sure she didn't have some squirreled away somewhere?" he asked. "You're sure she couldn't have been sneaking some?"

If looks could have killed, the one my daughter gave him would have removed one great doctor from the world on the spot.

"You see the trouble is," he explained, "that her blood has been thinned out way too much. We try to keep the protime count stabilized around twenty-two, but hers is seventy-seven, and there's been seepage into the brain. I can't understand how it could have happened."

Later I checked the Coumadin the hospital had given me—a month's supply, thirty pills. Julia had had one a night for ten nights, and there were twenty pills left in the bottle.

For my wife, from the moment she had suffered that splitting headache, there was virtually no hope. The hospital residents, learning that she had had open-heart surgery only three weeks previously, expected her heart to collapse at any moment; but—a tribute to Dr. Ebert's surgical skill—it didn't. It kept pounding away until her condition was stabilized enough for her to be removed from the emergency room and placed in intensive care.

All the resources of the hospital were now thrown into the futile battle to undo the damage neglect had done. On the hospital's part, it was a magnificent effort. According to staff members, never in their recollection had so many nurses, residents, and specialists labored on one person. It was all too late, of course; and, as if some grim jester were making sport of us, the medical foul-ups continued.

When I phoned the hospital early Monday

third-party payments, and they have thrived as a result.

The third factor encouraging the growth of the hospitals is a change in the prestige structure of American medicine. The once revered "family doctor" now tends to be thought of as someone who merely prescribes pills for aches and pains;

prestige and glamour go instead to the medical researcher and the specialist. Naturally the most appropriate place for advanced research, diagnosis, and treatment is a large, urban, university-based teaching hospital, where the necessary skilled colleagues, patients, grants, equipment, and other facilities are available. Although these

morning, the information desk told me my wife's condition was "fair." Reprieve. The miracle we had not dared to hope for must have happened during the night, we thought. But when I double checked later with The Great Doctor's office, I found there had been no miracle. My wife's condition was unchanged, critical; the doctor did not know how the hospital could possibly have reported "fair."

Then, on Monday afternoon, the doorbell rang. There stood a black woman technician in her white coat, with her tray of tubes and paraphernalia—the representative of Friday's immobile mobile laboratory, now reactivated and come to take my wife's blood count. It was too much. My nerves snapped, and I was brutal.

"Your patient," I told the young woman, "is now dying in intensive care in the hospital because you couldn't get here Friday to test her blood."

The poor girl looked as stunned as if I had hit her with a baseball bat. "What happened?" she asked, and I told her. She explained that, on Friday, there had been only one person on duty in the office. There was a rigid rule that the office must be kept open at all costs, and so no one could leave to make the blood test.

Early that evening, I went to the hospital to see Julia. I felt that I was saying good-bye to her. She lay there unconscious, a nurse beside her constantly siphoning off mucus that gathered in her throat. I took Julia's hand; it was cold to my touch, and she did not know, of course, that I was holding it. I looked down at her as she lay there, a faint reddish discoloration across her forehead above the eyebrows. The long surgical scar down her chest had healed beautifully and was already beginning to fade—and all for nothing. I knew without being told that she was dying.

The heart that Dr. Ebert had fixed so well kept pounding away for some thirty hours before it gave out around two-thirty A.M. on Tuesday, July 23. The operation that we had hoped would prolong Julia's life had cut it short.

Even then, the medical system could not right itself to get the plain fact of death straight. A lawyer neighbor of mine, worried about Julia, telephoned the hospital about six-thirty A.M. Though my wife had been dead for four hours, the cheery voice of the girl on the information desk told him that her condition was "fair."

In accordance with Julia's repeatedly expressed wishes, we held the funeral the next day; and on Thursday morning about ten-thirty I telephoned Dr. Ebert's office. I had already determined to investigate what had happened; to do something, if I could, to help prevent such needless tragedies from happening to others. It was, I had decided, the only possible compensation, the only thing that I could do for Julia now.

"Oh, how are you, Mr. Cook?" Dr. Ebert's secretary asked when I called.

"I'm all right," I told her. "But my wife isn't."

"Oh," the secretary asked, "what's the matter?"

"She's dead," I said.

There was an audible gasp on the phone, then the secretary asked, "What happened?" I explained.

Julia had now been dead for some fifty-six hours, but Dr. Ebert had been unaware until I called. Nobody had talked to anybody; the fact of death, it seemed, had not been all that important.

great hospitals are not profit-making, they are out to make money, as much as they possibly can, because they are in competition with one another: the more lavish their facilities and funding, the better they are able to attract top researchers, teachers, and students, and thus climb in the prestige hierarchy. The lesser institutions in the surrounding area scurry to become affiliated in one way or another with the major teaching hospitals, so that they too can share in its prestige and the facilities it offers.

The effect of these changes is that medical care has become increasingly bureaucratized and impersonal, and more concerned with remedying illness than preventing it.[24] In fact, preventive health care—involving regular checkups, x-rays, Pap tests, and so on—is not a specialty or even a particular interest of modern American medicine. Increasingly, the focus of medical interest is on research into rare and exotic diseases or illnesses that may respond to treatment with dramatic cures. As we saw in Chapter 11 ("Aging"), only a tiny fraction of the money and energies spent on teaching and research goes into routine, widespread complaints such as the chronic health problems of the elderly.

Hospital costs account for the greater part of the inflation in the nation's health-care bill. These costs represent 40 percent of health-care expenditures, and during the past decade have risen four times as fast as the consumer price index. In 1965 the average cost of a day in the hospital was $40 and the nation's hospital bill was $9.1 billion; by 1976 the cost of a day in the hospital was around $200 and the total bill was $45.1 billion, and still rising rapidly. In addition to the factors already mentioned, this increase in hospital costs is partly the result of the often needless acquisition and duplication of facilities, which are "funded" by the third-party method of payment and promoted by a huge medical-supplies industry that offers hospitals a wide variety of high-cost, low-utilization medical equipment, from electronic thermometers to hyperbaric chambers. Hospitals compete with one another to have the very latest in fashionable and expensive—if little used—medical hardware. In addition, doctors often demand much of this equipment not because it is medically essential, but simply because it will make their lives easier.

The most outstanding example of wasteful duplication, however, is the surplus of hospital beds in the United States. On any given day there are around 100,000 empty beds, representing a loss to hospitals of about $2 billion a year—a cost that is indirectly passed on to the public.[25] An empty bed costs a hospital money because the hospital must maintain the same facilities and staff that would be required if it were filled. As a result, there is always the risk of some pressure for patients to be hospitalized unnecessarily or to be kept in the hospital longer than necessary. Insurance programs such as Blue Cross compound the problem because they reimburse hospitals for care at a flat daily rate, based on the average charges for all patients treated. The first few days of hospitalization are usually the most expensive, because this is when most diagnostic tests, surgery, and other treatments are conducted; the last few days, when the patient is recovering, are the least expensive. There is therefore a strong incentive to keep the patient in the hospital for a few extra days to increase income and fill surplus beds.

The need for income-producing patients has led to two practices that, although taken for granted in the United States, are viewed with sheer amazement by foreign observers. The first practice, which is, mercifully, not very widespread, is "body-snatching" by ambulance crews attached to particular hospitals. These crews are supposed to respond only to emergency calls channeled directly to them, but in many instances they are encouraged to listen in to radio transmissions of the police and other ambulance services, so that they can race to the scene of an emergency and claim the sick or injured for their own hospital. It is not unknown for two or more ambulance crews to arrive simultaneously at the scene of an accident and start quarreling over possession of the injured. The second practice is that of attempting to find out how a sick person proposes to pay his or her bill before hospital admission is granted or any treatment is given. Hospital administrative staff commonly question incoming patients, even in emergency rooms, about whether they are covered by any form of insurance before admitting them. Perhaps nothing better illustrates the commercial rather then the service orientation of American medicine than these two rituals.

In 1977 the Carter administration decided to make a frontal assault on rising medical costs, and singled out the hospitals as the main target. A bill was introduced into Congress to force the nation's 6,000 acute-care hospitals to hold their

[24]See David Mechanic, *The Growth of Bureaucratic Medicine: An Inquiry into the Dynamics of Patient Behavior and the Organization of Medical Care* (New York: Wiley, 1976).

[25]*New York Times*, May 7, 1978, p. 69; see, also, *Newsweek*, May 9, 1977, p. 90.

annual average increases in charges to 9 percent, hardly a miserly figure. Under the provisions of the bill, hospitals that exceeded this limit would face penalties, and Medicaid, Medicare, and private insurers would be prohibited from making reimbursements in excess of the limit. The bill also restricted the construction of new facilities and the purchase of costly new medical technology. The administration estimated that if the bill were passed, it would save about $5.5 billion by 1980.

As conflict theory would predict, the doctors, hospitals, and medical suppliers interpreted this $5.5 billion saving to others as a $5.5 billion loss to themselves, and the AMA and the American Hospitals Association launched an intensive lobbying campaign against the bill. Largely as a result of their efforts, the legislation was killed in the two committees that first considered it. One of these, the congressional Health Subcommittee, had thirteen members, eleven of whom had received contributions from the AMA during the 1974 and 1976 elections. On the recommendation of its chairman—who had received $5,000 from the AMA in each of these years—the committee voted the bill down. The second committee, the House Interstate and Foreign Commerce Committee, voted 22 to 21 to reject the bill. Of the twenty-two members who voted against the bill, nineteen had received a total of $85,150 in contributions from the AMA in the three preceding years. These facts do not prove, of course, that legislators were unduly influenced by the generosity of the AMA. Indeed, some members of Congress who had received AMA handouts voted for the bill. But it is perhaps significant that the average gift to members voting against the bill was $4,482, whereas the average for those voting for it was only $1,000; and the ten members who received the largest donations during this period, ranging from $5,500 to $16,050, all voted against the bill.[26]

The Physicians

The physician has long been highly regarded in American society. In one classic survey the public

[26]Common Cause, *op. cit.*

ranked physicians second in prestige only to Supreme Court justices, placing them ahead of dozens of other occupations such as bankers, state governors, members of Congress, priests, federal cabinet members, and authors.[27] Part of the traditionally high prestige of doctors no doubt stems from respect for their learning and the income that it commands, but much of the prestige is probably also the result of the doctor's established image as nurturing helper, healer, and confidant. In more recent years, however, the public has come to realize that physicians are probably no more nor less greedy, self-seeking, or corrupt than most other people. There may still be some surprise today when members of the

[27]Robert W. Hodge *et al.*, "Occupational Prestige in the United States, 1925–1963," *American Journal of Sociology*, 70 (November 1964), 286–302.

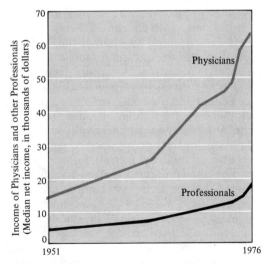

FIGURE 12.2 **Income of physicians and other professionals.** The income of physicians has been rising so rapidly in recent decades that it now far outpaces that of other professionals. Unlike other professionals, physicians have a captive market, in that people cannot choose whether or not to be ill. The "ethics" of the profession prevent competition among doctors, and many simply set a target income for themselves each year, increasing their charges until they achieve it.

(Council on Wage and Price Stability.)

profession are caught with their hands in the Medifraud cookie jar, but there are unmistakable signs of a decline of public confidence in the profession. The Harris poll, for example, found that those with a "great deal" of confidence in the medical profession had dropped from 73 percent in 1966 to 43 percent in 1977.

Of course, many of the nation's physicians are men and women of high ideals and great dedication, but the extent of idealism among doctors should not be overestimated. Many medical students choose their career out of motives linked more to money than compassion. Many others are dedicated to helping the sick when they start their training, but, as Howard Becker and his colleagues discovered in a classic study of the socialization of medical students, this early idealism tends to be modified.[28] Some medical students become cynical, ready to view medicine primarily as a means of achieving social status and seeking their own fortune.

A career in medicine is certainly a financially rewarding one. Doctors earn five times more than the average male wage earner and 3.5 times more than the average professional. In 1978 the median income of American doctors was $65,000. The President's Council on Wage and Price Stability pointed out in a 1978 report that doctors' incomes were rising at a faster rate than that of any other occupational group; since 1950 the increase in the price of doctors' services has been nearly double the increase in prices generally. The council claimed that doctors' fees are "unjustifiably high by established economic standards," and alleged that some doctors set "target incomes" for themselves, simply raising their fees until they achieve the income they want.[29] Competition among doctors, which might have the effect of driving prices down, is condemned as "unethical" by the AMA. Among the acts specifically banned have been such competitive practices as advertising and charging less than prevailing fees.

One factor that has contributed to the escala-

tion in physicians' fees is the need of doctors to insure themselves against *medical malpractice suits*—lawsuits in which doctors are sued for damages allegedly resulting from incompetent care. It is estimated that about 5 percent of the nation's 350,000 doctors are unfit to practice their profession, being either ignorant of modern medicine, mentally disordered, or addicted to alcohol or other drugs (physicians have a higher rate of narcotics addiction than any other occupational group).[30] Each year 30,000 people die as a result of faulty prescriptions, and ten times that number suffer from dangerous side effects of these prescriptions. Apart from the errors committed by medical incompetents, even the most skilled doctors sometimes make genuine mistakes. Juries have recently started to award huge damages against doctors, and insurance against malpractice suits now costs the individual physician several thousand dollars a year. This cost is of course passed on to the patient in the form of increased fees. To compound the problem, many doctors practice "defensive medicine" to protect themselves against possible malpractice suits: that is, they order far more tests and offer much more elaborate treatment than they consider necessary, to prevent any later accusations that they incompetently overlooked a medical problem. "Defensive medicine" also increases doctors' fees.

Until fairly recently there was a national shortage of doctors in the United States. The reason can be traced to a long campaign by the AMA to restrict the number of doctors in accordance with the classic economic theory of supply and demand: if there were fewer doctors, their incomes would be higher. In the late nineteenth century the AMA prevailed on state legislatures to stiffen the licensing requirements for physicians, particularly through the use of examinations prepared and judged by other doctors. The proportion of doctors relative to the population immediately began to decline. In particular, the number of female physicians dropped rapidly—so much so that there were fewer women doctors in 1940 than in 1910. Early

[28]Howard S. Becker *et al.*, *Boys in White: Student Culture in Medical School* (Chicago: University of Chicago Press, 1961).

[29]*New York Times*, May 7, 1978, p. 69.

[30]David Makofsky, "Malpractice and Medicine," *Society*, (January–February 1977), 25–29.

in the twentieth century the AMA used its influence to limit the number of medical schools, and in the 1930s it pressured the schools to reduce the number of students admitted. In that decade the total number of medical students fell by 17 percent, with the number of black and Jewish medical students dropping by nearly a third.[31] In the early 1960s, the United States had fewer doctors per 100,000 members of the population than such countries as Russia, Bulgaria, and Argentina.

Since then the AMA has changed its attitude, for it has become apparent at last that doctors' incomes are not subject to the classical supply-and-demand theory, inasmuch as sick people do not choose to need the attention of a physician. In fact, doctors' fees tend to be highest in the areas where the supply of doctors is the greatest, such as Los Angeles and New York City. The AMA has now ended its opposition to expanded medical-school admissions, and the ratio of doctors to the population has improved for over a decade: from 156 per 100,000 in 1966 to 174 per 100,000 in 1976.

Although there is no national shortage of doctors, the services of doctors are unevenly delivered, resulting in shortages both in some areas of the country and in some areas of medicine. Doctors are increasingly concentrated in affluent urban and surburban areas. High-income Westchester County in New York, for instance, has 260 doctors per 100,000 people; the state of Mississippi, relatively poor and rural, has only 82 doctors per 100,000 people. Over 87 percent of doctors practice in metropolitan areas, which hold only 68 percent of the population. In fact, some 5,000 towns in 135 counties of the United States have no doctor at all.[32]

There is also a shortage of doctors involved in primary care—that is, general practitioners, internists, and pediatricians—and a surplus of specialists, particularly surgeons. In 1930 only 17 percent of doctors were specialists; today the figure is an astounding 72 percent. Part of the

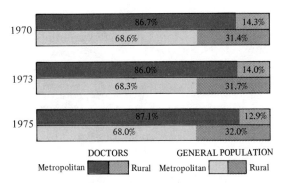

FIGURE 12.3 **Where the doctors are.** Physicians are becoming more concentrated in metropolitan areas, which consequently have an oversupply of doctors in comparison with small town and rural areas.
(U.S. Bureau of the Census; American Medical Association.)

reason for the increase, of course, is that medical knowledge has become more specialized, but another factor is that a specialist can command much higher fees than a primary-care doctor.

One effect of the surplus of surgeons appears to be a surplus of surgery. The United States has twice as many surgeons per capita as Britain, for example, and it has twice as many operations per capita as well. During the 1970s the number of operations rose by 23 percent, whereas the population as a whole grew by only 5 percent.[33] Only about 20 percent of surgical operations performed in the United States are necessary, in the sense that they save or extend life. The remainder are optional, and it is calculated that about 2 million of these 25 million operations performed each year are unnecessary and result in about 15,000 deaths.[34] There is strong evidence that many surgeons recommend operations of doubtful value—particularly certain

[31]A. F. Ehrbar, "A Radical Prescription," *Fortune,* (February 1977), p. 169.

[32]*New York Times,* May 7, 1978, p. 69; see, also, *Newsweek,* May 9, 1977, p. 90.

[33]*New York Times,* January 26, 1976, p. 20; "Too Much Surgery?" *Newsweek,* April 10, 1978, pp. 65–67; Bruce C. Paton, "Who Needs Coronary Bypass Surgery?" *Human Nature,* 1 (September 1978), 76–83.

[34]*Cost and Quality of Medical Care: Unnecessary Surgery,* Report of the Subcommittee on Oversight and Investigations of the Committee on Interstate and Foreign Commerce, House of Representatives, 94th Congress, 2nd Session (Washington, D.C.: U.S. Government Printing Office, 1976).

tonsillectomies, hysterectomies, and coronary-bypass operations—on the principle that the more surgery you do, the more income you get.

The Nursing Homes

As recently as the 1930s there were only a handful of nursing homes in the United States, most of them run on a nonprofit basis by church groups or local authorities. After World War II, however, the demand for places in nursing homes grew rapidly. People were living longer than ever before, so there was an increase in the number of aged people who could not fully manage on their own. These people were generally poor (the aged over sixty-five have less than half the income of adults under that age). Moreover, they often had no immediate relatives or, if they did, were not living with them for one reason or another. Private health insurance never covers long-term home care, so most of this growing group of the aged had no real means of paying the high costs of nursing-home care.

In 1965 Congress included provisions in the Medicaid and Medicare legislation to pay the nursing-home fees of the poor and the aged. Medicare provides federal financing for most health care for people over sixty-five, including up to one hundred days in a nursing home after hospitalization. Medicaid pays for the health care of the poor of any age, including the costs of unlimited nursing home stays. As a result, money suddenly flooded into the financially starved nursing homes—and almost overnight created one of the most sordid industries in the United States.[35]

The prospect of the profits to be made by providing nursing-home care attracted to the industry a host of shady entrepreneurs with little or no background in medicine and certainly with no previous record of concern for the elderly. Nursing-home stocks soared as the owners of new and converted homes racked up annual returns of well over 20 percent on their investments.

The financial appeal of the nursing homes to these entrepreneurs lies, once again, in the fact that Medicaid and Medicare guarantee to pay most of the bills. The more these bills can be inflated and the more costs can be kept down, the greater the profits will be. Almost inevitably the nursing homes have become the locus for new varieties of Medifraud. Among the more common are supplying and billing for unnecessary services; establishing kickback arrangements with pharmacies; billing for expensive brand-name drugs while supplying patients with cheap generic drugs; feeding patients on less than a dollar a day while billing several times that amount for food; arranging with medical suppliers to bill for equipment that is never delivered, then splitting the profit with them; giving kickbacks to local physicians who recommend that old people enter the nursing home in question; hiring untrained assistants at or below the minimum wage and billing for the services of skilled nurses; and arranging for "gang visits" with local physicians, who see dozens of nursing-home patients in a few hours, bill for extensive services supposedly rendered, and split the fees with the nursing-home operators. Not very surprisingly, the nursing homes have attracted the attention of organized crime: in 1978 the House Committee on Aging reported that law-enforcement officials in thirty-one states had evidence of organized-crime involvement in Medicare and Medicaid fraud, related most often to the ownership or operation of nursing homes.

Mary Mendelson, a critic of the nursing homes, has visited hundreds of these institutions and has found very few that meet even the minimum standards required by the law and the relevant regulations: "It is the same everywhere. All over the country, nursing homes are similar, and similarly bad. Excellent homes are rare, and most of those that are considered good are good only by comparison to the majority that are worse."[36] During her investigations she found, among other things, aged patients washing their

---

[33]See Subcommittee on Long-Term Care, Special Committee on Aging, United States Senate, *Nursing Home Care in the United States: Failure in Public Policy* (Washington, D.C.: U.S. Government Printing Office, 1974); Mendelson, *op. cit.*; and Frank E. Moss and Val J. Halamandaris, *Too Old, Too Sick, Too Bad: Nursing Homes in America* (Germantown, Md.: Aspen Systems Corp., 1977).

[36]Mendelson, *op. cit.*, p. 22.

Conditions in many American nursing homes can be described only as scandalous; these institutions are often little more than places where the elderly are warehoused while the owners reap rich profits from Medicaid and Medicare.

sheets by hand; beds without blankets; expensive medical equipment stored away unused; dreadful food bearing little correspondence to the posted menu; choice meat kept on hand in the refrigerator to show visiting inspectors, then taken home for consumption by the nursing-home owners; bathrooms without soap or toilet paper; permanently locked fire-exit doors; patients kept constantly drugged for the convenience of the staff; systematic theft or embezzlement of senile or frightened patients' Social Security checks; physical abuse of patients by untrained staff; and even a fake sprinkler system, with spouts set into the ceiling but not connected to any water supply, its only purpose being to fool inspectors.

CONFRONTING THE PROBLEM

What can be done about the problems posed by health care in the United States?

Organizing for change. For decades, attempts at reform of the American health-care system have been thwarted or distorted by influential representatives of those who benefit financially from the existing system. Until these pressure groups are effectively counterbalanced, significant reform is unlikely. At present much of the pressure for change has come from organizations and social movements representing the aged; the sick as such have no real social movement, although smaller groups are beginning to organize around such issues as patients' right. There is a genuine and widespread anger in the United States about the failings of the health-care system, and not only Congress but also Blue Cross, Blue Shield and other interest groups are beginning to take account of the mood for change. If this diffuse feeling of frustration and resentment can be organized into a positive program for reform, changes will be more rapid and more far-reaching.

Reform of Medicaid and Medicare.   Assuming that the Medicaid and Medicare programs are to be retained in some form or another, one significant reform is essential: the fees for medical services must be set by a more impartial authority than the doctor or hospital receiving them, and there must be built-in incentives against, rather than in favor of, extravagance and waste.

Reducing Unnecessary Surgery.   Several moves are already afoot to curb needless operations. Over a hundred Blue Cross, Blue Shield, and other health-insurance plans now pay for a second opinion before consenting to meet the costs of an operation; in about 18 percent of cases the second opinion is against the operation. In addition, Professional Standards Review Organizations composed of physicians have been at work all over the country since 1978 monitoring medical treatment, including surgery, that is covered by Medicare and Medicaid programs. If surgery and specialist care that are unnecessary can be eliminated, there might be pressure for doctors to practice instead in primary medicine, where the need is far greater.

Encouraging Primary Care and Preventive Medicine.   The health of Americans would improve markedly if there were more emphasis on preventive medicine and primary care. Stimulated by insurance programs that cover only inpatient care, the American medical system has focused on hospitals, which by their nature are concerned with acute problems and curative medicine. There is a need for an extension of emphasis to outpatient care, in which regular checkups can be used to detect problems before they become serious. If part of the money currently flowing into the hospitals were made available instead for outpatient care, preventive medicine would receive an important boost.

There is a need, too, for more research into the behavioral and environmental causes of many diseases, and for people to become more aware of their own responsibility for maintaining good health. As Thomas McKeown notes,

> The role of individual medical care in preventing sickness and premature death is secondary to that of other influences, yet society's investment in health care is based on the premise that it is the major determinant. It is assumed that we are ill and are made well, but it is nearer the truth to say that we are well and are made ill. Few people think of themselves as having the major responsibility for their own health. . . .
>
> The public believes that health depends primarily on intervention by the doctor and that the essential requirement for health is the early discovery of disease. This concept should be replaced by recognition that disease often cannot be treated effectively, and that health is determined predominately by the way of life individuals choose to follow. Among the important influences on health are the use of tobacco, the misuse of alcohol and drugs, excessive or unbalanced diets, and lack of exercise. With research, the list of significant behavioral influences will undoubtedly increase.[37]

A Crackdown on Medifraud.   It seems vital that there be a concerted crackdown on the rampant corruption in the health-care system, particularly in such institutions as the "Medicaid mills" and nursing homes. Although Medifraud cases and other abuses are difficult to prove, it is essential that law-enforcement officials show that they mean business and that swindlers and embezzlers can no longer exploit the system with impunity. The Department of Health, Education, and Welfare has set up a "Project Integrity" to track down instances of Medifraud, and by 1979 had over 1,800 such cases under investigation.

---

[37]Thomas McKeown, "Determinants of Health," *Human Nature,* 1 (April 1978), 66; for a discussion of a new Canadian program, see, also, Eugene Vayda, "Keeping People Well: A New Approach to Medicine," *Human Nature,* 1 (July 1978), 64–71.

Generic Drugs. The chemical formulae of generic (nonpatent) drugs and patent drugs are identical: the only differences are in the trade name and the price, typically around twice as much for the patent drug. One obvious means of reducing the costs of health care, then, would be to encourage the use of generic drugs. New York State, for example, passed a law in 1977 that requires pharmacists to fill all prescriptions with the cheaper generic counterparts of patent drugs unless the physician specifically directs otherwise.

Health-Maintenance Organizations (HMOs). Health-maintenance organizations are a form of prepaid health-care service. Subscribers to an HMO pay a fixed annual sum, usually in installments, and in return receive comprehensive medical care with an emphasis on preventive medicine. HMOs vary in size, but most include specialists and general practitioners and offer a service that includes some hospital and home care, diagnostic and laboratory facilities, and drugs. The federal Health Maintenance Organization Act of 1973 provided funds for the creation of HMOs and obliged employers to offer HMO plans where available as an alternative to other health-insurance programs. Although more than 60 percent of American doctors are opposed to them, HMOs show lower consumer costs and hospitalization rates than other forms of medical insurance.[38]

Major Reform. The proposals so far discussed are essentially aimed at tinkering with the present system so as to make it more workable.[39] In the long run, however, a total, root-and-branch overhaul of the American health-care system seems necessary and inevitable. In the eighty-fourth Congress no fewer than eighteen bills to reform the system were offered. Some of the bills, sponsored by groups such as the AMA or the American Hospitals Association, called for relatively few changes; others, such as the bill proposed by Senator Edward Kennedy, visualized more radical reforms involving automatic health-care insurance for everyone, with the medical profession stripped of its right to unilaterally determine the level of fees.[40]

The ultimate shape of a new health-care system will probably be that of national health insurance, in which everybody is covered at least to some extent for most medical expenses, rather than a British-type system of free "socialized medicine" in which the government owns hospitals, employs doctors, and even nationalizes drug companies. The tradition of medicine as a field for private profit is so deeply ingrained in American culture that the new system is likely to be a compromise, granting the medical profession and its industrial allies their profits while insisting that medical services be more equitably delivered to the American people. Precisely what such a system will offer to the consumers and how well it will work to satisfy the nation's health-care needs will depend on the course of the political struggle that lies ahead.

SUMMARY

1. Health care in the United States presents a social problem in that its costs are excessively high and it is very unevenly delivered. The underlying problem is that health care is a business run for profit, not a service run for the public. Sickness is a social problem because the determinants of illness are often social and cultural. Ill people play the sick role, seeking the help of professionals. The social organization of American health care often reflects the priorities of the medical profession itself.

2. From the functionalist approach, the prob-

[38]Paul Starr, "HMOS: The Undelivered Health System," *The Public Interest* (Winter, 1976), 66–85, and R. W. Birnbaum, *Health Maintenance Organizations* (New York: Halstead Press, 1976).

[39]Victor Sidel and Ruth Sidel, *A Healthy State* (New York: Pantheon, 1977).

[40]See Avedis Donabedian, "Issues in National Health Insurance," *American Journal of Public Health*, 66 (April 1976), 345–350; and Margolis, *op. cit.*, pp. 12–43.

lem is one of social disorganization caused by such changes as the rapid growth of hospitals and third-party medical payments, combined with increasing public demand for health services. From the conflict approach, the problem is largely caused by the self-interest pursuits of organized medical groups, such as the AMA.

3. The British system contrasts sharply with the American system in that the British health care is offered free as a public service.

4. Most Americans are partially covered against medical expenses through private insurers such as Blue Cross, Blue Shield, and commercial companies. Medicare offers some coverage to the aged and Medicaid extends assistance to the poor. Third-party payments have contributed to rising medical costs, and the government programs have become the target for extensive fraud.

5. The focus of American medicine has shifted from the solo practitioner to the larger urban hospital. Care has thus become more impersonal

and more concerned with research and cures than with preventive medicine. Extravagant use of third-party funds by the hospitals has been a major source of increased costs.

6. Physicians enjoy high prestige and incomes in the United States. There is no longer a national doctor shortage, but there is a shortage of doctors in some areas and in primary-care medicine. An excess of surgeons appears to have led to extensive unnecessary surgery.

7. The nursing-home industry has taken advantage of Medicare and Medicaid to reap huge and sometimes fraudulent profits.

8. The problem can be confronted by organizing for change; reforming Medicare and Medicaid payment methods; reducing unnecessary surgery; encouraging primary care and preventive medicine; cracking down on Medifraud; using generic rather than patent drugs; using health-maintenance organizations; and making health-care services freely available to the American people.

GLOSSARY

Medicaid. A public health-assistance program financed from federal and state taxes and designed to cover the medical expenses of people with very low incomes.

Medical malpractice suit. A lawsuit brought against a doctor for damages allegedly resulting from incompetent care.

Medicare. A public health-insurance program financed from Social Security taxes and designed to cover some of the medical expenses of people over the age of sixty-five.

Profession. An occupation requiring extensive knowledge or training in an art or science.

Sick role. The pattern of behavior society expects of a person who is ill.

FURTHER READING

EHRENREICH, BARBARA, and JOHN EHRENREICH. *The American Health Empire: Power, Profits, and Politics.* New York: Vintage, 1971. A useful critical analysis of the American health-care system, with emphasis on the political processes and interests involved.

ENOS, DARRYL D., and PAUL SULTAN. *The Sociology of Health Care.* New York: Praeger, 1977. A good sociological overview of all the major aspects of health care in the modern United States.

EPSTEIN, SAMUEL S. *The Politics of Cancer.* San Francisco: Sierra Club Books, 1978. A powerful but controversial discussion of how various cancer-causing agents have been introduced into the environment by modern industry.

FREEMAN, HOWARD E., *et al.* (eds.) *Handbook of Medical Sociology.* 2nd edition. Englewood Cliffs, N.J.: Prentice-Hall, 1972. A good, comprehensive survey of theory and research in medical sociology.

ILLICH, IVAN. *Limits to Medicine.* London: Marion

Boyars, 1976. A highly controversial attack on modern medicine, by a provocative thinker who asserts that medicine as currently practiced makes little contribution to health.

KOTELCHUCK, DAVID (ed.). *Prognosis Negative: Crisis in the Health Care System.* New York: Vintage, 1976. An excellent collection of short articles covering almost every aspect of the health-care problem.

KRAUSE, ELLIOT A. *Power and Illness: The Political Sociology of Health and Medical Care.* New York: Elsevier, 1977. An important radical critique of the American health-care system, relying heavily on insights from conflict theory.

MAYNARD, ALAN. *Health Care in the European Community.* Pittsburgh: University of Pittsburgh Press, 1975. A useful study of the health-care systems of several other Western industrial nations.

MENDELSON, MARY ADELAIDE. *Tender Loving Greed.* New York: Vintage, 1976. A disturbing and highly readable firsthand account of the author's investigations into the American nursing-home industry.

TWADDLE, ANDREW C., and RICHARD M. HESSLER. *A Sociology of Health.* St. Louis: Mosby, 1977. This up-to-date text provides a good introduction to the study of health from a sociological perspective.

13
Mental Disorders

THE PROBLEM

The extent of mental disorder in the United States is far greater than is commonly realized. The President's Commission on Mental Health reported in 1978 that about 6.7 million people were receiving specialized mental-health care and that each year about 1.5 million are actually hospitalized for mental disorders.[1] In addition, about 1 American in 8 suffers depression serious enough to require psychiatric treatment during his or her lifetime; over 300,000 people are treated for acute depression annually, and an estimated 4 to 8 million are in need of treatment but do not seek it. Of the more than 50,000 suicides that take place every year in the United States, about half are committed by people suffering from serious depression.[2]

The statistics of people who receive treatment do not tell the whole story. Only a small proportion of mental disorders are actually treated. Many Americans, including some who have severe symptoms, do not know they need help, or refuse to seek it, or cannot find it. In fact, the President's Commission on Mental Health estimated that at any given time between 20 and 30 million Americans need some kind of mental-health care. In addition, the commission suggested that as many as 25 percent of the population suffers from mild to moderate depression, anxiety, or other symptoms of emotional dis-

order. These less acute difficulties do not show up in hospital and similar official statistics, but their impact is significant. The people affected may expend immense energy in trying to preserve a façade of happiness and normality despite their underlying tension, and this effort involves a further toll in job inefficiency, personal anguish, and problems with family and friends.

This basic social problem of excessive psychological stress and mental disorder is compounded by other social factors, one of which, as we shall see, is the absence of any real consensus on the exact nature and causes of mental disorders. Another factor is that those who have been labeled mentally disordered tend to be viewed with suspicion by others, even if they have been pronounced cured—a stigma that makes many people reluctant to seek treatment and complicates social readjustment once treatment has been initiated. In addition, the problem is intensified by the high cost of treatment and by the inadequacy of many facilities, particularly those for outpatients and ex-patients living in the community. Finally, some methods of treatment raise important questions about the civil liberties of those who have been diagnosed as mentally disordered. In sum, the social reaction to the problem has further complicated it in many respects.

WHAT IS MENTAL DISORDER?

In practical terms, people may be said to be suffering from *mental disorder* if they are psychologically unable to cope realistically and effectively with the ordinary challenges and tasks

---

[1]The President's Commission on Mental Health, *Report to the President from the President's Commission on Mental Health*, Vol. 1 (Washington, D.C.: U.S. Government Printing Office, 1978), p. 8.

[2]"Coping with Depression," *Newsweek*, January 8, 1973, pp. 51–54.

of the real world. If this definition seems rather vague, it is only because the concept of mental disorder is itself a vague one. How can we establish in particular cases if someone is suffering from a mental disorder? How, for example, do we tell if someone is "mad"?

There is no easy answer to that question, because "madness" is more a matter of subjective judgment than an objective fact. It is difficult, if not impossible, to draw a line between sanity and insanity. Behavior that would seem antisocial or eccentric in a rural village might be considered unimportant or even normal in the more tolerant climate of a large city. In the seventeenth century, religious leaders who had heretics burned at the stake were considered well-adjusted members of the community; any religious leader who attempted to do the same today would be committed to an institution as an obvious lunatic. Praying to God is regarded by most people as perfectly natural, but talking to spirits—which is not so very different—is considered very odd behavior indeed. Some subjective judgment is always involved in any decision about whether or not someone is mentally disordered, because what is considered bizarre or irrational depends on the standards of the culture, of the subculture, and of the individual observer. This problem is often illustrated in the criminal courts, where, after studying the same

In 1978, over 900 American members of the People's Temple cult committed mass suicide at the order of their leader, the Reverend Jim Jones. Were they mad? Many people would think so, but there is little clinical evidence of widespread insanity among them. Certainly they were under extraordinary psychological pressure, but judgments about their sanity (or anyone else's) rest to a large extent on subjective rather than objective criteria.

evidence, expert psychiatrists frequently disagree about the sanity of the accused.

In fact, there is no real consensus on how to classify or diagnose mental disorders. For years psychiatrists in different countries used a variety of terms to describe many different mental disorders they believed they had diagnosed, but there was little general agreement on the classification of particular symptoms. Since 1968 there has been an accepted agreement in the form of the International Classification of Diseases, but there is still a great deal of inconsistency in diagnosis from country to country or even from psychiatrist to psychiatrist within each society.

In the United States and Western Europe mental disorders are generally grouped into two broad categories, *neuroses* and *psychoses*. Neuroses are less serious and usually do not require hospitalization, whereas psychoses typically involve a severe break with reality. It is not always possible in practice, however, to establish a definite borderline between normality and neurosis or between neurosis and psychosis.

Neuroses

A neurosis is generally regarded not as a disease but as a personality disturbance, its chief characteristic being anxiety, which is believed in most cases to have its origins in childhood experiences. Despite their anxiety, neurotic people still have a firm grasp on reality and are able on the whole to function in life. The neurotic impairment is often limited to a particular area, and neurotics may be normal in all other respects. Neurotic people often know they have a problem and wish to overcome it, although they may not know its cause. There are several subtypes of neurosis:

Anxiety reaction: a deep, generalized anxiety about life. The person affected finds the ordinary routines of life highly stressful, but usually has no conscious awareness of the reasons for anxiety.
Hypochondria: an obsessive belief that one is physically ill—for example, that one has a brain tumor—even though no such illness is present.
Neurotic depression: feelings of deep depression, often lasting for long periods; in extreme cases the depression can lead to suicide.

Obsessive neurosis: a compulsion to behave in a particular way without any rational reason—for example, repeatedly washing one's hands throughout the day.
Phobia: an unreasonable fear of a specific situation or thing. Some of these fears are very common, such as acrophobia (the fear of heights) and claustrophobia (the fear of enclosed spaces). But even such unterrifying objects as butterflies can provoke intense phobias in some people.
Psychosomatic illness: a physical ailment that originates from a psychological problem; symptoms include, among other things, headache, backache, rashes, or even, in extreme cases, blindness or paralysis. The afflicted person usually does not realize that the illness is caused by psychological stress.

Psychoses

The essential difference between the neurotic and psychotic is that the psychotic experiences a sharp break with reality. The mental processes of psychotics are so grossly deranged that they are unable to evaluate external reality: they are out of touch with their own situation and do not attempt to adapt to the world. There are two main types of psychosis. *Organic psychoses* are those with an identifiable physical basis. They result from damage to the brain tissues resulting from physical injury, senility, alcoholism, advanced syphilis, brain tumors, or other causes. *Functional psychoses* are those that have no obvious physical basis and whose origin is presumed to be partly or wholly psychological.

We shall place particular emphasis on functional psychoses in this chapter, for they are the most severe mental disorders (patients suffering from them constitute about 80 percent of first admissions to mental hospitals) and are at the core of the social problem of mental disorder. There are three main subtypes of functional psychosis.

Paranoia is a relatively rare form of psychosis, which is characterized by persistent delusions of persecution or grandeur (paranoid people may believe, for example, that someone is trying to poison or kidnap them). These paranoid delusions are often organized into logical systems focused on specific areas and are impervious to rational arguments. In other respects, the paranoid person's intellectual and emotional functions need not be impaired, and there are usually no hallucinations or other abnormal behavior patterns. In fact, delusions aside, the paranoid may appear quite normal.

Affective psychosis encompasses a wide category of disorders characterized by extremes of mood rather than by bizarre behavior, although in some cases there may be hallucinations and delusions. In the *manic* form, the person may be highly excitable and occasionally violent; in the *depressive* form, he or she may be depressed and withdrawn, even suicidal. Sufferers who fluctuate between these extremes are called manic-depressive. Their cycles of moods vary in length and regularity, but the depressive phase of the cycle usually predominates over the manic phase.

Schizophrenia is the most common form of functional psychosis. The word itself means "split personality"—not, as seems commonly thought, in the sense that schizophrenics have two different personalities, but in the sense that their intellectual and emotional functions are separated: they may laugh or cry at inappropriate moments, speak to inanimate objects, or talk in an incoherent fashion; they may suffer delusions, feelings of persecution, and visual and auditory hallucinations. There are several types of schizophrenia, of which the most common are *simple schizophrenia*, characterized by general withdrawal from reality into a world of disordered thought processes; *hebephrenia*, characterized by giggling, infantile behavior, hallucinations, and seclusion; *catatonia*, characterized by episodes of stupor and immobility which may persist for hours or even decades; and *chronic undifferentiated schizophrenia*, a residual category used when the individual's symptoms are not clear and cannot be fitted into one of the other categories. Schizophrenia is the psychosis that afflicts young people most frequently: about two-thirds of the schizophrenics who come into treatment for the first time are between the ages of fifteen and thirty-five. About three-fifths of all mental-hospital patients under the age of sixty-five are schizophrenics, and about one American in a hundred will suffer from some form of this functional psychosis. In many respects, schizophrenia is the single most serious mental disorder in American society.

The diagnoses are based on the main symptoms displayed by the patients, but they tend to be unreliable in the long run, since many people may exhibit symptoms from several different categories, either simultaneously or one after another. Psychiatrists often fail to reach agreement not only on questions of diagnosis, but even on the crucial question of whether someone is psychotic or not: in one study, psychiatrists disagreed in 20 percent of the cases of possible psychosis they were asked to judge. On the question of exactly what form of psychosis someone is suffering from, agreement among psychiatrists rarely exceeds 50 percent.[3] As one psychiatrist, D. L. Rosenhan, observes:

> Whenever the ratio of what is known to what needs to be known approaches zero, we tend to invent "knowledge" and assume that we understand more than we actually do. We seem unable to acknowledge that we simply don't know. The needs for diagnosis and remediation of behavioral and emotional problems are enormous. But rather than acknowledge that we are just embarking on understanding, we continue to label patients . . . as if in those words we had captured the essence of understanding. The facts of the matter are that we have known for a long time that diagnoses are not useful or reliable. . . .[4]

In a similar vein, the psychologist Joseph Church comments that "the attempts of mental health experts to define and diagnose these 'diseases,' and to prescribe specific treatments, lie somewhere between low farce and high tragedy. Their learned pronouncements lead one to wonder whether the inmates have indeed taken charge of the asylum."[5]

[3]Myron G. Sandifer, Charles Pettus, and Dana Quade, "A Study of Psychiatric Diagnosis," *Journal of Nervous Mental Disease,* 139 (October 1964), 350–356.

[4]David L. Rosenhan, "On Being Sane in Insane Places," *Science,* January 19, 1973, pp. 250–258.

[5]Joseph Church, "Two Fly Over the Cuckoo's Nest," *New York Times Book Review,* March 26, 1978, p. 11; see, also, the extensive critique of psychiatry in Martin L. Gross, *The Psychological Society* (New York: Random House, 1978); and "Psychiatry on the Couch," *Time,* April 2, 1979, pp. 74–82.

This state of uncertainty has far-reaching implications. For as we shall see, some critics of our current approaches to mental disorders have argued that "mental illness" is simply a social definition, not a pathological (diseased) state.

They have claimed, for example, that schizophrenia may be simply a variant state of consciousness (like dreaming, transcendental meditation, religious ecstasy, or a psychedelic trip), and not really a disease at all.

ANALYZING THE PROBLEM

The social problem of mental disorders can be usefully analyzed from the functionalist, conflict, and deviance approaches; each offers a complementary viewpoint on the issue.

The Functionalist Approach

The functionalist approach views the high rate of mental disorder in American society as being rooted in the very structure of the society. In other words, social disorganization is present to the extent that social conditions exert sufficient pressure on some people or groups to cause them to become emotionally or psychologically impaired. As we shall see, sociological research has shown that mental disorders are not randomly distributed throughout the society: they have a higher incidence in densely populated, rapidly changing, impoverished areas—such as socially disorganized, deteriorating urban slums—and among certain social groups—particularly those with lower social and economic status—who seem to be subjected to more personal and psychological stress than others. In addition, the structure of American society is such that these groups are less likely to seek early treatment and are less likely to receive the best care.

The functionalist approach thus locates the source of the problem within a large, rapidly changing society that places some of its members at greater psychological risk than others and fails to offer the appropriate services or other remedial measures that might reduce the incidence of mental disorder.

The Conflict Approach

The conflict approach has been applied to the problem of mental disorders only relatively re-

cently, but it sensitizes us to the fact that mental disorder is more than a medical matter: it can also be a social issue, and even a political one, since there are clear class differences in the incidence and quality of treatment for mental disorders. But the area for potential conflict extends even further. Many critics have pointed out that the label "mentally disordered" can be used as a means of social control, as a convenient way of dealing with those who disrupt the established order. Joseph Church suggests:

> The student who cannot or will not learn, the welfare recipient, the criminal, the psychologically disturbed, and even alcoholics and homosexuals and political dissidents are coming to be seen as sick people, to be cured by the magic of modern psychiatry and psychology . . .

> The translation of education, social-welfare, mental-health, criminal and ideological issues into medical problems effectively removes them from the ordinary constitutional protections such as due process and the right to privacy. The logic here is that the deviant is now a *patient* receiving medical *therapy* that is for his own individual good. No one in his right mind would object to curing sick people, and the recalcitrant patient is only demonstrating just how sick he really is. The authority of the psychiatrist reigns supreme, and unwanted people are humanely neutralized as threats to the social order.[6]

There is a danger, some critics suggest, that modern society is becoming a "therapeutic state," in which criminal and other nonconformist or deviant behaviors are defined as sicknesses and treated accordingly.[7] And of course

---

[6]Church, *op. cit.*, p. 11.

[7]See Nicholas N. Kittrie, *The Right to Be Different: Deviance and Enforced Therapy* (Baltimore: Penguin,

the power to determine who is "sick" rests with those who hold high social, economic, and political status. The definitions of mental normality are socially constructed, as Robert Coles points out, by those who exert authority in society:

> What indeed is mental health? Who indeed is normal? Were slave holders normal? . . . If a man tells me he is going to kill himself, I call him "suicidal" and want to hospitalize him. If a man in Vietnam runs into a burst of machine gun fire, urging his comrades to do likewise, I call him a hero. If a man wants to kill someone, he is homicidal and needs confinement. If a man drops a bomb on people he doesn't even see or know, he is doing his duty.[8]

The Deviance Approach

Sociologists have generally used the deviance approach for the analysis of mental disorders in the past, and this approach remains fruitful today. The mentally disordered person is socially deviant in the sense that he or she is defined as a violator of basic social norms relating to the very nature of reality. In some cases, of course, this violation of norms arises from factors over which the individual has no control whatever, for the source of the disorder lies in the organic processes of the brain. In many other cases, however, there is strong evidence that mentally disordered behavior, like other forms of deviance, is learned.

Labeling theory has probably had the greatest influence on sociological analysis of how people learn mentally disordered behavior.[9] Although they may disagree over the exact details of the process, many social scientists accept that this behavior is unconsciously adopted by some people as a way of escaping from social situations

they find intolerable. The development of certain forms of mental disorder thus involves a complex, continuing interaction between the individual concerned and the surrounding society.[10] Perceiving various behaviors of a person under stress as socially incompetent—as "odd," or "strange"—other people label the individual as emotionally or psychologically disturbed and make allowances for his or her behavior. Exempted from some social responsibilities, the individual is tempted to repeat or extend the behavior, and others apply the label more firmly. Eventually the individual comes to play the social role of a mentally disordered person, and society responds accordingly.

Because mentally disordered people are often regarded as deviants, their plight is complicated by a factor that is not present in the case of ordinary physical illnesses: a *stigma*, or mark of "disgrace," is applied to them by society. This stigma, which sets them apart from "normal" people even when they have been pronounced cured, is made worse by the cultural stereotypes of mentally disordered behavior that we learn during the socialization process—stereotypes that tend to emphasize bizarre behavior patterns such as violent outbursts, foaming at the mouth, delusions of being Napoleon, and so forth. Although most patients are returned to their communities within a matter of months or even weeks, treatment for mental disorder—like imprisonment for crime—carries with it a label, one that may remain for years afterward, affecting the way the individual is viewed by employers, friends, and even family. As Erving Goffman observes, the victims of mental disorder have a "spoiled identity."[11]

An example of this stigmatization occurred when presidential candidate George McGovern selected Senator Thomas Eagleton of Missouri as the vice-presidential candidate in 1972. The choice was warmly received until some newspa-

1973); Thomas S. Szasz, "Toward the Therapeutic State," in William J. Chambliss (ed.), *Sociological Readings in the Conflict Perspective* (Reading, Mass.: Addison-Wesley, 1973); Gresham M. Sykes, *Criminology* (New York: Harcourt Brace Jovanovich, 1978), pp. 568–581; and Peter Shrag, *Mind Control* (New York: Random House, 1978).

[8]Robert Coles, "A Fashionable Kind of Slander," *Atlantic* 226 (November 1970), 54.

[9]See Thomas J. Scheff (ed.), *Labeling Madness* (Englewood Cliffs, N.J.: Prentice-Hall, 1974).

[10]A classic analysis of such a process is Edwin M. Lemert, "Paranoia and the Dynamics of Exclusion," *Sociometry* 25 (March 1962), 2–20.

[11]Erving Goffman, *Stigma: Notes on the Management of a Spoiled Identity* (Englewood Cliffs, N.J.: Prentice-Hall, 1963).

pers revealed that earlier in his career the senator had been treated for acute depression. Public reaction was so severe that Senator Eagleton was forced to withdraw from the ticket; McGovern's personal judgment was called into question, and his entire campaign suffered a setback from which it never recovered. There was, of course, no way of knowing if Thomas Eagleton's mental health at the time was any better or worse than that of the other candidates, Richard Nixon and Spiro Agnew, who were duly elected but who later had to resign in disgrace. It was the label from Eagleton's past, rather than his current behavior, that damned him. Interestingly, one United States president was almost certainly a sufferer from an acute manic-depressive disorder, but because he was not treated, his condition did not arouse any public concern. That president was Abraham Lincoln, whose depression was so severe his friends feared he might commit suicide. In 1841 Lincoln wrote: "If what I feel were equally distributed to the whole human family, there would not be one cheerful face on earth."[12]

THE MEDICAL MODEL

Our earlier discussion of the classification and diagnosis of mental disorders makes it clear that they are conceived primarily according to a *medical model*; that is, as though they were analogous to physical ailments like appendicitis or smallpox. The disorders are referred to as mental "illness"; the sufferers become "patients" in "hospitals" where they are given "treatment" by "doctors." This approach stems from a belief that, to a greater or lesser extent, mental disorder has some organic basis in heredity, in the chemistry of the brain, or both. If, in fact, mental disorders are simply a form of physical illness, then the medical model is appropriate. If, however, many mental disorders have some quite different origin, then rigid adherence to this model may be a waste of effort. How valid, then, is the medical model?

There is persuasive evidence that at least some mental disorders may have a hereditary basis. Children of schizophrenics have an increased probability of becoming schizophrenic as well. About 10 percent of children who have one schizophrenic parent and nearly half the children who have two schizophrenic parents become schizophrenic themselves. This finding in itself does not prove that the schizophrenia is genetically transmitted: the children might have learned to become schizophrenic through being raised by schizophrenic parents. But other evidence is more persuasive. Children who are removed from schizophrenic mothers at birth are more likely to develop schizophrenia than children taken from normal mothers at birth.[13] The same is true of children whose mother is normal but whose father is schizophrenic.[14] Studies of identical twins show that if one twin suffers from schizophrenia, the chances are 69 percent that the other twin will also be affected. The likelihood of this happening in nontwin siblings is 11 percent.[15] These findings seem to indicate that heredity may predispose some people to schizophrenia. But we cannot conclude that heredity is the main or the only factor: if it were, then any pair of identical twins would be either both normal or both schizophrenic, since they have identical heredity.

There is also persuasive evidence that chemical factors may underlie some mental disorders. Ever since scientists discovered the "flight or fight" hormone, adrenalin, we have known that certain chemicals in the body can cause marked alterations in mood and behavior. The hormonal changes of menstruation and menopause, for example, can strongly affect a woman's emotional state. We also know that many chemicals,

[12]Rona Cherry and Laurence Cherry, "Depression, the Common Cold of Mental Ailments," *New York Times Magazine*, November 25, 1973, p. 38.

[13]Leonard I. Heston, "Psychiatric Disorders of Foster-Home-Reared Children and Schizophrenic Mothers," *British Journal of Psychiatry*, 112 (August 1966), 819–825.
[14]Paul H. Wender, David Rosenthal, and Seymour S. Kety, "A Psychiatric Assessment of the Adoptive Parents of Schizophrenics," in David Rosenthal and Seymour S. Kety (eds.), *The Transmission of Schizophrenia*, (London: Pergamon, 1968), pp. 235–250.
[15]Franz J. Kallman, "The Genetic Theory of Schizophrenia," *American Journal of Psychiatry*, 103 (November 1946), 309–322.

The son of popular novelist Kurt Vonnegut, Jr., describes his treatment with Thorazine, a frequently prescribed tranquilizing drug, following his second hospitalization for schizophrenia in Vancouver, British Columbia. Also mentioned in the account are his wife Virginia and his doctor Dale.

. . .

Taking Thorazine was part of doing things right. I hated Thorazine but tried not to talk about hating it. Hating Thorazine probably wasn't a healthy sign. But Thorazine has lots of unpleasant side effects. It makes you groggy, lowers your blood pressure, making you dizzy and faint when you stand up too quickly. If you go out in the sun your skin gets red and hurts like hell. It makes muscles rigid and twitchy.

The side effects were bad enough, but I liked what the drug was supposed to do even less. It's supposed to keep you calm, dull, uninterested and uninteresting. No doctor or nurse ever came out and said so in so many words, but what it was was an antihero drug. Dale kept saying to me, "You mustn't try to be a hero." Thorazine made heroics impossible.

What the drug is supposed to do is keep away hallucinations. What I think it does is just fog up your mind so badly you don't notice the hallucinations or much else.

My father sent me an article in *Psychology Today* on an experiment with schizophrenics to evaluate the effectiveness of Thorazine. The conclusion was that patients who before their illness had been well socialized, able to make friends and function effectively on a social level, actually recovered more quickly without Thorazine than with it.

I managed to cheat on the Thorazine some. Very whimpy unheroic cheating. I deliberately misinterpreted what some nurse had said and skipped a few days. I felt great. My mother and Virginia both remarked on how fast I was recovering and how chipper I was getting. The spirit of our little apartment jumped a hundredfold. I

wasn't cramping anyone's style any more. I even got chipper enough to tell them why I was so chipper. They were a little worried about that, but I was so obviously in a good state of mind they almost started questioning Dale's judgment.

When I went to see Dale that week it was far and away the nicest visit we'd ever had. He said I was making a remarkable recovery, I was putting on much-needed weight, color was coming back into my face, I was in better shape than he had ever seen me. If I just stuck with his regimen and kept improving, I could maybe visit the farm for a few days in a couple of weeks.

He was so pleased. I was so pleased. Virginia and my mother and all my friends were so pleased. In this atmosphere of seemingly unanimous, universal pleasedness, I told him I didn't need so much Thorazine. I told him, in fact, that at least part of the reason everyone was so pleased was that I had stopped taking it and I was sure I could recover much more quickly without it.

He became a lot less pleased and came on with his antiheroics theme again. I showed him the article my father had clipped from *Psychology Today*. He wasn't impressed.

He called my mother and Virginia into the office. He explained that under no circumstances was he going to take any chances with my health. "Remember what happened last time?" Blah, blah, blah, etc.

So I was back on Thorazine again.

On Thorazine everything's a bore. Not a bore, exactly. Boredom implies impatience. You can read comic books and *Reader's Digest* forever. You can tolerate talking to jerks forever. Babble, babble, babble. The weather is dull, the flowers are dull, nothing's very impressive. Muzak, Bach, Beatles, Lolly and the Yum-Yums, Rolling Stones. It doesn't make any difference.

. . .

Source: Mark Vonnegut, *The Eden Express* (New York: Bantam, 1976), pp. 251–253. Copyright 1975 by Praeger Publishers, Inc.

from tranquilizers to industrial pollutants, can affect brain function. Lead poisoning can cause severe and permanent changes in behavior—and in our cities lead intake is about ten thousand times normal, as a result of pollution from automobile emissions. Carbon monoxide in the atmosphere, mostly from the same source, can markedly reduce efficiency in many areas of mental functioning. Insecticides, now found in virtually everything we eat, can lead to mental disturbance if the concentration is sufficiently great.

The workings of the human brain are staggeringly complex. The brain consists of approximately 10 billion nerve cells, each connected with as many as a thousand of the others, each acting as a tiny computer, receiving, processing, and transmitting information through chemical changes and electrical impulses. Some scientists believe that disordered behavior is the result of the presence or lack of certain chemical substances in specific regions of the brain, and the effectiveness of some drugs in chemically combatting some disorders does lend support to this view. So far, however, there seems to be no conclusive evidence of consistent differences in the brain chemistry of functional psychotics and normal people.

Criticisms of the Medical Model

The medical model may yet prove to be the most effective approach. But there are also several points at which the analogy between mental and physical disorders breaks down.

1. In physical disorders, such as measles or a broken leg, there is general agreement on symptoms and diagnosis. This is not so in the case of mental disorders, where there is often disagreement even on the basic question of whether someone is "ill" or not—let alone what form of "illness" he has.
2. In physical disorders, there is general agreement on the appropriate methods of treatment, and there is usually an understanding of how the treatment works. In the case of mental disorders, there is little agreement on appropriate treatment and little understanding of how some forms of treatment work, or of why they work in some cases and not in others.
3. In physical disorders the symptoms are the same in all cultures. But in the case of mental disorders the symptoms vary in acordance with local stereotypes of how a mentally disordered person is supposed to

behave.[16] In parts of Malaysia, for example, a standard schizophrenic symptom is to "run amok" in a public place after formally announcing to an authority figure—father or village headman—that one intends to do so. A teen-age girl in a pious, Catholic community in rural France would be more likely to hear voices and see visions.
4. The relationship between physician and patient in cases of physical disorder is fundamentally different from that in cases of mental disorder. In the former the patients usually define themselves as ill; the doctor confirms the diagnosis and then, with the patients' consent, initiates treatment, from which the patients can withdraw at any time. But in the latter instance, the physician defines the patients as ill (even though they may define themselves as healthy) and in some cases treats them against their will—perhaps by drugging them, locking them up, giving them electric shocks, or even severing their brain tissues. It is often not clear to whom the physician is responsible—to the family, to the state, or to the patient.

These difficulties have led to strong attacks on the medical model. One of its most outspoken critics is Thomas Szasz, a psychiatrist who asserts that "the traditional definition of psychiatry . . . places it alongside such things as alchemy and astrology, and commits it to the category of a pseudo-science."[17] In books with titles such as *The Myth of Mental Illness, The Manufacture of Madness,* and *The Myth of Psychotherapy,* Szasz insists that there is no such thing as mental illness.[18] He does not deny that the *behaviors* labeled as "mental illness" exist. He asserts only that these behaviors are not *illnesses* but merely deviations from accepted moral, legal, and social norms. Other writers have also suggested that the medical model is too

---

[16]See, for example, John Marshall Townsend, *Cultural Conceptions and Mental Illness: A Comparison of Germany and America* (Chicago: University of Chicago Press, 1978); John S. Strauss, "Social and Cultural Influences on Psychopathology," in Mark R. Rosenzweig and Lyman W. Porter, *Annual Review of Psychology* (Palo Alto, Calif.: Annual Reviews, 1979).

[17]Thomas S. Szasz, *The Myth of Mental Illness* (New York: Harper & Row, 1974), p. 1.

[18]Szasz, *ibid.; The Manufacture of Madness* (New York: Harper & Row, 1970); and *The Myth of Psychotherapy* (New York: Doubleday, 1978).

narrowly conceived. Schizophrenia and other mental disorders that lack any obvious physical basis, they argue, can be fully understood only in the social context in which they emerge. These criticisms imply a different, social-psychological model to acount for these mental disorders.

THE SOCIAL-PSYCHOLOGICAL MODEL

Whereas the traditional medical model focuses on mental disorder as a matter of individual "illness," the *social-psychological model* takes into account the wider human context: both the social factors that might drive people "mad" and the factors that might influence other people to define or label them as "mad." The most effective statements of this perspective have been those of Gregory Bateson, Thomas Scheff, Thomas Szasz, and R. D. Laing. Common to all their writings is the idea that people become mentally disordered as a result of unbearable social pressures and demands—or rather, that because of these pressures and demands, some people may take on the *sick role* that their culture has created for "mentally disturbed" persons. As we have seen elsewhere, when someone takes on the role of a sick person, many of that person's social duties are suspended. In the case of someone who is physically sick, for example, there is no expectation that he or she will turn up for work or undertake household chores. When people are mentally "sick," there is similarly no longer any expectation that they should perform their normal interpersonal duties, such as displaying love to other family members. The social-psychological theorists thus argue that some people adopt the role of a mentally disordered person as an unconscious strategy for escaping from the realities of daily living.

Bateson's Theory

The anthropologist Gregory Bateson offered a "double-bind" theory of schizophrenia.[19] Bate-

son claimed that certain patterns of family behavior can confuse and disturb children to such an extent that, in extreme cases, they may become mentally disordered. A specific form of this kind of interaction within the family is the double-bind situation, in which the child is under the pressure of two contrary demands; to obey either is to act wrongly—and there is no way of escaping the situation. For example, a father may insist that he will respect his son only if he "acts like a man," but will then punish the son for standing up to him. The bind may be made worse if another member of the family, such as the mother, is unconsciously manipulating the situation for her own ends. If the family interaction patterns consistently take this form, argues Bateson, then the individual—intellectually confused but emotionally involved with the other family members—may become severely disturbed and adopt the stereotyped role of a "sick" person.

Scheff's Theory

Thomas Scheff uses the labeling theory of deviance, and argues that the mentally disordered are social deviants of a special type.[20] In addition to the standard norms of a society—violation of which carries such labels as "criminal," "drug addict," "delinquent," and so on—there are, says Scheff, certain "residual norms" that are so much taken for granted they appear to be almost a part of nature. One does not, for example, talk to someone who is not present, or make a completely irrelevant response to every question one is asked. Violation of these residual norms is frightening to people; they assume that the violators have taken leave of their senses, so they label them as mentally ill. Thus, although a person's original violation of residual norms may have been simply a temporary deviance caused by inability to deal with a particular social situation, the individual finds that as a result of this "offense" a label has been applied by others. The person may willingly or unwillingly accept the label and continue to behave in ways consid-

[19]Gregory Bateson *et al.*, "Toward a Theory of Schizophrenia," *Behavioral Science*, 1 (October 1956), 251–264.

[20]Thomas J. Scheff, *Being Mentally Ill: A Sociological Theory* (Chicago: Aldine, 1966).

ered appropriate to the "mentally sick" role. There are, says Scheff, certain behaviors that mentally disordered people follow, the rules for which are learned in childhood from a variety of sources—anecdotes, films, comics, books, TV. Accepting the label and following these rules gives someone an opportunity to escape many personal responsibilities. Once the person has gone this far, however, it is hard to turn back; the label is not cast aside as easily as it was taken on. Scheff thus regards mental disorder as a form of learned behavior, although he sees it, of course, as a real and serious condition.

Szasz's Theory

Thomas Szasz acknowledges that mental disorders exist, but claims that they are not illnesses: they are simply "a problem in living."[21] He sees mental disorders as defective strategies that people adopt in order to handle unbearable personal and emotional situations. Human relationships are fraught with tensions and problems, and some people simply use "illness" at an unconscious level as an excuse for avoiding unpleasant reality. Those who become mentally "ill" do so because they do not have effective ways of handling their problems. Their disorder is nothing more than defective social behavior, unconsciously adopted either because other behavior has not been learned well enough or because this behavior happens to be especially useful. Psychiatrists are not physicians in a real sense; they are merely interpreters of social norms who unwittingly penalize people who have defective strategies for dealing with their problems and with other people.

Laing's Theory

The psychiatrist R. D. Laing offers a still more radical critique.[22] In his early work Laing felt that the mentally disordered were "ill" and that it was the psychiatrist's task to readapt them to

reality.[23] The problem with the mentally disordered, he suggested, is that they suffer from insecurity in their very being. As a result of social pressures, both from the family and from an unsympathetic society, some people feel their basic selves to be divided into an inner, true, authentic self and an outer, false, social front. As the boundaries between these selves collapse, the person feels the essential self to be in danger. In his early work Laing also argued strongly that the behavior of schizophrenics makes sense if viewed in the social and familial context in which the disorder arose. The seemingly rambling and irrelevant speech of schizophrenics has inner meaning to anyone who takes the trouble to learn about their previous experience and then listen with an open mind to what they say.

In his later work Laing has taken a much more radical approach[24]—so radical that many orthodox psychiatrists seem to wonder whether Laing himself isn't insane. He has rejected the conventional concept of insanity, arguing instead that "insanity" is simply one of many differing forms of consciousness, each of which is equally valid. Sane, normal leaders who boast that they have doomsday weapons, comments Laing, are as divorced from "reality" as the worst raving lunatic. He argues that psychiatrists merely interfere with a natural healing process when they try to "cure" the "mentally ill." In Laing's view, the schizophrenic experience can be a voyage into a different state of consciousness, and if the psychiatrist has any role at all, it should be as "priest," to escort the individual on this voyage. Pleads Laing, "Can we not see that *this voyage is not what we need to be cured of, but that it is itself a natural way of healing our own appalling state of alienation called normality.*"[25] Laing does not argue, however, that this different state of consciousness is a particularly blissful one. Because it has its origins in our "normal" reality, it is in a sense as "sick" as our normality is "sick":

[21]Szasz, *The Myth of Mental Illness, op. cit.*

[22] See Martin Howarth-Williams, *R. D. Laing: His Work and Its Relevance for Sociology* (Boston: Routledge & Kegan Paul, 1977).

[23]R. D. Laing, *The Divided Self* (New York: Pantheon, 1969). This book was originally published some years before in England.

[24]R. D. Laing, *The Politics of Experience* (New York: Pantheon, 1967).

[25]*Ibid.*, p. 116.

Our sanity is not "true" sanity. Their madness is not "true" madness. The madness of our patients is an artifact of the destruction wreaked on them by us and by them on themselves. . . . The madness that we encounter in "patients" is a gross travesty, a mockery, a grotesque caricature of what the natural healing of that estranged integration we call sanity might be.[26]

On the basis of studies he and his colleagues have made of schizophrenic subjects, Laing concludes that they have unconsciously adopted the "illness" as the only meaningful strategy open to them—with tragic results for themselves:

It seems to us that *without exception* the experience that gets labeled schizophrenic is a *special strategy that a person invents in order to live in an unlivable situation.* In his life situation the person has come to feel he is in an untenable position. He cannot make a move, or make no move, without being beset by contradictory and paradoxical pressures and demands, pushes and pulls, both internally from himself, and externally from those around him. . . . There is no such "condition" as schizophrenia, but the label is a social fact. . . . The person labeled is inaugurated not only into a role, but into a career of patient. . . . The "committed" person labeled as patient, and specifically as "schizophrenic," is degraded from full existential and legal status as a human agent. . . . After being subjected to a degradation ceremonial known as a psychiatric examination, he is bereft of his civil liberties in being imprisoned in a total institution known as a "mental" hospital.[27]

Evaluation

These views are emphatically rejected by most orthodox psychiatrists.[28] However compelling the arguments of the social-psychological theorists may be, they provide only a critique of the medical model, not a total refutation of it. Rather, their views offer an additional perspective. Perhaps in the future, scientists will find

some physical basis for all mental disorders. All psychological states must have some physical basis in the mental processes of the brain, and at least in principle it ought to be possible to intervene chemically and modify behavior. But the social-psychological approach implies that the *ultimate* causes of mental disorders may lie in social context, not in brain chemistry: in other words, the emotional state of the individual may influence brain chemistry, which may in turn influence behavior.[29] Because of what we already know, it is probably better to combine the approaches into a broader, sociomedical perspective: some people may be vulnerable to mental disorders because of their genetic heritage or brain chemistry, but social influences are extremely important in determining which individuals will actually be affected and how they will react.

THE TREATMENT OF MENTAL DISORDERS

The treatment of mental disorders has varied a great deal in the past and remains controversial today: indeed, the social response to mental disorder has sometimes become a problem in itself.

Historical Attitudes

Some preliterate communities regarded the mentally disordered with awe and interpreted their disjointed statements as messages from the supernatural. More commonly, traditional societies attributed the behavior of the mentally disordered to the presence of some evil spirit that had entered the body. One of the earliest types of surgery of which we have evidence, in the form of mutilated skull bones, is called trephining. The operation, used by the Egyptians 4,000 years ago, consisted of chipping a hole in the skull to allow an evil spirit to escape. In medieval Europe the Church began to define the mentally disor-

---

[26]*Ibid.,* p. 101.

[27]*Ibid.,* pp. 78–79, 83–84.

[28]See Miriam Siegler and Humphrey Osmond, *Models of Madness, Models of Medicine* (New York: Macmillan, 1974).

[29]R. D. Laing now accepts this view, in "R. D. Laing Interviewed by Ian Robertson," *Granta* (Cambridge University), October 1977, pp. 4–8.

The "crib" was a device used in the United States at the end of the last century for the purpose of restraining and punishing mental patients. Its use reveals how far the hospitals had departed from their initial purpose of providing care and asylum for the mentally disordered. *(The Bettmann Archive)*

dered as heretics and witches: the clergy reasoned that if an evil spirit was visiting the body, it must have been invited there through a pact with the devil. In order to make the body a less habitable place the afflicted were flogged or starved, and if that brought no results, in many cases they were hanged or burned at the stake. The Church also used elaborate rituals of exorcism to drive out the spirits. Up to the late eighteenth century, both church and state held the mentally disordered at least partly responsible for their condition, which was seen as a form of moral degeneracy. Considered dangerous to society, they were kept chained in cells. Gradually, specialized institutions developed for the control of lunatics. One of the earliest (c. 1400) was St. Mary of Bethlehem Hospital in London—"Bedlam" for short, a name that soon became a common word for the conditions that prevailed there. The hospital even sold tickets to public viewings of the more violent inmates in their cells. The less violent were allowed out to beg on the streets.

The first great change in attitudes toward the mentally disordered came during the French Revolution, when the physician Philippe Pinel took charge of the Paris institution for the insane. Pinel was a humane reformer, and his first act was to release the inmates from their chains. By handling them with kindness and concern, he demonstrated that they could respond to treatment. His approach became known as "moral treatment" and inspired social movements to campaign for safe, humane places of refuge—"asylums"—for mentally disordered persons.

In colonial America there were no special facilities for the mentally disordered until the time of the War of Independence, when a few private organizations began to establish asylums.

State mental institutions were created only in the mid-nineteenth century, largely as a result of the campaigns of a social movement led by the New England humanitarian Dorothea Dix. But demand for places far exceeded the supply, and the asylums faced many problems. The mentally disordered did not always respond to treatment, the institutions were overcrowded, many patients were unruly, and the staffs were overworked. As a result, the asylums eventually became institutions for the custody of, rather than the treatment of, the mentally disordered—little more than places where people were committed, often involuntarily and often for life, as a means of ridding society of their troublesome presence.

The federal government began to provide mental health care facilities only after World War II. During the war some 1.8 million men among the 15 million examined were rejected by the Selective Service because of alleged psychiatric problems, and a further 750,000 were discharged for similar reasons.[30] Public concern at the previously unsuspected extent of mental disorders led to the establishment of the National Institute of Mental Health three years later. Yet conditions in the mental hospitals improved very little; as late as the 1950s they were widely described as "snake pits." The number of patients in the mental hospitals grew rapidly until by 1955 it peaked at a total of 559,000. Since then there have been consistent efforts to find alternatives to mental institutions,

---

[30]David Mechanic, *Mental Health and Social Policy* (Englewood Cliffs, N.J.: Prentice-Hall, 1969), p. 55; Nina Ridenour, *Mental Health in the United States: A Fifty-Year History* (Cambridge, Mass.: Harvard University Press, 1961), p. 60.

chiefly through the treatment of the mentally disordered by private psychiatrists or in general hospitals and outpatient clinics (today there are more psychiatric admissions to general hospitals than to the state mental hospitals). Another alternative was offered by the Community Mental Health Centers Act of 1963, which created a system of centers in which the mentally disordered can be treated in the context of their own community.

Contemporary Treatment

The contemporary treatment of mental disorders, both inside and outside the state mental hospitals, is usually based on one or more of three broad approaches: psychotherapy, somatic therapy, and chemotherapy.

Psychotherapy. This term refers to all treatment involving personal interaction between the patient and a psychiatrist. There are many forms of psychotherapy, but most are based to some extent on Sigmund Freud's theory that mental disorders are unconscious strategies, or "defense mechanisms," that people adopt to avoid emotional pain, even though the strategies may cause more pain than the problems they were meant to evade. Psychotherapists usually assume that the patients are the victims of unconscious conflicts that influence their behavior and interpretation of reality. The intention of psychotherapy is to bring understanding of the reasons for the condition, in the hope that this understanding will help the patient to modify the behavior. Psychotherapy is often successful, particularly with neurotics, but the overall recovery rate of those who have been treated with psychotherapy is not significantly higher than the rate for those who have received no treatment at all. Psychotherapy is also an expensive and time-consuming form of treatment.

Somatic Therapy. This term refers to all physical treatment administered directly to the body. One such technique is psychosurgery, which involves the severing or removal of brain tissue for the purpose of changing the patient's behavior. The most controversial form of psychosur-

gery is lobotomy, an operation in which nerves in the frontal lobes of the brain are severed. During the 1950s about 50,000 lobotomies were performed, mostly on violent patients. The operation subdued them—but in some cases it also turned them into little more than vegetables. The use of lobotomies has been much restricted since that time, but even so, hundreds are still performed each year.

Another form of somatic therapy is electroshock treatment in which electrodes are placed on either side of the head and a bolt of electric current of between 150 and 170 volts is sent into the patient's brain for a period of a second or less. When this method was originally introduced in the 1930s, patients were given electric shocks while fully conscious, and a team of attendants was needed to hold them down so that they would not break their limbs or spines during their writhings and convulsions. Despite these precautions, fractures were frequent and deaths not uncommon. Patients often needed a dose of strychnine to get them breathing again after the treatment. Today an injection containing a mixture of anesthetic and muscle relaxant is administered to render the patients unconscious and reduce the convulsions. The treatment is particularly effective for cases of depression, which can usually be cured after six or eight sessions, and is sometimes helpful in treating schizophrenia. The use of electroshock treatment is very controversial, however. Patients often hate and fear the method and complain that it causes confusion and loss of memory. No one knows exactly how electroshock treatment works or what temporary or permanent effects it has on the brain.[31]

Chemotherapy. Treatment of mental disorder through the use of drugs was initiated in 1954, when tranquilizers were first introduced into mental hospitals. Since then chemotherapy has revolutionized the therapeutic approach and has been a major factor in reducing the number of mental patients in hospitals in recent years; many patients who might have spent their lives in institutions have been released, and many

[31]See Samuel Chavkin, *The Mind Stealers: Psychosurgery and Mind Control* (Boston: Houghton Mifflin, 1978).

others have been made more amenable to psychotherapeutic treatment. Two main types of drugs are used in chemotherapy: tranquilizers, which calm excitable or violent patients, and antidepressants, which relieve extreme depressive symptoms. About 20 million prescriptions for antidepressants are written each year; they appear to be effective in about 60 percent of cases. Psychiatrists do not know precisely how these drugs work, nor why they work on some people but not on others who seem to have identical symptoms. Moreover, drugs do not cure mental disorders; they merely suppress the symptoms. For this reason their use is sometimes criticized as being merely a form of "psychic first aid," alleviating the symptoms without getting to the underlying causes.[32]

THE INCIDENCE OF MENTAL DISORDERS

Who are most likely to be affected by mental disorder, and what do we know about their social characteristics? At first this question might seem easy to answer: a sociologist would simply have to find the figures for the incidence of mental disorder and then correlate them with particular variables such as social class, population density, race, and so on. But there are severe methodological problems. How do we determine, for example, the incidence of schizophrenia? Mental-hospital statistics alone are misleading. Different hospitals have different criteria for admission, and different psychiatrists have different criteria for diagnosis. It may also be that members of one social class are more likely to seek treatment than members of another class, and this would bias the data. Moreover, there is evidence that people are more likely to be hospitalized if there is a mental hospital in their vicinity, so the number and location of these institutions influence the number of recorded cases in particular regions. Statistics on patients in private nursing homes or outpatient clinics are often difficult to obtain. It is even more difficult to get facts and figures on

people who are being treated privately, not to mention the people who have mental disorders but are not being treated at all. Despite these methodological problems, however, the evidence is overwhelming that susceptibility to mental disorders and the likelihood of hospitalization are strongly linked to social class.

Mental Disorders and Social Class

One of the earliest investigations into the social correlates of mental disorder was conducted by Robert Faris and Warren Dunham in Chicago in the 1930s.[33] They obtained information on all the patients in both private and public mental hospitals in Chicago and then plotted the residential distribution of the patients. The results showed clearly that mental disorders were not randomly distributed throughout the area. Instead, the highest rates were in the city center, in areas of high population density and poor socioeconomic conditions. The affluent suburbs had much lower rates. The figures were influenced by the fact that many "skid row" alcoholics and others suffering from organic psychoses had congregated in the inner city, but even allowing for their presence, there was little doubt that mental disorder was linked to place of residence and social class. Faris and Dunham attributed this fact to the social disorganization of the city center, with its high crime rates, lack of employment, social instability, and extremely crowded living conditions.

A. B. Hollingshead and F. Redlich conducted another revealing study in New Haven, Connecticut, in the late 1950s.[34] They were able to get data not only from the public and private hospitals in the area but also from private psychiatrists. They found that schizophrenia was eleven times more prevalent for the lower class than for the upper class if measured in terms of hospitalization rates. This difference was largely due to the fact that people of lower social status were more likely to be kept in institutions for a

---

[32]See Peter Shrag, *Mind Control* (New York: Pantheon, 1978).

[33]Robert E.L. Faris and H. Warren Dunham. *Mental Disorders in Urban Areas* (Chicago: University of Chicago Press, 1939).

[34]August B. Hollingshead and Frederick Redlich, *Social Class and Mental Disorder* (New York: Wiley, 1958).

longer period. For private treatment, however, the upper class had a much higher rate than the lower strata. It seemed that the upper-class people were far more likely to define their problems in psychological terms and to seek treatment. Both the nature and length of treatment varied with social class. Upper-class patients were more likely to be treated with psychotherapy and to be institutionalized only for brief periods; lower-class patients were more likely to be treated with drugs or electroshock therapy, and they took longer to recover. Over 70 percent of the lower-class patients were referred for treatment by courts or welfare agencies, whereas some 70 percent of the upper-class patients were referred by their families or sought treatment themselves.

Leo Srole and his associates undertook a more ambitious study in midtown Manhattan in the 1950s.[35] Investigating a random cross section of the entire population of the area, they conducted extensive interviews with 1,660 people to find out if they had ever had a nervous breakdown, sought psychotherapy, or shown neurotic symptoms. They then gave the information to a team of psychiatrists, who rated each case on the degree of psychiatric impairment. The findings were surprising and disturbing. Over 23 percent of the population were considered "significantly" impaired in mental functioning, and only 18 percent were considered healthy. The degree of mental health correlated very closely with social class. The psychiatrists considered nearly one person in every two in the lowest stratum psychologically impaired, but the rate fell to one in eight for the highest stratum. It was also clear that members of the upper class tended to seek early treatment. A fifth of the upper-class people who were rated as impaired were receiving therapy at the time, and over half had received psychiatric treatment at one time or another—usually as outpatients. However, only 1 percent of the lower-status groups were receiving therapy at the time, and only 20 percent of them had ever had psychiatric treatment—al-

most always in mental hospitals. Thus the lowest socioeconomic group was the one most in need of attention but the one receiving the least of it.

Twenty years later, in 1974, Srole traced 695 members of his original sample and reinterviewed them. He compared the mental-health ratings of those subjects then in their forties with those who were in their forties twenty years before, and found that the proportion in need of psychiatric help had dropped by half. The reason for this change, Srole believes, lies not in social changes since the 1950s but rather in changes that took place when those who were in their forties in the 1970s were in their formative years. The generation that was in its forties in the 1950s had experienced the Great Depression and harsh child-rearing practices, whereas the generation in its forties in the 1970s escaped these influences. Also, Srole's analysis of comparative data rejects as a myth the prevalent view that mental disorders are more common in cities than in small communities or rural areas, a view that his original study had mistakenly been interpreted as supporting.

The poor and the deprived, then, seem more prone to mental disorders than those who are better off. The reasons are presumably linked to their social status, which influences attitudes, values, education, personality development, job satisfaction, economic well-being, and sense of personal autonomy.[36] The poor are much less likely to seek treatment, which means that their condition may well deteriorate before they receive attention; and they are more likely to become institutionalized and receive less individual attention than upper-class people.

Other Correlates of Mental Disorders

Although social class seems to be the crucial variable, other social characteristics are also linked to mental disorder.[37]

[35]Leo Srole *et. al.*, *Mental Health in the Metropolis: The Midtown Manhattan Study*, Books I and II, rev. ed. (New York: Harper & Row, 1978).

[36]Melvin L. Kohn, "Social Class and Schizophrenia: A Critical Review and a Reformulation," *Schizophrenia Bulletin*, no. 7 (Winter 1973), 60–79.

[37]For discussions of some correlates of mental disorder, see *The Journal of Health and Social Behavior*, vols. 16 (December 1975) and 17 (September 1976).

Age. The aged are more likely to suffer some forms of mental disorder, particularly organic psychoses. Degeneration of the brain cells is one reason for this, but it is also likely that the sick role commonly offered to the old in our society has an effect. Since we have no rewarding social role to offer the elderly, they are often left with a crushing sense of isolation and uselessness.

Race. Blacks are more likely than whites to suffer mental disorders, and their hospitalization rate is about 33 percent higher than that of whites. There seem to be two main reasons for this trend: first, blacks are more likely to have lower social status; second, their problems are more likely to be treated through hospitalization than through private therapy. If these factors are taken into account, the different rate of mental disorder for blacks and whites virtually disappears.[38] Minorities do suffer the additional problem that they are unlikely to be treated by health-care practitioners who come from similar cultural backgrounds. Of all the psychiatrists and other doctoral-level providers of services in psychology, only 0.9 percent are black, 0.7 percent Asian, 0.4 percent Hispanic, and 0.1 percent American Indian.[39]

Marital Status. Married people of both sexes have lower rates of mental disorder than people who are single, widowed, or divorced. The rate of mental disorder is somewhat higher for unmarried men than unmarried women.[40]

Sex. Men and women are equally likely to be treated for mental disorder, but the nature of the diagnosis and treatment tends to vary according to sex. Men are more likely to be diagnosed as psychotic; women, as neurotic. Women are also more likely to be admitted to mental hospitals, and they have higher rates of depression. There is

some evidence that psychiatrists—who are overwhelmingly male—apply different standards to men and women. For example, sexual promiscuity or aggressive behavior in a man might be overlooked, but might be considered signs of mental disturbance in a woman.[41]

Research findings thus consistently show that mental disorders recur in particular social contexts among particular social groups—presumably those that are most subject to stress. This finding lends support to a social-psychological view of the origins of at least some forms of mental disorder.

MENTAL DISORDER AND SOCIAL CONTROL

Society has always tried to exercise at least minimal control over persons defined as mentally disordered, since some of them are a danger to themselves and others, and some are incapable of taking care of themselves. But the social control of people labeled as mentally disordered has sometimes taken on sinister implications.

In the Soviet Union, many dissenters in recent years have been sent not to concentration camps in Siberia but to insane asylums. The list of poets, writers, and intellectuals who have been defined by the Soviet authorities as mentally ill rather than criminal is a lengthy one, and includes people who would be highly respected in the West. Soviet psychiatrists may not be as cynical as we might think; given that their "reality" is a Marxist-Leninist one, it may seem obvious to them that people who are not adapted to that reality are psychologically impaired. But whether they are fully aware of the political implications of their diagnoses or not, these Soviet psychiatrists are clearly using the label of mental illness as a method of social control.[42]

[38]George J. Warheit, Charles E. Holzer, and Sandra A. Arey, "Race and Mental Illness: An Epidemiological Update," *Journal of Health and Social Behavior*, 16 (September 1975), 243–356.

[39]President's Commission on Mental Health, *Report to the President*, p. 6.

[40]National Institute of Mental Health, *Statistical Note 104*, 1974.

[41]See Phyllis Chesler, *Women and Madness* (New York: Avon, 1972); President's Commission on Mental Health, *Report to the President, op. cit.*, p. 6.

[42]For a graphic account of Soviet political psychiatry, see Ludmilla Thome, "Inside Russia's Psychiatric Prisons," *New York Times Magazine*, June 12, 1977, pp. 26–71.

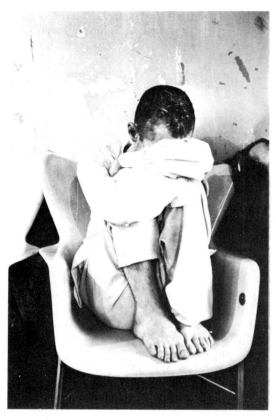

Is this mental patient immersed in some other, private reality—or simply disordered? The work of radical psychiatrists has made the issue a highly controversial one.

The Labeling of Nonconformists

Does anything similar to what happens in Russia occur in the United States? We certainly do not have an officially sponsored system for labeling political dissenters as mad. But do we use the label of mental illness, perhaps unintentionally, as a means of social control over people who do not conform to social expectations? As we have seen, Thomas Szasz argues that this form of social control is a major function of modern psychiatry: "I have long maintained that the psychiatrist impersonates a medical role; actually he is an interpreter of moral rules and an enforcer of social laws and expectations."[43]

Certain violations of established moral and legal norms, says Szasz, are liable to be defined as "sick"; the officials who make the definitions assume that their own standards are somehow natural and healthy. In the late nineteenth and early twentieth century, for instance, masturbation was considered a symptom of mental disorder, and some asylums had separate wards for patients supposedly suffering from "masturbatory insanity." Or to take a more modern example, it was only in 1974 that the American Psychiatric Association finally removed homosexuality from its official list of mental disorders.[44] To make his point, Szasz quotes from a handbook for college psychiatrists written by Dana L. Farnsworth, a Harvard psychiatrist and leading authority on college psychiatric services in the United States.

> Library vandalism, cheating and plagiarism, stealing in the college or community stores or in the dormitories, unacceptable or anti-social sexual practices (overt homosexuality, exhibitionism, promiscuity), and the unwise and unregulated use of harmful drugs, are examples of behavior that suggest the presence of emotionally unstable persons. . . . [45]

Such a view of deviant behavior, Szasz suggests, has no medical basis whatsoever. The acts involved are simply violations of certain established social norms. Criminal penalties seem inappropriate because the violators are young and often privileged, so the label of "emotionally unstable" is used instead. Szasz believes that just as the clergy once labeled certain deviants "heretics," so the psychiatrist now labels them "mentally ill": psychiatrists may not fully understand their role, but what they too are doing in effect is exerting social control and ensuring conformity

[43]Thomas S. Szasz, "The Psychiatrist as Double Agent," Trans-action, 4 (October 1967), 16.

[44]For a case study of how American psychiatrists voted this "mental illness" out of existence, see Malcolm Spector, "Legitimizing Homosexuality," Society, 14 (July–August 1977), 52–56.

[45]Dana L. Farnsworth, Psychiatry, Education, and the Young Adult, quoted in Szasz, "The Psychiatrist as Double Agent," op. cit., p. 17.

to the norms of society. The label "deviant" serves as an implied threat to restrain deviant behavior. If deviance does take place, the label at least defines the deviant as being outside the "normal" community. And as conflict theory would suggest, the right to apply these definitions to others depends very largely on the power and influence of the people concerned:

> Administrators and faculty members have the privilege of incriminating students as mentally ill; students have the privilege of incriminating their fellow students as mentally ill; but students do not have the privilege of incriminating administration and faculty members as mentally ill.[46]

The psychiatrist Robert Coles takes a similar view. In the early days of the civil rights movement in the South, Coles obtained firsthand experience of how black "troublemakers," whom he considered quite normal, could be regarded as mentally disordered. The courts, he found, would "summon all the authority of medicine and science to the task of defending the status quo—which meant putting firmly in their place (a hospital or clinic) those who chose to wage a struggle against the status quo."[47]

Coles detects the same type of attitude in the reaction to student protestors in the late 1960s and early 1970s. Instead of considering the demands of the students and evaluating their citicisms of society, people in positions of power assume there is something wrong with the students rather than society. Since there is really nothing to protest about, the students must be "immature," or "out of touch with reality," or have "exhibitionist tendencies," or suffer from "authority problems." They are described as "acting out their fantasies" or having "poor ego controls," which make them "rebel against parent surrogates" and issue "unrealistic" statements. Coles notes that psychiatric labels such as these are not used indiscriminately against everyone who has antisocial or aggressive tendencies; they are applied only to those who challenge the existing order:

What are we to say, for instance, about the "early childhood" or "mental state" of political leaders or business leaders or labor leaders who lie or cheat or order thousands to go off to fight and kill? What kind of "psychological conflict" enables a man to be an agent of the Central Intelligence Agency, or a pilot who drops napalm bombs? . . . Moreover, if students are out to kill their "parent surrogates," what indeed of our desires as grown-ups to squelch the young, subtly and not so subtly degrade them, be rid of them— because they inspire envy in us; because they confront us with all the chances we forsook, all the opportunities we have lost, all the tricks and compromises and duplicities we have long since *rationalized* or *repressed* or *projected?*[48]

Involuntary Commitment

In 1971 five inmates were released from an Ohio mental institution for the criminally insane. They had never been convicted of any crime—in fact, they had been sent there merely for observation—yet they had been kept in the institution for periods of from twenty-two to forty-one years because, literally, they had been forgotten. They were released only because one psychiatrist had noticed them, considered them fit to be discharged, and taken up their case. He estimated at the time that there were over one hundred other patients in the institution who were in a similar position.[49] Since then many similar cases have been discovered in mental hospitals all over the United States. How can this happen?

For one thing, people whose behavior seems odd are frequently referred by the police and courts to mental hospitals for psychiatric examination. Until 1975 it was possible for such people to be confined against their will for long periods—even for life—if they were judged mentally ill. In most states the legal procedures, if any existed, were entirely inadequate. And because they were suspected of being mentally disordered, the protection offered persons facing involuntary incarceration was far less than that granted persons facing a similar fate in the courts

---

[46]Szasz, "The Psychiatrist as Double Agent,"*op. cit.*, p. 16.
[47]Robert Coles, "A Fashionable Kind of Slander," *Atlantic*, 226 (November 1970), 54.

[48]*Ibid.*, p. 55.
[49]*Los Angeles Times*, April 24, 1971, p. 6.

because they were suspected of being criminals. In 1975 the Supreme Court ruled that people may be committed to mental institutions against their will only if they are dangerous to others or are incapable of looking after themselves. This was a significant step forward, but the possibility still remains that people may be committed against their will without sufficient cause or that, like their predecessors before 1975, they may gradually become forgotten once they have spent some time within the institutional walls.

It may be that much of the case against psychiatry as a form of social control is overstated. But the situation is serious enough for the American Psychological Association, representing over 30,000 psychologists, to have made an official statement on the subject in 1972. The association declared that it

> condemns the practice, wherever it may occur, of suppressing or neutralizing political dissenters by diagnosing them as mentally ill and committing them to mental hospitals. We consider it the responsibility of individual psychologists to oppose such practices within the organization in which they are employed and, if they do not succeed in changing the practices, to dissociate themselves from personal complicity in them.[50]

THE MENTAL HOSPITALS

Since the mid-1950s many efforts have been made to reform mental hospitals, yet the criticisms continue. The focus of criticism has changed, however, from an earlier ethical concern about what went on inside mental hospitals to questioning whether these hospitals can deal appropriately with mental disorders at all.

The main objection to mental hospitals is that, however benign their intentions, they tend to adapt individuals to the needs of the system rather than the other way around. Isolation from the community seems a poor preparation for inmates who, on release, will have to continue their lives in the communities from which they have been separated—and it seems especially

poor when it is dramatically intensified by the physical conditions of these institutions. The architecture of mental hospitals, most of which are many decades old, is usually forbiddingly bleak: long gloomy corridors, dormitories without privacy, day rooms monitored by administrators boxed off in glass observation cubicles, and factory-type lighting are common features. In addition, most hospitals currently hold many more patients than they were designed for; and because a small minority may attempt to escape, doors and windows are usually kept locked.

Since hospital authorities must maintain close control over those inmates who might be prone to violence or suicide, everyone tends to come under surveillance. Officials find their jobs easier if there are straightforward regulations applicable to all patients, and staff members enforce these rules by a system of punishments and rewards (such as granting or withholding permission to see films). A great deal of attention is devoted to record-keeping, food preparation, administering drugs, restraining difficult patients, and scheduling daily activities; there is not much time left for interpersonal relationships or therapy. The patients have little time with psychiatrists: most of their contact with hospital personnel is with the aides who control the wards and the access of patients to clinical staff. More than half of the aides have not completed high school and most of them have had no prior training in mental-health care.

The Mental Hospital as a "Total Institution"

One of the most influential research studies of mental hospitals is that of Erving Goffman, [51] who did his research while working for a year as a hospital aide. Moving freely among the patients, talking to them and noting down his impressions, Goffman analyzed mental hospitals in terms of his concept of the *total institution*, a place of work or residence in which a number of people in a similar situation are cut off from the

---

[50]*American Psychological Association Monitor*, 4 (1973), 1.

[51]Erving Goffman, *Asylums: Essays on the Social Situation of Mental Patients and Other Inmates* (Garden City, N.Y.: Anchor, 1961).

wider society and lead an enclosed, formally administered life. In the total institution there is an absolute cleavage between the inmates and the administrators. A hierarchy of officials has control over the inmates, whose activities are scheduled and monitored from above. Entry into a total institution is a process of transition, in which the individual gives up a former, self-determining role and takes on the role of inmate. On entry the inmates are identified, examined, and coded; their personal possessions and clothes are taken from them and uniforms are substituted. All experience of the institution impresses on the inmates their sense of personal inadequacy. Behavior is controlled by rewards and punishments and the inmates are entirely dependent on the institution for all physical needs.

To be successful in the total institution, the inmate has to learn to play by the rules: the mental patient or prisoner who makes trouble is immediately defined as being unfit for release.

Goffman found that mental patients tended to be treated in terms of the institution's expectations of them: normal behavior was not considered significant and was not entered on their records, but a single episode of abnormal behavior was immediately noted. Individual patients, he found, tended to adopt one of three strategies: they would withdraw into themselves and ignore the institutional setting; they would openly challenge the system and "make trouble"; or they would conform to the rules and surrender their personal autonomy.

Goffman's conclusion is now widely accepted:

Many social scientists and medical practitioners are concerned that mental hospitals may worsen rather than improve the condition of some patients. A prolonged stay in one of these institutions could prove a depressing and depersonalizing experience.

many patients are suffering not so much from their original condition as from the depersonalizing effects of the mental hospital themselves. The atmosphere of the institutions aggravates their mental problems, and they learn the sick role from other inmates around them. The longer they remain confined, the less the chance of their being released (when release does occur, it is usually within the first six months). Once a person has been inside an institution continuously for more than two years, the chances of being released are very small indeed.[52] The danger is particularly acute for young schizophrenics. If they are not discharged quickly, they are apt to remain in the institutions for very long periods, and are more likely to suffer periodic recurrences even if they are released. The problem of the long-term effects of hospitalization is now widely recognized, and in most hospitals every effort is made to release new patients before they suffer a loss of hope and personal responsibility. Since 1955 there has been a steady decline in the number of resident patients, even though the number of admissions has been rising. Most people admitted to a mental hospital for the first time with a diagnosis of schizophrenia are now discharged within one month.

"Pseudopatients" in the Mental Hospital

A study of mental hospitals published in 1973 attracted national attention. A California psychiatrist, D. L. Rosenhan, who had long been skeptical of the way people are categorized as mentally ill, decided to find out what would happen if perfectly sane people tried to gain admission to mental hospitals. He reasoned that if the imposters behaved normally but were still diagnosed as mentally disordered, serious questions would be raised about traditional methods of diagnosis and about the state of our mental hospitals.[53]

Rosenhan arranged for eight of his associates, none of whom had any previous history of mental disorder, to present themselves at twelve different mental hospitals in five states on the East Coast and the West Coast. The hospitals were carefully selected to include some of the most prestigious institutions in the United States. On arriving at the hospitals, the pseudopatients told interviewers that they had one symptom: they heard a voice saying a single word (such as "thud," "empty," or "hollow"). Apart from giving this information and falsifying their names and jobs, they provided completely accurate life histories.

All the pseudopatients were diagnosed as schizophrenics and admitted. Once inside the hospital, they behaved normally and no longer claimed to hear voices. In not a single case was their normality detected by a staff member. However, many of the inmates approached the pseudopatients and accused them of being perfectly sane journalists or academics who were "checking up on the place." The pseudopatients were held for an average of nineteen days—the shortest stay was a week and the longest was fifty-two days—and they were released not as cured but as schizophrenics "in remission."

All the behavior of the pseudopatients was interpreted on the basis of the diagnosis, rather than the other way around. For example, when one pseudopatient took notes of his experiences, this fact was noted in his record as "engages in note-taking behavior" and treated as a pathological symptom—by an attendant who was herself taking notes of the note-taking. Details of the pseudopatients' life histories were evaluated in the light of the false diagnosis and were interpreted as reasons for their subsequent schizophrenic condition. The staff tended to treat the patients as though they were scarcely aware of their presence. They avoided eye contact and personal conversation:

> A nurse unbuttoned her uniform to adjust her brassiere in the presence of an entire ward of viewing men. One did not have the sense that she was being seductive. Rather, she didn't notice us. A group of staff members might point to a patient in the day room and discuss him animatedly, as if he were not there.[54]

[52]Morton Kramer, *et al.*, "A Historical Study of the Disposition of First Admissions to a State Mental Hospital," *Public Health Monographs*, no. 32 (Washington, D.C.: U.S. Government Printing Office, 1955).

[53]Rosenhan, *op. cit.*

The problem was not that the staff were inefficient or unkind; on the contrary, they usually seemed dedicated and concerned. But the mental hospitals were simply not organized to deal adequately with the problems of the patients:

> Powerlessness was evident everywhere. The patient is deprived of many of his legal rights by dint of his psychiatric commitment. He is shorn of credibility by virtue of a psychiatric label. His freedom of movement is restricted. He cannot initiate contact with the staff, but may only respond to such overtures as they make. Personal privacy is minimal. Patient quarters and possessions can be entered and examined by any staff member, for whatever reason. His personal history and anguish are available to any staff member who chooses to read his folder, regardless of their therapeutic relationship to him. His personal hygiene and waste evacuation are monitored. . . . Psychological categorization of mental illness is useless at best and downright harmful, misleading and pejorative at worst. . . . How many are wrongly thought to be mentally ill? How many have been stigmatized by well-intentioned, if erroneous, diagnoses?[55]

There is an interesting postscript to Rosenhan's experiment. Officials at a mental hospital that was not included in his study were skeptical of his findings, and felt that in their hospital, at least, pseudopatients would be detected. Rosenhan announced that he would try to infiltrate pseudopatients into this hospital, and members of the staff were warned to be on the lookout for them. In fact, Rosenhan did not attempt to send any pseudopatients to the hospital—but over a three-month period at least forty-one genuine patients were judged by the staff to be Rosenhan's imposters.

Few would deny that mental hospitals have their uses and that in many cases they may offer the most appropriate treatment available. But the shortcomings of mental hospitals are also being recognized, and it is accepted that hospitalization may create problems for many patients as well as solve them. Mental hospitals are increasingly being regarded as a last resort. The present goal is to admit all patients voluntarily if possible: committing agencies have to show why the patient cannot be better dealt with in an ordinary hospital, in an outpatient ward, or under the care of a private psychiatrist. The population of mental hospitals has dropped from the peak of over 559,000 in the mid-1950s to less than 200,000 today.

The release of so many mental patients has led to further problems, however, as facilities for their care in the community are often hopelessly inadequate. In a classic case of a solution to a social problem causing a new problem, the massive discharges of patients from state mental hospitals over the last few years has created a

---

[54]*Ibid.*, p. 256.
[55]*Ibid.*, pp. 251, 256–257.

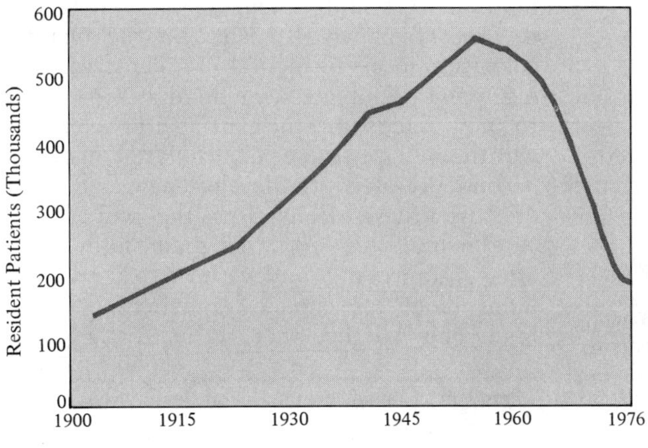

FIGURE 13.1 **Inpatient population of state and county medical hospitals: 1900–1976.** The inpatient population of state and county mental hospitals rose steadily from the turn of the century until 1955, since when it has decreased sharply. The downward trend has occurred because hospitals now keep patients for much shorter periods than before, and are even releasing long-term residents into the community whenever possible.

(Ellen L. Bassuk and Samuel Gerson, "Deinstitutionalization and Mental Health Services,"*Scientific American* 238 [February 1978], p 46; Bureau of the Census, *Statistical Abstract*, 1978, p 116.)

series of "psychiatric ghettos" in inner cities.[56] Thousands of patients have been turned out to live in poverty in run-down hotels—unwanted, unemployed, and victimized by criminals. Many of these patients, it seems, are being discharged for economic reasons. Each patient in a state mental hospital costs the taxpayers an average of $15,000 a year; some state officials are thus strongly tempted to encourage the discharge of as many patients as possible, so that the federal welfare system assumes the burden of supporting them instead. Some of the discharged patients have been institutionalized for many years—in some cases, for most of their adult lives. They are capable of surviving in the community, but only if they receive help and support—in finding a place to live, in getting a job, in receiving continuing mental-health services. Yet all too often, this help is lacking. As the President's Commission on Mental Health reported:

A basic premise of the movement toward commu-

nity-based services was that care would be provided in halfway houses, family and group homes, private hospitals and offices, residential centers, foster care settings, and community mental health centers. . . .

In the few communities that had this broad range of services, many patients made effective transitions from state hospitals to the community. The majority of communities, however, did not have the necessary services, were not given proper assistance to develop them, or enough time to prepare to receive returning patients.

Time and again we have learned . . . of people with chronic mental disabilities who have been released from hospitals but who do not have the basic necessities of life. They lack adequate food, clothing, or shelter. . . . We have seen evidence that half the people released from large hospitals are being readmitted within a year of discharge . . . Many of the readmissions to state hospitals could have been avoided if comprehensive assistance had existed in their communities.[57]

CONFRONTING THE PROBLEM

Mental disorders constitute a complex problem for which there are no easy solutions. Our existing methods of diagnosis and treatment need careful reexamination, and social policy on mental disorders must now be seen to have ramifications beyond the field of medicine. How can we confront the problem in the future?

Improved Drug Therapy. One significant trend is the increasingly sophisticated use of drugs. Although drugs are sometimes criticized as "chemical straitjackets" used to control the mentally disordered person while avoiding the

"real" problem, they have had dramatic effects on the lives of millions of neurotic and psychotic people, and they have greatly eased the burden on staffs in mental institutions. But drug therapy cannot as yet cure mental disorders; it simply represses the symptoms, making possible the use of other therapies. Research on the pharmacological aspects of mental disorder is continuing, with three objectives in mind. First, we need to know exactly how the existing drugs work and why they work on some people but not on others. Second, we need to develop new and more effective drugs—ideally, drugs that will actually cure mental disorders rather than simply alleviate symptoms. And third, we need to know much more about the chemical functioning of the brain and whether there is in fact a purely

[56]Ellen L. Bassuk and Samuel Gerson, "Deinstitutionalization and Mental Health Services," *Scientific American*, 238 (February 1978), 46–53; Antonio G. Olivieri, "Mentally Ill, Dumped and Isolated," *New York Times*, March 11, 1978, p. 23; Jack Anderson, "Release of Patients Is Creating Psychiatric Ghettos," *Daily News* (New York), February 18, 1978, p. 8.

[57]President's Commission on Mental Health, *Report to the President, op. cit.*, p. 5.

chemical basis for all types of mental disorder. If this is the case, then in theory at least, we should be able to combat any neurosis or functional psychosis with the appropriate chemical treatment.

The Therapeutic Community. Another important development is that of the "therapeutic community," an innovation that is now widely used in mental hospitals. Under the traditional system, the staff could spend very little time in therapy with patients; an hour a day would be considered generous. But if the entire community of the institution is mutually involved in therapy, a more supportive and constructive environment can be created. Group therapy is not just an economy measure. It encourages the development of interpersonal relationships by giving patients the opportunity to take an interest in one another, and it helps them to see their own problems more clearly. This development is typical of the general change taking place in the climate of the mental hospitals.

Behavior Modification. A technique that is being used with some success in many cases is behavior modification, a form of treatment based on fundamental learning principles. The assumption behind the technique is that abnormal behavior, unless it has an organic origin, is learned and can therefore be unlearned. Accordingly, appropriate behavior is rewarded and inappropriate behavior mildly punished. The nature of the rewards and punishments varies from individual to individual, but might include the granting or withholding of social approval or small luxuries. There has been some criticism of behavior modification, however, on the grounds that although it may eliminate inappropriate behavior, it does nothing to deal with the original causes of the disorder. There is also concern that there may be an overemphasis on punishment rather than rewards—punishments that include solitary confinement, nausea-inducing drugs, and painful electric shocks.[58]

Community Mental Health Centers. Another development, which in the long run could revolutionize our treatment of, and attitudes toward, mental disorder, is the community mental-health center. In the 1950s a social movement arose to release as many patients as possible from state mental hospitals and to treat them in the community from which they came—if possible, without actual hospitalization. The movement won strong support, and in 1963, Congress passed the Community Mental Health Centers Act. The goal is to integrate mental-health services and social services so that a wide range of resources can be made available to the troubled individual. Schools, hospitals, labor organizations, courts, police, welfare agencies, and interested citizens can participate in a variety of programs that emphasize the prevention of mental disorders or their cure through rapid community intervention. It is also hoped that, in addition to providing facilities for the mentally disordered, the centers will offer other services, such as marriage counseling; in this way, the stigma of attending the centers may be lessened. The centers are located in "catchment areas" of between 75,000 and 200,000 persons and are required to be "comprehensive"; that is, they must offer inpatient care, outpatient care, day hospitalization, twenty-four-hour emergency care, and "consultation and education." Over 700 of these centers are now in operation, and it is hoped that by the early 1980s there will be a center for every 100,000 members of the population. The centers have faced many early difficulties, ranging from shortages of funds to entanglement in community political issues,[59] but their very flexibility gives them the potential to develop new and effective ways of confronting the problems of mental disorder. In particular, these centers or other similar facilities must develop a range of readily accessible services for the patients who are being released in such large numbers from the state mental hospitals.

Changing Attitudes and Values. Whatever their potential, these new approaches may have

[58]Church, *op. cit.*, p. 11; Seymour L. Hallek, "Legal and Ethical Aspects of Behavior Control," *American Journal of Psychiatry* 131 (April 1974), 381–385.

[59]David F. Musto, "Whatever Happened to Community Mental Health?" *The Public Interest*, no. 39 (Spring 1975).

relatively little effect unless there are accompanying changes in public attitudes and values. We need to acknowledge how very little we know about mental disorders, and we need to recognize that we should not allow old assumptions to stand in the way of progress. At the same time, we should not accept new approaches uncritically, however appealing. We need to remove the stigma from mental disorder because this stigma makes people reluctant to look for help and, if they do undertake treatment, makes their readjustment to society much more difficult. Finally, we must have the courage to ask what it is about the very structure and nature of American society that gives us such a high incidence of mental disorders compared to other nations. Are we prepared to identify and change those aspects of our society and our relationships with one another that can drive people to that state we call madness?

SUMMARY

1. Mental disorder is a serious problem in American society. Because many victims go untreated or are treated privately, the problem is more widespread than official statistics suggest.

2. Whether someone is mentally disordered is to some extent a matter of definition. The current practice is to divide mental disorders into two broad categories, neuroses (involving relatively mild personality disturbance) and psychoses (involving severe impairment of mental functions). Organic psychoses are caused by damage to brain tissues; neuroses and functional psychoses, such as schizophrenia, are thought to be partly or wholly caused by social and psychological factors.

3. From the functionalist approach the problem is related to social disorganization: the structure of society is such that certain individuals or groups are under undue psychological stress or have inadequate access to mental-health care. The conflict approach notes that incidence rates and quality of treatment vary accordingly to social class and emphasizes that the label of mental disorder may be used as a means of social control. The deviance approach sees the mentally disordered as deviants who violate social norms concerning reality; this behavior may be learned through labeling, and the stigma of mental disorder may hamper the patients' adjustment to society.

4. Mental disorder has been regarded for some time as an "illness" and treated in terms of a medical model. The analogy between physical and mental "disease" is an imperfect one, however, and theorists such as Bateson, Scheff, Szasz, and Laing have proposed a social-psychological model that sees mental disorder as a form of learned behavior. In this model, people unconsciously play a sick role in order to escape intolerable social pressures, but then become trapped in the role.

5. Mental hospitals and improved care facilities have been created largely as a result of pressure from social movements. The three principal methods of treatment today are psychotherapy, somatic therapy, and chemotherapy.

6. As a result of methodological problems, the incidence of mental disorders is not easy to determine. It is clear, however, that social class is a crucial factor. Other important variables are age, race, marital status, and sex.

7. Some writers have argued that the label "mentally disordered" is sometimes used as a means of applying social control to deviants, particularly those who challenge the existing political order.

8. There is growing realization that commitment to mental hospitals may actually worsen rather than improve the condition of patients, largely because the mental hospital is, in Goffman's terms, a "total institution." Rosenhan's study of pseudopatients in a mental hospital

raises disturbing questions about professionals' ability to distinguish the sane from the insane. The release of many patients from hospitals into communities unprepared to receive them has created a new problem.

9. Important trends in confronting the problem of mental disorders are improved drug therapy; the use of the therapeutic community; behavior modification; and community mental-health centers. It is important, however, that social attitudes toward the mentally disordered also change.

GLOSSARY

Chemotherapy. Medical treatment of a disorder through the use of drugs.

Functional psychosis. A psychosis that has no obvious physical basis and whose origin is presumed to be partly or wholly psychological.

Medical model. A model of mental disorders in which they are viewed and treated as though they were analogous to physical ailments.

Mental disorder. A psychological inability to cope realistically and effectively with the ordinary challenges and tasks of the real world.

Neurosis. A personality disturbance, usually involving anxiety but not a sharp break with reality.

Organic psychosis. A psychosis that has an identifiable physical basis resulting from damage to brain tissues.

Psychosis. A serious form of mental disorder involving a sharp break with reality.

Psychotherapy. Treatment of a mental disorder through interaction between the patient and psychiatrist aimed at improving the patient's understanding of, and ability to solve, the problem.

Schizophrenia. The most common form of functional psychosis, involving a separation of intellectual and emotional functions and disordered behavior.

Sick role. The pattern of behavior society expects of a person who is ill.

Social-psychological model. A model of mental disorders in which they are viewed not as illnesses but as an unconscious strategy for escaping intolerable social pressures.

Somatic therapy. Medical treatment of a disorder through the use of surgery or other techniques applied directly to the body.

Stigma. The mark of social disgrace applied to deviants by those who consider themselves normal.

Total institution. A place of work or residence in which a number of people are cut off from the wider society and lead an enclosed, formally administered life.

FURTHER READING

CHESLER, PHYLLIS. *Women and Madness.* New York: Avon, 1972. An argument that psychiatric diagnosis and practice are influenced by our cultural heritage of sexism. Chesler relates various forms of alleged mental disorder in women to sexual inequality in our society.

COLEMAN, JAMES C. *Abnormal Psychology and Modern Life.* 5th ed. Glenview, Ill.: Scott, Foresman, 1976. The standard introductory text on abnormal psychology, with a comprehensive and up-to-date discussion of the various forms of mental disorder and the methods of treating them.

GOFFMAN, ERVING. *Asylums: Essays on the Social Situation of Mental Patients and Other Inmates.* New York: Doubleday, 1961. A sensitive account of life in a mental hospital, written by an acute participant-observer. Goffman suggests that the routines of life in a "total institution," such as a mental hospital, can worsen rather than improve the condition of inmates.

————, *Stigma: Notes on the Management of a Spoiled Identity*. Englewood Cliffs, N.J.: Prentice-Hall, 1963. An exploration of the concept of stigma and its meaning for those who are regarded as abnormal by other members of society.

GROSS, MARTIN L. *The Psychological Society*. New York: Random House, 1978. An important and controversial analysis of psychiatry, psychotherapy, and psychoanalysis; the book offers a well-documented critique of the excesses and failures of the mental-health industry and its professionals.

LAING, R. D. *The Politics of Experience*. New York: Pantheon, 1967. A powerful and often poetic book in which Laing presents his controversial argument that "insanity" is simply another form of consciousness—and that "sane" behavior is in reality dehumanizing and alienating.

PERRUCI, ROBERT. *Circle of Madness*. Englewood Cliffs, N.J.: Prentice-Hall, 1974. A critical account of the mental hospital, by an author who contends that mental illness is a myth.

PRESIDENT'S COMMISSION ON MENTAL HEALTH. *Report to the President from the President's Commission on Mental Health*. Washington, D.C.: U.S. Government Printing Office, 1978. A useful survey of the state of American mental-health services, with a series of recommendations for improvements in the system.

ROSEN, GEORGE. *Madness and Society*. London: Routledge & Kegan Paul, 1968. A historical perspective on mental disorder in which the author discusses earlier beliefs about the disorders and the methods that were used to treat them.

SCHEFF, THOMAS J. *Being Mentally Ill: A Sociological Theory*. Chicago: Aldine, 1966. Scheff analyzes mental illness in terms of a labeling theory of deviance and argues that certain people become "boxed in" to a socially defined role as a "sick" person.

SCHRAG, PETER. *Mind Control*. New York: Pantheon, 1978. A comprehensive critique of the modern American psychiatric establishment. The book challenges many popular assumptions about mental disorders and psychiatric goals and methods.

SIEGLER, MIRIAM, and HUMPHREY OSMOND. *Models of Madness, Models of Medicine*. New York: Macmillan, 1974. A work that offers a strong argument in favor of the medical model of such illnesses as schizophrenia and provides a useful critique of other, nonmedical models.

SZASZ, THOMAS. *The Myth of Mental Illness*. Rev. ed. New York: Harper & Row, 1974. A hard-hitting book in which Szasz, a radical critic of contemporary psychiatry, outlines his argument that mental disorder is not an illness and that the psychiatrist is simply an agent of social control.

14
Crime and Violence

THE PROBLEM

For at least a decade, Americans have perceived crime as one of the most serious social problems facing the country. Although a 1963 Harris poll found that only 2 percent of Americans regarded crime as a serious issue, attitudes had changed dramatically five years later: in 1968 no less than 65 percent of the population regarded crime as the most important problem confronting the nation. By 1971 some 70 percent of those surveyed expressed the view that "law and order have broken down in the country," and in 1974 another poll found that more than half of the population is afraid to walk alone at night.[1] Since then, the rates for most forms of crime have continued to rise, and the issue remains one of the most worrying and intransigent of our social problems.

American crime statistics certainly give cause for concern. On average, a serious crime is committed in the United States every three seconds. There is a burglary every ten seconds, a larceny-theft every five seconds, and a motor-vehicle theft every thirty-three seconds. A violent crime—the type the public fears most—takes place every thirty-one seconds on average: an aggravated assault every minute, a robbery every seventy-eight seconds, a forcible rape every eight minutes, and a murder every twenty-seven minutes.[2]

Compounding the problem of the sheer prevalence of crime, particularly violent crime, is the state of the entire criminal-justice system, which many Americans seem to believe is little more than a shambles—a cumbersome, ineffectual, irrational, and unjust system in which, more often than not, crime pays. A 1978 Gallup poll, for example, found that only 47 percent of the public had favorable attitudes toward the police, only 19 percent had such attitudes toward the courts, and only 14 percent had them toward the prisons and other correctional facilities.[3]

The efficiency of the police is in doubt, for only about a fifth of all serious crimes result in an arrest,[4] and the arrest rate for less serious crimes is even lower. Some groups, particularly among racial minorities and the poor, remain suspicious of the police and fear that they may abuse their powers; other groups, particularly among the white middle class, feel that the police are needlessly hampered in their work by an undue concern for the civil rights of suspected offenders. The courts also are criticized, both for their interminable delays in bringing cases to a conclusion, and for their sentencing practices. Opinion polls during the 1970s have consistently shown that over 80 percent of the public believe that the courts do not treat criminals harshly enough.[5] In addition, there is concern about wide discrepancies in sentences meted out in apparently similar cases, about the disparities between the harsher sentences received by "ordi-

[1]Louis Harris, *The Anguish of Change* (New York: Norton, 1973), p. 169; Bureau of the Census, *Statistical Indicators, 1976* (Washington, D.C.: U.S. Government Printing Office, 1977), p. 6.
[2]Federal Bureau of Investigation, *Crime in the United States: Uniform Crime Reports, 1977.* (Washington, D.C.: U.S. Government Printing Office, 1978), p. 6.

[3]*New York Times*, April 10, 1978.
[4]*Crime in the United States, op. cit.*, p. 160.
[5]*Statistical Indicators, 1976, op. cit.*, p. 238.

nary" criminals in contrast to the light fines typically imposed on "white collar" offenders such as industrial polluters, corporate price-fixers, wealthy tax-evaders, or high-ranking embezzlers. The prisons, too, have become a focus of public attention, for they and other correctional facilities are clearly failing in what Americans believe to be their main function: the rehabilitation of their inmates. The rate of *recidivism*—that is, of a convicted person's return to crime—is disturbingly high. Nearly two-thirds of those arrested each year have been convicted at least once before in the previous five years. Far from reforming criminals, it seems, the prisons are breeders of crime. The social problem of crime and justice is thus a twofold one: how to reduce crime as far as possible while maintaining a criminal justice system that is efficient and fair.

Before we look at the problem of crime and violence in more detail, we must first ask what exactly a crime is, and who the criminals are. We must also consider the accuracy of our crime statistics, for they are highly relevant both to public perceptions of crime and to the shaping of public policy toward the problem.

What Is Crime?

An important element in social control in all modern societies is law. Unlike informal norms, a *law* is a formal social rule that is enforced by a political authority. A *crime* is simply an act prohibited by a law. Generally speaking, the state—or the dominant class that controls the state—designates as crime those acts that violate certain strongly held norms and values. The laws serve to make social reaction to these violations more orderly by defining the specific offenses, the persons to whom each law applies, and the kind of punishment a violation entails.

However, not all behavior that violates important norms is prohibited by law: in some cases the regulation of such conduct is left to the informal process of public disapproval; in other cases laws are simply drafted poorly, resulting in "legal loopholes" that may come as a surprise to those who made the laws. At the same time, on the other hand, there are laws prohibiting behavior

that, because of changing norms, is no longer regarded as wrong by the society. These obsolete laws—such as those that forbid card-playing on Sundays or the sale of contraceptives—often remain on the statute book but tend not to be applied. Without the sentiment of a community behind it, a law loses its moral and practical force, as the American experiment with Prohibition so effectively demonstrated.

Some acts, such as murder, are regarded as criminal in virtually every human society because they involve conduct that, if tolerated, would make preservation of social order impossible. Other acts, however, are not universally regarded as evil, and laws prohibiting them are simply a reflection of the values of a particular society or its rulers at a particular point in time. These offenses may seem trivial or even laughable to outsiders. In medieval Iceland, for example, it was a criminal offense to write verses about another person—even verses of praise—beyond a certain length.[6] In modern South Africa it is a serious offense, punishable by imprisonment and whipping, for persons of different races to have or to attempt to have sexual intercourse with one another.[7] In many Arab countries the use of marijuana is acceptable, but the use of alcohol is illegal; in the United States the reverse is generally true. In short, laws are relative to the societies that create them. All laws are thus in a sense political, for it takes a deliberate act of political authority to define what conduct is punishable by the state.

Who Are the Offenders?

The likelihood of arrest for criminal activity in the United States is not equally distributed throughout the population. The person arrested for a crime is disproportionately likely to be young, male, a city resident, and a member of a racial minority.

Young people appear to commit far more than

[6]Edwin H. Sutherland and Donald R. Cressey, *Principles of Criminology*, 7th ed. (Philadelphia: Lippincott, 1966), p. 16.
[7]Ian Robertson and Phillip Whitten, "Sexual Politics in South Africa," in Glen Gaviglio and David E. Raye (eds.), *Society As It Is: A Reader*, 2nd ed. (New York: Macmillan, 1976).

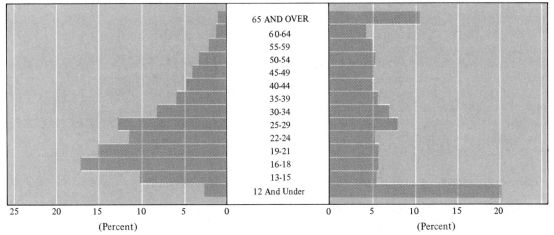

Persons Arrested
Distribution by age, 1977

Total Population
Distribution by age, 1977

65 AND OVER
60-64
55-59
50-54
45-49
40-44
35-39
30-34
25-29
22-24
19-21
16-18
13-15
12 And Under

25   20   15   10   5   0
(Percent)

0   5   10   15   20
(Percent)

FIGURE 14.1 **Persons arrested compared with total population.** Young people commit far more than their share of crime. A major reason for the increased crime rate of recent years has been the sharp increase in the proportion of young people in the population. Unless other factors intervene, the crime rate should stabilize or even drop in the future as the proportion of young people shrinks once more. (Federal Bureau of Investigation, *Uniform Crime Reports,* 1978, p. 171)

their share of crime, including the crimes that the FBI regards as the most serious—murder, rape, auto theft, aggravated assault, larceny, burglary, arson, and robbery. In 1977, persons under fifteen years of age accounted for 8 percent of all arrests; those under eighteen, for 24 percent; those under twenty-one, for 40 percent; and those under twenty-five, for 56 percent. Youths under eighteen committed 21 percent of the serious violent crime and 46 percent of the serious property crime.[8] Some 73 percent of all serious crimes are committed by persons under twenty-five. Convicted juvenile offenders are far more likely than other juveniles to become adult offenders.

Young or old, the offender is likely to be male. Males are arrested about five times as often as females. Only in juvenile runaway cases do female offenders feature in the statistics as often as their male peers. There are probably two reasons for this differential arrest rate. One is the aggressiveness that American society encourages in males, in contrast to the passivity and conformity that it expects of females. The second is the tendency of law-enforcement agencies to deal more leniently with female offenders. Nevertheless, crime among females is increasing at a much faster rate than among males. Between 1973 and 1977, arrests for serious crimes increased 11 percent for males under age eighteen, but 19 percent for females under that age. However, males account for 90 percent of arrests for violent crime; in terms of serious crimes, women are arrested primarily for larceny.[9]

Both the crime rate and the arrest rate increase with the size of the community. Over 50 percent of all serious crimes against the person take place in twenty-six major cities, containing less than a fifth of the population. Cities with more than 250,000 inhabitants have twice the arrest rate of suburbs and three times the arrest rate of rural areas.[10] Within the city, crime tends to be concentrated in particular sections. Those parts of the city that are changing rapidly and have a poor, transient population have much higher

[8]*Crime in the United States, op. cit.,* pp. 169–171, 180.

[9]*Crime in the United States, op. cit.,* p. 171. See, also, Freda Adler, *Sisters in Crime: The Rise of the New Female Criminal* (New York: McGraw-Hill, 1976).

[10]President's Commission on Law Enforcement and the Administration of Justice, *The Challenge of Crime in a Free Society* (Washington, D.C.: U.S. Government Printing Office, 1967), p. 28.

crime rates than more stable, residential areas. The fact that, until very recently, the American population was growing steadily younger and more urban probably accounts for much of the increased crime rate of the past several years. It does not provide a full explanation, however, since the crime rate has increased even faster than these two forces.[11]

One other group that is disproportionately vulnerable to arrest is the black population. Black adults are arrested five times as often as white adults.[12] One reason for this high arrest rate is that blacks apparently do commit more than their share of such crimes as assault and robbery.[13] The black community is a poor one, and there is a high correlation between unemployment, poverty, and the arrest rate for these kinds of crime. (In the past, other minority groups—such as immigrant Irish or Poles—have had a similarly high rate of arrest, but as the economic position of these groups has improved, their arrest rates have come to conform to the national rate.) An additional reason for the higher arrest rate of blacks may be prejudice against minority and lower-class groups: many studies have shown that the likelihood of arrest, prosecution, conviction, and imprisonment for an offense decreases as the social status of the offender rises. Even judges are not immune to such prejudice. In one experiment some three dozen judges were given fact sheets on a hypothetical case and asked to determine an appropriate sentence. The sheets contained the following basic information:

> "Joe Cut," 27, pleaded guilty to battery. He slashed his common-law wife on the arms with a switchblade. His record showed convictions for disturbing the peace, drunkenness, and hit-run driving. He told a probation officer that he acted in self-defense after his wife attacked him with a

broom handle. The prosecutor recommended not more than five days in jail or a $100 fine.[14]

On half the sheets, however, "Joe Cut" was identified as white and the other half as black. The judges who thought he was white gave him a jail sentence of three to ten days; the judges who thought he was black gave him a sentence from five to thirty days.

How Accurate Are Crime Statistics?

American arrest statistics yield a profile of the "typical" criminal as young, male, urban, perhaps black. But, in fact, the statistics give us only a very partial view of who the offenders really are. The basic source for crime statistics is the Uniform Crime Reports (UCR) that the FBI issues each year based on data collected from local police forces. Naturally, the UCR covers only reported crimes and actual arrests. Furthermore, the UCR deals with certain categories of crime, concentrating—for reasons known only to the FBI—on the serious crimes mentioned earlier: murder, rape, robbery, arson, aggravated assault, auto theft, burglary, and larceny of $50 and over. The UCR thus focuses on crimes that are more likely to be committed by persons of lower social and economic status, and in so doing, probably omits the great majority of the crimes committed in the United States. In particular, the FBI report does not cover the many crimes more typically committed by middle- and upper-class people: tax evasion, fraud, bribery, embezzlement, false advertising, industrial pollution, corporate price-fixing, stock manipulation, and so on. The inclusion of the respectable corporate executives, lawyers, stockbrokers, politicians, shopkeepers, physicians, and others who are usually responsible for such crimes would significantly alter the profile of the "typical" criminal, who would become markedly older, whiter, and more suburban.

Equally important is the fact that the UCR statistics exclude the most successful criminal, the one who escapes arrest—and at one time or

---

[11]Gresham M. Sykes, *Criminology* (New York: Harcourt Brace Jovanovich, 1978), p. 143.

[12]President's Commission on Law Enforcement and the Administration of Justice, *op. cit.*, p. 44.

[13]Michael J. Hindelgang, "Race and Involvement in Common Law Personal Crimes," *American Sociological Review* 43 (February 1978), 93–109.

[14]Donald Jackson, "Justice for None," *New Times*, January 11, 1974, p. 51.

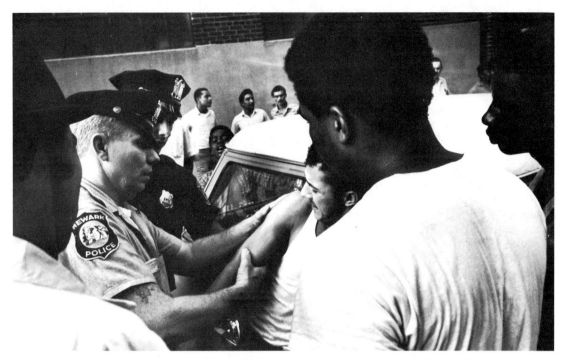

The likelihood of arrest and conviction is far greater for lower-class than for middle-class people, even though many studies have shown that the actual crime rate is similar for both groups (although they tend to commit different kinds of crime).

another that includes most of us. A large number of self-report studies, in which people are asked to give anonymous details of any crimes they may have committed, have shown that "close to 100 percent of all persons have committed some kind of offense, although few have been arrested."[15] The great majority of juveniles and adults have committed one or more crimes. In what way, then, do these people—the supposedly law-abiding majority—differ from the criminal minority who actually get arrested? One possibility is that for most people, criminal acts are very few and far between; those who get arrested are more likely to be making a career of crime, or at least to be breaking the law more regularly. But the main difference is probably in the kind of crime committed. The poor tend to commit the only type of crimes that are available to them—high-risk, low-yield crimes such as burglary, larceny, or robbery. The criminal better-off have no need to engage in such crimes, for they can indulge in more appealing, low-risk, high-yield crimes such as "padding" expense accounts or evading income taxes.

Data on many of these white-collar crimes are not even collected, and many such crimes go either undetected or unreported to the police. Careful surveys suggest that the actual crime rate in the United States is at least twice as high as the reported figures indicate, and perhaps even higher.[16]

---

[15]Eugene Doleschal and Nora Kapmuts, *Toward a New Criminology* (Hackensack, N.J.: National Council on Crime and Delinquency, 1973), p. 4.

[16]See President's Commission on Law Enforcement and the Administration of Justice, *Task Force Report: Assessment of Crime* (Washington, D.C.: U.S. Government Printing Office, 1967); and "Unreported Crime Twice as High," *LEAA Newsletter*, 3 (March 1974), 1–11.

One other factor distorts the crime statistics: the manipulation of data by the police and public officials. Politicians and police are under great pressure to keep the crime rate low, and one way to do this is to include serious crimes in different, less serious categories. In 1974, for example, the federal National Crime Panel found that in Philadelphia, where the mayor was the former commissioner of police, the actual crime rate was five times as high as the official statistics indicated. But the classic example of how reporting procedures can influence the apparent crime rate occurred in Chicago between 1928 and 1931. The Chicago Crime Commission, believing that the true crime rate was being obscured by police reporting methods, had insisted on a change in the way data were collected and presented. In those three years the number of robberies increased from 1,263 to 14,544 per year, and the number of burglaries soared from 879 to a spectacular 18,689 per year.[17] Most criminologists believe that much of the apparent increase in crime during the 1960s was actually the result of more accurate police reporting methods, combined with a greater willingness of the poor and minority-group members to report crimes to the police, whom they did not fear as much as they had before the civil rights legislation of the 1960s.[18] The "typical" criminal, then, is in reality the criminal who typically gets arrested for committing one of the select category of crimes that the FBI includes in its reports.

ANALYZING THE PROBLEM

A major concern of sociologists and criminologists has been to find the causes of criminal behavior. In this quest the functionalist, conflict, and deviance approaches have all been helpful, particularly as there is no single theory that seems able to explain all forms of crime.

The Functionalist Approach

The functionalist approach sees crime largely as the product of social disorganization caused by the breakdown of social control in large urban communities within a rapidly changing industrial society. Sociologists have long contrasted the small, stable, traditionalist communities of the past, centered around the kinship group and local parish, with the impersonal, urban societies of the modern world. Crime in small, traditional communities appears to have been relatively rare: deeply embedded in social relationships with family and neighbors, most people behaved in a conventional manner, and any criminal impulses were quickly noted and curbed by the community as a whole. In a large, modern, urbanized society, however, the social environment becomes disorganized. Traditionalism gives way to uncertainty; kinship ties, to the fleeting, anonymous contacts of the city; the shared values of the small community, to the different and often clashing values of a heterogeneous mass society. Deviance of every kind is the result, and the high rates of crime and violence in large cities is one of the more striking symptoms of this social disorganization.

An early functionalist theorist, Emile Durkheim, commented that crime was part of the price that a free society must pay. What Durkheim meant was that the vastly greater individual liberty that a modern society offers its members encourages some of them to violate social norms, including those that prohibit various criminal acts. The very loosening of social controls that makes a modern society so much more free than a traditional one is also an invitation for some people to abuse that freedom. Many of the social changes that urbanization and industrialization have brought about have been beneficial, or functional, for the maintenance of society; but they may also have had the unanticipated dysfunction of creating a climate in which crime can flourish.

[17]Donald R. Cressey, "The State of Criminal Statistics," *National Probation and Parole Journal.* 3 (July 1957), 232.
[18]Sykes, *op. cit.*, pp. 143–144.

The Conflict Approach

The conflict approach emphasizes that the law is the outcome of a political process.[19] It is only because some groups try to impose their will on others, and have enough power to do so successfully, that there are laws—and therefore criminals—at all. While there may be a social consensus on the need for laws against some acts, such as murder, there is much less agreement on the need for other laws, such as those that attempt to regulate private conduct with regard to, say, smoking marijuana or engaging in homosexual activity. Legal definitions of right and wrong are the prerogative of the group or groups that enjoy power in society, and these groups are inclined to make criminal those acts that conflict with their own interests and values. As Karl Marx pointed out, the laws in every society tend inevitably to favor the interest of the "haves" rather than the "have-nots."

The conflict approach can also be usefully applied to the entire criminal-justice process. We have seen that criminal activity occurs at every level of society, but that it is the poor, the young, and the powerless who are disproportionately likely to be arrested, charged, convicted, and imprisoned. At every stage in the process, those who have a higher social and economic status have an advantage over those who do not: their crimes are less likely to be detected or reported; they are more likely to be granted, and to be able to afford, bail; they can better afford to hire skilled lawyers and can pay for expert defense witnesses; and even if they are convicted, their sentences are likely to be significantly milder than those meted out to people of lower status. Without a conflict analysis of the issue, the fact that our prisons are disproportionately filled with younger, urban, male, minority-group members would be inexplicable.

The issue of crime and violence is also deeply embroiled in conflicts of values and arouses more heated controversy over the best public policies to follow than nearly all other social problems. There are value conflicts, for example, over whether the police should have greater or less power; over whether the law should regulate private morality; over whether tougher sentences would reduce crime or brutalize criminals still further. Such conflicts make concerted social action against the problem all the more difficult to achieve.

The Deviance Approach

Sociologists have always seen crime as one of the most obvious and socially damaging forms of deviance, and the deviance approach has provided the umbrella for most theoretical and research work on the problem of why some people become criminals. The question has been answered in many ways over the centuries. Traditionally, criminals have been regarded as innately wicked, their criminality the result of some inherited and ineradicable vice. The culmination of this tradition occurred at the turn of the century in the work of Cesare Lombroso, who tried to discover physical criteria that could be used to distinguish criminals from noncriminals. After extensive studies of the inmates of prisons, Lombroso claimed to have identified certain physical signs common to "born criminals," such as long lower jaw, a flattened nose, and insensitivity to pain.[20] Later research has shown, of course, that there are no differences in physical appearance between criminals and noncriminals.

The problem with these traditional theories was that they did not take into account the relative nature of crime, that is, that each society defines crime differently and that a crime in one society might be a virtue in another, or even in the same society at a different time. Supposed inborn characteristics are thus useless as an explanation of a culturally relative phenomenon. Sociologists now accept that criminal behavior is learned behavior. The criminal is simply a so-

[19] See William Chambliss, *Law, Order, and Power* (Reading, Mass.: Addison-Wesley, 1971); Ian Taylor, Paul Walton, and Jock Young (eds.), *Critical Criminology* (London: Routledge & Kegan Paul, 1975); William Chambliss and Milton Mankoff (eds.), *Whose Law? What Order?* (New York: Wiley, 1976); and Richard Quinney, *Class, State, and Crime: On the Theory and Practice of Criminal Justice* (New York: McKay, 1977), and *Criminology*, 2nd ed. (Boston: Little, Brown, 1979).

[20] Cesare Lombroso, *Crime: Its Causes and Remedies* (Boston: Little, Brown, 1911).

cial deviant who violates certain norms that are encoded in law. In answer to the question of why some individuals rather than others become deviants, four main theories have been proposed: anomie, labeling, differential association, and control theory.

The Criminal as Product of Anomie. The theory of *anomie* as an explanation of deviance was developed by the functionalist theorist Robert Merton and is an attempt to link deviant behavior to the presence of social disorganization.

Anomie is essentially a state of normlessness. An anomic person is one who has failed to learn, or who has rejected, important social norms and whose behavior is therefore unregulated by them. Anomie arises from a form of social disorganization in which there is a discrepancy between social goals and the social opportunities available to achieve them. The United States is a materialistic society in which a high value is placed on acquiring wealth, a value strongly reinforced by the myth that great rewards are equally available to those who work hard. The fact is, of course, that the social structure puts some people at a distinct disadvantage in the competition for success. Consequently, people who accept the goal of economic success but who lack approved means of achieving it (such as a high-paying job) may fall into a state of anomie, continuing to accept the socially approved goal but resorting to socially disapproved means of achieving it, such as theft or embezzlement.

Deviance is therefore intimately linked to the norms and values of society as a whole. If a society prizes material goods but denies people equal access to them, it invites theft. If a society prizes sexual experience but restricts sexual relations to marriage, it invites prostitution. If a society prizes novelty and entertainment but offers them only to those who can pay for them, it invites delinquency among penniless juveniles in search of kicks. As Merton explains:

> It is only when a system of cultural values extols, virtually above all else, certain *common* success-goals for the population at large while the social structure restricts or completely closes access to approved modes of reaching these goals for a

considerable part of the same population, that deviant behavior ensues on a large scale.[21]

Anomie theory is particularly useful in explaining property crimes, such as theft or robbery, although it is less useful when applied to certain other crimes, such as murders committed in a moment of passion. But the theory does show how the very structure of society places greater pressure on some people than on others to deviate from the norms encoded in the law.

The Criminal as Product of Labeling. The labeling theory of deviance, as outlined by sociologists such as Howard Becker, views deviance as a social process rather than as a characteristic of the deviant. The deviant, Becker argues, is simply someone to whom the label of deviant has been successfully applied by society.[22]

Labeling theorists point out that many people occasionally engage in deviant, criminal behavior, such as inflating insurance claims or using illicit drugs, but because these people are not discovered and labeled, they do not regard themselves as criminals. Most young people, for instance, take part at some time or another in mild forms of juvenile delinquency—breaking curfews, shoplifting, violating drinking laws, and so on. Generally this behavior is not maintained for any length of time. It is often merely an exploratory adventure in the process of growing up, and it usually passes almost unnoticed. But if significant people such as teachers, parents, or even the police become aware of the behavior, they may label the offenders "delinquent" and treat them accordingly. Gradually the individuals concerned may come to accept this definition of themselves, and to construct their behavior, choice of companions, and interests on the basis of this self image. The imposed label thus becomes a prophetic one, and the deviant behavior eventually becomes habitual.

---

[21]Robert K. Merton, *Social Theory and Social Structure,* 2nd ed. (Glencoe, Ill.: Free Press, 1957), p. 146.

[22]Howard S. Becker, *Outsiders: Studies in the Sociology of Deviance* (New York: Free Press, 1963). See, also, Walter Grove (ed.), *The Labeling of Deviance* (New York: Wiley, 1975); and Edwin M. Schur, *Labeling Deviant Behavior: Its Sociological Implications* (New York: Harper & Row, 1971).

Many radical sociologists combine the labeling theory with the conflict approach, pointing out that the labeling process frequently involves a difference of interests and values between the labelers and the labeled. To understand why some acts are defined as crimes and why some crimes are defined as more serious than others, we have to look at the people who have the power to define criminal behavior and to label others in terms of this definition. For example, the reason that the minor larcenies of the lower class are often regarded as more serious than white-collar, middle-class crimes involving much greater sums may be that the laws and the courts reflect middle-class rather than lower-class interests. In the same way, the fact that in the United States the consumption of alcohol is permitted but the use of marijuana has generally been prohibited in the past may be explained on the grounds that alcohol, though potentially addictive and dangerous, is the favored drug of the powerful, whereas marijuana has been the favored drug of the powerless young. As people in positions of power and influence become more tolerant of marijuana, the laws are gradually being eased, and what was once a serious crime is becoming either a minor offense or no offense at all. The characteristics of marijuana have not changed: the significant change is in the attitudes of those who have the power to apply labels that will stick.

The Criminal as Product of Differential Association. Another influential theory to account for criminal deviance is that of Edwin Sutherland, who argued that people may become criminals if their socialization provides instruction in criminal techniques or encourages a defiant attitude toward prevailing social norms and laws. Just as one youth might learn conformist, nondelinquent behavior from intimate associates, so might another youth learn deviant, delinquent behavior by growing up among people who are contemptuous of the law.

Sutherland's theory is essentially a sophisticated version of the old "bad companions" formula; as he put it "a person becomes delinquent because of an excess of definitions favorable to violation of the law over definitions unfavorable to violation of the law."[23] The number of contacts with people who are contemptuous of the law is a major factor in determining whether a person will tend toward delinquency; but the intensity, duration, and frequency of the contacts are also relevant, along with the age at which the contacts are experienced. Thus, prolonged contact at an early age with law-abiding people may see someone safely through an adolescence surrounded by delinquent peers, but a less favorable early environment followed by further socialization in a delinquent subculture might predispose that person to criminal behavior.

The theory of differential association lends strong support to the view that imprisonment may have counterproductive effects, particularly on juveniles. Separated from society and thrown into the company of experienced criminals, the young person encounters "an excess of definitions favorable to violation of the law" and is quite likely to learn new ways to burgle, rob, or defraud. Imprisonment may thus "harden" criminals rather than rehabilitate them.

One problem with differential-association theory is that it does not lend itself to empirical research and therefore is difficult to validate. How does one analyze in practice such concepts as the duration, frequency, and intensity of contacts, and which gets the most weight? Nonetheless, the theory does offer a common-sense explanation of some kinds of crime, and particularly of the tendency for certain ex-convicts to become habitual offenders.

The Criminal as Product of Inadequate Social Control. Another approach to the problem sees crime as the result of a lack of social control over individual behavior. According to Travis Hirschi, the crucial element in social control is the bond that exists between individual and society.[24] If that bond is weak, people feel little pressure to conform; but if the bond is strong, people have too much to lose by deviating and therefore tend to obey the law.

---

[23]Sutherland and Cressey, *op. cit.*, p. 81.

[24]Travis Hirschi, *Causes of Delinquency* (Berkeley, Calif.: University of California Press, 1969).

Hirschi suggests that there are three elements in the bond between individual and society. The first is *attachment*. The more strongly the individual feels attachment to others, the more that person takes their attitudes into account, and the less likely he or she is to engage in criminal deviance. Delinquency among young people, for instance, is typically most intense at the time when parent-child attachments are at their weakest; conversely, juvenile delinquents tend to become more law-abiding when they become romantically attached and especially when they marry. The second element is *commitment*. The more a person is committed to conventional society—by holding a job, attending school, taking part in the social life of the community—the greater stake that person has in conventional behavior, and the more prohibitive the risks of criminal activity: there is too much to lose. By the same token, many crimes are committed by people who have little commitment to conventional society. This is especially true of street crimes, particularly those involving needless violence: the offenders lack commitment to society and feel they have virtually nothing to lose. The third element in the social bond is *involvement*. The more deeply and actively involved a person is in the social and economic life of the community, the less time and opportunity there is for deviant behavior. Those who are trying to raise families, win promotion at work, or pass examinations seem less likely to become involved in criminal deviance than those who are habitually unemployed or otherwise uninvolved in the community.

Social-control theory does seem persuasive, although it perhaps underestimates the amount of crime committed by white-collar workers who are in fact attached, committed, and involved in society. The theory does have the advantage of containing a prescription for reducing crime: create job opportunities and other ways of cementing the bond between individual and society.

THE FORMS OF CRIME IN AMERICA

Each of the theories discussed above seems to provide only a partial explanation of crime: none of them can be convincingly applied to all crimes. Yet this situation is perhaps inevitable, for crime takes many diverse forms. As the President's Commission on Law Enforcement and Administration of Justice pointed out:

> A skid-row drunk lying in the gutter is crime. So is the killing of an unfaithful wife. A Cosa Nostra conspiracy to bribe public officials is a crime. So is a strong-arm robbery by a 15-year-old-boy. The embezzlement of a corporation's funds by an executive is a crime. So is the possession of marijuana cigarettes by a student. . . . Thinking of "crime" as a whole is futile.[25]

Let us examine some of the major forms of crime in America.

Juvenile Delinquency

To both the public and to sociologists juvenile delinquency is a major issue. Its importance arises partly because juveniles account for such a high proportion of all arrests and partly from a concern for the juveniles themselves, simply because they are young. Social policy faces the difficult task of simultaneously protecting the public from acts of juvenile delinquency and treating the delinquents in such a way that their chances of acquiring a criminal record and becoming persistent offenders are minimized.

Most research on juvenile delinquency has focused on gang members in lower-class urban neighborhoods. For example, Albert Cohen[26] analyzes juvenile delinquency in terms of Merton's theory of anomie, seeing delinquency as a reaction to the discrepancy between socially approved goals and opportunities for achieving them. In short, lower-class juveniles have little chance to become successful in the middle-class world and may experience "status frustration" as a result. The dominant society expects them to be ambitious, responsible, achievement-oriented, respectful of property, self-disciplined,

---

[25]President's Commission on Law Enforcement and the Administration of Justice, *The Challenge of Crime, op. cit.*, p. 3.

[26]Albert Cohen, *Delinquent Boys: The Culture of the Gang* (Glencoe, Ill.: Free Press, 1955).

gainfully employed, and willing to plan ahead and defer gratification. Lacking the opportunity or ability to meet these requirements, delinquents reject them by behaving in an exactly opposite way: they value an act precisely to the degree that it violates the norms of the larger culture. Status in the gang is achieved by "hell-raising," behavior which provides the opportunities for prestige, at least within that subculture, that are unattainable by legitimate means.

Of course, not all delinquents express their "status frustration" in the same "hell-raising" way. Richard Cloward and Lloyd Ohlin suggest that there are three distinct delinquent subcultures, all of which result from the discrepancy between socially approved goals and the lower-class juvenile's opportunities for achieving them. The first type, the *criminal subculture*, is organized for the purpose of material gain through systematic theft, extortion, robbery, and fraud. This subculture often has links with adult crime and sometimes serves as an avenue into a criminal career. The second type of subculture, the *conflict-oriented subculture*, usually involves battles and territorial disputes between rival gangs (the gang member does not aspire, however, to adult forms of violence or to adult forms of criminality). The third type, the *retreatist subculture* is made up of those who cannot succeed in, or are denied access to, the other subcultures. They retreat into a private world and seek solace in drugs, alcohol, or other forms of "kicks" that are less publicly visible than the activities of the other two subcultures. Cloward and Ohlin also found that boys who become members of delinquent gangs explicitly attribute their failures to the social order rather than to any inadequacies of their own. They are highly critical of society and consider themselves justified in rejecting the dominant social norms and values.[27]

Other sociologists argue that lower-class life itself generates delinquent behavior, since mere adherence to some lower-class values can lead to trouble with the law. Walter Miller identifies certain "focal concerns" of this lower-class sub-

culture. *Trouble* is a major concern, whether one gets into it or stays out of it; ideally, one walks the line between doing what one wants and becoming entangled with middle-class institutions such as the law or welfare agencies. Other focal concerns are *toughness*, or what we might call male chauvinism or machismo (an emphasis on physical strength and endurance and a disdain for anything "effeminate"); *smartness*, (the capacity to be street-wise, to hold one's own in the world); *excitement* (perhaps in the form of fighting or gambling, to relieve the dismal routine of working without ever "getting ahead"); *autonomy* (the desire to be free of external social controls and authority); and *fate* (the sense that the ups and downs of life are beyond one's control). Miller argues that the gang provides an environment in which these concerns can be expressed; at the same time it offers security, stability, and support for its members. Miller acknowledges that not all lower-class youths are prone to delinquency, particularly because some will identify with middle-class rather than with lower-class values. The delinquent, however, is the one who embraces the lower-class values.[28]

David Matza has challenged all the theorists who emphasize the delinquent subculture. He believes that the distinction between delinquents and nondelinquents is at best a tenuous one and that most juveniles behave conventionally a great deal of the time, with only sporadic lapses into misbehavior. He describes this state of balance between delinquency and crime as *drift*.[29]

Matza's view is supported by recent research, which seems to be undermining the notion that gangs provide the basic environment for juvenile delinquency. Self-report studies indicate that juveniles frequently commit delinquent acts on their own, not in groups.[30] More important,

[27]Richard S. Cloward and Lloyd E. Ohlin, *Delinquency and Opportunity: A Theory of Delinquent Gangs* (Glencoe, Ill.: Free Press, 1960).

[28]Walter B. Miller, "Lower Class Culture as a Generating Milieu of Gang Delinquency," *Journal of Social Interest*, 14, (1958), 5–19.

[29]David Matza, *Delinquency and Drift* (New York: Wiley, 1964).

[30]Maynard L. Erickson, "Group Violations, Socioeconomic Status and Official Delinquency," *Social Forces*, 52 (September 1973), 51; and "The Group Context of Delinquent Behavior," *Social Problems*, 19 (Summer 1971), 114–129.

In the past, sociologists concentrated on the gang as the breeding ground for juvenile delinquency. Recent research, however, indicates that middle-class juveniles commit at least as many crimes as gang members, but the gang is more visible and attracts more police attention.

research is casting severe doubt on whether delinquency is even found primarily among lower-class juveniles. The juveniles in the arrest statistics are overwhelmingly from the lower class, but this does not mean that they commit the most delinquent acts, only that they are the most often arrested. One national self-report survey of teen-agers found little relationship between delinquency and social class, except that higher-status boys were slightly more delinquent than lower-status boys. The higher-status boys committed more thefts and even more assaults than the lower-status boys.[31] A careful study by William J. Chambliss of two teen-age gangs, the middle-class Saints and the lower-class

Roughnecks, turned up a far greater number of delinquent acts on the part of the Saints. Yet the Roughnecks were the ones in constant trouble and were universally considered to be delinquent; the behavior of the Saints, on the rare occasions when it was noticed, was more apt to be considered as youthful high spirits:

> The local police saw the Saints as good boys who were among the leaders of the youth in the community. Rarely, the boys might be stopped in town for speeding or for running a stop sign. When this happened the boys were always polite, contrite, and pled for mercy. As in school, they received the mercy they asked for. None ever received a ticket or was taken into the precinct by the local police. . . . Townspeople never perceived the Saints' high level of delinquency. The Saints were good boys who just went in for an occasional prank. . . . The Roughnecks were a

[31]Eugene Doleschal and Nora Klapmuts. *Toward a New Criminology* (Hackensack, N.J.: National Council on Crime and Delinquency, 1973).

different story. . . . Everyone agreed that the not-so-well-dressed, not-so-well-mannered, not-so-rich boys were heading for trouble. . . . From the community's viewpoint, the real indication that these kids were in for trouble was that they were constantly involved with the police. . . . There was a high level of mutual distrust and dislike between the Roughnecks and the police. The boys felt very strongly that the police were unfair and corrupt.[32]

Why, if the Saints were more delinquent than the Roughnecks, did the police, school, and community hold a distorted impression of the behavior of the two gangs? Chambliss believes that a labeling process was responsible:

Differential treatment of the two gangs resulted in part because one gang was infinitely more visible than the other. This differential visibility was a direct function of the economic standing of the families. The Saints had access to automobiles and were able to remove themselves from the sight of the community. . . . Through necessity the Roughnecks congregated in a crowded area where everyone in the community passed frequently, including teachers and law enforcement officers. They could easily see the Roughnecks hanging around the drugstore. . . .

To the notion of visibility must be added the difference in the responses of group members. . . . If one of the Saints was confronted with an accusing policeman . . . his demeanor was apologetic and penitent. A Roughneck's attitude was almost the polar opposite . . . the Roughneck's hostility and disdain were clearly observable.

Selective perception and labeling—finding, processing and punishing some kinds of criminality and not others—means that visible, poor, non-mobile, outspoken, undiplomatic "tough" kids will be noticed, whether their acts are seriously delinquent or not. Other kids . . . disciplined and involved in respectable activities, who are mobile and monied, will be invisible when they deviate from sanctioned activities. They'll sow their wild oats—perhaps even wider and thicker than their lower-class cohorts—but they won't be noticed.[33]

Crimes Without Victims

Most crimes have an identifiable victim who suffers in a definable way as a direct result of the criminal act. But certain crimes have no victims: in cases of prostitution, gambling, or vagrancy, for example, there is no one who suffers directly from the act, except perhaps the person who commits it. Laws that make such behavior criminal are designed not to protect some citizens from others but rather to regulate peoples' private lives in the supposed interests of public morality. The laws exist because society, or powerful groups within society, regards these acts as morally repugnant.

The United States invests enormous resources in controlling victimless crime, as reflected by the high proportion of such crime among the 10.2 million arrests recorded in the FBI UCR for 1977. There were over 85,000 arrests for prostitution and commercialized vice; over 640,000 prosecutions for drug abuse (about 70 percent for possession of marijuana); over 58,000 arrests for gambling; more than 1,360,000 arrests for drunkenness; more than 49,000 for vagrancy; and 96,000 for curfew violations and loitering.

Many of those arrested for victimless crimes are never prosecuted: arrest and overnight lockup are used simply as a means of exerting social control over the drunk or the prostitute without going to the bothersome lengths of creating a convincing prosecution case. As a result, habitual drunks may build up formidable "criminal" records even though they may never have harmed anyone, except possibly themselves.[34] One study found that two-thirds of repeatedly arrested alcoholics had been charged with nothing more than public intoxication and related offenses, such as vagrancy, throughout their long "criminal" careers.[35]

The people who are affected by these laws, however, may not regard their behavior as im-

---

[32]William J. Chambliss, "The Saints and the Roughnecks," *Society* (November–December 1973), 26, 27.

[33]*Ibid.*, pp. 29, 30, 31.

[34]Wayne R. La Fave, *Arrest: The Decision to Take a Suspect into Custody* (Boston: Little, Brown and the American Bar Foundation, 1965), p. 439.

[35]David Pittman, as cited in Stephan Landsman, "Massachusetts' Comprehensive Alcoholism Law: Its History and Future," *Massachusetts Law Quarterly*, 58 (Fall 1973), p. 288.

moral and may deeply resent the attempts of other groups to impose the dominant morality upon them: their attitude to the law is simply pragmatic. The college student who smokes marijuana or the business executive who gambles most likely feels no guilt at violating the law; each is only concerned with escaping detection. If enough people adopt this attitude of moral indifference to a law, it gradually falls into disuse, as has happened, for example, with laws against adultery. Often in such cases, attempts to repeal the law would evoke outcries from interest groups that still support it, so controversy is avoided by leaving the law on the books but simply not enforcing it. In times of rapid social change, however, groups that are considered deviant are often reluctant to wait for the laws affecting them to fall into disuse, and instead resort to open protest. But in the meantime there are millions of arrests each year as the police and the courts continue to apply laws against such groups as homosexuals, drug users, prostitutes, gamblers, and pornography sellers— laws that large sections of the community do not recognize as legitimate and simply refuse to obey.[36]

It is fair to say that organized crime in the United States owes its existence largely to laws against victimless crimes, since it makes the bulk of its money by satisfying consumer demands for goods and services that have been made illegal in the supposed interests of the moral regulation of society. Prohibition is the outstanding historical example of this process: the attempt to ban alcohol resulted in a massive criminal network that supplied alcohol at inflated prices. Likewise, a good deal of the gambling facilities, drug supply, and prostitution in the United States today is controlled by organized crime.

An additional problem with victimless crimes is that most corruption of police and courts is associated with these offenses. Few police are willing to accept bribes from murderers, burglars, or other criminals whose acts are patently harmful and have identifiable victims. However, many police officers feel that victimless crime is not

particularly serious and that, in any case, it is impossible to eradicate. Hence, organized crime is often readily able to buy police protection for many of its activities.

A further problem is that during attempts to obtain evidence against criminals who have no victims, the police frequently violate the civil liberties of the suspects. Prostitutes and drug pushers, for example, are regularly victims of police entrapment, for the simple reason that there often is no other means by which the police can obtain evidence to secure a conviction. As Alexander Smith and Harriet Pollack point out:

> The prostitute's client has not been forcibly seduced; the housewife who bets a quarter on the numbers has not been robbed; the dope user has harmed only himself. Because there are no victims available to testify for the state, the burden of producing enough evidence for the prosecution rests entirely on the police. It is this need for evidence to make morals offense violations "stick" that traditionally has produced the greatest number of civil liberties violations by the police. . . . If their customers cannot testify, who besides the plainclothesman can? And what better way of establishing a case than by offering an obviously willing girl a little "encouragement"? Official police records indicate that an incredible number of gamblers and drug pushers "drop" gambling slips and narcotics at the mere approach of a policeman. This so-called dropsie evidence is frequently a euphemism for an illegal search. . . .[37]

Because so many problems are connected with the enforcement of laws against victimless crimes and because enforcement takes up so much time and money that police and courts could be devoting to the reduction of more serious crime, there has recently been increasing support for the repeal of at least some of these laws. As Smith and Pollack note:

> For every murderer arrested and prosecuted, literally dozens of gamblers, prostitutes, dope pushers and derelicts crowd our courts' dockets. If we took the numbers runners, the kids smoking pot, and winos out of the criminal justice system, we would substantially reduce the burden on the courts and

[36]Alexander B. Smith and Harriet Pollack, "Crimes Without Victims," *Saturday Review*, December 4, 1971, pp. 27–29.

[37]*Ibid.*, pp. 28–29.

the police. . . . Moral laws that do not reflect contemporary mores or that cannot be enforced should be removed from the penal code through legislative action because, at best, they undermine respect for the law.[38]

White-Collar Crime

When the public demands "law and order," and when newspaper editorials bemoan the "rising tide of crime," they have in mind mostly street crime committed by the poor. Even the massive report of the President's Crime Commission, *The Challenge of Crime in a Free Society*, devoted only two pages to the entire subject of white-collar offenders and business crimes. The deep concern with street crime is understandable. Unlike a swindler, who merely takes the victim's money, an armed mugger threatens physical injury and even death. Yet the fact remains that a great deal of crime in American society—perhaps most crime, and certainly the most costly crime—is committed by respectable middle-class and upper-class citizens.[39] The term "white-collar crime" was first used by Edwin Sutherland in an address to the American Sociological Association in 1939. "White-collar crime," he declared, "may be defined approximately as a crime committed by a person of respectability and high status in the course of his occupation."[40] Sutherland documented the existence of this form of crime with a study of the checkered careers of 70 large, reputable corporations, which together had amassed 980 violations of the criminal law, or an average of 14 convictions apiece. Behind the offenses of false advertising, unfair labor practices, restraint of trade, price-fixing agreements, stock manipulation, copyright infringement, and outright swindles, were perfectly respectable middle-class executives. Sociologists now use the term "white-collar crime" to refer not only to crimes committed in the course of business activities for corporate benefit but also to crimes, such as embezzlement, typically committed by persons of high status for personal benefit.

As Sutherland pointed out, the full extent of white-collar crime is difficult to assess. Many corporate malpractices go undetected, and many wealthy people are able to commit crimes like expense-account fraud for years without being found out. More important, white-collar crimes are usually regarded as somehow less serious than the crimes of the lower class, and attract less attention from police and prosecutors. Even the victims may be unwilling to prosecute, often preferring to take account of the offender's "standing in the community" and to settle the matter out of court. A company that finds its safe has been burgled in the night will immediately summon the police, but it may be more circumspect if it finds that one of its executives has embezzled some of its funds. To avoid unwelcome publicity, the company officials may simply allow the offender to resign after making an arrangement to repay the missing money.

On the whole, American society is remarkably tolerant of white-collar crime. A pickpocket who steals $100 may well go to prison, but imprisonment of a person evading payment of a similar sum in taxes is almost unheard of; indeed, tax evasion has to reach massive proportions before the IRS refers the matter to the FBI rather than settling it privately. The main reason for this tolerance seems to be that most white-collar crime involves large, impersonal organizations: there is little sense that a specific individual has been unjustly victimized. Thus, many people who would never dream of stealing items from a private home are quite willing to take "souvenirs" in the form of ashtrays, towels, sheets, and accessories from hotels. In fact, about one hotel guest in three steals something from his or her hotel room, to a total annual loss of over $500 million.[41] In commercial activity as well, we accept a certain amount of deception as the norm; the most striking examples of this tacit

---

[38] *Ibid.*, pp. 27–28.

[39] See John M. Johnson and Jack Douglas (eds.), *Crime at the Top: Deviance in Business and the Professions* (Philadelphia: Lippincott, 1978).

[40] Edwin Sutherland, *White Collar Crime* (New York: Dryden, 1949), p. 9. For a more modern statement, see Gilbert Geis and Robert F. Meier (eds.), *White Collar Crime* (New York: Free Press, 1977).

[41] *New York Times,* January 27, 1974, p. 1.

tolerance of deceit may be found in the field of advertising. As Edwin Schur points out:

> Modern mass advertising at its heart represents a kind of institutionalization of deception and misrepresentation. . . . The cumulative effect of advertising is to nurture a disposition both to engage in and to succumb to fraudulent practices . . . at all social levels of our society. . . . Mass advertising promotes a philosophy of behavior and of man's nature which cannot help but exert indirect influence on the value patterns and dominant activities of our society.[42]

Because most white-collar crime is unrecorded, its total economic impact is difficult to ascertain. Even when it is detected, the cost is not easily measured. How do we evaluate the social and economic cost of illegal pollution of air and water, of the inclusion of illegal additives in food, of the marketing of insufficiently tested new drugs, of the use of false advertising, or of a major stock swindle? We do have some indications, however, of just how great the economic impact of some white-collar crime can be. The President's Commission on Law Enforcement and the Administration of Justice compared the annual cost of four categories of white-collar crime—embezzlement, forgery, tax evasion, and fraud—with the annual cost of four categories of property crime—auto theft, robbery, burglary, and larceny of sums exceeding $50. The total cost in 1967 of the white-collar crimes was almost three times that of the property crimes—$1,730,000,000 as opposed to $614,000,000.[43] To cite another example, short-weighting may cost American consumers as much as $10 billion a year.[44]

These facts raise serious questions about our traditional conceptions of crime and criminals. So long as the typical criminal is stereotyped as a member of the depressed lower class, it is possible to regard criminality as stemming from personal pathology, disorganized surroundings, or discrepancies between goals and opportunities. But if, as is possible, the typical criminal is a middle-class person who does not even regard himself or herself as a criminal, our theories of the causes of crime may seem inadequate. Sutherland, however, believed that white-collar crime arises through the same process of differential association that generates lower-class crime: since business executives or professionals associate with others who regard white-collar crimes as normal, defensible practices, they are also likely to begin conforming to these illegal norms.

Theorists who regard a good deal of criminal deviance as the result of a labeling process have been quick to point out the implications of white-collar crime. A single price-fixing arrangement, for instance, may present consumers with a bigger bill than thousands of burglaries, yet it is the burglar who receives the stigma and the severe penalties, whereas the offending business executive receives only mild disapproval and a nominal fine—often to be paid by the company. The explanation of this discrepancy, labeling theorists assert, is to be found in the power structure of society; the offenses that are considered least serious are those that are most likely to be committed by members of the dominant group.

Organized Crime

Unlike most other forms of crime, organized crime does not necessarily steal from or defraud the public: indeed, it offers goods and services for which there is obviously a wide public demand. The existence of organized crime therefore depends on two social factors: the criminalization of certain activities, such as gambling and prostitution, and the willingness of large numbers of citizens to pay for these services even if they are illegal. And pay they do: organized crime is one of America's largest industries, with a gross income estimated to be twice that of all other kinds of illegal activity combined.[45]

---

[42]Edwin M. Schur, *Our Criminal Society* (Englewood Cliffs, N.J.: Prentice-Hall, 1969), pp. 168–170.

[43]"White Collar Crime: Huge Economic and Moral Drain," *Congressional Quarterly*, May 7, 1971, p. 1048.

[44]Ralph Nader (ed.), *The Consumer and Corporate Accountability* (New York: Harcourt Brace Jovanovich, 1973), p. 6.

[45]President's Commission on Law Enforcement and the Administration of Justice, *The Challenge of Crime, op. cit.,* p. 32.

Some years before his death in a gang murder, "the Hawk" describes in a police interview his early involvement with crime.

. . .

And I stood in school awhile and then when I was twelve I had in mind to get out of school. I schemed for my birth certificate to be forged. I erased my date of birth, I made myself fifteen years old and I brought it to the school, brought it to the Board of Health, and the school fell for it, and I got my working papers and got out of school. I got out of school and I started what I always wanted to do, a career of crime.

I started by burglarizing. We called it the bucket racket, myself and one other boy about eighteen. What we used to do is ring a bell and if a woman came out we'd have a car outside and we'd say, "Can we have a bucket of water? The car's steaming." And if nobody answered the bell, we'd break in. We'd ransack the house, go for the bedrooms, jewelry, money. The jewelry, we'd get rid of it, take it to a pawnshop or sell it to people out on the street that we knew. I was twelve. We did about seventy-five or a hundred burglaries. Then I was arrested, me and this other fella. Then I was thirteen, but I told them I was sixteen and they believed me. I got a suspended sentence of three years.

So I kept on burglarizing. There were three of us now. I was arrested again, coming out of a home. We were all shot at by detectives, caught red-handed. I was sentenced to one day and three years in the New York City reformatory. I was still thirteen. I did ten months. Then I went out and this time I went on with crime, but no burglaries. I did robberies with three other fellas, older than me. I bought a gun off another hoodlum. I was fourteen.

One day we were given chase by two cops in a radio car. While they were chasing us, we threw the guns out of the car. They got up to us, stopped us, searched us and took us in. I was held for violation of parole and went back for another eight months.

Then I went back to the neighborhood. I was out a couple of weeks, and I got a letter from my brother, that he was in trouble, to go and see him at Raymond Street jail. He was in trouble for robbery. He asked me to help him out, to go to New York [Manhattan] and get in touch with these fellas that he associated with, to join them, to join their outfit, to help my brother, join them in what they were doing, committing robberies. I went to New York, I joined them and any robbery we did I put my share on the side for my brother, to help him with his lawyer. So what happened was that my brother received five to ten years in state prison and I was shot, which I almost died.

When I used to go out with these fellas, one of the fellas was taking a share out for a girl he was living with at his apartment. There were four of us. He wanted to put the girl in for a share. And he did put her in a few times. So I had an argument with him. I told him I wouldn't take it from him. I called him names. So I was going on and on and he told me to shut up, "or I'll shoot you right in the head." And I told him, foolishly, that he hadn't got the guts enough to shoot me in the head.

Well, the first thing you knew, I was shot. As I'm falling down, the girl started screaming. The two other fellas scrambled out and this fella told the girl, "Let's throw him out the window." So she hollered, "No," and that's all I could remember.

. . .

Source: James Mills, *On the Edge* (Garden City: Doubleday, 1975), pp. 67–68. Copyright 1971, 1972, 1975 by James Mills.

Strictly speaking, any group of cooperating criminals may be called "organized crime." But the term is usually restricted to large-scale organizations—supposedly complete with bureaucracies and specialized officers—that, illegalities aside, operate in much the same way as any other commercial organization.

The very existence of organized crime in the United States was much questioned, thanks chiefly to assertions to the contrary by J. Edgar Hoover, longtime head of the FBI. More recent investigations, however, show that syndicated crime is a reality, largely organized around the Mafia, or Cosa Nostra. Donald Cressey describes the Mafia not as an international syndicate of Sicilian crooks but as a loose network of American regional syndicates, coordinated by a "commission" composed of the heads of the most powerful crime "families." According to Cressey, there are 24 of these families, ranging in size from 20 to 700 members and each having a similar basic organization. At the head of every family is the boss (*don*), who has absolute authority over his family unless overruled by the commission. He is assisted by an underboss (*sottocapo*) and a counselor (*consigliere*). Next in the hierarchy are the "lieutenants" (*capidecina*), each of whom supervises a group of "soldiers" (*soldati*), who, in turn, take the responsibility for specific illegal enterprises. The leadership of the Mafia is Italian American, but lower ranks may be drawn from all ethnic groups.[46]

Although some sociologists feel that some details of this picture are mythical and that organized crime is a good deal less organized than Cressey would allow, there can be little doubt about the existence of powerful criminal syndicates.[47] The Mafia seems to have developed during the Prohibition era, when criminal groups were organized to supply illegal alcohol. When Prohibition was ended, the groups invested their vast profits in other forms of crime, primarily gambling. Always tailoring their activities to popular demand, organized crime has more recently become deeply involved in the supply of narcotics and other illicit drugs.

The organizational chart of the Mafia leaves out one important participant: the public official who is corrupted by organized crime. By paying off police, prosecutors, judges, and politicians, the Mafia is able to ensure minimal interference from the law. The American public is well aware of this fact: a Harris poll showed that 80 percent of the population believe that "organized crime has corrupted and controls many politicians in this country." The continu-

ing relative impunity with which the Mafia is able to operate in the United States inevitably undermines public confidence in the integrity of the entire law-enforcement system.

Violent Crime

Violent crime—that is, murder, forcible rape, assault, and robbery (defined as theft through the use of threat of force)—is the category of crime that is most played-up by the news media, most railed against by politicians, and most feared by the public. Yet it accounts for only 9 percent of all serious crime and a much smaller proportion of all offenses. Of every 100,000 Americans in 1977, some 5,055 were the victims of serious crimes, 466 of which were violent. The aggravated-assault rate per 100,000 inhabitants was 241.5; the robbery rate, 187.1; the forcible-rape rate, 29.1; and the murder rate, 8.8[48] (three times as many people are killed each year in auto accidents as are murdered).

The risk for all violent crimes is significantly greater in metropolitan areas than in rural areas or in small towns. More than half of all robberies in big cities occur on the streets, a fact that has contributed to the public perception of street crime as a major problem and which, indeed, has made many people fearful to walk the streets at night. Part of the fear of street violence stems from a dread of being attacked by a total stranger, but in fact, most people who are murdered or assaulted have at least a passing acquaintance with their attacker. A high proportion of murders and assaults arise in the course of family arguments or romantic entanglements (see Chapter 10, "Family Problems"). In nearly 60 percent of all homicides, the murderer and the victim are acquainted.[49] Firearms are used in 63 percent of all murders (48 percent of these cases involve handguns). Of those persons arrested for murder, 10 percent are under eighteen and 43 percent are under twenty-five. The police are more successful in making arrests in homicide cases (some 75 percent) than they are with any other crime—partly because they devote special

[46]Donald R. Cressey, *Theft of the Nation: The Structure and Operations of Organized Crime in America* (New York: Harper & Row, 1969), p. 6.

[47]See Francis A. J. Ianni and Elizabeth Reuss-Ianni (eds.), *The Crime Society* (New York: New American Library, 1976); and John E. Conklin (ed.), *The Crime Establishment* (Englewood Cliffs, N.J.: Prentice-Hall, 1973).

[48]*Crime in the United States, op. cit.*, p. 35.

[49]*Ibid.*, pp. 9–10.

1977

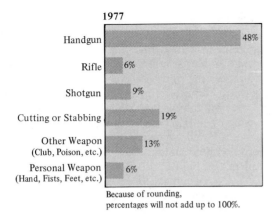

Because of rounding,
percentages will not add up to 100%.

FIGURE 14.2 **Murder by type of weapon used.** Most homicides committed in the United States each year involve guns—most commonly, handguns. Given that there are over 100 million privately owned firearms in the country, this statistic is hardly surprising.
(Federal Bureau of Investigation: *Uniform Crime Reports*, 1978, p. 10.)

attention to homicides, but also because the "murder mystery" of TV drama is relatively uncommon: in most cases, questioning of neighbors, friends, and relatives soon turns up the killer.

The violent crime that shows the most rapid apparent increase in rates in recent years is rape, from 15.9 cases per 100,000 population in 1968 to 29.1 per 100,000 in 1977.[50] Much of this apparent increase is undoubtedly due to a greater willingness of the victims to report the attacks. Nevertheless, the actual rate is probably much higher because many women are still unable to face the various ordeals commonly associated with pressing rape charges.

As suggested, violent crimes, measured in strictly numerical terms, are probably less common than most people assume. But this fact is no consolation to the victims of the crimes; and in any case, violence at anything like the current level seems intolerable in a civilized society. The United States ranks far above all other modern industrial nations in its rates of violence, and its homicide rate is more comparable to that of

socially disorganized developing nations than to those of the other more advanced nations of the world. In fact, its homicide rate is roughly ten times that of such countries as Austria, France, Australia, Poland, and Sweden, and roughly twenty times that of Denmark, Greece, Spain, or Norway.[51]

What are the causes of violence? Three general theories have been proposed: the biological, the frustration-aggression, and the cultural.

Biological theories of violence assume that human beings are innately aggressive. Writers such as Konrad Lorenz,[52] Robert Ardrey,[53] and Desmond Morris[54] have argued that we are descended from "killer apes" or other aggressive animal forebears, and that we still retain an "instinct" to attack or even kill our fellows under certain circumstances. Few social scientists accept this view.[55] If violence were innate in our nature, we would expect to find it—as we find instincts in any other animal—in all normal members of the species under the same conditions. But we do not. Some societies are extremely violent; others (all of them small tribal communities) have little or no place for violence.[56] (The Tasaday, a recently discovered Stone Age tribe in the Philippines, do not even have words in their language to express hostility or aggression.) At the individual level, even within these violent United States, there are vast variations in the degree of violence found among the population, and millions of people are never violent. It therefore seems highly unlikely that we have a residual "instinct" for violence, but even if we do, it is clear that it can be readily

---

[51]U.S. Bureau of the Census, *Statistical Abstract of the United States, 1978* (Washington, D.C.: U.S. Government Printing Office, 1978) p. 174.

[52]Konrad Lorenz, *On Aggression* (New York: Bantam, 1967).

[53]Robert Ardrey, *The Territorial Imperative* (New York: Atheneum, 1967), and *The Hunting Hypothesis* (New York: Atheneum, 1976).

[54]Desmond Morris, *The Naked Ape* (New York: McGraw-Hill, 1968).

[55]See Ashley Montagu, *The Nature of Human Aggression* (New York: Oxford University Press, 1976).

[56]See Ashley Montagu, *Learning Nonaggression: The Experience of Preliterate Societies* (New York: Oxford University Press, 1978).

controlled. Biological theories thus cannot explain the incidence of violence in American society.

Frustration-aggression theory is based on the common-sense observation that frustration often provokes an aggressive response. More specifically, this view sees violence as an expressive reaction, a release of the tension produced by the frustrating situation. A student who cannot solve a math problem may react by throwing the math book at the wall; a husband who cannot find a job may respond by beating his wife; ghetto dwellers, as they did in American cities during the 1960s, may riot out of frustration at a society that promises equality but does not deliver it. It remains to be determined, however, why frustration should lead to aggression only in some people and situations and not in others. It is likely that an individual's or group's reaction depends on the resources that are available for dealing with the frustration: violence may be a last resort, the only resource left when other resources such as money, self-respect, and hope are gone.

Cultural theories of violence assume that violent behavior is learned whenever a culture or subculture offers violence as an appropriate response to the world under certain circumstances. For example, in America aggression is considered more acceptable among the working class than among the middle class: a young working-class male may be expected to "stand up and fight" in a dispute, whereas a young middle-class male would be expected to resolve it verbally. In addition, American culture as a whole seems exceptionally tolerant of aggression in the male. The United States is probably the only industrial society in which the word "aggressive" can be used in a favorable sense. (In job advertisements, companies often specify that they want an "aggressive" executive.)

The United States has a long history of domestic mayhem, from the subjugation of the American Indian to the nineteenth-century vigilante violence of the Old West, from the immense sufferings of the Civil War through to the bloody conflicts of the labor movement and the urban riots of the 1960s.[57] That violence is accepted as part of the American way is further

suggested by a Harris poll that found a substantial majority of Americans agreeing with such statements as "justice may have been a little rough and ready in the days of the Old West, but things worked better than they do with all the legal red tape"; "human nature being what it is, there will always be wars and conflict"; and "when a boy is growing up, it is important he have a few fist fights."[58] Our mass media, too, often present violence as an approved method of solving problems.

A clear appreciation of cultural and subcultural approval of violence can thus be helpful in understanding some of the violent crime in the United States. For example, rape cannot be interpreted as simply the satisfaction of sexual lust. The motivation goes much deeper: as Gresham Sykes comments, "the causes of rape are likely to be found not in a sick psyche but in a complex of accepted cultural values in which masculinity, violence, and aggressive sexuality are entwined."[59] In other words, rape is at least as much an expression of aggressive power as it is of sexual desire.[60]

Charles Silberman uses cultural theory to help explain the fact that blacks are disproportionately arrested for crimes of violence. Although 90 percent of violent crimes involve a victim and an offender of the same race, some black youths, Silberman suggests, are delighting in their newfound ability to terrorize whites. These young people are drawn almost entirely from the ranks of the ghetto poor, and their future prospects are bleak. Reviewing a history of oppression that

[57]See Richard Hofstadter and Michael Wallace (eds.), *American Violence: A Documentary History* (New York: Knopf, 1970); and James A. Inciardi and Anne E. Pottieger (eds.), *Violent Crime: Historical and Contemporary Issues* (Beverly Hills, Calif.: Sage, 1978).

[58]Harris, *op. cit.*, p. 159.

[59]Sykes, *op. cit.*, p. 142.

[60]See Nancy Gager and Cathleen Schurr, *Sexual Assault: Confronting Rape in America* (New York: Grosset and Dunlap, 1976); Le Roy G. Schultz (ed.), *Rape Victimology* (Springfield, Ill.: Charles C. Thomas, 1975); Susan Brownmiller, *Against Our Will: Men, Women, and Rape* (New York: Simon and Schuster, 1975); and Duncan Chappell, Robley Geis, and Gilbert Geis (eds.), *Forcible Rape: The Crime, the Victim, and the Offender* (New York: Columbia University Press, 1978).

included slavery, lynchings, and pervasive discrimination, Silberman claims that what is remarkable is not how much but rather how little black violence there has always been in the United States. In part of the ghetto youth subculture, however, the cultural devices that kept violence under control have broken down. The whites are "running scared," and a delinquent subculture approves the threat or use of violence to maintain a situation in which the tables are turned.[61]

It is probable that there is no single explanation for all forms of violence. The question to be

[61]Charles E. Silberman, *Criminal Violence, Criminal Justice* (New York: Random House, 1978); see, also, Anthony R. Harris, "Race, Commitment to Deviance, and Spoiled Identity," *American Sociological Review*, 41 (June 1976), 432–442.

addressed, then, is, under what conditions do human beings tend to wreak violence on others? Once we have answers to this question, we can begin to confront the problem. But even when solutions seem obvious, implementation is not always, or even often, an easy matter. For example, after such violent and nationally traumatic events as the assassinations of John Kennedy, Robert Kennedy, and Martin Luther King, Jr. in the 1960s, support has always risen for gun-control legislation, but so far Americans have balked at taking the crucial step of prohibiting or even seriously restricting the private possession of firearms. The argument against this step—an argument widely championed by firearms manufacturers and the National Rifle Association—is that it would leave law-abiding citizens unarmed while criminals remained in possession of their

Violence is a recurrent feature of American life. One reason for its prevalence may be that our culture tolerates a certain measure of aggression, particularly in males. Some people come to rely on aggressiveness as a resource in interpersonal relations.

weapons. Interestingly, the British reverse this argument: British police, who do not carry guns, have always resisted any suggestion that they be armed, on the grounds that this would encourage criminals to carry arms as well. At present, Britain, with a population of over 55 million, has fewer homicides each year than the city of Philadelphia, with a population of about 2 million. The British start with the advantage, however, that they have always had stringent gun control, so that weapons are not readily available to criminals in the first place.

THE POLICE

American society places an enormous burden on its 437,000 police officers. They are the link between the public and those who make the law, and within limits they have considerable discretion in determining whether or not the law should be applied. Not everyone who commits an offense within a police officer's sight will be arrested. The number of laws is immense—over 30,000 local, state, and federal statutes, most of them containing numerous clauses and subclauses specifying various categories of offenses. Many of these laws are ambiguous, many directly contradict one another, and many are hopelessly outdated. The decision to act upon or ignore an offense is therefore often in the hands of the individual police officer on patrol.

The question of how the police can be made more effective in maintaining "law and order" has been debated in many communities as the crime rate has risen. One common demand is for more police. Surprisingly, however, the evidence indicates that the number of police officers does not significantly affect the crime or arrest rate; the President's Commission on Law Enforcement and the Administration of Justice reported that "there appears to be no correlation between the differing concentrations of police and the amount of crime committed or the percentage of known crimes solved in the various cities."[62] This

statement refers to the number of police on duty, not to the number who are on patrol. Actually, the number on patrol is often only a small proportion of policemen on duty. (One reason for this is that it takes almost ten hours of an officer's time to process an arrested suspect through the courts.[63]) The evidence on whether high visibility of police has any effect on crime is mixed. When uniformed policemen were stationed in every subway train in New York City in 1979, the number of subway crimes dropped dramatically. In Kansas City, however, the police were taken off patrol in some areas for an entire year without any significant increase in the crime rates in these areas.[64] Preliminary evidence suggests that police patrols probably do more to make people feel safe than to ensure their safety.

Another and more divisive question is whether police should be given increased powers, even if this means limiting the various civil rights of accused suspects. In their desire for protection, sections of the public often demand that "the handcuffs be taken off the police." The "handcuffs" in this case are Supreme Court rulings on the rights of the accused. In *Mapp* v. *Ohio* the court ruled that evidence illegally obtained was inadmissible, and in *Miranda* v. *Arizona*, the court set free a confessed criminal because the police had not advised him of his right to counsel during police interrogation. As a result of such decisions the police in recent years have had to take considerable care not to infringe the civil liberties of suspects.

Naturally, these restrictions annoy some members of the public, and especially the police. But the restrictions are imposed for a reason: to balance the concern for law and order with a due respect for the rights of a suspect who may well be innocent. The Anglo-American legal tradition regards it as an intolerable wrong that an innocent person be punished: far better, it is held, to

---

[62]President's Commission on Law Enforcement and the Administration of Justice, *The Challenge of Crime, op. cit.,* p. 106.

[63]"Study on Police: Some Things Just Never Change," *New York Times*, February 24, 1974, p. 5.

[64]Patrick J. Murphy, "Courts, Police and Individuals," *Philanthropy in a Changing Society: Proceedings of the 16th Annual Conference of the National Council on Philanthropy* (New York: National Council on Philanthropy, 1974), p. 36.

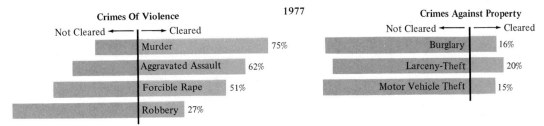

FIGURE 14.3 **Crimes cleared by arrest.** The police are modestly successful in making arrests in crimes of violence, but most property crimes do not result in an arrest. These data relate only to serious offenses recorded by the FBI; the arrest rate for white-collar and other crimes is even lower.
(Federal Bureau of Investigation, *Uniform Crime Reports,* 1978, p. 161.)

let the guilty go free. Consequently, our legal system insists that a suspect be considered innocent until proved guilty, and it accords a suspect a variety of legal rights which inevitably make the task of the police more difficult. It is true, no doubt, that the police could catch more criminals if they did not have to honor the rights of suspects; but catching crooks is not the only purpose of the law. The law and the agencies that enforce it are also expected to maintain a decent respect for human rights, for the plight of the innocent, and for the atmosphere of freedom that our society values.[65] The experience of numerous countries in which the rule of law has been undermined through the granting of undue authority to the police serves as a strong reminder of the virtues of a balance between the power of the police and the rights of the citizen.

THE COURTS

Above the entrance to the Supreme Court building in Washington are inscribed the words "Equal Justice under the Law." The motto reflects a high ideal, but the reality of the American judicial system is often different. In theory the defendant has every possible safeguard: privilege against self-incrimination and rights to pretrial bail, to counsel for defense, to a jury trial, to appeal in higher courts. But in practice many suspects cannot afford bail and end up spending days, weeks, or even months in jail awaiting trial. If they cannot afford to hire their own lawyers and have to settle for the more perfunctory services of an overworked court-appointed lawyer, they are put under strong pressure to plead guilty. (Over 90 percent of the people who appear in lower courts plead guilty and are sentenced on the spot.) Those who do insist on a jury trial and are eventually convicted receive, on the average, heavier sentences than those who forego the trial; they are punished, in effect, for wasting the court's time by insisting on their right to a trial. And although the length of a sentence depends in great part on the discretion of one fallible individual, the judge, there is usually no right of appeal against the sentence itself; only the conviction may be appealed.

No more than a privileged few are able to take advantage of the formal system of "adversary" justice in which the truth about the alleged offense is supposed to emerge, in the style of "Perry Mason," from the formalized courtroom clash of prosecution and defense.[66] In the lower courts, where nearly every defendant pleads guilty, a single judge may hear 200 to 400 cases a day. Even the right to a lawyer, guaranteed in more serious matters by the Supreme Court in 1963, was not extended to people charged with misdemeanors until 1973. Prior to that a defendant who could not afford a lawyer but who still wanted to contest a misdemeanor charge was obliged to enter the lists on his or her own behalf against a prosecutor trained in law and experienced in courtroom procedure. Even in federal

---

[65]Sykes, *op. cit.,* p. 324.

[66]See Stephen Arons and Ethan Katch, "How TV Cops Flout the Law," *Saturday Review,* March 19, 1977, pp. 10–14+.

courts, where crimes are serious and penalties severe, only 10 percent of all cases actually go to trial. The rest of the accused plead guilty, partly to escape a heavier sentence and partly to avoid the expense of a lawyer's fee.

The process of pleading guilty is facilitated by a curious feature of the American legal system known as plea-bargaining, a practice whereby the prosecutor, in return for a plea of guilty from the defendant, agrees to reduce the charges or to recommend leniency to the judge. Although it is an informal procedure having no official recognition in law or in court rules, plea-bargaining is very widespread, for several reasons. The prosecutor may have a weak case, and may prefer to accept a plea of guilty to a lesser charge rather than risk a verdict of innocent if the case goes to trial on a more serious charge. Or the prosecutor may feel that the harsh penalty attached to the more serious charge would do more harm than good in a particular case, and so may be willing to reduce charges. The main reason, however, is administrative convenience, to save courtroom time and expense. Even with merely 10 percent of cases actually coming to trial, the courts are hopelessly overburdened. If only an additional 10 percent of suspects chose to go to trial rather than plea-bargain, the burden on the courts would be doubled, and the criminal justice system might face collapse.

Plea-bargaining has serious disadvantages, however. The defendants who consent to it deprive themselves of the opportunity to have the fair, open trial to which they are constitutionally entitled. They also surrender the right to have the court review the handling of their case by the police and the prosecutor. Innocent people may be induced to plead guilty out of fear that if they do not, they might be convicted of a more serious offense. Those who insist on trial run the risk of far heavier sentences, a fact that seems to represent deliberate encouragement by the courts for the defendants to plead guilty. And there is always the possibility that a corrupt prosecutor can extort money in return for modifying the charges.[67]

In most countries the penalties for various offenses are fairly specific, and the judges have little flexibility in determining sentences. American judges, however, have a very wide latitude in this area. As a result of this freedom—and also perhaps as a result of the fact that sentences are seldom open to review—there are extremely wide variations in sentences for similar offenses. The race and the social status of the defendant are two factors that often make a difference.[68] Another is pretrial imprisonment; prisoners who are not released on bail before the trial are more likely to be convicted and more likely to receive heavier sentences. The severity of the sentence may also be dependent on the tendencies of the particular judge who hears the case: one judge may give probation less than 10 percent of the time, whereas another judge in the same system may give probation 40 percent of the time.[69] One federal judge never gave a sentence of more than seven years during his thirty-seven years on the bench; others believe in stiff punitive and deterrent measures and hand out maximum sentences regularly. Judge John Sirica, the federal judge who heard many of the Watergate cases, was known in legal circles as "Maximum John." In one recent year, 1974, the average federal sentence was 42.2 months, but in the Southern District of Georgia it was only 18.4 months and in the Western District of Michigan it was no less than 94.4 months. And in a study conducted by the Federal Judicial Center of how different judges react to the same set of facts, the sentences in one extortion case ranged from three years and no fine to twenty years and a $65,000 fine.[70]

In some states judges may give an indeterminate sentence—that is, they leave the length of

---

[67]See Arthur Rosett and Donald R. Cressey, *Justice by Consent: Plea Bargaining in the American Courthouse*

(Philadelphia: Lippincott, 1976); and Lloyd L. Weinreb, *Denial of Justice: Criminal Process in the United States* (New York: Free Press, 1977).

[68]Whitney North Seymour, Jr., "Social and Ethical Considerations in Assessing White Collar Crime," *American Criminal Law Review*, 11 (Summer 1973), 821–834.

[69]Sutherland and Cressey, *op. cit.*, p. 438; see, also, President's Commission on Law Enforcement and the Administration of Justice, *Task Force Report: The Courts* (Washington, D.C.: U.S. Government Printing Office, 1967), p. 23.

[70]*New York Times*, March 10, 1977, p. 34.

the sentence up to a parole board, which periodically reviews the progress of the prison inmates. The original intention of the indeterminate sentence was to allow the early release of prisoners who appeared motivated to rehabilitate themselves. In practice, however, the system has actually lengthened sentences by subjecting prisoners to the whims of parole board members and of public opinion. In California, a state which pioneered the system of indeterminate sentences, the median term served by felons up to the point of their first release rose from twenty-four months in 1960 to thirty-six months in 1970. One former inmate pleaded: "Don't give us steak and eggs . . . Free us from the tyranny of the indeterminate sentence."[71]

CORRECTIONS

The term "corrections" refers to the various means by which society handles convicted offenders: means such as imprisonment, probation, and parole. The objectives of the corrections process are many, and include *punishment* for

---

[71]Jessica Mitford, *Kind and Unusual Punishment* (New York: Knopf, 1973), pp. 86–87.

The prison is a "total institution" in which inmates are stripped of their individuality, segregated from the outside world, and subjected to control of every aspect of their lives. Is rehabilitation possible in such an environment?

the crime, *deterrence* of others through the example of punishment, *incapacitation* of offenders by excluding them from society, and *rehabilitation* of offenders by giving them the attitudes and skills that will enable them to become law-abiding members of society.

Over a hundred years ago, the nation's leading prison officials met in Cincinnati and declared that "reformation, not vindictive suffering,

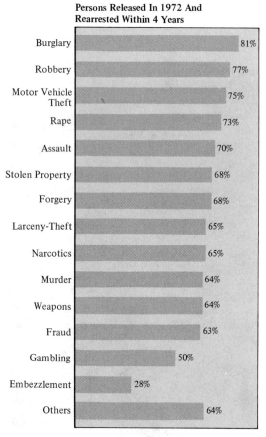

Persons Released In 1972 And Rearrested Within 4 Years

Burglary	81%
Robbery	77%
Motor Vehicle Theft	75%
Rape	73%
Assault	70%
Stolen Property	68%
Forgery	68%
Larceny-Theft	65%
Narcotics	65%
Murder	64%
Weapons	64%
Fraud	63%
Gambling	50%
Embezzlement	28%
Others	64%

FIGURE 14.4 Percent repeaters. The corrections process in the United States is none too successful at reforming or rehabilitating convicts. As this graph shows, the majority of convicted offenders in almost every major category of crime are rearrested (not necessarily for the same offense) within four years. (Federal Bureau of Investigation: *Uniform Crime Reports*, 1978, p 45.)

should be the purpose of the penal treatment of prisoners." That remains the ideal to this day. A Harris poll showed that 78 percent of the American public believes that rehabilitation, rather than punishment, deterrence, or incapacitation, should be the basic aim of the prisons. But the prisons are failing in that task. Forty percent of released prisoners are rearrested within five years. We spend over a billion dollars a year to produce this high failure rate, but most of the money does not go for rehabilitation. Out of every dollar spent in the entire corrections system, approximately some 95 cents goes toward feeding, clothing, housing, and guarding prisoners; the remaining 5 cents is spent on rehabilitation.[72] In many states, prisons offer no suitable job training for prisoners, partly because unions and local businesses have lobbied against the development of prison industries that might compete in the marketplace and hold down wages and profits.

The United States has about 5,000 local and county jails and 400 state and federal prisons. On an average day about half a million adults and juveniles are confined in these institutions. Over half of these inmates have not been convicted of any crime, and of these many are eligible for bail but cannot raise the cash. The very nature of the prison as an institution makes it difficult for much attention to be devoted to rehabilitation; the chronic problem of control takes priority over all else. The result is that the prison is organized as what Erving Goffman calls a *total institution*, a place of residence and work where all the inmates are in a similar situation, are cut off from the wider society, and lead an enclosed, formally administered life.[73] (Other examples of "total institutions" are mental hospitals, traditional boarding schools, and army camps.) The inmate, kept under the absolute control of the administrative authorities, is deprived of liberty, possessions, heterosexual outlets, and personal

---

[72]James P. Campbell *et al.*, "A Survey of American Corrections," Leonard Orlando (ed.), in *Justice, Punishment, Treatment: The Correctional Process* (New York: Free Press, 1973), p. 139.

[73]Erving Goffman, *Asylums: Essays on the Social Situation of Mental Patients and Other Inmates* (Garden City, N.Y.: Anchor, 1961).

autonomy. The psychological effects of prolonged imprisonment under these conditions can be devastating, and there is evidence that some long-term inmates become incapable of adjusting to the responsibilities of life in the society beyond. Even when they are released, they, their fellow inmates, and the custodial staff all know that they will soon be back, unable to "make it" in the outside world.

A frightening experiment by social psychologist Philip Zimbardo gives some insights into the prison as a "total institution." Zimbardo created a mock prison and selected two dozen college-educated, emotionally stable young volunteers to participate in the experiment. He divided them at random into "prisoners" and "guards" and paid them to participate in the study, which he expected would last for two weeks. Zimbardo arranged for the "prisoners" to be picked up at their homes by a city police officer in a squad car; they were then searched, handcuffed, fingerprinted, and taken blindfolded to the "jail." There they were stripped, deloused, put into prison dress, given a number, and locked up. The "guards," meanwhile, were equipped with uniforms, wrap-around reflective sunglasses, whistles, clubs, and handcuffs. They were put on eight-hour shifts and were allowed to improvise rules for the maintenance of order and of respect for authority. The results of the experiment were very disturbing:

At the end of only six days we had to close down our mock prison because what we saw was frightening. It was no longer apparent to most of the subjects . . . where reality ended and their roles began. The majority had indeed become prisoners or guards, no longer able to clearly differentiate between role-playing and self. There were dramatic changes in virtually every aspect of their behavior, thinking, and feeling. In less than a week the experience of imprisonment undid (temporarily) a lifetime of learning; human values were suspended, self-concepts were challenged and the ugliest, most base, pathological side of human nature surfaced. We were horrified because we saw some boys (guards) treat others as if they were despicable animals, taking pleasure in cruelty, while other boys (prisoners) became servile, dehumanized robots who thought only of escape, of

their own individual survival and of their mounting hatred for the guards.

We had to release three prisoners in the first four days because they had such acute situational traumatic reactions as hysterical crying, confusion in thinking and severe depression. Others begged to be paroled, and all but three were willing to forfeit all the money they had earned if they could be paroled. . . .

About a third of the guards became tyrannical in their arbitrary use of power, in enjoying their control over other people. They were corrupted by the power of their roles and became quite inventive in their techniques of breaking the spirit of the prisoners and making them feel they were worthless. . . .[74]

Zimbardo concludes that the prisons are breeding grounds for hatred of society, and argues that the prison experience contributes to the high rate of recidivism among inmates by hardening rather than rehabilitating them.

Some prisoners may be so dangerous, so unreformable, that imprisonment may be the only way society can deal with them. But for many other criminals, imprisonment may have little positive value, either to themselves or, in the long run, to society.

Probation and Parole

Although prisons get the lion's share of whatever public attention and resources we devote to corrections, two-thirds of convicted offenders serve all or part of their sentences outside prison under the supervision of a probation or parole officer. In theory these officers give counsel to their charges, help them through difficult periods, and generally work with them toward their rehabilitation. In practice, however, the probation and parole officers are so burdened with cases that they can devote very little time to any one individual: two-thirds of all felons and three-quarters of all misdemeanants report to parole or probation officers with a caseload of one hundred or more. Juvenile offenders receive somewhat more attention, but nearly 90 percent of them report to officers with a caseload of fifty

[74]Philip G. Zimbardo, "Pathology of Imprisonment," *Society*, 9 (April 1972), 4–9.

or more.[75] Typically, officers see the offenders assigned to them only once a month for a brief ritual visit. There is little evidence that supervision by a probation or parole officer has any effect on the rehabilitation of offenders. One large-scale federal study did not find a single individual, even among those receiving intensive supervision, who attributed any effect to the officers. Instead, credit for keeping the offender out of trouble was given to family, friends, and the offender's own personal efforts.[76]

CONFRONTING THE PROBLEM

The prospects for reducing crime and violence in the United States in the future are uncertain, largely because we do not yet know enough about why people engage in criminal activity, how to discourage them from doing so, and how to reform them if they do become criminal. Although appeals for "law and order" often include demands for stiffer penalties, there is no conclusive evidence relating severity of sentence either to the incidence of crime or to the rate of recidivism among former convicts. There is a strong possibility that the rates for some forms of crime will level off in the early 1980s as the tail end of the postwar "baby boom" moves into more mature adulthood. When this happens, the age category that contributes so disproportionately to crime will have shrunk significantly. But this is only a hope. What can be done by way of concerted social action to improve the situation?

A Goal: Swift and Certain Punishment. It is generally agreed that if punishment for crime is to have any real deterrent effect, then it must be both swift and certain. The longer the time lag between the crime and the ultimate punishment, and the more uncertain the penalty for an offense (probation? a plea-bargained reduced sentence? imprisonment for three months? for five years?), the less the deterrent effect of punishment must be. As Lance Morrow suggests:

> To be told the law, and to be told the punishment, and to be punished if one breaks the law, is a sounder and more reliable system of justice than

the confusing and ineffective process now operating. A society can be subverted by a system that appears to be not only inconsistent but almost whimsical in its workings. A huge sense of grievance festers. . . . If a law has meaning, it must carry predictable consequences. And the law for some years has not been certain whether it means to be a guilt-ridden social worker or a hanging judge.[77]

Swift and certain punishment cannot be legislated overnight, but it must be a major goal. Any measures that will speed the criminal justice process and make punishment more certain can only advance the fight against crime.

Confronting White-Collar Crime. White-collar crime must receive far more attention in the future than it has in the past. The Watergate scandals—in which many high-ranking members of an administration pledged to "law and order" were accused of such abuses as extortion, bribery, illegal wiretapping, conspiracy to violate civil rights, conspiracy to pervert the course of justice, perjury, destruction of evidence, tax fraud, and misappropriation of campaign funds—focused public attention on the issue of white-collar crime as never before. The discrepancies between the sentences received by these criminals and the much harsher sentences meted out to ordinary thieves and burglars aroused comment,

---

[75]President's Commission on Law Enforcement and the Administration of Justice, *The Challenge of Crime, op. cit.,* p. 169.

[76]Richard F. Sparks, "The Effectiveness of Probation: A Review," in Leon Radzinowicz and Marvin E. Wolfgang (eds.), *The Criminal in Confinement,* vol. 3, *Crime and Criminal Justice* (New York: Basic Books, 1971), p. 214; see, also, Richard McCleany, *Dangerous Men: The Sociology of Parole* (Beverly Hills, Calif.: Sage, 1978).

[77]Lance Morrow, "On Crime and Much Harder Punishment," *Time,* September 18, 1978, pp. 54–59.

and the pardoning of former President Nixon, who faced a number of possible criminal charges, excited a major controversy. The existence of white-collar crime, especially if it goes largely unpunished, undermines public respect for those in positions of economic and political influence and creates a climate in which all violations of the law seem less reprehensible. As organized crime comes more and more to resemble white-collar crime in its operations, demands for effective control of white-collar crime are likely to increase.

Incapacitate Serious Offenders.   The growing public revulsion against serious crimes of violence, often committed by juveniles, seems a justified one. Striking as they do at the physical and psychological integrity of the person, these crimes cannot be tolerated in a civilized society. In some cases, perhaps in most, it may be possible to reform the offenders. But other offenders are so dangerous or so incorrigible that the protection of society must become an overriding concern. In these cases it seems reasonable that the offenders should be incapacitated through imprisonment, if necessary for very long periods of time. Where the offenders are juveniles, it may be necessary to try them as adults so that they can be given sentences commensurate with the gravity of the offenses rather than the lenient treatment usually reserved for minors. Several states, in fact, have already made provision for juveniles convicted of homicide and other violent crimes to be charged and tried as adults. In a sense, the proposal that serious offenders be locked up for long periods is an admission of failure: we simply have no better suggestions for dealing with them. But the actual and potential victims of these violent criminals have rights, too, and these rights are paramount.[78]

Uniform Sentencing.   The wide variations in sentences received by different criminals for the same crime also require urgent attention. If justice is to be equal for all, then the race, sex, and economic status of the defendant ought not to influence sentencing. One way to confront this problem of differentials would be to make sentences subject to appeal. This would increase the amount of court time spent on appeal cases, but if we are to take our commitment to equal justice seriously, the inconvenience is one we may have to accept. Legislative changes could also make sentences more uniform by reducing some of the latitude given to judges in this matter.

Decriminalize Victimless Crimes.   If some or all of the crimes that have no victims could be decriminalized, immense resources of time and money could be diverted to confronting the crimes that do have victims. The police would be freed from their obligation to deal with these victimless crimes—an obligation they heartily dislike—and much of the logjam in the courts would be removed. Certainly we can anticipate continuing controversy over the existence of these laws. Some groups, such as the gay liberation movement, regard the campaign to repeal some of this legislation as nothing less than a moral crusade; other groups, such as marijuana smokers, simply violate the laws applying to their preferences—on such a large scale that in many areas the police fail to apply them. Prostitution is legal only in one state, Nevada, but many other countries allow prostitutes to ply their trade without criminal sanctions, so long as they do not create a public nuisance by importuning customers in the streets. Current changes in American attitudes toward sexual activity and drug use are creating a climate in which laws regulating these acts are being continually reviewed and amended. Gambling laws, too, are likely to change in the future: these statutes do not seem to have widespread public sentiment behind them, and already several cities and states have set up legal gambling activities, such as lotteries. With public institutions engaged in the gambling business, it seems unlikely that private groups can be severely restricted for much longer.

Gun Control.   According to a 1978 report by the National Council for a Responsible Firearms

[78]See James Q. Wilson, "Lock 'em Up!" *New York Times Magazine*, March 9, 1975, pp. 11–48, and *Thinking About Crime* (New York: Basic Books, 1975).

Policy, in the fifteen years between 1963, when President Kennedy was assassinated with a mail-order rifle, and 1978, 190,000 Americans were killed within their own country by gunfire. Another 150,000 killed themselves with guns, over a million were wounded by gunfire, and at least 1.7 million were robbed at gunpoint. Under conditions of perfect gun control, virtually none of these weapons would have been in use, and much or most of this slaughter and maiming might have been prevented. There are currently so many firearms, particularly handguns, in circulation in the United States that perfect gun control, or anything resembling it, is probably impossible.[79] Yet some steps can be taken—for example, preventing the importation, manufacture, or sale of handguns except for approved and limited purposes; issuing gun permits only under exceptional circumstances; and recalling all unlicensed guns under threat of heavy penalties.

Reform the Prisons. Although prisons presently do very little in the way of successfully rehabilitating offenders, it is important that there be continuing experiments with various kinds of rehabilitation programs, in an effort to find principles and methods that can be widely applied within the prison community. One of the various reforms that have been proposed, for example, is the use of behavior-modification techniques to reform prisoners. These techniques are based on the assumption that criminal behavior is learned through positive rewards to the criminal, and therefore can be unlearned—by giving negative sanctions for undesirable behavior and positive rewards for desirable behavior. Patuxent Institution in Maryland is one prison that has pioneered these methods: by improved behavior, prisoners work their way up from one tier of rewards to the next, receiving on the various levels such positive reinforcements as vocational training, picnics with their families, and parole. Although most of the prisoners in Patuxent are hardened cases, recidivism is lower

than average.[80] This and many other programs have had limited achievements, but no rehabilitation program has yet been devised that has universal or even very significant success. The main reason may be that it is not so much the content of the program as the motivation of the individual prisoner that influences the prospects for rehabilitation; if this is the case, then more work must be done on motivating prisoners to "go straight" when they are released.

Transitional Programs.   It is likely that the best prospects for rehabilitation might occur in the context of the community rather than the prison, in situations where the offender can establish firm bonds with conventional society. Transitional devices such as short-term furloughs, work-release programs, and halfway houses all have this objective, being specifically designed to ease adjustment problems and to permit families to stay together to some extent. The furlough system allows the prisoner to make short home visits. Although it is objected that furloughs facilitate escape, Michigan and Mississippi, the two states making the most use of furloughs, report that only 1 percent of prisoners escape while on home leave.[81] Work-release programs use the resources of the community to free prisoners from the suffocating boredom and idleness of prison: those who can go back to the jobs they held before imprisonment are permitted to do so; others are given training and sent out to new jobs. Most states still do not have work-release programs, however, and even in those that do, most of the prison population is considered ineligible. Halfway houses are residential institutions that allow prisoners a certain degree of freedom, while providing a structured environment in which rehabilitation can take place. They are designed to provide a transition between prison and complete release; however, if the prisoner misbehaves while in the halfway house, he or she may be returned to prison. In

[79]Douglas R. Murray, "Handguns, Gun Control Laws and Firearm Violence," *Social Problems*, 22 (October 1975), 81–93.

[80]Daniel L. Goldfarb, "American Prisons: Self-Defeating Concrete," *Psychology Today*, Vol. 7 no. 8 (January 1974), p. 85.

[81]President's Commission on Law Enforcement and the Administration of Justice, "The Challenge of Crime in a Free Society, " pp. 176–177.

some cases, particularly those involving juvenile delinquents, the halfway house can also be used an an alternative, rather than a supplement, to incarceration. Convicts serving life terms at Rahway prison in New Jersey have developed a widely publicized program to discourage certain juvenile delinquents from further crime. The delinquents are taken on a visit to the prison, where they can talk freely to the convicts and observe prison .conditions first-hand. For their part, the convicts urge the juveniles not to make the same mistakes that they did in breaking the law. The idea is that the juveniles, faced with a glimpse of the harsh reality of prison life, will be strongly motivated to reform. It is too early to tell whether this program will be successful, however, as early reports show mixed results.

While many of these reforms seem promising, the very concept of the prison, reformed or not, is likely to be challenged in the future. Many people are adopting the view that imprisonment is counterproductive and inappropriate for a majority of offenders. California, in an effort to find an alternative to confinement, is currently experimenting with a program for nonresidential community treatment for juvenile offenders. The delinquents are required to come at regular intervals to community centers, where their progress is followed and where support, therapy, and training are available. Preliminary results show a significantly lower rate of recidivism among these delinquents than among those who are institutionalized. Other states, such as Massachusetts, Iowa, and Wisconsin, have been transferring juvenile and adult offenders from penal institutions to community rehabilitation centers, and they too report encouraging results. It seems likely that in the future our corrections system will come to rely more and more on combinations of different types of facilities rather than on a uniform policy of incarceration for those who violate the criminal code.

SUMMARY

1. Crime and violence are perceived as a major problem in American society. Part of the problem is the prevalence and rising rate of crime, especially violent crime; part of it is the ineffectual, irrational, and often unjust criminal-justice system.

2. A crime is an act prohibited by law. According to FBI statistics, the typical criminal is disproportionately likely to be young, male, urban, and black, but FBI statistics omit most white-collar crime and therefore provide a distorted picture.

3. The functionalist approach sees crime and violence as the result of social disorganization caused by the breakdown of social control in large, urbanized societies. The conflict approach emphasizes that the law and the criminal-justice process reflect the interests of the dominant group in society. The deviance approach tries to explain why certain people become criminals. Several theories have been offered: anomie, labeling, differential association, and inadequate social control.

4. The major forms of crime in the United States are juvenile delinquency, crimes without victims, white-collar crime, organized crime, and violent crime. Violence has been explained as the result of biological factors, frustration-aggression, and cultural factors.

5. The police operate under many restraints, but these seem necessary to protect the rights of the innocent. The courts rarely follow the procedures seen in TV dramas: plea-bargaining allows 90 percent of cases to be settled without a trial. There is a great discrepancy in sentences, not only between white-collar crime and other crimes but also between different persons accused of the same crime.

6. The objectives of corrections are punishment, deterrence, incapacitation, and rehabilitation. The latter is often seen as the most important goal, but is it rarely achieved, perhaps because of the nature of the prison as a "total institution." Probation and parole also seem to have little rehabilitative effect.

7. The problem can be confronted by establishing the goal of swift and certain punishment; confronting white-collar crime; incapacitating serious offenders; establishing uniform sentences; decriminalizing victimless crimes; gun control; reforming the prisons; and developing transitional programs.

GLOSSARY

Anomie. A state in which social norms have ceased to be meaningful or effective, often resulting in deviant behavior.

Crime. An act prohibited by a law.

Criminology. The scientific study of crime.

Law. A formal social rule that is enforced by a political authority.

Recidivism. A convicted person's return to crime.

Total institution. A place of residence and work where all the inmates are in a similar situation, are cut off from the wider society, and lead an enclosed, formally administered life.

FURTHER READING

CHAMBLISS, WILLIAM, and MILTON MANKOFF (eds.). *Whose Law? What Order?* New York: Wiley, 1976. A useful collection of readings that explore issues of crime and justice primarily from a conflict perspective.

CRESSEY, DONALD R. *Theft of the Nation: The Structure and Operations of Organized Crime in America.* New York: Harper & Row, 1969. An interesting sociological analysis of the Mafia and its workings.

FOUCAULT, MICHAEL. *Discipline and Punish: The Birth of the Prison.* New York: Pantheon, 1978. An ambitious and sophisticated analysis of the prison. Foucault traces the cultural and historical origins of the prison and its implications for social control in modern society.

GEIS, GILBERT, and ROBERT F. MEIER (eds.). *White Collar Crime.* New York: Free Press, 1977. The various articles in this collection give an excellent overview of the nature and extent of white-collar crime in the United States.

MITFORD, JESSICA. *Kind and Unusual Punishment.* New York: Knopf, 1973. A comprehensive and readable critique of the sentencing and correctional process in the modern United States.

NETTLER, GWYNN. *Explaining Crime.* 2nd ed. New York: McGraw-Hill, 1978. A clearly written introductory survey of the major theories of the causes of crime.

SILBERMAN, CHARLES E. *Criminal Violence, Criminal Justice.* New York: Random House, 1978. An important and provocative discussion of crime in the United States, with particular emphasis on violent crime and its relationship to urban poverty and race.

SYKES, GRESHAM M. *Criminology.* New York: Harcourt Brace Jovanovich, 1978. A splendid introductory text on criminology. Recommended for the student who wants a comprehensive overview of the field.

WEINREB, LLOYD L. *Denial of Justice: Criminal Process in the United States.* New York: Free Press, 1977. A critical analysis of criminal procedure in the United States; Weinreb exposes many of the inefficiences and inequities that the system produces.

WILSON, JAMES Q. *Thinking about Crime.* New York: Basic Books, 1975. A controversial, well-argued analysis by one of the more conservative of modern criminologists. Wilson challenges many established assumptions and urges a more pragmatic and tougher approach to certain forms of crime.

15
Sexual Variance

THE PROBLEM

All over America there are people who take part in variant forms of sexual behavior; and there are other people who regard this behavior as a social problem. There seems to be an unprecedented amount of pornography circulating in the United States, displayed more openly than at any time in the past. City authorities are constantly opening new campaigns against prostitution in their downtown areas, but after decades of effort they seem no nearer to success; in fact, prostitutes appear to be operating more freely than ever before. A gay liberation movement, demanding that homosexuals be allowed to pursue their life style as freely as anyone else, has made a hitherto forbidden topic an issue of public controversy.

A decade or two ago the source of this social problem seemed self-evident to almost everyone: it was the wicked behavior of a small, deviant minority. Americans had long taken it for granted that variant forms of sexual behavior are depraved and engaged in only by those who are in a profound sense abnormal. Recently, however, this traditional view has been vociferously challenged. Many individuals and groups argue that the social problem of sexual variance lies not in the behavior itself but rather in society's reaction to it. They question whether it is legitimate to penalize people for purely private acts that have no identifiable victims or adverse social consequences. Although some people urge the tightening of laws prohibiting variant sexual acts in order to preserve the moral fiber of the nation, others are calling for the repeal of these

laws on the grounds that they harass people for conduct that falls within the range of normal and harmless human behavior.

In this chapter we shall not deal with those sexually variant acts that have victims, such as rape. Acts of this kind are covered in Chapter 14, "Crime and Violence," and there is a general social consensus that criminal sanctions should be applied against those who commit them. Nor shall we be concerned with forms of sexual variance that are not penalized by law and that affect such a relatively small proportion of the population that they are not usually considered social problems, such as sadomasochism or transsexualism. Instead, we shall focus on the three most widespread and visible forms of variance: homosexuality, prostitution, and pornography.

THE NATURE OF HUMAN SEXUALITY

To see the problem in its proper context, we must consider the nature of human sexuality and the question of why variant forms of sexual behavior should exist at all. To most people it seems self-evident that males and females are biologically programmed to mate with one another in a specific way. Yet research has clearly indicated that human sexual preferences are learned, not instinctive. We are born with an innate "drive" for sexual expression—but not for the precise form it takes. Each society develops its own norms of sexual behavior, and people who are socialized in that society generally take these norms for granted as part of "human nature." It often comes as a shock to find that a form of behavior which seems "natural" is in fact merely a social product, found in one society but absent or even condemned in another. Human sexuality is highly flexible; people are capable of learning to attach their erotic desires to almost anything.

Even in many higher primates, mating behavior is learned. Harry F. Harlow's experiments[1] have revealed that if young rhesus monkeys are reared in isolation and prevented from observing adults mating, they will be incapable of mating in later years, and it is almost impossible to teach them how to do so. The same is true of human beings. Kingsley Davis, a sociologist who has devoted much of his career to the study of marriage and family, observes: "Like other forms of behavior, sexual activity must be learned. Without socialization, human beings would not even know how to copulate." The human sex drive can best be compared to the human hunger drive. Although we all have an innate tendency to feel hungry periodically, we have to learn through the socialization process what we may eat and what we may not eat. Some items are inedible, as the infant discovers when it bites a chair or a rock. Some are edible but taboo: Zulus learn not to eat fish, Jews learn not to eat pork; similarly, Americans learn not to eat snakes, dogs, or roaches—indeed, we have what we think is an "instinctive" aversion to the idea of these creatures as food, though they are considered extremely suitable fare by the inhabitants of some other societies.

The way we learn our sexual norms is similar: we start with a basic, undirected drive and through the socialization process learn to recognize some stimuli as being nonsexual, some as sexual, and some as sexual but taboo. The very fact that the human sex drive is potentially so flexible is one reason why every society makes its

particular norms explicit and rigid. Otherwise, the range of variance might threaten reproduction and the family system. If any particular form of sexual behavior were "natural" or "instinctive," it would appear in all members of the species, and there would be no need for the regulations and taboos that every society uses to channel sexual desires into socially approved outlets.

The flexibility of the human sexual impulse is demonstrated by anthropological research on sexual norms in various societies. Clellan S. Ford and Frank A. Beach conducted a major cross-cultural study of sexual behavior in 190 different societies and concluded:

> Men and women do not develop their individual patterns of sexual behavior simply as a result of biological heredity. Human sexual responses are not instinctive. . . . On the contrary, from the first years of life every child is taught about sex, either directly or indirectly. And most significant is the fact that different societies teach different lessons in this regard. In some cultural settings children learn that sex is a subject to be avoided and that any form of sexual expression during childhood is wrong. In other societies boys and girls are taught that certain sexual activities are permissible whereas others are not. As a result of such divergent experiences in early life, the adult members of different societies have quite different opinions as to what is proper or normal in sexual relations, and what is immoral or unnatural.[3]

Ford and Beach found wide cultural variations in sexual behavior. Most societies, they found, are permissive rather than restrictive in their attitudes toward sex (of the 190 societies studied, only 10 wholly disapprove of both extramarital and premarital sexual intercourse). Even the approved position for intercourse varies from culture to culture, and the position considered "normal" in America is deviant or unknown in some other societies. Notions of personal beauty also vary considerably: in some societies the eyes

---

[1]See Harry F. Harlow, "The Affectional Systems," in Allan Schrier et al. (eds.), Behavior of Nonhuman Primates: Modern Research Trends (New York: Academic Press, 1965).

[2]Kingsley Davis, "Sexual Behavior," in Robert K. Merton and Robert Nisbet (eds.), Contemporary Social Problems (New York: Harcourt Brace Jovanovich, 1971), p. 315.

[3]Clellan S. Ford and Frank A. Beach, Patterns of Sexual Behavior (New York: Harper & Row, 1951), p. 14; see, also, Vern L. Bullough, Sexual Variance in Society and History (New York: Wiley, 1976).

and mouth are significant determinants of attractiveness, but in others the shape of the ears is more important. In some societies female breasts are highly eroticized, but in many others, particularly in the tropics, the breasts are not considered a sexual feature at all. Among some peoples, kissing is unknown, and among others, such as the Siriono of Bolivia, it is regarded as a particularly disgusting act. Prostitution is relatively rare in the societies studied by Ford and Beach, probably because most of them are sexually permissive and other outlets are more readily available. Portrayals that might be considered pornographic in America are common in some other societies; many, for example, display paintings or sculptures of the human penis in public places, usually as a symbol of fertility.

Attitudes toward homosexual behavior vary widely. In some of the societies in the Ford and Beach sample, homosexuality is punishable by ridicule, beatings, or even death. In 64 percent of the societies, however, homosexuality is regarded as acceptable either for a minority of the community or for all members of the community at particular times. In a few societies homosexuals are accorded high social status, and some societies—such as the Lango of Uganda, the Koniag of Alaska, and the Tanala of Madagascar—make provision for a man to take another man as his "wife" along with his female wives. There are several societies—including the Siwans of Africa, the Aranda of Australia, and the Keraki of New Guinea—in which every male is expected to engage in homosexual activities as an exclusive outlet during adolescence. Among the Keraki, for example, adolescent males are required to take the passive role in anal intercourse for a full year after their initiation ceremony; thereafter they take the active role for the remainder of their adolescence, until they enter heterosexual marriage. All cultures, however, institutionalize heterosexuality even if they also accept homosexuality.[4] There are, nonetheless, a very small number of predominantly homosexual societies. The Etoro people of New Guinea, for example, place a taboo on heterosexual intercourse for 295 days a year—and have considerable difficulty

maintaining their population numbers.[5] The neighboring Marindanim people, who are primarily homosexual and who segregate husbands from wives in sleeping quarters, have to kidnap children from surrounding tribes in order to maintain their own population.[6]

The evidence, then, points to the extremely flexible and exploratory nature of the human sexual impulse. Every society finds it necessary, in the interests of social cohesion and stability, to institutionalize certain norms to regulate the sexual behavior of its members, but every society is faced to a greater or lesser extent with the variations from those norms that will inevitably occur. Thus arises the potential for a social problem.

Sexual Behavior in America

Like those that govern our social behavior, the norms relating to sexual behavior are well-known, explicit, and often encoded in law. They derive from a particular interpretation of the ancient Judeo-Christian sexual morality, which regards only one form of sexual behavior as morally legitimate: genital heterosexual intercourse, limited to the context of marriage. Deviations from this pattern are considered to be depraved and sometimes sinful, and are often illegal as well.[7]

To a greater extent than any other Western society, the United States has tried to legislate the sexual morality of its citizens. Traces of the predominant morality are to be found on the statute books of every state. Adultery, for example, is still considered a criminal offense in nearly forty states. Cohabitation—repeated sexual intercourse between unmarried partners—is illegal in over twenty states. Fornication—a single act of intercourse between unmarried partners—is also illegal in over twenty states, and in some of

---

[4]Ford and Beach, *op. cit.*, pp. 132–141.

[5]Raymond C. Kelly, *Etoro Social Structure* (Ann Arbor, Mich.: University of Michigan Press, 1977).

[6]Conrad Phillip Kottak, *Anthropology: Exploration of Human Diversity*, 2nd ed. (New York: Random House, 1978), pp. 286, 409–411.

[7]See Vern and Bonnie Bullough, *Sin, Sickness, and Sanity: A History of Sexual Attitudes* (New York: New American Library, 1977).

A lesbian mother of two boys, living with her own mother following separation from her husband, describes her dual life and the furtiveness necessitated by her efforts to win custody of her sons.

. . .

I couldn't leave the name and number of a club where I would be, because it was in my mind, always, that someone would find out. For three and a half months I was living two different existences. I was living with my mother and two sons and going to college, full time. That was one life. When I left the house to meet Ann, I lived another life that my family and friends at work knew nothing about. The other nurses knew me as a mother, a nurse, a daughter living at home and a college student. Whenever my social life came up I would give the names of men I had gone with when I was first divorced. When someone would question me about my dating I would say, 'In fact, I just went out with So-and-So last night.' Yet it was not with any of these men I was going with; it was Ann. At this point 'she' became 'he' and names of clubs were not identified. In the heterosexual world you could give names of clubs freely. In the realm of the homosexual life you couldn't give names of places for fear that someone would pick up on it and know that they were gay clubs. It was hard to live that way, very hard. I never had to lie before and this was what I was forced to do. It was a world, and until you were there, you didn't know how hard it was to live in. I became a different person. I was much more quiet in the dual life. In the period of a month I went from an outgoing, lively, talkative person to someone who put up barricades to almost everyone at work, for fear they would find out.

The one out I had was college. I was midway through my degree program and I could say the college severely hampered my social life. Most everyone understood this and they wouldn't press me so much about who I was going with or whether or not I was serious, or would remarry. At home, Rose and Barbara were my way out, my alibi. The only stipulation was that whenever I used them as an excuse to be away from home, I would have to let them know in advance. And I would never use them unless, indeed, they would be at home so my family could reach me in an emergency. I did spend time with my family; the boys got to see me and talk with me every day. Jimmy, of course, as a teenager, was always on the go and didn't rely on me for emotional support and love the way Richard did. When I got home from work, at around 3:45 I would spend time with the boys. Mother would prepare dinner and we would be together until shortly before seven when I would go to school. After class I would go to Ann's for thirty to forty-five minutes and then return home, except on the weekends. Richard was always in bed by nine, so he didn't miss any of my time in the evening, and Jimmy was occupied with TV or his stereo by then anyway. At this point I think Mother was beginning to suspect, but she didn't want a firm answer. Didn't want to know the truth. At one point during these three months she did come right out and ask me if I was seeing Lisa. I was truthfully able to say no. I saw her at class but never went out with her or spent any time with her after or before class. That seemed to hold Mother's questions. She couldn't quite figure out what else to ask.

. . .

Source: Gifford Guy Gibson with the collaboration of Mary Jo Risher, *By Her Own Admission: A Lesbian Mother's Fight to Keep Her Sons* (Garden City: Doubleday, 1977). pp. 56–57. Copyright 1977 by Gifford Guy Gibson.

them carries penalties of up to five years' imprisonment. Oral-genital contacts are prohibited by law in nearly forty states, in some of which offenders are liable to up to twenty years' imprisonment. Anal intercourse is against the law in over forty states, and in several of these carries a sentence of up to twenty years' imprisonment. Prostitution is illegal in every state except Nevada, where local counties are permitted to decide for themselves whether or not to allow it.

Homosexual acts were illegal in every state until recently, but several states have repealed, or are in the process of repealing, these statutes. Many of the laws governing these various "deviations" have, of course, fallen into almost complete disuse, but prosecutions under some of them are by no means uncommon.

Most Americans learn the official norms of sexual behavior from the family, the school, and a host of other agencies of socialization. Yet actual research into the sexual practices of Americans has demonstrated consistently and conclusively that there is a wide discrepancy between the moral norms specifying how Americans *ought* to behave and the statistical norms revealing how they *actually* behave. In fact, the great majority of Americans have violated one or more of our traditional sexual norms.

Research into the sex lives of Americans is at best sketchy; like other citizens, social scientists have been affected by the taboos surrounding the subject. The first major study of sexual behavior was published by Alfred C. Kinsey and his associates in the late 1940s and early 1950s, and their work, for all its flaws, remains the most comprehensive source of data on the topic. When Kinsey published his massive volumes *Sexual Behavior in the Human Male* and *Sexual Behavior in the Human Female*,[8] they evoked an uproar. The *New York Times* refused to carry publisher's advertisements for the books on the grounds that Kinsey's scrupulously scientific works were obscene. The general public was both shocked and fascinated to discover just how varied the sexual lives of Americans really are.

Kinsey found, for example, that nearly 70 percent of American men had frequented prostitutes. One man in six had as much homosexual as heterosexual experience. Some 85 percent of all men had experienced premarital intercourse, and 50 percent of married men had had extramarital sexual experience. Kinsey found that 40 to 50 percent of the boys reared on farms had participated in sexual activities with animals.

Some 92 percent of men had masturbated, and 59 percent had engaged in heterosexual oral-genital contacts. Of the women, 48 percent had engaged in premarital intercourse and 26 percent had experienced extramarital intercourse. Some 58 percent of women had masturbated, 43 percent had engaged in oral-genital activity, and 28 percent had had lesbian experience or desires.

Caution must be exercised in comparing Kinsey's findings with those of later studies, because the various surveys do not employ the same sampling techniques or ask precisely the same questions. The indications are, however, that there has been a substantial increase in many forms of variant sexual behavior, largely because of the more permissive attitudes adopted by younger Americans in the postwar years. In one recent study, Robert Sorensen found that 44 percent of all males between thirteen and fifteen have had sexual intercourse, 36 percent of them experiencing their first episode by the age of twelve. By the age of nineteen, some 72 percent of boys and 57 percent of girls have experienced intercourse.[9] Another study, reported in 1974, found that only a quarter of all men and women in a national sample considered anal intercourse "wrong," and nearly a quarter of married couples under the age of thirty-five had used the technique.[10] Even in conservative "middle America" there are signs of change. The practice of "swinging"—the consensual exchange of marital partners—is practiced by a substantial number of Americans, most of them middle-aged suburban residents. One study of "swingers" found that they were overwhelmingly right-wing in their political attitudes.[11]

---

[8]Alfred C. Kinsey, *et al.*, *Sexual Behavior in the Human Male* (Philadelphia: W. B. Saunders, 1948), and *Sexual Behavior in the Human Female* (Philadelphia: W. B. Saunders, 1953).

[9]Robert Sorensen, *Adolescent Sexuality in Modern America: Personal Values and Sexual Behavior, Ages 13 to 19* (Cleveland: World, 1972).

[10]Morton Hunt, *Sexual Behavior in the 1970s* (Chicago: Playboy Press, 1974), pp. 32, 204.

[11]Gilbert Bartell, "Group Sex Among the Mid-Americans," *Journal of Sex Research*, 6 (May 1970) 113–130; see, also, Charles Palson and Rebecca Palson, "Swinging in Wedlock," *Society*, 9 (February 1972), 28–37; and Duane Denfield and Michael Gordon, "The Sociology of Mate-Swapping: or The Family That Swings Together Clings Together," in James R. Smith and Lynn C. Smith (eds.), *Beyond Monogamy* (Baltimore: John Hopkins Press, 1974).

ANALYZING THE PROBLEM

The social problem arising from variant sexual behavior can be usefully analyzed from the functionalist, conflict, and deviance approaches.

The Functionalist Approach

The functionalist approach is useful in that it helps to explain why some forms of sexual behavior attract a great deal of social stigma. For instance, given that a large majority of Americans violate most of our supposed norms of sexual behavior, one might wonder why homosexuality, prostitution, and pornography create the controversy that they do. Part of the reason seems to stem from the fact that in the past a society usually had to ensure a very high birth rate in order to maintain its population; in addition, all societies have to maintain a stable family system in order to provide optimally for the care of children. The death rate in traditional, preindustrial societies was very high, with as many as half of the children dying in the first few years of life. Large families were an economic advantage, and large populations were often regarded as a military resource. For these societies, then, a norm insisting on genital, heterosexual intercourse was highly functional. Any sexual activity that was nonreproductive would tend to depress the birth rate, and thus be dysfunctional: if it were sufficiently widespread, social disorganization would result and the society might face collapse.

Some traditional societies, it is true, permitted various forms of nonreproductive sexual behavior—but only as a supplement to, not a substitute for, genital heterosexual intercourse. Societies that allow or approve widespread homosexuality, for example, always insist on some degree of bisexuality; there has never been a society that approved homosexuality exclusively. Other traditional societies were much more restrictive, permitting no deviation from the central norm of genital heterosexuality. This was true of the ancient Israelites, from whose sexual norms our own are ultimately derived. Even masturbation is condemned in the Old Testament as the "wasting of seed."

The social reaction to certain forms of sexual variance becomes more understandable in the light of this ancient cultural tradition. The gratification of sexual desires through homosexuality is nonreproductive, and exclusive homosexuality cannot be reconciled with the family system. Exclusive gratification through pornography is also nonreproductive, and many people feel that pornography encourages other nonreproductive forms of sexual experience. Intercourse with prostitutes, too, is essentially nonreproductive, since both partners are anxious to avoid pregnancy; and by definition, prostitution operates outside the family system. To make matters worse, homosexuality, prostitution, and pornography are publicly visible—in the first case, because homosexuals form their own subculture, and in the latter two cases because prostitutes and pornographic merchandise are on open display in the streets of our cities. In contrast, other variant outlets—such as heterosexual oral-genital contacts—are no less private than heterosexual intercourse; and although they are nonreproductive in themselves, they can more readily be used as supplements to marital intercourse. Consequently they are subject to relatively little active public regulation. It is only when these acts are used chronically as a substitute for genital intercourse that they risk being regarded as severely deviant.

In the modern world of exploding populations, of course, nonreproductive forms of sexual behavior are no longer dysfunctional. In as far as they limit population growth, they are functional. Much of the increased social acceptance of variant forms of sexual behavior (and indeed of abortion and contraception) is probably related to this fact. Societies that are desperately trying to limit their populations can hardly object to nonreproductive sexual behaviors on the grounds that they constitute a "wasting of seed." But the old attitudes and values—often entrenched in law—have been slow to change. Most people continue to internalize the dominant cultural attitude that certain sexual acts are perverted, unnatural, sinful, or repellent.

The Conflict Approach

The conflict approach emphasizes the many clashes of interests and values that are involved in the problem of sexual variance in society. In the more permissive climate of the post-World War II years, there has been an extensive and unprecedented public debate about the nature of sexual morality and the right of the state to regulate the private sexual lives of consenting adults. The problem of sexual variance is thus becoming an arena of conflict between those who adhere to, and those who are critical of, the traditional norms.

The question of pornography, for example, has aroused complex arguments based on conflicting values. There is controversy over the effects, if any, that pornography might have on children or on public morality generally. There is debate about the extent to which the censorship of pornography might clash with the deeply held American value of freedom of speech, of the press, and of other forms of expression. And it is not only conservatives who are critical of pornography; some radical feminists have also denounced it on the grounds that it debases women.

Prostitution arouses similar value conflicts. To some, it is an evil practice that undermines family life, weakens social morality, and should be eradicated with the full force of the law. To others, it is a private commercial arrangement between consenting adults and, whatever one might personally think of the practice, it should be of no concern to the state or the public.

Homosexuality has become increasingly controversial since the late 1960s, when the gay liberation movement launched its campaign to end prejudice and discrimination against homosexuals. Other social movements, with titles such as "Save Our Children," have arisen to oppose the new movement for homosexual rights. The issue of gay rights has been debated in cities and states across the nation as legislation to protect homosexuals from discrimination has been proposed, passed, defeated, repealed, or endorsed by voters and legislators. Again, there is a fundamental conflict between those who abhor sexual variance and those who resent the attempt of the dominant group to impose its values on others.

The Deviance Approach

The deviance approach has often been applied to the problem of sexual variance. From this approach, people who participate in homosexuality, prostitution, or the use of pornography are social deviants: they have either failed to learn, or have rejected, the relevant norms of the dominant society. The members of the dominant society apply stigma to these people, partly as a punishment for the deviance and partly as a warning to others.

The deviance approach also attempts to understand the actual process by which people come to learn deviant sexual behaviors. Thus the anomie theory, for example, explains a great deal of deviance in terms of a discrepancy between culturally approved values and the availability of culturally approved means of achieving them. The theory points to the fact that American society has a culturally approved value of sexual satisfaction but that the approved means of achieving that satisfaction—marriage to an appealing spouse—is not available to everyone. Those who adhere to the value but lack the approved means of achieving it may resort to other, disapproved means, such as the use of prostitutes or pornography. The pressure on some individuals to deviate is thus located within the values of the dominant culture.

The labeling theory of deviance, on the other hand, focuses on the ways in which some people come to be labeled as deviant by others. The process of becoming a prostitute or of identifying oneself as a homosexual rarely consists of a sudden, immediate act. Rather, the individual gradually comes to accept the label of deviant— either because he or she has been actively labeled as such by others or because he or she anticipates the label that others would apply if they knew of the deviant behavior. Once people are actually labeled as sexual deviants, they tend to structure their later behavior in terms of the label. In other words, they come to think of themselves as homosexuals or prostitutes, to associate with others of similar interests, and to have their behavior patterns further reinforced. The labeling theory also emphasizes that deviance is a relative matter: any group is deviant from the point of view of another group with different norms. The more powerful group, however, is able to impose its own values and label the less powerful group as deviant.

Let us look more closely at those sexual variations that are considered a social problem in the United States.

HOMOSEXUALITY

Homosexuality, which refers to sexual acts or sexual feelings directed toward members of the same sex, is perhaps the most stigmatized of the main forms of sexual variance in the United States. American attitudes toward male homosexuality are reflected in laws against homosexual conduct that are among the most stringent in the world. *Lesbianism*, or female homosexuality, has generally escaped the attention of legislatures both in America and elsewhere in the world, perhaps because lesbians do not form such obvious subcultures as male homosexuals. Lesbianism has also been largely neglected by social scientists, and sociological research on the subject is very limited.[12]

Public attitudes toward homosexuality are currently in a state of considerable flux, primarily because of the efforts of the gay liberation movement. Some decades ago, homosexuals were widely considered to be morally depraved. This attitude gradually gave way to the view that they are psychologically "sick"—that is, that homosexuality is a form of mental illness. The problem with this formulation, in the view of many social scientists, is that it is difficult to regard as "sick" someone who would be regarded as "healthy" in another society or context: people with smallpox are indisputably sick wherever they may be, but, as we have seen, there have been and are many cultures where homosexual behavior would be considered normal and even desirable. For a long time the American Psychiatric Association (APA) listed homosexuality in its official schedule of mental illnesses, but after extensive debates in 1973, all sixty-eight district branches of the APA resolved to remove it. In a 1974 referendum, American psychiatrists voted by a large majority to eliminate homosexuality from the list of mental illnesses.[13] Instead, psychiatrists now recognize a "sexual-orientation disturbance" stemming not from homosexuality itself but from the anxiety aroused in some individuals by the social reactions to it.

Gay liberation spokespeople, with the backing of most social scientists, contend that homosexuality is simply a different life style, not a "perversion" or "sickness." Their arguments have met with a mixed reaction: some states, such as Illinois and Connecticut, have repealed antihomosexual legislation, and several cities, such as San Francisco and Seattle, have passed homosexual civil rights bills to prevent discrimination against homosexual teachers, police officers, and other city employees. Other states and cities, however, have emphatically rejected proposed reforms, and the federal government continues to discriminate against homosexuals. One reason for the lack of clarity or consistency in public policy is the substantial ignorance about homosexuality that exists in America as the result of generations of treating it as unmentionable.

Incidence

Trying to determine how common homosexuality is in America is not an easy task. One problem is that surveys may underestimate the number of homosexuals, largely because people may be reluctant to admit to homosexual inclinations or activities. A second problem is the extreme difficulty of defining what, in practice, a "homosexual" is. It is commonly supposed that the population falls into two neat sexual categories,

---

[12]See, however, Barbara Ponse, *Identities in the Lesbian World: The Social Construction of Self* (Westport, Conn.: Greenwood Press, 1978); Betty-Wysor, *The Lesbian Myth* (New York: Random House, 1974); Donna M. Tanner, *The Lesbian Couple* (Lexington, Mass.: D. C. Heath, 1978); and Deborah Goleman Wolf, *The Lesbian Community* (Berkeley, Calif.: University of California Press, 1979).

[13]Malcolm Spector, "Legitimizing Homosexuality," *Society*, 41 (July–August 1977), 52–56.

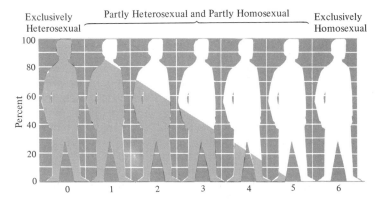

Exclusively Heterosexual | Partly Heterosexual and Partly Homosexual | Exclusively Homosexual

FIGURE 15.1 **Kinsey sexual rating scale.** Alfred Kinsey's research on human sexual behavior established that homosexuality and heterosexuality are not mutually exclusive categories: elements of both are found in most people in varying degrees. Kinsey's seven-point scale measures this balance, from the one extreme to the other.

(Adapted from Alfred C. Kinsey et al., *Sexual Behavior in the Human Male* [Philadelphia: W. B. Saunders, 1948], p. 638.)

homosexual and heterosexual, but in fact most people probably fall somewhere on a continuum between the two, presenting researchers with an array of tricky questions. For example, how do we categorize those who alternate between both forms of behavior? Or those whose behavior is exclusively heterosexual but whose fantasies are exclusively homosexual? Or those who are currently exclusively heterosexual but who have a long history of homosexuality? Or those who, because they are unconsciously fearful of their own latent homosexuality, brag about their heterosexual interests and express extreme hostility to homosexuals? Clearly, different researchers may handle these and other anomalies in very different ways, and may produce different statistics as a result.

In his massive study of American sexual behavior, Kinsey found that 4 percent of males were exclusively homosexual throughout their lives. He also found that an additional 6 percent of males were primarily homosexual for at least three years between the ages of sixteen and fifty-five. Moreover, some 37 percent of American males and 13 percent of American females had, after adolescence, at least one homosexual experience resulting in orgasm, and 30 percent of all males had been brought to orgasm through oral stimulation by another male. Another 13 percent of males reacted erotically to other males but had had no homosexual experience. Of those males who were predominantly homosexual, 80 percent had experienced heterosexual intercourse and 10 percent were married. Some 2 to 3 percent of females were exclusively homosexual, but 13 percent of women had had homosexual

experience and another 15 percent had experienced erotic feelings toward other women.

There is some debate about how accurate these figures are, because no comparable survey has since been undertaken. A 1970 survey by *Psychology Today* found exactly the same figures as those in Kinsey's survey—4 percent of males were exclusively homosexual throughout their lives and 37 percent had experienced at least one homosexual act.[14] The survey used very different sampling procedures, however, and the identical findings may be only a coincidence. A 1974 national survey commissioned by *Playboy* found a significantly lower incidence of homosexuality, but this survey used a very unreliable sampling procedure which specifically omitted "strongly deviant groups."[15]

Kinsey himself was surprised at the high incidence of homosexual experience and rigorously checked his data; finding the same pattern emerging from group after group in his sample, he proposed a seven-point rating scale, with exclusive heterosexuality at one end and exclusive homosexuality at the other (Figure 15.1). Kinsey concluded:

> The world is not divided into sheep and goats. . . . Only the human mind invents categories and tries to force facts into separated

---

[14]Robert Athanasiou, Phillip Shaver, and Carol Travis, "Sex," *Psychology Today*, 4 (July 1970), 39–52.

[15]Hunt, *op. cit.*, see Appendix on methodology; see, also, Douglas Kirby, "Methods and Methodological Problems of Sex Research," in Joann S. DeLora and Carol A. B. Warren (eds.), *Understanding Sexual Interaction* (Boston: Houghton Mifflin, 1977).

pigeon holes. The living world is a continuum in each and every one of its aspects. The sooner we learn this concerning human sexual behavior the sooner we will reach a sound understanding of the realities of sex.[16]

Myths

Several myths surround the issue of homosexuality in America.[17] One of the most common is that homosexuals suffer from gender confusion, that is, that male homosexuals are typically "effeminate" and female homosexuals typically "masculine." Although a very small number of homosexuals may adopt the mannerisms associated with the public homosexual stereotype, the great majority are indistinguishable in manner and appearance from their heterosexual counterparts. There is no objective evidence that a "feminine" appearance in men is any more common among homosexuals than among heterosexuals, and the same is true of "masculine" women. The myth probably derives from widespread confusion between homosexuality and *transvestism*—the wearing of the clothing of the opposite sex for one's own sexual arousal. Many otherwise normal heterosexuals who have no homosexual impulses whatever engage in transvestite behavior, and there is no evidence to suggest that transvestism is any more common among homosexuals than among heterosexuals.[18] And although in our culture male homosexuality is commonly associated with effeminacy, historically it has frequently been associated with aggressive masculinity, as in the case of military commanders like Julius Caesar and Alexander the Great, or militarist groups such as

the warrior Spartans and the Japanese Samurai. Perhaps in reaction to the "effeminate" stereotype, the American homosexual community is rapidly becoming "masculinized," with many homosexuals adopting a ruggedly masculine dress and appearance.[19] It should be noted, incidentally, that the scorn that "effeminacy" in men evokes is closely linked to the general devaluation of women in American society. That is why an effeminate boy is more likely to be the object of criticism or even contempt than a tomboyish girl—the girl is at least aspiring to a higher status, whereas the boy is stooping to a status of less value.

Another myth is that both male and female homosexuals typically play either an "active" or a "passive" role in their sexual relations. The evidence is, however, that most homosexuals play both roles. As is the case with heterosexuals, any specific preferences they may have cannot be deduced from their physical appearance. The great majority of both men and women who identify themselves as homosexual have had some heterosexual experience; their sexual orientation thus seems to be a matter of preference and not the result of a lack of experience of the opposite sex. Most homosexuals form long-lasting, affectionate relationships with other people of the same sex at some time in their lives; this is particularly true of lesbians. Male homosexuals, however, do tend to be more promiscuous than heterosexual males. Another myth is that male homosexuals are a particular threat to young boys. The fact is that most homosexuals, like most heterosexuals, are not sexually attracted to children, and homosexuals are proportionately less likely to attempt to seduce children than are heterosexuals.

Yet another persistent myth is that homosexuals share a distinct and consistent personality type. In fact, they are, like heterosexuals, a heterogeneous group who may have little in common other than their sexual orientation.[20] In one study, Evelyn Hooker matched a selected group of homosexuals with a group of heterosex-

[16]Kinsey, *Sexual Behavior in the Human Male, op. cit.,* p. 639.

[17]See Alan P. Bell and Martin S. Weinberg, *Homosexualities: A Study of Diversity Among Men and Women* (New York: Simon and Schuster, 1978), for a comparison of several of these myths against actual research data. See, also, Martin S. Weinberg and Colin J. Williams, *Male Homosexuals: Their Problems and Adaptations* (New York: Oxford University Press, 1974); William Masters and Virginia Johnson, *Homosexuality in Perspective* (Boston: Little, Brown, 1979).

[18]H. T. Buckner, "The Transvestic Career Path," *Psychiatry*, 33 (1970), 381–389; Esther Newton, *Mother Camp: Female Impersonation in America* (Englewood Cliffs, N.J.: Prentice-Hall, 1972).

[19]Laud Humphreys, "New Styles in Homosexual Manliness," *Transaction*, 8 (March–April 1971), 38–46.

[20]Bell and Weinberg, *op. cit.*

uals for age, IQ, and educational attainment. She gave extensive personality and other psychological tests to both groups, then had the results of the tests evaluated by a panel of experienced clinical psychologists. The experts were unable to determine the sexual orientation of the subjects. In addition, there was no difference in score between the homosexuals and the heterosexuals in general personality adjustment. A wide range of personality types existed in both groups.[21]

Causes

Why do some people become predominantly homosexual in the face of powerful social norms specifying heterosexual conduct as the only legitimate expression of sexuality? The problem has vexed social scientists for decades, and several theories have been put forward.

Biological Determinism. Certain researchers have tried to find a genetic or physiological basis for homosexuality, but their supporting evidence is extremely limited. Studies of twins have shown that if one twin is homosexual, the chances are significantly greater than average that the other will also be homosexual. But since twins share much more similar learning experiences than other children, their common environment is at least as likely as their common heredity to be responsible for their sexual orientation. Other attempts to find hormonal correlates of homosexuality have been inconclusive at best. Most scientists now reject the biologically determinist view, for it cannot account for the changes in orientation that take place over an individual's lifetime, or for the different incidence of homosexuality in different cultures at different times. Like heterosexual behavior, homosexual behavior is learned.

Early Experiences. Some researchers believe that early childhood or adolescent experience of homosexuality may cause someone to become predominantly homosexual later in life. This may be the case in some instances, but the fact is that the great majority of American preadolescents and a substantial proportion of adolescents do engage in homosexual activity, yet only a small minority of these become adult homosexuals. Then, too, others who have not had early homosexual experience also become homosexual later in life. The theory therefore cannot provide a comprehensive account for individual cases of homosexuality in adulthood.

Family Environment. Psychoanalytic theorists have concentrated on the early environment of homosexuals and have tried to isolate factors common to their home backgrounds. The main advocate of this view is Irving Bieber, whose studies led him to believe that male homosexuals typically had cold, domineering mothers and ineffectual or hostile fathers.[22] Bieber's views have been much criticized, however, on the grounds that his research sample consisted entirely of subjects receiving psychiatric care, making it unrepresentative of the general homosexual population. It is quite possible that a study of heterosexuals in psychiatric treatment would reveal a similar or equally disturbed home background—but such a finding could hardly be used to explain their heterosexuality. Other studies have failed to find any consistent differences in the parental background of homosexuals and heterosexuals, and it is clear that many homosexuals have home environments quite unlike those that Bieber described.[23]

Social Learning. Another explanation is derived from the behaviorist, or social-learning, school of psychology, which holds that virtually all behavior is learned through a process of rewards and punishments.[24] In this view a person

---

[21]Evelyn Hooker, "The Adjustment of the Male Overt Homosexual," *Journal of Projective Techniques*, 21 (1957), 18–31.

[22]Irving Bieber *et al.*, *Homosexuality: A Psychoanalytic Study* (New York: Basic Books, 1962).

[23]Evelyn Hooker, "Parental Relations and Male Homosexuality in Patient and Nonpatient Samples," *Journal of Consulting and Clinical Psychology*, 33 (April 1969), 140–142.

[24]See Ronald L. Akers, *Deviant Behavior: A Social Learning Approach*, 2nd ed. (Belmont, Calif.: Wadsworth, 1977).

A woman describes her growing awareness of her own bisexuality beginning at age twenty-eight.

. . .

Even prior to that age I'd acknowledged I'd been a woman-watcher, not a man-watcher, but I'd never really done anything. At a party or a restaurant when a lovely woman walked into the room, no matter how good-looking the man with her was, I always wound up staring at her. After countless discussions with some of my gay friends, I was still adamant that I had no intention of joining their ranks. I was very much attracted to men as well as women. It never dawned on me I could be bisexual. A further concern was society's attitude that if you had one homosexual experience you were obviously gay. It's as if with that single move you were declaring all of your past or future relations with men null and void. With the conditioning we're all exposed to, we learn there are only peaks and valleys. We have to get on one end of the pole or the other rather than shinny up and down.

My feelings about women scared me in the beginning, because I felt society's pressure. Slowly some thoughts came to my mind, and this was prior to any heavy experiences with women. I decided anything I do on this earth I'd have to do because I wanted to and not because I was pressured into doing it by anyone else. If I were sleeping with both men and women because I wanted to, then that's where I was. I couldn't feel guilty about it. Also I think our sexuality is tied up with genetics, and there's certainly nothing I could do to change that.

It's funny because suddenly I sensed a contentment with myself when I reached those con-clusions. I even noticed I started man-watching a lot in addition to woman-watching. What the psychological context is I don't know, but it's worked well for me. Maybe it's always been a case of the bisexuality in me struggling to get out, saying, "Hey, appreciate both men and women." It's overkill, I suppose, like anything we do in life. Let me give you an example. If you get a little bit angry at someone about something and you don't air your views about it but hold them in, the day is going to come when you explode for some minor reason. By refusing to recognize my bisexuality for a long time, I went to the complete other extreme and convinced myself that if I ever slept with any woman at all, I was going to instantly turn into a lesbian. It was irrational. I feel I wasted a lot of years and the possibilities of good relationships by having that hang-up.

After all that thought, I was completely ready for my first actual exploring with a woman. It took me a long time to get there, but when I did it was satisfying. The other woman hadn't gone through any extended period of introspection, and for her it was probably much more frightening. She was a complete closet case who was afraid of appearing as anything but exclusively straight. Because she was confused about her own feelings, she acted like someone in the movie *The Boys in the Band*. The next morning she greeted me with one of those lines, "God, I was so drunk last night, what did I do?" From there I've gone on to good, solid relationships with both men and women.

. . .

who finds an early homosexual experience pleas-ant may repeat the experience, reinforce the homosexual orientation further, and so on. This approach is helpful, but it also has defects. First, it does not explain why only a handful of those who have homosexual experiences find the activity so rewarding that they repeat it until they become fully homosexual. Second, the overall balance of punishments and rewards in our society strongly favors a heterosexual orientation, and it is difficult to see how limited homosexual experience can outweigh the intense heterosexual conditioning to which every member of our society is subjected. Third, some homosexuals clearly do not find their sexual orientation rewarding and may even wish to change it—yet they are unable to do so. In view of these factors an explanation based purely on rewards and punishments is inadequate.

Self-Definition. A more plausible theory, which is attracting increased attention, is that homosexuals adopt their sexual orientation as a result of an early definition—often unconscious and involuntary—of themselves as homosexual.[25] Some individuals may internalize the social belief that homosexuality and heterosexuality are mutually exclusive categories, but may fail to internalize fully the social prohibition on homosexual behavior. Consequently, when they engage in exploratory homosexual acts they may come to think of themselves as homosexuals, become trapped within their own definition, and structure their subsequent experiences in accordance with this view of themselves. If they are labeled as homosexuals by others, this definition of the self is further reinforced. As Edward Sagarin observes:

> It might be useful to start from a premise . . . that there is no such thing as *a homosexual,* for such a concept is . . . an artificially created entity that has no basis in reality. What exists are people with erotic desires for their own sex, or who engage in sexual activities with same-sex others, or both. The desires constitute feeling, the acts constitute doing, but neither is being. Emotions and actions are fluid and dynamic, learnable and unlearnable, exist to a given extent . . . but are constantly in a state of change, flux, development, and becoming.

> However, people become entrapped in a false consciousness of identifying themselves as *being* homosexuals. They believe that they discover what they are. . . . Learning their "identity," they become involved in it, boxed into their own biographies. . . . There is no road back because they believe there is none. . . . [26]

A particular advantage of this theory is that instead of looking for a specific account of how homosexual behavior is learned, it suggests a basically similar process for the learning of all sexual behavior: the theory can be applied successfully to heterosexuality and bisexuality as well as homosexuality, because it recognizes that it is only the precise content of any of these behaviors that varies from one person to another.

The Homosexual Community

The stresses on a homosexual in American society can be severe. Unless he or she is prepared to make an overt declaration of sexual preference and accept any adverse social reaction that follows, the homosexual must at all times be on guard against doing or saying anything that would give friends, employer, or others any reason to suspect his or her true sexual orientation. To these stresses may often be added feelings of guilt and shame, the constant embarrassments of leading a double life, and fear of the criminal penalties that could be applied to one's sexual acts.[27]

The homosexual community provides an escape from these pressures and serves to socialize new entrants into the homosexual subculture and its norms and values.[28] These communities are found primarily in large cities, where attitudes toward sexual variance are usually more tolerant than elsewhere. These cities often have definable homosexual areas, containing an almost exclusively homosexual population and a high concentration of restaurants, shops, hotels, and other amenities that cater primarily to homosexual customers. An important element in these communities is the "gay bar." Large cities such as New York, San Francisco, and Los Angeles have several hundred such bars, which

---

[25]See Edward Sagarin, *Deviants and Deviance* (New York: Praeger, 1975); and Philip Blumstein and Pepper Schwartz, "The Acquisition of Sexual Identity: The Bisexual Case," paper presented at the Annual Meetings of the American Sociological Association, August 25–29, 1974, Montreal.

[26] Edward Sagarin, "The Good Guys, the Bad Guys, and the Gay Guys," *Contemporary Sociology,* 2 (January 1973), 10.

[27]See Edward William Delph, *The Silent Community: Public Homosexual Encounters* (Beverly Hills, Calif.: Sage, 1978).

[28]Laud Humphreys, *Out of the Closets: The Sociology of Homosexual Liberation* (Englewood Cliffs, N.J.: Prentice-Hall, 1972); Carol A. B. Warren, *Identity and Community in the Gay World* (New York: Wiley, 1974); Joseph Harry and William B. DeVall, *The Social Organization of Gay Males* (New York: Praeger, 1978).

Several churches in the United States are now willing to marry homosexual couples, although these marriages have no force in law. Gay organizations are arguing, however, that marriage or some other legal union between same-sexed partners should be officially recognized.

often serve as an environment in which the individual can accept his or her behavior as natural and as a source of pride. As Evelyn Hooker notes:

> The young man who may have had a few isolated homosexual experiences in adolescence, or indeed none at all . . . may find the excitement and opportunities for sexual gratification appealing and thus begin active participation in the community life. Very often, the debut, referred to by homosexuals as "coming out," of a person who believes himself to be homosexual but who has struggled against it, will occur in a bar when he, for the first time, identifies himself publicly as a homosexual in the presence of other homosexuals. . . . he may be agreeably astonished to discover a large number of men who are physically attractive, personable, and "masculine"-appearing, so that his hesitancy in identifying himself as a homosexual is greatly reduced. . . . he becomes convinced that far from being a small minority, the "gay" population is very extensive indeed. Once he has "come out," that is, identified himself as a homosexual to himself and to some others . . . they assist him in providing justifications for the homosexual way of life as legitimate.[29]

In a study of the "coming out" process, Barry Dank found that the gay community served the important function of giving homosexuals an acceptable view of themselves and a feeling of normality. One of his subjects, for example, reported:

> I knew that there were homosexuals, queers and whatnot: I had read some books, and I was

[29]Evelyn Hooker, "The Homosexual Community," in *Proceedings of the XIV International Congress of Applied Psychology*, vol. 2, *Personality Research* (Copenhagen: Munksgaard, 1962), pp. 52–53.

resigned to the fact that I was a foul, dirty person, but I wasn't actually calling myself a homosexual yet. . . . The time I really caught myself coming out is the time I walked into this bar and saw a whole crowd of groovy, groovy guys. And I said to myself, there was the realization, that not all gay men are dirty old men or idiots, silly queens, but there are some just normal-looking and acting people, as far as I could see. I saw gay society and I said, "Wow, I'm home."[30]

The impact of the gay liberation movement is likely to make the homosexual community and life style more visible in the future. Strong pressures will continue to be exerted to redefine the problem as being not homosexuality but society's attitude toward it.

PROSTITUTION

Prostitution is the relatively indiscriminate exchange of sexual favors for economic gain. Termed "the world's oldest profession," it is highly resistant to all attempts at elimination. Prostitution is illegal, and flourishing, in nearly every state in this country. The penalties of the law are usually applied only to the prostitute and rarely to her client, however—probably because the clients are likely to include respectable citizens of high status and because men, not women, make the laws. To many people, prostitution is a social problem simply because it is seen as immoral, institutionalizing the use of sex for pleasure alone rather than for expressive or reproductive ends. Other people are concerned by the social problems associated with prostitution—the spread of venereal disease, the existence of organized crime based on prostitution, and the robbery and blackmail to which clients are sometimes subjected. There is debate, however, over whether prostitution can or should be controlled by law. Many people insist that the removal of criminal penalties would tend to undermine moral standards by legitimizing prostitution in the eyes of the public. Others take the

view that since prostitution will continue to exist whether it is unlawful or not, many of the problems surrounding prostitution could be better solved if it were legal but socially regulated. It is also often argued that the state has no business interfering in the private lives of its citizens by making crimes of acts that have no victims.

Forms of Prostitution

Not all exchanges of sexual favors for rewards are considered to be prostitution. Because they do not offer their sexual services in a relatively indiscriminate way, the woman who "marries for money" and the permanent "mistress" who is supported by a married man are not considered prostitutes. The true prostitute accepts a number of customers, feels no emotional tie to most or all of them, and uses prostitution as a major or sole source of income. Estimates of the number of prostitutes in the United States range from a quarter of a million to about half a million, but many of them practice their profession only intermittently or on a part-time basis.

Prostitution takes several main forms: the streetwalker, the housegirl, the call girl, and various types of male prostitutes.[31]

The Streetwalker. The streetwalker has the lowest status and earnings among prostitutes. She solicits clients in public places, such as streets, bars, and the lobbies of cheap hotels, and her fee is often under $20. Some streetwalkers are young novices in the profession, but many others are older women who are no longer able to make

---

[30]Barry M. Dank, "Coming Out in the Gay World," *Psychiatry*, 34 (May 1971), 187; see, also, Warren, *op. cit.*

[31]See Harold Greenwald, *The Call Girl* (New York: Ballantine, 1958), and *The Affluent Prostitute* (New York: Walker, 1970); Harry Benjamin and R. E. L. Masters, *Prostitution and Morality* (New York: Julian Press, 1964); Barbara S. Heyl, *The Madame as Entrepreneur: Political Economy of a House of Prostitution* (Brunswick, N.J.: Transaction Books, 1977); Charles Winick and Paul M. Kinsie, *The Lively Commerce: Prostitution in the United States* (Chicago: Aldine, 1971); Paul K. Rasmussen and Lauren H. Kuhn, "The New Masseuse: Play for Pay," in *Urban Life*, special issue, "Sexuality: Encounters, Identities and Relationships" (October 1976); Mary Riege Laner, "Prostitution as an Illegal Vocation: A Sociological Overview," in Clifton D. Bryant (ed.), *Deviant Behavior* (Chicago: Rand McNally, 1974).

a living in the higher-status forms of prostitution. The streetwalker is particularly subject to harassment by the police: uniformed officers may arrest her for loitering, and plainclothes vice officers may entrap her by posing as potential clients.

The Housegirl. The housegirl, who is usually younger and more attractive than the streetwalker, has somewhat higher status. She works and sometimes lives in a brothel, an organized house of prostitution run by a "madam," generally an older retired prostitute who hires the women and supervises their activities. The madam takes a considerable percentage of the housegirl's fees, and quickly fires women who fail to attract clients. Although much publicity has been given to brothels that have sprung up disguised as "massage parlors" or "clubs," the indications are that the number of brothels in the United States has been declining for many years. Urban "red light" districts containing dozens of brothels are a feature of the past.

The Call Girl. One reason for the decline of the brothel has been the rise of the call girl, who has the highest status and earnings in the profession. The call girl works from her own room or apartment, is relatively selective in her choice of customers, and usually makes contact with them by telephone. Her clientele consists largely of regulars who have been introduced to her through the private recommendations of other customers. Many call girls occupy rooms in fashionable hotels and contact prospective clients through members of the hotel staff. Call girls may earn considerable sums, sometimes charging several hundred dollars for one night's services. In some instances they may find wealthy clients who are prepared to maintain them in separate apartments as mistresses or even to marry them. Many call girls see their profession as a possible avenue to economic security and high social status.

The Male Prostitute. Male prostitution attracts very little attention in the United States, largely because many statutes against prostitution are directed only at females. Heterosexual male prostitution is very rare; even the "gigolo" usually serves only as a social companion to the wealthy woman who pays him. Homosexual prostitution, however, is common in large cities.

Despite endless campaigns to eliminate it, prostitution seems to be here to stay. There is debate about whether the United States should continue to apply criminal sanctions to prostitutes or follow other industrial societies that have legalized its practice.

The lowest status is accorded to the "hustler," who is usually adolescent and solicits customers on the streets of certain areas of the city. Many if not most of the hustlers consider themselves heterosexual and see their activities as a relatively temporary means of making money.[32] The "bar hustler" is usually somewhat older and solicits clients in certain gay bars. The "houseboy" works but rarely lives in a male house of prostitution, of which there are a few in most large cities. The "call boy" has the highest status and earnings in the profession and, like the call girl, operates out of his apartment or hotel room for a select group of clients. A male prostitute may hope to become a "kept boy," the homosexual equivalent of the mistress maintained by a wealthy man.

Reasons for Prostitution

Why does prostitution exist in our society, and why is it so difficult to eradicate?

From the point of view of the prostitute, the occupation offers the opportunity for earnings far in excess of those available in most other occupations open to women. To some women, the work of the prostitute may seem preferable to that of laboring for long hours as a factory machinist or key-punch operator for much lower rates of pay.

From the point of view of the client, prostitution offers the advantages of sexual variety free from the troublesome obligations of more socially acceptable relationships. For the older or physically handicapped man, prostitution provides perhaps the only opportunity for sexual experience with a young and attractive woman. For the man who is temporarily deprived of his usual sexual outlets—such as the traveler or the sailor—prostitution offers a convenient source of sexual gratification. The norms governing sexual expression in our society make no provision for men in these situations, and prostitution is functional in that it provides an alternative outlet for those dissatisfied with their existing opportunities. Kingsley Davis, who seems more concerned with the function of the prostitutes for men than with the effects of this service on the prostitutes themselves, observes:

> Enabling a small number of women to care for the needs of a large number of men, it is the most convenient sexual outlet for armies and for the legions of strangers . . . and physically repulsive in our midst. It performs a role which apparently no other institution fully performs.[33]

Davis points out that prostitution could be eliminated only in a society that was totally permissive and in which sexual relations were freely available to all. Such a society would be impossible, he contends, because total permissiveness would be incompatible with the family system, without which there might be no effective means of socializing children and the society would tend to collapse.

Is prostitution on the increase? Certainly it is becoming more visible. Paradoxically, however, the growing permissiveness of American society that has allowed this increased visibility may have led to a decrease in the number of prostitutes and the number of men who use their services. In his 1948 survey Kinsey found that 22 percent of college males had visited prostitutes; a 1968 study found that only 4.2 percent had done so.[34] The decrease is presumably linked to the much greater availability of other sexual outlets to contemporary college males. The *Playboy* survey in 1974 found a sharp decrease, as compared to Kinsey's figures, in the number of males who had experienced premarital intercourse with prostitutes and in the frequency with which they had such experiences.[35] And although prostitutes may have become more blatant in their soliciting and thus more visible to the public, their number also appears to be declining; a 1945 estimate put the total number of prostitutes at 1,200,000, more than twice as many as the current maximum estimates.[36]

---

[32]Albert J. Reiss, Jr., "The Social Integration of Peers and Queers," *Social Problems*, 9 (Fall 1961), 102–120.

[33]Davis, *op. cit.*, p. 351.

[34]Vance Packard, *The Sexual Wilderness* (New York: McKay, 1968), p. 509.

[35]Hunt, *op. cit.*, p. 142.

[36]"Vice, Regulation of," *The Encyclopedia Americana*, vol. 28 (New York: Americana Corp., 1945), p. 58.

Prostitution as an Occupation

What limited studies of female prostitutes there are indicate that most come from lower-class or lower-middle-class home backgrounds and that they often have histories of considerable promiscuity in adolescence. One study of fifteen streetwalkers concluded that they were alienated from their parents and particularly their fathers.[37] Another study found that prostitutes tended to have histories of family instability, usually involving an alcoholic, violent, or absentee parent; more than half of the prostitutes had spent at least one year of their childhood in foster homes.[38] Another study of twenty-four call girls, all of them earning very high incomes, found that every one of them had suffered emotional deprivation in childhood; bonds of affection and love seemed to have been lacking in all their families.[39] The indications are that most prostitutes have disturbed backgrounds and relatively low self-esteem (indeed, it would be difficult to reconcile high self-esteem with the choice of so stigmatized an occupation).

Many prostitutes, however, regard themselves as performing a valuable service. One comments:

> We get 'em all. The kids who are studying to be doctors and lawyers and things, and men whose wives hate the thought of sex. And men whose wives are sick or have left them. What are such men going to do? Pick on married women . . . or run around after underage girls? They're better off with us. That's what we're here for.[40]

Prostitutes also rationalize their own position by pointing to the immorality and hypocrisy of society at large. They may contend, for example, that the woman who marries an older man for money is not morally superior to a prostitute—

and neither is the prostitute's "respectable" client. The prostitute can derive some self-esteem from the certainty that she is not a hypocrite:

> We come into continual contact with upright, respected citizens whose voices are loudly raised against us in public, yet who visit us in private. . . . If they are afraid at all . . . their fear is not that they are sinning against the laws of God or decency, or even so much that they may pass on to their wives and families whatever disease we may be suffering from . . . but rather that they will somehow be discovered consorting with us and lose thereby the respect of their fellows.[41]

Despite the stigma of their profession, there seems to be a reasonable degree of job satisfaction among prostitutes; a study by Wardell B. Pomeroy found that two-thirds of them expressed no regrets about their choice of occupation, although only one-fifth would advise others to enter it.[42]

Entry into prostitution typically appears to involve a slow transition rather than an abrupt decision. Most prostitutes drift into the profession, usually through contact with another prostitute who teaches them professional techniques—how to solicit in public, how to handle difficult customers, how to recognize plainclothes police officers, and the like.[43] Others, however, are recruited by a pimp, a male who finds clients for the prostitute, arranges meetings, safeguards the prostitute against assault by customers, pays bail when she is arrested, and generally acts as her business manager—in exchange for a hefty percentage of her earnings. A high proportion of streetwalkers and call girls work for pimps, and a successful pimp may "own" an entire "string" or "stable," of prostitutes and may enjoy considerable affluence as a result of their efforts, especially since there is a tendency for the prostitute to take pride in providing well for her pimp, whose ostentatious

[37]Norman R. Jackman, Richard O'Toole, and Gilbert Geis, "The Self-Image of the Prostitute," *The Sociological Quarterly,* 4 (April 1963), 150–161.

[38]Nanette J. Davis, "The Prostitute: Developing a Deviant Identity," in James M. Henslin (ed.) *Studies in the Sociology of Sex* (New York: Appleton-Century-Crofts, 1971), pp. 297–322.

[39]Greenwald, *The Call Girl, op. cit.*

[40]Quoted in John Gosling and Douglas Warner, *City of Vice* (New York: Hillman, 1961), p. 82.

[41]Quoted in Travis Hirschi, "The Professional Prostitute," *Berkeley Journal of Sociology,* 7 (Spring 1962), 45.

[42]Wardell B. Pomeroy, "Some Aspects of Prostitution," *Journal of Sex Research,* 1 (December 1965), 177–187.

[43]James H. Bryan, "Apprenticeship in Prostitution," *Social Problems,* 12 (Winter 1965), 278–297.

Erotic displays are a commonplace feature of the downtown areas of all large cities. Many citizens consider these advertisements deeply offensive, while others eagerly patronize the establishments that display them.

life style provides evidence of her own professional success.[44]

A good deal of prostitution, particularly that involving brothels, is under the control of organized crime. Criminal syndicates have the resources to pay off police and city authorities to ensure that the brothels do not receive undue attention from the vice officers; instead, the common streetwalker bears the brunt of official attention.

PORNOGRAPHY

Pornography—written or pictorial material designed to cause sexual excitement—is as old as civilization. There is general agreement that the amount of pornography circulating in the United States is increasing, and there have been many fears about its effect on American society in general and on young people in particular. Again, however, opinion is divided. As James McCary observes:

The attitude of American men and women to pornography is varied indeed. Many consider it informative or entertaining; others believe that it leads to rape or moral breakdown, or that it improves the sexual relationship of married couples, or that it leads to innovation in a couple's coital techniques, or that it eventually becomes only boring, or that it causes men to lose respect for women, or that it serves to satisfy normal curiosity. More people than not report that the effects on themselves of erotica have been beneficial. Among those who feel pornography has detrimental effects, the tendency is to see those bad effects as harming others—but not one's self or personal acquaintances.[45]

[44]Wayland Young, "Prostitution," in Jack Douglas (ed.), *Observations of Deviance* (New York: Random House, 1970).

[45]James Leslie McCary, *Human Sexuality*, 2nd ed. (New York: Van Nostrand Reinhold, 1973), pp. 379–380.

To many people, pornography is disgusting: they feel that it presents a shameless and degrading view of human beings, contributes to the spread of sexual variance, and stimulates sex crimes. Others take the view that pornography is harmless, even if it is distasteful, that it appeals only to those who are already predisposed to use it, and that it may reduce the number of sex crimes by serving as a substitute for criminal acts rather than as a stimulus to commit them.[46]

The Problem of Censorship

The issue is further complicated by value conflict over the question of censorship. Some Americans believe that the public must be protected from pornographic material, but others— including many who find the material offensive—are reluctant to accept censorship. They object that it deprives citizens of the right to make up their own minds, and thereby interferes with their personal liberty; moreover, censorship is easily abused. History is littered with attempts at censorship that seem ridiculous today: such works as *Huckleberry Finn, Alice in Wonderland, Robinson Crusoe, On the Origin of Species*, and even the Bible have run afoul of censors in the past, as have many paintings and sculptures by great artists. Pornography is very much in the eye of the beholder. To most Americans, William Shakespeare is a literary genius, but in some communities his plays have been banned from schools on the grounds that they are obscene. Any system of censorship lends itself to the imposition on the many of the prejudices of the few.

The courts in the United States have held that pornographic material is not protected by the First Amendment, which guarantees freedom of speech and expression. The courts, however, have had to confront the problem of defining pornography. The guidelines laid down by the Supreme Court specify that material can be considered pornographic if "to the average person, applying contemporary community stan-

dards, the dominant theme of the material taken as a whole appeals to prurient interests . . . [and is] utterly without redeeming social importance." The difficulty of interpreting what the "contemporary community standards" actually are has been a severe one. In 1964 the Supreme Court ruled that "community standards" referred to national standards—a decision much resented by conservative local communities that did not share the more permissive attitudes of the nation as a whole. In 1973, however, the court changed its decision, ruling that local community standards would apply. This decision was resented by those who feared that genuine works of art would be repressed in what they regard as the cultural backwaters of the nation. Local communities are now exercising much more censorship than they could in the past.[47]

Findings of the Commission on Pornography

In 1967 Congress determined that the amount of pornography circulating in the United States was "a matter of national concern." The president appointed the National Commission on Obscenity and Pornography, consisting of nineteen experts on the subject. The commission investigated the problem for two years, and finally issued its report in 1970. Congress and most Americans expected that the report would recommend more stringent controls over pornography. Instead, the commission urged the relaxation of the laws; the only restrictions recommended were those designed to prevent children from gaining access to pornographic material.[48]

The commission's report provided a great deal of evidence about pornography in the United States. More than 85 percent of adult men and 70 percent of adult women have been exposed to pornographic material, mainly through friends (only 3 percent have received it unsolicited through the mail). About 75 percent of these

[46]See Ray C. Rist (ed.), *The Pornography Controversy: Changing Moral Standards in American Life* (New Brunswick, N.J.: Transaction Books, 1975).

[47]See Louis Z. Zurcher, Jr., and George Kirkpatrick, *Citizens for Decency: Antipornography Crusades as Status Defense* (Austin: University of Texas Press, 1976).

[48]*Report of the President's Commission on Obscenity and Pornography* (New York: Bantam, 1970).

people had their first exposure before the age of twenty-one. In general, the likelihood of exposure is greater for men than for women, for the young rather than for the old, and for the well-educated rather than the poorly educated. Young adults, the commission found, rarely patronize the bookstores that sell pornography; the typical customers are male, white, middle-class, middle-aged, and married. Between a fifth and a quarter of the adult male population has regular experience with pornographic material.

The commission found that a small majority of police chiefs believe that pornography plays a significant role in juvenile delinquency. On the other hand, a large majority of psychologists, psychiatrists, sex educators, and social workers believe that the materials are not harmful to either adolescents or others. The commission itself took the latter view:

> Research indicates that erotic materials do not contribute to the development of character defects, nor operate as a significant factor in antisocial behavior or in crime. In sum, there is no evidence that exposure to pornography operates as a cause of misconduct in either youths or adults.[49]

The commission also found, to the surprise of many, that "there is no evidence to suggest that exposure of youngsters to pornography has a detrimental impact upon moral character, sex orientation, or attitudes."[50] The commission nonetheless recommended retention of legislation preventing the sale or distribution of pornographic materials to minors. This recommendation is perhaps inconsistent, but probably reflects the commission's awareness that American public opinion strongly favors retention of these laws. Whatever the findings of social science research, many people feel that their "common sense" is a better guide to action, and their intuition tells them, rightly or wrongly, that pornography is a corrupting influence. This attitude was adopted by President Nixon, who simply rejected out of hand the commission's entire report and conclusions. In fact, Nixon announced before the commission made its report, and before he had seen any of the evidence, that he would not accept any conclusion that favored relaxation of the law.

Pornography and Crime

One of the most serious worries about pornography is that it may encourage some people to commit sex crimes. Most psychologists take the opposite view, contending that the use of pornography may actually provide sexual gratification to these individuals, thereby lessening the chances of their committing offenses against others. The president's commission accepted this position, largely on the basis of the existing research on the correlation between sex crimes and the use of pornography. A survey of the major studies in this field shows that in most cases convicted sex offenders had significantly less exposure to pornography, and had been exposed to it at a much later age, than control groups of nonoffenders.[51]

The experience of Denmark provides a further interesting insight into the relationship between sex crimes and the availability of pornography. In 1967 the Danes liberalized their laws on pornography. Within two years the number of reported sex crimes dropped by 40 percent. In 1969, largely as a result of this finding, the Danes abolished all remaining laws restricting the sale and distribution of pornography. Within a year there was a further 31 percent drop in the number of reported sex crimes: rape decreased by a small margin, but exhibitionism and child-molestation rates fell by very large margins.[52]

Whatever the findings of social science research, there is still a great deal of public concern about pornography. Nevertheless, the evidence does suggest, as James McCary notes, that the chief objection to pornographic materials "must lie in their literary, theatrical or pictorial worthlessness, rather than their power to corrupt."[53]

[49]Ibid.

[50]Ibid.

[51]W. Cody Wilson, "Facts Versus Fears: Why Should We Worry About Pornography?" *Annals of the American Academy of Political and Social Science*, 397 (September 1971), 105–117.

[52]Ibid.

[53]McCary, *op. cit.*, p. 387.

CONFRONTING THE PROBLEM

Sexual variance is a permanent feature of the American scene; whether it will remain a social problem will depend very much on the attitudes and values of Americans in the years ahead. If Americans become more tolerant of variant sexual behavior (as they did, say, with premarital intercourse), the laws regulating it will tend to be repealed or to fall into disuse, and the issue may no longer be considered a serious social problem. But as long as American society continues to regard heterosexual monogamy as the ideal context for sexual expression, other forms will continue to attract a certain measure of stigma and those who practice them will experience some personal difficulties in consequence.

Homosexuality. What exactly is the social problem of homosexuality in America that must be confronted? A few years ago the answer would have been homosexuality itself; as recently as 1969 a Harris poll found that over 60 percent of adults regarded homosexuality as "harmful to the American way of life." Since then, attitudes have changed rapidly, and it is becoming increasingly apparent that the real social problem

is discrimination against homosexuals. In 1977 the Gallup poll found that 56 percent of Americans believed homosexuals should have equal job rights; the Harris poll found that Americans favored the outlawing of "discrimination against homosexuals in any job for which they are qualified" by 54 to 28 percent; and *The New York Times*–CBS News poll found that the public felt it wrong by 61 to 20 percent to deny a qualified person a job because he is homosexual. There is still considerable hostility, however, to the idea of allowing homosexuals to work with young people in such jobs as teaching (although, of course, many homosexuals discreetly hold such jobs already).

Several states have repealed laws that made homosexual behavior illegal, and about forty cities have passed gay rights bills that prevent discrimination against city employees such as police officers, fire fighters, and, in some cities, teachers. In 1977, antigay movements in several cities and in Dade County, Florida, initiated referenda in which the voters repealed gay rights laws that had been passed earlier by elected officials. In 1978, however, American voters supported gay rights legislation for the first time—reaffirming a gay rights bill in Seattle and rejecting a proposal to fire homosexual teachers in the state of California. The gay liberation movement is presently meeting the same kind of opposition that the civil rights and women's liberation movements initially faced, but there can be little doubt that legal restraints on homosexuals will be reduced and eventually eliminated in the United States in the future. The Carter administration has been sympathetic to demands that discrimination on the grounds of sexual orientation be abolished, and the president indicated that he would sign federal legislation to guarantee the civil rights of homosexuals.

Public attitudes and values may change more slowly than the law, but as the climate becomes more tolerant, and larger numbers of homosexuals declare themselves to friends, relatives, and employers, it will be increasingly difficult to discriminate against them. In addition, changes

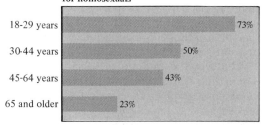

Percentage, by age, saying that the Government should pass laws to guarantee job rights for homosexuals

18-29 years	73%
30-44 years	50%
45-64 years	43%
65 and older	23%

FIGURE 15.2 Opinions on job rights for homosexuals. Since 1977 opinion polls have shown that a substantial majority of the public favors laws to prevent discrimination against homosexuals. Differences of opinion on the subject are greatest among different age groups: there is little support for homosexual rights among the aged, but overwhelming support among the young.
(New York Times/CBS News Poll, August 3, 1977.)

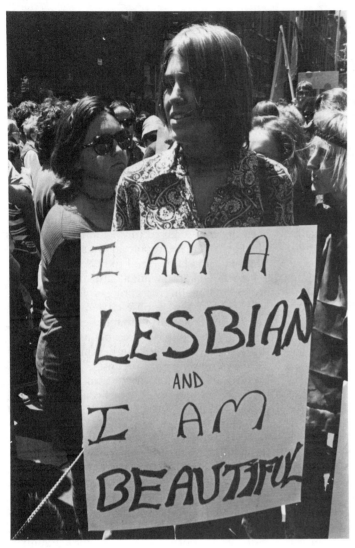

The active campaign for gay rights by members of the gay liberation movement provides an excellent example of the role social movements can play in confronting social problems and bringing about change. Without the efforts of the movement, it is doubtful whether any of the progress in attaining gay rights over the past decade would have been achieved.

in values and attitudes should be facilitated by the public availability, for the first time, of nonantagonistic and objective information about homosexuality. (It is easy to forget that only a quarter of a century ago no American newspaper would dare put the word "homosexual" in print.)

Prostitution. In an increasingly permissive society like the United States there is likely to be a decrease in prostitution, simply because so many other opportunities for sexual gratification are available. However, there is no chance that prostitution will disappear because there will always be those who cannot conveniently find the gratification they seek in any other way, and there will always be those willing to provide the service for financial reward. Essentially, then, there are two basic ways to approach the problem: try to control prostitution by keeping it illegal, or make it legal and then try to regulate it.

Public policy will undoubtedly continue along its present lines for some time—with authorities ignoring the problem for the most part but periodically launching symbolic attempts to "clean up vice." Such attempts have failed for centuries and are unlikely to succeed in the future. It is difficult to get convictions in prostitution cases, because there is no aggrieved "victim" to press charges or give evidence. Since imprisonment is generally considered too heavy a penalty for what is really a minor crime, fines are imposed—but prostitutes can pay the fines only by further prostituting themselves. Legal harassment of prostitutes does keep their activity in check, however, and thus restrains some of the public nuisance associated with prostitution.

If American attitudes and values change in the future, there may be greater pressures to legalize prostitution. Following the model of most Western European countries, Nevada has already taken this step, and now formally regulates the operations of its brothels, reaping from this commercial enterprise a tax profit that formerly went to organized crime. An alternative method of decriminalizing prostitution was introduced in Britain in the 1960s. Under British law, prostitution itself is not illegal, but it is illegal to solicit for the purposes of prostitution, and it is illegal for other parties—such as pimps—to live off the proceeds of prostitution. This law has the virtue of not interfering in the private affairs of citizens while at the same time curbing the public nuisance of solicitation on the streets.

Pornography. The great volume of pornography in the United States today clearly meets a public demand that will not subside simply because action is taken against pornography. Moreover, the civil libertarian tradition in the United States probably runs so deep as to preclude the success of any major efforts to censor the reading and viewing preferences of Americans. The object of public policy, it seems then, should be not the elimination of pornography but rather the ensuring that the only ones exposed to it are those who want to be.

The Supreme Court ruling that local community standards rather than national standards should apply in determining whether material is pornographic is likely to lead to both an increase in the amount of banned material and an increase in the number of court cases aimed at overturning these bans. The ruling does mean, however, that smaller, conservative communities need not be subjected to the more liberal tastes of the larger metropolitan areas, where the "national standards" tend to be set.

Future legislation might also be directed at unsolicited mailings of pornography and at sidewalk displays that expose citizens to pornography against their will. Through their zoning laws, several American cities are now using two basic strategies to limit the number and location of "adult entertainment" premises. The first is to concentrate these activities within small areas of the city and to refuse them licenses elsewhere: Boston, for example, has created a small district (known as the "combat zone") for this purpose. The second strategy is to disperse these premises throughout the commercial (but not residential) areas of the city while restricting their number. Detroit, for example, permits only three such establishments within designated 1,000-foot zones; other cities prevent "adult entertainment" premises from being close to schools, churches, and other amenities. Pornography itself will thrive as long as there are people willing to pay for it, but zoning measures such as these could have a cosmetic effect on the urban scene.

SUMMARY

1. Sexual variance is widely perceived as a problem in America, although some people are now claiming that the problem is not so much the behavior as society's attitude toward it.

2. Human sexuality is extremely flexible; it does not follow "instinctive" patterns but is learned through socialization in a particular culture. Practices that would be considered highly abnormal in the United States are approved in other societies.

3. Sexual behavior in America is marked by discrepancy between ideal and real norms. Although the "official" morality sanctions only genital, heterosexual intercourse between married partners, most Americans have violated this norm.

4. The functionalist approach emphasizes that sexual variance would tend to be dysfunctional in traditional societies, where a high birth rate was needed. Although it need not be dysfunctional in this respect in modern society, traditional cultural attitudes still persist. The conflict approach focuses on the conflict of interests and especially values in the area of sexual variance: to some, sexual variance is a problem; to others, the problem is that some people are trying to impose their values on others. The deviance approach sees those engaging in variant sexual acts as deviants from social norms; both the anomie and labeling theories can help explain how some forms of sexual deviance arise.

5. Exclusive homosexuality is fairly rare in the United States, but a large part of the population has had some homosexual experience or desires since adolescence. Social science research has refuted many earlier myths about homosexuality. Theories of the causes of homosexuality include biological determinism, early experiences, family environment, social learning, and self-definition. There are organized homosexual communities in urban America, in which homosexuals interact and learn favorable definitions of themselves.

6. Prostitution in the United States takes the basic forms of the streetwalker, the housegirl, the call girl, and various types of male prostitute. Prostitution exists because it appeals to some women for economic reasons and offers some men sexual satisfaction. Entry into prostitution is usually a process of "drift," sometimes involving recruitment by a pimp.

7. The amount of pornography circulating in the United States has been increasing rapidly. Repression of pornographic material raises problems concerning free speech and censorship, since pornography is difficult to define. A national commission on pornography reviewed the evidence and concluded that pornography does not contribute to character defects or crime; in fact, use of pornography may gratify urges that might otherwise find more antisocial expression. The principal objection to pornography is perhaps its vulgarity and literary and artistic worthlessness.

8. Public attitudes toward homosexuality are changing, as are the laws regulating homosexual conduct; this trend will probably continue. Prostitution may be more visible today, but the number of prostitutes and of the men who resort to them is unlikely to increase in a permissive society in which other immediate nonmarital sexual outlets are available. There will be continued attempts to restrict pornography, particularly through city zoning regulations, but these cannot be fully successful as long as people are prepared to pay for the material.

GLOSSARY

Homosexuality. Sexual acts or feelings directed toward a member of the same sex.

Pornography. Written or pictorial material designed to cause sexual arousal.

Prostitution. The relatively indiscriminate exchange of sexual favors for economic gain.

Stigma. The mark of social disgrace applied by society to those who deviate from important norms.

FURTHER READING

BELL, ALAN P., and MARTIN S. WEINBERG. *Homosexualities: A Study of Diversity Among Men and Women*. New York: Simon and Schuster, 1978. An important study of homosexual behavior, personality, and life style in the modern United States, solidly based on extensive research.

BULLOUGH, VERN L. *Sexual Variance in Society and History*. New York: Wiley, 1976. A useful survey of sexually variant behavior and the social response to it, both in the past and in contemporary society.

FORD, CLELLAN S., and FRANK A. BEACH. *Patterns of Sexual Behavior*. New York: Harper & Row, 1951. A classic on sexual behavior by an anthropologist and a psychologist. The book is objective and readable and covers a tremendous range of anthropological, psychological, and biological data.

HENSLIN, JAMES M., and EDWARD SAGARIN (eds.). *The Sociology of Sex: An Introductory Reader*. 2nd ed. New York: Schocken, 1978. A collection of articles on various aspects of human sexuality; the book provides a good and interesting overview of sociological work in the field.

HUMPHREYS, LAUD. *Out of the Closets: The Sociology of Homosexual Liberation*. Englewood Cliffs, N.J.: Prentice-Hall, 1972. A useful sociological analysis of the homosexual community and the gay liberation movement.

HYDE, JANET SHIBLEY. *Understanding Human Sexuality*. New York: McGraw-Hill, 1979. A factual, up-to-date, and well-written college textbook that covers most aspects of human sexual behavior. The book integrates material from several disciplines.

KINSEY, ALFRED C. et al. *Sexual Behavior in the Human Male*. Philadelphia: W. B. Saunders, 1948. *Sexual Behavior in the Human Female*. Philadelphia: W. B. Saunders, 1953. Classic studies of the sexual behavior of Americans that cover almost every aspect of the topic and include a wealth of statistical detail. Kinsey's work is still the most comprehensive research on the subject.

Report of the President's Commission on Obscenity and Pornography. New York: Bantam, 1970. A comprehensive report on the problem of pornography by a group of experts from many different fields. The report includes summaries of social science research findings on the subject and concludes that there is no evidence that pornography has harmful effects on adults or even on children.

RIST, RAY C. (ed.). *The Pornography Controversy*. New Brunswick, N.J.: Transaction Books, 1975. A collection of articles covering legal, moral, and social scientific aspects of pornography.

TRIPP, C. A. *The Homosexual Matrix*. New York: McGraw-Hill, 1975. An important discussion of various aspects of homosexuality; the book includes theoretical and descriptive material and summarizes major research findings.

WINICK, CHARLES, and PAUL M. KINSIE. *The Lively Commerce: Prostitution in the United States*. Chicago: Aldine, 1971. A useful sociological analysis of prostitution. The book includes both historical material and contemporary information.

16
Drug Abuse

THE PROBLEM

Drug abuse in the United States has come to be regarded as one of the most challenging social problems facing the nation. Indeed, the very word "drug" excites strong emotions, and opinion polls since the late 1960s have shown that the "drug problem" is perceived by most Americans as a major threat to our society, particularly to its younger members.

For our purposes we can define a *drug* as any chemical that is psychoactive, or capable of modifying a person's behavior through its effect on emotions, thinking, or consciousness. Strictly speaking, many familiar substances such as aspirin or tea are drugs, but when most Americans think of drugs, they have in mind only outlawed substances such as heroin or LSD. A characteristic of many psychoactive chemicals is that they lead to *dependence;* that is, the user develops a recurrent craving for them. Dependence may be psychological, physical, or both. In the case of psychological dependence, the user feels psychologically discomforted if cut off from the drug. In the case of physical dependence, or *addiction,* bodily withdrawal symptoms may occur, taking many forms and ranging in severity from slight trembling to fatal convulsions. Users develop a *tolerance* for some drugs: that is, they have to take steadily increasing amounts to achieve a given level of effect.[1]

Drug use is almost universal in human societies. The only peoples who do not use drugs

belong either to religious communities that prohibit such substances or to groups, like the Eskimo, who live in places so barren that no drug-yielding plants can be cultivated. Because the use of a drug may have socially undesirable effects—incapacitation of its users, for example—each society, through social norms and often by law as well, regulates drug usage, specifying which drugs are acceptable, who may legitimately use them, how much of a given drug it is permissible to consume, and the circumstances under which drug use is appropriate. Failure to conform to these norms constitutes *drug abuse* in the society in question. In many parts of North Africa and the Middle East, for example, marijuana is acceptable, whereas alcohol is not (in Saudi Arabia, alcohol users are still publicly flogged). In India, opium is freely available in street bazaars, but alcohol is prohibited by the constitution. Many countries impose severe penalties for the use of cocaine, but in parts of the Andes Mountains its use is nearly universal. No reliable global estimate of the number of marijuana smokers is currently available, but a rough United Nations estimate in the 1950s set the figure at more than 200 million. In modern industrialized societies, alcohol, tobacco, and caffeine are the most commonly used drugs, and the use of synthetic chemicals, such as stimulants and sedatives, is also widespread.

The sociologist is interested in why people choose the drugs they do, why some abuse drugs, and why particular societies permit certain drugs but not others. Also of interest is the social reaction to various forms of drug use, because this reaction serves to define the status of the

[1]For a detailed discussion of these terms, see Reginald G. Smart, "Addiction, Dependency, Abuse or Use: Which Are We Studying with Epidemiology?" in Eric Josephson and Eleanor E. Carroll (eds.), *Drug Use: Epidemiological and Sociological Approaches* (New York: Wiley, 1974).

drug-takers—in some cases, by labeling them as criminals.

THE SOCIAL COST OF DRUG USE

Drug abuse in the United States is a social problem because it has a wide range of social costs, or dysfunctions—some obvious and measurable, some hidden and difficult to quantify.

Crime.   There is a strong association between some forms of drug use and crime. The use of alcohol, for example, is highly correlated with violent crime; more than half of those committing murder and other violent assaults have consumed alcohol immediately before the crime.[2] Heroin addiction, too, is related to crime, although not so directly to violence. Heroin addicts may need as much as $100 a day to support their habit, and most addicts find that they must steal in order to raise these sums. In addition, users of illegal drugs have to rely directly or indirectly on criminal networks that manufacture, smuggle, and distribute these drugs. The profits from this illicit commerce are vast, and the Mafia and other criminal syndicates have become deeply involved in the supply of heroin and, more recently, of cocaine. (Technically, the profits of organized crime are not an economic "cost" to society: they are business profits, no less than those of General Motors, and are actually an unrecorded part of the nation's gross national product. But they are social costs in that this huge, untaxed income is generated by, and used to support, a variety of criminal activities, thus diverting resources that might be put to more socially useful ends.)

Not all drugs, however, are related to crime. Contrary to what some Americans believe, marijuana is not associated with aggressive behavior of any kind. The drug's calming effects are not conducive to violent acts, and because marijuana is nonaddictive, there is little motive for the user to resort to theft to obtain it. LSD and other hallucinogenic drugs, too, have little or no relationship to violent or criminal behavior.

Automobile Accidents.   Alcohol use is directly responsible for tens of thousands of highway accidents and injuries; the drug is blamed for half of the annual total of road traffic fatalities.[3] Some 60 percent of all drivers fatally injured in auto accidents have a blood-alcohol concentration of over .05 percent, a level that the National Safety Council considers sufficient to impair driving ability, and over 35 percent have a concentration of over .15 percent, a level high enough to cause intoxication. The cost of property damage and medical expenses due to alcohol-related automobile accidents totals about $1 billion each year.

There is little information on the effects of other drugs on highway accidents, but it is reasonable to suppose that most psychoactive substances, taken in sufficient doses, will impair driving ability. In simulated driving tests, marijuana has been found to affect performance by slowing down reaction time, reducing the driver's attention, and impairing judgment.[4] Amphetamines, too, which are sometimes used by drivers to increase alertness, can reduce driving performance when fatigue sets in as the effect of the drug wears off.

Disrespect for the Law.   Existing laws that regulate drug use define many millions of American citizens as criminals. A majority of American students, for example, have broken laws relating to marijuana use, and hundreds of thousands of Americans have acquired criminal records and in some cases served jail sentences for acts that many do not believe should be regulated by the criminal law at all. When laws are applied that many citizens regard as irrational, hypocritical, or outmoded, widespread disrespect for the legal system may result.

---

[2]Second Report of the National Commission on Marijuana and Drug Abuse, *Drug Use in America: Problem in Perspective* (Washington, D.C.: U.S. Government Printing Office, 1973), p. 157.

[3]"Rising Toll of Alcoholism: New Steps to Combat It," *U.S. News & World Report,* October 29, 1973.

[4]A. B. Dott, *Effect of Marijuana on Risk Acceptance in a Simulated Passing Test,* Public Health Service Publication (Washington, D.C.: U.S. Government Printing Office, 1972).

Economic Losses. The cost of alcohol abuse alone totals over $43 billion a year in accidents, medical bills, lost production, and so on. It is difficult, however, to estimate the total economic costs of drug use.[5] One reason is that there are many indirect costs society must pay to support drug-dependent persons. Treatment and control of drug abuse constitute a major drain on law-enforcement and other public resources. Chronic drug abusers, for example, may become unemployable and end up on the welfare rolls. By the mid-1970s, federal and state governments were spending over $1 billion per year on the treatment of various drug abusers. Another half billion dollars annually goes into processing drug users through the criminal justice system (well over a third of the arrests in the United States each year are for alcohol and other drug-related offenses). The economic losses resulting from criminal activities associated with drug use are also enormous.[6]

Effects on Individuals. Drug dependence takes a significant toll in terms of personal health and safety. The heavy user of drugs is much more likely than a member of the general population to be killed or to commit suicide, either deliberately or accidentally. Alcoholics, for example, have a death rate nearly three times higher than that of the general population; they represent a third of all suicides and are seven times more likely than nonalcoholics to suffer fatal accidents. Use of heroin increases one's chances of premature death through overdose, infectious diseases such as hepatitis and endocarditis, or suicide. Barbiturates also cause several thousand deaths in the United States every year. Many drugs have severe and sometimes irreversible effects on mental as well as physical health. Drug dependency, too, may affect other areas of the individual's life, ranging from the home to the work place to personal relationships with friends.

ANALYZING THE PROBLEM

Although the deviance approach is the one most often used to analyze the problem of drug abuse, the functionalist and conflict approaches have also proved useful. Drug abuse takes many forms, and different aspects of the problem can be explained in different ways.

The Functionalist Approach

The functionalist approach emphasizes that some measure of drug use is functional for a society: that is why it is sanctioned, even encouraged, by social norms. Drug use can have many beneficial effects, or functions, both for society as a whole and for subcultures within it. The most obvious instance is the contribution that drug use makes to the vitally important

social institution of leisure: in moderation, drugs such as alcohol can act as a "social lubricant," encouraging feelings of sociability and relaxation. Within subcultures, particularly religious groups, the use of drugs can have important ritual and symbolic functions, enhancing the social solidarity of the members. Social disorganization for the society or some part of it arises, however, when drug use turns into drug abuse, that is, when drug use has dysfunctional rather than neutral or functional effects.

One source of this social disorganization may be rapid social change in the form of the introduction of new drugs for which norms of usage have not yet evolved. This was the case with synthetic drugs such as LSD, which were initially used without the aid of reliable knowledge about their effects and dangers. Similarly, American adults have developed norms governing the moderate use of prescription amphetamines and barbiturates, but when these drugs become avail-

[5]See National Institute on Alcohol Abuse and Alcoholism, *Alcohol and Health* (Third Report) (Washington, D.C.: U.S. Government Printing Office, 1978).

[6]*Drug Use in America, op. cit.,* p. 175.

Value conflicts are deeply embroiled in the social problem of drug use, for different groups have very different values and interests to defend.

able to schoolchildren who do not share these norms, extensive abuse is more likely to follow.

The Conflict Approach

The conflict approach to the problem emphasizes both a conflict of values and a conflict of interests, pointing out that different groups value different drugs, but that the users of some drugs are stigmatized as deviants whereas the users of others are regarded as perfectly normal. Which groups are to be labeled as deviant is decided by those who have power and influence in society. In the United States, alcohol and tobacco are the approved drugs of those who have social, economic, and political power, so naturally the use of these drugs is regarded as normal, acceptable, and legal. Those who prefer marijuana (which appears less dangerous than alcohol or tobacco) have as a group lacked this power, so marijuana is widely considered unacceptable, and its users may be considered deviant and even criminal.

As we shall see, the dominant social reaction to drugs is influenced not so much by the dangers of the particular substances concerned as by the social characteristics, and the motives, of the group that uses them. It is acceptable, for example, for a middle-aged person to use pills for "nerves," but not acceptable for college students to use the same pills for "fun." Similarly, concern about marijuana use seems to stem not from any demonstrated dangers of the drug but from the fact that in the past its use has been popularly associated with youthful rebellion. Conflict theorists tend to regard this clash of values as a potentially healthy one because, like other social conflicts, it is likely to generate necessary changes; it has, in fact, already led to a relaxation of the absurdly severe penalties that have been applied against marijuana users in the past, and, increasingly, use of the drug is being regarded as conventional rather than deviant behavior.

The conflict approach also emphasizes that a society's patterns of drug use and abuse must be interpreted in the light of conflicts of interest. For example, in any social decision about permitting or restricting the use of a drug, there are some groups that stand to win and some that stand to lose. Consider the case of tobacco, a drug that is estimated to be responsible for one death in the United States every minute and a half. The American Cancer Society and other organizations have worked hard for the passage of antismoking legislation, but most of their efforts have been frustrated by the tobacco industry, which spends over $400 million a year on advertising and constantly lobbies in Washington through the industry's organization, the Tobacco Institute. Senator Edward Kennedy has commented that "hour for hour, and dollar for dollar, they're probably the most effective lobby on Capitol Hill." The Tobacco Institute spends huge sums of money challenging the research motives and objectivity of the American Cancer Society and other antismoking groups. Between 1975 and 1979 it had sent officials to speak against antismoking legislation in more than 400 cities in 48 states, gaining coverage on over 1,300 radio and TV shows. The industry has donated hundreds of thousands of dollars to candidates for public office. The outcomes of proposals to restrict smoking in public places, to increase tobacco taxes, and so on, are not decided simply on their merits but emerge from conflicts among organized groups defending their own values and interests.[7] The same is true of other drugs: one group's "solution" to a drug issue— such as prohibiting or permitting the use of the drug—is a "problem" to another group.

The Deviance Approach

From the deviance approach, a social problem arises when some people violate the social norms that govern drug use in their society—perhaps by consuming too much of a drug, perhaps by using an illegal drug, or perhaps by using a drug that is permitted to another category of the population but not to their own. The drug abuser is thus someone who has failed to internalize, or has rejected, the society's drug-use norms.

In the popular mind, people who abuse drugs do so either because of personal irresponsibility or because they have been corrupted by the malevolent "pusher." This view tends to be encouraged by law-enforcement officials and newspaper editorial writers, who are apt to see the spread of drug abuse as an "epidemic" analogous to the spread of a disease through the population, with the drug as the germ and the pusher as the carrier. Most sociologists consider this view rather simplistic, particularly since it tells us nothing about why people should resort to drug abuse in the first place. What, then, are the social sources of deviant drug use?

One theory is that drug abuse arises through *differential association*. According to this theory, people will tend to learn the drug-use norms of the subculture into which they are socialized. There are, for example, marked differences between the alcohol-use norms of American Italians and Jews, on the one hand, and American Irish, on the other. In both Italy and the Italian subculture in the United States alcohol is used primarily at mealtimes. The use of wine at meals is an integral part of Italian dietary customs in which even the young participate. Drunkenness at mealtimes is rare, however, partly because of the low alcohol content of wine and partly because the effect of the wine is lessened by the presence of large amounts of food in the stomach. Thus, although alcohol is used extensively in the Italian community, alcohol abuse and alcoholism are relatively rare.[8] Similarly, alcohol is commonly used by both adults and the young of the Jewish community (particularly among Orthodox Jews) as part of religious ritual, where there are strong norms preventing abuse. Among American Jews, alcoholism is also rare.[9] In Ireland, however, there is no such custom of closely regulated alcohol consumption within the family, but the culture tolerates periodic bouts of excessive drinking by single males as a way for them to relieve frustration and tension. This

[7]Michael E. Jensen, "Tobacco: A Potent Lobby," *New York Times*, February 19, 1978.

[8]Giorgio Lolli *et al.*, *Alcohol in Italian Culture* (Glencoe, Ill.: Free Press, 1958); U.S. Department of Health, Education, and Welfare, *Alcohol and Health* (Rockville, Md.: Public Health Service, 1975), pp. 15–16.

[9]Charles R. Snyder, *Alcohol and the Jews* (New York: Free Press, 1958).

cultural norm was brought to the United States by Irish immigrants, and to this day there is a relatively high rate of alcoholism among Irish American males.[10] It is possible, too, for people socialized in one subculture to be resocialized into the drug-use norms of another subculture: by differential association, for example, a high-school student who has had no previous contact with marijuana may be socialized into its use by a new subculture of peers.

Another theory is that some forms of drug abuse may result from *anomie*, the situation that arises when there is a discrepancy between culturally approved goals (such as making money) and the availability of culturally approved means of achieving them (such as good jobs). This theory is strongly influenced by the functionalist approach, for it sees drug abuse as a result of an imbalance in the social system: if the society is so organized that many people are prevented from realizing their goals, they may be "driven to drink" or may seek solace in drug experiences that provide the gratification their society denies them. Heroin addiction, for example, has long been primarily a problem of the black ghettos, which have high rates of poverty, unemployment, and other symptoms of social disorganization. Similarly, marijuana use is commonest among young people—particularly college students—largely for the reason that it offers the kinds of experience and "kicks" that are not easily available through approved channels.[11]

A third theory is that drug abuse comes about largely through *labeling*, the process by which one group applies the label "deviant" to another. According to this theory, some people may occasionally indulge in disapproved drug use, perhaps by smoking marijuana or by getting drunk. Such people, who do not consider themselves deviant and are not so considered by others, are "primary" deviants. But if significant other people—such as parents, high-school principals, or even the police—discover this behavior, the individual may be publicly labeled a "dope user" or "drunkard." Close surveillance of the person results, so further lapses are more likely to be detected and the label is confirmed. The person may accept the label, come to think of himself or herself in terms of it, and then embark on a "career" as a drug abuser. The deviance becomes habitual, and the person becomes a confirmed, or "secondary," deviant.

THE UNITED STATES AS A DRUG-TAKING SOCIETY

We noted earlier that drug-taking is a pervasive feature of American society. Let us look more closely at drug use in the United States.

Historical Background

When the Pilgrims set sail for the New World, they took with them 14 tons of water—plus 42 tons of beer and 10,000 gallons of wine. The use and abuse of drugs in America has continued unabated ever since, although the issue has been considered a serious problem only at intermittent points in our history.

Widespread narcotics addiction was a feature of American society from the middle of the nineteenth century to the first decade of the twentieth. After the Civil War tens of thousands of men who had been treated with narcotics to relieve the pain of their wounds were left addicted. The narcotics addiction rate increased steadily until the turn of the present century, when about 1 percent of the population was addicted—a much higher rate than at any time since.[12] One reason for this high rate was the general availability of opiates, such as heroin and morphine, for medical purposes. Grocery stores, pharmacies, and even mail-order houses did a flourishing sale in opiates, which were used to combat minor ailments such as stomach pain and to ease the distress of infants during teething.

[10]Robert F. Bales, "Cultural Differences in Rates of Alcoholism," *Quarterly Journal of Studies on Alcohol*, 6 (March 1946), 480–499; Richard Stivers, *A Hair of the Dog: Irish Drinking and the American Stereotype* (University Park, Pa.: Pennsylvania University Press, 1976).

[11]See Stanley Cohen and Laurie Taylor, *Escape Attempts: The Theory and Practice of Resistance to Everyday Life* (London: Allen Lane, 1976).

[12]See Leon G. Hunt and Carl D. Chambers, *The Heroin Epidemics* (New York: Spectrum, 1976).

The chewing of tobacco was common in the United States during early colonial times, but after 1870, when the drug came to be widely smoked, the use of tobacco began to be regarded by many people as a social problem. It was variously claimed that smoking led to impotence, sexual deviance, and insanity, and that it was a "stepping stone" to the use of alcohol. As a result of pressure from antitobacco social movements, the sale of the drug was banned in fourteen states in the early part of the present century, but the ban proved ineffective, and the laws were repealed after World War I. Now that we realize the serious hazards that it poses to the health of smokers, the use of tobacco is once more regarded as a social problem.

The use of marijuana has a long history in the United States. There were no laws prohibiting its use until the early part of the twentieth century, and marijuana was commonly smoked by artists and writers in the urban centers of the mid-nineteenth century. The drug became illegal only when its use became associated in the public mind with "unruly" behavior among blacks and Mexican Americans. Laws prohibiting the drug were quickly passed in some Southern and Southwestern states, and all the other states soon followed suit. The federal government did not act against marijuana until 1937, when a vigorous campaign against the drug was launched by Harry J. Anslinger, then head of the Federal Bureau of Narcotics. Marijuana had attracted relatively little national attention up to that time, but Anslinger claimed that the drug was the "assassin of youth." The mass media took up the issue and printed many stories of "marijuana atrocities"—and the stereotype of the crazed "drug fiend" was born. There is some evidence that Anslinger started his sudden campaign against marijuana because his bureau's budget had been cut by 25 percent in the preceding four years; by finding a new drug issue, he ensured the flow of funds to the bureau and the preservation of its prestige. As a result of this campaign, Congress passed legislation against marijuana without any attempt to form an objective opinion about its effects or addictive potential. As late as the 1950s Anslinger was putting forward a new version of the "stepping

stone" theory: "The danger is this: over 50 percent of these young addicts started on marijuana. They started there and graduated to heroin; they took the needle when the thrill of marijuana was gone."[13]

Within a few years after the Pilgrims landed, the governor of Massachusetts was complaining in his diaries of excessive drunkenness in the town of Plymouth. Since that time the abuse of alcohol has been recognized as a serious problem in this country. A strong social movement against alcohol, the American Temperance Union, appeared in the early part of the nineteenth century. Later movements, such as the Women's Christian Temperance Union and the Anti-Saloon League, joined the campaign. After the middle of the past century a number of states began to pass legislation against alcoholic beverages, and by the start of World War I about half the population lived in "dry" areas. The social movement against alcohol was so successful that in 1919 national prohibition was introduced with the ratification of the Eighteenth Amendment to the Constitution by every state except Rhode Island and Connecticut. Americans lived under Prohibition until 1933, when the amendment was repealed by a resounding majority. The experiment in prohibition was a total failure; it may have temporarily reduced alcohol consumption, but it also helped to create a vast network of organized crime—a system of criminal syndicates that have since moved into other fields and become so powerful that they now seem a permanent feature of American life. The attempt at prohibition showed convincingly that laws cannot eliminate drug use that is endorsed by the norms of a large part of the community.[14]

Contemporary Patterns

The use of drugs remains almost universal in American society. The great majority of Ameri-

---

[13]Donald Dickson, "Bureaucracy and Morality: An Organizational Perspective on a Moral Crusade," *Social Problems*, 16 (Fall 1968), 146–156. See, also, Richard J. Bonnie and Charles H. Whitebread, *The Marihuana Conviction* (Charlottesville, Va.: University of Virginia Press, 1974).

[14]See Norman H. Clark, *Deliver Us From Evil: An Interpretation of American Prohibition* (New York: Norton, 1976).

cans have at one time or another used psychoactive drugs. Each year we spend over a billion dollars on more than 225 million prescriptions for stimulants, sedatives, and tranquilizers. The alcohol industry sells over a billion gallons of spirits, wine, and beer each year, at a cost of more than $24 billion to some 100 million consumers. Despite the acknowledged link between cigarette smoking and such illnesses as lung cancer and heart disease, 54 million adults still continue to smoke.

However, cultural patterns of drug use have shifted in one very important respect—from legal to illegal drugs. In the past the use of illegal drugs was largely restricted to small subcultures, primarily among minority groups. Today the use of illegal drugs, particularly marijuana, has become a norm among a substantial proportion of the younger generation (although only 7 percent of adults over the age of thirty-five have used the drug, it has been used by 8 percent of those aged twelve to thirteen, by 29 percent of those fourteen to fifteen, by 47 percent of those sixteen to seventeen, and by 60 percent of those aged eighteen to twenty-five.)[15] In the late 1970s it was estimated that a total of 42 million Americans had smoked marijuana and that approximately 8 million had taken a psychedelic drug, such as LSD or mescaline. In addition, there are several hundred thousand heroin users in the United States, many of whom are addicted to the drug.

At present there are continual shifts in the specific drugs that are favored—LSD, for example, was significantly more popular in the early 1970s than it is at present; alcohol is far more commonly used by young people now than it was in the 1960s; and cocaine, a drug that was little used in the 1960s, is more popular today.[16]

Moreover, the use or abuse of any drug can take many forms. The National Commission on Marijuana and Drug Abuse identified at least

five distinct forms of use in which the motives and conduct of the user may differ:

Experimental use is short-term and of a trial nature: a person uses a drug once or twice simply to experience its effects and may never use it again.

Social-recreational use is occasional and occurs among friends or acquaintances: a drug is taken as part of a shared experience to support and enhance social interaction among group members.

Circumstantial-situational use is restricted to particular pressing circumstances: a student may use a drug to keep alert for examinations; or a person may take a drug because of peer-group pressure.

Intensified use refers to long-term, patterned drug taking, as when a person uses a drug habitually and regularly.

Compulsive use refers to high-frequency use of a drug: the individual has great difficulty in facing life without the drug and becomes physiologically and/or psychologically dependent upon it.[17]

Social attitudes, and indeed the law, often fail to distinguish among these forms of drug use. Disapproval or legal penalties may be applied indiscriminately to all types of users, from the experimental to the compulsive. Public concern about drug use has also been increased by the common belief that there is a relationship between crime and the abuse of illegal drugs—either because the drugs cause people to commit crimes or because users commit crimes to pay for the drugs. And the fact that the older generation, as many surveys have shown, has little experience or even accurate knowledge of the illegal drugs used by the young has made the problem more complex.[18]

Attitudes Toward Drugs

Value conflicts are deeply implicated in social policies on drug use. In certain cases, such as the abuse of alcohol or heroin, hostile social reaction is based largely on the universally acknowledged dangers of the drugs. In other cases, as William Goode suggests, "much of the social disapproval

[15]U.S. Bureau of the Census, *Statistical Abstract of the United States, 1978* (Washington, D.C.: U.S. Government Printing Office, 1978), p. 123.

[16]Ann Crittenden and Michael Ruby, "Cocaine: The Champagne of Drugs," *New York Times Magazine*, September 1, 1974, p. 14.

[17]*Drug Use in America, op. cit.*, pp. 30–32, 93–98.

[18]See *Drug Use in America, op. cit.*, and Michael R. McKee, "Main Street, USA: Fact and Fiction About Drug Abuse," *Journal of Drug Education*, 3 (Fall 1973), 275–295.

of drugs is based on a judgment, in most cases correct, that the user withdraws either into his or her own world or into a world that is deviant in other ways, and thus rejects or is unable to discharge his or her role obligations."[19] But in many cases there is no obvious connection between the dangers of the drugs and the severity of social reaction to their use. The National Commission on Marijuana and Drug Abuse acknowledged this fact when it reported that "it is no longer satisfactory to defend social disapproval of a particular drug on the ground that it is a mind altering drug or a means of escape. For so are they all."[20] The commission went on to point out that

> . . . chemically induced mood alteration is taken for granted and generally acceptable in contemporary America. The degree of acceptability, however, is defined by the source and type of substance taken as well as by certain characteristics of the individual, such as age and socio-economic status. This society is not opposed to all drug taking but only to certain forms of drug use by certain persons.
> . . . This variation in the acceptability of drug-using behavior is regarded by many young people as hypocritical. The Commission recognizes that contemporary social attitudes are indeed inconsistent, reflecting the special status which this society accords its youth. . . . [21]

Surveys conducted by the commission found a great deal of ignorance and even irrationality on the part of older people about the drugs used by young people, particularly marijuana. The commission found, for example, that 57 percent of adults believed that "if marijuana were legal, it would lead to teen-agers' becoming irresponsible and wild." Some 56 percent of adults considered that "many crimes are committed by persons who are under the influence of marijuana." Although only 4 percent of marijuana smokers have ever tried heroin, no less than 70 percent of adults believed that "marijuana makes people

want to try stronger drugs like heroin." The belief that marijuana smokers can die from an overdose of the drug was held by 48 percent of adults, although in fact no such death has ever been recorded. Only 9 percent of the population over fifty years of age believed that "marijuana smokers lead a normal life."[22] Moreover, only 39 percent of adults regarded alcohol as a drug, and only 27 percent regarded tobacco as a drug—but 80 percent regarded marijuana as a drug.[23] A majority of adults believed that even if marijuana were legalized, smoking it would still constitute "drug abuse."[24]

How can we account for such social attitudes? Many sociologists believe that the critical determinant of the social response to a specific drug is the social attitude toward the group that chooses to use it. Throughout this century, and particularly in the 1940s and 1950s, narcotics addiction has been common in urban black ghettos, but because it was largely invisible beyond these areas, and because the rest of society was little concerned about conditions in the ghettos, the problem was ignored. But in the 1960s, when heroin spread to the white suburbs, it became a matter of intense public concern; President Nixon declared before Congress that heroin addiction was "public enemy number one."

The adverse social reaction to marijuana also seems to be connected with the fact that in the mid-1960s its use was associated with a youthful social movement that challenged established norms and values—the "hippie" counterculture. Indeed, many adults felt that the use of marijuana actually caused young people to reject the values and life styles of their parents in favor of "dropping out" into a subculture that embraced instant gratification, lack of motivation, political radicalism, and sexual liberation.[25] Although marijuana use is no longer so closely correlated with antiestablishment values, some of the old attitudes have lingered on, and marijuana smok-

[19]William J. Goode, *Principles of Sociology* (New York: McGraw-Hill, 1977), p. 166.
[20]*Drug Use in America, op. cit.*, p. 23.
[21]*Ibid.*, pp. 42–43.
[22]The Official Report of the National Commission on Marijuana and Drug Abuse, *Marijuana: A Signal of Misunderstanding* (New York: New American Library, 1972).
[23]*Drug Use in America, op. cit.*, p. 10.
[24]*Ibid.*, p. 13.
[25]*Marijuana, op. cit.*, p. 10.

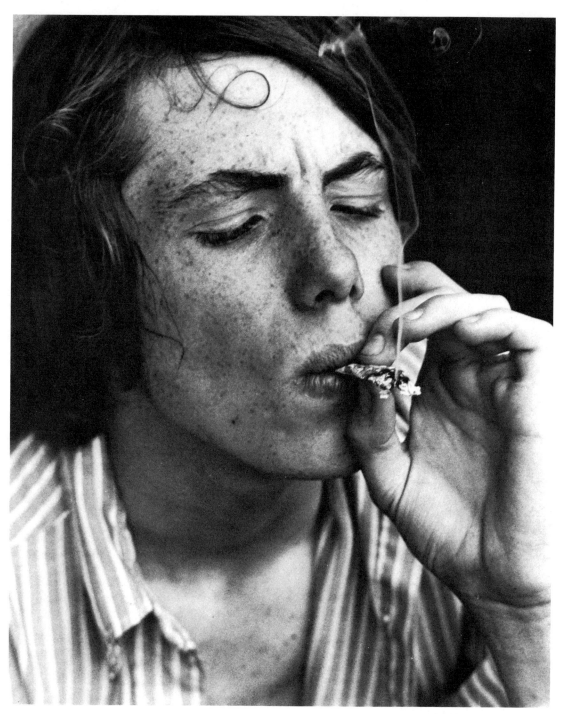

The social response to a particular drug depends less on the characteristics of the drug itself than on the social attitudes toward those who use it. Many adult Americans still associate marijuana with cultural and political radicalism among adherents of the "hippie" counterculture in the sixties and therefore remain suspicious of the drug primarily for this reason.

ers are still often viewed as a threat to society and to themselves. For similar reasons, any drug that is associated with rebellious youth remains forbidden, and even drugs that are considered acceptable when used by adults are disapproved of when used by young people for purely pleasurable purposes.[26]

The Role of Drug Subcultures

The fact that someone uses or abuses drugs is often explained in psychological terms that focus on the individual's personal history, qualities of character, reactions to stress, or strength of will in the face of temptation. Some psychologists have tried to link particular personality types with particular patterns of drug use—suggesting, for example, that the marijuana smoker has a mildly disturbed personality and that the heroin user is severely maladjusted.[27]

Although sociologists accept that psychological factors may predispose certain individuals to experiment with particular drugs, they find a purely psychological explanation of drug use inadequate. Drug use does not take place in isolation from society: the drugs that are used, the incidence of their use, and the social definition of drug users all vary from place to place and from time to time. Particular social contexts may offer opportunities for drug use, or they may present problems for which drug use appears as a potential solution. The fact that narcotics abuse is more common in urban than in rural areas, for example, does not necessarily mean that rural inhabitants are better adjusted psychologically than their urban counterparts: it may simply mean that people in cities are more likely to be exposed to narcotics and are therefore more likely to use them.

Moreover, many sociologists are reluctant to believe that the users of illegal or even dangerous drugs are necessarily psychologically maladjusted. Certainly the mere fact that someone engages in dangerous behavior largely for the experience it offers is not in itself an indication of maladjustment—the charge is not made, for example, against mountaineers, professional soldiers, stunt drivers, or astronauts. Some drug abusers, of course, may be highly disturbed people, but psychological factors cannot provide a comprehensive explanation of drug abuse.

The main agency for the socialization of individuals into a pattern of drug use or abuse is the *drug subculture*, usually composed of peers. Although a few addicts of alcohol or heroin may habitually take their drug alone, most drug-taking occurs in the context of a social group that approves the use of the drug in question. This point was first made by Howard S. Becker in 1953 in a classic article, "Becoming a Marijuana User."[28] Becker found that the novice does not simply smoke marijuana and get "high"; he or she is introduced to the drug by a group, and learns to recognize the experience as a pleasant one through the reassurances of group members. Membership in the drug subculture serves to define the nature of the drug experience, to sustain drug use, and to influence further behavior. New members, Becker argues, have to be partly resocialized by the group: they must learn to discard established norms governing drug use and to accept the norms of the drug subculture.

Similar processes appear to take place when people are initiated into the use of other types of drugs. New users of alcohol, for example, learn about the drug in the presence of other alcohol users, where they internalize the group norms pertaining to the drug. Similarly, the user of LSD is usually introduced to the drug by others who have had experience with it; they explain its use and effects and define the nature of the experience. Although the drug subculture may be dysfunctional for society because it encourages drug-taking, it does serve an important positive function for the individual user. The subculture

---

[26]See Jock Young, *The Drugtakers* (London: Paladin, 1971) and Thomas Szasz, *Ceremonial Chemistry: The Ritual Persecution of Drugs, Addicts, and Pushers* (New York: Doubleday, 1974).

[27]See David P. Ausubel, "Causes and Types of Narcotics Addiction: A Psychosocial View," *Psychiatric Quarterly*, 35 (Fall 1961), 523–531.

[28]Howard S. Becker, "Becoming a Marijuana User," *American Journal of Sociology*, 59 (November 1953), 235–242; see, also, Denise Kandel, "Adolescent Marijuana Use: Role of Parents and Peers," *Science*, September 14, 1973, pp. 1067–1070; and Bruce D. Johnson, *Marijuana Users and Drug Subcultures* (New York: Wiley, 1974).

provides a stock of knowledge about the drug and a set of norms regulating its use; the common experience of the members allows them to determine the safety limits of dosages and any adverse effects of high-frequency use. The solitary individual who uses LSD or heroin for the first time runs much higher risks than the person who first experiences the drug in the context of a subculture whose members know how to administer the drug and how to structure the subsequent drug experience.[29]

THE DRUGS AMERICANS USE

In analyzing the social problem of drug use, it is important to realize that the United States does not have a single drug problem but, rather, several separate problems. Each drug has a unique set of psychological and physical effects, each draws users from a different segment of society, each has its own social, economic, and personal consequences, and each is viewed differently by society. The drugs arousing most concern in America are alcohol, tobacco, narcotics, hallucinogens, marijuana, stimulants, and depressants. Let us look at each of these drugs in turn.

Alcohol

Medical and social scientists are almost unanimous in the view that alcohol is the most damaging drug in American society. The National Commission on Marijuana and Drug Abuse reported that "alcohol dependence is without question the most serious drug problem in this country today."[30] Most Americans, however, do not consider alcohol a problem; in one survey only 7 percent mentioned it as a serious social problem.[31]

Alcohol acts on the central nervous system as an anesthetic and as a depressant. Its effects vary with the amount of alcohol in the bloodstream when it passes through the brain. The rate of absorption depends not only on the amount consumed but also on the speed at which it is

drunk, the weight of the of the drinker, and the amount of food in the stomach. Generally the effects become apparent when the concentration of alcohol in the blood reaches .1 percent; extreme intoxication occurs when it reaches .2 percent; loss of consciousness results from concentrations of over .4 percent; and a concentration of over .7 percent causes death.

Alcohol affects behavior in two ways: it tends to reduce psychological and emotional inhibitions and it hinders task performance by impeding coordination, reaction time, and reasoning ability. The first of these effects makes alcohol generally accepted as a "social lubricant." But when this effect occurs to excess, especially in combination with the second, the results may be highly undesirable. About a third of all arrests in the United States every year are related to abuse of the drug. Moreover, about half of the traffic fatalities, half of the homicides, and nearly a third of the suicides are alcohol-related.[32] A survey of sex offenders revealed that alcohol was reported as a factor in 67 percent of sexual crimes against women.[33] A 1977 Gallup poll found that 18 percent of adults complain of the effect that alcohol has on their family life—an increase of 50 percent since 1974.

Most American adults are light drinkers, consuming up to five alcoholic beverages a week. About a fourth of the adult population are heavier drinkers, taking more than six drinks in seven days.[34] In addition, between 5 million and 9 million Americans are compulsive alcoholics.[35] Alcohol use begins earlier than other kinds of drug use, and continues longer. Some 40 percent of American youth report having tried alcohol before their eleventh birthday, and about 90 percent of high-school seniors have used the drug. The incidence of use rises rapidly from the middle teens to early adulthood: 66 percent of those between the ages of twenty-two and

[29]Young, op. cit.

[30]Drug Use in America, op. cit., p. 143.

[31]Ibid., p. 144.

[32]Alcohol and Health, op. cit.

[33]Ibid., pp. 157–158.

[34]Ibid., p. 45.

[35]Edward M. Brecher et al., Licit and Illicit Drugs: The Consumers Union Report on Narcotics, Stimulants, Depressants, Inhalants, Hallucinogens, and Marijuana—Including Coffee, Nicotine, and Alcohol (Boston: Little, Brown, 1972), p. 260.

twenty-five use the drug on a regular basis. Throughout the remainder of the adult years, use remains considerable, but it gradually tapers off until less than 40 percent of those over fifty continue to drink. Men are considerably more likely to use alcohol than are women, and the better educated are more likely to use it than are the less educated: 71 percent of those with a college education drink, compared with only 38 percent of those with no more than a high-school education. Urban residents are more likely to drink than rural residents. Among adults, alcohol use is highest in the Northeast, where 65 percent of adults use the drug, and lowest in the South, where only 37 percent do so. Use among young people is more evenly distributed.

Alcoholism may be defined as the compulsive and excessive use of alcohol to the extent that it is harmful to the drinker's health, job performance, and interpersonal relations. This definition is perhaps rather imprecise, but there is no way of making a clear-cut distinction between the "problem drinker" and the true alcoholic. The process of becoming a problem drinker and then being defined as an alcoholic is influenced to a large extent by the reactions of one's family, peers, associates, and community. For example, the "drier" the community in which one lives, the less alcohol and the fewer personal problems it takes for someone to be labeled an alcoholic; the "wetter" the community, the more it takes. Nor can alcoholism be defined pure in terms of the amount or frequency of a person's drinking. Some people are able to drink relatively large amounts quite regularly, but show no overt symptoms of alcoholism—although they have a high likelihood of becoming alcoholics. On the other hand, some people who have not touched a drop for years may be alcoholics; if they start to drink again, a prolonged "binge" or series of binges is almost inevitable. It is widely believed that "once an alcoholic, always an alcoholic," but there is evidence—still controversial—that some alcoholics may be able, after treatment, to take up normal drinking habits.[37]

Alcoholics are not necessarily physically addicted to the drug, although prolonged excessive use tends to lead to addiction. The addicted alcoholic has an insatiable desire for the drug, and if unable to obtain it, develops symptoms of physical withdrawal—rapid heartbeat, profuse sweating, uncontrollable trembling and severe nausea. Some people become chronic alcoholics quite soon after they start drinking, but the time between the first experience of alcohol and ultimate addiction may be quite long, ranging up to about eighteen years. Most alcoholics are male, but the proportion of female alcoholics has been rising sharply—from one in every six in 1966 to one in every three in 1976.[38] Very few alcoholics—perhaps 5 percent at most—fit the public stereotype of the down-and-out "skid-row bum." Most are ordinary people from every walk of life, indistinguishable from their fellows except for their alcoholism and the problems it causes for them.

Prolonged use of alcohol can cause irreversible damage to the liver and the brain; in major United States cities, alcoholic cirrhosis of the liver (the replacement of cells with scar tissue) is the third or fourth leading cause of death among those aged twenty-five to forty-five. The combination of drinking and smoking increases enormously the risk of cancer of the mouth and throat—to fifteen times the rate for people who neither drink nor smoke.

Alcohol use and abuse are very much on the increase among young persons. A 1977 study found that 90 percent of both male and female college students drink, compared with 80 percent of college men and 61 percent of the women in 1950.[39] A survey by the National Institute of Alcohol Abuse and Alcoholism showed that 30 percent of high-school students had been "pretty drunk" at least once during the previous month, and 7 percent get drunk every week.[40] The institute believes that about 1.3 million adolescents have a drinking problem. If this trend

[36]*Drug Use in America, op. cit.*, pp. 44–48.

[37]See David J. Armor, J. Michael Polich, and Harriet G. Stambul, *Alcoholism and Treatment* (New York: Wiley Interscience, 1978).

[38]"Women Alcoholics," *Newsweek*, November 15, 1976, p. 73.

[39]Edward B. Fiske, "Study Finds Use of Alcohol Is Up Sharply at Colleges," *New York Times*, March 11, 1978.

[40]"Young People and Alcohol," *Alcohol Health and Research World* (Summer 1975), 2–10.

continues, the social problem of alcohol abuse and alcoholism is likely to become much more severe in the future.

Tobacco

Tobacco is probably the most physiologically damaging of all the drugs used in the United States. Cigarette smoking reduces life expectancy, can cause lung cancer and emphysema, and greatly increases the risk of heart disease and stroke, particularly in women who use birth-control pills. If a pregnant woman smokes, her child is likely to be born underweight, and the chances of premature birth or miscarriage are doubled. Yet in spite of these facts, millions of citizens persist in using the drug; some 35 percent of American adults smoke cigarettes, and three-quarters of them picked up the habit before the age of twenty-one.[41] The extent of tobacco use

among these smokers varies, but consumption generally tends to increase over time (whereas only 5 percent of youthful smokers use one pack a day or more, 25 percent of adult smokers have reached this level).[42] The incidence of tobacco use increases with age until it reaches a peak in middle adulthood; nearly half of those between the ages of twenty-six and thirty-four smoke. More men than women smoke, although among young smokers there are as many females as males. The incidence of smoking is highest in the South and in metropolitan areas, and is somewhat more common among nonwhites than whites.[43] There is also a strong relationship between smoking and other types of drug use; the person who smokes is much more likely than

[41]U.S. Department of Health, Education, and Welfare, *Surgeon-General's Report on Smoking and Health* (Washington, D.C.: U.S. Government Printing Office, 1979).

[42]*Drug Use in America, op. cit.*, pp. 44–45.

[43]*Ibid.*, p. 47.

Alcohol is by far the most personally and socially damaging drug in America. There are at least 9 million alcoholics, and the drug is a major contributor to crime, marital breakdown, and highway fatalities. Unfortunately, the abuse of alcohol among teen-agers is rapidly increasing.

a nonsmoker to use alcohol, stimulants, sedatives, and marijuana.[44]

Tobacco is a highly habit-forming drug. The active ingredient is nicotine, a remarkable chemical that can act as a stimulant, a depressant, or a tranquilizer. Cigarette smokers rapidly develop a tolerance for nicotine, and therefore tend to increase consumption from a few cigarettes a day to one or more packs. Even a few trial experiments with cigarettes are enough to start a person on a smoking career, as Hamilton Russell points out:

> It requires no more than three or four casual cigarettes during adolescence virtually to ensure that a person will become a regular dependent smoker. . . . If we bear in mind that only 15 percent of adolescents who smoke more than one cigarette avoid becoming regular smokers and that only about 15 percent of smokers stop before the

age of 60, it becomes apparent that of those who smoke more than one cigarette during adolescence, some 70 percent continue smoking for the next 40 years.[45]

Other studies have shown that even among those who have attended special clinics and tried very seriously to stop smoking, more than 80 percent fail to do so.[46]

Why do many people, especially young people, take up cigarette smoking in the face of the widespread knowledge of its adverse effects? One reason is a barrage of advertisements that subtly associate cigarette smoking with sexual attractiveness, rugged manliness, or social sophistica-

[44]*Ibid.*, pp. 44–47.

[45]M. A. Hamilton Russell, "Cigarette Smoking: Natural History of a Dependence Disorder," *British Journal of Medical Psychology*, 44 (March 1971), 9.

[46]William A. Hunt and Joseph D. Matarazzo, "Habit Mechanisms in Smoking," in William A. Hunt (ed.), *Learning Mechanisms of Smoking* (Chicago: Aldine, 1970), p. 76.

tion, all in an attempt to maintain and increase the profits of the large tobacco corporations. Another reason seems to be that young people simply do not appreciate quite how strong dependence on tobacco can become, and how very difficult the smoking habit is to break. In one study of teen-age smokers it was found that only 21 percent thought it "very likely" that they would still be smoking five years later; the majority, with unjustified optimism, confidently expected that they would stop before then.[47]

Narcotics

The word "narcotic" literally means "sleep-inducing," although, in fact, the narcotic drugs are correctly classified as analgesics, or pain-killers. Their principal effect is to create feelings of euphoria. The narcotics most commonly used in the United States are the opiates—opium, morphine, and heroin—which are all derived from the opium poppy. Opium, a drug renowned for centuries for its soothing, dreamlike effects, is the dried form of a milky substance that oozes from the seed pods after the petals fall from the white or purple flower. Morphine, which is the main active ingredient of opium, was first isolated in 1803 and has been used extensively as a painkiller ever since. Heroin is, in turn, derived from morphine, and is an even more potent drug. Opium can be taken orally, but it is usually smoked. Both morphine and heroin can be sniffed or they can be injected into the skin, into a muscle, or —for maximum effect—directly into a vein ("mainlining"). Heroin is the most commonly abused opiate. The purity of heroin sold in the streets rarely exceeds 7 percent and is often as low as 2 percent, because dealers mix, or "cut," the drug with other substances, such as milk sugar, to increase their profits.[48]

Narcotics act primarily on the central nervous system and may produce feelings of drowsiness, tranquility, or even euphoria. An excessive dose,

however, may result in a coma or even in death by respiratory failure. All narcotics are highly addictive. Contrary to popular belief, however, most users of heroin are sporadic users and are not addicted.[49] Addiction develops after the user has taken the drug at regular intervals for a period of time, the length of which—sometimes only a few weeks—depends on the particular narcotic, the strength of the dosages, and the regularity of use. Users rapidly develop a tolerance for narcotics, after which they require steadily increasing doses to achieve the original effect of the drug: opium addicts, for example, may eventually need up to one hundred times a dose that would have been fatal during their initiation to the drug. If deprived of narcotics, the addict may suffer unpleasant withdrawal symptoms, including sweating, running of the nose, watering of the eyes, chills, cramps, and sometimes acute nausea. An intense craving for the drug may recur intermittently for several months thereafter. Narcotics also induce strong psychological dependence, perhaps because the various rituals of "copping" the drug and "shooting up" provide a habit and focus to the lives of the addicts.[50]

Addiction to narcotics is extremely difficult to break, particularly among young people. As the Consumers Union noted in a report on drug use in America, the narcotic drug

> is one that most users continue to take even though they want to stop, decide to stop, try to stop, and actually succeed in stopping for days, weeks, months, or even years. It is a drug for which men and women will prostitute themselves. It is a drug to which most users return after treatment. . . . It is a drug which most users continue to use despite the threat of long-term imprisonment for its use—and to which they promptly return after experiencing long-term imprisonment.[51]

For reasons that are not clearly understood, it seems to be much more difficult for persons

[47]Lieberman Research, Inc., "The Teenager Looks at Cigarette Smoking," survey conducted for the American Cancer Society, September 1969, Table 108, p. 212.

[48]Gary Hoenic, "The Infinite Resilience of Drug Abuse," New York Times, February 9, 1975, p. 16.

[49]Leon G. Hunt and Norman E. Zinberg, Heroin Use: A New Look (Drug Abuse Council, 1976).

[50]Stanton Peele, "Addiction: The Analgesic Experience," Human Nature, 1 (September 1978), 61–67. .

[51]Brecher et al., op. cit., p. 84.

under thirty to break the heroin habit than for those in their mid-thirties and above. It appears that a majority of addicts do not continue to use the drug beyond their mid-thirties, but it is not certain why they are successful in breaking a habit they could not beat a few years earlier.[52]

Most narcotics addicts are male, under thirty, poorly educated, and of low socioeconomic status; and the likelihood of addiction is significantly higher for blacks than for whites. Addiction is found primarily in large urban centers. Throughout most of the past few decades heroin addiction was largely confined to black urban ghettos, but in the late 1960s the drug spread to white middle-class suburbs, and its abuse among the young was rapidly defined as a major social problem. The ready availability of cheap heroin in Southeast Asia contributed to considerable addiction among American soldiers in Vietnam, further intensifying the problem. At the end of the 1960s the number of heroin addicts in the United States was estimated to be 600,000. It seems certain that the incidence of heroin addiction has stabilized or even dropped slightly since then; in 1977 the National Institute of Drug Abuse estimated the number of addicts at a maximum of 559,000, most of them living in large cities, with the greatest number—at least 70,000, and perhaps many more—being concentrated in New York City. San Francisco and Los Angeles, however, have the highest per capita incidence of addiction.

Heroin abuse continues to be regarded by many Americans as the gravest drug problem in the United States, although this attitude bears very little relationship to the incidence of heroin use or to the drug's pharmacological effects. Heroin has by far the lowest rate of use of all the drugs mentioned in this chapter; only .8 percent of adults over thirty-five, 3.6 percent of youths aged eighteen to twenty-four, and 1.1 percent of those aged twelve to seventeen have ever tried the drug, and the percentage of regular users is far lower still.[53] Of those who have never used

the drug, only 1 percent expressed any interest in trying it, even if it were legal.[54]

If widespread abuse is not the basis for public concern about the drug, why does it excite such a strong social reaction? One important reason is the "dope fiend" mythology that pictures addicts committing violent crimes. The public is also alarmed by frequent reports of deaths due to heroin overdose, but there seems to be much less alarm over the number of fatalities linked to abuse of barbiturates, alcohol, and tobacco—although these drugs directly or indirectly claim hundreds of thousands of lives each year, in

---

[54]*Drug Use in America, op. cit.*, p. 69.

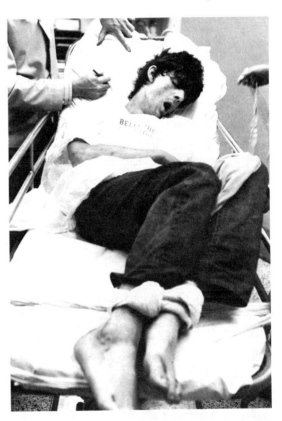

Heroin is probably the most dreaded drug in American society, although drugs like alcohol and barbiturates have far more addicts, contribute to many more deaths, and cause much more severe withdrawal symptoms.

---

[52]See Lee N. Robins and G. E. Murphy, "Drug Use in a Normal Population of Young Negro Men," *American Journal of Public Health*, 57 (September 1967), pp. 1580–1596.

[53]*Statistical Abstract of the United States, 1978*, p. 123.

comparison with a few hundred heroin overdose deaths. Also, although heroin withdrawal symptoms are extremely unpleasant, they often receive exaggerated publicity and are typically less severe than those experienced by chronic alcoholics or barbiturate addicts who are deprived of their drugs. Heroin withdrawal is never fatal, whereas alcohol or barbiturate withdrawal often is. It is also commonly believed that narcotics addiction has adverse physical effects on the user, but, in fact, alcohol and tobacco are unquestionably more damaging to the human body than is heroin. So long as the heroin addict maintains a supply of the drug and avoids excess doses, there are no detectable physical ill effects, and an addict may continue for decades without any signs of physical deterioration.

In its report on drugs in America, the Consumers Union came to the conclusion that almost all of the undesirable effects usually attributed to the opiates are in fact the effects of the narcotics laws: by labeling and treating users as deviants, political and legal authorities create new problems.

> By far the most deleterious effects of being a narcotics addict in the United States today are the risks of arrest and imprisonment, infectious disease, and impoverishment—all traceable to the narcotics laws, to vigorous enforcement of those laws, and to the resulting excessive black-market prices for narcotics.[55]

Because the possession of narcotics is illegal and severely penalized in the United States, the demand for illicit narcotics has inevitably led to the development of a black market in which the drugs, often diluted with dangerous impurities, are sold at grossly inflated prices. Organized crime has been attracted by the high profits in the narcotics trade and has become deeply involved in the smuggling and distribution of the drugs. The addicts, meanwhile, frequently have to resort to illegal means to finance their drug habits, and the constant search for a daily supply of the narcotic makes it almost impossible for them to lead normal lives.

Hallucinogens

The three types of hallucinogens most commonly used in the United States are mescaline (peyote), psilocybin, and LSD. All are taken orally. Peyote, which is derived from a cactus plant, has been used in the Americas for centuries and formed the basis for the "peyote cult" among American Indians in the late nineteenth century. Members of the Native American Church, a contemporary religious movement descended from the peyote cult, are still legally entitled to use peyote on ceremonial occasions. Mescaline, the synthetic form of peyote, is illegally manufactured in the United States and is more commonly used than peyote. Psilocybin is derived from a small mushroom found in the southwestern United States; it too has a long history of use by American Indians. Virtually all hallucinogens sold on the streets as mescaline or psilocybin, however, prove on chemical analysis to be lysergic acid diethylamide, or LSD. This drug was first synthesized in 1938, but researchers did not realize its hallucinogenic effects until one of them accidentally inhaled some in 1943. The researcher, Dr. Albert Hoffman, recorded in his notebook the extraordinary "illness" that overcame him:

> Last Friday . . . I had to interrupt my laboratory work in the middle of the afternoon and go home, because I was seized with a feeling of great restlessness and mild dizziness. At home, I lay down and sank into a not unpleasant delirium, which was characterized by extremely excited fantasies. In a semiconscious state, with my eyes closed (I felt the daylight to be unpleasantly dazzling), fantastic visions of extraordinary realness and with an intense kaleidoscopic play of colors assailed me.[56]

LSD is a colorless, tasteless substance of much higher potency than the other hallucinogens; a dose of 100 micrograms—an almost invisible speck—will produce dramatic effects. Relatively easy to manufacture, LSD is by far the most

[55]Brecher *et al.*, p. 22.

[56]Quoted in John Cashman, *The LSD Story* (Greenwich, Conn.: Fawcett, 1966), p. 31.

readily available hallucinogen in the United States today.

The effects of hallucinogenic drugs vary a great deal depending on the psychological state and expectations of the user and on the context in which the drug is taken. A typical "trip" lasts for about eight hours, during which the user often has vivid hallucinations and may "see" sounds as colors, experience heightened perception, and feel an enhanced awareness. In some cases, however, the user may have a "bad trip," involving panic, loss of self-control, or paranoid reactions. These negative effects are more likely to occur if the user is in a disturbed or anxious state at the time of taking the drug.[57]

The hallucinogenic drugs are not addictive. However, users develop a tolerance for them, usually so rapidly that sustained, high-frequency use of the drugs quickly produces virtually no effect, however high the dose. In any case, the hallucinogens are typically used as experimental drugs: the novelty of "tripping" seems to wear off fairly rapidly, and few people use the drugs regularly for long periods. No deaths directly due to the use of hallucinogens have ever been recorded, although there have been a very few highly publicized instances of indirect fatalities resulting, for example, from users' attempts to fly from upper-story windows. There are no confirmed long-term physical effects of the use of the drug; one experimenter suggested that LSD (like aspirin, caffeine, and many other drugs) might cause chromosome damage and perhaps lead to genetic defects, but other researchers have established that there is no relationship between use of LSD and birth defects.[58]

Nevertheless, there do appear to be some long-term psychological effects of the use of hallucinogens. LSD in particular produces a "flashback" effect in a small minority of users. Some of the reactions associated with an LSD experience recur days, weeks, or even months later. There is also evidence that in some people prolonged high-frequency use of hallucinogens is followed by periods of depression. It seems, too, that hallucinogenic drugs may have adverse long-term effects on people who are already psychologically disturbed.

LSD and similar hallucinogens have been used by 4.6 percent of those aged twelve to seventeen, by 19.1 percent of those fifteen to twenty-five, and by 2.6 percent of those over thirty-five.[59] The incidence of use of these drugs increased from the late 1960s, when they were eulogized by rock stars and used in the "hippie" movement, to a peak in the early 1970s. Use of the drugs appears to have declined since the mid-1970s.

Marijuana

The hemp plant, *cannabis sativa*, which originated in central Asia, has long been cultivated in the United States. In the seventeenth century more than half the winter clothing was made from hemp, and after cotton it was probably the most important cash crop in the South during the post-Revolutionary War period. Today the main interest in the plant centers on its dried leaves—marijuana—and its dried resin—hashish. Both may be taken orally but are more commonly smoked. The resin is about six times more potent than the leaf. The potency of both forms increases steadily from year to year, since the growers—mostly in Mexico and Colombia—use selective-breeding techniques to produce plants with an ever greater concentration of the active ingredient.

Marijuana is widely used by Americans from a variety of backgrounds, but its use varies most significantly with age and drops off rapidly among older men and women. Surveys reveal that men are more likely to use the drug than women, students are more likely to use it than any other occupational group, and the wealthy are more likely to use it than poorer groups. Geographically, marijuana use is disproportion-

[57]A useful overview of the effect of LSD is to be found in Richard Ashley, "The Other Side of LSD," *New York Times Magazine*, October 19, 1975, pp. 40–62.

[58]William H. McGlothlin, Robert S. Sparkes, and David O. Arnold, "Effects of LSD on Human Pregnancy," *Journal of the American Medical Association*, 212 (June 1970), 1483–1487; See, also, Norman I. Dishotsky *et. al.*, "LSD and Genetic Damage," *Science* 172 (April 30, 1971), 431–440.

[59]*Statistical Abstract of the United States, 1978, op. cit.*, p. 123.

ately more common in metropolitan areas and the Northeast and West.[60] Marijuana smoking is now so widespread that Americans spend about $6 billion a year on the drug—more than they spend on ice cream, hot dogs, and apple pie combined.[61] In addition, Americans spend some $50 million a year on rolling papers and a further $150 million on such paraphernalia as hash pipes and roach clips—all for a drug whose use is almost everywhere a criminal offense.

The psychological effects of marijuana include relaxation, intensification of sensory stimulation, increase in self-confidence, and feelings of enhanced awareness and creativity. The drug has little observable impact on the performance of simple mental tasks, although more complex tasks such as driving may be somewhat impaired. The effects of the drug are influenced by the user's mood, expectations, and the social context in which it is taken. Heavy dosages, particularly of hashish taken orally, can lead to psychotic episodes similar to a "bad trip," but this kind of effect is rare.

The short-term physical effects of marijuana are minor: a slight rise in heart rate, a reddening of the eyes, and a dryness of the throat and mouth. The drug is not physically addictive, and even chronic users do not experience withdrawal symptoms when deprived of the drug. Nor does the marijuana user develop tolerance for the drug, so there is no need for increasing dosages. Some researchers have suggested that there may be serious health hazards associated with long-term marijuana use—hazards involving brain damage, irritation of the bronchial tract and lungs, chromosome damage, and disruption of cell metabolism. These findings have not been confirmed by other researchers, however, and remain controversial.[62]

The attempt to regulate marijuana use has

been described as a "second Prohibition"[63] that is unlikely to be any more successful than the first, simply because a very substantial section of the population does not regard the attempt to forbid marijuana as legitimate. Laws that regulate crimes without victims are notoriously difficult to apply, especially when they criminalize the private acts of citizens who are otherwise law-abiding. In 1972 the National Commission on Marijuana and Drug Abuse—like similar commissions established in Canada, Britain, and Scandinavia—recommended that possession of marijuana for personal use should no longer be a criminal offense. Several states have now decriminalized the possession of small quantities of marijuana, and more are likely to follow suit.

Stimulants

Many natural substances contain drugs that stimulate the central nervous system. Caffeine, which is found in coffee, tea, Coca-Cola, and cocoa, is a widely used stimulant in American society. It is even commercially available in tablet form, such as No-Doz. Caffeine reduces fatigue, hunger, and boredom and improves intellectual and motor activity. There is considerable evidence that the drug is addictive, and many users find that they develop a tolerance for it. When a person is accustomed to drinking large quantities of coffee each day, withdrawal symptoms—primarily mild irritability and depression—occur if caffeine use is stopped. When taken to excess, the drug may cause restlessness, disturbed sleep, and gastrointestinal irritation. In doses of ten grams or more, the drug can have fatal results.

Caffeine is undoubtedly the most widely used of all psychoactive substances in the United States: 91 percent of Americans drink either coffee or tea, and enough coffee is sold every year to provide over 180 billion doses of the drug to American consumers. Nevertheless, because coffee has the status of a "nondrug" in our society, coffee drinkers are not categorized as criminals, there is no black market for coffee, and no deviant subculture of coffee drinkers exists. Be-

---

[60]*Drug Use in America, op. cit.,* pp. 63–67; *Statistical Abstract of the United States, 1978, op. cit.,* p. 123.

[61]ABC TV Special Report, "Marijuana: The Grass is Getting Greener," April 11, 1977.

[62] See Thomas H. Maugh, II, "Marihuana: The Grass May No Longer Be Greener," *Science,* 74 (August 23, 1974), 683–865; and Edward M. Brecher, "Marijuana: The Health Questions," *Consumer Reports,* March 1975, pp. 143–149.

[63]John Kaplan, *Marijuana: A New Prohibition* (New York: World, 1970).

cause the use of coffee is legal, its price is low compared to other drugs, and coffee drinkers are not tempted to adopt a life of crime to support their habit. Many sociologists believe that the experience of our society in dealing with caffeine may have implications for our responses to other, currently illegal, drugs.[64]

Cocaine is another natural stimulant. The drug, which is also a local anesthetic, is derived from the leaves of a mountain shrub indigenous to the Andes mountain region of South America, where the inhabitants consider the drug a gift from the gods. Cocaine may be injected, but is more commonly sniffed. The drug stimulates the central nervous system and produces feelings of great confidence, well-being, and euphoria. It may also reduce pain and fatigue. But excessive dosages, particularly if they are injected, can lead to psychotic reactions involving impulsive and paranoid behavior, and in some cases can cause convulsions, heart and respiratory failure, and death. Prolonged use by sniffing can also wear away the nasal tissues, causing the nose itself to collapse.

In the past, cocaine has been misclassified by the federal government as a narcotic, but in fact it is not related to the opiates at all. The drug is not physically addictive, but some users seem to become psychologically dependent on it and may become depressed if they are deprived of it. Although cocaine use is illegal in the United States, the drug has rapidly become more popular since the early 1970s. The fact that it is illegal has inevitably led to the emergence of a black market in which vast profits are made. At a street price of up to $100 per heavily "cut" gram, cocaine is by far the most expensive of the illegal drugs, and its habitual use is largely restricted to more affluent sections of the country's young adults.[65] About 2 million Americans now pay $20 billion annually for more than 66,000 pounds of cocaine, most of it smuggled in from Colombia.[66]

The group of drugs called amphetamines ("speed") are synthetic stimulants. Their effects are similar to those of natural stimulants but are longer-lasting. Usually available as pills, the amphetamines increase alertness and improve physical skills; for these reasons they may be used by athletes, truckdrivers, students, astronauts, and others who want to maintain high levels of performance for relatively short periods of time. An amphetamine high, however, is often followed by mental depression and fatigue. The drug rapidly produces tolerance; a user may eventually swallow an entire handful of tablets rather than one or two. Heavy use of amphetamines may produce serious psychoses.

Amphetamines may be taken legally only if they are issued on prescription, but many of the prescriptions that are written each year find their way onto the black market and are used by people other than those for whom they are intended. One of the most destructive of all forms of drug abuse is the intravenous injection of large amounts of amphetamines. A "speed freak" may inject the drug several times a day, remaining awake for three to five days at a stretch and becoming progressively more tense, nervous, and paranoid. The speed freak typically loses his or her appetite and may suffer malnutrition as a result. Insomnia and psychotic reactions may also occur for many weeks or months after long-term use of high doses of the drug. Many people become psychologically dependent on amphetamines, but there is little evidence that the drugs are physically addictive as well. The use of amphetamines, with or without a prescription, has declined drastically during the 1970s—not so much because demand has slackened as because of new federal restrictions on their prescription and the reluctance of responsible physicians to prescribe them. Even so, the drugs have been used by 8 million men and 12 million women.

Another kind of stimulant that has a limited but rapidly increasing popularity among young

---

[64]John Timson, "Is Coffee Safe to Drink?" *Human Nature,* 1 (December 1978), 57–59.

[65]*Newsweek,* December 20, 1978, p. 51. See, also, a report of the National Institute for Drug Abuse, *Cocaine: 1977* (Washington, D.C.: U.S. Government Printing Office, 1977); and Lester Grinspoon and James B. Bakalar, *Cocaine: A Drug and Its Social Evolution* (New York: Basic Books, 1976).

[66]"The Colombia Connection," *Time,* January 29, 1979, pp. 24–30.

Table 16.1 Facts About Drugs (question marks indicate conflict of opinion)

Name	Slang Name	Source	Classification	How Taken
Heroin	H., Horse, Junk, Smack, Scag, Dope	Semisynthetic (from morphine)	Narcotic	Injected or sniffed
Morphine	White Stuff, M.	Natural (from opium)	Narcotic	Swallowed or injected
Methadone	Dolly	Synthetic	Narcotic	Swallowed or injected
Cocaine	Coke, Snow, Toot, Blow	Natural (from coca, not cocoa)	Stimulant, local anesthetic	Sniffed, injected, or swallowed
Amphetamines	Speed, Ups, Bennies, Dexies, Pep Pills, Black Beauties, etc.	Synthetic	Sympatho-mimetic	Swallowed or injected
Amyl nitrate, Butyl nitrate	Poppers, Locker Room, Rush	Synthetic	Stimulant, vascular dilatant	Sniffed
Marijuana	Pot, Grass, Hash, Dope, Joints, Reefer, Smoke	Natural	Relaxant, euphoriant; in high doses, hallucinogen	Smoked, swallowed, or sniffed
Barbiturates	Downs, Downers, Barbs, Reds, Yellow Jackets, Tooies, etc.	Synthetic	Sedative-hypnotic	Swallowed or injected
Methaqualone	Ludes	Synthetic	Sedative-hypnotic	Swallowed
Phencyclidine	Angel Dust, Superjoint, etc.	Synthetic	Anesthetic	Smoked, swallowed, sniffed, injected
LSD	Acid, Sugar, Trips, Blotter	Semisynthetic (from ergot alkaloids)	Hallucinogen	Swallowed
Mescaline	Mesc	Natural (from péyote)	Hallucinogen	Swallowed
Psilocybin	Magic Mushroom	Natural (from psilocybe)	Hallucinogen	Swallowed
Alcohol	Booze, Juice, etc.	Natural (from grapes, grains, etc., via fermentation)	Sedative-hypnotic	Swallowed
Tobacco	Cancer Tube, Coffin Nail, etc.	Natural	Stimulant-sedative	Smoked, sniffed, chewed

*Persons who inject drugs under nonsterile conditions run a high risk of contracting hepatitis, abscesses, or circulatory disorders. Barbiturates and most amphetamines are not water-soluble and may cause abscesses and other lesions if injected.
Source: Adapted 1980 from Today's Education: NEA Journal (February 1971).

Effects Sought	Long-Term Symptoms	Physical Dependence Potential	Mental Dependence Potential	Organic Damage Potential
Euphoria, prevent withdrawal discomfort	Addiction, constipation, loss of appetite	Yes	Yes	No*
Euphoria, prevent withdrawal discomfort	Addiction, constipation, loss of appetite	Yes	Yes	No*
Prevent withdrawal discomfort	Addiction, constipation, loss of appetite	Yes	Yes	No*
Exhilaration, excitation, talkativeness	Depression, convulsions	No	Yes	Yes
Alertness, activeness	Loss of appetite, delusions, hallucinations, toxic psychosis	No?	Yes	Yes*
Mental and physical exhilaration, excitation; intensification of sexual pleasure.	Usually none?	No	No	No?
Relaxation; euphoria, increased perceptions, sociability	Usually none	No	Yes?	No
Anxiety reduction, euphoria	Addiction with severe withdrawal symptoms, possible convulsions, toxic psychosis	Yes	Yes	Yes*
Anxiety reduction, euphoria	Addiction with severe withdrawal symptoms, possible convulsions, toxic psychosis	Yes	Yes	Yes
Euphoria, distortion of senses.	Coma; psychosis, including paranoid delusions; violence	No?	Yes?	Yes
Insightful experiences, exhilaration, distortion of senses	May intensify existing psychosis, panic reactions	No	No?	No?
Insightful experiences, exhilaration, distortion of senses		No	No?	No?
Insightful experiences, exhilaration, distortion of senses		No	No?	No?
Sense alteration, anxiety reduction, sociability	Cirrhosis, toxic psychosis, neurologic damage, addiction	Yes	Yes	Yes
Calmness, sociability	Emphysema, lung cancer, mouth and throat cancer, cardiovascular damage, loss of appetite	Yes?	Yes	Yes

people is a drug prescribed for patients who risk certain forms of heart failure. This drug is amyl nitrate ("poppers"), a volatile liquid that is sold either bottled in small containers or enclosed in a breakable ampule. As soon as the container is opened the chemical begins to evaporate; if the pungent vapor is sniffed, the user experiences an almost instantaneous dilation of blood vessels and increase in heart rate, and for a minute or two has feelings of physical and mental excitation (a "body rush" and a "head rush"). The drug is supposedly available only by prescription, but the great majority of units that are manufactured each year find their way onto the illicit drug market. Another drug, butyl nitrate, has a similar effect, and is still available without a prescription. In recent years commercial enterprises have manufactured this drug under such trade names as Locker Room and Rush, and it is now widely sold in novelty stores, "head shops," and sexual-aid shops. Butyl nitrate is used in the same way as amyl nitrate, but it is highly poisonous if swallowed.

Until the end of the 1970s the use of these drugs was restricted almost entirely to the homosexual community, where they were commonly used as stimulants during sexual activity and while dancing in discotheques. In the late 1970s the discotheque phenomenon spread rapidly from the gay to the heterosexual community, with many of the more fashionable discos catering to a clientele of both sexual persuasions, and the use of "poppers" is now becoming more widespread among young people. The drugs, however, can sometimes have some unpleasant short-term side effects, including dizziness, headaches, and fainting. Death has also been reported in a few rare cases of excessive overdose. The long-term effects, if any, of persistent nonmedical use of the drugs are not yet known, since adequate studies have yet to be made.[67]

Depressants

The depressants are a class of drugs consisting mainly of sedatives and hypnotics—chemicals that tranquilize or induce sleep. The best-known of these drugs are the barbiturates, which are commonly used to relieve insomnia and anxiety. There are over 2,500 different synthetic barbiturates. Some are prescribed mainly for nocturnal use as sleeping pills and others for daytime use to sedate anxious or tense patients. The use of barbiturates is illegal unless they are obtained through a physician's prescription.

The barbiturates are widely used for nonmedical purposes and are highly addictive; abuse of these drugs has been called America's "hidden drug problem." Taken in sufficient doses, barbiturates produce effects similar to those of alcohol. They remove inhibitions, with some users becoming calm and relaxed, and others aggressive and hyperactive. Regular use of barbiturates leads to physical addiction, and withdrawal may be accompanied by anxiety, profuse sweating, body tremors, fever, and hallucinations. In many cases fatal convulsions occur, sometimes even when withdrawal takes place under medical supervision.

Barbiturates are particularly dangerous when taken with alcohol, because alcohol increases the potency of the barbiturate and hence the likelihood that the user will take an overdose. Accidental deaths due to excessive doses are frequent, and deliberate overdose is a common means of suicide in America.[68] Another dangerous method of abuse is taking amphetamines with barbiturates, a combination that produces an alternating pattern of artificially induced "ups" and "downs."

Barbiturates are relatively easy to obtain, despite the laws prohibiting possession without a prescription. Over 3.5 billion doses of barbiturates are manufactured in the United States every year, and many of them reach users through illegal channels. In the average year about 11 percent of all adult Americans use

[67]See Guy M. Everett, "Amyl Nitrate ("Poppers") as an Aphrodisiac," in M. Sandler and G. L. Gessa (eds.), *Sexual Behavior: Pharmacology and Biochemistry* (New York: Raven Press, 1975); Donald B. Louria, "Sexual Use of Amyl Nitrate," *Medical Aspects of Human Sexuality* (January 1970), 89; and Hardin Jones and Helen Jones, *Sensual Drugs* (New York: Cambridge University Press, 1977).

[68]Dan J. Lettieri, *Drugs and Suicide: When Other Coping Strategies Fail* (Beverly Hills, Calif.: Sage, 1978).

barbiturates, legally or illegally; and 3 percent take them on a regular basis.

In recent years there has been a shift among young people from the nonmedical use of barbiturates to a drug that is chemically different but has broadly similar effects—methaqualone, commonly known by the patent name Quaalude. Quaaludes are medically prescribed for such purposes as calming manic or psychotic patients, but "bootleg" versions of the drug are manufactured in massive quantities, mostly in Mexico and Colombia, and then smuggled into the United States to meet the large and growing demand. One reason for the drug's popularity is its reputation as a "love drug": it supposedly makes users more eager for sex and enhances their sexual pleasure. If methaqualone has these effects at all, it is not because of any magical property of the drug but rather because, like barbiturates and alcohol, it lessens inhibitions. Like the barbiturates, methaqualone induces both physical and psychological dependence, with severe and unpleasant symptoms when the drug is withdrawn. Abuse of the drug can aggravate liver damage, cause headaches, hangovers, fatigue, and temporary paralysis of the limbs. Overdose can result in delirium, convulsions, coma, and death (most deaths occur accidentally when methaqualone is consumed with alcohol, which—as it does with the barbiturates—vastly increases the drug's potency).

Another depressant that is chemically very different from those just discussed is phencyclidine, usually known as PCP or by its more popular street name, "angel dust." PCP was first developed in the late 1950s as an anesthetic, but its use on human beings was soon discontinued when many patients were found to display psychotic symptoms after being given the drug. The only legal use of PCP today is for tranquilizing monkeys and elephants, whose systems seem to be immune to the drug's side effects.

PCP is used mainly by teen-agers, especially those who are unsophisticated about drug use in general and who are ignorant of the dangers of PCP in particular. The drug may be swallowed, sniffed, or injected, but is most commonly smoked, typically after it has been sprinkled on a marijuana joint. Many young people thus seem to regard PCP as little more than a "superjoint," something to potentiate the effect of marijuana. In fact, however, PCP is a highly dangerous drug. The user who "gets dusted" with even a small quantity of PCP experiences a distortion of the senses and an inability to think clearly; there may also be a marked loss of the sense of balance and other physical capacities. Larger amounts of PCP sometimes cause effects similar to psychosis, a frequent form of which is a paranoid reaction that may spark aggressive behavior and even homicidal violence on the part of the user.

It is not yet clear whether PCP induces physical or psychological dependence. An overdose, however, can lead to coma and even death, and sustained use of smaller amounts can produce long-term psychotic reactions. Unfortunately, PCP is easy to manufacture in a home laboratory, and the necessary chemical ingredients and recipes for making the drug are readily available. The abuse of "angel dust" is likely to present a serious problem for some time to come, at least until American teen-agers have a wider appreciation of the dangers of the drug.

CONFRONTING THE PROBLEM

It is doubtful if the United States will ever be without a drug problem, but the nature of the problem and of the social responses to it is likely to be different in the future. Patterns of drug use will continue to alter because of changes in tastes and in norms, values, and attitudes, and because of the continual introduction of new synthetic psychoactive agents.

Abuse of alcohol is likely to remain America's major drug problem in terms both of the number of addicts and also of the social and economic costs associated with the drug; and if the present trend toward increased alcohol consumption among young Americans is maintained, the dimensions of the problem will become much more serious in the years ahead. The failure of

Elaine is trying to kick alcohol and drugs. Thirty-eight years old, she is on welfare and has a seventeen-year old son.

. . .

I haven't had a drink for six months. I used to drink heavily. And they gave me nerve pills. Librium. And sleeping pills. I used to drink and then take one sleeping pill because I couldn't sleep. But then I couldn't go to sleep on one sleeping pill. So I took another one and I almost died. I knew I was passing out. I got dizzy. So I called my mother and some friends, and they called an ambulance. I was living alone. They took me to Kingsbrook Hospital to pump my stomach. The doctor told my sister five minutes more and I would have been dead.

If I didn't have money to go to the liquor store, I would take some nerve pills. It wasn't exactly like taking a drink, but it calms you. I took two, three Libriums. One didn't have enough effect. So I took two or three and then I took a drink. I'd feel myself dozing off. I'd be blacking out. I'd say 'Ah, I'm just tired.' So I'd drink some more to keep me awake and the next thing I know I was passed out.

I'm not divorced, but I had to put my husband out, you know? I have a lot of problems, man. Try to keep myself high and drunk to forget them. I had problems with my son not going to school. I would send him to school. He wasn't goin'. And then the welfare was aggravating me. So I'd start drinking and my mind would tell me that I could feel better if I took a Librium. Then the drinking and the pills sometimes would make me mad. Sometimes my friends come over to drink and I'm taking these pills and I want them to leave. But they don't want to leave, right? We get into an argument. So I get a knife and I go out in the street and stab their tires.

I started drinking when I was 17. I took a drink to talk to somebody. I was at a party. I'm an ex-addict. I was on heroin. I got on methadone in '68 and I got off it in '70. I was also shooting coke. Everything that I did I was drinking along with it.

. . .

Karen, a woman in her late 30s, lived for twelve years with a man who was also an addict, before she moved out.

. . .

Frank was a heavy drinker for years before his problem developed. He could consume up to a fifth of Scotch a day, but his drinking didn't affect

Prohibition demonstrated that alcohol abuse cannot be legislated out of existence. The use of alcohol is currently regulated primarily through social norms against excessive consumption of the drug, but these norms clearly fail to govern the behavior of millions of Americans. What can be done?

No fully effective method for the treatment of alcoholism has yet been found, but high success rates have been achieved by Alcoholics Anonymous, a voluntary association of over half a million alcoholics who offer moral encouragement to heavy drinkers to break the habit. Often the first task of AA, curiously enough, is to convince alcoholics that that is what they are: alcoholics are notoriously reluctant to accept the fact that they have a drinking problem, even when the drug has been disrupting their lives for years on end. Once this hurdle is surmounted,

members begin work with newcomers to help them stay off alcohol "one day at a time." In addition to Alcoholics Anonymous, there is also an Al-Anon organization for the spouses of alcoholics, and an Alateen organization to help children face the problems posed by alcoholic parents.

Another promising development is the introduction of the drug Antabuse (also known as disulfiram). If a person who is taking Antabuse drinks alcohol, the result is a nausea so violent that it virtually precludes repeating the experience ever again. Many alcoholics find the regular use of Antabuse helpful, for it gives them an immediate and powerful reason not to drink. The success of the drug does depend, however, on the alcoholic's willingness to take it regularly, rather than abandon it in favor of alcohol.

Another hopeful development is the growing

his ability to function as far as work or social life was concerned.

In his late 30's and early 40's, he began to develop acute feelings of anxiety. That was when he started taking Valium. This was about 12 years ago. Frank has never been someone who likes taking medication, so I guess his problem could have been worse. I think at some point he became aware intellectually that there is a reaction between alcohol and these tranquilizers, but emotionally I don't think he recognized for a long time what was happening to him. Maybe he still doesn't.

At any rate, curious things began to happen when he started taking tranquilizers. He was taking 20 to 30 milligrams of Valium a day, which is a lot. Here was a man who had been able to handle a lot of alcohol and still function. And here he was suddenly at the point where if he had two or three drinks he would be drunk, really drunk. He would be incoherent, unable to remember anything the next day.

I began to be more and more frightened about it because he had a couple of accidents with the car. He had always been an excellent driver even with a lot of alcohol in him. And now with a

couple of drinks he was running off the road or being picked up for drunken driving.

Driving with him became a big issue in our relationship. If we went anywhere in the evening together, I would insist we go in separate cars. Our friends began to joke about the two cars. I made up excuses about why I had to go home early in my own car.

Frank got his prescription of Valium renewed regularly by his doctor. He was always very careful not to drink before 5 P.M. and it got to the point where when I heard the ice cubes clinking in the glass at 5 P.M. I knew I had about 30 minutes more to talk to him before he was blotto for the rest of the evening. Ultimately, it ruined the relationship.

The interaction seems so obvious now. In my mind the drinking was always the problem. I never thought of telling him he should stop the tranquilizers. I wish I had. It all might have turned out differently.

. . .

Source: "Dual Addiction," by William Stockton. *The New York Times Magazine,* August 6, 1978, pp. 36–37, 40–41. Copyright 1978 The New York Times.

social tendency to see alcoholism not as an untreatable curse but as a problem that can be confronted and dealt with. An important outcome of this new approach was the Comprehensive Alcohol Abuse and Alcoholism Prevention, Treatment and Rehabilitation Act of 1970, which created the National Institute on Alcohol Abuse and Alcoholism and provided for the expenditure of $300 million for research into the problems and treatment of alcoholics. The act also established the National Advisory Council on Alcohol Abuse and Alcoholism to recommend national policy. As a result, many new projects for the treatment of alcoholism, such as community-care programs, are being developed. Continuing research may yield new understanding of alcoholism and new methods of treatment.

Tobacco, unfortunately, will continue to ravage the health of millions of Americans for the

foreseeable future. Certainly "prohibition" of tobacco would be unsuccessful, since no society into which tobacco has been introduced has ever managed to rid itself of the drug, although many have imposed harsh penalties on smokers. The Sultan Murad of Constantinople even decreed the death penalty for smoking, but to no avail:

> Whenever the Sultan went on his travels or on a military expedition his haunting-places were always distinguished by a terrible increase in the number of executions. Even on the battlefield he was fond of surprising men in the act of smoking, whom he would punish by beheading, hanging, quartering, or crushing their hands and feet and leaving them helpless. . . . Nevertheless, in spite of all the horrors of this persecution. . . the

[6,9]Count Egon Caesar Corti alla Catene, *A History of Smoking,* trans. Paul England (London: Harrap, 1931), pp. 138–139.

passion for smoking still persisted. . . . Even the fear of death was of no avail with the passionate devotees of the habit.[69]

Although the milder methods of persuasion used in the United States are unlikely to be any more successful, the percentage of adults who smoke has dropped since the Surgeon General reported in 1964 that there seems to be a link between smoking and lung cancer. In 1966, 41 percent of adults smoked; in 1978, 33 percent did. Some 30 million Americans stopped smoking during these years. It may be that some new means can be found to help the remaining smokers give up their habit—perhaps a chemical that eliminates the desire for nicotine but has no adverse effects itself. However, future policy is likely to concentrate on dissuading young people from starting on a smoking career. An obvious target is the advertising of the tobacco industry; it seems intolerable that the use of this dangerous drug should be publicly encouraged, particularly when people are jailed for using other drugs that are far less harmful. TV advertising of cigarettes has been banned, and the restrictions may be extended to other media, although powerful economic interests will oppose any such measures. It is indicative of the conflict of interests involved that the federal government simultaneously spends tens of millions of dollars to subsidize tobacco farmers, and tens of millions of

dollars to persuade Americans not to smoke.

Another possibility would be to reduce federal subsidies to tobacco growers, providing them instead with subsidies to grow other crops so as to prevent economic hardship. A further possibility would be to impose much heavier taxes on tobacco as a means of discouraging people from smoking. There is also a good deal of public support for antismoking laws that prevent smoking in at least some public places; in fact, the Tobacco Institute estimated in 1978 that more than a hundred such bills were pending in state legislatures. So far, some 33 states and 225 municipalities have some restriction on smoking.[70]

Marijuana is almost certainly a permanent fixture of American society: too many people use the drug and regard the law as an unenforceable one for attempts at its suppression to be successful. The effect of such efforts is not so much to control marijuana use as to create victims of law enforcement.[71] Unless strong evidence of severe adverse effects of marijuana is found—and it is certainly possible that it might be—the drug will probably be fully legalized in the United States at some time in the future. Many states have already reduced penalties for possession, and in many areas the police tend to turn a blind eye to minor marijuana offenses. The laws against marijuana are, in fact, coming to be seen as more of a social problem than the drug itself, since the enforcement of marijuana laws diverts the efforts of police and courts from more important problems. Equally counterproductive have been some of the efforts to prevent the drug from reaching consumers. At the end of the 1960s President Nixon launched "Operation Intercept," under which customs officers, instead of making selective searches of people entering the United States, opened virtually every piece of luggage of almost every entrant, and searched nearly every car crossing the Mexican border. Delays of many hours were common at all customs points, but very little marijuana was

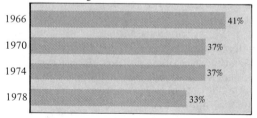

FIGURE 16.1 **Percentage of adults who smoke cigarettes.** The percentage of American adults who smoke cigarettes has declined steadily since 1966, when the Surgeon General's first report linking tobacco smoking and cancer was published. More recent research has further strengthened the evidence that smoking can cause cancer.
(Department of Health, Education, and Welfare, 1979.)

[70]*Newsweek*, October 2, 1978, p. 61.

[71]Erich Goode, "Notes on the Enforcement of Moral Crimes," in H. A. Faberman and Erich Goode (eds.), *Social Reality* (Englewood Cliffs, N.J.: Prentice-Hall, 1973).

confiscated during this period. Instead, organized-crime smugglers concentrated on bringing heroin through customs in small, easily concealed, and far more valuable packages. Similarly, in the mid-1970s the United States government supported a program under which Mexican authorities sprayed marijuana fields with the deadly weed-killer paraquat. However, Mexican farmers harvested the plants anyway, and by 1978 more than a third of samples of marijuana in the United States had residues of this dangerous chemical. The maximum paraquat residue permitted on farm crops in the United States is 0.05 parts per million; the average in the marijuana samples from Mexico was 450 parts per million. In trying to save users from the supposed hazards of marijuana, the federal government had exposed them to much greater dangers, and the Department of Health, Education, and Welfare was obliged to launch major publicity campaigns to warn smokers of the threat.[72]

The abuse of prescription drugs such as amphetamines and barbiturates can be sharply checked if physicians refuse to prescribe the drugs as indiscriminately as they have often done in the past. The overprescription of these drugs is a reflection of basic attitudes and values of American society: we are a nation of drug-takers, conditioned by advertising to believe that happiness, relief from pain or boredom, and various other desirable ends are obtainable by simply taking a suitable pill. From a strictly medical point of view most amphetamine and barbiturate prescriptions are probably unnecessary, and the nation's health would be improved rather than worsened if millions fewer of these pills were prescribed each year. Of course, any attempt to curtail the manufacture and distribution of these drugs would invite strong opposition from the big drug companies.

Narcotics addiction will probably continue to decline in the United States in the future. The abrupt increase in the use of narcotics in the late 1960s occurred at a time when old social norms and values were being widely challenged by young people; it was a period of considerable confusion, and new norms regulating novel forms

of drug behavior had not fully evolved. The use of heroin was not viewed as negatively by young people as it is today, especially since experimentation with narcotics was then often a source of prestige with peers.

The traditional punitive approach to narcotics addiction is rapidly being replaced by a concern for rehabilitation, but there is much debate about how best to help heroin addicts. One method that has had considerable success is the use of therapeutic communities—sometimes residential centers where the addicts live until they have overcome their problems, sometimes "halfway houses" where they spend part of their time while trying to reconstruct their lives in the community beyond. These centers often feature a rigid, busy schedule to keep addicts occupied throughout the day, and a grueling form of encounter-group therapy aimed at getting to the root of any personal problems that may have driven them to addiction. Some successful communities are staffed partly by ex-addicts and partly by professionals. The ex-addicts provide proof to the newcomers that addiction is curable, and they have a better initial rapport with the addicts than the "straight" professional staff might have.[73]

An approach to narcotics addiction that has been successful in some respects is the British one, which regards a heroin addict as "sick" rather than "criminal." Instead of jailing heroin addicts, the British give them their drug. Like any other medically prescribed drug in Britain, heroin is available either at a nominal charge or, if the patient cannot afford it, free. To qualify, the heroin user must satisfy a specially certified physician that he or she is an addict. The addict is then officially registered as such, and thereafter may receive a steady supply of the drug—but only enough of it to prevent withdrawal symptoms, not enough to get "high." If a registered addict is found with heroin from any other source, he or she will be prosecuted. Similarly, anyone found with heroin who is not a registered

[72]*New York Times*, July 5, 1978, p. 10.

[73]David Caplovitz, *The Working Addict* (White Plains, N.Y.: M. E. Sharpe, Inc., 1978); Patrick H. Hughes, *Behind the Wall of Respect: Community Experiments in Addiction Control* (Chicago: University of Chicago Press, 1977).

addict will also be prosecuted. Attempts are made to rehabilitate the addict, either by gradually decreasing the amount of heroin on prescription, or by switching the addict to the less dangerous drug methadone.

The main effect of the British method has been to keep narcotics abuse down to minuscule levels compared with the United States, and to virtually eliminate narcotics-related crime. Because addicts can get their drug free, they do not have to steal to buy it. Because there is little black market demand for heroin, organized crime has no incentive to smuggle the drug into the country. Because the addicts need their entire prescription supply for themselves, there is little heroin available for nonaddicts to experiment with. And because the prescription drug is of uniform strength, the possibility of deaths through overdoses or lethal impurities is drastically reduced. This entire system works because it fits very well with British values; conversely, it is unlikely ever to be widely adopted in the United States because it runs so counter to American values, which are steadfastly against the idea of giving "something for nothing"—especially when that something would be heroin provided at public expense to youthful addicts.

There are some programs in the United States, however, that provide addicts with the synthetic narcotic methadone as a legally available substitute for heroin. Methadone usually does not give addicts much of a "high," so they can function normally in a social or work situation. The drug can be taken orally, helps to eliminate craving for other narcotics, and has few undesirable side effects if taken in moderate doses. However, its use does constitute the substitution of one addictive drug for another.[74] A further problem with methadone is that supplies of the drug are entering the narcotics black market, with unfortunate effects: in 1974 New York City medical authorities found that, for the first time, narcotics deaths involving methadone were more common than those involving heroin.[75] About 80,000 narcotics addicts are currently involved in methadone maintenance programs.

The use of hallucinogenic drugs will probably continue to be confined to a small minority of Americans who are attracted by the potential that the drugs are believed to offer for the exploration of human awareness. The widespread and indiscriminate use of the drugs that occurred in the late 1960s and early 1970s is unlikely to be repeated because a good deal more is now known about the undesirable short- and long-term psychological effects that the drugs have in some cases.

A drug-free America is almost certainly an impossibility. Future policy will have to concentrate on honest and effective drug education to make the population, and particularly its younger members, fully aware of the dangers of certain drugs, particularly tobacco and alcohol. Drug use will have to be regulated in the future, but this will be better done through rationally based and widely accepted social norms rather than through the application of criminal sanctions to drug abusers. Ultimately, both the social norms and the laws will have to correspond much more closely to the intrinsic dangers of the drugs they regulate than they do at present.

SUMMARY

1. Drug abuse is widely seen as a major social problem in the United States. A drug is a psychoactive chemical, and many drugs produce dependence in their users—psychological dependence, physical dependence (addiction), or both. Some drugs also induce tolerance, or the need for steadily increasing dosages. Drug use is found in virtually all societies; drug abuse occurs when people violate the social norms that regulate drug use.

---

[74]For a useful discussion of methadone treatment, see James V. deLang, "The Methadone Habit," *New York Times Magazine*, March 16, 1975, pp. 16–93.

[75]*Enquirer* (Cincinnati), August 18, 1974.

2. The social costs of drug use include crime, automobile accidents, disrespect for the law, economic losses, and undesirable physical or psychological effects on individuals.

3. From the functionalist approach, the problem arises when drug use becomes dysfunctional rather than functional as a result of social disorganization caused, for example, by the introduction of new drugs to groups that have no norms regulating their use. From the conflict approach, the problem involves clashes of drug-related values and interests, in which the stronger parties are able to impose their values or interest on the weaker groups. From the deviance approach, the problem arises when some people violate social norms regulating drug use. This deviance may be explained through the theories of differential association, anomie, and labeling.

4. The United States has always been a drug-using society, but in recent years there has been a major shift, especially among young people, from the use of legal drugs to illegal drugs. There are several distinct forms of drug use, ranging from the experimental to the compulsive. Social attitudes toward particular drugs appear to be influenced by attitudes toward the group that uses them rather than by the properties of the drugs concerned. Most drugs are taken in the context of a subculture that approves the drug in question and initiates novices into use of the drug.

5. The drugs most commonly used in the United States are alcohol, tobacco, narcotics, hallucinogens, marijuana, stimulants, and depressants. The characteristics of the drugs and of their users vary widely.

6. There is no prospect of "solving" the drug problem in the foreseeable future. Instead, social policy must concentrate on ways of preventing the use of the more dangerous drugs and rehabilitating those who use them, and on developing more rational attitudes toward those drugs whose use is disproportionately penalized.

GLOSSARY

Addiction. A state of physical dependence on a drug, in which physical withdrawal symptoms will appear if use of the drug is discontinued.

Alcoholism. The compulsive and excessive use of alcohol to the extent that it is harmful to the drinker's health, job performance, or interpersonal relationships.

Dependence. A state of recurrent desire or craving for a drug whose use has become a habit.

Drug. Any chemical that is psychoactive, or capable of modifying a person's behavior through its effect on emotions, thinking, or consciousness.

Drug abuse. Use of a drug that does not conform to social norms prescribing the appropriate use of that drug.

Drug subculture. A subculture distinguished from the rest of society primarily by its focus on the use of a particular drug or drugs.

Tolerance. The tendency for users of particular drugs to require steadily increasing dosages to achieve a consistent level of effect.

FURTHER READING

BRECHER, EDWARD et al. Licit and Illicit Drugs: The Consumers Union Report on Narcotics, Stimulants, Depressants, Inhalants, Hallucinogens, and Marijuana—Including Coffee, Nicotine, and Alcohol. Boston: Little, Brown, 1972. A report prepared for the Consumers Union of the United States. Written in a clear and interesting style, this book contains a great deal of information on all the drugs commonly used and abused in the United States. The report adopts a liberal attitude toward reform of the drug laws.

FORT, JOEL. *Alcohol: Our Biggest Drug Problem*. New York: Knopf, 1973. A physician's examination of the use and abuse of alcohol in America, with recommendations for the prevention and treatment of alcoholism.

GOODE, ERICH. *Drugs in American Society*. New York: Knopf, 1972. A valuable and comprehensive sociological discussion of each of the main forms of drug abuse in the United States.

GRINSPOON, LESTER. *Marijuana Reconsidered*. 2nd ed. Cambridge, Mass.: Harvard University Press, 1977. A physician's thorough investigation of the social and medical implications of marijuana use.

JOSEPHSON, ERIC, and ELEANOR E. CARROLL (eds.). *Drug Use: Epidemiological and Sociological Approaches*. New York: Wiley, 1974. An important collection of articles on problems and patterns of drug use.

KAPLAN, JOHN. *Marijuana: The New Prohibition*. New York: New American Library, 1975. A critical account of the laws against marijuana, by a law professor who has campaigned for reform of these laws.

MCGRATH, JOHN H. and FRANK R. SCARPITTI (eds.). *Youth and Drugs: Perspectives on a Social Problem*. Glenview, Ill.: Scott, Foresman, 1970. A collection of articles exploring various aspects of youthful experimentation with drugs.

NATIONAL COMMISSION ON MARIJUANA AND DRUG ABUSE. OFFICIAL REPORT. *Marijuana: A Signal of Misunderstanding*. Washington, D.C.: U.S. Government Printing Office, 1972. Second Report. *Drug Use in America*. Washington, D.C.: U.S. Government Printing Office, 1973. Two important, objective, and wide-ranging federal reports on drug use in America. Written in clear, nontechnical language, these authoritative reports contain surveys of research findings on drugs and offer recommendations for reform of the drug laws.

YOUNG, JOCK. *The Drugtakers*. London: Paladin, 1971. A sociologist's critical view of social attitudes toward drugs. Young argues strongly that the social reaction to drugs depends more on who uses them than on the properties of the drugs themselves.

EPILOGUE

Solving Social Problems

There is surely general agreement that we would be better off without the social problems that this book has discussed. In their different ways, these problems impose major strains on the society, and the quality of all our lives suffers as a result. We might reasonably ask, therefore: "If things are that bad, why isn't something more done about it?" And indeed we have seen, in chapter after chapter, that potential solutions do exist, even if some of them are only partial. Yet the social problems persist, and some of them even seem to grow worse in certain respects. Unhappily, it seems that solving social problems can become a problem in itself. It would be useful, then, as we complete this survey of American problems, for us to address two related questions. What special difficulties hinder the solution of social problems? And what are the prospects, realistically speaking, for actually solving them?

The answer to the first question is that four recurrent features make social problems difficult to solve, even when the stage has been reached where public opinion favors action and government is ready to act.

First, *major social problems are deeply embedded in culture and social structure.* They do not suddenly appear, full-grown, from nowhere; rather, they develop imperceptibly, nourished by the social environment. Although sociologists and other observers may notice emerging (or "latent") problems at this stage, it is hard to mobilize public opinion about them, and collective action to solve them is therefore unlikely. By the time a social problem is widely recognized as a serious and urgent one, it has usually become deeply rooted in the institutional arrangements and culture of the society. At this stage, attempts to confront the problem can cause massive disruptions of existing social and cultural patterns. For example, a decade or more of warnings about an impending energy crisis fell on generally deaf ears until 1979. In the summer of that year, gasoline shortages played havoc with social and economic life throughout the nation, and millions of Americans finally realized, during their long waits on the gas lines, how serious the problem was. But although the energy crisis is now recognized as a social problem that threatens the very foundations of the society, it is anything but solved. The causes of the energy shortage—overdependence on foreign sources, profiteering by the oil companies, poor conservation practices, careless disposal of wastes, the American love-affair with the private automobile, and the past lack of a national energy policy—are all so deeply embedded in our way of life that they cannot be eliminated overnight (or in a month or a year), no matter how strong the will to find a solution may be.

A second and related difficulty is that *all solutions to all social problems have their own costs, too.* There are many ways that the energy crisis could be resolved, if the nation were willing to bear the social, political, economic, or personal costs that are inevitably involved. For example, we could have an abundance of electricity by building a profusion of nuclear reactors across the nation—if communities would allow the plants to be located near their own neighborhoods, rather than in someone else's. We could strip-mine vast quantities of coal from the nation's huge reserves and burn it to provide energy—if the citizens of coal-bearing areas like

467

Wyoming would permit us to literally tear up their states, and if the rest of us could tolerate the atmospheric pollution the coal fires would cause. We could end the gasoline shortage by permitting cars to be driven on alternate days of the month only, or by taxing gas until its price doubles or triples to its price level in other industrial societies—if members of Congress were foolhardy enough to risk their seats by supporting such proposals. The point is that so little progress has been made in solving the energy problem because Americans, so far, are not prepared to pay the necessary costs in terms of a changed lifestyle. Indeed, public debate about the energy shortage has centered not on the problem of how to adjust to reduced consumption, but rather on how we can increase supplies so as to maintain the energy-abundant way of life we have known for so long.

A third difficulty is implied by the one we have just discussed: *all solutions to social problems are controversial.* Even if the gravity of a problem is universally recognized, general agreement on its solution is unlikely. The costs of solving a problem translate into gains for some groups and losses for others—and when the proposals of one social movement or interest group are perceived as a threat by another, the latter will use all its power to stall that proposal and impose one of its own. This is why Congress has butchered virtually every energy program that it has been asked to consider. As partisans of different interests and as representatives of different regions, members of Congress vigorously defend their own positions, often to the detriment of the nation as a whole. On the issue of gasoline allocation, for example, state delegations typically argue that their own particular state is a "special case" that deserves favored treatment. On the issues of fuel pricing and resource development, representatives of coal-rich states argue one view; those from oil-rich states argue another; those from energy-poor states argue a third. In the long run this kind of conflict will clarify the issues, but until the controversies are resolved, efforts to solve the problem are crippled by indecision and inertia.

A fourth difficulty is that *all social problems are interrelated and highly complex.* Although interest groups are quick to reduce complex issues to catchy slogans, social problems are never simple, never amenable to quick and easy solutions. Because various aspects of different social problems are interrelated, any attempt at solution will have multiple impacts—some unforeseen, and some even affecting problems other than the one they were applied to. For example, any solution to the shortage of energy and other resources will have extensive impact on the environment, because the production and use of energy always causes some form of pollution. Similarly, if the solution adversely affects the automobile industry, there may be further impacts on the areas of work, government and corporations, and poverty. Table 1 illustrates these complex relationships: drawing examples from each chapter of the book, it shows how solutions to specific problems have created other problems.

Let us turn to our second question, about the chances for actually solving social problems. In the face of all these difficulties, is the task a hopeless one?

The answer, of course, is no. An awareness of the difficulties should not discourage us; rather, it should make us realize that facile "solutions" probably will not work. High expectations of easy results can lead to cynicism and disillusion—as happened in the late 1960s with the failure of the Johnson administration's apparent policy of "throwing money at problems" in the hope that they would somehow vanish. Instead, an awareness of the difficulties should equip us to confront social problems more effectively. It can enable us to recognize that they are rarely "solved" in the sense of being completely eliminated. Rather, undesirable social conditions can be steadily *ameliorated*, or made better, through a coherent plan of attack that takes account of social realities. Thus, the fact that a proposed solution has its own costs does not mean that the solution is useless: it could be that the costs are worth bearing. The federal government made just such a judgment when it decided that cleaner air is worth the cost of the lower gas mileage obtained by cars that meet federal auto-emission standards. Our energy problem will probably be ameliorated and perhaps even-

Table 1   The Complexity of Social Problems: Solutions Can Cause New Problems

General Area	Specific Problem	Specific Solution	New Problem
Population	High infant mortality rate in developing countries.	Improve health care, especially through childhood vaccinations.	Infant mortality drops, resulting in a population explosion.
Environment and resources	Auto emissions cause hazardous air pollution.	Require cleaner EPA standards for auto emissions.	Autos that meet EPA standards use more gas, worsening energy shortage.
Work	High unemployment, especially among blue-collar and unskilled workers.	Encourage economic growth to create new jobs in industry.	New industrial production depletes scarce resources and increases pollution.
The cities	Urban tax base shrinks as middle class moves to the suburbs.	Increase city taxes to make up lost revenue.	Remaining residents and businesses have even more reason to leave.
Government and corporations	Corporations engage in unethical or fraudulent practices; produce shoddy or dangerous products.	Create federal regulatory agencies to protect the consumer.	Federal bureaucracy grows; business complains of red tape and government interference.
Poverty	Millions of Americans live below the poverty line.	Provide welfare payments to the poor.	Many taxpayers see payments to supposed "free-loaders" as a problem.
Race and Ethnic Relations	Urban schools are segregated as a result of residential segregation.	Integrate schools through busing.	Many whites see busing as a problem; probably as a result, white students enroll outside of the city schools, increasing the overall degree of segregation.
Sex Roles	Job discrimination against women (and racial minorities).	Create affirmative action programs to enhance job opportunities for women (and racial minorities).	White male workers complain of job discrimination against them.
Family Problems	Illegitimate children suffer stigma through no fault of their own, partly because laws discriminate against them.	Repeal laws that discriminate against illegitimate children.	Illegitimacy rate soars, largely because unwed parents have less motive to make children legitimate.

(Cont. on next page)

Table 1   (Continued)

General Area	Specific Problem	Specific Solution	New Problem
Aging	Many older workers resent enforced retirement at age 65.	Extend mandatory retirement age to 70.	Slower promotion for younger workers; fewer job openings for the unemployed poor.
Health Care	The aged and the poor cannot afford the high cost of medical care.	Create Medicaid and Medicare to pay all or part of their costs.	Influx of public money into the health care system drives up costs higher and faster than before.
Mental Disorders	Prolonged stay in mental hospitals may worsen the condition of the patients.	Release patients into the community whenever their hospitalization is no longer essential.	Lacking adequate community support facilities, many poor and unemployed expatients languish in urban "psychiatric ghettos."
Crime and Violence	Gambling, prostitution, vagrancy, and marijuana smoking offend public morals.	Arrest and prosecute gamblers, prostitutes, vagrants, marijuana smokers.	Resources of police, court, and correctional facilities are diverted from crimes with victims to crimes without victims.
Sexual Variance	Homosexual behavior violates traditional norms.	Legislate against homosexual behavior; prevent homosexuals from holding certain jobs.	Prejudice and discrimination against homosexuals becomes a problem.
Drug Abuse	Heroin addiction has undesirable social or individual effects.	Make possession of heroin illegal.	Heroin becomes obtainable only on the black market: organized crime profits as the price soars; addicts must rob and steal to support their habits.

tually solved through a series of realistic partial solutions rather than through one sweeping stroke: thus, several new energy sources may be developed, energy conservation may be encouraged, dependence on foreign sources may be reduced, the greed of the oil companies may be checked, public transport systems may be extended, and so on.

There is no social problem in this book that cannot be ameliorated; and in the long run, there is probably none that cannot be solved. Aspects of some of the problems, certainly, seem worse than they were ten or twenty years ago: global population is greater, crime rates are higher, resource depletion is increasing. In the case of other problems, such as health care, there is a sense that the forces for change are now irresistable, and that marked improvements are in the offing. In many other instances, social conditions have been greatly ameliorated: for example, the aged, the poor, women, gays, racial minorities, or the mentally disordered are all significantly better off in some respects than they were only a few years ago.

In fact, despite nostalgic talk of the "good old days," the overall quality of our lives is surely far higher than it was in the past. The changes that have taken place are perhaps better seen in a longer time perspective than that of a few years, and Table 2 compares selected social problems at the turn of the present century with the same problems today. The comparison yields a powerful sense of progress—although, from the point of view of those who compaigned for change some eight decades ago, the obstacles must have seemed overwhelming.

Although our society still has many problems and imperfections, there is much to value and appreciate. Yet we can enjoy its better features only because of the efforts of committed men and women of the past, who tackled immense problems in the faith that conditions could be improved for future generations like our own. Recognizing the difficulties, but equipped with a scientific understanding of society and its problems, we should be able to do at least as much: to improve social conditions in our lifetime, and to leave a more worthy, decent, and humane society to the generation that follows.

Table 2   American Social Problems: in 1900 and in the 1980s

Problem	Then	Now
Population	The birth rate was very high and large families were the norm. A new social movement advocated birth control, but its members were persecuted and even imprisoned.	The birth rate is very low, and small families are the norm. Most married couples use birth control during their child-bearing years, and the government strongly favors population limitation.
Environment	Pollution went virtually unchecked, and a new conservation movement struggled to protect areas of scenic beauty from industrial and commerical exploitation.	An Environmental Protection Agency sets and monitors standards for all forms of pollution. National and state parks protect vast areas of the country from careless development.
Work	The labor movement was locked in a bitter and bloody struggle for the right to form unions and to take strike action, for the abolition of child labor, for unemployment benefits, and for a living wage.	Labor unions are virtually part of the establishment, and their early goals are long since achieved. New concerns have emerged that would have seemed a luxury in earlier decades, such as the problem of alienation and unsatisfying work.
Poverty	Grinding poverty was widespread, particularly among new immigrants to the country. There was no system of social security or public welfare for the sick, the disabled, the young, the old, or the unemployed to fall back on.	Despite the persistence of poverty, a far smaller proportion of the population lives in poverty today. Although it is still inadequate in some respects, there is now an extensive system of public assistance for those who can show that they need it. (Cont. on next page)

Table 2   (*Continued*)

Problem	Then	Now
Race and Ethnic Relations	Strict racial segregation was enforced throughout the United States, either by law or by custom. Blacks were denied such elementary civil rights as the vote.	Spurred by the civil rights movement, government and courts have outlawed enforced segregation and discrimination, and now guarantee the civil rights of minorities.
Sex Roles	Women were regarded, in practice and indeed in law, as the property of their fathers or husbands. A woman's movement campaigned for such basic rights as the vote.	Legal barriers to full female participation in the economy and society have collapsed. Traditional sex roles are changing, and women are achieving steadily greater equality with men.
Aging	The aged had to rely on their own resources or those of their relatives; if this were not possible, their only recourse was to charity—if they could get it.	The aged can now rely on social security pensions for an income, and they receive public assistance for many of their medical expenses, including extended nursing home stays.
Mental Disorders	The mentally disordered were severely stigmatized. They were often incarcerated, with little or no treatment, in asylums that were called "snake pits" because of the conditions within them.	Thanks largely to the efforts of the mental health movement, there is much less stigma attached to mental disorder, and hospital conditions and methods of treatment have greatly improved.
Sexual Variance	Laws against various forms of supposed variance—adultery, fornication, homosexuality, cohabitation, interracial sex, oral-genital sex, even masturbation—were rigorously enforced throughout the nation.	Most of these statutes have either been repealed or have fallen into disuse. The gay liberation movement is successfully challenging the remaining laws, which no longer have the same degree of support among the public.

Glossary

Absolute deprivation. A lack of the basic necessities of life.

Achieved status. A status that is gained by the individual at least partly through his or her own efforts or failings.

Addiction. A state of physical dependence on a drug, in which physical withdrawal symptoms will appear if use of the drug is discontinued.

Ageism. A set of beliefs that justifies systematic discrimination against the elderly by supposing that inequalities between the young and the old are the natural outcome of biological and not social factors.

Age structure. The proportion of different age groups within a given population.

Alcoholism. The compulsive and excessive use of alcohol to the extent that it is harmful to the drinker's health, job performance, or interpersonal relationships.

Alienation. The sense of powerlessness and meaningless that people experience when confronted by social institutions that they consider oppressive, and feel they cannot control.

Anomie. A state in which social norms have ceased to be meaningful or effective, often resulting in deviant behavior.

Ascribed status. A status assigned to the individual by society on arbitrary grounds over which the individual has little or no control.

Automation. The use of self-regulating machines that monitor and control a production process.

Birth rate. The number of births per year per thousand members of a population.

Bureaucracy. An organizational structure in which officials have specific tasks and work under a formal system of rules to maximize the efficiency of the organization as a whole.

Case study. An intensive examination of a particular social phenomenon.

Chemotherapy. Medical treatment of a disorder through the use of drugs.

City. A permanent concentration of large numbers of people who do not produce their own food.

Conflict approach. A theoretical approach that emphasizes conflict among competing groups as an important influence on social and cultural arrangements and as a source of social change.

Crime. An act prohibited by a law.

Criminology. The scientific study of crime.

Culture. All the shared products of human society, comprising its total way of life.

Culture lag. The tendency for society to be disorganized because some of its parts have not adjusted to changes elsewhere in society.

Culture of poverty. A set of values, norms, and other cultural characteristics alleged to exist among the poor in industrialized societies.

Death rate. The number of deaths per year per thousand members of a population.

Demographic transition. The tendency for the growth rate of a population to decrease and then stabilize once a certain level of economic development has been achieved.

Demography. The scientific study of the size, composition, growth rates, and distribution of human populations.

Dependence. A state of recurrent desire or craving for a drug whose use has become a habit.

Developed country. A society that is fully industrialized, such as the United States, Japan, and the countries of Europe.

Developing country. A country that is in transition from a predominantly agricultural to a predominantly modern industrial economy, such as most nations of Africa, Asia, and Latin America.

Deviance. Any behavior that violates important social norms and is therefore negatively valued by large numbers of people.

Discrimination. Action against others on the grounds of their group membership and supposed group characteristics.

Division of labor. The division of economic activity into specialized tasks that are performed by specific people.

Doubling time. The time it will take for a population to double in size.

Drug. Any chemical that is psychoactive, or capable of modifying a person's behavior through its effect on emotions, thinking, or consciousness.

Drug abuse. Use of a drug that does not conform to social norms prescribing the appropriate use of that drug.

Drug subculture. A subculture distinguished from the rest of society primarily by its focus on the use of a particular drug or drugs.

Dysfunction. A negative effect that one element in a system has on the rest of the system or on some other part of the system.

Ecological approach. An approach to social phenomena that focuses on the relationships between human beings and their social and physical environment.

Ecology. The science of the mutual relationships between organisms and their environment.

Ecosystem. A self-sustaining community of organisms in its natural environment.

Ethnic Group. A large number of people who have had a high level of mutual interaction over a long period of time and who share distinctive cultural traits; as a result, they regard themselves and are regarded by others as a cultural unity.

Ethnocentrism. The tendency for members of one group to assume that their own values, attitudes, and norms are superior to those of other groups, and to judge other groups by their own standards.

Experiment. A carefully controlled method for tracing the influence of one variable on another.

Exponential growth. A type of growth in which the increase in a given period is based not on the original figure but on the figure for the previous period.

Extended family. A family system in which several generations of the same kinship line live together.

Family. A group of people who live together and who are related by ancestry, marriage, or adoption.

Folkways. The ordinary customs and conventions of society; conformity to these norms is expected, but people are not morally outraged by violations of them.

Formal organization. A group that is deliberately and rationally structured in order to achieve specific goals.

Function. The effect that one element in a system has on the rest of the system or on some other part of the system.

Functionalism. A theoretical approach that sees society as an organized system, in which each part ideally has a useful function in maintaining social stability.

Functional psychosis. A psychosis that has no obvious physical basis and whose origin is presumed to be partly or wholly psychological.

Gemeinshaft. A term used to describe a small community marked by intimate relationships, strong feelings of solidarity, and loyalty to traditional values.

Gender. Refers to cultural concepts of masculinity and femininity, as distinct from the biological fact of maleness and femaleness.

Geriatrics. The scientific study of the medical problems of the elderly.

Gerontology. The scientific study of aging.

Gesellschaft. A term used to describe a society marked by impersonal contacts, an emphasis on individualism rather than group loyalty, and solidarity based on utility rather than affection or shared traditions.

Growth rate. A measure of population growth obtained by subtracting the number of deaths from the number of births and expressing this figure as an annual percentage.

Homosexuality. Sexual acts or feelings directed toward a member of the same sex.

Hypothesis. A tentative theory that has not been confirmed by research.

Ideology. A set of ideas and beliefs that justifies the perceived interests of those who hold it; the ideology of the dominant group in any unequal society therefore justifies the inequality.

Institution. A stable pattern of norms, statuses, and roles that centers on some social need.

Institutionalized discrimination. Discriminatory acts and policies that are not necessarily encoded in law but are nonetheless pervasive in the major institutions of society

Kinship. A network of people related by ancestry, marriage or adoption.

Labeling. The social process by which some people successfully attach the label of "deviant" to others.

Law. A formal rule that is backed by the power of the state.

Legal discrimination. Discriminatory acts and policies that are encoded in the law of the land.

Life expectancy. The number of years of life that the average newborn will enjoy.

Marriage. A socially approved sexual union of some permanence between two people.

Medicaid. A public health-assistance program financed from federal and state taxes and designed to cover the medical expenses of people with very low incomes.

Medical malpractice suit. A lawsuit brought against a doctor for damages allegedly resulting from incompetent care.

Medical mode. A model of mental disorders in which they are viewed and treated as though they were analogous to physical ailments.

Medicare. A public health-insurance program financed from Social Security taxes and designed to cover some of the medical expenses of people over the age of sixty-five.

Megalopolis. A virtually unbroken urban tract consisting of two or more adjacent metropolises.

Mental disorder. A psychological inability to cope realistically and effectively with the ordinary challenges and tasks of the real world.

Metropolis. An urban area including a city and its surrounding suburbs.

Migration rate. The number of people entering or leaving a population per year per thousand members of the population.

Military-industrial complex. An interlocking network of politicians, Pentagon bureaucrats, military chiefs, and executives of corporations that supply military equipment.

Mores. Morally significant social norms, violations of which are considered a serious matter.

Multinational corporation. A large business enterprise that is based in one country but owns subsidiary corporations in many other countries.

Neurosis. A personality disturbance, usually involving anxiety but not a sharp break with reality.

Norms. Formal or informal rules that prescribe the appropriate behavior in a given situation.

Nuclear family. A family system in which a single married couple and their dependent children live apart from their other relatives.

Oligarchy. A situation in which power is concentrated in the hands of a few officials of an organization or group.

Organic psychosis. A psychosis that has an identifiable physical basis resulting from damage to brain tissues.

Pornography. Written or pictorial material designed to cause sexual arousal.

Prejudice. A "prejudged" negative attitude toward other groups.

Primary group. A group consisting of a small number of people who interact in direct, personal, and intimate ways, usually over a long period of time.

Primary industry. Economic activity involving the gathering or the extracting of undeveloped natural resources.

Profession. An occupation requiring extensive knowledge or training in an art or science.

Prostitution. The relatively indiscriminate exchange of sexual favors for economic gain.

Psychosis. A serious form of mental disorder involving a sharp break with reality.

Psychotherapy. Treatment of a mental disorder through interaction between the patient and psychiatrist aimed at improving the patient's understanding of, and ability to solve, the problem.

Race. A large number of people who have interbred over a long period of time; as a result, they share distinctive physical features and regard themselves and are regarded by others as a biological unity.

Rationalization. The process by which traditional, spontaneous, methods of social organization are replaced by routine, systematic procedures.

Recidivism. A convicted person's return to crime.

Relative deprivation. A lack of the living standards considered customary in the society.

Role. The part that a person occupying a particular status plays in society.

Role structure. The relative numbers and the types of roles that a society makes available to its members.

Schizophrenia. The most common form of functional psychosis, involving a separation of intellectual and emotional functions and disordered behavior.

Secondary group. A group consisting of a small or large number of people who have few if any emotional ties with one another, who do not know one another well, and who usually come together for a specific, practical purpose.

Secondary industry. Economic activity involving the transformation of raw materials into manufactured goods.

Sex. Refers to the biological fact of maleness and femaleness, as distinct from cultural concepts of gender.

Sexism. An ideology or set of values and beliefs that justifies the domination of women by men on the grounds that inequality results from inborn differences.

Sex roles. The learned patterns of behavior expected of the sexes in a given society.

Sick role. The pattern of behavior society expects of a person who is ill.

Social disorganization. A situation in which society is imperfectly organized for the maintenance of social stability and the achievement of social goals.

Social mobility. Movement from one social status to another.

Social movement. A large number of people who join together to bring about or to resist some social or cultural change.

Social problem. Whatever a significant part of the population perceives as an undesirable gap between social ideals and social realities and believes can be eliminated by collective action.

Social stratification. The division of a society into social classes that enjoy varying degrees of access to the rewards the society offers.

Social structure. The underlying pattern of social relationships in a society.

Socialization. The lifelong experience through which the individual acquires personality and learns the culture of the society.

Sociology. The scientific study of human society and social behavior.

Stagflation. A combination of stagnation (low growth, low investment, high unemployment) and inflation.

Standard Consolidated Area. A term used by the Bu-

reau of the Census to refer to a megalopolis, an urban tract consisting of two or more metropolises.

Standard Metropolitan Statistical Area. A term used by the Bureau of the Census to refer to a city or cities and their surrounding suburbs that have a population of over 50,000.

Stigma. The mark of social disgrace applied by society to those who deviate from important norms.

Suburb. A less densely populated, primarily residential area that lies beyond the boundary of a city.

Status. A position in society.

Stereotype. A rigid mental image of a group that is applied indiscriminately to all its members.

Structural unemployment. Persistent unemployment that is built into the structure of the economy.

Subculture. A group that participates in the overall culture of a society but also has its own distinctive life styles and values.

Survey. A method of discovering facts or opinions by questioning members of a population.

Taboo. A powerful social prohibition against behavior that is considered loathsome or unthinkable.

Tertiary industry. Economic activity involving the provision of various services.

Thanatology. The scientific study of death and dying.

Theory. A statement that explains a relationship between facts or concepts.

Total institution. A place of residence and work where all the inmates are in a similar situation, are cut off from the wider society, and lead an enclosed, formally administered life.

Underemployment. A situation in which people are working only for short or irregular periods or for wages so low that they cannot adequately support themselves.

Values. Socially shared ideas about what is desirable, right, and proper.

Variable. Any characteristic that can vary across time or space or from one person to another.

Zero population growth. A situation in which population size remains stable over time.

INDEX

Credits and Acknowledgments

PHOTO CREDITS

Chapter 1
2—Paolo Koch;
5—Charles Gatewood;
7—Bob Combs/Rapho/Photo Researchers, Inc.;
11—Peter Angelo Simon;
18—Leonard Speier.

Chapter 2
30—Peter Menzel/Stock, Boston;
40—Thomas Hopker/Woodfin Camp & Assoc.;
45—Rene Burri/Magnum;
49—Vivienne/DPI.

Chapter 3
56—Rick Smolan;
59—Robert A. Isaacs/Photo Researchers, Inc.;
65—Arthur Tress/Photo Researchers, Inc.;
69—Bruce Davidson/Magnum;
78—George Hall/Woodfin Camp & Assoc.

Chapter 4
84—DPI;
88—Jan Lukas/Rapho/Photo Researchers, Inc.;
91—Inge Morath/Magnum;
102—Sherry Suris/Rapho/Photo Researchers, Inc.;
107—Ken Heyman.

Chapter 5
118—Elliot Erwitt/Magnum;
124—Paul Sequeira/Rapho/Photo Researchers, Inc.;
127—J. P. Laffont/Sygma;
132—Leonard Speier;
137—Carl Frank/Photo Researchers, Inc.

Chapter 6
142—Michael Evans/Liaison;
151—Ken Heyman;
156—George W. Gardner;

165—UPI;
165—Gerhard E. Gscheidle/Peter Arnold, Inc.

Chapter 7
174—James R. Holland/Stock, Boston;
181—H. Kubota/Magnum;
185—Ken Heyman;
190—Paul Fusco/Magnum;
195—Arthur Tress/Photo Researchers, Inc.

Chapter 8
204—Ken Heyman;
211—Dennis Stock/Magnum;
(left) 214—Joel Gordon;
(right) 214—Nicholas Sapieda/Stock, Boston;
218—Martin J. Dain/Magnum;
222—Ginger Chih/Peter Arnold, Inc.;
226—Bob Adelman/Magnum.

Chapter 9
234—Judy Dater;
237—Leif Skoogfors/Woodfin Camp & Assoc.;
244—Fred Mayer/Woodfin Camp & Assoc.;
249—Ken Heyman;
251—Courtesy, Christian Dior.

Chapter 10
262—Tim Eagen/Woodfin Camp & Assoc.;
266—Ron Sherman/Nancy Palmer;
271—Culver Pictures;
279—Thomas Hopker/Woodfin Camp & Assoc.

Chapter 11
290—Hella Hammed/Rapho/Photo Researchers, Inc.;
292—Bernard Pierre Wolff/Magnum;
304—Joel Gordon;
311—Hella Hammed/Rapho/Photo Researchers, Inc.

Chapter 12
314—Stephen L. Feldman/Photo Researchers, Inc.;
317—Marc & Evelyne Bernheim/Woodfin Camp & Assoc.;
318—Culver Pictures;
327—Spencer Carter/Woodfin Camp & Assoc.;
335—Sepp Seitz/Woodfin Camp & Assoc.

Chapter 13
340—Ken Heyman;
342—(c) The Washington Post 1978/Frank Johnston/ Woodfin, Camp & Assoc.;
353—The Bettmann Archive;
358—Mary Ellen Mark/Magnum;
361—Paul Fusco/Magnum.

Chapter 14
370—Charles Gatewood;
375—Ken Heyman;

382—Paul Conklin/Monkmeyer Press Photo;
391—J. Berndt/Stock, Boston;
395—Danny Lyon/Magnum.

Chapter 15
404—Leonard Freed/Magnum;
418—Mimi Forsyth/Monkmeyer Press Photo;
420—Eric Kroll/Taurus Photos;
423—Joel Gordon;
427—Harvey Stein.

Chapter 16
432—Charles Gatewood;
436—Anna Kaufman Moon/Stock, Boston;
442—Paul Conklin/Monkmeyer Press Photo;
446—Charles Gatewood;
447—Jim Anderson/Woodfin Camp & Assoc.;
449—Leonard Freed/Magnum.

TEXT CREDITS

Chapter 1
From Howard S. Becker "Whose Side Are We On?" *Social Problems*, 14:3 (Winter 1967). Copyright © 1967 by The Society for the Study of Social Problems. Reprinted by permission of the author and publisher; Figure 1.2, from Joan H. Rytina, "Income and Stratification Ideology." *American Journal of Sociology*, 75 (January 1970). Copyright © 1970 by the University of Chicago. Reprinted by permission of the publisher.

Chapter 2
From Nathaniel Wander, unpublished paper. Copyright © 1979 by Nathaniel Wander. Reprinted by permission of the author; Table 2.1, adapted from *1978 World Population Data Sheet*, The Population Reference Bureau, Inc., Washington, D.C. Reprinted by permission; Figure 2.2, adapted from *1973 World Population Data Sheet*, Population Reference Bureau, Inc., Washington, D.C. Reprinted by permission.

Chapter 3
From Norman Cousins, "Affluence and Effluence," *Saturday Review*, May 2, 1970. Copyright © 1970 by *Saturday Review*. Reprinted by permission; From John G. Mitchell, *Losing Ground*. Copyright © 1975 by the Sierra Club. Reprinted by permission; Figure 3.3, from John McHale, *World Facts and Trends*. Orginally appeared in *Time*, July 11, 1969. Copyright © 1969 by *Time*, the Weekly Newsmagazine. Reprinted by permission.

Chapter 4
From Jeremy Brecker and Tim Costello, *Common Sense for Hard Times*. Copyright © 1976 by Jeremy Brecker and Tim Costello. Reprinted by permission; From Robert Lekachman, "The Specter of Full Employment," *Harper's Magazine* (February 1977). Copyright © 1977 by *Harper's Magazine*. All rights reserved. Reprinted by permission; From Studs Terkel, *Working: People Talk About What They Do All Day and How They Feel About What They Do*. Copyright © 1972, 1974 by Studs Terkel. Reprinted by permission of Pantheon Books, a Division of Random House, Inc.; From Robert Coles and Jane Hallowell Coles, *Women of Crisis: Lives of Struggle and Hope*. Copyright © 1978 by Robert Coles and Jane Hallowell Coles. Reprinted by permission of Delacorte Press. A Merloyd Lawrence Book.

Chapter 5
From Studs Terkel, *Working: People Talk About What They Do All Day and How They Feel About What They Do*. Copyright © 1972, 1974 by Studs Terkel. Reprinted by permission of Pantheon Books, a Division of Random House, Inc.

Chapter 6
From Richard J. Barnet, Ronald E. Müller, and Joseph Collins, "Global Corporations: Their Quest for Legitimacy," in *Exploring Contradictions: Political Economy in the Corporate State*, eds. Philip Brenner, Robert Borosage, and Bethany Weider. Copyright © 1974 by Longman Inc. Reprinted by permission; From Studs Terkel, *Working: People*

Talk About What They Do All Day and How They Feel About What They Do. Copyright © 1972, 1974 by Studs Terkel. Reprinted by permission of Pantheon Books, a Division of Random House, Inc.; From A. Ernest Fitzgerald, *The High Priests of Waste.* Copyright © 1972 by A. Ernest Fitzgerald. Reprinted by permission of the author; From Anthony Sampson, *The Sovereign State of ITT.* Copyright © 1973 by Anthony Sampson. Reprinted by permission of Stein and Day, Publishers; Table 6.1, adapted from *The Fortune Directory.* Copyright © 1979 by Time, Inc. Reprinted by permission; Figure 6.1, from the *New York Times,* August 3, 1977. Copyright © 1977 by The New York Times Company. Reprinted by permission.

Chapter 7

From Kenneth E. Boulding, "Reflections on Poverty," in *The Social Welfare Forum: 1961.* Copyright © 1961 by Columbia University Press. Reprinted by permission; From Earl and Miriam Selby, *Odyssey: Journey Through Black America.* Copyright © 1971 by Earl and Miriam Selby. Reprinted by permission of G. P. Putnam's Sons; From Herbert J. Gans, "The Uses of Poverty: The Poor Pay All." *Social Policy* (July/August 1971). Copyright © 1971 by Social Policy Corporation. Reprinted by permission; From Robert Coles, *Children of Crisis: Vol. II: Migrants, Sharecroppers, Mountaineers.* Copyright © 1971 by Robert Coles. Reprinted by permission of Little, Brown and Company; From A. Dale Tussing, "The Dual Welfare System," *Society,* Vol. II, No. 2 (January/February 1974). Copyright © 1974 by Transaction, Inc. Reprinted by permission; Figure 7.5, from *The New York Times,* August 3, 1977. Copyright © 1977 by The New York Times Company. Reprinted by permission.

Chapter 8

From Robert Coles, *Children of Crisis: Vol. IV: Eskimos, Chicanos, Indians.* Copyright © 1977 by Robert Coles. Reprinted by permission of Little, Brown and Company; Figure 8.2, from *A Study of Attitudes Toward Racial and Religious Minorities,* conducted by Louis Harris and Associates, Inc., for the National Conference of Christians and Jews. (November 1978). Reprinted by permission.

Chapter 9

From Miriam Schapiro, "Notes From a Conversation on Art, Feminism and Work," in *Working It Out,* eds. Sarah Ruddick and Pamela Daniels. Copyright © 1977 by Sarah Ruddick and Pamela Daniels. Reprinted by permission of Pantheon Books, a Division of Random House, Inc.; Table 9.1. Adapted from George P. Murdock, "Comparative Data on the Division of Labor by Sex," *Social Forces* (May 1937). Copyright 1937 by The University of North Carolina Press. Reprinted by permission.

Chapter 10

From Lillian Breslow Rubin, *Worlds of Pain: Life in the Working Class Family.* Copyright © 1976 by Basic Books, Inc., Publishers. Reprinted by permission; From Eloise Taylor Lee, "Raising a Child Alone," *The Christian Science Monitor,* August 14, 1978. Copyright © 1978 by The Christian Science Publishing Society. All rights reserved. Reprinted by permission; From Leslie Westoff, "Kids With Kids," *The New York Times Magazine,* February 22, 1976. Copyright © 1976 by The New York Times Company. Reprinted by permission.

Chapter 11

From Elisabeth Kübler-Ross, "Facing Up to Death," *Today's Education* (January 1972). Reprinted by permission of the author and publisher; From Studs Terkel, *Working: People Talk About What They Do All Day and How They Feel About What They Do.* Copyright © 1972, 1974 by Studs Terkel. Reprinted by permission of Pantheon Books, a Division of Random House, Inc.; Table 11.1 and p. 309, from *The Myth and Reality of Aging in America,* a study prepared by Louis Harris and Associates, Inc. for the National Council on the Aging, Inc., Washington, D.C. Copyright © 1975 by Louis Harris and Associates Inc. Reprinted by permission.

Chapter 12

From Studs Terkel, *Working: People Talk About What They Do All Day and How They Feel About What They Do.* Copyright © 1972, 1974 by Studs Terkel. Reprinted by permission of Pantheon Books, a Division of Random House, Inc.; From Fred J. Cook, *Julia's Story: The Tragedy of an Unnecessary Death.* Copyright © 1974, 1976 by Fred J. Cook. Reprinted by permission of Holt, Rinehart and Winston; From Thomas McKeown, "Determinants of Health," *Human Nature* (April 1978). Copyright © 1978 by Human Nature, Inc. Reprinted by permission of Harcourt Brace Javanovich, Inc.

Chapter 13

From David L. Rosenhan, "On Being Sane in Insane Places," *Science,* Vol. 179, January 19, 1973. Copyright © 1973 by The American Association for the Advancement of Science. Reprinted by permission of the author and publisher; From Joseph Church, "Two Fly Over the Duckoo's Nest." *The New York Times Book Review,* March 26, 1978. Copyright © 1978 by The New York Times Company. Reprinted by permission; From Robert Coles, "A Fashionable Kind of Slander," *Atlantic* (November 1970). Copyright © 1970 by The Atlantic Monthly Company, Boston, Mass. Reprinted by permission; From Mark Vonnegut, *Eden Express.* Copyright © 1975 by Praeger Publish-

ABOUT THE AUTHOR

Ian Robertson received his B.A. in Political Science from the University of Natal in South Africa. Because of his activities against apartheid in that country, he was "banned" by the government. After his departure from South Africa, he lived in England, where he obtained a Diploma in Education in English and Latin from Oxford University and a First-Class Honors degree and M.A. in Sociology from Cambridge University. At Cambridge, he was elected Senior Scholar in Sociology for King's College.

Subsequently, in the United States, he took both a master's degree and a doctorate in the Sociology of Education at Harvard University.

Dr. Robertson has taught Sociology of Education at the graduate level to Harvard students and sociology to Cambridge University undergraduates. At present, he is devoting himself to various research and writing projects.

In addition to articles on social problems that were published by the *Times* and *Guardian* in England and the *New Republic* and *Nation* in the United States, Dr. Robertson has written *Sociology* (Worth, 1977). He has also edited *Readings in Sociology: Contemporary Perspectives* (Harper & Row, 1976) and *Race and Politics in South Africa* (Transaction Books, 1978).